S0-BYN-805

TAKING SIDES

Clashing Views on

Educational Issues

FOURTEENTH EDITION, EXPANDED

TAKING SIDES

Clashing Views on
Educational Issues
FOURTEENTH EDITION, EXPANDED

Selected, Edited, and with Introductions by

James Wm. Noll
University of Maryland

McGraw Hill **Contemporary Learning Series**
2460 Kerper Blvd., Dubuque, IA 52001

Visit us on the Internet
http://www.mhcls.com

For Stephanie and Sonja

Photo Acknowledgment
Cover image: Rim Light/PhotoLink/Getty Images
Christopher Merrigan/The McGraw-Hill Companies, Inc.
Punchstock
Photodisc/Getty Images

Cover Acknowledgment
Maggie Lytle

Copyright © 2008 by McGraw-Hill Contemporary Learning Series,
A Division of The McGraw-Hill Companies, Inc., Dubuque, Iowa 52001

Copyright law prohibits the reproduction, storage, or transmission in any form by any means of any
portion of this publication without the express written permission of McGraw-Hill Contemporary
Learning Series and of the copyright holder (if different) of the part of the publication to be
reproduced. The Guidelines for Classroom Copying endorsed by Congress explicitly
state that unauthorized copying may not be used to create, to replace, or to
substitute for anthologies, compilations, or collective works.

Taking Sides ® is a registered trademark of the McGraw-Hill Companies, Inc.

Manufactured in the United States of America

Fourteenth Edition, Expanded

123456789DOCDOC987

Library of Congress Cataloging-in-Publication Data
Main entry under title:
Taking sides: clashing views on educational issues/selected, edited, and
with introductions by James Wm. Noll.—14th ed.
Includes bibliographical references and index.
1. Education-United States. I. Noll, James Wm., *comp.*
370.973

MHID: 0-07-339717-2
ISBN: 978-0-07-339717-7
ISSN: 1091-8817

Printed on Recycled Paper

Preface

Controversy is the basis of change and often of improvement. Its lack signifies the presence of complacency, the authoritarian limitation of viewpoint expression, or the absence of realistic alternatives to the existing circumstances. An articulate presentation of a point of view on a controversial matter breathes new life into abiding human and social concerns. Controversy prompts reexamination and perhaps renewal.

Education is controversial. Arguments over the most appropriate aims, the most propitious means, and the most effective control have raged over the centuries. Particularly in the United States, where the systematic effort to provide education has been more democratically dispersed and more varied than elsewhere, educational issues have been contentiously debated. Philosophers, psychologists, sociologists, professional educators, lobbyists, government officials, school boards, local pressure groups, taxpayers, parents, and students have all voiced their views.

This book presents opposing or sharply varying viewpoints on educational issues of current concern. Part 1 offers consideration of four basic theoretical issues that have been discussed by scholars and practitioners in past decades and are still debated today: the purpose of education, curriculum content and its imposition upon the young, the motivational atmosphere of schools, and the philosophical underpinning of the process of education. Part 2 features six issues that are fundamental to understanding the present circumstances that shape American education: citizenship training, school desegregation, religion in public schools, federal efforts to improve the system, high-stakes testing, and the definition of "public" schooling. Part 3 examines more specific issues currently being discussed: vouchers and choice plans, charter schools, home schooling, inclusion policies, the factor of school size and class size, bilingual education, discipline policies, homework, computer use, merit pay for teachers, and alternative teacher certification.

I have made every effort to select views from a wide range of thinkers—philosophers, psychologists, sociologists, professional educators, political leaders, historians, researchers, and gadflies.

Each issue is accompanied by an *introduction*, which sets the stage for the debate, and each issue concludes with a *postscript* that considers other views on the issue and suggests additional readings. I have also provided relevant Internet site addresses (URLs) on the *On the Internet* page that accompanies each part opener. By combining the material in this volume with the informational background provided by a good introductory textbook, the student should be prepared to address the problems confronting schools today.

My hope is that students will find challenges in the material presented here—provocations that will inspire them to better understand the roots of educational controversy, to attain a greater awareness of possible alternatives in dealing with the various issues, and to stretch their personal powers of creative thinking in the search for more promising resolutions of the problems.

Changes to this edition This 14th edition offers five new issues (two of which were featured in the expanded version of the previous edition): Is Constructivism the Best Philosophy of Education? (Issue 4), Can the Public Schools Produce Good Citizens? (Issue 5), Has Resegregation Diminished the Impact of *Brown?* (Issue 6), Should "Public Schooling" Be Redefined? (Issue 10), and Is Home Schooling a Danger to American Society? (Issue 13). In addition, new selections have been placed in Issue 9 on high-stakes testing, Issue 17 on zero-tolerance policies, and Issue 19 on computer technology. In all there are 14 new articles in this edition.

A word to the instructor An *Instructor's Manual With Test Questions* (multiple choice and essay) is available through the publisher for the instructor using *Taking Sides* in the classroom. A general guidebook, called *Using Taking Sides in the Classroom*, which discusses methods and techniques for integrating the procon approach into any classroom setting, is also available. An online version of *Using Taking Sides in the Classroom* and a correspondence service for Taking Sides adopters can be found at http://www.mhcls.com/usingts/.

Taking Sides: Clashing Views on Controversial Educational Issues is only one title in the Taking Sides series. If you are interested in seeing the table of contents for any of the other titles, please visit the Taking Sides Web site at http://www.mhcls.com/takingsides/.

Acknowledgments I am thankful for the kind and efficient assistance given to me by Susan Brusch, Larry Loeppke, and the other members of the production staff at McGraw-Hill Contemporary Learning Series.

James Wm. Noll
University of Maryland

Contents In Brief

Contents

Child development professor David Elkind contends that the philosophical positions found in constructivism, though often difficult to apply, are necessary elements in a meaningful reform of educational practices. Jamin Carson, an assistant professor of education and former high school teacher, offers a close critique of constructivism and argues that the philosophy of objectivism is a more realistic and usable basis for the process of education.

PART 2 CURRENT FUNDAMENTAL ISSUES 67

Issue 5. Can the Public Schools Produce Good Citizens? 68

Princeton politics professor Stephen Macedo expresses confidence in the public schools' ability to teach students to become active participants in our democracy, suggesting that naysayers may wish to undermine all public institutions. Thomas B. Fordham Foundation president Chester E. Finn, Jr., contends that the diversity of the American population makes the public schools ill-equipped to produce the engaged citizens our democracy requires.

Issue 6. Has Resegregation Diminished the Impact of *Brown*? 84

Harvard professor Gary Orfield and his research associates present evidence that school resegregation has been increasing almost everywhere in recent years, placing a cloud over the fiftieth anniversary celebration of the *Brown* decision. Journalist and commentator Juan Williams, while recognizing the slow pace and backward steps involved in school desegregation, argues that the social and cultural changes inaugurated by *Brown* mark it as a monumental ruling.

Issue 7. Have Public Schools Adequately Accommodated Religion? 98

Edd Doerr, executive director of Americans for Religious Liberty, asserts that a fair balance between free exercise rights and the obligation of

Professor of education Charles L. Glenn argues that the Supreme Court's decision in *Zelman v. Simmons-Harris* is an immediate antidote to the public school's secularist philosophy. Professor of government Paul E. Peterson, while welcoming the decision, contends that the barricades against widespread use of vouchers in religious schools will postpone any lasting effects.

Former assistant secretaries of education Chester E. Finn, Jr., and Bruno V. Manno, along with Gregg Vanourek, vice president of the Charter School Division of the K12 education program, provide an update on the charter school movement, which, they contend, is reinventing public education. School superintendent Marc F. Bernstein sees increasing racial and social class segregation, church-state issues, and financial harm as outgrowths of the charter school movement.

Education professor Michael W. Apple examines the larger context of the "conservative restoration" in which much of the home schooling movement is lodged and sounds a number of socio-cultural warnings. Brian D. Ray, president of the National Home Education Research Institute, feels that in the historical struggle over the control of influences on the younger generation, home schooling has strengthened the side of freedom and democracy.

Education consultant Richard A. Villa and education professor Jacqueline S. Thousand review the implementation of the Individuals with Disabilities Education Act and suggest strategies for fulfilling its intentions. Education professor Karen Agne argues that legislation to include students with all sorts of disabilities has had mostly negative effects and contributes to the exodus from public schools.

Education dean Patricia A. Wasley contends that schools and class-rooms must be small if they are to be places where students' personal and learning needs are met. Policy analyst Kirk A. Johnson, of the Heritage Foundation, argues that while small scale is a popular concept when it comes to class size, the cost is not justified by research findings.

Rosalie Pedalino Porter, director of the Research in English Acquisition and Development Institute, offers a close examination of the major research studies and concludes that there is no consistent support for transitional bilingual education programs. Richard Rothstein, a research associate of the Economic Policy Institute, reviews the history of bilingual education and argues that, although many problems currently exist, there is no compelling reason to abandon these programs.

Albert Shanker, president of the American Federation of Teachers (AFT), advocates a "get tough" policy for dealing with violent and disruptive students in order to send a clear message that all students are responsible for their own behavior. Alfie Kohn, author of numerous books on education, contends that heavy-handed disciplinary procedures fail to get at the causes of aggression and are detrimental to the building of a school culture of safety and caring.

Biology teacher and science department administrator Mark Terry warns of the so-called Wedge Strategy being employed by the Discovery Institute to incorporate the "intelligent design" approach into the public school science curriculum. Attorney Dan Peterson presents fact-based arguments that separate "intelligent design" from previous campaigns for inclusion of "creation science" in the biology curriculum and cause evolution theorists to possibly adjust their standard positions.

Issue 23.   Is There a Crisis in the Education of Boys?   421

Michael Gurian and Kathy Stevens, researchers in gender differences and brain-based learning at the Gurian Institute, contend that our schools, structurally and functionally, do not fulfill gender-specific needs and that this is particularly harmful to boys. Sara Mead, a senior policy analyst at Education Sector in Washington, D.C., assembles long-term data from the federally sponsored National Assessment of Educational Progress to show that the "crisis" emphasis is unwarranted and detracts from broader social justice issues.

Introduction

Ways of Thinking About Educational Issues

James Wm. Noll

Concern about the quality of education has been expressed by philosophers, politicians, and parents for centuries. There has been a perpetual and unresolved debate regarding the definition of education, the relationship between school and society, the distribution of decision-making power in educational matters, and the means for improving all aspects of the educational enterprise.

In recent decades the growing influence of thinking drawn from the humanities and the behavioral and social sciences has brought about the development of interpretive, normative, and critical perspectives, which have sharpened the focus on educational concerns. These perspectives have allowed scholars and researchers to closely examine the contextual variables, value orientations, and philosophical and political assumptions that shape both the status quo and reform efforts.

The study of education involves the application of many perspectives to the analysis of "what is and how it got that way" and "what can be and how we can get there." Central to such study are the prevailing philosophical assumptions, theories, and visions that find their way into real-life educational situations. The application situation, with its attendant political pressures, sociocultural differences, community expectations, parental influence, and professional problems, provides a testing ground for contending theories and ideals.

This "testing ground" image applies only insofar as the status quo is malleable enough to allow the examination and trial of alternative views. Historically, institutionalized education has been characteristically rigid. As a testing ground of ideas, it has often lacked an orientation encouraging innovation and futuristic thinking. Its political grounding has usually been conservative.

As social psychologist Allen Wheelis points out in *The Quest for Identity* (1958), social institutions by definition tend toward solidification and protectionism. His depiction of the dialectical development of civilizations centers on the tension between the security and authoritarianism of "institutional processes" and the dynamism and change-orientation of "instrumental processes."

The field of education seems to graphically illustrate this observation. Educational practices are primarily tradition bound. The twentieth-century reform movement, spurred by the ideas of John Dewey, A. S. Neill, and a host of critics who campaigned for change in the 1960s, challenged the structural rigidity of schooling. In more recent decades, reformers have either attempted to restore uniformity in the curriculum and in assessment of results or campaigned for the support of alternatives to the public school monopoly. The latter group comes from both the right and the left of the political spectrum.

We are left with the abiding questions: What is an "educated" person? What should be the primary purpose of organized education? Who should control the decisions influencing the educational process? Should the schools follow society or lead it toward change? Should schooling be compulsory?

Long-standing forces have molded a wide variety of responses to these fundamental questions. The religious impetus, nationalistic fervor, philosophical ideas, the march of science and technology, varied interpretations of "societal needs," and the desire to use the schools as a means for social reform have been historically influential. In recent times other factors have emerged to contribute to the complexity of the search for answers—social class differences, demographic shifts, increasing bureaucratization, the growth of the textbook industry, the changing financial base for schooling, teacher unionization, and strengthening of parental and community pressure groups.

The struggle to find the most appropriate answers to these questions now involves, as in the past, an interplay of societal aims, educational purposes, and individual intentions. Moral development, the quest for wisdom, citizenship training, socioeconomic improvement, mental discipline, the rational control of life, job preparation, liberation of the individual, freedom of inquiry—these and many others continue to be topics of discourse on education.

A detailed historical perspective on these questions and topics may be gained by reading the interpretations of noted scholars in the field. R. Freeman Butts has written a brief but effective summary portrayal in "Search for Freedom—The Story of American Education," *NEA Journal* (March 1960). A partial listing of other sources includes R. Freeman Butts and Lawrence Cremin, *A History of Education in American Culture*; S. E. Frost, Jr., *Historical and Philosophical Foundations of Western Education*; Harry Good and Edwin Teller, *A History of Education*; Adolphe Meyer, *An Educational History of the American People*; Robert L. Church and Michael W. Sedlak, *Education in the United States: An Interpretive History*; Merle Curti, *The Social Ideas of American Educators*; Henry J. Perkinson, *The Imperfect Panacea: American Faith in Education, 1865–1965*; Clarence Karier, *Man, Society, and Education*; V. T. Thayer, *Formative Ideas in American Education*; H. Warren Button and Eugene F. Provenzo, Jr., *History of Education and Culture in America*; David Tyack and Elisabeth Hansot, *Managers of Virtue: Public School Leadership in America, 1820–1980*; Joel Spring, *The American School, 1642–1990*; S. Alexander Rippa, *Education in a Free Society: An American History*; John D. Pulliam, *History of Education in America*; Edward Stevens and George H. Wood, *Justice, Ideology, and Education*; and Walter Feinberg and Jonas F. Soltis, *School and Society*.

These and other historical accounts of the development of schooling demonstrate the continuing need to address educational questions in terms of cultural and social dynamics. A careful analysis of contemporary education demands attention not only to the historical interpretation of developmental influences but also to the philosophical forces that define formal education and the social and cultural factors that form the basis of informal education.

Examining Viewpoints

In his book *A New Public Education* (1976), Seymour Itzkoff examines the interplay between informal and formal education, concluding that economic and technological expansion have pulled people away from the informal culture by placing a premium on success in formal education. This has brought about a reactive search for less artificial educational contexts within the informal cultural community, which recognizes the impact of individual personality in shaping educational experiences.

This search for a reconstructed philosophical base for education has produced a barrage of critical commentary. Those who seek radical change in education characterize the present schools as mindless, manipulative, factory-like, bureaucratic institutions that offer little sense of community, pay scant attention to personal meaning, fail to achieve curricular integration, and maintain a psychological atmosphere of competitiveness, tension, fear, and alienation. Others deplore the ideological movement away from the formal organization of education, fearing an abandonment of standards, a dilution of the curriculum, an erosion of intellectual and behavioral discipline, and a decline in adult and institutional authority.

Students of education (whether prospective teachers, practicing professionals, or interested laypeople) must examine closely the assumptions and values underlying alternative positions in order to clarify their own viewpoints. This tri-level task may best be organized around the basic themes of purpose, power, and reform. These themes offer access to the theoretical grounding of actions in the field of education, to the political grounding of such actions, and to the future orientation of action decisions.

A general model for the examination of positions on educational issues includes the following dimensions: identification of the viewpoint, recognition of the stated or implied assumptions underlying the viewpoint, analysis of the validity of the supporting argument, and evaluation of the conclusions and action-suggestions of the originator of the position. The stated or implied assumptions may be derived from a philosophical or religious orientation, from scientific theory, from social or personal values, or from accumulated experience. Acceptance by the reader of an author's assumptions opens the way for a receptive attitude regarding the specific viewpoint expressed and its implications for action. The argument offered in justification of the viewpoint may be based on logic, common experience, controlled experiments, information and data, legal precedents, emotional appeals, and/or a host of other persuasive devices.

Holding the basic model in mind, readers of the positions presented in this volume (or anywhere else, for that matter) can examine the constituent elements of arguments—basic assumptions, viewpoint statements, supporting evidence, conclusions, and suggestions for action. The careful reader will accept or reject the individual elements of the total position. One might see reasonableness in a viewpoint and its justification but be unable to accept the assumptions on which it is based. Or one might accept the flow of argument from assumptions to viewpoint to evidence but find illogic or impracticality in the stated conclusions and suggestions for action. In any event, the reader's personal view is tested and honed through the process of analyzing the views of others.

Philosophical Considerations

Historically, organized education has been initiated and instituted to serve many purposes-spiritual salvation, political socialization, moral uplift, societal stability, social mobility, mental discipline, vocational efficiency, and social reform, among others. The various purposes have usually reflected the dominant philosophical conception of human nature and the prevailing assumptions about the relationship between the individual and society. At any given time, competing conceptions may vie for dominance-social conceptions, economic conceptions, conceptions that emphasize spirituality, or conceptions that stress the uniqueness and dignity of the individual, for example.

These considerations of human nature and individual-society relationships are grounded in philosophical assumptions, and these assumptions find their way to such practical domains as schooling. In Western civilization there has been an identifiable (but far from consistent and clear-cut) historical trend in the basic assumptions about reality, knowledge, values, and the human condition. This trend, made manifest in the philosophical positions of idealism, realism, pragmatism, and existentialism, has involved a shift in emphasis from the spiritual world to nature to human behavior to the social individual to the free individual, and from eternal ideas to fixed natural laws to social interaction to the inner person.

The idealist tradition, which dominated much of philosophical and educational thought until the eighteenth and nineteenth centuries, separates the changing, imperfect, material world and the permanent, perfect, spiritual or mental world. As Plato saw it, for example, human beings and all other physical entities are particular manifestations of an ideal reality that in material existence humans can never fully know. The purpose of education is to bring us closer to the absolute ideals, pure forms, and universal standards that exist spiritually, by awakening and strengthening our rational powers. For Plato, a curriculum based on mathematics, logic, and music would serve this purpose, especially in the training of leaders whose rationality must exert control over emotionality and baser instincts.

Against this tradition, which shaped the liberal arts curriculum in schools for centuries, the realism of Aristotle, with its finding of the "forms" of things *within* the material world, brought an emphasis on scientific investigation and on environmental factors in the development of human potential. This fundamental view has influenced two philosophical movements in education: naturalism, based on following or gently assisting nature (as in the approaches of John Amos Comenius, Jean-Jacques Rousseau, and Johann Heinrich Pestalozzi), and scientific realism, based on uncovering the natural laws of human behavior and shaping the educational environment to maximize their effectiveness (as in the approaches of John Locke, Johann Friedrich Herbart, and Edward Thorndike).

In the twentieth century, two philosophical forces (pragmatism and existentialism) have challenged these traditions. Each has moved primary attention away from fixed spiritual or natural influences and toward the individual as shaper of knowledge and values. The pragmatic position, articulated in America by Charles Sanders Peirce, William James, and John Dewey, turns from metaphysical abstractions toward concrete results of action. In a world of change and relativity, human beings must forge their own truths and values as they interact with their environments and each other. The European-based philosophy of existentialism, emerging from such thinkers as Gabriel Marcel, Martin Buber, Martin Heidegger, and Jean-Paul Sartre, has more recently influenced education here. Existentialism places the burdens of freedom, choice, and responsibility squarely on the individual, viewing the current encroachment of external forces and the tendency of people to "escape from freedom" as a serious diminishment of our human possibilities.

These many theoretical slants contend for recognition and acceptance as we continue the search for broad purposes in education and as we attempt to create curricula, methodologies, and learning environments that fulfill our stated purposes. This is carried out, of course, in the real world of the public schools in which social, political, and economic forces often predominate.

Power and Control

Plato, in the fourth century B.C., found existing education manipulative and confining and, in the *Republic*, described a meritocratic approach designed to nurture intellectual powers so as to form and sustain a rational society. Refor-moriented as Plato's suggestions were, he nevertheless insisted on certain restrictions and controls so that his particular version of the ideal could be met.

The ways and means of education have been fertile grounds for power struggles throughout history. Many educational efforts have been initiated by religious bodies, often creating a conflict situation when secular authorities have moved into the field. Schools have usually been seen as repositories of culture and social values and, as such, have been overseen by the more conservative forces in society. To others, bent on social reform, the schools have been treated as a spawning ground for change. Given these basic political forces, conflict is inevitable.

When one speaks of the control of education, the range of influence is indeed wide. Political influences, governmental actions, court decisions, professional militancy, parental power, and student assertion all contribute to the phenomenon of control. And the domain of control is equally broad-school finances, curriculum, instructional means and objectives, teacher certification, accountability, student discipline, censorship of school materials, determination of access and opportunity, and determination of inclusion and exclusion.

The general topic of power and control leads to a multitude of questions: Who should make policy decisions? Must the schools be puppets of the government? Can the schools function in the vanguard of social change? Can cultural indoctrination be avoided? Can the schools lead the way to full social integration? Can the effects of social class be eradicated? Can and should the schools teach values? Dealing with such questions is complicated by the increasing power of the federal government in educational matters. Congressional legislation has broadened substantially from the early land grants and aid to agricultural and vocational programs to more recent laws covering aid to federally impacted areas, school construction aid, student loans and fellowships, support for several academic areas of the curriculum, work-study programs, compensatory education, employment opportunities for youth, adult education, aid to libraries, teacher preparation, educational research, career education, education of the handicapped, and equal opportunity for females. This proliferation of areas of influence has caused the federal administrative bureaucracy to blossom from its meager beginnings in 1867 into a cabinet-level Department of Education in 1979.

State legislatures and state departments of education have also grown in power, handling greater percentages of school appropriations and controlling basic curricular decisions, attendance laws, accreditation, research, and so on. Local school boards, once the sole authorities in policy making, now share the role with higher governmental echelons as the financial support sources shift away from the local scene. Simultaneously, strengthened teacher organizations and increasingly vocal pressure groups at the local, state, and national levels have forced a widening of the base for policy decisions.

Some Concluding Remarks

The schools often seem to be either facing backward or completely absorbed in the tribulations of the present, lacking a vision of possible futures that might guide current decisions. The present is inescapable, obviously, and certainly the historical and philosophical underpinnings of the present situation must be understood, but true improvement often requires a break with conventionality—a surge toward a desired future.

The radical reform critique of government-sponsored compulsory schooling has depicted organized education as a form of cultural or political imprisonment that traps young people in an artificial and mainly irrelevant environment and rewards conformity and docility while inhibiting curiosity and creativity. Constructive reform ideas that have come from this critique include the creation of open classrooms, the de-emphasis of external motivators, the diversification of educational experience, and the building of a true sense of community within the instructional environment.

Starting with Francis Wayland Parker's schools in Quincy, Massachusetts, and John Dewey's laboratory school at the University of Chicago around the turn of the twentieth century, the campaign to make schools into more productive and humane places has been relentless. The duplication of A. S. Neill's Summerhill model in the free school movement in the 1960s, the open classroom/open space experiments, the several curricular variations, and the emergence of schools without walls, charter schools, privatization of management, and home schooling across the country testify to the desire to reform the present system or to build alternatives to it.

The progressive education movement, the development of "life adjustment" goals and curricula, and the "whole person" theories of educational psychology moved the schools toward an expanded concept of schooling that embraced new subject matters and new approaches to discipline during the first half of this century. Since the 1950s, however, pressure for a return to a narrower concept of schooling as intellectual training has sparked new waves of debate. Out of this situation have come attempts by educators and academicians to design new curricular approaches in the basic subject matter areas, efforts by private foundations to stimulate organizational innovations and to improve the training of teachers, and federal government support of educational technology. Yet criticism of the schools abounds. The schools, according to many who use their services, remain too factorylike, too age-segregated, and too custodial. Alternative paths are still sought-paths that would allow action-learning, work-study, and a diversity of ways to achieve success.

H. G.Wells has told us that human history becomes more and more a race between education and catastrophe. What is needed in order to win this race is the generation of new ideas regarding cultural change, human relationships, ethical norms, the uses of technology, and the quality of life. These new ideas, of course, may be old ideas newly applied. One could do worse, in thinking through the problem of improving the quality of education, than to turn to the third-century philosopher Plotinus, who called for an education directed to "the outer, the inner, and the whole." For Plotinus, "the outer" represented the public person, or the socioeconomic dimension of the total human being; "the inner" reflected the subjective dimension, the uniquely experiencing individual, or the "I"; and "the whole" signified the universe of meaning and relatedness, or the realm of human, natural, and spiritual connectedness. It would seem that education must address all of these dimensions if it is to truly help people in the lifelong struggle to shape a meaningful existence. If educational experiences can be improved in these directions, the end result might be people who are not just filling space, filling time, or filling a social role, but who are capable of saying something worthwhile with their lives.

On the Internet . . .

The Center for Dewey Studies

Southern Illinois University site offers a wealth of source materials on the ideas of philosopher-educator John Dewey and the progressive education movement.

http://www.siu.edu/~deweyctr

The National Paideia Center

Promotes and supports efforts of educators who are implementing the long-term systemic school reform known as the Paideia Program based on the ideas of philosopher Mortimer J. Adler.

http://www.paideia.org

Coalition of Essential Schools

Offers facts and ideas on this national curriculum movement dedicated to improving teaching and enabling education reform.

http://www.essentialschools.org

Learn in Freedom!

Provides ideas, resources, and encouragement for unschoolers, homeschoolers, and all learners within or without school.

http://www.learninfreedom.org

Behaviorism

Stanford Encyclopedia of Philosophy offers articles on B. F. Skinner and other behaviorists plus links to other sites.

http://plato.stanford.edu/entries/behaviorism

The Association for Humanistic Psychology

Features material on the theories of Carl Rogers, Abraham Maslow, Rollo May, and others, as well as links to web resources.

http://ahpweb.org

Constructivism vs. Instructivism

Offers research on two dominant pedagogical approaches and the philosophical assumptions lying behind them.

http://www.ed.sc.edu/caw/webbarton.htm

PART 1

Basic Theoretical Issues

*W*hat *is the basic purpose of education? How should the curriculum be organized and how much control should students have over their own development? What is the best way to teach and motivate students to learn? What philosophy of education should guide the process of education? These questions have been discussed throughout the history of American education and continue to be debated today. In this section, some major figures from the 20th century— John Dewey, Robert M. Hutchins, Mortimer J. Adler, John Holt, B. F. Skinner, and Carl R. Rogers—and two current scholars in the field of education—David Elkind and Jamin Carson—address these basic questions.*

Issue 1. Should Schooling Be Based on Social Experiences?

Issue 2. Should the Curriculum Be Standardized for All?

Issue 3. Should Behaviorism Shape Educational Practices?

Issue 4. Is Constructivism the Best Philosophy of Education?

ISSUE 1

Should Schooling Be Based on Social Experiences?

YES: John Dewey, from *Experience and Education* (Macmillan, 1938)

NO: Robert M. Hutchins, from The *Conflict in Education in a Democratic Society* (Harper & Row, 1953)

ISSUE SUMMARY

YES: Philosopher John Dewey suggests a reconsideration of traditional approaches to schooling, giving fuller attention to the social development of the learner and the quality of his or her total experience.

NO: Robert M. Hutchins, noted educator and one-time chancellor of the University of Chicago, argues for a liberal arts education geared to the development of intellectual powers.

Throughout history, organized education has served many purposes-the transmission of tradition, knowledge, and skills; the acculturation and socialization of the young; the building and preserving of political-economic systems; the provision of opportunity for social mobility; the enhancement of the quality of life; and the cultivation of individual potential, among others. At any given time, schools pursue a number of such goals, but the elucidation of a primary or overriding goal, which gives focus to all others, has been a source of continuous contention.

Schooling in America has been extended in the last 100 years to vast numbers of young people, and during this time the argument over aims has gained momentum. At the turn of the century, John Dewey was raising serious questions about the efficacy of the prevailing approach to schooling. He believed that schooling was often arid, pedantic, and detached from the real lives of children and youths. In establishing his laboratory school at the University of Chicago, Dewey hoped to demonstrate that experiences provided by schools could be meaningful extensions of the normal social activities of learners, having as their primary aim the full experiential growth of the individual.

In order to accomplish this, Dewey sought to bring the learner into an active and intimate relationship with the subject matter. The problem-solving, or inquiry, approach that he and his colleagues at Columbia University in New York City devised became the cornerstone of the "new education"— the progressive education movement.

In 1938 Dewey himself (as expressed in the selection that follows) sounded a note of caution to progressive educators who may have abandoned too completely the traditional disciplines in their attempt to link schooling with the needs and interests of the learners. Having spawned an educational revolution, Dewey, in his later years, emerges as more of a compromiser.

In that same year, William C. Bagley, in "An Essentialists' Platform for the Advancement of American Education," harshly criticized what he felt were antiintellectual excesses promulgated by progressivism. In the 1950s and 1960s this theme was elaborated on by other academics, among them Robert M. Hutchins, Hyman Rickover, Arthur Bestor, and Max Rafferty, who demanded a return to intellectual discipline, higher standards, and moral guidance.

Hutchins' critique of Dewey's pragmatic philosophy was perhaps the best reasoned. He felt that the emphasis on immediate needs and desires of students and the focus on change and relativism detracted from the development of the intellectual skills needed for the realization of human potential.

A renewal of scholarly interest in the philosophical and educational ideas of both Dewey and Hutchins has resulted in a number of books, among which are *Hutchins' University: A Memoir of the University of Chicago* by William H. O'Neill (1991); *Robert M. Hutchins: Portrait of an Educator* by Mary Ann Dzuback (1991); *John Dewey and American Democracy* by Robert B.Westbrook (1991); *The End of Epistemology: Dewey and His Allies on the Spectator Theory of Knowledge* by Christopher B. Kulp (1992); and *The Promise of Pragmatism* by John Patrick Diggins (1994). Their continuing influence is charted by Rene Vincente Arcilla in "Metaphysics in Education After Hutchins and Dewey," *Teachers College Record* (Winter 1991).

More recent articles on the legacies of Dewey's progressivism and the traditionalism of Hutchins include "Education and the Pursuit of Happiness: John Dewey's Sympathetic Character," by Sam Stack, *Journal of Thought* (Summer 1996); "A Conversation Between John Dewey and Rudolph Steiner," by Jacques Ensign, *Educational Theory* (Spring 1996); "Toward a Theory of Progressive Education?" by Jurgen Herbst, *History of Education Quarterly* (Spring 1997); "Why Traditional Education Is More Progressive," by E. D. Hirsch, Jr., *The American Enterprise* (March 1997); "The Plight of Children Is Our Plight," by William H. Schubert, *Educational Horizons* (Winter 1998); and Diana Schaub's "Can Liberal Education Survive Liberal Democracy?" *The Public Interest* (Spring 2002).

In the following selections, Dewey charts what he considers a necessary shift from the abstractness and isolation of traditional schooling to the concreteness and vitality of the newer concept. Hutchins dissects the assumptions underlying Dewey's position and puts forth his own theory based on the premise that human nature is constant and functions the same in every society.

Experience and Education

Mankind likes to think in terms of extreme opposites. It is given to formulating its beliefs in terms of *Either-Ors*, between which it recognizes no intermediate possibilities. When forced to recognize that the extremes cannot be acted upon, it is still inclined to hold that they are all right in theory but that when it comes to practical matters circumstances compel us to compromise. Educational philosophy is no exception. The history of educational theory is marked by opposition between the idea that education is development from within and that it is formation from without; that it is based upon natural endowments and that education is a process of overcoming natural inclination and substituting in its place habits acquired under external pressure.

At present, the opposition, so far as practical affairs of the school are concerned, tends to take the form of contrast between traditional and progressive education. If the underlying ideas of the former are formulated broadly, without the qualifications required for accurate statement, they are found to be about as follows: The subject-matter of education consists of bodies of information and of skills that have been worked out in the past; therefore, the chief business of the school is to transmit them to the new generation. In the past, there have also been developed standards and rules of conduct; moral training consists of forming habits of action in conformity with these rules and standards. Finally, the general pattern of school organization (by which I mean the relations of pupils to one another and to the teachers) constitutes the school as a kind of institution sharply marked off from other social institutions. Call up in imagination the ordinary schoolroom, its time schedules, schemes of classification, of examination and promotion, of rules of order, and I think you will grasp what is meant by "pattern of organization." If then you contrast this scene with what goes on in the family, for example, you will appreciate what is meant by the school being a kind of institution sharply marked off from any other form of social organization.

The three characteristics just mentioned fix the aims and methods of instruction and discipline. The main purpose or objective is to prepare the young for future responsibilities and for success in life, by means of acquisition of the organized bodies of information and prepared forms of skill which comprehend the material of instruction. Since the subject-matter as well as standards of proper conduct are handed down from the past, the attitude of pupils must, upon the whole, be one of docility, receptivity, and obedience.

From John Dewey, *Experience and Education* (Macmillan, 1938). Copyright © 1938 by Kappa Delta Pi, an International Honor Society in Education. Reprinted by permission.

Books, especially textbooks, are the chief representatives of the lore and wisdom of the past, while teachers are the organs through which pupils are brought into effective connection with the material. Teachers are the agents through which knowledge and skills are communicated and rules of conduct enforced.

I have not made this brief summary for the purpose of criticizing the underlying philosophy. The rise of what is called new education and progressive schools is of itself a product of discontent with traditional education. In effect it is a criticism of the latter. When the implied criticism is made explicit it reads somewhat as follows: The traditional scheme is, in essence, one of imposition from above and from outside. It imposes adult standards, subject-matter, and methods upon those who are only growing slowly toward maturity. The gap is so great that the required subject-matter, the methods of learning and of behaving are foreign to the existing capacities of the young. They are beyond the reach of the experience the young learners already possess. Consequently, they must be imposed; even though good teachers will use devices of art to cover up the imposition so as to relieve it of obviously brutal features.

But the gulf between the mature or adult products and the experience and abilities of the young is so wide that the very situation forbids much active participation by pupils in the development of what is taught. Theirs is to do— and learn, as it was the part of the six hundred to do and die. Learning here means acquisition of what already is incorporated in books and in the heads of the elders. Moreover, that which is taught is thought of as essentially static. It is taught as a finished product, with little regard either to the ways in which it was originally built up or to changes that will surely occur in the future. It is to a large extent the cultural product of societies that assumed the future would be much like the past, and yet it is used as educational food in a society where change is the rule, not the exception.

If one attempts to formulate the philosophy of education implicit in the practices of the new education, we may, I think, discover certain common principles amid the variety of progressive schools now existing. To imposition from above is opposed expression and cultivation of individuality; to external discipline is opposed free activity; to learning from texts and teachers, learning through experience; to acquisition of isolated skills and techniques by drill, is opposed acquisition of them as means of attaining ends which make direct vital appeal; to preparation for a more or less remote future is opposed making the most of the opportunities of present life; to static aims and materials is opposed acquaintance with a changing world.

Now, all principles by themselves are abstract. They become concrete only in the consequences which result from their application. Just because the principles set forth are so fundamental and far-reaching, everything depends upon the interpretation given them as they are put into practice in the school and the home. It is at this point that the reference made earlier to *Either-Or* philosophies becomes peculiarly pertinent. The general philosophy of the new education may be sound, and yet the difference in abstract principles will not decide the way in which the moral and intellectual preference involved shall be worked out in practice. There is always the danger in a new movement that in rejecting the aims and methods of that which it would supplant, it may develop its principles negatively rather than positively and constructively. Then it takes its clew in practice from that which is rejected instead of from the constructive development its own philosophy.

I take it that the fundamental unity of the newer philosophy is found in the idea that there is an intimate and necessary relation between the processes of actual experience and education. If this be true, then a positive and constructive development of its own basic idea depends upon having a correct idea of experience. Take, for example, the question of organized subject-matter. . . . The problem for progressive education is: What is the place and meaning of subject-matter and of organization *within* experience? How does subject-matter function? Is there anything inherent in experience which tends towards progressive organization of its contents? What results follow when the materials of experience are not progressively organized? A philosophy which proceeds on the basis of rejection, of sheer opposition, will neglect these questions. It will tend to suppose that because the old education was based on ready-made organization, therefore it suffices to reject the principle of organization *in toto*, instead of striving to discover what it means and how it is to be attained on the basis of experience. We might go through all the points of difference between the new and the old education and reach similar conclusions. When external control is rejected, the problem becomes that of finding the factors of control that are inherent within experience. When external authority is rejected, it does not follow that all authority should be rejected, but rather that there is need to search for a more effective source of authority. Because the older education imposed the knowledge, methods, and the rules of conduct of the mature person upon the young, it does not follow, except upon the basis of the extreme *Either-Or* philosophy, that the knowledge and skill of the mature person has no directive value for the experience of the immature. On the contrary, basing education upon personal experience may mean more multiplied and more intimate contacts between the mature and the immature than ever existed in the traditional school, and consequently more, rather than less, guidance by others. The problem, then, is: how these contacts can be established without violating the principle of learning through personal experience. The solution of this problem requires a well thought-out philosophy of the social factors that operate in the constitution of individual experience.

What is indicated in the foregoing remarks is that the general principles of the new education do not of themselves solve any of the problems of the actual or practical conduct and management of progressive schools. Rather, they set new problems which have to be worked out on the basis of a new philosophy of experience. The problems are not even recognized, to say nothing of being solved, when it is assumed that it suffices to reject the ideas and practices of the old education and then go to the opposite extreme. Yet I am sure that you will appreciate what is meant when I say that many of the newer schools tend to make little or nothing of organized subject-matter of study; to proceed as if any form of direction and guidance by adults were an invasion of individual freedom, and as if the idea that education should be concerned with the present and future meant that acquaintance with the past has little or no role to play in education. Without pressing these defects to the point of exaggeration, they at least illustrate what is meant by a theory and practice of education which proceeds negatively or by reaction against what has been current in education rather than by a positive and constructive development of purposes, methods, and subject-matter on the foundation of a theory of experience and its educational potentialities.

It is not too much to say that an educational philosophy which professes to be based on the idea of freedom may become as dogmatic as ever was the traditional education which is reacted against. For any theory and set of practices is dogmatic which is not based upon critical examination of its own underlying principles. Let us say that the new education emphasizes the freedom of the learner. Very well. A problem is now set. What does freedom mean and what are the conditions under which it is capable of realization? Let us say that the kind of external imposition which was so common in the traditional school limited rather than promoted the intellectual and moral development of the young. Again, very well. Recognition of this serious defect sets a problem. Just what is the role of the teacher and of books in promoting the educational development of the immature? Admit that traditional education employed as the subject-matter for study facts and ideas so bound up with the past as to give little help in dealing with the issues of the present and future. Very well. Now we have the problem of discovering the connection which actually exists *within* experience between the achievements of the past and the issues of the present. We have the problem of ascertaining how acquaintance with the past may be translated into a potent instrumentality for dealing effectively with the future. We may reject knowledge of the past as the *end* of education and thereby only emphasize its importance as a *means.*When we do that we have a problem that is new in the story of education: How shall the young become acquainted with the past in such a way that the acquaintance is a potent agent in appreciation of the living present? . . .

In short, the point I am making is that rejection of the philosophy and practice of traditional education sets a new type of difficult educational problem for those who believe in the new type of education. We shall operate blindly and in confusion until we recognize this fact; until we thoroughly appreciate that departure from the old solves no problems. What is said in the following pages is, accordingly, intended to indicate some of the main problems with which the newer education is confronted and to suggest the main lines along which their solution is to be sought. I assume that amid all uncertainties there is one permanent frame of reference: namely, the organic connection between education and personal experience; or, that the new philosophy of education is committed to some kind of empirical and experimental philosophy. But experience and experiment are not self-explanatory ideas. Rather, their meaning is part of the problem to be explored. To know the meaning of empiricism we need to understand what experience is.

The belief that all genuine education comes about through experience does not mean that all experiences are genuinely or equally educative. Experience and education cannot be directly equated to each other. For some experiences are miseducative. Any experience is miseducative that has the effect of arresting or distorting the growth of further experience. An experience may be such as to engender callousness; it may produce lack of sensitivity and of responsiveness. Then the possibilities of having richer experience in the future are restricted. Again, a given experience may increase a person's automatic skill in a particular direction and yet tend to land him in a groove or rut; the effect again is to narrow the field of further experience. An experience may be immediately enjoyable and yet promote the formation of a slack and careless attitude; this attitude then operates to modify the quality of subsequent experiences so as to prevent a person from getting out of them what they have to give. Again, experiences may be so disconnected from one another that, while each is agreeable or even exciting in itself, they are not linked cumulatively to one another. Energy is then dissipated and a person becomes scatter-brained. Each experience may be lively, vivid, and "interesting," and yet their disconnectedness may artificially generate dispersive, disintegrated, centrifugal habits. The consequence of formation of such habits is inability to control future experiences. They are then taken, either by way of enjoyment or of discontent and revolt, just as they come. Under such circumstances, it is idle to talk of self-control.

Traditional education offers a plethora of examples of experiences of the kinds just mentioned. It is a great mistake to suppose, even tacitly, that the traditional schoolroom was not a place in which pupils had experiences. Yet this is tacitly assumed when progressive education as a plan of learning by experience is placed in sharp opposition to the old. The proper line of attack is that the experiences which were had, by pupils and teachers alike, were largely of a wrong kind. How many students, for example, were rendered callous to ideas, and how many lost the impetus to learn because of the way in which learning was experienced by them? How many acquired special skills by means of automatic drill so that their power of judgment and capacity to act intelligently in new situations was limited? How many came to associate the learning process with ennui and boredom? How many found what they did learn so foreign to the situations of life outside the school as to give them no power of control over the latter? How many came to associate books with dull drudgery, so that they were "conditioned" to all but flashy reading matter?

If I ask these questions, it is not for the sake of wholesale condemnation of the old education. It is for quite another purpose. It is to emphasize the fact, first, that young people in traditional schools do have experiences; and, secondly, that the trouble is not the absence of experiences, but their defective and wrong character—wrong and defective from the standpoint of connection with further experience. The positive side of this point is even more important in connection with progressive education. It is not enough to insist upon the necessity of experience, nor even of activity in experience. Everything depends upon the *quality* of the experience which is had. The quality of an experience has two aspects. There is an immediate aspect of agreeableness or disagreeableness, and there is its influence upon later experiences. The first is obvious and easy to judge. The *effect* of an experience is not borne on its face. It sets a problem to the educator. It is his business to arrange for the kind of experiences which, while they do not repel the student, but rather engage his activities are, nevertheless, more than immediately enjoyable since they promote having desirable future experiences. Just as no man lives or dies to himself, so no experience lives or dies to itself. Wholly independent of desire or intent, every experience lives on in further experiences. Hence the central problem of an education based upon experience is to select the kind of present experiences that live fruitfully and creatively in subsequent experiences.

. . . Here I wish simply to emphasize the importance of this principle [of the continuity of experience] for the philosophy of educative experience. A philosophy of education, like my theory, has to be stated in words, in symbols. But so far as it is more than verbal it is a plan for conducting education. Like any plan, it must be framed with reference to what is to be done and how it is to be done. The more definitely and sincerely it is held that education is a development within, by, and for experience, the more important it is that there shall be clear conceptions of what experience is. Unless experience is so conceived that the result is a plan for deciding upon subject-matter, upon methods of instruction and discipline, and upon material equipment and social organization of the school, it is wholly in the air. It is reduced to a form of words which may be emotionally stirring but for which any other set of words might equally well be substituted unless they indicate operations to be initiated and executed. Just because traditional education was a matter of routine in which the plans and programs were handed down from the past, it does not follow that progressive education is a matter of planless improvisation.

The traditional school could get along without any consistently developed philosophy of education. About all it required in that line was a set of abstract words like culture, discipline, our great cultural heritage, etc., actual guidance being derived not from them but from custom and established routines. Just because progressive schools cannot rely upon established traditions and institutional habits, they must either proceed more or less haphazardly or be directed by ideas which, when they are made articulate and coherent, form a philosophy of education. Revolt against the kind of organization characteristic of the traditional school constitutes a demand for a kind of organization based upon ideas. I think that only slight acquaintance with the history of education is needed to prove that educational reformers and innovators alone have felt the need for a philosophy of education. Those who adhered to the established system needed merely a few fine-sounding words to justify existing practices. The real work was done by habits which were so fixed as to be institutional. The lesson for progressive education is that it requires in an urgent degree, a degree more pressing than was incumbent upon former innovators, a philosophy of education based upon a philosophy of experience.

I remarked incidentally that the philosophy in question is, to paraphrase the saying of Lincoln about democracy, one of education of, by, and for experience. No one of these words, of, by, or for, names anything which is self-evident. Each of them is a challenge to discover and put into operation a principle of order and organization which follows from understanding what education experience signifies.

It is, accordingly, a much more difficult task to work out the kinds of materials, of methods, and of social relationships that are appropriate to the new education than is the case with traditional education. I think many of the difficulties experienced in the conduct of progressive schools and many of the criticisms leveled against them arise from this source. The difficulties are aggravated and the criticisms are increased when it is supposed that the new education is somehow easier than the old. This belief is, I imagine, more or less current. Perhaps it illustrates again the *Either-Or* philosophy, springing from the idea that about all which is required is not to do what is done in traditional schools.

I admit gladly that the new education is *simpler* in principle than the old. It is in harmony with principles of growth, while there is very much which is artificial in the old selection and arrangement of subjects and methods, and artificiality always leads to unnecessary complexity. But the easy and the simple are not identical. To discover what is really simple and to act upon the discovery is an exceedingly difficult task. After the artificial and complex is once institutionally established and ingrained in custom and routine, it is easier to walk in the paths that have been beaten than it is, after taking a new point of view, to work out what is practically involved in the new point of view. The old Ptolemaic astronomical system was more complicated with its cycles and epicycles than the Copernican system. But until organization of actual astronomical phenomena on the ground of the latter principle had been effected the easiest course was to follow the line of least resistance provided by the old intellectual habit. So we come back to the idea that a coherent *theory* of experience, affording positive direction to selection and organization of appropriate educational methods and materials, is required by the attempt to give new direction to the work of the schools. The process is a slow and arduous one. It is a matter of growth, and there are many obstacles which tend to obstruct growth and to deflect it into wrong lines.

. . . [W]e must escape from the tendency to think of organization in terms of the *kind* of organization, whether of content (or subject-matter), or of methods and social relations, that mark traditional education. I think that a good deal of the current opposition to the idea of organization is due to the fact that it is so hard to get away from the picture of the studies of the old school. The moment "organization" is mentioned imagination goes almost automatically to the kind of organization that is familiar, and in revolting against that we are led to shrink from the very idea of any organization. On the other hand, educational reactionaries, who are now gathering force, use the absence of adequate intellectual and moral organization in the newer type of school as proof not only of the need of organization, but to identify any and every kind of organization with that instituted before the rise of experimental science. Failure to develop a conception of organization upon the empirical and experimental basis gives reactionaries a too easy victory. But the fact that the empirical sciences now offer the best type of intellectual organization which can be found in any field shows that there is no reason why we, who call ourselves empiricists, should be "pushovers" in the matter of order and organization.

NO

Robert M. Hutchins

The Basis of Education

The obvious failures of the doctrines of adaptation, immediate needs, social reform, and of the doctrine that we need no doctrine at all may suggest to us that we require a better definition of education. Let us concede that every society must have some system that attempts to adapt the young to their social and political environment. If the society is bad, in the sense, for example, in which the Nazi state was bad, the system will aim at the same bad ends. To the extent that it makes men bad in order that they may be tractable subjects of a bad state, the system may help to achieve the social ideals of the society. It may be what the society wants; it may even be what the society needs, if it is to perpetuate its form and accomplish its aims. In pragmatic terms, in terms of success in the society, it may be a "good" system.

But it seems to me clearer to say that, though it may be a system of training, or instruction, or adaptation, or meeting immediate needs, it is not a system of education. It seems clearer to say that the purpose of education is to improve men. Any system that tries to make them bad is not education, but something else. If, for example, democracy is the best form of society, a system that adapts the young to it will be an educational system. If despotism is a bad form of society, a system that adapts the young to it will not be an educational system, and the better it succeeds in adapting them the less educational it will be.

Every man has a function as a man. The function of a citizen or a subject may vary from society to society, and the system of training, or adaptation, or instruction, or meeting immediate needs may vary with it. But the function of a man as man is the same in every age and in every society, since it results from his nature as a man. The aim of an educational system is the same in every age and in every society where such a system can exist: it is to improve man as man.

If we are going to talk about improving men and societies, we have to believe that there is some difference between good and bad. This difference must not be, as the positivists think it is, merely conventional. We cannot tell this difference by any examination of the effectiveness of a given program as the pragmatists propose; the time required to estimate these effects is usually too long and the complexity of society is always too great for us to say that the consequences of a given program are altogether clear. We cannot discover the difference between good and bad by going to the laboratory, for men and

From Robert M. Hutchins, *The Conflict in Education in a Democratic Society* (Harper & Row, 1953). Copyright © 1953 by Harper & Row Publishers, Inc.; renewed 1981 by Vesta S. Hutchins. Reprinted by permission of HarperCollins Publishers, Inc.

societies are not laboratory animals. If we believe that there is no truth, there is no knowledge, and there are no values except those which are validated by laboratory experiment, we cannot talk about the improvement of men and societies, for we can have no standard of judging anything that takes place among men or in societies.

Society is to be improved, not by forcing a program of social reform down its throat, through the schools, or otherwise, but by the improvement of the individuals who compose it. As Plato said, "Governments reflect human nature. States are not made out of stone or wood, but out of the characters of their citizens: these turn the scale and draw everything after them." The individual is the heart of society. . . .

Man is by nature free, and he is by nature social. To use his freedom rightly he needs discipline. To live in society he needs the moral virtues. Good moral and intellectual habits are required for the fullest development of the nature of man.

To develop fully as a social, political animal man needs participation in his own government. A benevolent despotism will not do. You cannot expect the slave to show the virtues of the free man unless you first set him free. Only democracy, in which all men rule and are ruled in turn for the good life of the whole community, can be an absolutely good form of government. . . .

Education deals with the development of the intellectual powers of men. Their moral and spiritual powers are the sphere of the family and the church. All three agencies must work in harmony; for, though a man has three aspects, he is still one man. But the schools cannot take over the role of the family and the church without promoting the atrophy of those institutions and failing in the task that is proper to the schools.

We cannot talk about the intellectual powers of men, though we can talk about training them, or amusing them, or adapting them, and meeting their immediate needs, unless our philosophy in general tells us that there is knowledge and that there is a difference between true and false. We must believe, too, that there are other means of obtaining knowledge than scientific experimentation. If knowledge can be sought only in the laboratory, many fields in which we thought we had knowledge will offer us nothing but opinion or superstition, and we shall be forced to conclude that we cannot know anything about the most important aspects of man and society. If we are to set about developing the intellectual powers of man through having them acquire knowledge of the most important subjects, we have to begin with the proposition that experimentation and empirical data will be of only limited use to us, contrary to the convictions of many American social scientists, and that philosophy, history, literature, and art give us knowledge, and significant knowledge, on the most significant issues.

If the object of education is the improvement of men, then any system of education that is without values is a contradiction in terms. A system that seeks bad values is bad. A system that denies the existence of values denies the possibility of education. Relativism, scientism, skepticism, and anti-intellectualism, the four horsemen of the philosophical apocalypse, have produced that chaos in education which will end in the disintegration of the West.

The prime object of education is to know what is good for man. It is to know the goods in their order. There is a hierarchy of values. The task of education is to help us understand it, establish it, and live by it. This Aristotle had in mind when he said: "It is not the possessions but the desires of men that must be equalized, and this is impossible unless they have a sufficient education according to the nature of things."

Such an education is far removed from the triviality of that produced by the doctrines of adaptation, of immediate needs, of social reform, or of the doctrine of no doctrine at all. Such an education will not adapt the young to a bad environment, but it will encourage them to make it good. It will not overlook immediate needs, but it will place these needs in their proper relationship to more distant, less tangible, and more important goods. It will be the only effective means of reforming society.

This is the education appropriate to free men. It is liberal education. If all men are to be free, all men must have this education. It makes no difference how they are to earn their living or what their special interests or aptitudes may be. They can learn to make a living, and they can develop their special interests and aptitudes, after they have laid the foundation of free and responsible manhood through liberal education. It will not do to say that they are incapable of such education. This claim is made by those who are too indolent or unconvinced to make the effort to give such education to the masses.

Nor will it do to say that there is not enough time to give everybody a liberal education before he becomes a specialist. In America, at least, the waste and frivolity of the educational system are so great that it would be possible through getting rid of them to give every citizen a liberal education and make him a qualified specialist, too, in less time than is now consumed in turning out uneducated specialists.

A liberal education aims to develop the powers of understanding and judgment. It is impossible that too many people can be educated in this sense, because there cannot be too many people with understanding and judgment. We hear a great deal today about the dangers that will come upon us through the frustration of educated people who have got educated in the expectation that education will get them a better job, and who then fail to get it. But surely this depends on the representations that are made to the young about what education is. If we allow them to believe that education will get them better jobs and encourage them to get educated with this end in view, they are entitled to a sense of frustration if, when they have got the education, they do not get the jobs. But, if we say that they should be educated in order to be men, and that everybody, whether he is ditch-digger or a bank president, should have this education because he is a man, then the ditch-digger may still feel frustrated, but not because of his education.

Nor is it possible for a person to have too much liberal education, because it is impossible to have too much understanding and judgment. But it is possible to undertake too much in the name of liberal education in youth. The object of liberal education in youth is not to teach the young all they will ever need to know. It is to give them the habits, ideas, and techniques that they need to continue to educate themselves. Thus the object of formal institutional liberal education in youth is to prepare the young to educate themselves throughout their lives.

I would remind you of the impossibility of learning to understand and judge many of the most important things in youth. The judgment and understanding of practical affairs can amount to little in the absence of experience with practical affairs. Subjects that cannot be understood without experience should not be taught to those who are without experience. Or, if these subjects are taught to those who are without experience, it should be clear that these subjects can be taught only by way of introduction and that their value to the student depends on his continuing to study them as he acquires experience. The tragedy in America is that economics, ethics, politics, history, and literature are studied in youth, and seldom studied again. Therefore the graduates of American universities seldom understand them.

This pedagogical principle, that subjects requiring experience can be learned only by the experienced, leads to the conclusion that the most important branch of education is the education of adults. We sometimes seem to think of education as something like the mumps, measles, whooping cough, or chicken pox. If a person has had education in childhood, he need not, in fact he cannot, have it again. But the pedagogical principle that the most important things can be learned only in mature life is supported by a sound philosophy in general. Men are rational animals. They achieve their terrestrial felicity by the use of reason. And this means that they have to use it for their entire lives. To say that they should learn only in childhood would mean that they were human only in childhood.

And it would mean that they were unfit to be citizens of a republic. A republic, a true *res publica*, can maintain justice, peace, freedom, and order only by the exercise of intelligence. When we speak of the consent of the governed, we mean, since men are not angels who seek the truth intuitively and do not have to learn it, that every act of assent on the part of the governed is a product of learning. A republic is really a common educational life in process. So Montesquieu said that, whereas the principle of a monarchy was honor, and the principle of a tyranny was fear, the principle of a republic was education.

Hence the ideal republic is the republic of learning. It is the utopia by which all actual political republics are measured. The goal toward which we started with the Athenians twenty-five centuries ago is an unlimited republic of learning and a worldwide political republic mutually supporting each other.

All men are capable of learning. Learning does not stop as long as a man lives, unless his learning power atrophies because he does not use it. Political freedom cannot endure unless it is accompanied by provision for the unlimited acquisition of knowledge. Truth is not long retained in human affairs without continual learning and relearning. Peace is unlikely unless there are continuous, unlimited opportunities for learning and unless men continuously avail themselves of them. The world of law and justice for which we yearn, the worldwide political republic, cannot be realized without the worldwide republic of learning. The civilization we seek will be achieved when all men are citizens of the world republic of law and justice and of the republic of learning all their lives long.

POSTSCRIPT

Should Schooling Be Based on Social Experiences?

Intellectual training versus social-emotional-mental growth-the argument between Dewey and Hutchins reflects a historical debate that flows from the ideas of Plato and Aristotle and that continues today. Psychologists, sociologists, curriculum and instruction specialists, and popular critics have joined philosophers in commenting on this central concern.

Followers of Dewey contend that training the mental powers cannot be isolated from other factors of development and, indeed, can be enhanced by attention to the concrete social situations in which learning occurs. Critics of Dewey worry that the expansion of effort into the social and emotional realm only detracts from the intellectual mission that is schooling's unique province.

Was the progressive education movement ruinous, or did it lay the foundation for the education of the future? A reasonably even-handed appraisal can be found in Lawrence Cremin's *The Transformation of the School* (1961). The free school movement of the 1960s, at least partly derived from progressivism, is analyzed in Allen Graubard's *Free the Children* (1973) and Jonathan Kozol's *Free Schools* (1972). Diane Ravitch's *Troubled Crusade* (1983) and Mary Eberstadt's "The Schools They Deserve," *Policy Review* (October/November 1999) offer effective critiques of progressivism.

Among the best general explorations of philosophical alternatives are Gerald L. Gutek's *Philosophical and Ideological Perspectives on Education* (1988); Edward J. Power's *Philosophy of Education: Studies in Philosophies, Schooling, and Educational Policies* (1990); and *Philosophical Foundations of Education* by Howard Ozmon and Samuel Craver (1990).

Also worth perusing are Philip W. Jackson's "Dewey's *Experience and Education* Revisited," *The Educational Forum* (Summer 1996); Jerome Bruner's 1996 book *The Culture of Education* (particularly chapter 3, "The Complexity of Educational Aims"); Robert Orrill's *Education and Democracy: Re-imaging Liberal Learning in America* (1997); Christine McCarthy's "Dewey's Ethics: Philosophy or Science?" *Education Theory* (Summer 1999); Debra J. Anderson and Robert L. Major, "Dewey, Democracy, and Citizenship," *The Clearing House* (November/December 2001); Julie Webber, "Why Can't We Be Deweyan Citizens?" *Educational Theory* (Spring 2001); and David B. Ackerman, "Taproots for a New Century: Tapping the Best of Traditional and Progressive Education," *Phi Delta Kappan* (January 2003).

Questions that must be addressed include: Can the "either/or" polarities of this basic argument be overcome? Is the articulation of overarching general aims essential to the charting of a worthwhile educational experience? And how can the classroom teacher relate to general philosophical aims?

ISSUE 2

Should the Curriculum Be Standardized for All?

YES: Mortimer J. Adler, from "The Paideia Proposal: Rediscovering the Essence of Education," *American School Board Journal* (July 1982)

NO: John Holt, from *Escape From Childhood* (E. P. Dutton, 1974)

ISSUE SUMMARY

YES: Philosopher Mortimer J. Adler contends that democracy is best served by a public school system that establishes uniform curricular objectives for all students.

NO: Educator John Holt argues that an imposed curriculum damages the individual and usurps a basic human right to select one's own path of development.

$\mathbf{C}$ontroversy over the content of education has been particularly keen since the 1950s. The pendulum has swung from learner-centered progressive education to an emphasis on structured intellectual discipline to calls for radical reform in the direction of "openness" to the recent rally to go "back to basics."

The conservative viewpoint, articulated by such writers as Robert M. Hutchins, Clifton Fadiman, Jacques Barzun, Arthur Bestor, and Mortimer J. Adler, arises from concerns about the drift toward informalism and the decline in academic achievement in recent decades. Taking philosophical cues from Plato's contention that certain subject matters have universal qualities that prompt mental and characterological development, the "basics" advocates argue against incidental learning, student choice, and diminution of structure and standards. Barzun summarizes the viewpoint succinctly: "Nonsense is at the heart of those proposals that would replace definable subject matters with vague activities copied from 'life' or with courses organized around 'problems' or 'attitudes.'"

The reform viewpoint, represented by John Holt, Paul Goodman, Ivan Illich, Charles Silberman, Edgar Friedenberg, and others, portrays the typical traditional school as a mindless, indifferent, social institution dedicated to producing fear, docility, and conformity. In such an atmosphere, the viewpoint holds, learners either become alienated from the established curriculum or learn to play the school "game" and thus achieve a hollow success. Taking cues from the ideas of John Dewey and A. S. Neill, the "radical reformers" have given rise to a flurry of alternatives to regular schooling during recent decades. Among these are free schools, which follow the Summerhill model; urban storefront schools, which attempt to develop a true sense of "community"; "schools without walls," which follow the Philadelphia Parkway Program model; "commonwealth" schools, in which students, parents, and teachers share responsibility; and various "humanistic education" projects within regular school systems, which emphasize students' self-concept development and choice-making ability.

The utilitarian tradition that has descended from Benjamin Franklin, Horace Mann, and Herbert Spencer, Dewey's theory of active experiencing, and Neill's insistence on free and natural development support the reform position. The ideology rejects the factory model of schooling with its rigidly set curriculum, its neglect of individual differences, its social engineering function, and its pervasive formalism. "Basics" advocates, on the other hand, express deep concern over the erosion of authority and the watering down of demands upon students that result from the reform ideology.

Arguments for a more standardized curriculum have been embodied most recently in Theodore R. Sizer's Coalition of Essential Schools and the Core Knowledge Schools of E. D. Hirsch, Jr., whose 1996 book *The Schools We Need and Why We Don't Have Them* summarizes the basic points of this view. An interview with Hirsch by Mark F. Goldberg titled "Doing What Works" appeared in the September 1997 issue of *Phi Delta Kappan*. A thorough critique of Hirsch's position is presented by Kristen L. Buras in "Questioning Core Assumptions," *Harvard Educational Review* (Spring 1999). In 1998 Terry Roberts and the staff of the National Paideia Center at the University of North Carolina released *The Power of Paideia Schools: Defining Lives Through Learning*.

A broad spectrum of ideas on the curriculum may be found in John I. Goodlad's *A Place Called School* (1984), Maxine Green's *The Dialectic of Freedom* (1987), Theodore R. Sizer's *Horace* trilogy, and Ernest L. Boyer's *The Basic School* (1995).

In the following selections, Mortimer J. Adler outlines his "Paideia Proposal," which calls for a uniform and unified curriculum and methodological approach—a common schooling for the development of a truly democratic society. In opposition, John Holt goes beyond his earlier concerns about the oppressiveness of the school curriculum to propose complete freedom for the learner to determine all aspects of his or her educational development.

Mortimer J. Adler  **YES**

The Paideia Proposal: Rediscovering the Essence of Education

In the first 80 years of this century, we have met the obligation imposed on us by the principle of equal educational opportunity, but only in a quantitative sense. Now as we approach the end of the century, we must achieve equality in qualitative terms.

This means a completely on-track system of schooling. It means, at the basic level, giving all the young the same kind of schooling, whether or not they are college bound.

We are aware that children, although equal in their common humanity and fundamental human rights, are unequal as individuals, differing in their capacity to learn. In addition, the homes and environments from which they come to school are unequal—either predisposing the child for schooling or doing the opposite.

Consequently, the Paideia Proposal, faithful to the principle of equal educational opportunity, includes the suggestion that inequalities due to environmental factors must be overcome by some form of preschool preparation at least one year for all and two or even three for some. We know that to make such preschool tutelage compulsory at the public expense would be tantamount to increasing the duration of compulsory schooling from 12 years to 13, 14, or 15 years. Nevertheless, we think that this preschool adjunct to the 12 years of compulsory basic schooling is so important that some way must be found to make it available for all and to see that all use it to advantage.

The Essentials of Basic Schooling

The objectives of basic schooling should be the same for the whole school population. In our current two-track or multitrack system, the learning objectives are not the same for all. And even when the objectives aimed at those on the upper track are correct, the course of study now provided does not adequately realize these correct objectives. On all tracks in our current system, we fail to cultivate proficiency in the common tasks of learning, and we especially fail to develop sufficiently the indispensable skills of learning.

The uniform objectives of basic schooling should be threefold. They should correspond to three aspects of the common future to which all the children are destined: (1) Our society provides all children ample opportunity

From *American School Board Journal,* July 1982. Copyright © 1982 by Paideia Group, Inc.

for personal development. Given such opportunity, each individual is under a moral obligation to make the most of himself and his life. Basic schooling must facilitate this accomplishment. (2) All the children will become, when of age, full-fledged citizens with suffrage and other political responsibilities. Basic schooling must do everything it can to make them good citizens, able to perform the duties of citizenship with all the trained intelligence that each is able to achieve. (3) When they are grown, all (or certainly most) of the children will engage in some form of work to earn a living. Basic schooling must prepare them for earning a living, but not by training them for this or that specific job while they are still in school.

To achieve these three objectives, the character of basic schooling must be general and liberal. It should have a single, required, 12-year course of study for all, with no electives except one—an elective choice with regard to a second language, to be selected from such modern languages as French, German, Italian, Spanish, Russian, and Chinese. The elimination of all electives, with this one exception, excludes what *should* be excluded—all forms of specialization, including particularized job training.

In its final form, the Paideia Proposal will detail this required course of study, but I will summarize the curriculum here in its bare outline. It consists of three main columns of teaching and learning, running through the 12 years and progressing, of course, from the simple to the more complex, from the less difficult to the more difficult, as the students grow older. Understand: The three columns (see Table 1) represent three distinct modes of teaching and learning. They do not represent a series of courses. A specific course or class may employ more than one mode of teaching and learning, but all three modes are essential to the overall course of study.

The first column is devoted to acquiring knowledge in three subject areas: (A) language, literature, and the fine arts; (B) mathematics and natural science; (C) history, geography, and social studies.

Table 1

The Paideia Curriculum

	Column One	Column Two	Column Three
Goals	Acquisition of Organized Knowledge	Development of Intellectual Skills and Skills of Learning	Improved Understanding of Ideas and Values
	by means of	*by means of*	*by means of*
Means	Didactic Instruction, Lecturing, and Textbooks	Coaching, Exercises, Supervised Practice	Maieutic or Socratic Questioning and Active Participation
	in these three subject areas	*in these operations*	*in these activities*
Subject Areas, Operations, and Activities	Language, Literature, and Fine Arts; Mathematics and Natural Science; History, Geography, and Social Studies	Reading, Writing, Speaking, Listening, Calculating, Problem Solving, Observing, Measuring, Estimating, Exercising Critical Judgment	Discussion of Books (Not Textbooks) and Other Works of Art; Involvement in Music, Drama, and Visual Arts

The three columns do not correspond to separate courses, nor is one kind of teaching and learning necessarily confined to any one class.

The second column is devoted to developing the intellectual skills of learning. These include all the language skills necessary for thought and communication—the skills of reading, writing, speaking, listening. They also include mathematical and scientific skills; the skills of observing, measuring, estimating, and calculating; and skills in the use of the computer and of other scientific instruments. Together, these skills make it possible to think clearly and critically. They once were called the liberal arts—the intellectual skills indispensable to being competent as a learner.

The third column is devoted to enlarging the understanding of ideas and values. The materials of the third column are books (*not* textbooks), and other products of human artistry. These materials include books of every variety—historical, scientific, and philosophical as well as poems, stories, and essays—and also individual pieces of music, visual art, dramatic productions, dance productions, film or television productions. Music and works of visual art can be used in seminars in which ideas are discussed; but as with poetry and fiction, they also are to be experienced aesthetically, to be enjoyed and admired for their excellence. In this connection, exercises in the composition of poetry, music, and visual works and in the production of dramatic works should be used to develop the appreciation of excellence.

The three columns represent three different kinds of learning on the part of the student and three different kinds of instruction on the part of teachers.

In the first column, the students are engaged in acquiring information and organized knowledge about nature, man, and human society. The method of instruction here, using textbooks and manuals, is didactic. The teacher lectures, invites responses from the students, monitors the acquisition of knowledge, and tests that acquisition in various ways.

In the second column, the students are engaged in developing habits of performance, which is all that is involved in the development of an art or skill. Art, skill, or technique is nothing more than a cultivated, habitual ability to do a certain kind of thing well, whether that is swimming and dancing, or reading and writing. Here, students are acquiring linguistic, mathematical, scientific, and historical *know-how* in contrast to what they acquire in the first column, which is *know-that* with respect to language, literature, and the fine arts, mathematics and science, history, geography, and social studies. Here, the method of instruction cannot be didactic or monitorial; it cannot be dependent on textbooks. It must be coaching, the same kind used in the gym to develop bodily skills; only here it is used by a different kind of coach in the classroom to develop intellectual skills.

In the third column, students are engaged in a process of enlightenment, the process whereby they develop their understanding of the basic and controlling ideas in all fields of subject matter and come to appreciate better all the human values embodied in works of art. Here, students move progressively from understanding less to understanding more—understanding better what they already know and appreciating more what they already have experienced. Here, the method of instruction cannot be either didactic or coaching. It must be the Socratic, or maieutic, method of questioning and discussing. It should not occur in any ordinary classroom with the students sitting in rows and the teacher in front of the class, but in a seminar room, with the students sitting around a table and the teacher sitting with them as an equal, even though a little older and wiser.

Of these three main elements in the required curriculum, the third column is completely innovative. Nothing like this is done in our schools, and because it is completely absent from the ordinary curriculum of basic schooling, the students never have the experience of having their minds addressed in a challenging way or of being asked to think about the important ideas, to express their thoughts, to defend their opinions in a reasonable fashion.

The only thing that is innovative about the second column is the insistence that the method of instruction here must be coaching carried on either with one student at a time or with very small groups of students. Nothing else can be effective in the development of a skill, be it bodily or intellectual. The absence of such individualized coaching in our schools explains why most of the students cannot read well, write well, speak well, listen well, or perform well any of the other basic intellectual operations.

The three columns are closely interconnected and integrated, but the middle column—the one concerned with linguistic, mathematical, and scientific skills—is central. It both supports and is supported by the other two columns. All the intellectual skills with which it is concerned must be exercised in the study of the three basic subject-matters and in acquiring knowledge about them, and these intellectual skills must be exercised in the seminars devoted to the discussion of books and other things.

In addition to the three main columns in the curriculum, ascending through the 12 years of basic schooling, there are three adjuncts: One is 12 years of physical training, accompanied by instruction in bodily care and hygiene. The second, running through something less than 12 years, is the development of basic manual skills, such as cooking, sewing, carpentry, and the operation of all kinds of machines. The third, reserved for the last year or two, is an introduction to the whole world of work—the range of occupations in which human beings earn their livings. This is not particularized job training. It is the very opposite. It aims at a broad understanding of what is involved in working for a living and of the various ways in which that can be done. If, at the end of 12 years, students wish training for specific jobs, they should get that in two-year community or junior colleges, or on the job itself, or in technical institutes of one sort or another.

Everything that has not been specifically mentioned as occupying the time of the school day should be reserved for after-hours and have the status of extracurricular activities.

Please, note: The required course of study just described is as important for what it *displaces* as for what it introduces. It displaces a multitude of elective courses, especially those offered in our secondary schools, most of which make little or no contribution to general, liberal education. It eliminates all narrowly specialized job training, which now abounds in our schools. It throws out of the curriculum and into the category of optional extracurricular activities a variety of things that have little or no educational value.

If it did not call for all these displacements, there would not be enough time in the school day or year to accomplish everything that is essential to the general, liberal learning that must be the content of basic schooling.

The Quintessential Element

So far, I have set forth the bare essentials of the Paideia Proposal with regard to basic schooling. I have not yet mentioned the quintessential element—the *sine qua non*—without which nothing else can possibly come to fruition, no matter how sound it might be in principle. The heart of the matter is the quality of learning and the quality of teaching that occupies the school day, not to mention the quality of the homework after school.

First, the learning must be active. It must use the whole mind, not just the memory. It must be learning by discovery, in which the student, never the teacher, is the primary agent. Learning by discovery, which is the only genuine learning, may be either unaided or aided. It is unaided only for geniuses. For most students, discovery must be aided.

Here is where teachers come in—as aids in the process of learning by discovery not as knowers who attempt to put the knowledge they have into the minds of their students. The quality of the teaching, in short, depends crucially upon how the teacher conceives his role in the process of learning, and that must be as an aid to the student's process of discovery.

I am prepared for the questions that must be agitating you by now: How and where will we get the teachers who can perform as teachers should? How will we be able to staff the program with teachers so trained that they will be competent to provide the quality of instruction required for the quality of learning desired?

The first part of our answer to these questions is negative: We *cannot* get the teachers we need for the Paideia program from schools of education as *they are now constituted*. As teachers are now trained for teaching, they simply will not do. The ideal—an impracticable ideal—would be to ask for teachers who are, themselves, truly educated human beings. But truly educated human beings are too rare. Even if we could draft all who are now alive, there still would be far too few to staff our schools.

Well, then, what can we look for? Look for teachers who are actively engaged in the process of *becoming* educated human beings, who are themselves deeply motivated to develop their own minds. Assuming this is not too much to ask for the present, how should teachers be schooled and trained in the future? First, they should have the same kind of basic schooling that is recommended in the Paideia Proposal. Second, they should have additional schooling, at the college and even the university level, in which the same kind of general, liberal learning is carried on at advanced levels—more deeply, broadly, and intensively than it can be done in the first 12 years of schooling. Third, they must be given something analogous to the clinical experience in the training of physicians. They must engage in practice-teaching under supervision, which is another way of saying that they must be *coached* in the arts of teaching, not just given didactic instruction in educational psychology and in pedagogy. Finally, and most important of all, they must learn how to teach well by being exposed to the performances of those who are masters of the arts involved in teaching.

It is by watching a good teacher at work that they will be able to perceive what is involved in the process of assisting others to learn by discovery.

Perceiving it, they must then try to emulate what they observe, and through this process, they slowly will become good teachers themselves.

The Paideia Proposal recognizes the need for three different kinds of institutions at the collegiate level: The two-year community or junior college should offer a wide choice of electives that give students some training in one or another specialized field, mainly those fields of study that have something to do with earning a living. The four-year college also should offer a wide variety of electives, to be chosen by students who aim at the various professional or technical occupations that require advanced study. Those elective majors chosen by students should be accompanied, for all students, by one required minor, in which the kind of general and liberal learning that was begun at the level of basic schooling is continued at a higher level in the four years of college. And we should have still a third type of collegiate institution—a four-year college in which general, liberal learning at a higher level constitutes a required course of study that is to be taken by all students. *It is this third type of college, by the way, that should be attended by all who plan to become teachers in our basic schools.*

At the university level, there should be a continuation of general, liberal learning at a still higher level to accompany intensive specialization in this or that field of science or scholarship, this or that learned profession. Our insistence on the continuation of general, liberal learning at all the higher levels of schooling stems from our concern with the worst cultural disease that is rampant in our society—*the barbarism of specialization.*

There is no question that our technologically advanced industrial society needs specialists of all sorts. There is no question that the advancement of knowledge in all fields of science and scholarship, and in all the learned professions, needs intense specialization. But for the sake of preserving and enhancing our cultural traditions, as well as for the health of science and scholarship, we need specialists who also are generalists—generally cultivated human beings, not just good plumbers. We need truly educated human beings who can perform their special tasks better precisely because they have general cultivation as well as intensely specialized training.

Changes indeed are needed in higher education, but those improvements cannot reasonably be expected unless improvement in basic schooling makes that possible.

The Future of Our Free Institutions

I already have declared as emphatically as I know how that the quality of human life in our society depends on the quality of the schooling we give our young people, both basic and advanced. But a marked elevation in the quality of human life is not the only reason improving the quality of schooling is so necessary—not the only reason we must move heaven and earth to stop the deterioration of our schools and turn them in the opposite direction. The other reason is to safeguard the future of our free institutions.

They cannot prosper, they may not even survive, unless we do something to rescue our schools from their current deplorable deterioration.

Democracy, in the full sense of that term, came into existence only in this century and only in a few countries on earth, among which the United States is an outstanding example. But democracy came into existence in this century, only in its initial conditions, all of which hold out promises for the future that remain to be fulfilled. Unless we do something about improving the quality of basic schooling for all and the quality of advanced schooling for some, there is little chance that those promises ever will be fulfilled. And if they are not, our free institutions are doomed to decay and wither away.

We face many insistently urgent problems. Our prosperity and even our survival depend on the solution of those problems—the threat of nuclear war, the exhaustion of essential resources and of supplies of energy, the pollution or spoilage of the environment, the spiraling of inflation accompanied by the spread of unemployment.

To solve these problems, we need resourceful and innovative leadership. For that to arise and be effective, an educated populace is needed. Trained intelligence—not only on the part of leaders, but also on the part of followers—holds the key to the solution of the problems our society faces. Achieving peace, prosperity and plenty could put us on the threshold of an early paradise. But a much better educational system than now exists also is needed, for that alone can carry us across the threshold. Without it, a poorly schooled population will not be able to put to good use the opportunities afforded by the achievement of the general welfare. Those who are not schooled to enjoy society can only despoil its institutions and corrupt themselves.

NO

John Holt

Escape From Childhood

Young people should have the right to control and direct their own learning, that is, to decide what they want to learn, and when, where, how, how much, how fast, and with what help they want to learn it. To be still more specific, I want them to have the right to decide if, when, how much, and by whom they want to be *taught* and the right to decide whether they want to learn in a school and if so which one and for how much of the time.

No human right, except the right to life itself, is more fundamental than this. A person's freedom of learning is part of his freedom of thought, even more basic than his freedom of speech. If we take from someone his right to decide what he will be curious about, we destroy his freedom of thought. We say, in effect, you must think not about what interests and concerns you, but about what interests and concerns *us*.

We might call this the right of curiosity, the right to ask whatever questions are most important to us. As adults, we assume that we have the right to decide what does or does not interest us, what we will look into and what we will leave alone. We take this right for granted, cannot imagine that it might be taken away from us. Indeed, as far as I know, it has never been written into any body of law. Even the writers of our Constitution did notmention it. They thought it was enough to guarantee citizens the freedom of speech and the freedom to spread their ideas as widely as they wished and could. It did not occur to them that even the most tyrannical government would try to control people's minds, what they thought and knew. That idea was to come later, under the benevolent guise of compulsory universal education.

This right to each of us to control our own learning is now in danger. When we put into our laws the highly authoritarian notion that someone should and could decide what all young people were to learn and, beyond that, could do whatever might seem necessary (which now includes dosing them with drugs) to compel them to learn it, we took a long step down a very steep and dangerous path. The requirement that a child go to school, for about six hours a day, 180 days a year, for about ten years, whether or not he learns anything there, whether or not he already knows it or could learn it faster or better somewhere else, is such gross violation of civil liberties that few adults would stand for it. But the child who resists is treated as a criminal. With this requirement we created an industry, an army of people whose whole work was to tell

From John Holt, *Escape From Childhood* (E. P. Dutton, 1974). Copyright © 1974 by Holt Associates. Reprinted by permission.

young people what they had to learn and to try to make them learn it. Some of these people, wanting to exercise even more power over others, to be even more "helpful," or simply because the industry is not growing fast enough to hold all the people who want to get into it, are now beginning to say, "If it is good for children for us to decide what they shall learn and to make them learn it, why wouldn't it be good for everyone? If compulsory education is a good thing, how can there be too much of it? Why should we allow anyone, of any age, to decide that he has had enough of it? Why should we allow older people, any more than young, not to know what we know when their ignorance may have bad consequences for all of us? Why should we not *make* them know what they *ought* to know?"

They are beginning to talk, as one man did on a nationwide TV show, about "womb-to-tomb" schooling. If hours of homework every night are good for the young, why wouldn't they be good for us all—they would keep us away from the TV set and other frivolous pursuits. Some group of experts, somewhere, would be glad to decide what we all ought to know and then every so often check up on us to make sure we knew it—with, of course, appropriate penalties if we did not.

I am very serious in saying that I think this is coming unless we prepare against it and take steps to prevent it. The right I ask for the young is a right that I want to preserve for the rest of us, the right *to decide what goes into our minds*. This is much more than the right to decide whether or when or how much to go to school or what school you want to go to. That right is important, but it is only part of a much larger and more fundamental right, which I might call the right to Learn, as opposed to being Educated, *i.e.*, made to learn what someone else thinks would be good for you. It is not just compulsory schooling but compulsory Education that I oppose and want to do away with.

That children might have the control of their own learning, including the right to decide if, when, how much, and where they wanted to go to school, frightens and angers many people. They ask me, "Are you saying that if the parents wanted the child to go to school, and the child didn't want to go, that he wouldn't have to go? Are you saying that if the parents wanted the child to go to one school, and the child wanted to go to another, that the child would have the right to decide?" Yes, that is what I say. Some people ask, "If school wasn't compulsory, wouldn't many parents take their children out of school to exploit their labors in one way or another?" Such questions are often both snobbish and hypocritical. The questioner assumes and implies (though rarely says) that these bad parents are people poorer and less schooled than he. Also, though he appears to be defending the right of children to go to school, what he really is defending is the right of the state to compel them to go whether they want to or not. What he wants, in short, is that children should be in school, not that they should have any choice about going.

But saying that children should have the right to choose to go or not to go to school does not mean that the ideas and wishes of the parents would have no weight. Unless he is estranged from his parents and rebelling against them, a child cares very much about what they think and want. Most of the time, he doesn't want to anger or worry or disappoint them. Right now, in families where the parents feel that they have some choice about their children's schooling, there is much bargaining about schools. Such parents, when their children are little, often ask them whether they want to go to nursery school or kindergarten. Or they may take them to school for a while to try it out. Or, if they have a choice of schools, they may take them to several to see which they think they will like the best. Later, they care whether the child likes his school. If he does not, they try to do something about it, get him out of it, find a school he will like.

I know some parents who for years had a running bargain with their children. "If on a given day you just can't stand the thought of school, you don't feel well, you are afraid of something that may happen, you have something of your own that you very much want to do—well, you can stay home." Needless to say, the schools, with their supporting experts, fight it with all their might—Don't Give in to Your Child, Make Him Go to School, He's Got to Learn. Some parents, when their own plans make it possible for them to take an interesting trip, take their children with them. They don't ask the schools' permission, they just go. If the child doesn't want to make the trip and would rather stay in school, they work out a way for him to do that. Some parents, when their child is frightened, unhappy, and suffering in school, as many children are, just take him out. Hal Bennett, in his excellent book *No More Public School*, talks about ways to do this.

A friend of mine told me that when her boy was in third grade, he had a bad teacher, bullying, contemptuous, sarcastic, cruel. Many of the class switched to another section, but this eight-year-old, being tough, defiant, and stubborn, hung on. One day—his parents did not learn this until about two years later—having had enough of the teacher's meanness, he just got up from his desk and without saying a word, walked out of the room and went home. But for all his toughness and resiliency of spirit, the experience was hard on him. He grew more timid and quarrelsome, less outgoing and confident. He lost his ordinary good humor. Even his handwriting began to go to pieces—it was much worse in the spring of the school year than in the previous fall. One spring day he sat at breakfast, eating his cereal. After a while he stopped eating and sat silently thinking about the day ahead. His eyes filled up with tears, and two big ones slowly rolled down his cheeks. His mother, who ordinarily stays out of the school life of her children, saw this and knew what it was about. "Listen," she said to him, "we don't have to go on with this. If you've had enough of that teacher, if she's making school so bad for you that you don't want to go any more, I'll be perfectly happy just to pull you right out. We can manage it. Just say the word." He was horrified and indignant. "No!" he said, "I couldn't do that." "Okay," she said, "whatever you want is fine. Just let me know." And so they left it. He had decided that he was going to tough it out, and he did. But I am sure knowing that he had the support of his mother and the chance to give it up if it got too much for him gave him the strength he needed to go on.

To say that children should have the right to control and direct their own learning, to go to school or not as they choose, does not mean that the law would forbid the parents to express an opinion or wish or strong desire on the matter. It only means that if their natural authority is not strong enough the parents can't call in the cops to make the child do what they are not able to persuade him to do. And the law may say that there is no limit to the amount of pressure or coercion the parents can apply to the child to deny him a choice that he has a legal right to make.

When I urge that children should control their learning, there is one argument that people bring up so often that I feel I must anticipate and meet it here. It says that schools are a place where children can for a while be protected against the bad influences of the world outside, particularly from its greed, dishonesty, and commercialism. It says that in school children may have a glimpse of a higher way of life, of people acting from other and better motives than greed and fear. People say, "We know that society is bad enough as it is and that if children go out into the larger world as soon as they wanted, they would be tempted and corrupted just that much sooner."

They seem to believe that schools are better, more honorable places than the world outside—what a friend of mine at Harvard once called "museums of virtue." Or that people in school, both children and adults, act from higher and better motives than people outside. In this they are mistaken. There are, of course, some good schools. But on the whole, far from being the opposite of, or an antidote to, the world outside, with all its envy, fear, greed, and obsessive competitiveness, the schools are very much like it. If anything, they are worse, a terrible, abstract, simplified caricature of it. In the world outside the school, some work, at least, is done honestly and well, for its own sake, not just to get ahead of others; people are not everywhere and always being set in competition against each other; people are not (or not yet) in every minute of their lives subject to the arbitrary, irrevocable orders and judgement of others. But in most schools, a student is every minute doing what others tell him, subject to their judgement, in situations in which he can only win at the expense of other students.

This is a harsh judgement. Let me say again, as I have before, that schools are worse than most of the people in them and that many of these people do many harmful things they would rather not do, and a great many other harmful things that they do not even see as harmful. The whole of school is much worse than the sum of its parts. There are very few people in the U.S. today (or perhaps anywhere, any time) in *any* occupation, who could be trusted with the kind of power that schools give most teachers over their students. Schools seem to me among the most anti-democratic, most authoritarian, most destructive, and most dangerous institutions of modern society. No other institution does more harm or more lasting harm to more people or destroys so much of their curiosity, independence, trust, dignity, and sense of identity and worth. Even quite kindly schools are inhibited and corrupted by the knowledge of children and teachers alike that they are *performing* for the judgement and approval of others—the children for the teachers; the teachers for the parents, supervisors, school board, or the state. No one is ever free from feeling that he is being judged all the time, or soon may be. Even after the best class experiences teachers must ask themselves, "Were we right to do that? Can we prove we were right? Will it get us in trouble?"

What corrupts the school, and makes it so much worse than most of the people in it, or than they would like it to be, is its power—just as their power-lessness corrupts the students. The school is corrupted by the endless anxious demand of the parents to know how their child is doing—meaning is he ahead of the other kids—and their demand that he be kept ahead. Schools do not protect children from the badness of the world outside. They are at least as bad as the world outside, and the harm they do to the children in their power creates much of the badness of the world outside. The sickness of the modern world is in many ways a school-induced sickness. It is in school that most people learn to expect and accept that some expert can always place them in some sort of rank or hierarchy. It is in school that we meet, become used to, and learn to believe in the totally controlled society. We do not learn much science, but we learn to worship "scientists" and to believe that anything we might conceivably need or want can only come, and someday will come, from them. The school is the closest we have yet been able to come to Huxley's *Brave New World*, with its alphas and betas, deltas and epsilons—and now it even has its soma. Everyone, including children, should have the right to say "No!" to it.

POSTSCRIPT

Should the Curriculum Be Standardized for All?

The free/open school movement values small, personalized educational settings in which students engage in activities that have personal meaning. One of the movement's ideological assumptions, emanating from the philosophy of Jean-Jacques Rousseau, is that given a reasonably unrestrictive atmosphere, the learner will pursue avenues of creative and intellectual self-development. This confidence in self-motivation is the cornerstone of Holt's advocacy of freedom for the learner, a position he elaborates upon in his books *Instead of Education* (1988) and *Teach Your Own* (1982). The argument has gained some potency with recent developments in home-based computer-assisted instruction.

Adler's proposal for a unified curricular and methodological approach, released in 1982 by the Institute for Philosophical Research, was fashioned by a group of distinguished scholars and practitioners and has its roots in such earlier works as Arthur Bestor's *Educational Wastelands* (1953), Mortimer Smith's *The Diminished Mind* (1954), and Paul Copperman's *The Literacy Hoax* (1978). The proposal has been widely discussed since its release, and it has been implemented in a number of school systems. See, for example, "Launching Paideia in Chattanooga," by Cynthia M. Gettys and Anne Wheelock, *Educational Leadership* (September 1994) and Terry Roberts and Audrey Trainor, "Performing for Yourself and Others: The Paideia Coached Project," *Phi Delta Kappan* (March 2004).

Holt's plea for freedom from an imposed curriculum has a champion in John Taylor Gatto, New York City and New York State Teacher of the Year. Gatto has produced two provocative books, *Dumbing Us Down: The Hidden Curriculum of Compulsory Schooling* (1992) and *Confederacy of Dunces: The Tyranny of Compulsory Schooling* (1992). Two other works that build upon Holt's basic views are Lewis J. Perelman's *School's Out: The New Technology and the End of Education* (1992) and George Leonard's "Notes: The End of School," *The Atlantic Monthly* (May 1992). A less ideological appraisal can be found in Paul Gagnon's "What Should Children Learn?" *The Atlantic Monthly* (December 1995). Theodore R. Sizer offers a plea for individualized instruction in "No Two Are Quite Alike," *Educational Leadership* (September 1999).

Among recent provocative books and articles dealing with the topic are Susan Ohanian, *Caught in the Middle: Nonstandard Kids and a Killing Curriculum* (2001): John Berlau, "What Happened to the Great Ideas?"

Insight on the News (August 27, 2001); and Elliott W. Eisner, "The Kind of Schools We Need," *Phi Delta Kappan* (April 2002), which is a balanced and thoughtful presentation of needed alterations. Excellent articles by E. D. Hirsch, Jr., and Alfie Kohn may be found in *Principal Leadership* (March 2003).

ISSUE 3

Should Behaviorism Shape Educational Practices?

YES: B. F. Skinner, from *Beyond Freedom and Dignity* (Alfred A. Knopf, 1971)

NO: Carl R. Rogers, from *Freedom to Learn for the Eighties* (Merrill, 1983)

ISSUE SUMMARY

YES: B. F. Skinner, an influential proponent of behaviorism and professor of psychology, critiques the concept of "inner freedom" and links learning and motivation to the influence of external forces.

NO: Professor of psychology and psychiatry Carl R. Rogers offers the "humanistic" alternative to behaviorism, insisting on the reality of subjective forces in human motivation.

$\mathbf{I}$ntimately enmeshed with considerations of aims and purposes and determination of curricular elements are the psychological base that affects the total setting in which learning takes place and the basic means of motivating learners. Historically, the atmosphere of schooling has often been characterized by harsh discipline, regimentation, and restriction. The prison metaphor often used by critics in describing school conditions rings true all too often.

Although calls to make schools pleasant have been sounded frequently, they have seldomly been heeded. Roman rhetorician Marcus Fabius Quintilian (ca. A.D. 35–100) advocated a constructive and enjoyable learning atmosphere. John Amos Comenius in the seventeenth century suggested a gardening metaphor in which learners were given kindly nurturance. Johann Heinrich Pestalozzi established a model school in the nineteenth century that replaced authoritarianism with love and respect.

Yet school as an institution retains the stigma of authoritarian control—attendance is compelled, social and psychological punishment is meted out, and the decision-making freedom of students is limited and often curtailed. These practices lead to rather obvious conclusions: the prevailing belief is either that young people are naturally evil and wild and therefore must be tamed in a restricting environment or that schooling as such is so unpalatable that people must be forced and cajoled to reap its benefits—or both.

Certainly, philosopher John Dewey (1895–1952) was concerned about this circumstance, citing at one time the superintendent of his native Burlington, Vermont, school district as admitting that the schools were a source of "grief and mortification" and were "unworthy of patronage." Dewey rejected both the need for "taming" and the defeatist attitude that the school environment must remain unappealing. He hoped to create a motivational atmosphere that would engage learners in real problem-solving activities, thereby sustaining curiosity, creativity, and attachment. The rewards were to flow from the sense of accomplishment and freedom, which was to be achieved through the disciplined actions necessary to solve the problem at hand.

More recent treatment of the allied issues of freedom, control, and motivation has come from the two major camps in the field of educational psychology: the behaviorists (rooted in the early-twentieth-century theories of Ivan Pavlov, Edward L. Thorndike, and John B. Watson) and the humanists (emanating from the Gestalt and field theory psychologies developed in Europe and America earlier in the twentieth century).

B. F. Skinner has been the dominant force in translating behaviorism into recommendations for school practices. He and his disciples, often referred to as "neobehaviorists," have contributed to widely used innovations such as behavioral objectives in instruction and testing, competency-based education, mastery learning, assertive discipline, and outcome-based education. The humanistic viewpoint has been championed by Carl R. Rogers, Abraham Maslow, Fritz Perls, Rollo May, and Erich Fromm, most of whom ground their psychological theories in the philosophical assumptions of existentialism and phenomenology.

Skinner believes that "inner" states are merely convenient myths, that motives and behaviors are shaped by environmental factors. These shaping forces, however, need not be negative, nor must they operate in an uncontrolled manner. Our present understanding of human behavior allows us the freedom to shape the environmental forces, which in turn shape us. With this power, Skinner contends, we can replace aversive controls in schooling with positive reinforcements that heighten the students' motivation level and make learning more efficient.

Recent manifestations of the continuing interest in Skinner's behaviorism and the humanistic psychology of Rogers include Virginia Richardson's "From Behaviorism to Constructivism in Teacher Education," *Teacher Education and Special Education* (Summer 1996) and Tobin Hart's "From Category to Contact: Epistemology and the Enlivening and Deadening of Spirit in Education," *Journal of Humanistic Education and Development* (September 1997).

Skinner deals with the problem of freedom and control in the selection that follows. In the second selection, Carl R. Rogers critiques Skinner's behaviorist approach and sets forth his argument supporting the reality of freedom as an inner human state that is the wellspring of responsibility, will, and commitment.

B. F. Skinner

Beyond Freedom and Dignity

Almost all living things act to free themselves from harmful contacts. A kind of freedom is achieved by the relatively simple forms of behavior called reflexes. A person sneezes and frees his respiratory passages from irritating substances. He vomits and frees his stomach from indigestible or poisonous food. He pulls back his hand and frees it from a sharp or hot object. More elaborate forms of behavior have similar effects. When confined, people struggle ("in rage") and break free. When in danger they flee from or attack its source. Behavior of this kind presumably evolved because of its survival value; it is as much a part of what we call the human genetic endowment as breathing, sweating, or digesting food. And through conditioning similar behavior may be acquired with respect to novel objects which could have played no role in evolution. These are no doubt minor instances of the struggle to be free, but they are significant. We do not attribute them to any love of freedom; they are simply forms of behavior which have proved useful in reducing various threats to the individual and hence to the species in the course of evolution.

A much more important role is played by behavior which weakens harmful stimuli in another way. It is not acquired in the form of conditioned reflexes, but as the product of a different process called operant conditioning. When a bit of behavior is followed by a certain kind of consequence, it is more likely to occur again, and a consequence having this effect is called a reinforcer. Food, for example, is a reinforcer to a hungry organism; anything the organism does that is followed by the receipt of food is more likely to be done again whenever the organism is hungry. Some stimuli are called negative reinforcers; any response which reduces the intensity of such a stimulus—or ends it—is more likely to be emitted when the stimulus recurs. Thus, if a person escapes from a hot sun when he moves under cover, he is more likely to move under cover when the sun is again hot. The reduction in temperature reinforces the behavior it is "contingent upon"—that is, the behavior it follows. Operant conditioning also occurs when a person simply avoids a hot sun—when, roughly speaking, he escapes from the *threat* of a hot sun.

Negative reinforcers are called aversive in the sense that they are the things organisms "turn away from." The term suggests a spatial separation—moving or running away from something—but the essential relation is temporal. In a standard apparatus used to study the process in the laboratory, an

From B. F. Skinner, *Beyond Freedom and Dignity* (Hackett Publishing Company, 2002). Copyright © 1971 by B. F. Skinner. Reprinted by permission of Hackett Publishing Company, Inc. All rights reserved.

arbitrary response simply weakens an aversive stimulus or brings it to an end. A great deal of physical technology is the result of this kind of struggle for freedom. Over the centuries, in erratic ways, men have constructed a world in which they are relatively free of many kinds of threatening or harmful stimuli—extremes of temperature, sources of infection, hard labor, danger, and even those minor aversive stimuli called discomfort.

Escape and avoidance play a much more important role in the struggle for freedom when the aversive conditions are generated by other people. Other people can be aversive without, so to speak, trying; they can be rude, danger-ous, contagious, or annoying, and one escapes from them or avoids them accordingly. They may also be "intentionally" aversive—that is, they may treat other people aversively because of what follows. Thus, a slave driver induces a slave to work by whipping him when he stops; by resuming work the slave escapes from the whipping (and incidentally reinforces the slave driver's behavior in using the whip). A parent nags a child until the child performs a task; by performing the task the child escapes nagging (and reinforces the par-ent's behavior). The blackmailer threatens exposure unless the victim pays; by paying, the victim escapes from the threat (and reinforces the practice). A teacher threatens corporal punishment or failure until his students pay atten-tion; by paying attention the students escape from the threat of punishment (and reinforce the teacher for threatening it). In one form or another inten-tional aversive control is the pattern of most social coordination—in ethics, religion, government, economics, education, psychotherapy, and family life.

A person escapes from or avoids aversive treatment by behaving in ways which reinforce those who treated him aversively until he did so, but he may escape in other ways. For example, he may simply move out of range. A person may escape from slavery, emigrate or defect from a government, desert from an army, become an apostate from a religion, play truant, leave home, or drop out of a culture as a hobo, hermit, or hippie. Such behavior is as much a product of the aversive conditions as the behavior the conditions were designed to evoke. The latter can be guaranteed only by sharpening the contingencies or by using stronger aversive stimuli.

Another anomalous mode of escape is to attack those who arrange aver-sive conditions and weaken or destroy their power. We may attack those who crowd us or annoy us, as we attack the weeds in our garden, but again the struggle for freedom is mainly directed toward intentional controllers—toward those who treat others aversively in order to induce them to behave in particu-lar ways. Thus, a child may stand up to his parents, a citizen may overthrow a government, a communicant may reform a religion, a student may attack a teacher or vandalize a school, and a dropout may work to destroy a culture.

It is possible that man's genetic endowment supports this kind of struggle for freedom: when treated aversively people tend to act aggressively or to be reinforced by signs of having worked aggressive damage. Both tendencies should have had evolutionary advantages, and they can easily be demonstrated. If two organisms which have been coexisting peacefully receive painful shocks, they immediately exhibit characteristic patterns of aggression toward each other. The aggressive behavior is not necessarily directed toward the actual source of stimulation; it may be "displaced" toward any convenient person or object. Vandalism and riots are often forms of undirected or misdirected aggression. An organism which has received a painful shock will also, if possible, act to gain access to another organism toward which it can act aggressively. The extent to which human aggression exemplifies innate tendencies is not clear, and many of the ways in which people attack and thus weaken or destroy the power of intentional controllers are quite obviously learned.

What we may call the "literature of freedom" has been designed to induce people to escape from or attack those who act to control them aversively. The content of the literature is the philosophy of freedom, but philosophies are among those inner causes which need to be scrutinized. We say that a person behaves in a given way because he possesses a philosophy, but we infer the philosophy from the behavior and therefore cannot use it in any satisfactory way as an explanation, at least until it is in turn explained. The literature of freedom, on the other hand, has a simple objective status. It consists of books, pamphlets, manifestoes, speeches, and other verbal products, designed to induce people to act to free themselves from various kinds of intentional control. It does not impart a philosophy of freedom; it induces people to act.

The literature often emphasizes the aversive conditions under which people live, perhaps by contrasting them with conditions in a freer world. It thus makes the conditions more aversive, "increasing the misery" of those it is trying to rescue. It also identifies those from whom one is to escape or those whose power is to be weakened through attack. Characteristic villains of the literature are tyrants, priests, generals, capitalists, martinet teachers, and domineering parents.

The literature also prescribes modes of action. It has not been much concerned with escape, possibly because advice has not been needed; instead, it has emphasized how controlling power may be weakened or destroyed. Tyrants are to be overthrown, ostracized, or assassinated. The legitimacy of a government is to be questioned. The ability of a religious agency to mediate supernatural sanctions is to be challenged. Strikes and boycotts are to be organized to weaken the economic power which supports aversive practices. The argument is strengthened by exhorting people to act, describing likely results, reviewing successful instances on the model of the advertising testimonial, and so on.

The would-be controllers do not, of course, remain inactive. Governments make escape impossible by banning travel or severely punishing or incarcerating defectors. They keep weapons and other sources of power out of the hands of revolutionaries. They destroy the written literature of freedom and imprison or kill those who carry it orally. If the struggle for freedom is to succeed, it must then be intensified.

The importance of the literature of freedom can scarcely be questioned. Without help or guidance people submit to aversive conditions in the most surprising way. This is true even when the aversive conditions are part of the natural environment. Darwin observed, for example, that the Fuegians seemed to make no effort to protect themselves from the cold; they wore only scant clothing and made little use of it against the weather. And one of the most striking things about the struggle for freedom from intentional control is how often it has been lacking. Many people have submitted to the most obvious religious, governmental, and economic controls for centuries, striking for freedom only sporadically, if at all. The literature of freedom has made an essential contribution to the elimination of many aversive practices in government, religion, education, family life, and the production of goods.

The contributions of the literature of freedom, however, are not usually described in these terms. Some traditional theories could conceivably be said to define freedom as the absence of aversive control, but the emphasis has been on how the condition *feels*. Other traditional theories could conceivably be said to define freedom as a person's condition when he is behaving under nonaversive control, but the emphasis has been upon a state of mind associated with doing what one wants. According to John Stuart Mill, "Liberty consists in doing what one desires." The literature of freedom has been important in changing practice (it has changed practices whenever it has had any effect whatsoever), but it has nevertheless defined its task as the changing of states of mind and feelings. Freedom is a "possession." A person escapes from or destroys the power of a controller in order to feel free, and once he feels free and can do what he desires, no further action is recommended and none is prescribed by the literature of freedom, except perhaps eternal vigilance lest control be resumed.

The feeling of freedom becomes an unreliable guide to action as soon as would-be controllers turn to nonaversive measures, as they are likely to do to avoid the problems raised when the controllee escapes or attacks. Nonaversive measures are not as conspicuous as aversive and are likely to be acquired more slowly, but they have obvious advantages which promote their use. Productive labor, for example, was once the result of punishment: the slave worked to avoid the consequences of not working. Wages exemplify a different principle; a person is paid when he behaves in a given way so that he will continue to behave in that way. Although it has long been recognized that rewards have useful effects, wage systems have evolved slowly. In the nineteenth century it was believed that an industrial society required a hungry labor force; wages would be effective only if the hungry worker could exchange them for food. By making labor less aversive—for instance, by shortening hours and improving conditions—it has been possible to get men to work for lesser rewards. Until recently teaching was almost entirely aversive: the student studies to escape the consequences of not studying, but nonaversive techniques are gradually being discovered and used. The skillful parent learns to reward a child for good behavior rather than punish him for bad. Religious agencies move from the threat of hellfire to an emphasis on God's love, and governments turn from aversive sanctions to various kinds of inducements. . . . What the layman calls a reward is a "positive reinforcer," the effects of which have been exhaustively studied in the experimental analysis of operant behavior. The effects are not as easily recognized as those of aversive contingencies because they tend to be deferred, and applications have therefore been delayed, but techniques as powerful as the older aversive techniques are now available. . . .

The literature of freedom has never come to grips with techniques of control which do not generate escape or counterattack because it has dealt with the problem in terms of states of mind and feelings. In his book *Sovereignty*, Bertrand de Jouvenel quotes two important figures in that literature. According to Leibnitz, "Liberty consists in the power to do what one wants to do," and according to Voltaire, "When I can do what I want to do, there is my liberty for me." But both writers add a concluding phrase: Leibnitz, ". . . or in the power to want what can be got," and Voltaire, more candidly, ". . . but I can't help wanting what I do want." Jouvenel relegates these comments to a footnote, saying that the power to want is a matter of "interior liberty" (the freedom of the inner man!) which falls outside the "gambit of freedom."

A person wants something if he acts to get it when the occasion arises. A person who says "I want something to eat" will presumably eat when something becomes available. If he says "I want to get warm," he will presumably move into a warm place when he can. These acts have been reinforced in the past by whatever was wanted. What a person *feels* when he feels himself wanting something depends upon the circumstances. Food is reinforcing only in a state of deprivation, and a person who wants something to eat may feel parts of that state—for example, hunger pangs. A person who wants to get warm presumably feels cold. Conditions associated with a high probability of responding may also be felt, together with aspects of the present occasion which are similar to those of past occasions upon which behavior has been reinforced. Wanting is not, however, a feeling, nor is a feeling the reason a person acts to get what he wants. Certain contingencies have raised the probability of behavior and at the same time have created conditions which may be felt. Freedom is a matter of contingencies of reinforcement, not of the feelings the contingencies generate. The distinction is particularly important when the contingencies do not generate escape or counterattack. . . .

The literature of freedom has encouraged escape from or attack upon all controllers. It has done so by making any indication of control aversive. Those who manipulate human behavior are said to be evil men, necessarily bent on exploitation. Control is clearly the opposite of freedom, and if freedom is good, control must be bad. What is overlooked is control which does not have aversive consequences at any time. Many social practices essential to the welfare of the species involve the control of one person by another, and no one can suppress them who has any concern for human achievements. . . . [I]n order to maintain the position that all control is wrong, it has been necessary to disguise or conceal the nature of useful practices, to prefer weak practices just because they can be disguised or concealed, and—a most extraordinary result indeed!—to perpetuate punitive measures.

The problem is to be free men, not from control, but from certain kinds of control, and it can be solved only if our analysis takes all consequences into account. How people feel about control, before or after the literature of freedom has worked on their feelings, does not lead to useful distinctions.

Were it not for the unwarranted generalization that all control is wrong, we should deal with the social environment as simply as we deal with the nonsocial. Although technology has freed men from certain aversive features of the environment, it has not freed them from the environment. We accept the fact that we depend upon the world around us, and we simply change the nature of the dependency. In the same way, to make the social environment as free as possible of aversive stimuli, we do not need to destroy that environment or escape from it; we need to redesign it.

Man's struggle for freedom is not due to a will to be free, but to certain behavioral processes characteristic of the human organism, the chief effect of which is the avoidance of or escape from so-called "aversive" features of the environment. Physical and biological technologies have been mainly concerned with natural aversive stimuli; the struggle for freedom is concerned with stimuli intentionally arranged by other people. The literature of freedom has identified the other people and has proposed ways of escaping from them or weakening or destroying their power. It has been successful in reducing the aversive stimuli used in intentional control, but it has made the mistake of defining freedom in terms of states of mind or feelings, and it has therefore not been able to deal effectively with techniques of control which do not breed escape or revolt but nevertheless have aversive consequences. It has been forced to brand all control as wrong and to misrepresent many of the advantages to be gained from a social environment. It is unprepared for the next step, which is not to free men from control but to analyze and change the kinds of control to which they are exposed.

Freedom to Learn

One of the deepest issues in modern life, in modern man, is the question as to whether the concept of personal freedom has any meaning whatsoever in our present-day scientific world. The growing ability of the behavioral scientist to predict and to control behavior has brought the issue sharply to the fore. If we accept the logical positivism and strictly behavioristic emphases which are predominant in the American psychological scene, there is not even room for discussion. . . .

But if we step outside the narrowness of the behavioral sciences, this question is not only *an* issue, it is one of the primary issues which define modern man. Friedman in his book (1963, p. 251) makes his topic "the problematic of modern man—the alienation, the divided nature, the unresolved tension between personal freedom and psychological compulsion which follows on 'the death of God'." The issues of personal freedom and personal commitment have become very sharp indeed in a world in which man feels unsupported by a supernatural religion, and experiences keenly the division between his awareness and those elements of his dynamic functioning of which he is unaware. If he is to wrest any meaning from a universe which for all he knows may be indifferent, he must arrive at some stance which he can hold in regard to these timeless uncertainties.

So, writing as both a behavioral scientist and as one profoundly concerned with the human, the personal, the phenomenological and the intangible, I should like to contribute what I can to this continuing dialogue regarding the meaning of and the possibility of freedom.

Man Is Unfree

. . . In the minds of most behavioral scientists, man is not free, nor can he as a freeman commit himself to some purpose, since he is controlled by factors outside of himself. Therefore, neither freedom nor commitment is even a possible concept to modern behavioral science as it is usually understood.

To show that I am not exaggerating, let me quote a statement from Dr. B. F. Skinner of Harvard, who is one of the most consistent advocates of a strictly behavioristic psychology. He says,

> The hypothesis that man is not free is essential to the application of scientific method to the study of human behavior. The free inner man who is held

From Carl R. Rogers, *Freedom to Learn for the Eighties* (Merrill, 1983). Copyright © 1983 by Carl R. Rogers. Adapted by permission of Prentice Hall, Inc., Upper Saddle River, NJ.

responsible for his behavior is only a prescientific substitute for the kinds of causes which are discovered in the course of scientific analysis. All these alternative causes lie *outside* the individual (1953, p. 477).

This view is shared by many psychologists and others who feel, as does Dr. Skinner, that all the effective causes of behavior lie outside of the individual and that it is only through the external stimulus that behavior takes place. The scientific description of behavior avoids anything that partakes in any way of freedom. For example, Dr. Skinner (1964, pp. 90-91) describes an experiment in which a pigeon was conditioned to turn in a clockwise direction. The behavior of the pigeon was "shaped up" by rewarding any movement that approximated a clockwise turn until, increasingly, the bird was turning round and round in a steady movement. This is what is known as operant conditioning. Students who had watched the demonstration were asked to write an account of what they had seen. Their responses included the following ideas: that the pigeon was conditioned to *expect* reinforcement for the right kind of behavior; that the pigeon *hoped* that something would bring the food back again; that the pigeon *observed* that a certain behavior seemed to produce a particular result; that the pigeon *felt* that food would be given it because of its action; that the bird came to *associate* his action with the clock of the food dispenser. Skinner ridicules these statements because they all go beyond the observed behavior in using such words as *expect, hope, observe, felt,* and *associate*. The whole explanation from his point of view is that the bird was reinforced when it emitted a given kind of behavior; the pigeon walked around until the food container again appeared; a certain behavior produced a given result; food was given to the pigeon when it acted in a given way; the click of the food dispenser was related in time to the bird's action. These statements describe the pigeon's behavior from a scientific point of view.

Skinner goes on to point out that the students were undoubtedly reporting what they would have expected, felt and hoped under similar circumstances. But he then makes the case that there is no more reality to such ideas in the human being than there is in the pigeon, that it is only because such words have been reinforced by the verbal community in which the individual has developed, that such terms are used. He discusses the fact that the verbal community which conditioned them to use such terms saw no more of their behavior than they had seen of the pigeon's. In other words the internal events, if they indeed exist, have no scientific significance.

As to the methods used for changing the behavior of the pigeon, many people besides Dr. Skinner feel that through such positive reinforcement human behavior as well as animal behavior can be "shaped up" and controlled. In his book *Walden Two*, Skinner says,

> Now that we know how positive reinforcement works and how negative doesn't, we can be more deliberate and hence more successful in our cultural design. We scan achieve a sort of control under which the controlled, though they are following a code much more scrupulously than was ever the case

under the old system, nevertheless *feel free*. They are doing what they want to do, not what they are forced to do. That's the source of the tremendous power of positive reinforcement—there is no restraint and no revolt. By a careful cultural design we control not the final behavior but the *inclination* to behave—the motives, the desires, the wishes. The curious thing is that in that case *the question of freedom never arises* (1948, p. 218).

. . . I think it is clear from all of this that man is a machine—a complex machine, to be sure, but one which is increasingly subject to scientific control. Whether behavior will be managed through operant conditioning as in *Walden Two* or whether we will be "shaped up" by the unplanned forms of conditioning implied in social pressure, or whether we will be controlled by electrodes in the brain, it seems quite clear that science is making out of man an object and that the purpose of such science is not only understanding and prediction but control. Thus it would seem to be quite clear that there could be no concept so foreign to the facts as that man is free. Man is a machine, man is unfree, man cannot commit himself in any meaningful sense; he is simply controlled by planned or unplanned forces outside of himself.

Man Is Free

I am impressed by the scientific advances illustrated in the examples I have given. I regard them as a great tribute to the ingenuity, insight, and persistence of the individuals making the investigations. They have added enormously to our knowledge. Yet for me they leave something very important unsaid. Let me try to illustrate this, first from my experience in therapy.

I think of a young man classed as schizophrenic with whom I had been working for a long time in a state hospital. He was a very inarticulate man, and during one hour he made a few remarks about individuals who had recently left the hospital; then he remained silent for almost forty minutes. When he got up to go, he mumbled almost under his breath, "If some of *them* can do it, maybe I can too." That was all—not a dramatic statement, not uttered with force and vigor, yet a statement of choice by this young man to work toward his own improvement and eventual release from the hospital. It is not too surprising that about eight months after that statement he was out of the hospital. I believe this experience of responsible choice is one of the deepest aspects of psychotherapy and one of the elements which most solidly underlies personality change.

I think of another young person, this time a young woman graduate student, who was deeply disturbed and on the borderline of a psychotic break. Yet after a number of interviews in which she talked very critically about all of the people who had failed to give her what she needed, she finally concluded: "Well, with that sort of a foundation, it's really up to *me*. I mean it seems to be really apparent to me that I can't depend on someone else to *give* me an education." And then she added very softly: "I'll really have to get it myself." She goes on to explore this experience of important and responsible choice. She finds it a frightening experience, and yet one which gives her a feeling of strength. A force seems to surge up within her which is big and strong, and yet she also feels very much alone and sort of cut off from support. She adds: "I am going to begin to do more things that I know I should do." And she did.

I could add many other examples. One young fellow talking about the way in which his whole life had been distorted and spoiled by his parents finally comes to the conclusion that, "Maybe now that I *see* that, it's up to *me.*" . . .

For those of you [who] have seen the film *David and Lisa*—and I hope that you have had that rich experience—I can illustrate exactly what I have been discussing. David, the adolescent schizophrenic, goes into a panic if he is touched by anyone. He feels that "touching kills," and he is deathly afraid of it, and afraid of the closeness in human relationships which touching implies. Yet toward the close of the film he makes a bold and positive choice of the kind I have been describing. He has been trying to be of help to Lisa, the girl who is out of touch with reality. He tries to help at first in an intellectually contemptuous way, then increasingly in a warmer and more personal way. Finally, in a highly dramatic movement, he says to her, "Lisa, take my hand." He *chooses,* with obvious conflict and fear, to leave behind the safety of his untouchableness, and to venture into the world of real human relationships where he is literally and figuratively in *touch* with another. You are an unusual person if the film does not grow a bit misty at this point.

Perhaps a behaviorist could try to account for the reaching out of his hand by saying that it was the result of intermittent reinforcement of partial movements. I find such an explanation both inaccurate and inadequate. It is the *meaning* of the *decision* which is essential to understanding the act.

What I am trying to suggest in all of this is that I would be at a loss to explain the positive change which can occur in psychotherapy if I had to omit the importance of the sense of free and responsible choice on the part of my clients. I believe that this experience of freedom to choose is one of the deepest elements underlying change.

The Meaning of Freedom

Considering the scientific advances which I have mentioned, how can we even speak of freedom? In what sense is a client free? In what sense are any of us free? What possible definition of freedom can there be in the modern world? Let me attempt such a definition.

In the first place, the freedom that I am talking about is essentially an inner thing, something which exists in the living person quite aside from any of the outward choices of alternatives which we so often think of as constituting freedom. I am speaking of the kind of freedom which Viktor Frankl vividly describes in his experience of the concentration camp, when everything—possessions, status, identity—was taken from the prisoners. But even months and years in such an environment showed only "that everything can be taken from a man but one thing: the last of the human freedoms—to choose one's own attitude in any given set of circumstances, to choose one's own way" (1959, p. 65). It is this inner, subjective, existential freedom which I have observed. It is the realization that "I can live myself, here and now, by my own choice." It is the quality of courage which enables a person to step into the uncertainty of the unknown as he chooses himself. It is the discovery of meaning from within oneself, meaning which comes from listening, sensitively and openly to the complexities of what one is experiencing. It is the burden of being responsible for the self one chooses to be. It is the recognition of a person that he is an emerging process, not a static end product. The individual who is thus deeply and courageously thinking his own thoughts, becoming his own uniqueness, responsibly choosing himself, may be fortunate in having hundreds of objective outer alternatives from which to choose, or he may be unfortunate in having none. But his freedom exists regardless. So we are first of all speaking of something which exists within the individual, something phenomenological rather than external, but nonetheless to be prized.

The second point in defining this experience of freedom is that it exists not as a contradiction of the picture of the psychological universe as a sequence of cause and effect, but as a complement to such a universe. Freedom rightly understood is a fulfillment by the person of the ordered sequence of his life. The free man moves out voluntarily, freely, responsibly, to play his significant part in a world whose determined events move through him and through his spontaneous choice and will.

I see this freedom of which I am speaking, then, as existing in a different *dimension* than the determined sequence of cause and effect. I regard it as a freedom which exists in the subjective person, a freedom which he courageously uses to live his potentialities. The fact that this type of freedom seems completely irreconcilable with the behaviorist's picture of man is something which I will discuss a bit later. . . .

The Emergence of Commitment

I have spoken thus far primarily about freedom. What about commitment? Certainly the disease of our age is lack of purpose, lack of meaning, lack of commitment on the part of individuals. Is there anything which I can say in regard to this?

It is clear to me that in therapy, as indicated in the examples that I have given, commitment to purpose and to meaning in life is one of the significant elements of change. It is only when the person decides, "I am someone; I am someone worth being: I am committed to being myself," that change becomes possible.

At a very interesting symposium at Rice University recently, Dr. Sigmund Koch sketched the revolution which is taking place in science, literature and the arts, in which a sense of commitment is again becoming evident after a long period in which that emphasis has been absent.

Part of what he meant by that may be illustrated by talking about Dr. Michael Polanyi, the philosopher of science, formerly a physicist, who has been presenting his notions about what science basically is. In his book, *Personal Knowledge*, Polanyi makes it clear that even scientific knowledge is personal knowledge, committed knowledge. We cannot rest comfortably on the belief that scientific knowledge is impersonal and "out there," that it has nothing to do with the individual who has discovered it. Instead, every aspect of science is pervaded by disciplined personal commitment, and Polanyi makes the case very persuasively that the whole attempt to divorce science from the person is a completely unrealistic one. I think I am stating his belief correctly when I say that in his judgment logical positivism and all the current structure of science cannot save us from the fact that all knowing is uncertain, involves risk, and is grasped and comprehended only through the deep, personal commitment of a disciplined search.

Perhaps a brief quotation will give something of the flavor of his thinking. Speaking of great scientists, he says:

> So we see that both Kepler and Einstein approached nature with intellectual passions and with beliefs inherent in these passions, which led them to their triumphs and misguided them to their errors. These passions and beliefs were theirs, personally, even universally. I believe that they were competent to follow these impulses, even though they risked being misled by them. And again, what I accept of their work today, I accept personally, guided by passions and beliefs similar to theirs, holding in my turn that my impulses are valid, universally, even though I must admit the possibility that they may be mistaken (1959, p. 145).

Thus we see that a modern philosopher of science believes that deep personal commitment is the only possible basis on which science can firmly stand. This is a far cry indeed from the logical positivism of twenty or thirty years ago, which placed knowledge far out in impersonal space.

Let me say a bit more about what I mean by commitment in the psychological sense. I think it is easy to give this word a much too shallow meaning, indicating that the individual has, simply by conscious choice, committed himself to one course of action or another. I think the meaning goes far deeper than that. Commitment is a total organismic direction involving not only the conscious mind but the whole direction of the organism as well.

In my judgment, commitment is something that one *discovers* within oneself. It is a trust of one's total reaction rather than of one's mind only. It has much to do with creativity. Einstein's explanation of how he moved toward his formulation of relativity without any clear knowledge of his goal is an excellent example of what I mean by the sense of commitment based on a total organismic reaction. He says:

> "During all those years there was a feeling of direction, of going straight toward something concrete. It is, of course, very hard to express that feeling in words but it was decidedly the case and clearly to be distinguished from later considerations about the rational form of the solution" (quoted in Wertheimer, 1945, p. 183–184).

Thus commitment is more than a decision. It is the functioning of an individual who is searching for the directions which are emerging within himself. Kierkegaard has said, "The truth exists only in the process of becoming, in the process of appropriation" (1941, p. 72). It is this individual creation of a tentative personal truth through action which is the essence of commitment.

Man is most successful in such a commitment when he is functioning as an integrated, whole, unified individual. The more that he is functioning in this total manner the more confidence he has in the directions which he unconsciously chooses. He feels a trust in his experiencing, of which, even if he is fortunate, he has only partial glimpses in his awareness.

Thought of in the sense in which I am describing it, it is clear that commitment is an achievement. It is the kind of purposeful and meaningful direction which is only gradually achieved by the individual who has come increasingly to live closely in relationship with his own experiencing—a relationship in which his unconscious tendencies are as much respected as are his conscious choices. This is the kind of commitment toward which I believe individuals can move. It is an important aspect of living in a fully functioning way.

The Irreconcilable Contradiction

I trust it will be very clear that I have given two sharply divergent and irreconcilably contradictory points of view. On the one hand, modern psychological science and many other forces in modern life as well, hold the view that man is unfree, that he is controlled, that words such as purpose, choice, commitment have no significant meaning, that man is nothing but an object which we can more fully understand and more fully control. Enormous strides have been and are being made in implementing this perspective. It would seem heretical indeed to question this view.

Yet, as Polanyi has pointed out in another of his writings (1957), the dogmas of science can be in error. He says:

> In the days when an idea could be silenced by showing that it was contrary to religion, theology was the greatest single source of fallacies. Today, when any human thought can be discredited by branding it as unscientific, the power previously exercised by theology has passed over to science; hence science has become in its turn the greatest single source of error.

So I am emboldened to say that over against this view of man as unfree, as an object, is the evidence from therapy, from subjective living, and from objective research as well, that personal freedom and responsibility have a crucial significance, that one cannot live a complete life without such personal freedom and responsibility, and that self-understanding and responsible choice make a sharp and measurable difference in the behavior of the individual. In this context, commitment does have meaning. Commitment is the emerging and changing total direction of the individual, based on a close and acceptant relationship between the person and all of the trends in his life, conscious and unconscious. Unless, as individuals and as a society, we can make constructive use of this capacity for freedom and commitment, mankind, it seems to me, is set on a collision course with fate. . . .

A part of modern living is to face the paradox that, viewed from one perspective, man is a complex machine. We are every day moving toward a more precise understanding and a more precise control of this objective mechanism which we call man. On the other hand, in another significant dimension of his existence, man is subjectively free; his personal choice and responsibility account for the shape of his life; he is in fact the architect of himself. A truly crucial part of his existence is the discovery of his own meaningful commitment to life with all of his being.

POSTSCRIPT

Should Behaviorism Shape Educational Practices?

The freedom-determinism or freedom-control argument has raged in philosophical, political, and psychological circles down through the ages. Is freedom of choice and action a central, perhaps *the* central, characteristic of being human? Or is freedom only an illusion, a refusal to acknowledge the external shaping of all human actions?

Moving the debate into the field of education, John Dewey depicted a developmental freedom that is acquired through improving one's ability to cope with problems. A. S. Neill (*Summerhill: A Radical Approach to Child Rearing*, 1984), who advanced the ideas of early-twentieth-century progressive educators and the establishment of free schools, sees a more natural inborn freedom in human beings, which must be protected and allowed to flourish. Skinner refuses to recognize this "inner autonomous man" but sees freedom resulting from the scientific reshaping of the environment that influences us.

Just as Skinner has struggled to remove the stigma from the word *control*, arguing that it is the true gateway to freedom, John Holt, in *Freedom and Beyond* (1972), contends that freedom and free activities are not "unstructured"—indeed, that the structure of an open classroom is vastly more complicated than the structure of a traditional classroom.

If both of these views have validity, then we are in a position, as Dewey counselled, to go beyond either-or polemics on these matters and build a more constructive educational atmosphere. Jerome S. Bruner has consistently suggested ways in which free inquiry and subject matter structure can be effectively blended. Arthur W. Combs, in a report titled *Humanistic Education: Objectives and Assessment* (1978), helped to bridge the ideological gap between humanists and behaviorists by demonstrating that subjective outcomes can be assessed by direct or modified behavioral techniques.

Skinner's death in 1990 prompted a number of evaluations, among them "Skinner's Stimulus: The Legacy of Behaviorism's Grand Designer," by Jeff Meade, *Teacher* (November/December 1990); "The Life and Contributions of Burrhus Frederic Skinner," by Robert P. Hawkins, *Education and Treatment of Children* (August 1990); and Carson M. Bennett, "A Skinnerian View of Human Freedom," *The Humanist* (July/August 1990).

Other perspectives on the learning atmosphere in schools may be found in *In Search of Understanding: The Case for Constructivist Classrooms* by Jacqueline G. Brooks and Martin G. Brooks (1993); Dave Perkins, "The Many Faces of Constructivism," *Educational Leadership* (November 1999);

Robert J. Sternberg, "Ability and Expertise," *American Educator* (Spring 1999); Howard Gardner, *Intelligence Reframed: Multiple Intelligences for the Twenty-First Century* (1999); and John Steadman Rice, "The Therapeutic School," *Society* (January/February 2002), which is a critique of Rogers and other humanistic psychologists.

Is Constructivism the Best Philosophy of Education?

YES: David Elkind, from "The Problem with Constructivism," *The Educational Forum* (Summer 2004)

NO: Jamin Carson, from "Objectivism and Education: A Response to David Elkind's 'The Problem with Constructivism'," *The Educational Forum* (Spring 2005)

ISSUE SUMMARY

YES: Child development professor David Elkind contends that the philosophical positions found in constructivism, thought often difficult to apply, are necessary elements in a meaningful reform of educational practices.

NO: Jamin Carson, an assistant professor of education and former high school teacher, offers a close critique of constructivism and argues that the philosophy of objectivism is a more realistic and usable basis for the process of education.

For years the term *constructivism* appeared only in journals read primarily by philosophers, epistemologists, and psychologists. Nowadays, *constructivism* regularly appears in the teacher's manuals of textbook series, state education department curriculum frameworks, education reform literature, and education journals. Constructivism now has a face and a name in education.

So say educators Martin G. Brooks and Jacqueline Grennon Brooks in "The Courage to Be Constructivist," *Educational Leadership* (November 1999). According to them, the heart of the constructivist approach to education is that learners control their learning. This being the case, the philosophical orientation provided by John Dewey, John Holt, and Carl R. Rogers here in Part 1 would seem to feed into the development of David Elkind's ideas on this educational theory. The contrary positions taken by Hutchins, Adler, and Skinner would seem to contribute to the objectivist philosophy espoused by Jamin Carson.

Constructivism, which is additionally influenced by the theories of Jean Piaget, Lev Vygotsky, and Jerome Bruner, is an approach to learning in which students construct new understandings through active engagement with their past and present experiences. Constructivists contend that traditional instructional models emphasize knowledge transmission without producing deeper levels of understanding and internalization.

Objectivists and other critics of constructivism say that this approach to learning is imprecise, overly permissive, and lacking in rigor. This argument is quite well illustrated in a *Phi Delta Kappan* exchange between Lawrence A. Baines and Gregory Stanley on one hand and Lynn Chrenka on the other (Baines and Stanley, "We Want to See the Teacher: Constructivism and the Rage Against Expertise," in the December 2000 issue and Chrenka, "Misconstructing Constructivism," in the May 2001 issue). Baines and Stanley condemn the constructivists' adamant stand against direct instruction by lecturing and the sin of memorization. Chrenka replies that expertise is central in a constructivist classroom in which the teacher must develop "scaffolding strategies" needed for the learners to begin to construct their own meanings.

David N. Perkins of the Harvard Graduate School of Education, in "The Many Faces of Constructivism," *Educational Leadership* (November 1999), describes a tension between ideological constructivism and pragmatic constructionism, the former being seen as a rather rigid cure-all for traditional school ills and the latter as a flexible, circumstance-driven means of school improvement. While the constructivists' goal of producing active, collaborative, creative learners is certainly an antidote to the often prevalent emphasis on knowledge absorption by passive learners, the techniques for moving toward that goal are often difficult to implement and most always require more time than traditional methods.

These "theory-into-practice" difficulties have been elaborated upon by Mark Windschitl in "The Challenges of Sustaining a Constructivist Classroom Culture," *Phi Delta Kappan* (June 1999), and by Peter W. Airasian and Mary E. Walsh in "Constructivist Cautions," *Phi Delta Kappan* (February 1997). Windschitl sees constructivism as a culture, not a mere collection of practices, so its effectiveness as a guiding philosophy is realized only through major changes in curriculum, scheduling, and assessment. Airasian and Walsh insist that the "catch phrases" that flow from theorists to teachers are inadequate for dealing with implementation complexities.

These and similar concerns are addressed in the first of the following articles, in which constructivism advocate David Elkind examines three major barriers—societal, curricular, and pedagogical—that must be removed if the philosophy is to flourish in school settings. In the second article, Jamin Carson, an objectivist, attacks not only the practical aspects of constructivism's implementation but the very basic principles on which it is based.

David Elkind

YES

The Problem with Constructivism

Constructivism, in all of its various incarnations, is now a major educational philosophy and pedagogy. What the various interpretations of constructivism have in common is the proposition that the child is an active participant in constructing reality and not just a passive recorder of it. Constructivism thus echoes the philosophy implicit in Rousseau's *Emile* (1962) in which he argued that children have their own ways of knowing and that these have to be valued and respected. It also reflects the Kantian (Kant 2002) resolution of the nature/nurture controversy. Kant argued that the mind provides the categories of knowing, while experience provides the content. Piaget (1950) created the contemporary version of constructivism by demonstrating that the categories of knowing, no less than the contents of knowledge, are constructed in the course of development. Vygotsky (1978) added the importance of social context to the constructivist epistemology—a theory of knowledge and knowledge acquisition.

Constructivism in education has been approached at many different levels and from a variety of perspectives (e.g., Larochelle, Bednarz, and Garrison 1998). In this essay, I will limit the discussion to those writers who have attempted to translate constructivism into a practical pedagogy (e.g., Brooks and Brooks 1993; Fosnot 1996; Gagnon and Collay 2001; Lambert et al. 1997). Though many different models have been created and put to test, none have been satisfactorily implemented. The failure of the constructivist reform movement is yet another in the long list of ill-fated educational reform movements (Gibboney 1994).

The inability to implement constructivist reforms is particularly instructive with regard to the failures of educational reforms in general. Constructivist reforms start from an epistemology. This sets constructivism apart from those educational reforms inspired by political events (such as the curriculum reform movement spurred by the Russian launching of the Sputnik) or by social events (such as the school reforms initiated by the Civil Rights Movement) or by a political agenda (e.g., *A Nation at Risk* [National Commission on Excellence in Education 1983]; the No Child Left Behind initiative). That is to say, the constructivist movement is generated by genuine pedagogical concerns and motivations.

From *The Educational Forum*, vol. 68, Summer 2004, pp. 306–312. Copyright © 2004 by Kappa Delta Pi. Reprinted by permission.

The lack of success in implementing this widely accepted educational epistemology into the schools can be attributed to what might be called *failures of readiness*. Consider three types of readiness: teacher readiness, curricular readiness, and societal readiness. Teacher readiness requires teachers who are child development specialists with curricular and instructional expertise. Curriculum readiness requires courses of study that have been researched as to what, when, and how the subject matter should be taught. Societal readiness requires a nation that is willing—indeed eager—to accept educational change. For a reform movement to succeed, all three forms of readiness must be in alignment.

Teacher Readiness

Those who have tried to implement a constructivist pedagogy often argue that their efforts are blocked by unsupportive teachers. They claim that some teachers are wedded to an objectivist view that knowledge has an independent existence and needs only to be transmitted. Others have difficulty understanding how to integrate the learner's intuitive conceptions into the learning process. Still others are good at getting children actively involved in projects but are not able to translate them effectively into learning objectives. These problems are aggravated by an increasingly test-driven curriculum with little opportunity for creativity and innovation.

The problem, however, is not primarily with teachers but with teacher training. In the United States, many universities and colleges have done away with the undergraduate major in education. In Massachusetts, for example, a student with a bachelor's degree in any field can get a provisional certification after a year of supervised internship. After five years and the attainment of a master's degree, the candidate is eligible for permanent certification.

The demise of the undergraduate major in education can be attributed to a number of different factors that were enunciated in *Tomorrow's Schools of Education* (Holmes Group 1995) written by the deans of 80 of some of the nation's most prestigious schools of education. The report (1995, 45–46) targeted the education faculty who "ignore public schools to concentrate on theoretical research or to work with graduate students who do not intend careers as classroom teachers." In effect, the education faculty has failed to provide the kind of research that would be useful to teachers. As the report (1995, 45–46) argued, "Traditional forms of academic scholarship have a place in professional schools, but such institutions are obliged as well to learn from practice and to concern themselves with questions of applying knowledge." These observations are supported by the facts. Few teachers read the educational research journals, and few educational researchers read the journals directed at teachers such as *Educational Leadership* and *Young Children*. This also is true for researchers in the field of child development. Much of the research on children's cognitive, social, and emotional development is directly relevant to teaching. Yet, the educational implications of these studies are rarely, if ever, discussed in the literature.

The end result is that much of teaching as a profession has to be learned in the field. While this is true for all professions to a certain extent, it is particularly true of education. Indeed, one could make the case that teaching is, as yet, more art than profession. Professional training implies a body of knowledge and skills that are unique and that can be acquired only through a prescribed course of study. It is not clear that such a body of knowledge and skills exists for education. In fact, each educational reform movement challenges the practices currently in play. Perhaps it is because there is no agreed upon body of knowledge and skills that reform in education is so frequent and so unsuccessful. To be sure, all professions have disagreements but they all share some fundamental common ground, whether it is anatomy in medicine or legal precedence in the field of law. There is, however, no such common base in education.

Teaching will become a true profession only when we have a genuine science of education. Such a science will have to be multidisciplinary and include workers from traditional educational psychology, developmental psychology, sociology, and various subject matter disciplines. Researchers would investigate individual and group differences in learning styles in relation to the acquisition of the various tool subjects (i.e., reading, writing, arithmetic, science, and social studies) at different age levels. Teacher training would provide not only a solid grounding in child development but also would require domain specific knowledge as it applies to young people at different age levels. Teachers also would be knowledgeable about research and would have access to journals that serve both teachers and investigators.

The failure to treat education as a profession has a long history but was made patent by Flexner's (1910) report *Medical Education in the United States and Canada*. That report was critical of medical education in the United States and suggested that training in medicine should be a graduate program with an undergraduate major. It also argued for the establishment of teaching hospitals as a means of practical training under supervision. Though the report was mandated by the Carnegie Foundation for the Advancement of Teaching, no comparable critique and suggestions were made for teachers and teacher training. The only innovation taken from this report was the founding of lab schools which would serve the same function as teaching hospitals at various universities. These schools, however, were more often used for research than for training. Today, only a few lab schools remain in operation.

Before any serious, effective reform in education can be introduced, we must first reinvent teacher training. At the very least, teachers should be trained as child development specialists. But teachers need much more. Particularly today, with the technological revolution in our schools, teacher training should be a graduate program. Even with that, teaching will not become a true profession unless and until we have a true science of education (Elkind 1999).

Curricular Readiness

A constructivist approach to education presupposes a thorough understanding of the curriculum to be taught. Piaget understood this very well. Much of his research was aimed at shedding light on what might be called the *logical substructure* of the discipline. That is to say, to match the subject matter to the child's level of developing mental abilities, you have to understand the logical demands it makes upon the child's reasoning powers. In his research with Inhelder (1964), Piaget demonstrated that for a child to engage in the addition and multiplication of classes, relations, and numbers, children first need to attain concrete operations. Similarly, Inhelder and Piaget (1958) showed that true experimental thinking and dealing with multiple variables require the formal mental operations not attained until adolescence. Task analysis of this sort is required in all curricular domains. Only when we successfully match children's ability levels with the demands of the task can we expect them to reconstruct the knowledge we would like them to acquire.

In addition to knowing the logical substructure of the task, we also need research regarding the timing of the introduction of various subject matters. For example, the planets often are taught at second grade. We know that children of seven or eight do not yet have a firm grasp of celestial space and time. Does teaching the planets at grade two give the child an advantage when studying astronomy at the college level? Similar questions might be asked about introducing the explorers as a social study topic in the early elementary grades. I am not arguing against the teaching of such material; I am contending that we need to know whether this is time well spent. We have little or no research on these issues.

Another type of curriculum information has to do with the sequence of topics within any particular course of study. In elementary math, is it more effective to teach coins before or after we teach units of distance and weight? Some sequences of concepts are more effective for learning than others. In most cases, we don't have data upon which to make that kind of decision. In most public school textbooks, the order of topical instruction is determined more by tradition, or by the competition, than by research. We find this practice even at the college level. Most introductory courses begin with a chapter on the history of the discipline. Yet many students might become more engaged in the subject if the first topic was one to which they could immediately relate. Again, we have little or no research on such matters. This is true for teaching in an integrated or linear curriculum format.

The argument that there is little connection between academic research and practical applications has many exceptions. Nonetheless, as long as these remain exceptions rather than the rule, we will not move toward a true science of education.

Societal Readiness

If the majority of teachers are not ready to adopt a constructivist pedagogy, neither are educational policy makers and the larger society. To be successfully implemented, any reform pedagogy must reflect a broad and energized social consensus. John Dewey was able to get broad backing for his Progressive Education Reform thanks to World War I and the negative reaction to all things European. Up until the First World War, our educational system followed the European classical model. It was based on the doctrine of formal discipline whereby training in Greek and Latin, as well as the classics, rigorously trained the mind. In contrast, Dewey (1899) offered a uniquely American functional pedagogy. He wanted to prepare students for the demands and occupations of everyday life. There was general consensus that this was the way to go.

The launching of the Russian Sputnik in 1957 was another event that energized the nation to demand curriculum reform. Russia, it seemed, had outstripped us scientifically, and this reflected badly on our math and science education. The National Science Foundation embarked on a program of science and math curriculum reform. To this end, the foundation recruited leading figures in the fields of science and math to construct new, up-to-date curricula in these fields. These scholars knew their discipline but, for the most part, they did not know children. The new curricula, which included variable-base arithmetic and teaching the principles of the discipline, were inappropriate for children. When these curricula failed, a new consensus emerged to advocate the need to go "back to basics." The resulting teacher-made curricula dominated education prior to the entrance of the academicians. While "back to basics" was touted as a "get tough" movement, it was actually a "get easier" movement because it reintroduced more age-appropriate material.

Many of the educational reforms of any category have not had much success since that time. Though A Nation at Risk (NCEE 1983) created a number of reforms, the report itself did not energize the nation, and there was not sufficient motivation to bring about real change. In large part, I believe that this was because there was no national consciousness of a felt need for change. The current educational movement, No Child Left Behind, was introduced for political rather than pedagogical reasons. This legislation was avowedly for the purpose of improving student achievement and changing the culture of American schools. These aims are to be achieved by requiring the states to test all children every year from grades three through eight. Schools that do not meet statewide or national standards may be closed or parents given an opportunity to send their children to other schools.

This is an ill-conceived program based on a business model that regards education as akin to a factory turning out products. Obviously, children are not containers to be filled up to a certain amount at each grade level. The program forces schools to focus on tests to the exclusion of what is really important in the educational process. Testing is expensive and depletes already scarce educational resources. Students are being coached to do well on the tests without regard to their true knowledge and understanding. The policy is corrupt in that it encourages schools to cheat. The negative results of this policy already are being felt. A number of states are choosing to opt out of the program. The No Child Left Behind legislation is a good example of bad policy promoted for political gain that is not in the best interests of children.

Other than a national crisis, there is another way for social consensus to bring about educational reform. In Kuhn's (1996) innovative book on scientific revolutions, he made the point that such revolutions do not come about by the gradual accretion of knowledge. Rather they come about as a result of conflicts between opposing points of view with one eventually winning out over the other. Evolution, for example, is still fighting a rear-guard action against those who believe in the biblical account of the origin of man. In education, the long-running battle between nature and nurture (read development and learning) is not likely to be resolved soon by a higher order synthesis.

An alternative view was offered by Galison (1997), who argued that the history of science is one of tools rather than ideas. He used the history of particle physics as an example. The tools of particle physics are optical-like cloud chambers and electronic-like photographic emulsions that display particle interactions by way of images. One could make equal claims for the history of biology and astronomy. As both Kuhn and Galison acknowledged, scientific progress can come about by conflict or the introduction of new technologies.

Education seems likely to be changed by new tools rather than conflicting ideas. Computers are changing education's successive phases. In the first phase, computers simply replaced typewriters and calculators. In the second phase, computers began to change the ways in which we teach. The widespread use of e-mail, Blackboard, PowerPoint, and simulations are examples. And there is an active and growing field of computer education with its own journals and conferences (e.g., Advancement of Computer Education and Association for the Advancement of Computing in Education). The third phase already has begun, and we are now seeing changes in math and science curricula as a direct result of the availability of technology. Education is one of the last social institutions to be changed by technology, but its time has come.

Conclusion

In this paper, I have used the failure of the constructivist reform movement to illustrate what I believe is necessary for any true educational innovation to succeed. There must be teacher, curricular, and societal readiness for any educational innovation to be accepted and put into practice. In the past, reforms were generated by one or the other form of readiness, but without the support of the others. I believe that technology will change this. It is my sense that it will move us toward making teaching a true profession, the establishment of a multidisciplinary science of education, and a society ready and eager to embrace a technologically based education.

Education is, however, more than technology. It is, at its heart, people dealing with people. That is why any successful educational reform must build upon a human philosophy that makes clear its aims and objectives. Technology without a philosophy of education is mechanical, and a philosophy without an appropriate technology will be ineffective. Technology is forcing educational reform, but we need to harness it to the best philosophy of education we have available. I believe this to be constructivism. The current failure to implement constructivism is not because of its merits but because of a lack of readiness for it. We need to make every effort to ensure that the technological revolution in education creates the kinds of teachers, curricula, and social climate that will make constructivism a reality in our classrooms.

References

Brooks, J. G., and M. G. Brooks. 1993. *In search of understanding: The case for constructivist classrooms.* Alexandria, Va.: Association for Supervision and Curriculum Development.

Dewey, J. 1899. *The school and society.* Chicago: University of Chicago Press.

Elkind, D. 1999. Educational research and the science of education. *Educational Psychology* 11(3): 171–87.

Flexner, A. 1910. *Medical education in the United States and Canada.* New York: Carnegie Foundation for the Advancement of Teaching.

Fosnot, C. T. 1996. *Constructivism: Theory, perspectives, and practice.* New York: Teachers College Press.

Gagnon, G. W. J., and M. Collay. 2001. *Designing for learning: Six elements in constructivist classrooms.* Thousand Oaks, Calif.: Corwin Press.

Galison, P. L. 1997. *Image and logic: A material culture of microphysics.* Chicago: University of Chicago Press.

Gibboney, R. A. 1994. *The stone trumpet: A story of practical school reform.* Albany, N.Y.: State University of New York Press.

Holmes Group. 1995. *Tomorrow's schools of education.* Ann Arbor: University of Michigan.

Inhelder, B., and J. Piaget. 1958. *The growth of logical thinking from childhood to adolescence: An essay on the construction of formal operational structures,* trans. A. Parsons and S. Milgram. New York: Basic Books.

Inhelder, B., and J. Piaget. 1964. *The early growth of logic in the child, classification and seriation,* trans. E. A. Lunzer and D. Papert. New York: Harper and Row.

Kant, I. 2002. *Immanuel Kant: Theoretical philosophy after 1781,* trans. G. Hatfield and M. Friedman. New York: Cambridge University Press.

Kuhn, T. S. 1996. *The structure of scientific revolutions,* 3rd ed. Chicago: University of Chicago Press.

Lambert, L., M. Collay, M. Dietz, K. Kent, and A. E. Richert. 1997. *Who will save our schools? Teachers as constructivist leaders.* Thousand Oaks, Calif.: Corwin Press.

Larochelle, M., N. Bednarz, and J. Garrison. 1998. *Constructivism and education.* Cambridge, England: Cambridge University Press.

National Commission on Excellence in Education. 1983. *A nation at risk: The imperative for educational reform.* Washington, D.C.: U.S. Government Printing Office.

Piaget, J. 1950. *The psychology of intelligence,* trans. M. Piercy and D. E. Berlyne. London: Routledge and Paul.

Rousseau, J. J. 1962. *Emile,* trans. W. Boyd. New York: Teachers College Press.

Vygotsky, L. S. 1978. *Mind in society: The development of higher psychological processes,* ed. M. Cole. Cambridge, Mass.: Harvard University Press.

NO

Jamin Carson

Objectivism and Education: A Response to David Elkind's 'The Problem with Constructivism'

In "The Problem with Constructivism," David Elkind (2004) made several claims about why constructivism has not been implemented in schools. He argued that constructivism will be implemented only when we have *teacher*, *curricular*, and *societal readiness*; that teaching needs to become a science before it can be a true profession; and that constructivism is the only philosophy that will reform education. In this essay, I present counterarguments for each of these claims.

Constructivism is the theory that students learn by individually or socially transforming information (Slavin 1997). This theory necessarily entails certain metaphysical and epistemological assumptions. To accept constructivism, one must believe that:

- reality is dependent upon the perceiver, and thus constructed;
- reason or logic is not the only means of understanding reality, but one of many; and
- knowledge or truth is subjective and relative to the individual or community.

One philosophy of education that challenges this theory is objectivism, which asserts that students must be engaged actively in the subject matter to learn. This theory does not advocate, however, that students "transform" or "construct" reality, reason, knowledge, or truth. Objectivism holds that one reality exists independent of anyone perceiving it, humankind is capable of knowing this reality only by the faculty of reason, and objective knowledge and truth is possible (Peikoff 1993). I argue against Elkind's claims primarily from an objectivist viewpoint.

Failures of Readiness

Elkind's main thesis was that constructivism has not been implemented in schools because of failures of teacher, curricular, and societal readiness. Teacher readiness requires that a teacher be educated in a science of education such as

From *The Educational Forum,* vol. 69, Spring 2005, pp. 232–238. Copyright © 2005 by Kappa Delta Pi. Reprinted by permission.

child development. Curricular readiness involves knowing exactly when and how students are developmentally ready to learn specific information. Societal readiness is when society is eager for educational reform or change.

Elkind did not explain the causal relationship between these states of readiness and the implementation of constructivism. He only implied that a causal relationship exists. There is no reason to believe that a relationship exists or that any state of readiness would lead to a specific philosophy of education. A teacher must accept the metaphysical and epistemological assumptions of a pedagogic practice before he or she can implement it.

Elkind's definitions of readiness also were problematic. When defining teacher readiness as having good teacher "training"—which comes only from scientific knowledge (e.g., child development)—he stated (2004, 308), "Teaching will become a true profession only when we have a genuine science of education." Though education is not a true science, teachers generally are taught one unique body of knowledge. Most college and university teacher preparation programs, alternative certification programs, and professional development seminars teach the same information, and a great deal of it is constructivist in nature or a variant of it.

Elkind's definition of curricular readiness also has problems. He (2004, 307–08) defined curricular readiness as knowledge of "what, when, and how the subject matter should be taught" and then claimed that "only when we successfully match children's ability levels with the demands of the task can we expect them to reconstruct the knowledge we would like them to acquire." The phrase "we would like them to acquire" contradicts constructivist metaphysics and epistemology. If constructivism assumes that students construct their own knowledge, then how can a constructivist teacher choose the knowledge they would like students to acquire? The phrase "we would like them to acquire" presupposes an objective philosophy which holds that given a specific context, some knowledge is objectively superior to other knowledge. For a constructivist, this is a contradiction, if one views reality, reason, knowledge, and truth as subjective and relative to the perceiver, then what is the basis for arguing for any knowledge at all, let alone one over another? Any curricular choice, according to constructivist philosophy, should be as valid as any other. When constructivists make absolute claims about what, when, and how something should be taught, they are either objectivists or making arbitrary claims.

Finally, there are problems with societal readiness. Elkind (2004, 310) suggested that "to be successfully implemented, any reform pedagogy must reflect a broad and energized social consensus," which the United States currently does not have. Yet, a broad and energized social consensus in the United States does exist. The concensus is that public education has not adequately educated its students, particularly those of lower socioeconomic status. This societal readiness has paved the way for programs like No Child Left Behind. Progressive reform pedagogies like constructivism are usually prescribed by administrators to improve education or raise test scores. Despite the social consensus that education needs reform pedagogy and constructivism has been one of those pedagogies, education still has not closed the gap between rich and poor—assuming that is education's aim in the first place.

Science of Education

Most teachers receive the same education, but not all teachers readily accept what they are taught, whether it be constructivism or some other philosophy of education. Unlike medical practitioners, for example, educators disagree about nearly all issues within their field. Medical practitioners simply observe whether or not the treatment cured the patient. They may disagree about why or how a treatment worked, but at least they have objective and verifiable evidence of whether or not the treatment worked. Education, on the other hand, possesses many more points of disagreement. How do people learn? What should people learn? How do we measure learning? The complexity of these questions results in virtually no consensus about what works among all educators. Though education draws from a unique body of knowledge to prepare its teachers, it is not scientific and probably never will be because there is so much disagreement about the definition of education.

Assuming that Elkind is correct in believing that education must become a science, his argument is still flawed. It is contradictory for a constructivist to advocate a science of education. The philosophical foundation of constructivism rejects an objectively knowable reality. The philosophical foundation of science claims that one reality is objectively knowable through the senses and reason. Science, therefore, undermines constructivism rather than serves as a prerequisite to it.

If Elkind used Kuhn's (1996) definition of science—reality is observed by a perceiver who sees it through the lens of socially constructed paradigms that are periodically overthrown by new paradigms that are incommensurate with past paradigms—then any science of education still has no claim of truth over any other method of inquiry within education. Claims like "teaching will become a true profession only when we have a genuine science of education" are equivalent to saying that teaching will be a profession only when it becomes an art. If we construct our own reality, what is the difference?

If Elkind believes that most of what educators consider science comes from constructivists like Rousseau, Kant, Piaget, and Vygotsky, his argument is flawed. It is circular logic for a constructivist to claim that a science of education is needed and then to select only constructivists as the founders of that science. Though some beliefs are obtained in experiments, most are not—especially philosophical views about *literally* constructing reality, which are not testable or falsifiable and thus should not be accepted as scientific.

Philosophy of Education

Elkind seems to have overlooked the role of the educator's metaphysical and epistemological assumptions in accepting constructivism or any philosophy of education. He admitted that educators who "are wedded to an objectivist view that knowledge has an independent existence" have resisted constructivism, but he quickly dismissed this cause in favor of teacher readiness. Ironically, teacher readiness is more likely the cause of resistance to constructivism. For an educator to implement a pedagogical practice, he or she must consciously or unconsciously accept its metaphysical and epistemological assumptions. Constructivists possess certain metaphysical and epistemological assumptions that lead to constructivist practices, while objectivists possess other metaphysical and epistemological assumptions that lead to objectivist practices. Elkind overlooked the possibility that not everyone holds the same assumptions about reality, reason, knowledge, and truth that lead to constructivist practices. Some have other worldviews and, therefore, reject constructivism as a theory of learning because it contradicts their philosophical assumptions.

Elkind said that constructivism is the "best philosophy of education we have available," and that it has been "widely accepted." This is true only at the university level, where the majority of professors possess the metaphysical and epistemological assumptions that lead to constructivism. It is not true at other levels of education, where one is likely to encounter different metaphysical and epistemological assumptions that lead to other pedagogical practices.

Constructivism is not the best philosophy of education. Objectivism is more reasonable from a theoretical and practical perspective than constructivism. Objectivism holds that there is one reality independent of anyone perceiving it. This means that regardless of whether or not someone perceives something, it still exists. For example, I can leave the room with a table in it and be convinced that the table still exists. Most people probably would agree with this statement. Constructivism, on the other hand, holds that reality is dependent upon the perceiver. This means that something exists only if someone perceives it. From a constructivist perspective, if I leave a room with a table in it, the table ceases to exist. Most people would disagree with such a statement or at least have difficulty accepting it.

Objectivism also holds that humankind takes in data through the senses and uses reason to obtain knowledge. Constructivism does not deny the efficacy of reason completely, but does consider it as only one of many ways of knowing. This belief is another theory that does not stand up in practice. The theory of multiple intelligences, for example, proposes at least ten "intelligences" or ways of knowing: verbal, logical, musical, physical, spatial, inter- and intra-personal, natural, existential, and spiritual. When analyzed or reduced to their epistemological foundation, these intelligences seem more like specialized bodies of acquired knowledge than actual processors of information. Reason exists in all of them, which suggests that each is the *primary* way of knowing.

Objectivism also holds that we have objective knowledge and truth. A person observes reality via his or her senses, forms concepts through the use of noncontradictory (i.e., Aristotelian) logic, and thus acquires knowledge and truth. Constructivism posits that only subjective knowledge and relative truth are possible. If knowledge is subjective or relative to an individual or a group, then *any* knowledge could be true. Sacrificing virgins to appease the gods or believing that the universe revolves around the earth would count as knowledge and truth. Notable constructivists (Lawson 1989; Noddings 1998; Rorty 2003) have raised these criticisms about constructivist metaphysics and epistemology and have admitted that they have no answer to them.

Constructivism in Practice

Practically, objectivism is more reasonable than constructivism. As a high school English teacher, I implemented constructivism in my classes by allowing the students to construct what an English class is—choosing its purpose, curriculum, and instruction. Most of the students did not understand how they could "construct" an English class. They expected me to define the English class for them—a very reasonable assumption considering how young they were and how limited their experience. After a fair amount of prompting, a few bold students thought English should be spelling and grammar. Some might argue that the students' answer proves only that they had been prevented from constructing previous curriculums, and thus had not learned to think for themselves or to question the curriculum. I concede that the students' previous conception of what constitutes schooling was part of their inability to construct the course. However, perhaps children naturally look to adults to share with them their learned and acquired knowledge. They expect teachers to pass on to them a body of knowledge, imperfect though it may be, that they can update according to their discoveries. Many practicing constructivists refuse to do this, believing instead that a child's knowledge is equal to that of an adult's and a student is no less an authority on a subject than a teacher. This assumption is untrue and dangerous. It assumes that children are better off entering a world with no knowledge and creating their own rather than entering a world full of knowledge, learning it, and then updating it if it does not stand the test of their scrutiny.

The students in my English class could not be pure constructivists in the context of day-to-day assignments either. For example, when we read *Romeo and Juliet* by William Shakespeare, the reality of the story presented obstacles. If the students would have said that the story was about an aging salesman who imagines he is a success when he is not, a constructivist teacher would have to accept their response—right or wrong—because reality is constructed. For an objectivist English teacher, however, every claim must be supported by textual evidence and logic—by reality. *Romeo and Juliet*, therefore, must be about what the text supports and what logic dictates, not about the subjective feelings of the reader, which may not be in accordance with reality. Constructivist English teachers who tell students that there are no right-or-wrong answers or that their interpretation is as correct as anyone else's only encourage students to be careless and uncritical readers, writers, and thinkers.

I shifted to giving students a choice supported by evidence and logic because of the flaws in the practical application of constructivism. Students could choose the purpose, curriculum, and assignments of the course, but ultimately their choices had to conform to reality, not to their subjective whims. In other words, their choices had to have a compelling connection to their literacy development.

Conclusion

Constructivists must ask themselves whether they want to cling to the literal interpretation of constructivism that sees reality as constructed or simply believe that students learn best when they are actively engaged in the learning process.

The two definitions are not the same metaphysically or epistemologically. The former entails an untenable theory and practice and should be modified or rejected.

Noddings (1998, 117–18) addressed the distinction between moderate and radical constructivism in this way:

> [I]f radical constructivists are just saying that our perception and cognition are theory-laden, that all knowledge is mediated by our cognitive structures and theories, then they have lots of company among contemporary theorists. However, if they are saying that there is no mind-independent reality, then they seem to be arguing a line long ago rejected.

Though Noddings seemed to advocate a moderate constructivist view that denies a mind-dependent reality, I maintain that constructivists cannot be moderates. All constructivists necessarily must believe that reality is dependent upon the perceiver. It is logically impossible to believe that a person's perception and cognitive structures are theoryladen, while simultaneously believing that reality is independent of the perceiver. If reality is perceived by a theory-laden perceiver, then the reality is theory-laden too. The moment that one becomes theory-laden, one is prevented from knowing an objective reality.

Objectivists believe humans are not theory-laden in the pejorative sense of that word. Objectivists do not consider prior knowledge or cognitive structures as a subjective lens through which one views reality. Rather, one possesses prior knowledge that informs new knowledge and, consequently, makes the new knowledge meaningful. If the prior knowledge or cognitive structure is incorrect, eventually the new correct knowledge will conflict with it and a person will be forced to update his or her old knowledge. If constructivists believe in an independent reality, then they not only must believe in it, but also must possess an objective method of perceiving it and, therefore, have objective knowledge and truth. There is no middle ground.

References

Elkind, D. 2004. The problem with constructivism. *The Educational Forum* 68(4): 306–12.

Kuhn, T. S. 1996. *The structure of scientific revolutions*, 3rd ed. Chicago: The University of Chicago Press.

Lawson, H. 1989. Stories about stories. In *Dismantling truth: Reality in the post-modern world*, ed. H. Lawson and L. Appignanesi, xi–xxviii. London: Weidenfeld and Nicolson.

Noddings, N. 1998. *Philosophy of education*. Boulder, CO: Westview Press.

Piekoff, L. 1993. *Objectivism: The philosophy of Ayn Rand*. New York: Penguin Books.

Rorty, R. 2003. Dismantling truth: Solidarity versus objectivity. In *The theory of knowledge: Classical and contemporary readings*, 3rd ed., ed. L. P. Pojman, 324–30. Belmont, CA: Wadsworth/Thomson Learning.

Slavin, R. E. 1997. *Educational psychology: Theory and practice*, 5th ed. Boston: Allyn & Bacon.

POSTSCRIPT

Is Constructivism the Best Philosophy of Education?

So it can be seen that present-day constructivists like David Elkind draw a lot of inspiration from Dewey's portrayal of the active, probing learner immersed in social experience, Holt's learners who steer their own personal development unfettered by imposed curricula, and Rogers' self-exploring students whose subjective knowledge takes precedence. In contrast, objectivists like Carson most likely find comfort in Hutchins's timeless rationality, Adler's concept of a single best curriculum for all, and Skinner's use of scientific principles and quantitative methods to create effective learners.

Elkind responded to Carson's critique in the Summer 2005 issue of *Educational Forum*, primarily refuting the accusation that constructivists deny that a physical world exists outside our sensory experiences. He states that "it is not that an external reality does not exist, only that we have to reconstruct it to know it . . . it is because humans share a common sensory apparatus that we can agree upon an external reality existing outside our experience." Our senses can be mistaken but "objective" reasoning is fallible as well, he concludes.

In the past decade, the philosophy of constructivism has been widely treated by those who praise it and those who deplore it. A sampling of sources includes Jacqueline Grennon Brooks and Martin G. Brooks, *In Search of Understanding: The Case for Constructivist Classrooms* (1993); Susan Ohanian, *One Size Fits Few* (1999); Karen R. Harris and Steve S. Graham, "Memo to Constructivists: Skills Count, Too," *Educational Leadership* (February 1996); Tony Wagner, "Change as Collaborative Inquiry: A 'Constructivist' Methodology for Reinventing Schools," *Phi Delta Kappan* (March 1998); Heinrich Mintrop, "Educating Students to Teach in a Constructivist Way—Can It All Be Done?" *Teachers College Record* (April 2001); and Rhoda Cummings and Steve Harlow, "The Constructist Roots of Moral Education," *The Educational Forum* (Summer 2000).

Additional commentary may be found in Michael Glassman, "Running in Circles: Chasing Dewey," *Educational Theory* (August 2004); Donald G. Hackmann, "Constructionism and Block Scheduling: Making the Connection," *Phi Delta Kappan* (May 2004); Ian Moll, "Towards a Constructivist Montessori Education," *Perspectives in Education* (June 2004); and David Chicoine, "Ignoring the Obvious: A Constructivist Critique of a Traditional Teacher Education Program," *Educational Studies* (December 2004).

On the Internet . . .

Center for Civic Education

Offers articles, research papers, and speeches on topics related to civic education in American schools.

http://www.civiced.org

National Alliance for Civic Education

Dedicated to ensuring that the next generation understands and values democracy and participates in its processes.

http://www.civnet.net

Civil Rights Project

Harvard University organization generates and synthesizes research on key civil rights issues and equal opportunity policies.

http://www.civilrightsproject.harvard.edu

Americans United for Separation of Church and State

Organization that has worked since 1947 to protect the constitutional principle of church-state separation.

http://www.au.org

J. M. Dawson Institute of Church-State Studies

Baylor University site provides articles on church-state separation issues and offers links to other sites.

http://www3.baylor.edu/Church_State

No Child Left Behind

U. S. Department of Education site examines the implementation of the new Elementary and Secondary Education Act and provides links for parents.

http://www.ed.gov/nclb/landing.jhtml

Fair Test

National Center for Fair and Open Testing site offers articles, information, and links on standardized tests and school accountability.

http://www.fairtest.org/K-12.htm

PART 2

Current Fundamental Issues

*T*he issues discussed in this section cover a number of fundamental social, cultural, and political problems currently under consideration by education experts, social scientists, and politicians, as well as by parents and the media. Positions on these issues are expressed by Stephen Macedo, Chester E. Finn, Jr., Gary Orfield, Juan Williams, Edd Doerr, Warren A. Nord, Andrew Rotherham, Peter Schrag, Nina and Sol Hurwitz, Ken Jones, Frederick M. Hess, Linda Nathan, Joe Nathan, Ray Bacchetti, and Evans Clinchy.

ISSUE 5

Can the Public Schools Produce Good Citizens?

YES: Stephen Macedo, from "Crafting Good Citizens," *Education Next* (Spring 2004)

NO: Chester E. Finn, Jr., from "Faulty Engineering," *Education Next* (Spring 2004)

ISSUE SUMMARY

YES: Princeton politics professor Stephen Macedo expresses confidence in the public schools' ability to teach students to become active participants in our democracy, suggesting that naysayers may wish to undermine all public institutions.

NO: Thomas B. Fordham Foundation president Chester E. Finn, Jr., contends that the diversity of the American population makes the public schools ill-equipped to produce the engaged citizens our democracy requires.

Events here and abroad, combined with concerns about the level of preparation of the young for participation in democratic life have given impetus to current re-evaluations of the quality of civic education in American schools. The 9/11 terrorist attacks, the war in Iraq, and the passing of the Patriot Act by Congress have brought new urgency to the historic aim of education to produce knowledgeable and engaged citizens. At the same time, we are seeing a decline in voter participation among the young and persistently low scores on assessments of knowledge in areas essential to functioning in a democracy. Another factor to be considered is the increasing diversity of the population because the influx of Latin Americans and Asians, which raises new questions about the traditional assimilationist slant on citizenship preparation.

Civic education as a central purpose of schooling cannot be disputed. Thomas Jefferson made the principles of democratic government an essential element in the free basic education for the general citizenry. Horace Mann's common school was dedicated to producing people able to critically judge the political and social needs of the nation. Mann felt that only public schools could accomplish this because private schools tend to encourage students to develop a limited political perspective. Waves of European immigrants in the nineteeth century prompted a new emphasis on socialization strategies, the development of patriotism, and the requirements for full citizenship. As Joel Spring points out, in *Conflict of Interests: The Politics of American Education*, "in a totalitarian society it is possible to teach a single interpretation of the laws and government in the public schools, but in a society such as that of the United States, which fosters a variety of political beliefs . . . , attempts to teach principles of government can result in major political battles."

A further complication emerged in the 1980s with the push for stronger academic performance by American students to meet global economic competition. The current Bush administration emphasis on test performance to meet standards in certain academic areas may, according to the editors of *School: The Story of American Public Education* (2001), diminish the goal of building active and morally sensitive citizens who carry out their civic duties. Others have speculated that emphasis on parental choice in recent decades and the expansion of home schooling have had an effect on the goals of civic education. Charles N. Quigley of the Center for Civic Education has stated that formal instruction should provide students with an understanding of civic life, government, and the fundamental values underlying our democracy and that this should be abetted by informal instructional aspects of the school community. Every state notes the need for such civic education, but, Quigley contends, the goal is seldom given systematic attention in the K–12 public school curriculum and may well be missing in private schools or in home-schooling situations.

In "Civic Education and Political Participation," *Phi Delta Kappan* (September 2003), William A. Galston agrees that school-based civic education has been in decline over recent decades. He claims that every significant indicator of political engagement among the young has fallen. Community-service programs in high schools are on the increase, but there is no evidence that such "mandatory volunteerism" leads to wider civic participation. He states that "the surge of patriotic sentiment among young people in the immediate wake of September 11th has not yielded a comparable surge in engaged, active citizenship."

In the following debate, Stephen Macedo argues that the public schools should teach students to become active participants in democratic life and that this can be accomplished without resulting in political indoctrination. Chester E. Finn, Jr., counters that it may be impossible for government-run schools in such a diverse society to do a good job of forging citizens and that, indeed, some present attempts may well be harmful.

Stephen Macedo  **YES**

Crafting Good Citizens

Americans are rightly concerned that schools are not providing students with the knowledge and habits necessary to be good citizens. With the notable exception of volunteer activity, every form of civic engagement among the young has declined. About half of those aged 18 to 29 voted in the 1972 presidential election. By the 1996 election, however, the share had dropped to less than one-third. While 58 percent of college freshmen polled by UCLA in 1966 considered it important to keep up with politics, only 26 percent thought so by the end of the 1990s. Even though young Americans are more educated than ever before, they pay far less attention than previous generations did to traditional news sources like newspapers and network television. And few of them use new media such as the Internet to replace traditional sources of news about world events.

In response to these trends, increasing attention is being paid to civic education in the schools. But strangely, at a moment when the schools seem capable of becoming a bulwark against civic *dis*engagement among the young, a rising chorus of skeptics is casting doubt on the whole enterprise of civic education. In practice, they charge, civic education is ineffective and potentially harmful. The materials used in social studies courses, where most schooling about the political process occurs, are too often built on a foundation of moral relativism, cynicism toward received traditions, and, as Chester Finn puts it, "Undue deference to the *'pluribus'* at the expense of the *'unum.'*"

Critics also question the very idea of government-sponsored civic education, arguing that it threatens basic principles of intellectual freedom. It would be far better, they say, to leave the teaching of values to parents, churches, and private schools. Thus we would avoid the sorry spectacle of government's promoting some values at the expense of others.

So how should we assess civic education as public policy? Let's consider three fundamental questions:

- Is it true that civic education makes no difference or even undermines students' interest and participation in civic life?
- Have the efforts to promote civic engagement been sufficient to conclude that the experiment has failed?
- Are the differences in values among Americans truly so vast that it will be impossible to develop a reasonable public consensus on the goals of civic education?

From *Education Next*, Spring 2004, pp. 10, 12–15. Copyright © 2004 by Education Next. Reprinted by permission.

The answers to each of these questions, I will argue, give us substantial reasons to doubt the skeptical position on civic education. However, I am not at all sure that those who wish to eliminate civics from the public schools care much about finding out the facts. Their interest in maligning civic education may stem from a desire not to improve the content of public schooling but to undermine public institutions altogether.

Does Civic Education Work?

It is important, first, not to exaggerate what schools can accomplish in this sphere. After all, families are the primary socializers in our society, and the mass media shape children's attitudes in pervasive ways. We cannot expect schools by themselves to transform apathetic, self-absorbed consumers into active and engaged citizens. Nevertheless, the best available evidence suggests that teaching students about current events, the political process, and how to get involved can make them more willing and able to practice good citizenship.

Consider the findings summarized in an excellent recent report, *The Civic Mission of Schools*, issued by the Carnegie Corporation of New York and the Center for Information and Research on Civic Learning and Engagement:

- Formal instruction in the key elements of American history and the nation's governmental structure and processes is a crucial building block of civic education.
- Active discussion of current local, national, and international events should be incorporated into the classroom, especially issues of interest to young people. This can improve students' critical thinking and communication skills and promote the discussion of political issues outside the classroom.
- More than 80 percent of high-school seniors are already participating in some form of volunteer activity, which is one bright spot in the civic landscape. Nevertheless, more could be done to link community service with classroom instruction as well as other civic and political activities.
- Extracurricular activities have long been known to contribute to students' tendencies to become and remain civically engaged, even after decades have passed.
- Giving students a voice in the management of the classroom and the school may well increase civic skills and attitudes.
- Participating in simulations of democratic institutions may increase students' political knowledge, skills, and interest, though the data are not conclusive.

Despite these benefits of civic education, it turns out that the skeptics are already getting their way in many respects. Until the 1960s, it was common for high-school students to take as many as three courses in civics, democracy, and government. Today, however, most students take only one government-related course. According to the Carnegie report, social studies courses also appear to be in decline. Community service is widely encouraged in high schools, but it is too often separate from the rest of the curriculum. Meanwhile, the singular focus of high-stakes testing on students' math and reading scores largely ignores civic knowledge. Likewise, the National Assessment of Educational Progress (NAEP) offers a civics assessment only once every ten years. This sends the signal that civic education matters very little.

If public schools are failing to teach civic knowledge, it is at least partly because they are not trying. To simply throw up our hands and say that public education agencies should now withdraw from civic education seems nothing short of perverse.

Uncommon Values?

The critics' answer is that even if civic education does work, it is simply not a role that the state should undertake in a free society—or at least in a diverse society such as ours, where there are vast disagreements over political and moral values.

But do our differences make it impossible for us to arrive at reasonable consensus standards on the goals of civic education? To my mind, the answer is no. In fact, the nation has already developed reasonable national standards for the teaching of civics. The NAEP standards read:

> Twelfth-grade students performing at the Proficient level should have a good understanding of how constitutions can limit the power of government and support the rule of law. They should be able to distinguish between parliamentary systems of government and those based on separate and shared powers, and they should be able to describe the structure and functions of American government. These students should be able to identify issues in which fundamental democratic values and principles are in conflict—liberty and equality, individual rights and the common good, majority rule and minority rights, for example, and they should be able to take and defend positions on these issues.

On the 1998 NAEP civics exam, just 26 percent of high-school seniors qualified as "proficient." This is because the standards are genuinely demanding and because, as already noted, the schools are not making an adequate effort to teach civics. If anything, the NAEP civics standards, like the national standards formulated by the Center for the Study of Civic Education (a project in which I participated), might be criticized for being somewhat old-fashioned. Nevertheless, they are good mainstream standards, establishing an appropriate base of civic knowledge and competence that should be attained by all children. The same is true of the NAEP standards for the teaching of U.S. history. These standards do not emphasize indoctrination at the expense of critical thinking. On the contrary, the history standards say things like: students "should be able to communicate reasoned interpretations of past events, using historical evidence effectively to support their positions." What do critics find so bothersome there?

Critics rightly point to serious flaws in some guidelines offered for the teaching of social studies. The National Council for the Social Studies—the main professional organization in this field—has put forth guidelines that are less concerned with students' basic knowledge of civics and history than with encouraging students to develop a "personal perspective" so they can make "choices." Of course there are good and bad standards and practices for civic education. So why can't critics chip in and promote the good standards? It would be deeply unfortunate for them not to do so based on the misguided conviction that the whole enterprise of civic education is wrong in principle.

Education and Indoctrination

But what of the "Orwellian" paradox of the government of a free people dictating political values in the name of civic education? In the pages of *Education Next*, James B. Murphy has argued that all education should aim to instill only academic and intellectual virtues—the love of learning and the critical pursuit of truth—and that this is incompatible with efforts to inculcate particular convictions such as "my country is good" (see "Tug of War," *Research*, Fall 2003).

The assumption here seems to be that civic education will inevitably devolve into indoctrination—an assumption that is typically backed by some admittedly objectionable statements found in one social studies curriculum or another. However, most civic educators properly distinguish between empty propaganda and genuine education. To the extent that civic education involves teaching students about the structure of their government, the workings of the political process, and the issues that are debated in the public sphere, there is nothing essentially "Orwellian" about civic education or public schooling.

What of Murphy's argument that schooling should promote only intellectual virtues like love of learning, not moral values or other political virtues? This proposal has the twin defects of being impossible and unattractive. Civic education is inseparable from education: no teacher could run a classroom, no principal could run a school, without taking a stand on a wide range of civic values and moral and political virtues. How could you conduct a classroom without taking a stand on gender equality? Are you going to treat boys and girls the same or not? Are you going to treat all religions in a tolerant manner? Do you care equally about the education of rich kids and poor kids? It would be nothing short of bizarre for schools to confine themselves to promoting only "academic" or "intellectual" virtues while leaving aside democratic virtues such as basic equality of concern and respect for all people. Important moral and political values constrain and shape the way we conceive of and advance the intellectual enterprise.

Education and indoctrination are indeed two very different things, but to describe classroom learning as "academic" or "intellectual" as opposed to "civic" misses the extent to which our conception of learning is infused with democratic values. It is quixotic and misguided to think we should, or even can, get civic education out of the schools. Civic education is not only legitimate; it is inescapable. All education, properly undertaken, has a civic element.

Chester Finn's solution for the potentially indoctrinating effects of civic education is to allow parents to choose which schools—and thereby which civic traditions—they want for their children. But indoctrination is wrong in any school, whether public or private, secular or religious. Perhaps, however, the skeptics are not interested in civic education that teaches children about government and politics and encourages critical thinking about the major issues of the day. The argument that private schools are best equipped to deliver civic education may be driven by a different conception of what the term includes. It is sometimes argued that a *robust* civic and moral education requires the teaching of values and virtues about which parents disagree. Because a robust education is necessarily controversial, it can happen only if parents can choose schools that reflect their personal moral and religious convictions.

This argument is worrisome. It certainly throws the whole distinction between education and indoctrination out the window. Indoctrination is anti-educational whether it is undertaken by the government or by parents and churches. Parents already control much of what children learn. It may be that schooling would improve if parents were able to exercise more choices, but in the absence of common standards and accountability for the teaching of required subjects like civics, I would worry about whether nonpublic schools could be trusted to fulfill our aims for public education. The public has not only a right but also a responsibility to ensure that all publicly funded schools educate according to reasonable public standards.

The Persistence of Public Education

Previous research has shown that Catholic schools apparently do a better job than public schools of producing active and engaged future citizens. However, the "Catholic school advantage" with respect to civic education does not carry over to all private schools. Indeed, while the evidence is thin, it suggests that evangelical schools promote higher levels of civic engagement but also greater intolerance. In any case, enthusiasm for school choice should not lead us to ignore the importance of either civic education in public schools or public standards for civic education in all schools.

The fact is that we are not walking away from public schooling. The voucher revolution shows no sign of happening. The current system serves the interests of many if not most Americans, especially suburbanites removed from the problems of inner-city neighborhoods and schools. Therefore, we ought to think about how public schools can do a better job of promoting civic engagement. It makes no sense to simply trust private markets, private communities, or private choices to deliver on such an important public goal.

As publicly funded school choice expands incrementally—as I believe it will and (if properly regulated) should—there will need to be an increased focus on public standards and accountability for civic education. The public has a basic and legitimate interest in regulating what is taught in all publicly funded schools. And it is very hard for me to see how civic education—knowledge of how the political process works and of the major events and conflicts in American history—does not count among the essential branches of a child's education. In addition, the idea of civic education is popular with young people as well as adults—strong majorities of young people favor making civics classes mandatory in middle and high school. The extensive experience of other nations with publicly funded school choice also suggests that public dollars will inevitably be accompanied by extensive public expectations and regulations.

For all their admitted flaws, civic education courses and other school-based programs to promote civic engagement can and do make a positive difference. Moreover, research on civic education has expanded in recent years and become more sophisticated—we have begun to figure out what works. Meanwhile, good mainstream consensus standards for civic education have been articulated. These standards no doubt could be improved, but they have earned and deserve a reasonable bipartisan consensus. We have no reason for cynicism about civic education. Advocates of school choice should embrace the opportunity to demonstrate that private schools can do a good job at civic education, and common standards and testing are the only way to do so.

But do conservative critics care about civic education? The Bush administration came into office arguing for a renewed national commitment to service and citizenship (a fact that suggests civic education is not as ideologically contentious as critics charge). National service and volunteerism were keynotes of the president's 2002 State of the Union Address, following the tragic events of September 11, 2001. National service and civic education programs were reorganized, under an impressive leadership team, as the USA Freedom Corps. The White House called for a major increase in spending on service and programs for civic education. And where did all these noble efforts go? The current budget calls for a massive cut in the national service spending in order to help pay for tax cuts. So it's all a question of priorities.

In the end, critics of public schooling and civic education—and there is much to criticize—need to decide whether to join the efforts to fix what's broken or to continue simply trashing public institutions.

Chester E. Finn, Jr.

 **NO**

Faulty Engineering

Every society creates mechanisms for teaching its young what they must know to become contributing citizens. Yet in a liberal democracy such as the United States, the proper ordering of those mechanisms is beset by paradox: if free citizens are to rule the state, does the state have a legitimate role in shaping their values and beliefs via its public schools, universities, and other institutions?

Because Americans insist that government is the creature of its citizens, we are loath to rely on state decisions and institutions to instruct our children in how to think, how to conduct themselves, and what to believe. After all, civic education may sound like a good idea in theory, but in practice public schools could even do harm in this realm. Some educators harbor worrisome values: moral relativism, atheism, doubts about the superiority of democracy, undue deference to the "*pluribus*" at the expense of the "*unum*," discomfort with patriotism, cynicism toward established cultural conventions and civic institutions. Transmitting those values to children will gradually erode the foundations of a free society. Perhaps society would be better off if its schools stuck to the three Rs and did a solid job in domains where they enjoy both competence and wide public support.

However, a free society is not self-maintaining. Its citizens must know something about democracy and about individual rights and responsibilities. They must also learn how to behave in a law-abiding way, respecting basic societal norms and values. Thus all educational institutions, especially primary and secondary schools, would seem to have an obligation to help transmit these core ideas, habits, and skills. Indeed, we fret when we learn of schools that *neglect* this role—the more so in a dangerous world where attacks on American values and institutions (and people) make it more important than ever to rear children who understand and prize those values.

One of the more effective debating points scored against voucher plans, for example, is the charge that "Klan schools," "witchcraft schools," and "fundamentalist madrasas" will qualify for public subsidy while imparting malign values to their pupils. Yet should government define which values are sound? And how is that different from an Orwellian regime of authoritarianism and theocracy? A fine dilemma indeed.

From *Education Next*, Spring 2004, pp. 16, 18–21. Copyright © 2004 by Education Next. Reprinted by permission.

Standards and Civics

Our quandaries grow more vexing still as the standards movement transfers key decisions about the content of education from local neighborhoods and communities to distant policymakers in state and national capitals.

Under federal law, every state must now have statewide standards in reading, math, and science, and nearly every state has also developed standards in social studies and other important areas of the school curriculum. Social studies standards typically focus not only on history, geography, economics, and government, but also on citizenship, social norms, and the like. Here, for example, is the opening of New Jersey's description of its "core curriculum content standards for social studies":

> Citizen participation in government is essential in forming this nation's democracy, and is vital in sustaining it. Social studies education promotes loyalty and love of country and it prepares students to participate intelligently in public affairs. Its component disciplines foster in students the knowledge and skills needed to make sense of current political and social issues. By studying history, geography, American government and politics, and other nations, students can learn to contribute to national, state, and local decisionmaking. They will also develop an understanding of the American constitutional system, an active awareness and commitment to the rights and responsibilities of citizenship, a tolerance for those with whom they disagree, and an understanding of the world beyond the borders of the United States.

A worthy aspiration indeed, yet one that is rarely attained. There is ample evidence to demonstrate that U.S. schools have failed even to impart basic information to children about their country's history and how its government and civil institutions work. For example, just 26 percent of U.S. high-school seniors attained the "proficient" level on the 1998 National Assessment of Educational Progress civics exam. Just 11 percent reached that level on the 2001 assessment of U.S. history. (Fifty-seven percent scored below the "basic" level on that assessment.)

If young people don't know that their state has two senators, don't understand the separation of powers, cannot explain the causes of the Civil War, and have difficulty distinguishing the New Deal from a poker game, what chance is there that they are acquiring—from the schools, anyway—"an active awareness and commitment to the rights and responsibilities of citizenship"? Is it not imperative for schools to establish a solid foundation of basic knowledge on which values, attitudes, and behaviors can securely rest?

Outside the Classroom

There's good news, too, but of a perverse sort: the very limits of schooling—both its ineffectiveness and the relatively small place it occupies in children's lives—leave ample room for other influences to work on youngsters' civic values and behavior. Parents, neighbors, churches, scouts, girls and boys clubs, the media—all play a significant role in sculpting children's understanding of the world around them. America has a vibrant civil society that does a decent job of forging good citizens even if the schools don't. That's why so many young Americans do obey the law (if not necessarily the speed limit), do volunteer, do help old people across the street, do serve valiantly in the military, and so forth.

But we also know that many young Americans don't vote, don't read the newspaper, don't serve their communities, and show dwindling interest in current affairs. Worse, there is the huge problem of young people whose lives are influenced mainly by gangs, street culture, hip hop, and the worst of movies and television. These young people lack good role models at home and have few ties to civil society.

Which brings the problem into clearer focus. Let me recap. First, we are ambivalent about the role of the schools in teaching citizenship. Second, U.S. schools don't do a very good job today, either on the cognitive side or on the attitudinal and behavioral side. Third, though nearly all children suffer from the schools' shortcomings on the cognitive side, many fare reasonably well when it comes to the behavioral aspects of citizenship, thanks to other healthy influences in their lives. Fourth, young people without such influences are doubly victimized by the schools' failings—because they have little with which to compensate, either in acquiring knowledge or in forging decent civic values.

The Pitfalls of Civics Education

Can this knot of problems be untangled and solved? Many are trying. Innumerable foundations, commissions, state initiatives, and federal programs are now seeking to renew civic education in American schools. But solutions run headlong into a series of barriers. Four of these seem especially troublesome.

• First, efforts to develop a civics curriculum are snagged by a basic truth about America: beyond a narrow core of shared beliefs (honesty, tolerance, obeying the law), Americans hold strong but often divergent views about the values they want their children to acquire and about the role of teachers and schools in inculcating those values. It may, therefore, be impossible for the publicly operated schools of a society that is so diverse to do a good job of forging citizens. Consider the challenge of deciding what experiences constitute "service learning" for high-school students in jurisdictions where this is now expected as part of a civics class or social studies curriculum. Does volunteering in one's church qualify? In an abortion clinic? Bringing coffee and donuts to grateful GIs at the nearby military base? Leading a protest against military action? When adults heatedly disagree about the value of such activities, how can a democracy's public schools decide on their proper role in the lives and education of the young?

Fierce watchdog groups constantly scrutinize the public schools for signs of religiosity. Activists pressure schools to redefine "civic education" in terms of influencing public policy and engaging in political activity—while giving short shrift to being a good parent, dependable neighbor, and conscientious member of the nongovernmental institutions that compose civil society. And everybody gangs up on textbooks, which are afflicted by hypersensitivity to the possibility of bias or controversy. This baleful influence comes from both the left and the right.

Hence much gets omitted from class materials and much of what remains has been sanitized to the point of banality. This has the effect of depriving schools and teachers of many of the stories, books, poems, plays, and legends from which children might best learn the difference between good and evil, right and wrong, hero and villain, patriot and traitor. Moreover, the fear of being criticized by pressure groups encourages curriculum writers and textbook publishers to make their instructional materials value-free from the outset.

• Second, within the field of civics education, a battle rages between those who believe that the schools' responsibility is mainly cognitive (imparting specific knowledge to children) and those who insist that youngsters' behavior and attitudes are what schools should work on. It's one thing to explain the role of voting in a democracy, for example, but quite another to help young people acquire the habit of voting or internalize a sense of obligation that they must vote. For many civic educators, these habits, beliefs, and dispositions matter more than "book learning." For example, a recent Carnegie Corporation report, *The Civic Mission of Schools*, offers four takes on "competent and responsible citizens." The first of these says such citizens are "informed and thoughtful," which can mesh with a cognitive view of the school's role. But the other three—"participate in their communities," "act politically," and "have moral and civic virtues"—are harder to instill through conventional books and teaching. They rekindle old debates about the propriety and competency of schools' intruding into people's beliefs and behaviors.

Recall that, in the 1980s, a number of states poked into students' values and behavior through what was termed "outcomes-based" education. This began innocently and earnestly, as a logical response to the era's focus on school results rather than simply inputs. As it spread to include pupil attitudes, actions, and ideologies, however, many people balked at what they saw as government imposing patterns of behavior and thought on children under the guise of mandatory academic standards. For example, the Minnesota state board of education proposed in 1991 that high-school graduation should hinge on students' contributing to "global communities" and the "economic well-being of society," understanding the "interdependency of people," and "working cooperatively in groups." Rightly or not, some parents and religious leaders held that these smacked of socialism and one-worldism, if not Marxism, and that the state had no business imposing such things on its young people. The upshot was that most jurisdictions pulled back to the more strictly cognitive domains.

• Third, there are the limits of schooling itself. Between birth and age 18, a typical young American spends just 14 percent of waking hours beneath the school roof. That's barely enough time to cover reading, writing, and arithmetic well, much less to offset the harmful influences that may be at work on children during the other 86 percent of their lives. In response, one may want the school day or year to lengthen, and many good schools, especially those serving disadvantaged students, have striven to enlarge their portion of children's lives. But the overwhelming majority of schools start at about 8 a.m. and end around 2 p.m. Moreover, they are in session for only half the days in the year. Nor do children go near a public school until the age of five or six. How large a share of responsibility for shaping tomorrow's citizens is it practical for those schools to shoulder?

• Fourth and finally, the civic and pedagogical values of many educators differ from those of many parents. Faithful to "progressive" traditions and postmodern beliefs, too many education school professors signal to future teachers that they should abjure firm distinctions between right and wrong. Nowhere is this more evident than in the social studies—the part of the curriculum that is commonly held responsible for civics education.

The man in the street probably supposes that social studies consist mainly of history and civics, leavened with some geography and economics. At the end of a well-taught K–12 social studies sequence, one would expect young people to know at least who Abraham Lincoln and Theodore Roosevelt were, why World War II was fought, how to find Italy and Iraq on a map, and what "supply and demand" mean.

If that were so, school-based social studies would contribute to the forging of citizens, at least on the cognitive side. But that's not what animates the experts who rule this field. They are more concerned with imparting multiple "perspectives" to students, as described in a position paper of the National Council for the Social Studies (NCSS):

> Students should be helped to construct a personal perspective that enables them to explore emerging events and persistent or recurring issues, considering implications for self, family, and the whole national and world community. This perspective involves respect for differences of opinion and preference; of race, religion, and gender; of class and ethnicity; and of culture in general. This construction should be based on the realization that differences exist among individuals and the conviction that this diversity can be positive and socially enriching.

One may or may not find these to be valid goals for social studies, but it's reasonably safe to say that, as a framework for civics education in particular, they will stir dissent from American parents, voters, and taxpayers. Thus a clash is inevitable between what we can term the social studies view of civics and the popular view. Indeed, such a clash has been under way for decades. "During the 1930s," writes New York University scholar Diane Ravitch, "one national report after another insisted that social studies should replace chronological history and that young people should study immediate personal and social problems rather than the distant, irrelevant past."

Diversity in Civics Education

Can education reformers overcome these four barriers and place American schools on a sure-footed path to effective civics education? I think not, at least not through top-down reform strategies that emphasize uniform school practices, and certainly not as long as the real pressure for performance and accountability centers on reading and math.

There is, however, another possibility for strengthening civics education. It is to be found in the reform strategy known as school choice. Besides its other strengths, school choice sidesteps one of the big obstacles to better civic education: it accommodates the divergent views and priorities of ethnic and religious groups, parents, and educators, and allows them to tailor the approach to civics that they favor for their children rather than settling for awkward efforts at lowest-common-denominator consensus. Parents who decide that a given school's approach is not right for their daughters and sons are free to make other selections.

The accompanying risk is balkanization: discordant approaches to civic education as one school emphasizes Athenian values while another stresses those of Sparta. In response, choice proponents cite evidence that private school students are more civically engaged than their public school peers. They remind us that government-operated schools are doomed to do a lackluster job in this area. And they note that, as long as states retain the authority to establish core academic standards for all public schools, they have the opportunity to mitigate curricular balkanization, even in such fractious fields as social studies.

Although certain forms of school choice (tax credits, some voucher programs) abjure state academic standards and tests, others (such as charter schools and public school choice) normally take them for granted. Hence if the state—or other cognizant authority—can get its civics standards right, can attach decent assessments to them, and can steel itself to insist that student performance in this field "counts," it will go a considerable distance toward infusing both standards-based and choice-based education reform with a decent possibility of making a difference in this field.

But those are enormous ifs. All the aforementioned obstacles in society and within the education profession impede any large political unit (such as a state) from attaining consensus about what should be in its civics standards—much less tying an enforcement regimen to them. Today's pressure to boost math and reading achievement makes it less likely that the requisite political energy and resources can be mustered on behalf of a field like civics. The fractures within social studies and the ambivalence of parents will tend to deter public officials from even trying very hard. Moreover, the aspects of civics that can be spelled out in academic standards and accurately assessed through statewide tests are almost entirely cognitive: well worth learning, to be sure, even a necessary precondition for successful adult life, but not exactly what people have in mind when they say that schools should forge "responsible citizens."

In the end, we may need to accept the fact that the school's—and the state's—role in this domain is simply limited: by its meager portion of children's lives, by its pedagogical weakness, by the absence of political and intellectual consensus, and by the modest capabilities of state standards and tests. We may do well to acknowledge that the solemn duty of readying young people for successful participation in adult society depends at least as much—and perhaps quite a lot more—on what happens to them when they are not in school.

POSTSCRIPT

Can the Public Schools Produce Good Citizens?

Using the findings of the Carnegie report on *The Civic Mission of the Schools,* Stephen Macedo contends that teaching students about current events, the political process, and avenues of involvement can make them more willing and able to become good citizens. Citing National Assessment of Educational Progress standards and those formulated by the Center for the Study of Civic Education, he takes the position that our differences do not preclude arriving at a consensus about the goals of effective civic education. Chester E. Finn, Jr., worries that those who design and carry out civic education in the public schools may push certain values to the extent of indoctrination, emphasizing moral relativism, discomfort with patriotism, and doubts about the superiority of democracy. "America has a vibrant civil society that does a decent job of forging good citizens even if the schools don't," he claims, expressing his faith in school choice to accommodate diverse views. Education historian Diane Ravitch, in *Making Good Citizens: Education and Civil Society* (2001), shares Finn's fear of public schools controlled by "educational experts" and "progressive reformers" bent on "social engineering." Macedo, however, might be equally concerned about the risks of indoctrination and engineering in the private schools and charter schools operating under a parental choice plan.

One seemingly positive development in recent years on the civic education front has been the expansion of community-service programs. This attempt to generate altruism and engagement among youth has received encouragement at the national and state levels. Mandatory programs, however, have met with considerable opposition by those who feel that they sap the volunteer spirit. Some programs have been met with legal challenges, and the fact that many jurisdictions sentence white-collar criminals to periods of community service has certainly tainted the effort.

Among the many books available on this topic are Diane Ravitch and Joseph Viteritti, eds., *Making Good Citizens: Education and Civil Society,* (2001); Norman Nie, *Education and Democratic Citizenship in America* (1996); Amy Gutmann, *Democratic Education* (1999); David Tyack, *Seeking Common Ground: Public Schools in a Diverse Society* (2003); and James A. Banks, ed., *Diversity and Citizenship Education: Global Perspectives* (2004).

Articles of special interest include: Debra Henzey, "The Civic Mission of Schools," *Clearing House* (March–April 2003) and Harry C. Boyte, "Civic Education and the New American Patriotism Post 9/11," *Cambridge Journal of Education* (March 2003).

ISSUE 6

Has Resegregation Diminished the Impact of *Brown?*

YES: Gary Orfield, Erica D. Frankenberg, and Chungmei Lee, from "The Resurgence of School Segregation," *Educational Leadership* (December 2002/January 2003)

NO: Juan Williams, from "The Ruling That Changed America," *American School Board Journal* (April 2004)

ISSUE SUMMARY

YES: Harvard professor Gary Orfield and his research associates present evidence that school resegregation has been increasing almost everywhere in recent years, placing a cloud over the fiftieth anniversary celebration of the *Brown* decision.

NO: Journalist and commentator Juan Williams, while recognizing the slow pace and backward steps involved in school desegregation, argues that the social and cultural changes inaugurated by *Brown* mark it as a monumental ruling.

The fiftieth anniversary of the U.S. Supreme Court decision in *Brown* v. *Board of Education* in 2004 was a bittersweet celebration for many Americans, marking an occasion for societal self-appraisal. As Judith R. Kafka stated in her review of James T. Patterson's *Brown v. Board of Education: A Civil Rights Milestone and Its Troubled Legacy,* "The story of *Brown* is also its legacy—the years of Southern resistance, additional court cases, the Civil Rights Act of 1964, busing riots, white flight, as well as the debates on both the right and the left, in white communities and black, in scholarly works and popular writing about what *Brown* was all about, what it meant, what it accomplished, and what relevancy the Court decision and the integrationist liberal ideal it embodied have for us today."

A good deal of the soul-searching commentary of recent years was prompted by the 1996 publication of *Dismantling Desegregation: The Reversal of Brown v. Board of Education* by Gary Orfield and Susan E. Eaton of the Harvard Project on School Desegregation. "The nation is quick to celebrate *Brown* . . . as a sacred turning point in history . . . yet existing and in some cases increasing racial and economic isolation is overlooked," they claimed. They accused the Supreme Court of abandoning original desegregation plans. This sentiment is elaborated by Suzanne E. Eckes in "The 50th Anniversary of *Brown*: Is There Any Reason To Celebrate?" *Equity & Excellence in Education* (September 2004). She cites such cases as *Milliken* v. *Bradley* (1974), *Board of Education of Oklahoma* v. *Dowell* (1991), and *Missouri* v. *Jenkins* (1995) as evidence of the Supreme Court's path, claiming that because of these and lower court rulings, "school districts face racial divides almost as great as those of 1954."

One central factor that animates the current appraisals of the desegregation effort is the persistence of the achievement gap among the constituent racial groups. As Hugh B. Price, president of the National Urban League, points out in *Achievement Matters* (2002), "In virtually every school district across America, African-American children achieve at lower levels, earn lousier test scores, are placed more frequently into special education or remedial or less-challenging classes, and are discouraged from striving to excel academically or demanding excellence from themselves." The result is what he calls a "self-destructive mindset." Psychiatrist James P. Comer gets at this problem in *Leave No Child Behind* (2004), stating that because many poor black students "are not immersed in positive and protective family and community networks, many will embrace harmful nonmainstream habits and styles as 'our culture.' And because the habits do not promote school and life success, their involvement is not just an adolescent interlude but often a one-way ticket to marginality for themselves and generations to come." Charles T. Clotfelter, in *After Brown: The Rise and Retreat of School Desegregation* (2004), takes a different track, citing four factors impeding full desegregation: (1) white reluctance to accept racially mixed schools, (2) the multiplicity of options for avoiding such schools, (3) the willingness of local officials to accommodate these whites, and (4) the eventual loss of will on the part of the protagonists in the fight for integration.

The articles presented here examine the evolution of the desegregation effort launched by the *Brown* decision and civil rights legislation. Gary Orfield and his co-authors present a rather pessimistic portrayal of recent trends, while Juan Williams expresses a sense of optimism in the wide-ranging social and cultural gains that the effort has made possible.

Gary Orfield, Erica D. Frankenberg, and Chungmei Lee

YES

The Resurgence of School Segregation

Nearly half a century ago, the U.S. Supreme Court's decision in *Brown v. Board of Education* (1954) initiated decades of progress in the struggle to desegregate public schools. But now that progress has been reversed: Segregation has been increasing almost everywhere for a decade.

Traditionally, public schools have created a common preparation for citizenship. The fact that more students now attend separate and unequal schools portends serious consequences for our country's multiethnic future. Because elected officials and the courts have provided almost no leadership in addressing this issue since the 1970s, the responsibility for leadership is now falling on educators. As education leaders explore ways to reverse the growing separation of ethnic groups in U.S. schools, they need to understand the current ethnic composition of the school-age population, the status of resegregation, and the reasons for these trends.

The Public School Population Today

The United States has seen a rapid transformation in the racial composition of its public schools. In 1968, four of every five students were white, but since that time the student population has been growing consistently more diverse. In just a little more than 30 years, the Latino share of public school enrollment has almost tripled, reaching 7 million students, or 16.3 percent. During the same period, the African American proportion of total enrollment grew more modestly and now stands at about 8 million students, or 17.1 percent. As the second-fastest-growing minority group, Asians now number almost 2 million students and make up 4.1 percent of the total student population. The smallest racial group, Native Americans, number a little more than one-half million students and make up just over 1 percent of public school enrollment (The Civil Rights Project, 2002).

Until recently, the rapid growth in minority populations has been heavily concentrated in the South and West, two regions that together now enroll more than one-half of all students and have the largest concentrations of African American and Latino students, respectively. In the South, only 54 percent of all students are white, and in the West, only 51 percent.

From *Educational Leadership*, December 2002/January 2003, pp. 16–20. Copyright © 2002 by Association for Supervision & Curriculum Development. Reprinted by permission. The Association for Supervision & Curriculum Development is a worldwide community of educators advocating sound policies and sharing best practices to achieve the success of each learner. To learn more, visit ASCS at **www.ascd.org**

One-third of all students in the West are Latino, and they are a growing presence in a number of states in other regions. As both Latino and African American enrollments outpace the growth of white enrollment, every region is becoming more heavily minority (The Civil Rights Project, 2002).

Changing Levels of Segregation

Our recent study for The Civil Rights Project at Harvard University (Frankenberg & Lee, 2002) provides a portrait of the changing levels of segregation for African American and Latino students. We analyzed enrollment data collected by the U.S. Department of Education in the National Center for Education Statistics Common Core of Data from school year 2000–2001, examining school districts with enrollments greater than 25,000.

Despite the growing diversity of the school-age population, our research indicates an overwhelming trend toward school district resegregation. African American and Latino students became more racially segregated from whites in their schools from 1986 to 2000 in virtually every one of the 185 districts in our sample of public school districts with enrollment greater than 25,000.

In the United States, the average white student attends a school that is almost four-fifths white. Only 14 percent of white students attend schools where at least three races comprise 10 percent or more of the total student population.

African American students are twice as likely as white students to attend multiracial schools. The average African American student, however, attends schools that are less than one-third white.

The most segregated minority group by race and income (and, increasingly, by language) are Latino students. The average Latino student attends a school where less than half of the students are non-Latinos. More than three-fourths of Latino students are in predominantly minority schools, and three-eighths are in 90–100 percent minority schools. The isolation is even more extreme for the typical Latino English-language learner, who attends a school that is almost two-thirds Latino. Learning a second language is difficult enough; lack of opportunities to interact with native English-speaking peers makes this task even harder (Horn, 2002).

Why Do We See These Trends?

Some believe that minority exposure to whites is dropping just because the white student population is declining. Despite the continued decline of white students in the past 35 years, however, integration increased from the beginning of the 1960s until the late 1980s. Only in the past decade have we seen an unraveling of almost 25 years of increasing integration and a return toward segregation in our schools. What factors, then, have led to these trends?

Residential Patterns

The 2000 U.S. Census showed a pattern of increasing residential segregation for Latinos in most parts of the United States. For African Americans, however, most metropolitan areas in the United States are becoming more integrated.

Most of the declines in residential segregation resulted from the increased movement of African Americans into areas that were formerly overwhelmingly white. According to the Census, the suburbs, which have a long history of being largely white, are increasing in size and diversity. In fact, the suburbs are now over one-fourth minority, and their growth was fueled primarily by minorities during the past decade (Frey, 2001). Because we see an increase in African American school segregation at the same time that residential segregation is decreasing, residential patterns are clearly not responsible for the school trends.

School Choice

The data also suggest that private school choice does not play a large role in the trend toward increased public school segregation. In 2000, the vast majority of white students attended public schools, and the white share of overall private school enrollment was actually lower than half a century ago. Data from a recent private school study (Reardon & Yun, 2002) show that white enrollment in private schools fell after an initial rise during the post-*Brown* period; thus, the white private school enrollment rate in 2000 was comparable to that in 1968 (about 13 percent).

In some of the largest districts with high proportions of minority students, however, one-third or more of the white student population attends private schools, substantially affecting the racial composition of the public schools. Private schools in many city neighborhoods have long enrolled large numbers of white students; these schools may offer white parents a means to ensure that their children avoid attending public schools where they will be in the racial minority.

Public school choice also affects the overall segregation of students. More than 1.6 million students, or 3.5 percent of all public school students, attend either magnet or charter schools. Although a larger proportion of white students attend private schools, they are using public choice to a lesser extent: Whites are under-enrolled in both magnet and charter schools compared with their proportion of the general school population (The Civil Rights Project, 2002).

Magnet schools arose as a method to aid in desegregating schools. School systems hoped to attract white students by offering enhanced programs in inner-city areas. The success of magnet schools in achieving this goal varies from district to district, but evidence suggests that magnet schools may not have achieved their objectives in the largest districts. In almost half of school systems with enrollments greater than 60,000, the magnet schools have lower percentages of white students than the school system overall. For example, in Guilford County, North Carolina, the system's enrollment is almost half white, yet the magnet school enrollment is only 31 percent white (The Civil Rights Project, 2002).

Court Actions

An increasingly conservative judiciary, which has issued a series of rulings reversing earlier progress, has played a major role in the resegregation of U.S.

schools. To understand this role, we must look at the history of public school desegregation in the past half-century.

In 1954, the U.S. Supreme Court's *Brown v. Board of Education* decision outlawed the practice of legal segregation in public schools for African American and white students. Before this ruling was made, 17 states and the District of Columbia mandated separate schools. Desegregation evolved very slowly until the late 1960s, when both the federal court system and the executive branch worked to forcibly implement desegregation in Southern school districts (Orfield, Eaton, & The Harvard Project on School Desegregation, 1996).

In 1968, the Supreme Court ruled in *Green v. County School Board of New Kent County* that "freedom of choice" desegregation plans, which placed the onus of integration on African American students, did not go far enough in eradicating the dual system of segregated schools. By 1970, one-third of all African American students in the South attended predominantly white schools. One of the Court's strongest decisions regarding school desegregation was *Swann v. Charlotte-Mecklenberg Board of Education* in 1971, which mandated such remedies as busing to fully integrate schools.

But the tide of desegregation enforcement had begun to shift. The composition of the federal courts was transformed through the appointment of more conservative judges, and executive enforcement of desegregation became weaker.

In the early 1970s, the U.S. Supreme Court issued key decisions that blocked effective desegregation efforts outside the South. For example, the Court's ruling in *Milliken v. Bradley* (1974) restricted the use of inter-district desegregation remedies—that is, combining several school districts into one desegregation plan—unless the segregative practices of one system had an impact on another. The effect of this decision, combined with the continued expansion of urban minority communities, further diminished the actual desegregation that could occur in central city districts each year and meant that whites wishing to escape desegregation could simply move to the suburbs.

By the late 1980s, a solid conservative majority on the U.S. Supreme Court rolled back desegregation policies. Three Court decisions in the early 1990s dramatically relaxed the judicial desegregation standards required for school systems.

In 1991, the Court's ruling in *Board of Education of Oklahoma v. Dowell* created standards for dismissing long-running desegregation orders and allowing a return to neighborhood schools even if doing so meant returning to segregated schools. In two subsequent decisions, *Freeman v. Pitts* (1992) and *Missouri v. Jenkins* (1995), the Court further constricted the extent and duration of desegregation remedies.

The district courts have responded to the U.S. Supreme Court's rulings by dismissing desegregation plans for districts seeking to end oversight by the courts. In fact, some school districts that want to maintain their desegregation plans have had to fight in court to keep policies that earlier courts had imposed on them.

For a long time, educators could look to the courts and federal agencies to assume the burden of doing something about segregation. Now the courts, reconstructed in a 35-year period in which Democrats appointed only two Supreme Court justices, are dismantling desegregation orders. Segregation is spreading across the land.

Why Should Educators Care?

Resegregation would not matter so much if racial segregation were not linked to unequal education. Nine-tenths of intensely segregated schools for African Americans and Latinos have high concentrations of poverty (The Civil Rights Project, 2002).

The racial and poverty composition of schools is strongly linked to test scores, graduation rates, the ability to attract and retain talented and experienced teachers, the range of course offerings, student health, parental involvement, and many other factors that influence educational opportunity. After more than 60 years of trying to implement the 1896 mandate of "separate but equal," followed by a third of a century of Title I programs trying to improve high-poverty schools, both race and poverty remain powerfully linked to educational inequality. Schools faced with both high minority enrollments and high poverty rates rarely excel.

Segregated schools produce lower student achievement, controlling for other influences (Oakes, 1990). Some of the negative effects of segregation can be partially addressed, of course, by placing better teachers in such schools, enriching the curriculum, making the schools safer, and implementing other changes. Such schools rarely compete successfully for the best teachers and other scarce resources, however. In fact, good, experienced teachers tend to move away from segregated schools (Freeman, Scafidi, & Sjoquist, 2002).

Thus, educators find themselves in a bind. As the system becomes increasingly segregated, the No Child Left Behind Act will hold schools responsible for achieving equal results. If educators talk about segregation, they may be criticized. If they do not and the segregated schools fail, they will be blamed.

Some school district officials may believe that being released from a court order (by being declared "unitary") means that the district gains freedom to do what it wants. In fact, if the district wants to maintain integrated schools, a court order gives it the freedom to take conscious action, such as implementing desegregation goals for magnet schools. After the school system has been declared unitary and released from a court order, it may be forbidden to consider race in student assignment. In that case, the only good way to maintain diverse schools may be the kind of income desegregation now being explored in areas as diverse as Raleigh, North Carolina; Cambridge, Massachusetts; and La Crosse, Wisconsin.

Where Do We Go from Here?

In many places for long periods of time, African American students experienced substantial integration. (Latino students have largely been ignored in this struggle.) But today, U.S. public schools are more segregated than they were in the early 1970s, before the U.S. Supreme Court ordered busing for desegregation.

All the gains of desegregation have not been lost. Interracial exposure in schools remains high in many areas, despite the current judicial trends. In Kentucky, for example, the average African American student attends a school that is two-thirds white. Although the South has experienced the biggest increases in African American-white segregation in the past decade, because of the region's tremendous earlier progress it still has the lowest percentage of African American students in segregated schools (Frankenberg & Lee, 2002).

The issues today are different from those during the Civil Rights era. The problems are not in the small towns of the South, and they are not just about African Americans and whites. They are multiracial and metropolitan. Many of the immediate challenges are suburban.

In spite of its importance, desegregation is neither a cure-all nor feasible everywhere. But we should be concerned about the intensifying segregation and think about possible approaches to expand the number of successful interracial schools. We must replace the old model of integrating one minority group into a largely white school with a multiracial vision of school integration that fits our rapidly changing society. Education leaders need to preserve and expand integration where possible, and they need to invest strong leadership in making segregated schools less unequal. Both are urgent priorities.

References

Board of Education of Oklahoma v. Dowell, 498 U.S. 237 (1991).

Brown v. Board of Education of Topeka, 347 U.S. 483 (1954).

Civil Rights Project at Harvard University, The. (2002). Computations based on the National Center for Education Statistics Common Core of Data, 2000–01. Cambridge, MA: Author.

Frankenberg, E., & Lee, C. (2002). *Race in American public schools: Rapidly resegregating school districts*. Cambridge, MA: The Civil Rights Project at Harvard University.

Freeman, C., Scafidi, B., & Sjoquist, D. L. (2002). *Racial segregation in Georgia public schools, 1994–2001: Trends, causes, and impact on teacher quality*. Paper presented at the Resegregation of Southern Schools Conference, University of North Carolina at Chapel Hill, August, 2002.

Freeman v. Pitts, 503 U.S. 467 (1992).

Frey, W. H. (2001). *Melting-pot suburbs: A census 2000 study of suburban diversity*. (The Brookings Institution Center on Urban and Metropolitan Policy, census 2000 series). Washington, DC: Brookings Institution.

Green v. County School Board of New Kent County, 391 U.S. 430 (1968).

Horn, C. (2002). *The intersection of race, class and English learner status* (Working Paper). Cambridge, MA: The Civil Rights Project at Harvard University.

Milliken v. Bradley, 418 U.S. 717 (1974).

Missouri v. Jenkins, 115 S. Ct. 2038 (1995).

Oakes, J. (1990). *Multiplying inequalities: The effects of race, social class, and tracking on opportunities to learn math and science*. Santa Monica, CA: RAND.

Orfield, G., Eaton, S., & The Harvard Project on School Desegregation (Eds.). (1996). *Dismantling desegregation: The quiet reversal of* Brown v. Board of Education. New York: New Press.

Reardon, S., & Yun, J. T. (2002). *Private school racial enrollments and segregation*. Cambridge, MA: The Civil Rights Project at Harvard University.

Swann v. Charlotte-Mecklenburg Board of Education 402 U.S. 1 (1971).

 **NO**

The Ruling That Changed America

Fifty years later, the *Brown* decision looks different. At a distance from the volcanic heat of May 17, 1954, the real impact of the legal, political, and cultural eruption that changed America is not exactly what it first appeared to be.

On that Monday in May, the high court's ruling outlawing school segregation in the United States generated urgent news flashes on the radio and frenzied black headlines in special editions of afternoon newspapers. One swift and unanimous decision by the top judges in the land was going to end segregation in public schools. Southern politicians reacted with such fury and fear that they immediately called the day "Black Monday."

South Carolina Gov. James Byrnes, who rose to political power with passionate advocacy of segregation, said the decision was "the end of civilization in the South as we have known it." Georgia Gov. Herman Talmadge struck an angry tone. He said Georgia had no intention of allowing "mixed race" schools as long as he was governor. And he touched on Confederate pride from the days when the South went to war with the federal government over slavery by telling supporters that the Supreme Court's ruling was not law in his state; he said it was "the first step toward national suicide." The *Brown* decision should be regarded, he said, as nothing but a "mere scrap of paper."

Meanwhile, newspapers for black readers reacted with exultation. "The Supreme Court decision is the greatest victory for the Negro people since the Emancipation Proclamation," said Harlem's *Amsterdam News*. A writer in the *Chicago Defender* explained, "neither the atomic bomb nor the hydrogen bomb will ever be as meaningful to our democracy." And Thurgood Marshall, the NAACP lawyer who directed the legal fight that led to *Brown*, predicted the end of segregation in all American public schools by the fall of 1955.

Slow Progress, Backward Steps

Ten years later, however, very little school integration had taken place. True to the defiant words of segregationist governors, the Southern states had hunkered down in a massive resistance campaign against school integration. Some Southern counties closed their schools instead of allowing blacks and whites into the same classrooms. In other towns, segregationist academies opened, and most if not all of the white children left the public schools for the racially exclusive

From *American School Board Journal* by Juan Williams. Reprinted with permission from American School Board Journal, April 2004. Copyright 2004 National School Boards Association. All rights reserved.

alternatives. And in most places, the governors, mayors, and school boards found it easy enough to just ask for more time before integrating schools.

That slow-as-molasses approach worked. In 1957, President Eisenhower had to send troops from the 101st Airborne into Little Rock just to get nine black children safely into Central High School. Only in the late '60s, under the threat of losing federal funding, did large-scale school integration begin in Southern public schools. And in many places, in both the North and the South, black and white students did not go to school together until a federal court ordered schoolchildren to ride buses across town to bring the races together.

Today, 50 years later, a study by the Civil Rights Project at Harvard University finds that the percentage of white students attending public schools with Hispanic or black students has steadily declined since 1988. In fact, the report concludes that school integration in the United States is "lower in 2000 than in 1970, before busing for racial balance began." In the South, home to the majority of America's black population, there is now less school integration than there was in 1970. The Harvard report concluded, "At the beginning of the 21st century, American schools are now 12 years into the process of continuous resegregation."

Today, America's schools are so heavily segregated that more than two-thirds of black and Hispanic students are in schools where a majority of the students are not white. And today, most of the nation's white children attend a school that is almost 80 percent white. Hispanics are now the most segregated group of students in the nation because they live in highly concentrated clusters.

At the start of the new century, 50 years after *Brown* shook the nation, segregated housing patterns and an increase in the number of black and brown immigrants have concentrated minorities in impoverished big cities and created a new reality of public schools segregated by race and class.

The Real Impact of *Brown*

So, if *Brown* didn't break apart school segregation, was it really the earthquake that it first appeared to be?

Yes. Today, it is hard to even remember America before *Brown* because the ruling completely changed the nation. It still stands as the laser beam that first signaled that the federal government no longer gave its support to racial segregation among Americans.

Before *Brown*, the federal government lent its power to enforcing the laws of segregation under an 1896 Supreme Court ruling that permitted "separate but equal" treatment of blacks and whites. Blacks and whites who tried to integrate factories, unions, public buses and trains, parks, the military, restaurants, department stores, and more found that the power of the federal government was with the segregationists.

Before *Brown*, the federal government had struggled even to pass a law banning lynching.

But after the Supreme Court ruled that segregation in public schools was a violation of the Constitution, the federal attitude toward enforcing second-class citizenship for blacks shifted on the scale of a change in the ocean's tide or a movement in the plates of the continents. Once the highest court in the land said equal treatment for all did not allow for segregation, then the lower courts, the Justice Department, and federal prosecutors, as well as the FBI, all switched sides. They didn't always act to promote integration, but they no longer used their power to stop it.

An irreversible shift had begun, and it was the direct result of the *Brown* decision.

The change in the attitude of federal officials created a wave of anticipation among black people, who became alert to the possibility of achieving the long-desired goal of racial equality. There is no way to offer a hard measure of a change in attitude. But the year after *Brown*, Rosa Parks refused to give up her seat to a white man on a racially segregated bus in Montgomery, Ala. That led to a yearlong bus boycott and the emergence of massive, nonviolent protests for equal rights. That same year, Martin Luther King Jr. emerged as the nation's prophet of civil rights for all Americans.

Even when a black 14-year-old, Emmit Till, was killed in Mississippi for supposedly whistling at a white woman, there was a new reaction to old racial brutality. One of Till's elderly relatives broke with small-town Southern tradition and dared to take the witness stand and testify against the white men he saw abduct the boy. Until *Brown*, the simple act of a black man standing up to speak against a white man in Mississippi was viewed as futile and likely to result in more white-on-black violence.

The sense among black people—and many whites as well—that a new era had opened created a new boldness. Most black parents in Little Rock did not want to risk harm to their children by allowing them to join in efforts to integrate Central High. But working with local NAACP officials, the parents of nine children decided it was a new day and time to make history. That same spirit of new horizons was at work in 1962 when James Meredith became the first black student to enroll at the University of Mississippi. And in another lurch away from the traditional support of segregation, the federal government sent troops as well as Justice Department officials to the university to protect Meredith's rights.

The next year, when Alabama Gov. George Wallace felt the political necessity of making a public stand against integration at the University of Alabama, he stood only briefly in the door to block black students and then stepped aside in the face of federal authority. That was another shift toward a world of high hopes for racial equality; again, from the perspective of the 21st century, it looks like another aftershock of the *Brown* decision.

The same psychology of hope infected young people, black and white, nationwide in the early '60s. The Freedom Rides, lunch-counter sit-ins, and protest marches for voting rights all find their roots in *Brown*. So, too, did the racially integrated 1963 March on Washington at which Martin Luther King Jr. famously said he had a vision of a promised land where the sons of slaves and the sons of slave owners could finally join together in peace. The desire for change became a demand for change in the impatient voice of Malcolm X, the militant Black Muslim who called for immediate change by violent means if necessary.

THE FIVE CASES THAT LED TO *BROWN*

- *Belton (Bulah) v. Gebhart:* Two separate cases with the same issues—families frustrated by inequitable conditions in African-American schools—were filed in Delaware in 1951. At the state's request the cases were heard at the Delaware Court of Chancery, a move that backfired when the chancellor ruled that the plaintiffs were being denied equal protection under the law and ordered that the 11 children involved be immediately admitted to the white school. The school board appealed the decision to the Supreme Court. Even though the state's segregation law was not struck down, this was the only case of the five to bring relief to the plaintiffs at the state level.
- *Bolling v. Sharpe:* In 1950, a parent group sued to get 11 young African-American students admitted to John Philip Sousa Junior High School in Washington, D.C. The students were turned away, although the school had several empty classrooms. After the U.S. District Court ruled that segregated schools were constitutional in the District of Columbia, NAACP attorneys appealed. In 1954, the U.S. Supreme Court removed *Bolling v. Sharpe* from its *Brown* decision and rendered a separate opinion on the case because the 14th Amendment was not applicable in the District of Columbia.
- *Briggs v. Elliott:* Named for Harry Briggs, one of 20 parents who sued the Clarendon County, S.C., school board, the lawsuit was filed in November 1949 by the NAACP's Thurgood Marshall. Initially, block parents asked the county to provide school buses for their children, but Judge J. Waties Waring urged the plaintiffs to file a lawsuit to challenge segregation itself. Waring's 28-page dissent in an unsuccessful district court battle is considered a blueprint for much of the Supreme Court's decision in *Brown*.
- *Brown v. Board of Education:* Thirteen parents, working with local lawyers and representatives from the NAACP Legal Defense and Educational Fund, filed a lawsuit in February 1951 to force children to be admitted to their neighborhood schools. At the time, black children were required to attend schools that were designated for African Americans. While the request was denied in the U.S. District Court, the panel of judges agreed with psychological evidence that African-American children were adversely affected by segregation. The U.S. Supreme Court later quoted the findings in its 1954 opinion.
- *Davis v. Prince Edward County:* After 450 students participated in a two-week student strike to protest deplorable conditions at Robert R. Moton High School in Farmville, Va., the NAACP filed a lawsuit in May 1951 seeking the end to segregation in the state's schools. A three-judge panel at the U.S. District Court unanimously rejected the students' request, which was appealed to the Supreme Court. After *Brown and Brown II*, which required districts to desegregate with "all deliberate speed," were announced in 1954 and 1955, white Virginians launched a massive resistance campaign. In 1959, the Prince Edward County Board of Supervisors refused to appropriate funds to the school board; the public schools remained closed for five years.

Source: Brown v. Board of Education National Historic Site

In 1964, a decade after *Brown*, the Civil Rights Act was passed by a Congress beginning to respond to the changing politics brought about by the landmark decision. The next year, 1965, the wave of change had swelled to the point that Congress passed the Voting Rights Act.

Closer to the Mountaintop

This sea change in black and white attitudes toward race also had an impact on culture. Churches began to grapple with the Christian and Jewish principles of loving thy neighbor, even if thy neighbor had a different color skin. Major league baseball teams no longer feared a fan revolt if they allowed more than one black player on a team. Black writers, actors, athletes, and musicians—ranging from James Baldwin to the Supremes and Muhammad Ali—began to cross over into the mainstream of American culture.

The other side of the change in racial attitudes was white support for equal rights. College-educated young white people in the '60s often defined themselves by their willingness to embrace racial equality. Bob Dylan sang about the changing times as answers "blowing in the wind." Movies like "Guess Who's Coming to Dinner" found major audiences among all races. And previously all-white private colleges and universities began opening their doors to black students. The resulting arguments over affirmative action in college admissions led to the Supreme Court's 1978 decision in the *Bakke* case, which outlawed the use of quotas, and its recent ruling that the University of Michigan can take race into account as one factor in admitting students to its law school. The court has also had to deal with affirmative action in the business world, in both hiring and contracts—again as a result of questions of equality under the Constitution raised by *Brown*.

But the most important legacy of the *Brown* decision, by far, is the growth of an educated black middle class. The number of black people graduating from high school and college has soared since *Brown*, and the incomes of blacks have climbed steadily as a result. Home ownership and investment in the stock market among black Americans have rocketed since the 1980s. The political and economic clout of that black middle class continues to bring America closer to the mountaintop vision of racial equality that Dr. King might have dreamed of 50 years ago.

The Supreme Court's May 17, 1954, ruling in *Brown* remains a landmark legal decision. But it is much more than that. It is the "Big Bang" of all American history in the 20th century.

POSTSCRIPT

Has Resegregation Diminished the Impact of *Brown*?

The points made by Gary Orfield and Juan Williams provide a basic framework for the consideration of this dense and complicated issue. As Howard Fuller in "The Struggle Continues," *Education Next* (Fall 2004), states, "The *Brown* decision sent a powerful message by tearing down the legal structures of oppression, but there remains plenty of unfinished business." Focal issues needing discussion and action include the continuing achievement gaps, the expansion of the immigrant Hispanic population, the persistence of racial distrust and in some cases hatred, the impact of magnet schools and charter schools, the assessment of tracking as an instructional strategy, and the efforts to legislate more equitable approaches to school funding at federal, state, and local levels.

A partial listing of sources treating some of these sub-topics include: *Young, Gifted and Black: Promoting High Achievement Among African-American Students* (2003) by Theresa Perry, Claude Steele, and Asa Hilliard III; "A Wider Lens on the Black-White Achievement Gap" by Richard Rothstein in *Phi Delta Kappan* (October 2004); "Why Does the Gap Exist?" by Paul E. Barton in *Educational Leadership* (November 2004); "The Achievement Gap: Myths and Reality" by Mano Singham in *Phi Delta Kappan* (April 2003); "The New Diversity" by Lawrence Hardy in *American School Board Journal* (April 2004); "The Real Supply Side" by Robert B. Reich in *The American Prospect* (October 2003); "Confronting Racial Hatred to Make Schools Safer" by Sengsouvanh Soukamneuth in *Principal Leadership* (January 2004); and "Unrecognized Progress" by James B. Hunt, Jr., in *Education Next* (Spring 2003).

Some excellent insights into the black underachievement problem are provided by Gail L. Thompson in her book *Through Ebony Eyes: What Teachers Need to Know but Are Afraid to Ask About African-American Students* (2004). In Chapter One, titled "If African-American Kids Aren't Dumb or Lazy Why Are They Still Underachieving?" she specifies these factors for consideration: the deficit-deprivation theory, the theory of structural inequality, the effects of tracking, the "fourth grade failure syndrome," the theory of cultural discontinuity, the "acting white" theory, peer pressure and the lure of street life, the parents-are-at-fault theory, underprepared teachers, and low teacher expectations. Abigail and Stephan Thernstrom present a different take in their book *No Excuses: Closing the Racial Gap in Learning* (2003), claiming that the essence of disadvantage has little to do with poverty or economic class or school funding or class size. The real problem, they suggest, lies in a combination of school inertia, lack of high standards, and the learning-resistant cultures that students come from.

ISSUE 7

Have Public Schools Adequately Accommodated Religion?

YES: Edd Doerr, from "Religion and Public Education," *Phi Delta Kappan* (November 1998)

NO: Warren A. Nord, from "The Relevance of Religion to the Curriculum," *The School Administrator* (January 1999)

ISSUE SUMMARY

YES: Edd Doerr, executive director of Americans for Religious Liberty, asserts that a fair balance between free exercise rights and the obligation of neutrality has been achieved in the public schools.

NO: Warren A. Nord, a professor of the philosophy of religion, contends that the schools are still too secular and that a place in the curriculum must be found for religion.

The religious grounding of early schooling in America certainly cannot be denied, nor can the history of religious influences on the conduct of governmental functions. For example, U.S. Supreme Court decisions in the early decades of the twentieth century allowed certain cooperative practices between public school systems and community religious groups. However, it must also be recognized that many students, parents, and taxpayer organizations were distressed by some of these accommodating policies. Legal action taken by or on the behalf of some of the offended parties led to Supreme Court restrictions on prayer and Bible reading in the public schools in the 1960s. Particularly notable were the decisions in *Engel v. Vitale* (1962), *Murray v. Curlett* (1963), and *School District of Abington Township v. Schempp* (1963). These decisions curtailed the use of public school time and facilities for ceremonial and devotional religious purposes, but they did not outlaw the discussion of religion or the use of religious materials in appropriate academic contexts.

During the 1970s and 1980s religious activists, led by the Reverend Jerry Falwell's Moral Majority, campaigned against what they perceived to be the tyranny of a public education establishment dominated by the philosophy of secular humanism. Efforts were made to include creationism in the science curriculum as an antidote to the theory of evolution and to legalize voluntary organized prayer in the public schools. Despite these efforts, the courts have generally disallowed the teaching of "creation science," have vetoed organized moments of "silent meditation," and have declared unconstitutional the practice of including prayers in graduation ceremonies. Religious groups gained at least one major victory in the 1980s with the passage of the Equal Access Act, federal legislation that guarantees access to public school facilities for students wishing to engage in religious activities during nonschool hours. The legislation, which has been challenged in some localities, has been upheld by the U.S. Supreme Court.

And the battles continue. Recently, Kansans attempted to remove the theory of evolution from the science curriculum, Texans have pressed for approval of student-led invocations at high school football games, Virginians have tested a new version of daily "meditation moments," and several states have allowed the posting of the Ten Commandments in public schools. In the wake of the Columbine High School massacre and mounting evidence of "moral decay" among American youth, the pressure for further accommodation of religion seems to be growing. In December 1999 President Bill Clinton issued new guidelines promoting stronger partnerships between religious institutions and public schools in local communities, particularly in the areas of school safety, discipline, and literacy. Some national groups, such as Americans United for Separation of Church and State and People for the American Way, raised questions about the vagueness of these guidelines and the absence of clear limits on the extent of involvement. Another type of accommodation involves the providing or lending of secular learning materials and computer equipment to religious schools. A *Washington Post* editorial, "Church-State Muddle" (December 6, 1999), poses this dilemma: To disallow such aid programs discriminates against schools because of their religious affiliations, but to uphold these programs validates public support for religious institutions.

Some sources that examine the current status of this ongoing struggle include Perry Glanzer, "Religion in Public Schools: In Search of Fairness," *Phi Delta Kappan* (November 1998); Oliver S. Thomas, "Legal Leeway on Church-State in School," *The School Administrator* (January 1999); Gilbert T. Sewall, "Religion Comes to School," and Thomas Lickona, "Religion and Character Education," *Phi Delta Kappan* (September 1999); and Charles C. Haynes, "Seeking Common Ground," *American School Board Journal* (February 2000).

In the first of the following selections, Edd Doerr reviews what is permitted and what is forbidden on the basis of some 50 years of Supreme Court rulings and expresses belief that accommodation has gone as far as it can. Warren A. Nord, in the second selection, asserts that the study of religious thought and influence has been marginalized in the curriculum and that public school students are systematically taught to think about the world in secular ways only.

Edd Doerr  **YES**

Religion and Public Education

On 4 June 1998, the U.S. House of Representatives voted 224 to 203 for the so-called Religious Freedom Amendment, sponsored by Rep. Ernest Istook (R-Okla.) and more than 150 co-sponsors.[1] The measure fell well short of the two-thirds majority required to pass a constitutional amendment. In fact, the 52.4% vote dropped well below the 59.7% garnered on a similar proposal in 1971, the last time a school prayer amendment reached the House floor. The amendment's defeat is especially significant because it had strong backing from the House majority leadership and was the culmination of a massive four-year campaign led by televangelist Pat Robertson's Christian Coalition.

The Istook Amendment aroused strong opposition from education organizations, mainstream religious groups, and civil liberties organizations because it would have embroiled school districts and communities in prolonged, bitter, divisive conflicts over religious activities in the classroom or at graduations, athletic events, school assemblies, and other gatherings. In addition, the amendment's clause against "deny[ing] equal access to a benefit on account of religion" would have cleared the way for massive tax support of sectarian schools and other institutions. Opponents of the amendment correctly worried that it would weaken or wreck the First Amendment, taking the first major bite out of the Bill of Rights since its ratification in 1791.

Two weeks before the vote on the amendment, the U.S. Commission on Civil Rights held the first of three projected hearings on "Schools and Religion." Most of the 16 experts who spoke at the hearing (including this writer, I must disclose) agreed that the relevant Supreme Court rulings and other developments have pretty much brought public education into line with the religious neutrality required by the First Amendment and the increasingly pluralistic nature of our society. A fair balance has been established between the free exercise rights of students and the constitutional obligation of neutrality.

The speakers attributed the current reasonably satisfactory situation to 50 years of appropriate Supreme Court rulings plus two specific developments: passage by Congress in 1984 of the Equal Access Law, which allows student-initiated religious groups or other groups not related to the curriculum to meet, without school sponsorship, during noninstructional time; and the U.S. Department of Education's issuance in August 1995 of guidelines on "Religious Expression in Public Schools."

From Edd Doerr, "Religion and Public Education," *Phi Delta Kappan* (November 1998). Copyright © 1998 by Phi Delta Kappa International, Inc. Reprinted by permission of Phi Delta Kappa International, Inc., and the author.

A minority of speakers at the heating cited anecdotes about alleged violations of students' religious freedom. These turned out to be either exaggerations or cases of mistakes by teachers or administrators that were easily remedied by a phone call or letter. The occasional violations of student rights, like "man bites dog" stories, are few and far between and certainly do not point to any need to amend the Constitution.

Julie Underwood, general counsel designate for the National School Boards Association (NSBA), told the hearing that inquiries to the NSBA about what is or is not permitted in public schools declined almost to the vanishing point once the "Religious Expression in Public Schools" guidelines were published.

The guidelines grew out of a document titled "Religion in the Public Schools: A Joint Statement of Current Law," issued in April 1995 by a broad coalition of 36 religious and civil liberties groups.[2] The statement declared that the Constitution "permits much private religious activity in and around the public schools and does not turn the schools into religion-free zones." The statement went on to detail what is and is not permissible in the schools.

On 12 July 1995, President Clinton discussed these issues in a major address at—appropriately—James Madison High School in northern Virginia and announced that he was directing the secretary of education, in consultation with the attorney general, to issue advisory guidelines to every public school district in the country. This was done in August.

In his weekly radio address of 30 May 1998, anticipating the June 4 House debate and vote on the Istook Amendment, the President again addressed the issue and announced that the guidelines, updated slightly, were being reissued and sent to every district. This effort undoubtedly helped to sway the House vote.

The guidelines, based on 50 years of court rulings (from the 1948 *McCollum* decision to the present), on common sense, and on a healthy respect for American religious diversity, have proved useful to school boards, administrators, teachers, students, parents, and religious leaders. Following is a brief summary.

Permitted

"Purely private religious speech by students"; nondisruptive individual or group prayer, grace before meals, religious literature reading; student speech about religion or anything else, including that intended to persuade, so long as it stops short of harassment; private baccalaureate services; teaching *about* religion; inclusion by students of religious matter in written or oral assignments where not inappropriate; student distribution of religious literature on the same terms as other material not related to school curricula or activities; some degree of right to excusal from lessons objectionable on religious or conscientious grounds, subject to applicable state laws; off-campus released time or dismissed time for religious instruction; teaching civic values; student-initiated "Equal Access" religious groups of secondary students during noninstructional time.

Prohibited

School endorsement of any religious activity or doctrine; coerced participation in religious activity; engaging in or leading student religious activity by teachers, coaches, or officials acting as advisors to student groups; allowing harassment of or religious imposition on "captive audiences"; observing holidays as religious events or promoting such observance; imposing restrictions on religious expression more stringent than those on nonreligious expression; allowing religious instruction by outsiders on school premises during the school day.

Required

"Official neutrality regarding religious activity."

In reissuing the guidelines, Secretary Riley urged school districts to use them or to develop their own, preferably in cooperation with parents, teachers, and the "broader community." He recommended that principals, administrators, teachers, schools of education, prospective teachers, parents, and students all become familiar with them.

As President Clinton declared in his May 30 address, "Since we've issued these guidelines, appropriate religious activity has flourished in our schools, and there has apparently been a substantial decline in the contentious argument and litigation that has accompanied this issue for too long."

As good and useful as the guidelines are, there remain three areas in which problems continue: proselytizing by adults in public schools, music programs that fall short of the desired neutrality, and teaching appropriately about religion.

There are conservative evangelists, such as Jerry Johnston and the Rev. Jerry Falwell, who have described public schools as "mission fields." In communities from coast to coast, proselytizers from well-financed national organizations, such as Campus Crusade and Young Life, and volunteer "youth pastors" from local congregations have operated in public schools for years. They use a variety of techniques: presenting assembly programs featuring "role model" athletes, getting permission from school officials to contact students one-on-one in cafeterias and hallways, volunteering as unpaid teaching aides, and using substance abuse lectures or assemblies to gain access to students. It is not uncommon for these activities to have the tacit approval of local school authorities. Needless to say, these operations tend to take place more often in smaller, more religiously homogeneous communities than in larger, more pluralistic ones.

Religious music in the public school curriculum, in student concerts and theatrical productions, and at graduation ceremonies has long been a thorny issue. As Secretary Riley's 1995 and 1998 guidelines and court rulings have made clear, schools may offer instruction about religion, but they must remain religiously neutral and may not formally celebrate religious special days. What then about religious music, which looms large in the history of music?

As a vocal and instrumental musician in high school and college and as an amateur adult musician in both secular and religious musical groups, I feel qualified to address this issue. There should be no objection to the inclusion of religious music in the academic study of music and in vocal and instrumental performances, as long as the pieces are selected primarily for their musical or historical value, as long as the program is not predominantly religious, and as long as the principal purpose and effect of the inclusion is secular. Thus there should be no objection to inclusion in a school production of religious music by Bach or Aaron Copland's arrangements of such 19th-century songs as "Simple Gifts" or "Let Us Gather by the River." What constitutes "musical or historical value" is, of course, a matter of judgment and controversy among musicians and scholars, so there can be no simple formula for resolving all conflicts.

Certain activities should clearly be prohibited. Public school choral or instrumental ensembles should not be used to provide music for church services or celebrations, though a school ensemble might perform a secular music program in a church or synagogue as part of that congregation's series of secular concerts open to the public and not held in conjunction with a worship service. Sectarian hymns should not be included in graduation ceremonies; a Utah case dealing with that subject has been turned down for Supreme Court review. Students enrolled in music programs for credit should not be compelled to participate in performances that are not primarily religiously neutral.

As for teaching *about* religion, while one can agree with the Supreme Court that public schools may, and perhaps should, alleviate ignorance in this area in a fair, balanced, objective, neutral, academic way, getting from theory to practice is far from easy. The difficulties should be obvious. Teachers are very seldom adequately trained to teach about religion. There are no really suitable textbooks on the market. Educators and experts on religion are nowhere near agreement on precisely what ought to be taught, how much should be taught and at what grade levels, and whether such material should be integrated into social studies classes, when appropriate, or offered in separate courses, possibly electives. And those who complain most about the relative absence of religion from the curriculum seem to be less interested in neutral academic study than in narrower sectarian teaching.

Textbooks and schools tend to slight religion not out of hostility toward religion but because of low demand, lack of time (if you add something to the curriculum, what do you take out to make room for it?), lack of suitable materials, and fear of giving offense or generating unpleasant controversy.

The following questions hint at the complexity of the subject. Should teaching about religion deal only with the bright side of it and not with the dark side (religious wars, controversies, bigotry, persecutions, and so on)? Should instruction deal only with religions within the U.S., or should it include religions throughout the world? Should it be critical or uncritical? Should all religious traditions be covered or only some? Should the teaching deal only with sacred books—and, if so, which ones and which translations? How should change and development in all religions be dealt with?

To be more specific, should we teach only about the Pilgrims and the first Thanksgiving, or also about the Salem witch trials and the execution of Quakers? Should schools mention only the Protestant settlers in British North America or also deal with French Catholic missionaries in Canada, Michigan, and Indiana and with the Spanish Catholics and secret Jews in our Southwest? Should we mention that Martin Luther King was a Baptist minister but ignore the large number of clergy who defended slavery and then segregation on Biblical grounds?

Should teaching about religion cover such topics as the evolution of Christianity and its divisions, the Crusades, the Inquisition, the religious wars after the Reformation, the long history of anti-Semitism and other forms of murderous bigotry, the role of religion in social and international tensions (as in Ireland, in the former Yugoslavia, and in India and Pakistan), the development in the U.S. of religious liberty and church/state separation, denominations and religions founded in the U.S., controversies over women's rights and reproductive rights, or newer religious movements?

The probability that attempts to teach about religion will go horribly wrong should caution public schools to make haste very slowly in this area. In my opinion, other curricular inadequacies—less controversial ones, such as those in the fields of science, social studies, foreign languages, and word literature—should be remedied before we tackle the thorniest subject of all.

And let us not forget that the American landscape has no shortage of houses of worship, which generally include religious education as one of their main functions. Nothing prevents these institutions from providing all the teaching about religion they might desire.

The late Supreme Court Justice William Brennan summed up the constitutional ideal rather neatly in his concurring opinion in *Abington Township S.D. v. Schempp*, the 1963 school prayer case: "It is implicit in the history and character of American public education that the public schools serve a uniquely public function: the training of American citizens in an atmosphere free of parochial, divisive, or separatist influence of any sort—an atmosphere in which children may assimilate a heritage common to all American groups and religions. This is a heritage neither theistic nor atheistic, but simply civic and patriotic."

Notes

1. Text of H.J. Res. 78, Rep. Ernest Istook's Religious Freedom Amendment: "To secure the people's right to acknowledge God according to the dictates of conscience: Neither the United States nor any State shall establish any official religion, but the people's right to pray and to recognize their religious beliefs, heritage, or traditions on public property, including schools, shall not be infringed. Neither the United States nor any State shall require any person to join in prayer or other religious activity, prescribe school prayers, discriminate against religion, or deny equal access to a benefit on account of religion."
2. Copies of the statement are available free of charge from Americans for ReligiousLiberty, P.O. Box 6656, Silver Spring, MD 20916.

NO

Warren A. Nord

The Relevance of Religion to the Curriculum

For some time now, public school administrators have been on the front lines of our culture wars over religion and education—and I expect it would be music to their ears to hear that peace accords have been signed.

Unfortunately, the causes of war are deep-seated. Peace is not around the corner.

At the same time, however, it is also easy to overstate the extent of the hostilities. At least at the national level—but also in many communities across America—a large measure of common ground has been found. The leaders of most major national educational, religious and civil liberties organizations agree about the basic principles that should govern the role of religion and public schools. No doubt we don't agree about everything, but we agree about a lot.

For example, in 1988, a group of 17 major religious and educational organizations—the American Jewish Congress and the Islamic Society of North America, the National Association of Evangelicals and the National Council of Churches, the National Education Association and American Federation of Teachers, the National School Boards Association and AASA among them—endorsed a statement of principles that describes the importance of religion in the public school curriculum.

The statement, in part, says this: "Because religion plays significant roles in history and society, study about religion is essential to understanding both the nation and the world. Omission of facts about religion can give students the false impression that the religious life of humankind is insignificant or unimportant. Failure to understand even the basic symbols, practices and concepts of the various religions makes much of history, literature, art and contemporary life unintelligible."

A Profound Problem

As a result of this (and other "common ground" statements) it is no longer controversial to assert that the study of religion has a legitimate and important place in the public school curriculum.

From Warren A. Nord, "The Relevance of Religion to the Curriculum," *The School Administrator* (January 1999). Copyright © 1999 by The American Association of School Administrators. Reprinted by permission.

Where in the curriculum? In practice, the study of religion has been relegated almost entirely to history texts and courses, for it is widely assumed that religion is irrelevant to every other subject in the curriculum—that is, to understanding the world here and now.

This is a deeply controversial assumption, however. A profoundly important educational problem lingers here, one that is almost completely ignored by educators.

Let me put it this way. Several ways exist for making sense of the world here and now. Many Americans accept one or another religious interpretation of reality; others accept one or another secular interpretation. We don't agree—and the differences among us often cut deeply.

Yet public schools systematically teach students to think about the world in secular ways only. They don't even bother to inform them about religious alternatives—apart from distant history. That is, public schooling discriminates against religious ways of making sense of the world. This is no minor problem.

An Economic Argument

To get some sense of what's at issue, let's consider economics.

One can think about the economic domain of life in various ways. Scriptural texts in all religious traditions address questions of justice and morality, poverty and wealth, work and stewardship, for example. A vast body of 20th century literature in moral theology deals with economic issues. Indeed, most mainline denominations and ecumenical agencies have official statements on justice and economics. What's common to all of this literature is the claim that the economic domain of life cannot be understood apart from religion.

Needless to say, this claim is not to be found in economics textbooks. Indeed, if we put end to end all the references to religion in the 10 high school economics texts I've reviewed in the past few years, they would add up to about two pages—out of 4,400 pages combined (and all of the references are to premodern times). There is but a single reference to religion—a passing mention in a section on taxation and non-profit organizations—in the 47 pages of the new national content standards in economics. Moreover, the textbooks and the standards say virtually nothing about the problems that are the major concern of theologians—problems relating to poverty, justice, our consumer culture, the Third World, human dignity and the meaningfulness of work.

The problem isn't just that the texts ignore religion and those economic problems of most concern to theologians. A part of the problem is what the texts do teach—that is, neoclassical economic theory. According to the texts, economics is a science, people are essentially self-interested utility-maximizers, the economic realm is one of competition for scarce resources, values are personal preferences and value judgments are matters of cost-benefit analysis. Of course, no religious tradition accepts this understanding of human nature, society, economics and values.

That is, the texts and standards demoralize and secularize economics.

An Appalling Claim

To be sure, they aren't explicitly hostile to religion; rather they ignore it. But in some ways this is worse than explicit hostility, for students remain unaware of the fact that there are tensions and conflicts between their religious traditions and what they are taught about economics.

In fact, the texts and the standards give students no sense that what they are learning is controversial. Indeed, the national economics standards make it a matter of principle that students be kept in the dark about alternatives to neoclassical theory. As the editors put it in their introduction, the standards were developed to convey a single conception of economics, the "majority paradigm" or neoclassical model of economic behavior. For, they argue, to include "strongly held minority views of economic processes [would only risk] confusing and frustrating teachers and students who are then left with the responsibility of sorting the qualifications and alternatives without a sufficient foundation to do so."

This is an appalling statement. It means, in effect, that students should be indoctrinated; they should be given no critical perspective on neoclassical economic theory.

The problem with the economics texts and standards is but one aspect of the much larger problem that cuts across the curriculum, for in every course students are taught to think in secular ways that often (though certainly not always) conflict with religious alternatives. And this is always done uncritically.

Even in history courses, students learn to think about historical meaning and causation in exclusively secular ways in spite of the fact that Judaism, Christianity and Islam all hold that God acts in history, that there is a religious meaning to history. True, they learn a few facts about religion, but they learn to think about history in secular categories.

Nurturing Secularity

Outside of history courses and literature courses that use historical literature, religion is rarely even mentioned, but even on those rare occasions when it is, the intellectual context is secular. As a result, public education nurtures a secular mentality. This marginalizes religion from our cultural and intellectual life and contributes powerfully to the secularization of our culture.

Ignoring religious ways of thinking about the world is a problem for three important reasons.

It is profoundly illiberal.

Here, of course, I'm not using the term "liberal" to refer to the left wing of the Democratic Party. A liberal education is a broad education, one that provides students with the perspective to think critically about the world and their lives. A good liberal education should introduce students—at least older students—to the major ways humankind has developed for making sense of the world and their lives. Some of those ways of thinking and living are religious and it is illiberal to leave them out of the discussion. Indeed, it may well constitute indoctrination—secular indoctrination.

We indoctrinate students when we uncritically initiate them into one way of thinking and systematically ignore the alternatives. Indeed, if students are to be able to think critically about the secular ways of understanding the world that pervade the curriculum, they must understand something about the religious alternatives.

It is politically unjust.

Public schools must take the public seriously. But religious parents are now, in effect, educationally disenfranchised. Their ways of thinking and living aren't taken seriously.

Consider an analogy. A generation ago textbooks and curricula said virtually nothing about women, blacks and members of minority subcultures. Hardly anyone would now say that that was fair or just. We now—most of us—realize this was a form of discrimination, of educational disenfranchisement. And so it is with religious subcultures (though, ironically, the multicultural movement has been almost entirely silent about religion).

It is unconstitutional.

It is, of course, uncontroversial that it is constitutionally permissible to teach about religion in public schools when done properly. No Supreme Court justice has ever held otherwise. But I want to make a stronger argument.

The court has been clear that public schools must be neutral in matters of religion—in two senses. Schools must be neutral among religions (they can't favor Protestants over Catholics or Christians over Jews), and they must be neutral between religion and nonreligion. Schools can't promote religion. They can't proselytize. They can't conduct religious exercises.

Of course, neutrality is a two-edged sword. Just as schools can't favor religion over nonreligion, neither can they favor nonreligion over religion. As Justice Hugo Black put it in the seminal 1947 *Everson* ruling, "State power is no more to be used so as to handicap religions than it is to favor them."

Similarly, in his majority opinion in *Abington v. Schempp* in 1963, Justice Tom Clark wrote that schools can't favor "those who believe in no religion over those who do believe." And in a concurring opinion, Justice Arthur Goldberg warned that an "untutored devotion to the concept of neutrality [can lead to a] pervasive devotion to the secular and a passive, or even active, hostility to the religious."

Of course this is just what has happened. An untutored, naïve conception of neutrality has led educators to look for a smoking gun, an explicit hostility to religion, when the hostility has been philosophically rather more subtle—though no less substantial for that.

The only way to be neutral when all ground is contested ground is to be fair to the alternatives. That is, given the Supreme Court's longstanding interpretation of the Establishment Clause, public schools must require the study of religion if they require the study of disciplines that cumulatively lead to a pervasive devotion to the secular—as they do.

Classroom Practices

So how can we be fair? What would a good education look like? Here I can only skim the surface—and refer readers to *Taking Religion Seriously Across the Curriculum*, in which Charles Haynes and I chart what needs to be done in some detail.

Obviously a great deal depends on the age of students. In elementary schools students should learn something of the relatively uncontroversial aspects of different religions—their traditions, holidays, symbols and a little about religious histories, for example. As students mature, they should be initiated into that conversation about truth and goodness that constitutes a good liberal education. Here a two-prong approach is required.

First, students should learn something about religious ways of thinking about any subject that is religiously controversial in the relevant courses. So, for example, a biology text should include a chapter in which scientific ways of understanding nature was contrasted with religious alternatives. Students should learn that the relationship of religion and science is controversial, and that while they will learn what most biologists believe to be the truth about nature, not everyone agrees.

Indeed, every text and course should provide students with historical and philosophical perspective on the subject at hand, establishing connections and tensions with other disciplines and domains of the culture, including religion.

This is not a balanced-treatment or equal-time requirement. Biology courses should continue to be biology courses and economics courses should continue to be economics courses. In any case, given their competence and training, biology and economics teachers are not likely to be prepared to deal with a variety of religious ways of approaching their subject. At most, they can provide a minimal fairness.

A robust fairness is possible only if students are required to study religious as well as secular ways of making sense of the world in some depth, in courses devoted to the study of religion.

A good liberal education should require at least one year-long high school course in religious studies (with other courses, I would hope, available as electives). The primary goal of such a course should be to provide students with a sufficiently intensive exposure to religious ways of thinking and living to enable them to actually understand religion (rather than simply know a few facts about religion). It should expose students to scriptural texts, but it also should use more recent primary sources that enable students to understand how contemporary theologians and writers within different traditions think about those subjects in the curriculum—morality, sexuality, history, nature, psychology and the economic world—that they will be taught to interpret in secular categories in their other courses.

Of course, if religion courses are to be offered, there must be teachers competent to teach them. Religious studies must become a certifiable field in public education, and new courses must not be offered or required until competent teachers are available.

Indeed, all teachers must have a much clearer sense of how religion relates to the curriculum and, more particularly, to their respective subjects. Major reforms in teacher education are necessary—as is a new generation of textbooks sensitive to religion.

Some educators will find it unrealistic to expect such reforms. Of course several decades ago textbooks and curricula said little about women and minority cultures. Several decades ago, few universities had departments of religious studies. Now multicultural education is commonplace and most universities have departments of religious studies. Things change.

Stemming an Exodus

No doubt some educators will find these proposals controversial, but they will [be] shortsighted if they do. Leaving religion out of the curriculum is also controversial. Indeed, because public schools don't take religion seriously many religious parents have deserted them and, if the Supreme Court upholds the legality of vouchers, as they may well do, the exodus will be much greater.

In the long run, the least controversial position is the one that takes everyone seriously. If public schools are to survive our culture wars, they must be built on common ground. But there can be no common ground when religious voices are left out of the curricular conversation.

It is religious conservatives, of course, who are most critical of public Schooling—and the most likely to leave. But my argument is that public schooling doesn't take any religion seriously. It marginalizes all religion—liberal as well as conservative, Catholic as well as Protestant, Jewish, Muslim and Buddhist as well as Christian. Indeed, it contributes a great deal to the secularization of American culture—and this should concern any religious person.

But, in the end, this shouldn't concern religious people only. Religion should be included in the curriculum for three very powerful secular reasons. The lack of serious study of religion in public education is illiberal, unjust and unconstitutional.

POSTSCRIPT

Have Public Schools Adequately Accommodated Religion?

"Of all the groundless, hurtful attacks on public education, none is more painful than the charge that public schools are 'godless institutions of secular humanism.' . . . The public school day may not start with a Hail Mary or an Our Father, a mantra or a blood sacrifice, but public education does more of God's work for children every day than any other institution in America—and that includes the churches. So says journalist Frosty Troy in "Far From 'Godless' Institutions," *The School Administrator* (March 2000).

For more moderate positions on the issue, see Rachael Kessler, "Nourishing Students in Secular Schools," *Educational Leadership* (December 1998/ January 1999) and two articles in the December 1998 *American School Board Journal*, Jerry Cammarata's "We Haven't Got a Prayer" and Benjamin Dowling-Sendor's "Protecting Religious Vitality."

More recent opinions include the following: Charles A. Rohn, "Plenty of Religious Expression in Public Schools," *The School Administrator* (June 2000); Kenneth T. Murray and Craig S. Evans, "U.S. Supreme Court Revisits School Prayer," *NASSP Bulletin* (December 2000); Ralph D. Mawdsley, "Let Us Pray?" *Principal Leadership* (April 2001); Martha M. McCarthy, "Religious Influences in Public Education: Political and Judicial Developments," *The Educational Forum* (Spring 2001); Michael H. Romanowski, "Is School Prayer the Answer?" *The Educational Forum* (Winter 2002); and Joanne M. Marshall, "Religion and Education: Walking the Line in Public Schools," *Phi Delta Kappan* (November 2003).

Perhaps a reasonable summation of the total situation was provided by Charles C. Haynes in the *American School Board Journal* article cited in the issue introduction:

> The vast majority of educators are caring, dedicated professionals who want nothing more than to uphold the rights of all students and to address issues of religion and values with fairness and respect. But their training has left them ill-prepared to tackle religious-liberty questions or to teach substantively about religion in the curriculum, and they don't feel support from school boards and administrators to do so. Many school districts, in fact, have few or no policies concerning religion because school administrators and board members are often reluctant to address the underlying problems before a crisis erupts. Ironically, this avoidance is precisely what causes conflicts and lawsuits—either because religion is being ignored or because it is being improperly promoted by school officials.

ISSUE 8

Can Federal Initiatives Rescue Failing Schools?

YES: Andrew Rotherham, from "A New Partnership," *Education Next* (Spring 2002)

NO: Peter Schrag, from "Bush's Education Fraud," *The American Prospect* (February 2004)

ISSUE SUMMARY

YES: Education policy expert Andrew Rotherham argues that new federally imposed accountability standards will enhance opportunity and overhaul failing schools.

NO: Education writer-editor Peter Schrag finds the Bush administration's No Child Left Behind Act to be confusing, underfunded, and ultimately self-defeating.

While schooling in the United States has always been and remains primarily a state and local function, the federal government has played a significant role in initiating programs to meet specific needs and charting general goals. Beginning with the 1862 Morrill Act creating a land grant program to fund state agricultural and mechanical colleges, the legislative and executive branches of the federal government have provided support for vocational education (1917); educational assistance for veterans (1944); funds for strengthening instruction in science, math, and foreign languages (1958); funds to support school desegregation (1964 and 1972); mandates and partial funding for meeting the needs of children with disabilities (1975 and 1990); and assistance for drug abuse prevention (1986). President George Bush and the nation's governors set goals for American schools in 1989, and the Clinton administration continued this effort in 1994 with the Goals 2000: Educate America Act, which set standards and provided aid for state reforms.

In 1965 Congress passed the Elementary and Secondary Education Act (ESEA), a wide-ranging program emphasizing aid for disadvantaged students. Reauthorization of this law in 2002 under the George W. Bush administration as the No Child Left Behind Act has prompted a good deal of debate. Is the new ESEA a welcome increase in federal attention to school reform, or is it an expansion of bureaucratic red tape and a usurpation of state and local perogatives? While there is much agreement on the goals to be met, there is philosophical division over the means of achieving these goals. In the words of historian Diane Ravitch, "The most important national priority must be to redesign policies and programs so that education funding is used to educate children, not to preserve the system."

The new ESEA, a 1,080-page document authorizing $26.5 billion in fiscal year 2002 alone, sets standards and accountability measures aimed at closing the achievement gap over a period of 12 years. Richard F. Elmore, in "Unwarranted Intrusion," *Education Next* (Spring 2002), finds it ironic that Republicans have sponsored the single largest expansion of federal power over the nation's education system in history. While the most discussed portions of the new law are those dealing with mandates for annual statewide assessments in reading and mathematics (and later in science) and the requirements for yearly progress reports toward 100 percent proficiency, the law covers many more areas, among which are school and district report cards, bilingual education, teacher and principal quality, public charter schools, and military recruitment. Summaries of the law may be found at http://www.edweek.com and http://www.aft.org/ESEA.

Thomas Toch, in "Bush's Big Test," *The Washington Monthly* (November 2001), regrets that the federal administration has "punted the decision to the states," allowing states to set the passing grades on tests that will be used to parcel out rewards and sanctions. Another flaw Toch identifies is the plan's dependence on the U.S. Department of Education to police the testing efforts of the states. He feels that without a uniform test of achievement in reading and mathematics, the legislation will fail to meet its goals.

In the following selections, Andrew Rotherham offers a justification for federal enforcement of an accountability system to rescue disadvantaged students, while Peter Schrag sees this sweeping nationalization of school policy and procedures as a source of public and professional resentment.

Andrew Rotherham

 **YES**

A New Partnership

The issue of whether the federal government should outline and enforce an accountability system for states, school districts, and schools was essentially settled the day that George W. Bush took office as president. Bush had made "accountability" a cornerstone of his education platform, using his stated goal of ensuring equity for poor and minority children as a way of bolstering his credentials as a moderate. New Democrats, led by Democratic senators Joseph Lieberman and Evan Bayh, were also committed to the idea of accountability. They had made a results-based approach to federal education programs a major component of their "Three R's" proposal—on which much of the Bush plan and the final ESEA [Elementary and Secondary Education Act] legislation were based.

The legislation would build on the accountability measures first introduced during the 1994 reauthorization. That legislation required the states to develop academic standards and tests linked to the standards, but its accountability language was too vague and porous. For example, under the 1994 legislation, states were required to define "adequate yearly progress" in a way that resulted in "continuous and substantial yearly improvement" by schools and school districts toward the goal of getting all students to the proficient level. With states defining the adequate yearly progress standard and with no concrete timeline in place, practices varied widely from state to state. This led to great differences in results at the state level. Michigan and Arkansas identified 76 percent and 64 percent, respectively, of their Title I schools as low performing, while Connecticut and Maryland identified only 6 percent each. Regardless, the low-performing label is sadly almost meaningless: 41 percent of principals in these schools reported not even being aware of the designation. And for schools that were identified as low performing there was little in the way of sustained assistance. According to a Department of Education analysis, only 40 percent of schools identified as needing improvement received assistance from the state or their school district. This dismal statistic climbs to only 50 percent for schools that have been identified as low performing for three or more years.

In this system, what passed for accountability was the ability to provide detailed reports of planned and actual spending of federal funds—in other words, a system of accounting, not of accountability. In addition, the federal government was quite lax in enforcing the accountability provisions that were

From Andrew Rotherham, "A New Partnership," *Education Next* (Spring 2002). Copyright © 2002 by The Board of Trustees of Leland Stanford Junior University. Reprinted by permission.

in the law. As a result, as of this writing only 16 states had fully complied with the requirements of the 1994 ESEA reauthorization.

Critics have seized on the states' seeming inability to comply with the previous law as evidence of the folly of proceeding down the accountability route. In fact, critics warn, these federal efforts to demand results-based accountability are at best futile and at worst drive all sorts of perverse and unintended consequences, jeopardizing recent accomplishments at the state and local level. These arguments are the dullest yet most common arrows in the quivers of those fighting change. And they fall apart under close scrutiny. The critics' alternative to the accountability plan is to keep the federal dollars flowing regardless of the results. They have little to offer beyond tired bromides about needing more money for capacity building, innovative partnerships, and a host of other buzzwords that make no difference in the lives of children who attend failing schools.

Why Federal Accountability?

The states' haphazard results in complying with the 1994 requirements and improving low-performing schools overall are precisely why the law's accountability provisions ought to be strengthened and clarified. In a host of policy areas inside and outside of education, history shows that clear federal prescriptions accompanied by real consequences bring results. That's why, for example, you can't buy an alcoholic drink almost anywhere in the country if you're under 21. It's why our cars and airplanes are increasingly safe. And it's why the vestiges of discrimination are being eradicated from our schools and society, through laws like the Civil Rights Act and the Americans with Disabilities Act. Federal policymakers did not wait for states to address these issues on their own. Nor did they lament the states' incapacity to do so. Rather, they mandated clear standards and demanded results.

Increasing the rigor and specificity of the accountability provisions inESEA doesn't mean imposing the same system on every state, or a "one size fits all" approach in the political jargon. It means establishing clear criteria for improvement, specific indicators of success, and common goals. Such a system need not be incompatible with a variety of approaches at the state level, but it is at odds with the notion that wildly divergent results for students of various races, ethnic groups, and incomes are somehow acceptable.

Obviously there is a world of difference between a standard that says all cars must contain passenger-side airbags by a certain date and one that defines what it means to be academically proficient. Complicated issues of how to measure success or failure vex the process of education policymaking. Still, complicated doesn't mean futile. It doesn't mean we should just throw up our hands in collective frustration, because in the end it is simply irresponsible to continue pouring resources into systems that we know are failing without establishing clear benchmarks for their improvement and consequences if they do not reach them. To do otherwise essentially makes Washington the enabler in a terribly dysfunctional relationship that victimizes poor and minority children. It is ironic that many of the same interest groups and individuals that so readily look to Washington to address various ills suddenly resist federal intrusion in this particular area. Are they satisfied with a situation where African-American and Hispanic 12th graders read and do math as well as white 8th graders? Where, according to an analysis by Jay Greene of the Manhattan Institute, only 56 percent of African-American students and 54 percent of Hispanics graduate from high school?

Perhaps it's because white students score higher on achievement tests and graduate at substantially higher rates that many of the loudest voices in this debate aren't troubled by asking for patience and time to get things exactly right before proceeding. These critics can represent a powerful bloc. Consider that in states like Massachusetts, Virginia, and New York, resistance to the accountability system has come predominantly from affluent white suburbs. Call it the Scarsdale Syndrome. In Massachusetts, writes Georgia Alexakis in the *Washington Monthly*, the paradox of these reform efforts is, "The schools most likely to do poorly on the MCAS [the state test in Massachusetts] have also been most likely to embrace it, while those districts whose scores are already quite high are fighting hardest to get rid of it." The relative political strengths in such a fight are sadly obvious; this is one more reason why accountability can't be left solely to the states.

Listening to the critics' complaints, one is left wondering, What are the wondrous accomplishments that more rigorous accountability will place in jeopardy? It is clear that we have failed to successfully educate poor and minority students on a large-scale basis. It is also clear that despite their best intentions many teachers, principals, superintendents, and professors at schools of education do not know how to address these shortcomings on a meaningful scale. Federal requirements driving states to address these problems would be much more troubling if they were interfering with a variety of successful state and local approaches, but that is simply not the case. In fact, based on what we know, federal accountability provisions will complement the most successful state practices.

States Show Results

Will there be unintended consequences from the new federal accountability provisions? Undoubtedly. Will they all be perverse? No one knows, and unintended consequences that prove positive are certainly not unheard of. We do, however, know something of the intended consequences policymakers hope for. There is evidence that accountability systems with concrete goals change the behavior of school systems, at a minimum by refocusing efforts on disadvantaged students. Consider the experiences of Massachusetts, Virginia, and Texas. In Massachusetts and Virginia, where students are tested in key grades and will soon need to pass exit exams to graduate from high school, Cassandras predicted all kinds of pernicious results. They haven't materialized. In fact, although much work remains, test scores are steadily rising in both states.

During the past four years, the share of Virginia students passing the Algebra I and Algebra II Standards of Learning (SOL) assessments has risen by 34 and 43 percent, respectively. The pass rates for African-American students have gone from 20 percent to 59 percent in Algebra I and 13 percent to 58 percent in Algebra II since 1998. Virginia still needs to address a substantial achievement gap, but its minority students' scores have clearly improved.

In Massachusetts, test-score performance improved, once graduation requirements were imposed. In 2001, 75 percent of 10th graders passed the math portion of the state's MCAS test, and 82 percent passed the language-arts test. This is up from 55 percent and 66 percent, respectively, the previous year. The Massachusetts example is particularly encouraging in light of Achieve, Inc.'s recent finding that "The grade 10 tests are rigorous yet reasonable—and are, in fact, the most challenging of the exit-level tests Achieve has yet reviewed." Achieve also lauded Massachusetts for its work to align its standards, curriculum, and assessments, which has provided a model for other states.

In Texas, where the TAAS test is widely considered to be less rigorous than the SOLs or MCAS tests (although the state is revising the TAAS), minority students nonetheless have shown gains that are corroborated by the National Assessment of Educational Progress. There is considerable evidence that during the past decade in Texas the needs of minority students have received increased attention as a result of an accountability system that demands that a school show not only overall progress, but also progress among its most disadvantaged charges.

Accountability systems are no panacea, and there are certainly problems in Texas and elsewhere. But these results at least indicate that accountability systems can help to focus attention on poor and minority students whose needs have been ignored or neglected. These results also seem to prove the point that states, if left to their own devices, will take action. It's true that the accountability movement has been state-led, to a large extent. Yet most states have yet to meet the requirements of the 1994 law, and it's clear that some won't move forward in any aggressive way without federal action.

What Must Be Done

Obviously, designing an accountability system of this nature is complex. Any workable proposal must be clear to practitioners; fair in the sense of not holding educators accountable for things they can't control; technically sound; and supported and enforced. It also should not squelch promising approaches that the states are developing.

Perhaps the most contentious issue in this debate is the use of standardized tests to measure school performance. Much of the hostility to accountability is actually just hostility toward testing. While standardized tests are certainly not perfect (in fact, they're primitive from a technological point of view), they're still the best objective way to measure progress. They lay bare discrepancies in educational quality in a quantifiable way. Sure, too many state assessment systems are lacking in quality or rigor. Yet this is a case for improvement, not abandonment.

There are legitimate complaints about the ways in which states are using the results of standardized tests. As Thomas Kane and Douglas Staiger point out . . . , test scores bounce up and down from year-to-year for a variety of reasons that are unrelated to actual school performance. Thus no system should rely solely on the snapshot of a single year's test scores in making decisions about incentives or consequences. Accountability systems also need to include safeguards against the statistical unreliability of small classes and demographic groups that may include only a few students at a particular school.

Because some states are experimenting with value-added approaches to measuring school progress, it's important that federal accountability standards allow for this type of innovation. And while it may be desirable to have a purely technocratic system that makes no allowances for political and human impulses, it is not feasible. Because schools are human institutions shaped by a variety of forces and influences that may or may not be within their control, some "give" is required to address exceptional circumstances that will inevitably arise. States should have discretion to undertake and prioritize interventions and consequences. But such discretion (or "safe harbor" provisions) need not equal the vague 1994 language or allow states to use measures that are divorced from academic results or are purely subjective and porous. During the debate over the federal "adequate yearly progress" standard, many of the proposals that would have included other indicators as measures of a school's adequate yearly progress were simply thinly disguised attempts to eradicate any rigor from the system. There were proposals to, among other things, hold schools accountable only for the progress of the lowest-performing students in the bottom quintile; not disaggregate data by race and ethnicity; require states to deal only with the lowest-performing schools; or ignore test results altogether as an accountability tool.

The new law appears to have addressed all of these issues in a workable manner. In the end, it may well turn out that the president's mandate that states annually test all children in grades 3 through 8 will prove to be much more burdensome and troubling for states than the new accountability provisions. It's also entirely possible that the adequate yearly progress provisions will cause trouble, as more and more schools wind up on lists of the low performing and politicians take the heat. Nonetheless, there is reason for cautious optimism.

What Washington must avoid is simply demanding accountability and then walking away. The New Democratic Lieberman-Bayh approach on education was predicated not only on more accountability, but also on more investment, more flexibility for states and localities, and a strategic federal role aimed at helping states and localities solve these problems, serving almost as a consultant to states and localities. This argues for a more active but less programmatic federal role in education.

States are increasingly failing to reach their revenue targets as a result of the slowing economy. The reforms of the ESEA legislation, especially the testing requirements, will require an expenditure of state resources on issues that aren't tied directly to the day-to-day provision of education. In a tight fiscal climate, testing and accountability initiatives will be curtailed or put on hold before direct services. It's up to Washington to help see that states aren't forced to make this choice. It is also essential that funding for interventions in low-performing schools accompany the new requirements. President Clinton inaugurated an accountability fund as part of Title I as a way to focus resources specifically on this purpose. However, more money will not provide a solution without enforcing clear goals for results.

There must also be a greater emphasis on getting these new resources to underserved communities. Funds must be concentrated rather than spread as far and wide as possible for political advantage. Democratic senator Mary Landrieu, a cosponsor of the "Three R's" bill, worked tirelessly, and against considerable opposition from members of both political parties, to increase the targeting of federal education dollars to low-income communities and schools in an effort to better support their school reform efforts.

Unfortunately, this legislation does not do enough to define the federal role in terms of consolidating programs and increasing local flexibility to meet diverse circumstances. The law includes flexibility provisions and some streamlining that are improvements. However, if raising overall test-score performance and addressing the achievement gap are to be the main focus of federal policy, it is foolish to have a panoply of programs that direct state and local officials toward a host of other priorities, distracting them from their core mission.

Someone must enforce the new rules if they are to be workable. Washington will encounter resistance at both the federal and state levels. As Senator Bayh of Indiana aptly told the *Los Angeles Times* in the midst of the debate, "Everyone is for accountability until it actually gets put into place and applies to them." Washington has a dismal record of enforcing its dictates in education. Of course, considering some of those dictates, sometimes this is a blessing. But one lesson of the 1994 reforms is that without enforcement states will simply ignore or delay parts of federal education laws they don't like. Tightening and clarifying the accountability provisions and then failing to enforce them only means states will be ignoring a new set of requirements. That's not much of an improvement on the status quo.

It's worth remembering that an army of naysayers predicting adverse consequences, or at best futility, has accompanied every major federal policy shift in education. However, the positive impact of accountability systems, particularly for the poor and minority students who traditionally have been excluded from educational opportunities, outweighs the risks. Mistakes will be made, lessons will be learned, policies will be fine-tuned. But we shouldn't delay the good while waiting for the perfect.

Peter Schrag  **NO**

Bush's Education Fraud

Well before he became president, George W. Bush had made his education plan, the No Child Left Behind Act, the showcase of "compassionate conservatism"—meaning, in the conventional shorthand, a conservative route to liberal ends. Its objective was to force schools to close the huge racial achievement gaps in American education, to pay attention to the poor and minority kids they had so often neglected, and to make every child "proficient" in reading and math by the year 2014. The law's name itself was a rip-off of "Leave No Child Behind," the longtime rallying cry of Marian Wright Edelman's Children's Defense Fund. When Bush signed the legislation in January 2002, two liberal Democrats, Massachusetts Sen. Edward Kennedy and California Rep. George Miller, were the co-stars of the White House photo-op.

But in the past two years, No Child Left Behind (NCLB)—formally just an extension of the Johnson-era Elementary and Secondary Education Act of 1965, but in practice probably the most sweeping nationalization of school policy in the nation's history—has left a lot behind, including no end of confusion, uncertainty and resentment.

The law itself, the administration's failure to fund it as promised, and the uneven and sometimes incomprehensible way it's been managed by the U.S. Department of Education have begun to generate so many difficulties and so much backlash, particularly among state legislators, that the program could well implode and take down two decades of state educational reforms with it. In the process, it would also end the best hope—all the law's difficulties notwithstanding—that America's poor and minority children have for getting better schools, higher standards and the attention they deserve.

The law's basic objectives were simple:

- Create an accountability system of tests, graduation rates, and other indicators that would force individual schools and districts to make adequate yearly progress by raising not only school-wide test scores but the achievement levels of every major subgroup of students—African Americans, Latinos, English language learners, low-income students, special-education students—to a state-defined level of proficiency. Schools that don't make such progress two years running for each group in each subject and grade are to go into "Program Improvement," which triggers an escalating set of sanctions and "interventions,"

Reprinted with permission from *The American Prospect,* Volume 15, Number 2: February 1, 2004, pp. 38–41. The American Prospect, 11 Beacon Street, Suite 1120, Boston, MA 02108. All rights reserved.

ultimately including a state takeover until the school again makes its adequate yearly progress targets.

- Require schools and districts to issue annual "report cards," which would provide data on the performance and quality of each school. Children in low-performing schools would be allowed to transfer to better schools (for which the district must provide transportation), and extra help would be provided for those who needed it. At heart, it meant that kids wouldn't remain trapped in the nation's most horrible schools. Bush wanted private-school vouchers; the public-school transfer provision is what he got.
- Provide the necessary resources, including "highly qualified teachers," in every classroom by 2005–06. To fund those reforms, Bush agreed to a 27 percent boost in Elementary and Second Education Act funding, to $22 billion in the first year and more in the years thereafter.

All told, it was an agenda that seemed as noble as it was political.

But the law wasn't simple, and because its provisions were often laid on top of various state testing and accountability systems, it made things more complicated still. California, for instance, already reported each year's test scores in grades 2–11, scores on its high-school exit exam and each school's test-based Academic Performance Index. In addition, there are the periodically reported state breakdowns of scores on the National Assessment of Educational Progress, and the national sampling of educational achievement in major subjects, sometimes called "the nation's report card."

NCLB now also requires annual reporting of adequate yearly progress, plus an alphabet soup of other goals and criteria. As a consequence, parents and the public in many states receive a torrent of numbers purportedly rating school performance, few of them entirely consistent with the others and many wildly different. As Michael Cohen, who heads Achieve Inc., a business-backed group promoting higher school standards, told *Education Week,* there's "massive confusion, owing to the stapling together of state and federal accountability systems, and pretending we have one system."

To make things more confusing still, in the tortured political compromises between national requirements and state prerogatives that Congress was forced to make to pass the bill, it produced a law that was at once too rigid and meaninglessly flexible. It required schools to ensure that *every* student achieve "proficiency," yet it allowed the states to set their own proficiency standards and, within general limits—a four-year undergraduate degree, a teaching credential, subject matter knowledge—to write their own definitions of what makes a highly qualified teacher. Thus while Michigan reported that some 1,500 schools (40 percent of all the state's public ones) failed to make their adequate yearly progress goals in 2000–01, Arkansas and Wyoming, with lower proficiency standards, reported none. And while some states reported that more than half their teachers weren't highly qualified—Utah reported last year that only about a third of its teachers were "fully highly qualified"—others declared that every teacher in every classroom was. And because NCLB imposes costly remedial requirements on districts with large numbers of what are officially called underperforming schools, it creates strong incentives for states with high standards to lower them.

What makes those incentives particularly intense is that in its well-meaning attempt to make sure that no school could pass muster unless every major subgroup became proficient in reading and math, Congress created very high hurdles for many schools and districts. It meant, as many school officials vehemently complained, that some of the most highly regarded schools were suddenly in jeopardy of being labeled low performing. If a school tests less than 95 percent of its children and less than 95 percent of all major subgroups in every grade—meeting those numbers is itself a huge challenge, especially in high schools, where even a 90 percent attendance rate is extraordinary—and if any of those subgroups fail to make progress in both reading and math in any two succeeding years, the school and its staff get a black mark and go through a federally mandated shape up program. The principal and teachers are then subject to reassignment after four years.

If making the grade is statistically tough for many schools with lots of minority students, it's almost impossible in schools with large numbers of students who arrive speaking little English. Worse, for English learners, there's a catch-22: Because those who become proficient in English—and thus do well on tests—are "redesignated" as "English proficient," their numbers are no longer counted in the English-learner category. California and Illinois have gotten waivers allowing them to continue to count English-learning students for three years after redesignation. But that solves only part of the statistical problem, because any school that has a rising percentage of English-learning students, as many have, will never be able to show progress in that category. "It feels like you're being set up," said a veteran school administrator and federal official who is now a superintendent in a large city with a mushrooming immigrant population.

Until the federal government granted districts more flexibility in December 2003, the situation was even more surreal for special-ed students, who were being given the same tests as regular students even though they are so designated precisely because many can't manage the pace of the normal program.

Meanwhile, the Bush administration is largely ignoring the law's requirement that states get qualified teachers into those schools that are getting extra funding to serve their large numbers of children from low-income families. Many districts try to honor the law's intent, but its mandate that districts put a "highly qualified" teacher into every classroom was always a little like King Canute commanding the waves to stop. Worse, despite pleas from some of NCLB's strongest supporters, the government isn't enforcing even those provisions of the law that require states to report on the qualifications of teachers at such schools. This "conspiracy of silence," says the Education Trust, a private group that's been a longtime advocate for the education of poor and minority children and that supports NCLB, has made that requirement nearly meaningless.

The law's mandate that students in low-performing schools be allowed to transfer to better ones has also been honored more in the breach than in practice. In many districts, particularly in rural areas, there are no convenient alternatives. In others, the schools to which students might transfer are already overcrowded. But most often, parents prefer to keep their children in neighborhood schools, regardless of the school's performance. Of the 250,000 Chicago students eligible for choice slots in August 2003, for example, 19,000 applied and fewer than 1,100 were placed in other schools.

⋅◄◉►⋅

If you listen to state legislators from both parties, however, the most frequent complaint is the administration's failure to honor its funding commitments. While the White House argues that school funding is up, current year appropriations for NCLB fall $8 billion short of what was authorized by the bill. "We were all suckered into it," said Rep. Dick Gephardt (D-Mo.), who voted for the measure. "It's a fraud."

The underfunding complaints are accompanied by studies indicating that the states' costs of meeting NCLB requirements are running far beyond the money that the federal government is providing. In what's probably the most frequently cited report, published last year in *Phi Delta Kappan*, William J. Mathis, a Vermont school administrator, concluded that in seven of the 10 states he surveyed, school spending would have to increase 24 percent to comply with all the requirements of NCLB. According to Mathis, Texas, the largest of the states studied, would have to spend $6.9 billion more, roughly doubling the state's school budget. "We're being asked to do more with nothing," said Bob Holmes, who chairs the Georgia House Committee on Education.

Mathis' estimates are controversial: Parsing out real NCLB cost figures is a squishy process. But there's no doubt that at a time of extremely tight state budgets, the law has, said one school superintendent, made everybody crazy. In a survey of principals and superintendents published late in 2003, Public Agenda found that nearly 90 percent regarded NCLB as an unfunded mandate. More than 60 percent said NCLB "will require many adjustments before it can work"; 30 percent said it probably wouldn't work at all. Most significantly, perhaps, the Public Agenda report noted "a noteworthy discrepancy between what NCLB calls for in terms of 'highly qualified' teachers and what superintendents and principals say they need from new teachers." Among those qualifications: the ability to maintain order and discipline in the classroom, to work with students whose background is different from their own and to establish working relationships with parents.

All of that has generated increasing levels of backlash. In at least three states—Minnesota, New Hampshire and Hawaii—legislators passed or seriously debated resolutions urging those states to withdraw from NCLB even though it means losing the federal money that's tied to it. Otherwise, said a Hawaii Democrat, NCLB is "going to label a lot of excellent schools as failing." In Oregon, Gov. Ted Kulongoski was said to be considering joining up with the National Education Association, the nation's largest teachers' union, in a suit challenging the law as an unfunded mandate.

In most states, however, there's a subtler strategy. Some have lowered their proficiency benchmarks to make their numbers look better. Among them are Michigan, which claimed it really was just making its system more realistic and comparable to other states, and Colorado and Texas, which lowered the passing score on their own tests to reduce the failure rate. Because standards vary so widely, eighth-grade students labeled proficient in Wisconsin are ranked in the 89th percentile in one national survey; a proficient ranking in Montana puts you in the 36th percentile. More pervasive still: Because NCLB says all students must be proficient by 2014, some states have drawn—and the federal government has approved—their expected lines of progress so that the biggest required gains are deferred until further out, when they rise steeply toward what's been described as a balloon payment (and when, presumably, most of today's governors, state superintendents and legislators are gone).

Not surprisingly, NCLB is reinforcing the wave of adequacy lawsuits filed by students, community activists and local districts, demanding that states provide resources adequate to the standards and high-stakes tests they've imposed. If students who fail exit exams are denied diplomas, or if teachers and administrators face sanctions for failing to meet standards, the state presumably has a commensurate legal and moral responsibility to provide the resources to allow them to succeed. A recent adequacy decision in Kansas, which ordered that state to restructure its funding, explicitly cited NCLB; so have new suits filed by school districts and others in Nebraska, Missouri and North Dakota.

More broadly, the nonpartisan National Conference of State Legislatures (NCSL) has been warning that cash-strapped states are being squeezed by their own standards, the NCLB mandates and the threat of further lawsuits. Two years ago, said David Shreve, who tracks No Child Left Behind for the NCSL, the reaction to the bill was "very positive." Then, as now, most state officials supported the testing and accountability principles; some even said NCLB was giving them "a needed kick in the butt," as Shreve put it. But after the political costs of the long and extended battles in many other places to get all constituencies behind the states' own accountability plans—parents, the business community, teachers and administrators—many states, Shreve said, don't want to go through the process of getting their various constituencies to support another accountability system. And while the federal mandates were designed to create a single standard, what they've done is create enough confusion among different accountability measures that it could "cause the public to sour on the whole thing."

To compound the problem, neither Congress nor the administration is disposed to address the issues before the 2004 election, if then. Bush hopes to run on NCLB and doesn't want any high-profile debate about it in the meantime. And so the administration has sent out a parade of Education Department officials to laud the law as a perfect gem, to argue that funding is ample, and to brand as whiners those who want to send poor and minority kids back to what Bush called "the soft bigotry of low expectations." "For the last 25 years," said Assistant Education Secretary Laurie Rich, a veteran Texas Republican operative, at an NCSL meeting last year, "we've tried to solve problems with money alone." It was time, she said, to do something else.

From the start, the NCLB debates have echoed the classic American ambivalence about how much schools alone can be expected to do in closing historic achievement gaps and overcoming social and cultural disadvantages. But it has also had political overtones all its own: the belief, by some on the right, that people like Sen. Ted Kennedy (D-Mass.) signed on only to leverage more money from the federal government and would be happy to let the accountability system fade away; and the belief, in some circles on the left, that NCLB, like all accountability systems, was a conservative trick to show the schools as failures and open the door for vouchers. "The president's ultimate goal," said former Gov. Howard Dean (D-Vt.), one of the Democrats who now harshly attacks NCLB, "is to make the public schools so awful, and starve them of money, just as he's starving all the other social programs, so that people give up on the public schools." Vouchers remain very much on the conservative agenda.

What is certain is that Bush regarded the widely lauded "Texas Miracle"—which, as much as anything, gave him credibility as a moderate when he ran four years ago—as a model. [See Peter Schrag, "Too Good to Be True," *TAP*, Jan. 3, 2000.] Texas had shown substantial improvements and closed racial achievement gaps on its own high-stakes tests in the 1990s. But that success had come with major costs: Dropout rates rose, teachers had to emphasize tests and drills at the expense of the broader curriculum, and school bureaucrats were involved in rampant cheating and falsification of data in places like Houston, where Paige was superintendent before Bush made him U.S. secretary of education. And students often continued to test poorly on all but the mandated tests: On its own tests, more than 80 percent of Texas students are proficient in reading; on the National Assessment of Educational Progress tests, less than 25 percent are.

The real Texas record should long have been a cautionary signal, not only for NCLB but also for the states that copied it. Now, in state after state, the tough standards so hopefully adopted in the past decade are being rolled back, deadlines are being postponed and passing test scores lowered. That's driven in part by a fear of a backlash if lots of kids or schools don't make the grade, and, in part, by shortfalls in the funding that was supposed to accompany the higher standards. If local, state and federal budgets get still tighter, the same accountability-funding nexus that was supposed to get the schools more money may well drive the standards down. It's a two-way escalator.

Kennedy and Miller both feel snookered by Bush and angrily denounced the president's failure to fully fund NCLB as another example of a White House of four-flushers who talk big dollars and deliver nickels. (Miller issues periodic "Broken Promises" reports accusing Republicans of sabotaging school reform.) But both continue to support NCLB, as do liberal groups like the Education Trust and the Citizens' Commission on Civil Rights. "The federal government," said William Taylor, a veteran civil-rights lawyer and chairman of the Citizens' Commission, "is doing a hell of a lot more for the states now than in the early years. A lot of the whining and bitching and moaning is coming from people who don't like the accountability provisions, so they're saying they don't have the money to do this."

He's at least partly correct. Through most of the nearly 40 years since the passage of the Elementary and Secondary Education Act, Title I funds were dribbled into a politically driven form of general aid instead of going to the low-income children it was designed for. Clinton-era reforms started the process of requiring schools to focus it on poor kids—children who in many places were long neglected—and use it more effectively. NCLB took that process still further in making districts and schools accountable for the achievement of those children.

Given the lack of plausible political alternatives—the fact that nothing has ever put as much emphasis on the academic success of poor and minority children—it's the only real game in town. If NCLB goes, those who'll be most hurt will, once again, be the children who can least afford it. But NCLB badly needs fixing to provide more flexibility in some areas and more rigorous enforcement in others, especially of the provisions mandating better-qualified teachers for poor children. It needs to provide more help and fewer penalties to low-performing schools. And it desperately needs to be better funded. Otherwise it will be just another in a string of hollow promises.

POSTSCRIPT

Can Federal Initiatives Rescue Failing Schools?

> The history of struggles over schooling suggests that to make individual learning a subject of political conflict weakens the participation of individuals in their own education, reduces the professionalism of teaching, and undermines intellectual and cultural diversity.

So said Stephen Arons in his article "Constitutional Implications of National Curriculum Standards," *The Educational Forum* (Summer 1994). Similarly, James Moffett argued in his book *The Universal Schoolhouse* (1994) that political and economic considerations are obscuring practical knowledge about how to improve learning in the schools. These sentiments also flow through some of the concern over President George W. Bush's ideas on education reform. Some critics see a future progression from strict accountability to nationwide voucher plans to diversion of public funds to private schools. Michael C. Milam, in "G. W., the Privatization of Education, and American Values," *The Humanist* (May/June 2001), for example, states that "the implications of an expanded or even totally private educational system are awesome and contradict the spirit of the fundamental ideals upon which the U.S. was founded. Public schools dedicated to equal opportunity, where children study free of denominational bias and corporate influence and among fellow students representing a variety of religious and ethnic backgrounds, are essential for a democratic society based upon pluralism and tolerance."

Further questions about the federal role in school improvement are expressed in Stephen Metcalf, "Numbers Racket: W. and the Uses of Testing," *The New Republic* (February 12, 2001); Thomas Toch, "An Education Plan With the Right Goal, Wrong Yardstick," *The Washington Post* (November 18, 2001); Beverly Falk, "Standards-Based Reforms: Problems and Possibilities," *Phi Delta Kappan* (April 2002); and Juan Necochea and Zulmara Cline, "School Reform Without a Heart," *Kappa Delta Pi Record* (Spring 2002). Strong opinions are presented in an article by Monty Neill, "Leaving Children Behind," *Phi Delta Kappan* (November 2003) and two articles by Susan Ohanian, "Capitalism, Calculus, and Conscience," *Phi Delta Kappan* (June 2003) and "Bush Flunks Schools," *The Nation* (December 1, 2003).

In light of all the concern over wasted federal money, underfunded mandates, and anxiety-producing state testing programs, perhaps Rosetta Marantz Cohen has a good idea. In "Schools Our Teachers Deserve: A Proposal for Teacher-Centered Reform," *Phi Delta Kappan* (March 2002), she suggests putting teacher morale first in any reform efforts, offering sabbaticals, involving teachers in the evaluation process, making tenure mean something, and reallocating the use of time.

ISSUE 9

Do High-Stakes Assessments Improve Learning?

YES: Nina Hurwitz and Sol Hurwitz, from "Tests That Count,"
American School Board Journal (January 2000)

NO: Ken Jones, from "A Balanced School Accountability Model: An
Alternative to High-Stakes Testing," *Phi Delta Kappan* (April 2004)

ISSUE SUMMARY

YES: High school teacher Nina Hurwitz and education consultant
Sol Hurwitz assemble evidence from states that are leading the
movement to set high standards of educational performance and
cautiously conclude that it could stimulate long-overdue renewal.

NO: Teacher education director Ken Jones believes that much more
than test scores must be used to develop an approach to school
accountability that effectively blends federal, state, and local agencies and powers.

In the 1980s a number of national reports found America's public schools to
be seriously lacking in the production of students who were qualified to compete successfully in the emerging global economy. Among these reports were
the National Commission on Excellence in Education's *A Nation at Risk*, the
Education Commission of the States' *Action for Excellence*, the Twentieth Century Fund's *Making the Grade*, and the National Science Foundation's *Educating
Americans for the Twenty-First Century*. In response to these calls for higher standards, the Bush administration adopted the following national goals in its
"America 2000" plan: all children starting school prepared to learn, at least
90 percent of students graduating from high school, all students being able to
cope with challenging subject matter (particularly math and science), all adults
being literate and responsible citizens, and all graduates being able to compete
in a global economy.

To move toward these goals the Republican administration emphasized
more choice and competition, more influence from business leaders, and the
development of nationwide curriculum standards and testing programs. The
Clinton administration adopted the goals, renaming them "Goals 2000: Educate

America," but downplayed the role of the private sector and placed responsibility for assessing student progress on the individual states. The George W. Bush administration, while backing away from privatization and voucher issues, has strengthened the call for accountability and rigorous testing.

To date, many states have risen to the challenge, imposing statewide standardized tests of subject matter and mental skills. In some cases, states have set up procedures for taking over the administration of chronically underperforming local schools. In others, schools that dramatically increase student performance are rewarded in some tangible way.

Peter Sacks, in *Standardized Minds: The High Price of America's Testing Culture and What We Can Do to Change It* (1999), contends that "the case against standardized testing is as intellectually and ethically rigorous as any argument about social policy . . . and yet such testing continues to dominate the education system, carving further inroads into the employment arena as well." He further warns that "when thinking becomes standardized people are easily objectified, their skills and talents translated into the language and mechanisms of commercial enterprise." This sentiment is shared by Alfie Kohn, who, in "Unlearning How We Learn," *Principal* (March 2000), says that "raising standards has come to mean little more than higher scores on poorly-designed standardized tests," leading to abandonment of the best kind of teaching and learning.

This central concern about the direct impact of test mania on the nature of the learning process has been widely voiced by educators who advocate instructional approaches based on the theory of constructivism. Drawn from the thinking of John Dewey, Jean Piaget, Lev Vygotsky, Howard Gardner, and others, constructivism views learning as an active, group-oriented process in which students "construct" an understanding of knowledge utilized in problem-solving situations. Such sense-making activities can be time-consuming and therefore can get in the way of teachers and schools whose primary focus is on test performance.

Those who see the standards and testing movement as the clearest path to school improvement include Joan L. Herman, "The State of Performance Assessments," *The School Administrator* (December 1998); Jerry Jesness, "Why Johnny Can't Fail: How the 'Floating Standard' Has Destroyed Public Education," *Reason* (July 1999); and Mike Schmoker, "The Results We Want," *Educational Leadership* (February 2000). These and other advocates feel that a standardized testing program ensures acquisition of basic skills, holds schools accountable for results, and identifies problem areas.

In the following selections, Nina Hurwitz and Sol Hurwitz examine experiences with high-stakes testing in Texas, Chicago, and New York in order to identify crucial elements of successful implementation. Ken Jones argues that the current accountability approach, relying on the use of high-stakes tests mandated from above, is detrimental to local school improvement and erodes democratic principles.

**Nina Hurwitz and
Sol Hurwitz**

Tests That Count

They are tests that count, high-stakes tests that can deny promotion or graduation to students with failing scores. Schools with too many low-performing students can be exposed to the glare of publicity, placed on probation, or closed. A widening coalition of governors, business leaders, parents, and teachers—appalled that youngsters can advance through school, receive a diploma, and seek further education or a job without mastering basic skills—is promoting the use of these tests as a means of boosting standards and improving accountability in public education.

The movement is gaining national momentum. Forty-nine states have adopted performance standards for elementary and secondary education; 26 have high school exit exams in place or in process; 19 publicly identify failing schools. President Clinton is in the vanguard, calling for higher standards and a crackdown on social promotion. Last fall he urged the nation's governors, "Look dead in the eye some child who has been held back [and say], 'We'll be hurting you worse if we tell you you're learning something when you're not.'"

High Standards, High Stakes

High-stakes testing is forcing the debate over a fundamental question in American education—whether it is possible to achieve both excellence and equity. On one side are those who claim that tests with consequences are the only sure route to higher standards and stricter accountability. On the other are those who contend that high-stakes tests are a command-and-control instrument for "standardizing" education and punishing disadvantaged and minority children. But a more pragmatic middle position is evolving based on the experience of front-line practitioners: High-stakes testing can work with clear but limited goals, flexibility in meeting those goals, and the will to address head-on the problems of students at risk of failure.

Texas, Chicago, and New York City and state, discussed below, are being carefully watched by educators and decision makers nationwide for both positive and negative lessons. The states are driving the high-stakes movement: Kentucky, Maryland, Massachusetts, North Carolina, and Virginia are running noteworthy programs as well.

From Nina Hurwitz and Sol Hurwitz, "Tests That Count," *American School Board Journal* (January 2000). Copyright © 2000 by The National School Boards Association. Reprinted by permission of *American School Board Journal*.

Even as states and school districts attempt to raise standards and impose high-stakes tests, they are confronted with excessive numbers of their urban, minority, and disadvantaged students who are failing these tests. In urban districts, large-scale failure is inevitable, says *Education Week's* Ron Wolk, given the shoddy education these students are receiving. "For tens of thousands of urban youngsters, it's a kind of double jeopardy," Wolk declares. "The system failed to educate them adequately, and now it punishes them for not being educated." Schools and school districts might face punishment as well: Low scores could result in the reorganization of schools or a shift of resources to charter schools or private-school vouchers.

Parent advocacy and civil rights groups are challenging the tests on racial and equity grounds. The penalties, they claim, fall disproportionately on minority and at-risk students, who have been shortchanged in their education. Meanwhile, teachers and researchers are beginning to question the tests' educational validity: Do they, in fact, improve learning?

Educators are unanimous that high-stakes tests should be aligned with curriculum and instruction—they should measure what students have been taught and are expected to know—and that teachers should be involved in the process. But only gradually are states and school districts committing sufficient resources and time to achieve proper alignment with full teacher participation. The time lag, educators argue, makes it risky to impose consequences prematurely.

Disagreement between states and urban school districts over which test to use means students in the same grade might have to take two tests—in the same subject. Learning suffers, educators say, when teachers spend time preparing students for too many tests. "The first thing to go in a school or district where these tests matter," says education expert Alfie Kohn, "is a more vibrant, integrated, active, and effective kind of instruction." [See "Raising the Scores, Ruining the Schools," *ASBJ*, October 1999.] A fifth-grade teacher in Virginia concurs: "Sometimes, when I wish I could stay longer on a subject, I have to move on to prepare my kids for the tests."

A 1999 study titled *High Stakes* by the prestigious National Research Council sharply criticized the practice of relying solely on tests to determine promotion or graduation. Such decisions, the council argued, "should be buttressed by other relevant information about the student's knowledge and skills, such as grades, teacher recommendations, and extenuating circumstances." Many educators question the value of holding kids back *period*—but certainly not without a highly structured, and often costly, intervention and remediation strategy.

The growing public demand for standards with accountability has made high-stakes testing a tempting political issue. The public is fed up with low standards and courses that lack content—they want American students to be able to compete favorably with kids in other countries. Test scores provide an aura of businesslike accountability for superintendents, principals, and teachers and a stimulus for students. Initially, at least, testing seems easy and inexpensive compared with more deep-seated reforms such as hiring and training competent teachers, reducing class size, or repairing crumbling school buildings. But achieving accountability is neither simple nor cheap.

The states and school districts that have had the most success with highstakes testing share several common characteristics. They have maintained bipartisan political support and the backing of a broad coalition of interest groups, including the business community, over a sustained period. Highstakes tests have not only raised standards but have stimulated system-wide reform. Most important, there has been a heavy investment in addressing the academic performance of the weakest students.

Turnaround in Texas

Texas is a dramatic case in point. Once considered one of the nation's educational backwaters, the Texas public school system, according to the *New York Times*, is now viewed by educators as "a model of equity, progress and accountability." The state's education reforms have spanned the administrations of former Democratic governor Ann W. Richards and current Republican governor and presidential hopeful George W. Bush. In a system of 3.7 million students that is half African American and Hispanic, the scores of African-American and Hispanic students on national assessments in reading and mathematics in 1996 and 1998 outranked those of most other states, and scores on state assessments for all students have risen for the fourth straight year.

A unique feature of the Texas system is the Texas Assessment of Academic Skills (TAAS), the state's high-stakes exam program, introduced in 1990. The tests combine clearly stated educational standards with a detailed reporting of results by ethnicity and class. Scores are sorted according to white, African-American, Hispanic, and economically disadvantaged groups. Along with attendance and dropout rates, TAAS scores are used to identify a school as failing if any one of its four demographic cohorts falls below standard. "Disaggregation of scores has focused the schools' attention on kids that were once ignored," according to University of Texas professor Uri Treisman, who is director of the Charles A. Dana Center in Austin. Texas is gradually raising the passing bar to 50 percent for each cohort from the original 20 percent.

Until recently, the high stakes associated with the TAAS have consisted almost entirely of public disclosure of school-by-school test results, a process Gov. Bush calls "shining a spotlight of shame on failure." The ratings, published on the web, identify schools as exemplary, recognized, acceptable, or low-performing and provide strong incentives to improve for adults and students alike. For example, superintendents, principals, and teachers find it hard to get jobs if they come from failing schools. Although low-performing schools are bolstered by additional financial support, they are rarely closed. "There are no great ideas on what to do with really problematical schools," says Treisman.

Elementary and middle-school students are tested in grades three through eight on various combinations of reading, writing, and mathematics, with science and social studies added in the eighth grade. In response to political pressure, Texas will move to end social promotion by 2003. Hoping to avoid widespread retention, the state has instituted the Student Success

Initiative, an early-intervention program, starting with the current year's kindergarten class. A skeptic on retention, Treisman cautions that research on the dropout problem indicates that "being overage in your class has the single highest correlation for dropping out and is twice as high as for any other factor, including race." Also, as pressure mounts to pass the TAAS, state officials have become increasingly concerned over outbreaks of alleged cheating.

There is wide agreement that Texas high schools have not shown as much improvement as elementary schools. However, the state plans to beef up the content of the 10th-grade exit exam and move it to the 11th grade and to allow substitution of end-of-course exams in core subjects. The present 10th-grade exam is the subject of a lawsuit by the Mexican-American Legal Defense Fund in the U.S. District Court in San Antonio, which claims the test discriminates against minority students. Gov. Bush counters this claim: "Some say it is a racist test," he told the *New York Times* [recently]. "I strongly say it is racist not to test because by not testing we don't know, and by not knowing we are just moving children through the system." The outcome is sure to have an impact on other states, researchers agree.

Remarkably, the state's educational resurgence has occurred while expenditures remained below the national average: In 1998–99, Texas spent $5,488 per student compared with the national average of $6,407. Striking, too, is the autonomy that Texas gives its principals and teachers as long as test results remain positive. Bilingual education, for example, is a local option. However, scores for Spanish-speaking and special education students must now be included in overall ratings to ensure more accurate results.

Success in Chicago

Just as Texas has drawn raves for educational attainment at the state level, Chicago, with an enrollment of 431,000 students, has become the promised land for city reformers. Mayors, superintendents, and educators have flocked there to study the remarkable turnaround orchestrated by chief executive officer Paul Vallas, formerly budget director under Mayor Richard M. Daley. With no previous experience in education, Vallas has performed what many consider an educational miracle in a school district that U.S. Secretary of Education William J. Bennett in 1987 called "the worst in the country." Vallas achieved credibility largely through the selective but determined application of highstakes testing. Scores on Chicago's performance benchmark, the Iowa Test of Basic Skills in Reading and Mathematics, have risen for the fourth straight year.

When Vallas took charge in 1995, an earlier reform effort, which stressed decision making by local school councils, had virtually hit bottom. With high truancy, low standards, and rampant grade inflation, Vallas declared, "there was wide agreement that the earlier reform initiative had failed." Vallas exploited public dissatisfaction with the previous reform, while drawing grassroots support from a network of parents, community groups, foundations, and universities to fashion a new strategy.

Fundamental to his success was the solid backing of Mayor Daley and Gery Chico, president of the Chicago School Reform Board (successor to the former elected school board), whose members were all mayoral appointees. Vallas forged a close working relationship with Tom Reece, who heads both the Chicago Teachers Union and the Illinois Federation of Teachers, and together they have succeeded in avoiding strikes and confrontations by building communication and trust. In addition, he won points with the public for his skills as a financial manager by stamping out waste, ending deficits, and securing state funds for building and renovating schools.

Three years ago, Chicago gained national attention as the first big-city school system to end social promotion. Students who don't meet minimum standards on the Iowa Tests are at risk of retention, but the passing bar was set low at first to avoid massive failure and is only gradually being raised.

Chicago's promotion gates kick in for students in grades three, six, and eight. For those who fail, the city's mandatory Summer Bridge Program, staffed with experienced teachers, provides a scripted curriculum from the central administration with hour-by-hour guidelines. University of Chicago professor Melissa Roderick, a member of the Consortium on Chicago School Research, believes the program goads parents, students, and teachers to work harder to avoid retention. "Students love Summer Bridge," says Roderick, because they know it helps them. Of the estimated 25,000 students who attended summer school last year, two-thirds moved to the next grade. Chicagoans call the policy "retention plus" because it comes front-loaded with ample resources for intervention and remediation. "Retention is a last resort," Vallas maintains.

Chicago also provides tutoring during school, and in an after-school Lighthouse Program (with supper included), for students who fail. Cozette Buckney, the system's chief education officer, shares the prevailing view of education experts that students should not merely repeat the same curriculum once they are held back. "You must teach them differently, use different materials—give them a different experience," she says.

Finally, if students have not passed the eighth-grade test by age 15, they move to "academic prep centers" that offer small transitional classes and intensive test preparation, where expenditures per pupil are one-and-a-half times those for high schools. Most students move on to high school after one year, although some teachers believe the centers accentuate problems of self-esteem and increase the tendency to drop out.

So dazzling is Chicago's success in the lower grades that outside observers have hardly noticed that real achievement stops at the high school door. "In the high schools, we have been at a loss," Buckney admits. Standards remain low, and there is widespread disengagement of students, a weak curriculum, and meager support services. Half of the city's ninth-graders fail two or more courses.

The Chicago Academic Standards Exams (CASE), which are end-of-semester high school tests in core subjects, are currently being upgraded. Teachers now receive detailed content guides from the administration but complain about the rigidity that the guides impose on their teaching.

Although most teachers allow the exams to count for only 15 percent of the semester grade, a biology teacher contends that "the tests shape what I teach, what order I teach in, and how long I spend on each subject."

High school teachers have been more resistant to control from the central office than elementary school teachers, according to Vallas. "They view themselves as college professors—they're more set in their ways," he complains. Last year George Schmidt, an activist teacher, published parts of the CASE tests in protest, and students at top-rated Whitney Young High School boycotted the tests. Vallas dismisses such opposition, saying, "There is enough to be irritating but not enough to delay reform."

Recent efforts to close down and reconstitute Chicago's worst high schools have proved unsuccessful, and discharging low-performing administrators and teachers has been difficult. "The burden of proof [on the school administration] in removing failing teachers is pretty strong," Vallas admits.

Vallas is seeking to garner support for Chicago's high-stakes tests by allowing waivers and retesting. He is also identifying at-risk students early and conducting special programs for pregnant teens and teen mothers. "Good attendance, behavior, and grades" can help students get promoted, he says. The time will come, he predicts, when tests will become a diminishing factor in promotion decisions.

Disappointment in New York

Chicago's success in strengthening standards and ending social promotion in the early grades contrasts sharply with New York City's recent dismal experience with high-stakes testing. New York's gigantic scale—it is the nation's largest school system with 1.1 million students—and the fractured relationship between the schools chancellor and the mayor have vastly complicated attempts to impose high stakes on state and city tests. Unlike Chicago, where Paul Vallas and Mayor Daley work in blissful harmony, New York City's Schools Chancellor Rudy Crew has recently been at loggerheads with Mayor Rudolph W. Giuliani.

High-stakes testing [has been brought] to the boiling point. After months of cramming and intense pressure on students, teachers, and parents, the news came in May [1999] that 67 percent of New York City students had failed the state's new and more demanding fourth-grade language arts test. The test was given over three days and included passages to be read for comprehension and answered in essay form. Stunned by the low test scores, the mayor proposed the removal of principals from the bottom third of all city elementary schools and called for a major management shake-up. State Education Commissioner Richard P. Mills recommended summer school for all students who failed the test.

Then came the disappointing results on year-end city tests, administered and graded by CTB/McGraw-Hill, which showed only 44.6 percent of students reading at grade level, a five-point decline from the previous year. Mathematics scores were even lower, falling 10 percent. After this second dose of bad news, the mayor prescribed even stronger medicine. Impressed by Chicago's example, he called for abolishing the semi-independent board of education and placing the schools under his own control.

After constant badgering from the mayor, Crew responded in mid-June with a hastily arranged mandatory summer-school program starting in July for 37,000 third-, sixth-, and eighth-graders who had scored at or below the 15th percentile on the city's standardized reading test and the 10th percentile on the mathematics test, both taken in the spring. Students failing the tests a second time would be held back.

The summer-school program was plagued with problems. For six weeks the schools were forced to cope with thousands of youngsters who needed to pass the city tests to avoid retention. Many teachers were handicapped by a lack of student records and by inadequate course materials, and school buildings were stifling from a record-setting heat wave. Although paid at a lower rate than their school-year salaries, many teachers had to buy their own materials and bring fans from home. In some instances, students who were supposed to take only the mathematics test were drilled mainly for the reading test.

Chancellor Crew's pride in announcing that 64 percent of the students passed the tests was soon dampened when scoring errors by CTB/McGraw-Hill revealed that more than 8,600 students were sent to summer school by mistake. Lack of accurate summer-school attendance figures cast further doubt on the number of students who would be retained. The Puerto Rican Legal Defense Fund and Advocates for Children, a nonprofit legal services organization, have threatened court challenges, citing late warning of the new requirement to attend summer school and the use of a single test to determine promotion.

New York City's problems are likely to be exacerbated by Commissioner Mills' determined belief in high-stakes testing as a means of raising standards for the state's high schools. In a program that is unique in the nation, Mills and the State Board of Regents are requiring that by 2003, all students will have to receive a passing grade of at least 65 percent on the state's tough new Regents examinations in five subjects—English, mathematics, science, global studies, and American history—before they can graduate. Currently less than a quarter of New York City students qualify for a Regents diploma.

Turning aside his critics, Mills contended in a [recent] *New York Times* interview that without high standards, "You simply decide in advance that some students don't have access to the good life. They don't have access to jobs, they don't have access to enriched curriculum and everything that goes with it."

Mills understood the need for a structured program of remediation and support for those who fail the Regents tests. To this end, he proposed a $900 million program targeted toward poor districts, but Gov. George E. Pataki's budget came nowhere near to providing that amount. . . . [S]tate lawmakers—under pressure from parents, teachers, and school administrators who feared widespread failure on the Regents tests—argued for scaling down requirements. In October a consortium of parents and educators at 35 New York City alternative high schools asked legislators to compel the Regents to exempt its students from the new English Regents exams. With public opposition rising, it is doubtful the Regents will have enough public support to sustain such an extensive testing program with such high stakes over the long term.

As the results of [the] more rigorous six-hour, two-day English Regents tests were being released, accusations of deceptive scoring on the essay questions began to surface. According to a Harlem high-school teacher, "I never would have given points in a regular class for the kind of answers we were getting on those essays."

Many teachers had never seen the state's new standards; nor had they been trained to teach courses to the level of the Regents' demands. "No business or military organization would do that kind of campaign without adequate training," Thomas Sobol, former state education commissioner, asserted at a meeting in Purchase, N.Y. . . . For New York City's students, the stakes are overwhelming and probably unrealistic.

Making High-Stakes Testing Work

High-stakes tests are transforming the education landscape, and lawmakers and educators are learning to navigate in uncharted terrain. Conditions and requirements vary state-by-state, and progress in meeting the new standards requires patience. But some early lessons can be drawn from states and school districts that are beginning to achieve success:

Make sure that learning   not testing   is the goal   "Are we teaching for testing or teaching for knowledge?" a senior administrator asks. Tests can be important in identifying weaknesses. But too much testing in too many subjects overwhelms teachers, drains resources from enriched educational programs, stifles creativity, and increases cheating.

Give disadvantaged students special assistance   High-stakes tests can be a powerful tool for raising standards for at-risk students, but only if resources are reallocated to schools that serve them. And the testing program must be held accountable for ensuring that the tests are reliable, fair, and free of cultural bias.

Set failure rates at a realistic level   Most schools lack the resources and capacity to absorb masses of failing students in after-school and summer-school remediation programs and to conduct programs for students who repeatedly fail. But setting failure rates too low damages credibility in the system's standards. The right balance will vary according to circumstances, but finding it is crucial.

Invest in a wide range of educational reforms   not just tests   Tests don't work in a vacuum but in an environment that supports systemwide reform. Tests should be part of a program that encourages early childhood education; the recruitment, training, and development of capable teachers; smaller class size; and safer buildings.

Make retention a last resort   Most studies show that retention does more harm than good. Frequent failure erodes self-confidence, and students who are retained have a higher probability of dropping out. If retention helps at all, it does so only when students are supported by innovative learning strategies. Decisions to deny promotion should not be based on a single test and should involve the teacher.

Use publicity to force improvement   School rankings draw attention to the weakest schools and can be used to drive decisions regarding school reform, reorganization, or closure. School officials have an obligation to interpret test results to the public consistently and accurately and to be forthright about problems in the system.

Focus on urban high schools   Tests can be effective in raising standards but only if problems of school climate are addressed. Expect high school exit exams to be challenged in the courts by minority groups. Excessive testing narrows curriculum choice, and the need for remediation may lead to de facto tracking and high dropout rates.

Prepare for the long haul   It is the rare state or school district that gets high-stakes testing right the first time. Success takes time and requires experimentation. Be ready to adapt, adjust, and compromise in order to achieve long-term success.

On balance, high-stakes tests that are well-designed and carefully administered appear to be working, at least in the lower grades. But if their benefits are oversold and their dangers ignored, disenchantment could lead to diminished support for public education. If, on the other hand, they call attention to failure and encourage strategies to ensure success, they could stimulate a long-overdue educational renewal for the nation's neediest students.

NO

Ken Jones

A Balanced School Accountability Model: An Alternative to High-Stakes Testing

For some time now, it has been apparent to many in the education community that state and federal policies intended to develop greater school accountability for the learning of all students have been terribly counterproductive. The use of high-stakes testing of students has been fraught with flawed assumptions, oversimplified understandings of school realities, undemocratic concentration of power, undermining of the teaching profession, and predictably disastrous consequences for our most vulnerable students. Far from the noble ideal of leaving no child behind, current policies, if continued, are bound to increase existing inequities, trivialize schooling, and mislead the public about the quality and promise of public education.

What is needed is a better means for evaluating schools, an alternative to the present system of using high-stakes testing for school accountability. A new model, based on a different set of assumptions and understandings about school realities and approaches to power, is required. It must be focused on the needs of learners and on the goals of having high expectations for all rather than on the prerequisites of a bureaucratic measurement system.

Premises

In the realm of student learning, the question of outcomes has often been considered primary: what do we want students to know and be able to do as a result of schooling? Once the desired outcomes have been specified, school reform efforts have proceeded to address the thorny questions of how to attain them. Starting from desired outcomes is an important shift in how to think about what does or does not make sense in classroom instruction.

In the realm of school accountability, however, little attention has been paid to corresponding outcome-related questions. It has simply been assumed that schools should be accountable for improved student learning, as measured by external test scores. It has been largely assumed by policy makers that external tests do, in fact, adequately measure student learning. These and other assumptions about school accountability must be questioned if we are to

From *Phi Delta Kappan* by Ken Jones, pp. 584–590. Copyright © 2004 by Phi Delta Kappan. Reprinted by permission.

develop a more successful accountability model. It would be well to start from basic questions about the purposes and audiences of schools. For what, to whom, and by what means should schools be held accountable? The following answers to these questions provide a set of premises on which a new school accountability system can be based.

For what should schools be accountable?   Schools should be held accountable for at least the following:

- *The physical and emotional well-being of students.* The caring aspect of school is essential to high-quality education. Parents expect that their children will be safe in schools and that adults in schools will tend to their affective as well as cognitive needs. In addition, we know that learning depends on a caring school climate that nurtures positive relationships.
- *Student learning.* Student learning is complex and multifaceted. It includes acquiring not only knowledge of disciplinary subject matter but also the thinking skills and dispositions needed in a modern democratic society.
- *Teacher learning.* Having a knowledgeable and skilled teacher is the most significant factor in student learning and should be fostered in multiple ways, compatible with the principles of adult learning. Schools must have sufficient time and funding to enable teachers to improve their own performance, according to professional teaching standards.
- *Equity and access.* Given the history of inequity with respect to minority and underserved student populations, schools must be accountable for placing a special emphasis on improving equity and access, providing fair opportunities for all to learn to high standards. Our press for excellence must include a press for fairness.
- *Improvement.* Schools should be expected to function as learning organizations, continuously engaged in self-assessment and adjustment in an effort to meet the needs of their students. The capacity to do so must be ensured and nurtured.

To whom should schools be accountable?   Schools should be held accountable to their primary clients: students, parents, and the local community. Current accountability systems make the state and federal governments the locus of power and decision making. But the primary clients of schools should be empowered to make decisions about the ends of education, not just the means, provided there are checks to ensure equity and access and adherence to professional standards for teaching.

By what means should schools be held accountable?   To determine how well schools are fulfilling their responsibilities, multiple measures should be used. Measures of school accountability should include both qualitative and quantitative approaches, taking into account local contexts, responsiveness to student and community needs, and professional practices and standards. Because schools are complex and unique institutions that address multiple societal needs, there should also be allowances for local measures, customized to meet local needs and concerns. A standardized approach toward school accountability cannot work in a nation as diverse as the U.S.

Given these premises, what are the proper roles of a government-developed and publicly funded school accountability system?

- It should serve to improve student learning and school practices and to ensure equity and access, not to reward or punish schools.
- It should provide guidance and information for local decision making, not classify schools as successes or failures.
- It should reflect a democratic approach, including a balance of responsibility and power among different levels of government.

A Balanced Model

An accountability framework called the "balanced scorecard" is currently employed in the business world and provides a useful perspective for schools.[1] This framework consists of four areas that must be evaluated to give a comprehensive view of the health of an organization. The premise is that both outcomes and operations must be measured if the feedback system is to be used to improve the organization, not just monitor it. In the business context, the four components of the framework are: 1) financial, 2) internal business, 3) customer, and 4) innovation and learning.

Applying this four-part approach to education, we can use the following aspects of school performance as the components of a balanced school accountability model: 1) student learning; 2) opportunity to learn; 3) responsiveness to students, parents, and community; and 4) organizational capacity for improvement. Each of these aspects must be attended to and fostered by an evaluation system that has a sufficiently high resolution to take into account the full complexity and scope of modern-day schools.

1. Student learning.   Principles of high-quality assessment have been well articulated by various organizations and should be followed.[2] What is needed is a system that

- is primarily intended to improve student learning;
- aligns with local curricula;
- emphasizes applied learning and thinking skills, not just declarative knowledge and basic skills;
- embodies the principle of multiple measures, including a variety of formats such as writing, open-response questions, and performance-based tasks; and
- is accessible to students with diverse learning styles, intelligence profiles, exceptionalities, and cultural backgrounds.

Currently, there is a mismatch between what cognitive science and brain research have shown about human learning and how schools and educational bureaucracies continue to measure learning.[3] We now know that human intellectual abilities are malleable and that people learn through a social and cultural process of constructing knowledge and understandings in given contexts. And yet we continue to conduct schooling and assessment guided by the outdated beliefs that intelligence is fixed, that knowledge exists apart from culture and context, and that learning is best induced through the behaviorist model of stimulus/response.

Scientific measurement cannot truly "objectify" learning and rate it hierarchically. Accurate decisions about the quality and depth of an individual's learning must be based on human judgment. While test scores and other assessment data are useful and necessary sources of information, a fair assessment of a person's learning can be made only by other people, preferably by those who know the person best in his or her own context. A reasonable process for determining the measure of student learning could involve local panels of teachers, parents, and community members, who review data about student performance and make decisions about promotion, placement, graduation, and so on.

What is missing in most current accountability systems is not just a human adjudication system, but also a local assessment component that addresses local curricula, contexts, and cultures. A large-scale external test is not sufficient to determine a student's achievement. District, school, and classroom assessments must also be developed as part of a comprehensive means of collecting data on student learning. The states of Maine and Nebraska are currently developing just such systems.[4]

Most important, locally developed assessments depend on the knowledge and "assessment literacy" of teachers.[5] Most teachers have not been adequately trained in assessment and need substantial and ongoing professional development to create valid and reliable tasks and build effective classroom assessment repertoires. This means that an investment must be made in teacher learning about assessment. The value of such an investment is not only in the promise of improved classroom instruction and measurement. Research also shows that improved classroom assessment results in improved student achievement on external tests.[6]

Last, the need to determine the effectiveness of the larger state school system can either support or undermine such local efforts. If state or federal agencies require data to be aggregated from local to state levels, local decision making is necessarily weakened, and an undue emphasis is placed on standardized methods. If, however, the state and federal agencies do not rely on local assessment systems to gauge the health of the larger system, much may be gained. In New Zealand, for example, a system of educational monitoring is in place that uses matrix sampling on tasks that include one-to-one video-taped interviews, team tasks, and independent tasks.[7] No stakes are entailed for schools or students. The data are profiled and shared with schools for the purpose of teacher professional development and as a means of developing model tasks for local assessments. Such a system supports rather than undermines local assessment efforts.

2. Opportunity to learn.   How can students be expected to meet high standards if they are not given a fair opportunity to learn? This question has yet to be answered with respect to school accountability. Schools should be accountable for providing equitable opportunities for all students to learn, and we must develop ways to determine how well they do so.

At the heart of the matter is that the responsibility for opportunity to learn must be shared by the district and state. The inequitable funding of public schools, particularly the disparity between the schools of the haves and those of the have-nots, places the schools of disadvantaged students in unjust and often horrifying circumstances. Over the past decade, there have been lawsuits in various states attempting to redress this imbalance, which is largely a result of dependence on property taxes for school funding. Yet not a great deal of progress has been made.

How should we define and put into practice our understanding of opportunity to learn? How will we measure it? How can an accountability system foster it?

At a minimum, one might expect that schools and school systems will provide qualified teachers, adequate instructional materials, and sound facilities. This is the contention in a recent lawsuit, *Williams* v. *State of California*, in which the plaintiffs argued for an accountability system that is reciprocal—that is, while schools are held accountable for performance, the state is held accountable for ensuring adequate resources.[8]

But there is more to this issue than just funding. Jeannie Oakes describes a framework that includes opportunity-to-learn indicators for access to knowledge, professional teaching conditions, and "press for achievement."[9] Linda Darling-Hammond stresses the "fair and humane treatment" of students in a set of standards for professional practice.[10]

As such standards for opportunity to learn are articulated, the question arises as to how to monitor and report on them. Clearly, the degree of adherence to these standards cannot be determined through the proxy of testing. It is necessary to conduct observations in schools and classrooms and to evaluate the quality both of individual teachers and of the school as a whole.

Teacher evaluation has received a great deal of criticism for being ineffective. The hit-and-run observations that principals typically conduct do little to determine whether teachers are meeting established professional teaching standards. Unions have been described as more interested in protecting their membership than in ensuring high-quality teaching. A promising development that has potential for breaking through this impasse is the recent initiation of peer-review processes by a number of teacher unions. Adam Urbanski, president of the Rochester Teachers Association and director of the Teacher Union Reform Network (TURN), has been a leader in advocating for and implementing such teacher evaluation processes. In a recent unpublished manuscript, he describes how the process should work:

- Some classroom observation by peers and supervisors, structured by a narrative instrument (not a checklist) based on professional standards such as those of the National Board for Professional Teaching Standards (NBPTS) and framed by the teacher's goals for the lesson/unit;
- Information from previous evaluations and feedback, such as structured references from colleagues and other supervisors;

- Portfolios that might include examples of teaching syllabi, assignments made, feedback given to students and samples of student work, feedback received from parents and students as well as colleagues, data on student progress, teaching exhibitions such as videotaped teaching samples, professional development initiatives taken, and structured self-evaluation. All summative evaluation decisions about promotions or continued employment should be made by a specially established committee of teachers and administrators.

Urbanski goes on to describe safeguards for due process and for preventing malpractice. He also describes how such a process could be used in conjunction with professional development for improving teaching and school practice.[11]

In order to evaluate the performance of a school as a whole, a school review process will be necessary. Variations of inspectorates and school-quality reviews have been developed in New York, Rhode Island, Maine, and other states, as well as in Britain, New Zealand, Australia, and other countries.[12] In order for such reviews to serve the purpose of school improvement, the data should be collected in a "critical friend" manner, through a combination of school self-assessment and collegial visitations. Findings from such a process should not be employed in a bureaucratic and judgmental way but rather should be given as descriptions to local councils charged with evaluating school accountability. As with all aspects of any school renewal initiative, the quality and effectiveness of a review system will depend on the time, resources, and institutional support given to it.

Who will ensure that adequate opportunities to learn are present in schools? As described below, a system of reciprocal accountability must be set up so that both local accountability councils and the state itself serve to "mind the store" for all students. The issue of equitable funding will undoubtedly be resolved through the courts.

3. Responsiveness to students, parents, and community.   Current accountability systems move power and decision making away from the primary clients of the education system and more and more toward state and federal agencies. As high-stakes testing dictates the curriculum, less and less choice is available for students. Parent or community concerns about what is happening in the classroom and to the students have become less important to schools than meeting state mandates.

As the primary stakeholders in the schools, parents and communities must be made part of the effort to hold schools accountable. There are many examples of local community organizations, especially in urban areas, that have taken on the task of insisting that schools are responsive to the needs of children.[13]

To demonstrate responsiveness to students, parents, and the community, schools must go beyond sponsoring parent/teacher organizations or encouraging parent involvement as a means to gain support for existing school practices. They must also do more than gather survey information about stakeholders' satisfaction. True accountability to the primary clients for schools entails shifting power relationships.

Local school-based councils must be created that have real power to effect school change. These councils would review accountability information from state and local assessments as well as from school-quality review processes and make recommendations to school boards about school policies and priorities. They would hold school boards accountable for the development and implementation of school improvement plans. Phillip Schlechty discusses how such councils might work:

> Community leaders who are concerned about the futures of their communities and their schools should join together to create a nonprofit corporation intended to support efforts of school leaders to focus on the future and to ensure that lasting values as well as immediate interests are included in the education decision-making process. It would also be the function of this group to establish a small subgroup of the community's most trusted leaders who would annually evaluate the performance of the school board as stewards of the common good and would make these evaluations known to the community. . . .

> In a sense, the relationship between the school district and the monitoring function of the new corporation should be something akin to the relationship between the quality assurance division of a corporation and the operating units in the corporation. . . .

> When the data indicate that goals are not being met, the president of the corporation, working with the superintendent and the board of education, would seek to discover why this was the case, and would seek as well to create new approaches that might enhance the prospect of achieving the stated goals and the intended ends. It is not intended that the new corporation simply identify problems and weaknesses, it is intended that the leaders of this organization also participate in the creation of solutions and participate in creating support for solutions once they have been identified or created.[14]

Communities must determine how to sustain such councils and ensure that they do not pursue narrow agendas. The composition of councils in urban settings will probably be different from those in rural or suburban settings. Standards and acceptable variations for councils will be important topics for public discussion.

4. Organizational capacity. If schools are going to be held accountable to high levels of performance, the question arises: Do schools have the internal capacity to rise to those levels? To what degree are the resources of schools "organized into a collective enterprise, with shared commitment and collaboration among staff to achieve a clear purpose for student learning"?[15]

The issue of meaningful and ongoing teacher professional development is especially pertinent to whether or not schools are capable of enabling all students to meet higher standards of performance. A great deal of research has shed light on what kind of professional development is most effective in promoting school improvement.[16]

Schools must also attend to the issue of teacher empowerment. Teachers are increasingly controlled and disempowered in various ways. This leads to a declining sense of efficacy and professionalism and a heightened sense of job dissatisfaction and has become a factor in the attrition that is contributing to the growing teaching shortage.[17] Principals must share leadership with teachers and others as a means of sustaining capacity.

To be an effective collective enterprise, a school must develop an internal accountability system. That is, it must take responsibility for developing goals and priorities based on the ongoing collection and analysis of data, it must monitor its performance, and it must report its findings and actions to its public. Many schools have not moved past the stage of accepting individual teacher responsibility rather than collective responsibility as the norm.[18] States and districts must cooperate with schools to nurture and insist upon the development of such collective internal norms.

The New Role of the State

For a balanced model of school accountability to succeed, there must be a system in which states and districts are jointly responsible with schools and communities for student learning. Reciprocal accountability is needed: one level of the system is responsible to the others, and all are responsible to the public.

The role of state and federal agencies with respect to school accountability is much in need of redefinition. Agencies at these levels should not serve primarily in an enforcement role. Rather, their roles should be to establish standards for local accountability systems, to provide resources and guidance, and to set in place processes for quality review of such systems. Certainly there should be no high-stakes testing from the state and federal levels, no mandatory curricula, and no manipulation through funding. Where there are clear cases of faulty local accountability systems—those lacking any of the four elements discussed above (appropriate assessment systems; adequate opportunities to learn; responsiveness to students, parents, and community; or organizational capacity)—supportive efforts from the state and federal levels should be undertaken.

Are there any circumstances in which a state should intervene forcibly in a school or district? If an accountability system is to work toward school improvement for all schools, does that system not need such "teeth"? This question must be addressed in a way that acknowledges the multi-level nature of this school accountability model. One might envision at least three cases in which the state would take on a more assertive role: 1) to investigate claims or appeals from students, parents, or the community that the local accountability system is not meeting the standards set for such systems; 2) to require local schools and districts to respond to findings in the data that show significant student learning deficiencies, inequity in the opportunities to learn for all students, or lack of responsiveness to students, parents, or communities; and 3) to provide additional resources and guidance to improve the organizational capacity of the local school or district. Is it conceivable that a state might take over a local school or district in this model? Yes, but only after the most comprehensive evaluation of the local accountability system has shown that there is no alternative—and then only on a temporary basis.

It is of great importance to the health of our public schools that we begin as soon as possible to define a new model for school accountability, one that is balanced and comprehensive. Schools can and should be held accountable to their primary clients for much more than test scores, in a way that supports improvement rather than punishes deficiencies. The current model of using high-stakes testing is a recipe for public school failure, putting our democratic nation at risk.

Notes

1. Robert S. Kaplan and David P. Norton, "The Balanced Scorecard—Measures That Drive Performance," *Harvard Business Review*, January/February 1992, pp. 71–79.

2. National Forum on Assessment, *Principles and Indicators for Student Assessment Systems* (Boston: FairTest, 1993), available at www.fairtest.org/k-12.htm.

3. Lorrie A. Shepard, "The Role of Assessment in a Learning Culture," *Educational Researcher*, October 2000, pp. 4–14.

4. Debra Smith and Lynne Miller, *Comprehensive Local Assessment Systems (CLASs) Primer: A Guide to Assessment System Design and Use* (Gorham: Southern Maine Partnership, University of Southern Maine, 2003), available at www.usm.maine.edu/smp/tools/primer.htm; and "Nebraska School-Based, Teacher-Led Assessment Reporting System (STARS)," www.nde.state.ne.us/stars/index.html.

5. Richard J. Stiggins, *Student-Centered Classroom Assessment* (Columbus, Ohio: Merrill, 1997).

6. Paul Black and Dylan Wiliam, "Inside the Black Box: Raising Standards Through Classroom Assessment," *Phi Delta Kappan*, October 1998, pp. 139–48; and Paul Black et al., *Working Inside the Black Box: Assessment for Learning in the Classroom* (London, U.K.: Department of Educational and Professional Studies, King's College, 2002).

7. Terry Crooks, "Design and Implementation of a National Assessment Programme: New Zealand's National Education Monitoring Project (NEMP)," paper presented at the annual meeting of the Canadian Society for the Study of Education, Toronto, May 2002.

8. Jeannie Oakes, "Education Inadequacy, Inequality, and Failed State Policy: A Synthesis of Expert Reports Prepared for *Williams* v. *State of California*," 2003, available at www.decentschools.org/experts.php.

9. Jeannie Oakes, "What Educational Indicators? The Case for Assessing the School Context," *Educational Evaluation and Policy Analysis*, Summer 1989, pp. 181–99.

10. Linda Darling-Hammond, *Standards of Practice for Learning Centered Schools* (New York: National Center for Restructuring Education, Schools, and Teaching, Teachers College, 1992).

11. Adam Urbanski, "Teacher Professionalism and Teacher Accountability: Toward a More Genuine Teaching Profession," unpublished manuscript, 1998.

12. Jacqueline Ancess, *Outside/Inside, Inside/Outside: Developing and Implementing the School Quality Review* (New York: National Center for Restructuring Education, Schools, and Teaching, Teachers College, 1996); New Zealand

Education Review Office, *Frameworks for Reviews in Schools*, available at www.ero.govt.nz/EdRevInfo/Schedrevs/SchoolFramework.htm; Debra R. Smith and David J. Ruff, "Building a Culture of Inquiry: The School Quality Review Initiative," in David Allen, ed., *Assessing Student Learning: From Grading to Understanding* (New York: Teachers College Press,1998), pp. 164–82.

13. Kavitha Mediratte, Norm Fruchter, and Anne C. Lewis, *Organizing for School Reform: How Communities Are Finding Their Voice and Reclaiming Their Public Schools* (New York: Institute for Education and Social Policy, Steinhardt School of Education, New York University, October 2002).

14. Phillip Schlechty, *Systemic Change and the Revitalization of Public Education* (San Francisco: Jossey-Bass, forthcoming).

15. Fred M. Newmann, M. Bruce King, and Mark Rigdon, "Accountability and School Performance: Implications from Restructuring Schools," *Harvard Educational Review*, Spring 1997, p. 47.

16. Judith Warren Little, "Teachers' Professional Development in a Climate of Educational Reform," *Educational Evaluation and Policy Analysis*, vol. 15, 1993, pp. 129–51; and Milbrey W. McLaughlin and Joan Talbert, *Professional Communities and the Work of High School Teaching* (Chicago: University of Chicago Press, 2001).

17. Richard M. Ingersoll, *Who Controls Teachers' Work? Power and Accountability in America's Schools* (Cambridge, Mass.: Harvard University Press, 2003).

18. Charles Abelman et al., *When Accountability Knocks, Will Anyone Answer?* (Philadelphia: Consortium for Policy Research in Education, University of Pennsylvania, CPRE Research Report Series RR-42, 1999).

POSTSCRIPT

Do High-Stakes Assessments Improve Learning?

Whether standardized tests are a crucial tool in improving overall student performance or whether they rob teachers of the autonomy and creativity needed for lasting improvement of learning is among the most hotly debated topics on the current scene. Is Jerry Jesness correct in condemning "floating" standards that shield the status quo and guarantee the reign of mediocrity, or is Susan Ohanian right in demolishing high-stakes testing in her book *One Size Fits Few: The Folly of Educational Standards* (1999)?

Here are some further sources to tilt your thinking one way or the other: Mary E. Diez, "Assessment as a Lever in Education Reform," *National Forum* (Winter 1997); Elliot W. Eisner, "Standards for American Schools: Help or Hindrance?" *Phi Delta Kappan* (June 1995); Jack Kaufhold, "What's Wrong With Teaching for the Test?" *The School Administrator* (December 1998); Frederick M. Hess and Frederick Brigham, "None of the Above," *American School Board Journal* (January 2000); Jeff Berger, "Does Top-Down, Standards-Based Reform Work?" *NASSP Bulletin* (January 2000); Peter Schrag, "High Stakes Are for Tomatoes," *The Atlantic Monthly* (August 2000); Georgia Hedrick, "Real Teachers Don't Test," *Educational Horizons* (Winter 2002); Dale DeCesare, "How High Are the Stakes in High-Stakes Testing?" *Principal* (January 2002); Mary Ann Raywid, "Accountability: What's Worth Measuring?" *Phi Delta Kappan* (February 2002); Mark F. Goldberg, "The Test Mess," *Phi Delta Kappan* (January 2004); and Michael G. Gunzenhauser, "High-Stakes Testing and the Default Philosophy of Education," *Theory Into Practice* (Winter 2003).

Although most of the focus is now on state mandates, proposals for national testing are still under consideration. Long a practice in many foreign countries, high-stakes national examinations in valued subject matter areas are an explosive topic in the United States. Articles that examine the larger context of the issue include Richard Rothstein, "The Limits of Testing," *American School Board Journal* (February 2005); "Standards-Based Reform and Accountability: Getting It Right," a special section in *American Educator* (Spring 2005); and Joseph Casbarro, "The Politics of High-Stakes Testing," *Principal* (January/February 2005).

Multiple articles on the standards and testing movement can be located in the May 1999 issue of *Phi Delta Kappan*, the Winter 1999 issue of *Kappa Delta Pi Record*, the February 2000 issue of *Educational Leadership*, the January 2001 issue of *NASSP Bulletin*, the January 2001 issue of *Principal Leadership*, the December 2001 issue of *The School Administrator*, the February 2002 issue of *Phi Delta Kappan*, the Winter 2002 issue of *Kappa Delta Pi Record*, and the September 2003 issue of *American School Board Journal*.

ISSUE 10

Should "Public Schooling" Be Redefined?

YES: Frederick M. Hess, from "What Is a 'Public School?' Principles for a New Century," *Phi Delta Kappan* (February 2004)

NO: Linda Nathan et al., from "A Response to Frederick Hess," *Phi Delta Kappan* (February 2004)

ISSUE SUMMARY

YES: Frederick M. Hess, a resident scholar at the American Enterprise Institute, advocates a broadening of the definition of "public schooling" in light of recent developments such as vouchers, charter schools, and home schooling.

NO: Linda Nathan, Joe Nathan, Ray Bacchetti, and Evans Clinchy express a variety of concerns about the conceptual expansion that Hess proposes.

$$T$$he original public school crusade, led by Massachusetts education official Horace Mann (1796–1859) and other activists, built on the growing sentiment among citizens, politicians, and business leaders that public schools were needed to deal with the increase in immigration, urbanization, and industrialism, as well as to bind together the American population and to prepare everyone for participatory democracy. For the most part, the right of the government to compel school attendance, dating from Massachusetts legislation in 1852, went unchallenged, although Catholics formed their own private school system in reaction to the predominant Protestantism of public schools in certain areas. In the 1920s there were efforts to eliminate all alternatives to government-runpublic schools to ensure attendance compliance and curricular standardization. Such an effort in Oregon was challenged in court, and the U. S. Supreme Court ultimately ruled, in *Pierce v. Society of Sisters* (1925), that such legislation unreasonably interferes with parental rights. While this ruling preserved the private school option, it did not alter the governmental prerogative to compel school attendance.

This governmental authority met with sharp criticism from liberal writers in the 1950s and beyond, in works such as Paul Goodman's *Compulsory*

Mis-education (1964), Ivan Illich's *Deschooling Society* (1971), John Holt's *Instead of Education* (1976), and John Taylor Gatto's *Dumbing Us Down: The Hidden Curriculum of Compulsory Schooling* (1992). Gatto condemned the public school system for its emphasis on obedience and subordination rather than the unleashing of the intellectual and creative powers of the individual. Since the 1980s, a parallel attack has come from conservatives, such as William J. Bennett, E. D. Hirsch, Jr., Chester E. Finn, Jr., Charles J. Sykes, Grover Norquist, and Cal Thomas, and conservative groups, such as Parents for School Choice, the Cato Institute, and the Alliance for Separation of School and State. Building on the findings of the 1983 *A Nation at Risk* report, a significant segment of the American population continues to express disdain for the public education "establishment" (the U. S. Department of Education, the National Education Association, and teacher-training institutions) for its inability or unwillingness to improve public school performance. Their basic contention is that only choice-driven competition will bring about lasting improvement. William J. Bennett, in "A Nation Still at Risk," *Policy Review* (July/August 1998), has stated that although choices are spreading, charter schools are proliferating, privately managed public schools have long waiting lists, and home schooling is expanding, "the elephant still has most of the power." He concludes that "we must never again assume that the education system will respond to good advice. It will change only when power relationships change, particularly when all parents gain the power to decide where their children go to school."

Educator-reformer Deborah Meier, in "The Road to Trust," *American School Board Journal* (September 2003), argues that we must make public education feel like a public enterprise again. Hers is a call for the rebuilding of trust between public schools and the communities they directly serve. "Our school boards need to turn their eyes to their constituencies—not just to following the dictates of state and federal government micromanagers."

In the following articles, Frederick M. Hess makes the case that the time has come for a reconception of "public schooling" while four prominent educators challenge what they perceive to be an unproductive assault on public schooling.

Frederick M. Hess

 **YES**

What Is a 'Public School?' Principles for a New Century

T he phrase "public schooling" has become more a rhetorical device than a useful guide to policy. As our world evolves, so too must our conception of what "public" means. James Coleman eloquently made this point more than two decades ago, implying a responsibility to periodically reappraise our assumptions as to what constitutes "public schooling."[1] In a world where charter schooling, distance education, tuition tax credits, and other recent developments no longer fit neatly into our conventional mental boxes, it is clearly time for such an effort. Nonetheless, rather than receiving the requisite consideration, "public schooling" has served as a flag around which critics of these various reforms can rally. It is because the phrase resonates so powerfully that critics of proposals like charter schooling, voucher programs, and rethinking teacher licensure have at times abandoned substantive debate in order to attack such measures as "anti-public schooling."[2]

Those of us committed to the promise of public education are obliged to see that the ideal does not become a tool of vested interests. The perception that public schooling has strayed from its purpose and been captured by self-interested parties has fueled lacerating critiques in recent years. Such critics as Andrew Coulson and Douglas Dewey find a growing audience when they suggest that the ideal of public schooling itself is nothing more than a call to publicly subsidize the private agendas of bureaucrats, education school professors, union officials, and leftist activists.[3] While I believe such attacks are misguided, answering them effectively demands that we discern what it is that makes schooling public and accept diverse arrangements that are consistent with those tenets. Otherwise, growing numbers of reformers may come to regard public schooling as a politicized obstacle rather than a shared ideal.

While I do not aim to provide a precise answer as to what public schooling should mean in the early 21st century, I will argue that public schools are broadly defined by their commitment to preparing students to be productive members of a social order, aware of their societal responsibilities, and respectful of constitutional strictures; that such schools cannot deny access to students for reasons unrelated to their educational focus; and that the system of

From *Phi Delta Kappan,* February 2004, pp. 584–590. Copyright © 2004 by Phi Delta Kappan. Reprinted by permission.

public schools available in any community must provide an appropriate placement for each student. In short, I suggest that it is appropriate to adopt a much more expansive notion of public schooling than the one the education community holds today.

What Isn't Public?

Traditionally, "public schools" are deemed to be those directly accountable to elected officials or funded by tax dollars.[4] As a practical matter, such definitions are not very useful, largely because there are conventional "public" schools that do not fit within these definitions, while there are "private" providers that do.

We generally regard as "public schools" those in which policy making and oversight are the responsibility of governmental bodies, such as a local school board. Nongovernmental providers of educational services, such as independent schools or educational management organizations (EMOs), are labeled "nonpublic." The distinction is whether a formal political body is in charge, since these officials are accountable by election or appointment to the larger voting "public."

There are two particular problems here. First, how "hands on" must the government be for us to regard a service as publicly provided? The National Aeronautics and Space Administration, the Environmental Protection Agency, the U.S. Department of Education, and most other state, federal, and local government agencies contract with for-profit firms for support, to provide services, and to evaluate service delivery. Yet we tend to regard the services as "public" because they were initiated in response to a public directive and are monitored by public officials. It is not clear when government-directed activity ceases to be public. For instance, if a for-profit company manages a district school, is the school less public than it was when it purchased its texts from a for-profit textbook publisher and its professional development from a private consultant?

A second approach to defining "public" focuses on inputs. By this metric, any activity that involves government funds is public because it involves the expenditure of tax dollars. However, this distinction is more nebulous than we sometimes suppose. For instance, schools in the Milwaukee voucher program receive Wisconsin tax dollars. Does this mean that voucher schools ought to be regarded as de facto public schools? Similarly, Wisconsin dairy farmers receive federal subsidies. Does this make their farms public enterprises?

A particular complication is that many traditional public schools charge families money. For instance, during 2002–03, the families of more than 2,300 Indiana students were paying tuition of as much as $6,000 to enroll their children in a public school in another district. Public schools routinely charge fees to families that participate in interdistrict public choice plans, and they frequently charge families fees if a child participates in extracurricular activities. Would proponents of a revenue-based definition suggest that such practices mean that these schools are no longer "public"?

A third approach, famously advanced by John Dewey, the esteemed champion of "public" education, recognizes that private institutions may serve public ends and that public institutions may fail to do so.[5] Such a recognition suggests that public schools are those that serve public ends, regardless of the monitoring arrangements or revenue sources. This approach is ultimately problematic, however, because we do *not* have clear agreement on appropriate public purposes. I'll have more to say on this point shortly.

What Is Public Schooling?

Previously, I have posed five questions to guide our efforts to bring more precision to our understanding of "public schooling."[6] Here, I offer these questions as a way to sketch principles that may help shape a contemporary conception of "public schooling."

What are the purposes of public schooling? Schooling entails both public and private purposes, though we often fail to note the degree to which the private benefits may serve the public interest. In particular, academic learning serves the individual and also the needs of the state. Successful democratic communities require a high level of literacy and numeracy and are anchored by the knowledge and the good sense of the population. Citizens who lack these skills are less likely to contribute effectively to the well-being of their communities and more likely to be a drain on public resources. Therefore, in a real sense, any school that helps children master reading, writing, mathematics, and other essential content is already advancing some significant public purposes.[7] It is troubling that prominent educational thinkers, including Frank Smith, Susan Ohanian, Deborah Meier, and Alfie Kohn, have rejected this fundamental premise and encouraged "public schools" to promote preferred social values even at the expense of basic academic mastery.[8]

More fundamentally, there are two distinct ways to comprehend the larger public purposes of education. One suggests that schools serve a public interest that transcends the needs of individuals. This line of thought, understood by Rousseau as the "general will," can be traced to Plato's conviction that nations need a far-sighted leader to determine their true interests, despite the shortsighted preferences of the mob. A second way of thinking about the public purposes of education accepts the classically "liberal" understanding of the public interest as the sum of the interests of individual citizens and rejects the idea of a transcendent general will. This pragmatic stance helped shape American public institutions that protect citizens from tyrannical majorities and overreaching public officials.

While neither perspective is necessarily "correct," our government of limited powers and separate branches leans heavily toward the more modest dictates of liberalism. Despite our tendency to suffuse education with the sweeping rhetoric of a disembodied national interest, our freedoms are secured by a system designed to resist such imperial visions.

The "public" components of schooling include the responsibility for teaching the principles, habits, and obligations of citizenship. While schools of education typically interpret this to mean that educators should preach "tolerance" or affirm "diversity," a firmer foundation for citizenship education would focus on respect for law, process, and individual rights. The problem with phrases like "tolerance" and "diversity" is that they are umbrella terms with multiple interpretations. When we try to define them more precisely—in policy or practice—it becomes clear that we must privilege some values at the expense of others. For instance, one can plausibly argue that tolerant citizens should respectfully hear out a radical Muslim calling for jihad against the U.S. or that tolerance extends only to legalistic protection and leaves one free to express social opprobrium. If educators promote the former, as their professional community generally advises, they have adopted a particular normative view that is at odds with that held by a large segment of the public.

Promoting any one particular conception of tolerance does not make schools more "public." In a liberal society, uniformly teaching students to accept teen pregnancy or homosexuality as normal and morally unobjectionable represents a jarring absolutism amidst profound moral disagreement.

Nonetheless, many traditional "public" schools (such as members of the Coalition of Essential Schools) today explicitly promote a particular world view and endorse a particular social ethos. In advancing "meaningful questions," for instance, faculty members at these schools often promote partisan attitudes toward American foreign policy, the propriety of affirmative action, or the morality of redistributive social policies. Faculty members in these schools can protest that they have no agenda other than cultivating critical inquiry, but observation of classrooms or perusal of curricular materials makes clear that most of these schools are not neutral on the larger substantive questions. This poses an ethical problem in a pluralist society where the parents of many students may reject the public educators' beliefs and where the educators have never been clearly empowered to stamp out "improper" thoughts.

Public schools should teach children the essential skills and knowledge that make for productive citizens, teach them to respect our constitutional order, and instruct them in the framework of rights and obligations that secure our democracy and protect our liberty. Any school that does so should be regarded as serving public purposes.

How should we apportion responsibility between families and public schools? The notion that schools can or should serve as a "corrective" against the family was first promulgated in the early 19th century by reformers who viewed the influx of immigrants as a threat to democratic processes and American norms. In the years since, encouraged by such thinkers as George Counts, Paulo Freire, Michael Apple, Peter McLaren, and Amy Gutmann, educational thinkers have unapologetically called for schooling to free students from the yoke of their family's provincial understandings.

The problem is that this conception of the "public interest" rests uneasily alongside America's pluralist traditions. American political thought, dating back to Madison's pragmatic embrace of "faction," has presumed that our various prejudices and biases can constructively counter one another, so long as the larger constitutional order and its attendant protections check our worst impulses.

The notion that schools are more "public" when they work harder to stamp out familial views and impress children with socially approved beliefs is one that ought to give pause to any civil libertarian or pluralist. Such schools are more attuned to the public purposes of a totalitarian regime than those of a democratic one. While a democratic nation can reasonably settle upon a range of state/family relationships, there is no reason to imagine that a regime that more heavily privileges the state is more "public." The relative "publicness" of education is not enhanced by having schools intrude more forcefully into the familial sphere.

Who should be permitted to provide public schooling? Given publicly determined purposes, it is not clear that public schooling needs to impose restrictions on who may provide services. There is no reason why for-profit or religious providers, in particular, ought to be regarded as suspect.

While traditional public schools have always dealt with for-profit providers of textbooks, teaching supplies, professional development, and so on, profit-seeking ventures have recently emerged as increasingly significant players in reform efforts. For instance, the for-profit, publicly held company Edison Schools is today managing scores of traditional district schools across the nation. Yet these are still regarded as "public" schools. In fact, Edison is managing the summer school programs, including curricula and personnel, for more than 70 public school *districts*. Yet those communities continue to regard summer school as public schooling.

Such arrangements seem to run afoul of our conventional use of the term "public," but the conflict is readily resolved when we recognize that all public agencies, including public hospitals and public transit systems, routinely harness the services of for-profit firms. Just as a public university is not thought to lose its public status merely because portions of it enter into for-profit ventures with regard to patents or athletics, so the entry of for-profit providers into a K-12 public school does not necessarily change the institution's fundamental nature. What matters in public higher education is whether the for- profit unit is controlled and overseen by those entrusted with the university's larger public mission. What matters in public schooling is whether profit seekers are hired to serve public ends and are monitored by public officials.

The status of religious providers has raised great concern among such groups as People for the American Way and the Center on Education Policy. However, the nation's early efforts to provide public education relied heavily upon local church officials to manage public funds, to provide a school facility, and to arrange the logistics of local schooling. It was not until the anti-Catholic fervor of the mid- and late-19th century that states distanced themselves from religious schooling. It was not until the mid-20th century that advocacy groups such as the American Civil Liberties Union pushed the remnants of religion out of state-run schools.

In recent decades, the U.S. Supreme Court has made clear that the push for a "wall of separation" had overreached and run afoul of First Amendment language protecting the "free exercise" of religion. Moreover, contemporary America has continued to evolve since the anti- Catholic zeal of the 19th century and the anti-religious intellectualism of the mid-20th century. Those conflicts were of a particular time and place. Today, church officials have less local sway and lack the unquestioned authority they once held, while they are more integrated into secular society. Just as some onetime opponents of single-sex schools can now, because of changes in the larger social order, imagine such schools serving the public interest, so too we should not reflexively shrink from viewing religious schools in a similar light. In most industrial democracies, including such nations as Canada, France, and the Netherlands, religious schools operate as part of the public system and are funded and regulated accordingly.

What obligations should public schools have to ensure opportunity for all students? We have never imagined that providing opportunity to all students means treating all students identically. The existence of magnet schools, special education, gifted classes, and exam schools makes it clear that we deem it appropriate for schools to select some children and exclude others in order to provide desirable academic environments. Our traditional school districts have never sought to ensure that every school or classroom should serve a random cross-section of children, only that systems as a whole should appropriately serve all children.

Given the tension between families who want their child schooled in an optimal environment and public officials who must construct systems that address competing needs, the principle that individual schools can exclude children but that systems cannot is both sensible and morally sound. That said, this principle does mean that some children will not attend school with the peers their parents might prefer.

The dilemma this presents is that no solitary good school can serve all the children who might wish to attend and that randomly admitting students may impede a school's effectiveness. Demanding that a science magnet school accept students with minimal science accomplishments or that any traditional school accept a habitually violent student threatens the ability of each school to accomplish its basic purposes. This is clearly not in the public interest. The same is true when a constructivist school is required to admit students from families who staunchly prefer back-to-basics instruction and will agitate for the curricula and pedagogy they prefer. In such cases, allowing schools to selectively admit students is consistent with the public interest—so long as the process furthers a legitimate educational purpose and the student has access to an appropriate alternative setting. Such publicly acceptable exclusion must be pursued for some reasonable educational purpose, and this creates a gray area that must be monitored. However, the need to patrol this area does not require that the practice be preemptively prohibited.

Moreover, self-selected or homogeneous communities are not necessarily less public than others. For instance, no one suggests that the University of Wyoming is less public than the University of Texas, though it is less geographically and ethnically representative of the nation. It has never been suggested that elections in San Francisco or Gopher Springs, West Virginia, would be more public if the communities included more residents who had not chosen to live there or whose views better reflected national norms. Nor has it been suggested that selective public institutions, such as the University of Michigan, are less public than are community colleges, even though they are selective about whom they admit. Moreover, there is always greater homogeneity in self-selected communities, such as magnet schools, as they attract educators and families who share certain views. None of this has been thought to undermine their essential "publicness."

Even champions of "public education," such as Deborah Meier and Ted Sizer, argue that this shared sense of commitment helps cultivate a participatory and democratic ethos in self-selected schools. In other words, heightened familial involvement tends to make self-selected schools more participatory and democratic. Kneeling before the false gods of heterogeneity or nonselectivity undermines our ability to forge participatory or effective schools without making schools commensurately more "public."

Nowhere, after all, does the availability of a "public service" imply that we get to choose our fellow users. In every field—whether public medicine, public transportation, or public higher education—the term "public" implies our right to a service, not our right to have buses serve a particular route or to have a university cohort configured to our preferences. Even though such considerations influence the quality of the service, the need for public providers to juggle the requirements of all the individuals they must serve necessarily means that each member of the public cannot necessarily receive the service in the manner he or she would ultimately prefer. "Public schooling" implies an obligation to ensure that all students are appropriately served, not that every school is open to all comers.

What parts of public schooling are public? Debates about publicness focus on the classroom teaching and learning that is central to all schools. Maintenance, accounting, payroll, and food services are quite removed from the public purposes of education discussed above. Even though these peripheral services may take place in the same facility as teaching and learning, their execution does not meaningfully affect the "publicness" of schooling. Rather, we understand that it is sufficient to have ancillary services provided in a manner that is consistent with the wishes of a public education provider. For example, federal courts and state legislatures are indisputably public institutions, yet they frequently procure supplies, services, and personnel from privately run, for-profit enterprises. We properly regard these institutions as public because of their core purposes, not because of the manner in which they arrange their logistics.

Today's 'Public' Schools Often Aren't

Given the haphazard notion of public schooling that predominates today, it comes as little surprise that we offer contemporary educators little guidance in serving the public interest. This poses obvious problems, given that employment as an educator doesn't necessarily grant enhanced moral wisdom or personal virtue. If schools are to serve as places where educators advance purposes and cultivate virtues that they happen to prefer, it is not clear in what sense schools are serving "public purposes."

Blindly hoping that educators have internalized shared public purposes, we empower individuals to proselytize under the banner of "public schooling." This state of affairs has long been endorsed by influential educational theorists like George Counts, Paulo Freire, Henry Giroux, and Nel Noddings, who argue that teachers have a charge to use their classrooms to promote personal visions of social change, regardless of the broader public's beliefs. For these thinkers, "public schooling" ironically implies a community obligation to support schools for the private purposes of educators. The problem is that public institutions are not personal playthings. Just as it is unethical for a judge to disregard the law and instead rule on the basis of personal whimsy, so it is inappropriate for public school teachers to use their office to impose personal views upon a captive audience.

One appropriate public response is to specify public purposes and to demand that teachers reflect them, though we are reasonably cautious about adopting such an intrusive course. To the extent that explicit direction is absent, however, educators are left to their own devices. In such a case, our liberal tradition would recommend that we not subject children to the views of educators at an assigned school but allow families to avail themselves of a range of schools with diverse perspectives, so long as each teaches respect for our democratic and liberal tradition.

Conclusion

Today, our system of "public schooling" does little to ensure that our schools serve public purposes, while permitting some educators to use a publicly provided forum to promote their personal beliefs. Meanwhile, hiding behind the phrase's hallowed skirts are partisans who furiously attack any innovation that threatens their interests or beliefs.

There are many ways to provide legitimate public education. A restrictive state might tightly regulate school assignment, operations, and content, while another state might impose little regulation. However, there is no reason to regard the schools in the one state as more "public" than those in the other. The "publicness" of a school does not depend on class size, the use of certified teachers, rules governing employee termination, or the rest of the procedural apparatus that ensnares traditional district schools. The fact that public officials have the right to require public schools to comply with certain standards does not mean that schools subjected to more intrusive standards are somehow more public. The inclusion of religious schools in European systems, for instance, has been accompanied by intensive regulation of curricula and policy. Regulation on that order is not desirable, nor is it necessary for schools to operate as part of a public system; it is merely an operational choice made by officials in these relatively bureaucratic nations.

As opportunities to deliver, structure, and practice education evolve, it is periodically necessary to revisit assumptions about what constitutes public schooling. The ideology and institutional self-interest that infuse the dominant current conception have fueled withering attacks on the very legitimacy of public schooling itself. Failure to address this impoverished status quo will increasingly offer critics cause to challenge the purpose and justification of public education. Maintaining and strengthening our commitment to public schooling requires that we rededicate ourselves to essential principles of opportunity, liberal democracy, and public benefit, while freeing ourselves from political demands and historic happenstance.

In an age when social and technological change have made possible new approaches to teaching and learning, pinched renderings of "public schooling" have grown untenable and counterproductive. They stifle creative efforts, confuse debates, and divert attention from more useful questions. A more expansive conception is truer to our traditions, more likely to foster shared values, and better suited to the challenges of the new century.

Notes

1. James Coleman, "Public Schools, Private Schools, and the Public Interest," *Public Interest,* Summer 1981, pp. 19–30. See also idem, "Quality and Equality in American Education," *Phi Delta Kappan,* November 1981, pp. 159–64.

2. For the best empirical examination of the scope and nature of the "public school ideology," see Terry Moe, *Schools, Vouchers, and the American Public* (Washington, D.C.: Brookings, 2001).

3. See Andrew Coulson, *Market Education: The Unknown History* (New Brunswick, N.J.: Transaction Publishers, 1999); and Douglas Dewey, "An Echo, Not a Choice: School Vouchers Repeat the Error of Public Education," *Policy Review,* November/December 1996, www.policyreview.org/nov96/backup/dewey.html.

4. See Frederick M. Hess, "Making Sense of the 'Public' in Public Education," unpublished paper, Progressive Policy Institute, Washington, D.C., 2002.

5. John Dewey, *The Public and Its Problems* (1927; reprint, Athens: Ohio University Press, 1954).

6. See Frederick M. Hess, "What Is 'Public' About Public Education?," *Education Week,* 8 January 2003, p. 56.

7. An extended discussion of this point can be found in Paul T. Hill, "What Is Public About Public Education?," in Terry Moe, ed., *A Primer on America's Schools* (Stanford, Calif.: Hoover Institution, 2001), pp. 285–316.

8. Frank Smith, "Overselling Literacy," *Phi Delta Kappan,* January 1989, pp. 353–59; Alfie Kohn, *No Contest: The Case Against Competition* (Boston: Houghton Mifflin, 1986); Susan Ohanian, "Capitalism, Calculus, and Conscience," *Phi Delta Kappan,* June 2003, pp. 736-47; and Deborah Meier, "Educating a Democracy," in idem, ed., *Will Standards Save Public Education?* (Boston: Beacon Press, 2000).

NO

Linda Nathan et al.

A Response to Frederick Hess: The Larger Purpose of Public Schools

At times I want to cheer for Frederick Hess's words in "What Is a 'Public School'? Principles for a New Century." How true it is that many reformers "regard public schooling as a politicized obstacle rather than a shared ideal." How true that "those of us committed to the promise of public education are obliged to see that the idea does not become a tool of vested interests."

Yet there is also something chilling about his article that stops the cheer in my throat. His use of innuendo in place of evidence, his sloppy logic, and his attacks on some of the most effective public school reformers—painting them as the enemy—suggest that his real agenda is not strengthening public education but privatizing it through vouchers and for-profit takeover schemes.

Hess's labored analysis obscures a simple fact: public schools have a larger and more democratic purpose than private and parochial schools (although this is not to say that these schools contribute nothing to public life). Public school systems are open to everyone regardless of disability, wealth, status, race, or religion. Private and parochial schools are not. While some are more open than others, they can have entrance exams and can explicitly exclude students with disabilities or those who otherwise don't fit a preferred profile. And of course they can also exclude those who can't pay. They can expel students who cause trouble, at their sole discretion, without recourse.

Hess himself acknowledges this core principle of universal access, conceding that public schooling "implies an obligation to ensure that all students are appropriately served." But he seems indifferent to the inequities inherent in his "more expansive" notion of what makes a school public.

Hess makes a false analogy when he equates schools that buy textbooks from for-profit companies with schools that are managed by for-profit firms. Basic educational decisions should be made by citizens of the local school community—not by distant shareholders looking only at a corporate balance sheet. (It's ironic that Hess picks as his exemplar Edison Schools, Inc., which sold off the textbooks, computers, lab supplies, and musical instruments of the Philadelphia public schools it had been hired to manage just days before school was to open in 2002 in order to pay down the company's mounting debt.)

From *Phi Delta Kappan,* February 2004. Copyright © 2004 by Phi Delta Kappan. Reprinted by permission.

Hess objects to teaching "tolerance" and affirming "diversity" because, he says, these words are open to multiple interpretations. Then he states that "public schools should teach children the essential skills and knowledge that make for productive citizens" and "teach them to respect our constitutional order," as if these were absolute truths *not* open to interpretation. The example of tolerance he cites, wherein a radical Muslim is calling for jihad, slyly exploits a hot-button issue to imply that the "professional community" of educators condones terrorism. Similarly, he smears the notion of defending tolerance as "uniformly teaching students to accept teen pregnancy as normal" and implies that liberals equate these activities with their definition of "public schooling." Nonsense.

His attack on Deborah Meier, Alfie Kohn, and others is equally baseless. It's the classic straw man fallacy: he attributes a position to them—that they oppose the teaching of basic academic mastery in favor of promoting "preferred social values"—that they have in fact never espoused. Meier's argument, with which Hess is surely familiar, is that such a tradeoff is unnecessary and that strong academic habits and mastery of literacy are essential and are furthered by an intellectually open and challenging spirit of inquiry.

The Coalition of Essential Schools, another of Hess's targets, gets similar treatment. Without offering a single example or other evidence of any kind, he asserts that faculty members at Coalition schools routinely promote partisan political views and are determined to "stamp out 'improper' thoughts." Of course, he's right that some teachers and schools—including many private and religious schools—do have a "party line," whether they're conscious of it or not. But he wants to have it both ways. While he attacks Coalition teachers for promoting values he dislikes, he argues at the same time that there should be choice in education so that parents can select schools that reflect their values.

Hess's argument with regard to the personal views and political leanings of educators is simply a red herring. The underlying issue is his fear that his own preferred values are being "stamped out." He uses that phrase again in making the absurd claim that the goal of liberal educators is to subvert the influence of families on their children. If he were serious about the rights of parents, Hess would be attacking the idea of a federalized education system— with or without vouchers—in which the *state* defines which values, priorities, intellectual habits, and performance standards will dominate and in which schools must accept intrusive guidelines to receive a stamp of approval and public funding. It seems to me that his scorn should fall not on Deborah Meier and Ted Sizer but on George W. Bush and the other proponents of top-down standardization.

Hess wants teachers to promote respect for the law—unless the laws in question are those that guarantee equal rights to people regardless of sexual orientation. When I began teaching in the late 1970s, it was dangerous for a teacher to be homosexual, not because of students' or parents' reactions but because of administrative reprisals. And it was dangerous in those days to talk about the threat of nuclear war or to suggest that the U.S.-sponsored war in El Salvador was unjust or even to imply that there was another view of these issues than the government's. My colleagues daily taught their students that might was right and homosexuality was a sin. I had my tires slashed by colleagues who felt that desegregation had ruined the Boston Public Schools. That we have created schools in which more open dialogue is possible indeed represents progress.

In calling for more innovation and choice in public education, Hess is absolutely right. In diversity, after all, there is strength. The U.S. has tried many experiments in public schooling over the past two centuries. We are in the midst of yet another experiment with our charter schools. In many ways, this kind of exploration is healthy. It allows us to look at different models and seek out best practices. Yet the charter school experiment has largely ignored issues of equity. In Boston and many other districts, charter schools often make no provision for accepting students who require special educational services or facilities, while traditional public schools are required to do so. This is one reason that some see charter schools as less "public" than other public schools. The same inequities exist in many parochial schools.

We need schools that help young people and adults learn and practice the skills necessary to be participants in a vibrant democracy. Such schools will be messy places that must balance the public interest with America's pluralist tradition. In their classrooms everyone learns to ask probing questions, to use evidence well, to make legitimate arguments, and to recognize fallacies and lies. I invite Frederick Hess to come to the Boston Arts Academy, where we will be happy to give him the opportunity to practice these skills with our students.

Joe Nathan

A Response to Frederick Hess: Some Questions for Advocates of Public Education

T hree very specific questions for advocates of public education came to my mind as I read Frederick Hess's argument that we need to "reappraise our assumptions as to what constitutes 'public schooling.'" Let me pose them to *Kappan* readers, who no doubt are advocates for public education.

What is public about a suburban district in which the price of admission to the local public schools is the ability to purchase a home for more than one million dollars (and to pay tax-deductible property taxes on that home)?

What is public about an inner-city school with an admissions test that screens out all students with mental disabilities and more than 95% of the students in the surrounding district and so proclaims that it serves only the "cream of the crop"?

What is public about preventing some inner-city students from attending a magnet school just a few blocks from their homes that receives $1,500 per pupil more than the neighborhood school they attend? At the same time, in the name of integration, white students from wealthy suburbs are transported to this school—some via taxi.

These three questions form the basis for two larger questions that continue to trouble me even after being involved with public education for 33 years. I don't have definitive answers to these larger questions. But I share them with readers in the hope that they, too, will find them worth pondering. . . .

✦

. . . 1. *Since all public schools are not open to all kinds of students, what admissions standards should be acceptable for schools supported by public funds?* When my teachers in the Wichita public schools talked about public education, they stressed that a key difference between public and private schools was that public schools were open to all. Many of the authorities I read while I was at Carleton College, preparing to become a teacher, said the same thing.

This idea of "open to all" makes great sense to me. It seems like the right and just way to operate. Hess writes that he thinks it "appropriate" for some public schools to select some children and exclude others. I've disagreed with this position for more than 30 years. But lately, I'm not so sure.

When I began teaching I learned that many public schools were *not* open to all students. As I traveled the country, I learned that there were more than a thousand magnet schools and programs that have admissions tests. A study some years ago found that more than half of the nation's secondary magnet schools have admissions tests, as do about a quarter of the elementary magnets.[1]

Wisconsin Rep. Polly Williams, a Democrat and an African American state legislator, was enraged because most of the youngsters in her inner-city Milwaukee district were not able to get into exclusive magnet schools in the neighborhood, which brought in affluent, white, suburban students. Her frustration led her to fight successfully for the nation's first formal voucher plan.

Some opponents of vouchers insist that a level playing field isn't available when private schools can cherry-pick their students. I agree. But many educators, including me, have the same frustration about elite magnet schools: they have an unfair advantage over neighborhood public schools that are open to all in that they can screen out students with whom they don't wish to work.

I also learned that the country's single biggest choice system is called the suburbs. Millions of youngsters attend schools in the suburbs, and these schools clearly are *not* open to all students. They are open only to those whose families can afford to live in suburban communities.

A few years ago, I visited a school district on the northern coast of Long Island. Administrators there told me that the least expensive home in the district sold for $1,000,000. None of the district's teachers could afford to live there.

Today, some people argue that there should be publicly funded schools that are open only to young women. Two such schools have opened—one in New York, the other in Chicago. Even though I was not fond of this type of school, I visited the New York City district school, Young Women's Leadership Academy. I was impressed. The young women reported that, without boys around, they felt much more comfortable raising their hands in class and much more comfortable doing well on tests.

Should public funds go to some schools of choice that are only open to women? Or only to men? Five years ago, I would have said emphatically not. Today, I don't know.

2. *Shouldn't schools we describe as public accept and use some of the country's basic ideas to help improve education?* Americans generally endorse a number of ideas:

- choice of religion, job, neighborhood, places to obtain services, and so on;
- the provision of opportunities to try new ideas and approaches;
- the shared belief that this is a country not just of rights, but of responsibilities; and
- the notions that our cherished freedoms are not unlimited.

However, for three decades I've watched major public education groups vigorously oppose school choice programs, including public school choice programs, that are built on these principles. For example, there was intense opposition from educators in 1970 to the creation of the St. Paul Open School.

These organized groups ignore the professional and pedagogical rationales for public school choice, expressed best by veteran educator Deborah Meier:

> Choice is an essential tool in the effort to create . . . good public educa-
> tion. . . . We'll have to allow those most involved (teachers, administra-
> tors, parents) to exercise greater on-site power to put their collective
> wisdom into practice. Once we do all this, however, school X and school
> Y are going to start doing things differently. . . . Creating a school different
> from what any of those who work in the system are familiar with, one
> that runs counter to the experiences of most families, is possible only if
> teachers, parents, and students have time to agree on changes and a
> choice on whether or not they want to go along with them.[2]

Colleagues involved in other efforts to create new options over the last three decades have had similar experiences. During his tenure as president of the American Federation of Teachers, Al Shanker described what happened to teachers who proposed schools-within-schools:

> Many schools-within-schools were or are treated like traitors or outlaws
> for daring to move out of the lockstep and do something different. Their
> initiators had to move Heaven and Earth to get school officials to autho-
> rize them, and if they managed that, often they could look forward to
> insecurity, obscurity, or outright hostility.[3]

Over the past decade, with help from the Gates, Blandin, and Annenberg Foundations, the Center for School Change at the University of Minnesota has tried to help educators create new schools-within-schools in a number of communities. Shanker's words have often proved to be very accurate. The most intense, vigorous critics of offering a different kind of school—whether in a single building or in a district—have often been other educators.

Many educators have argued over the past 30 years that public, district schools serving racial minorities and students from low-income families are doing the best job they can with existing funds. According to the most recent Phi Delta Kappa/Gallup poll, 80% of the public thinks the achievement gap between white children and minority children is mostly related to factors other than the quality of schooling.[4]

Perhaps in part because some educators have helped to convince the public that inner-city schools are mostly not responsible for the achievement gap, 58% of the nation and 62% of public school parents think it is possible to narrow the achievement gap *without* spending more money than is cur-rently being spent on these students.[5] Unfortunately, many state legislators are opting not to raise taxes and not to give more to schools serving low-income, limited-English- speaking students.

Some of us vigorously disagree with these legislative actions and think that both more public school choice and more funding would help reduce the achieve-ment gap. We have seen—and in some cases have worked in—schools that have served the public interest by helping all youngsters achieve their potential and have done much to close the gap between students of different races.

Despite encouragement from such strong public school supporters as former President Bill Clinton, former Secretary of Education Richard Riley, and the late Sen. Paul Wellstone (D-Minn.), efforts to create independent charter public schools still face huge opposition from state teacher, school board, and superintendent groups. The opposition uses the same arguments used in 1970 against the St. Paul Open School: new options take away our money.

But it isn't their money. Legislatures allocate money for the education of children, not for the preservation of a system. If 50 students move from a city to a suburb or from a suburb to a city, the dollars follow them. The money doesn't belong to "the system."

Thousands of parents and educators are voting with their feet. The number of states with a charter law has gone from one in 1991 to 40 in 2003. The number of charter schools has gone from one school in 1991 to more than 3,000 in 2003. Federal statistics show that low-income students and racial minorities are overrepresented in charter schools. While the evidence is mixed—and almost certainly will be so when charter and district schools are compared—some charters are clearly producing major achievement gains. Shouldn't we learn from and replicate their best practices?

Starting new schools is extremely difficult work. But whether it's a Pilot School in the Boston Public Schools or a New Visions option in New York City or a charter school in any of 40 states, the opportunity to try new approaches is as vital for education as it is for medicine, business, or technology.

Some Tentative Conclusions

So Frederick Hess wants to "discern what . . . makes schooling public and accept diverse arrangements that are consistent with those tenets." I'm not sure what standards all publicly supported schools should meet. But after 33 years, I offer these as minimum requirements for schools that serve the public interest and are thus eligible to receive public funds. Public schools should:

- be open to all kinds of students and not use admissions tests;
- follow due process procedures with regard to students and educators;
- use state-approved, standardized, and other measures to help monitor student progress or lack thereof;
- have closing the achievement gap between white students and racial minority and low-income students as an explicit, measurable goal;[6] and
- be actively chosen by faculty, families, and students.

Thanks to Hess and to the *Kappan* for urging a timely reconsideration of the basic principles of public education. As social justice activist Leonard Fein states it:

> The future is not something we discover around the next corner. It is something we shape, we create, we invent. To hold otherwise would be to view ourselves as an audience to history, and not its authors. History, and even our own lives, cannot always be turned and twisted to make them

go exactly where we should like. But there is, for people of energy and purpose, more freedom of movement than most ever exercise.[7]

Notes

1.   Lauri Steel and Roger Levine, *Educational Innovation in Multiracial Contexts: The Growth of Magnet Schools in American Education* (Palo Alto, Calif.: American Institutes for Research, 1994). This study was prepared for the U.S. Department of Education under Contract No. LC 90043001.

2.   Deborah Meier, "Choice Can Save Public Education," *The Nation*, 4 March 1991.

3.   Al Shanker, "Where We Stand: Convention Plots New Course—A Charter for Change," *New York Times* (paid advertisement), 10 July 1988, p. E-7.

4.   Lowell C. Rose and Alec M. Gallup, "The 35th Annual Phi Delta Kappa/ Gallup Poll of the Public's Attitudes Toward the Public Schools," *Phi Delta Kappan*, September 2003, p. 48.

5.   Ibid.

6.   Student progress should be monitored using various measures, not just standardized tests. If there is not major improvement in narrowing the achievement gap in most areas over a five-year period, the school should be "reconstituted."

7.   Leonard Fein et al., *Reform Is a Verb: Notes on Reform and Reforming Jews* (New York: Union of American Hebrew Congregations, 1972), p. 152.

NO

Ray Bacchetti

A Response to Frederick Hess: An Ongoing Conversation

We don't look at the big issues of the principles and purposes of public schools often or carefully enough. Sadly, the political and philosophical conversation seems increasingly polarized. In Venn diagram terms, the two circles—labeled right/left, basics/constructivist, academic/child-centered, etc.—reveal at best a vanishingly thin region of overlap. When the true believers on either side look in the mirror, they see Dumbledore. Over their shoulders and gaining, they see Voldemort.

Frederick Hess's beefy rhetoric stakes out a position that reflects a more conservative world view than my own. In essence, he argues that the purposes of public education will be better served if we narrow the number of principles that define its publicness and expand the number of ways those principles can be implemented. In that expanded universe, religious schools, vouchers, for-profit ventures, and other alternatives would be welcome.

The principles advertised in Hess's title are woven through his essay, making it difficult to distinguish his main point from his subsidiary concerns. Here is what I take to be the core of his definition of what makes a school public. In addition to teaching skills and content, public schools should:

- prepare students to be "productive members of the social order";
- enable students to "become aware of their societal responsibilities," including the "principles, habits, and obligations of citizenship"; and
- educate students to be "respectful of constitutional strictures," including laws, process, and individual rights.

In carrying out these functions, public school systems should also:

- not "deny access to students for reasons unrelated to [a school's] educational focus"; and
- "provide an appropriate placement for each student" in every community.

Asserting by implication that the meanings of his key terms are inherently obvious, Hess goes on to argue that the terms others might use to set forth other principles are not. For example, he observes that "diversity" and "tolerance" are "umbrella terms with multiple interpretations." Therefore, they lie outside his cluster of principles because, when we try to define them more precisely, "it becomes clear that we must privilege some values at the expense of others." If he believes that a similar privileging of certain values might color his own key terms, such as "obligations of citizenship," "productive members of the social order," "societal responsibilities," "individual rights," and the like, he gives no indication.

Hess seems to arrive at his position partly for affirmative reasons (e.g., an emphasis on academic learning) and partly because of a surprisingly bitter view of educators (some of whom he names, but most of whom he only characterizes). In his view, these educators

- "explicitly promote a particular world view and endorse a particular social ethos";
- "promote partisan attitudes toward American foreign policy, the propriety of affirmative action, or the morality of redistributive social policies";
- teach students to "accept teen pregnancy or homosexuality as normal and morally unobjectionable";
- attempt to "stamp out familial views and impress children with socially approved beliefs"; and
- treat public institutions as their personal playthings.

To illustrate his more general points, Hess portrays the "meaningful questions" asked in the classrooms of the Coalition of Essential Schools as a herd of Trojan ponies surreptitiously unloading the teachers' agendas. It's not clear what "meaningful questions" might be in the classrooms he approves of, though readers might infer that they would be limited to the rational analysis of topics that arise from well-developed and authoritatively taught subject matter. There is nothing wrong with such questions, of course. But anyone who thinks that they—or the answers to them— would be value-free is likely to have slept through his or her undergraduate philosophy classes.

More to the point, however, a narrow and academic definition of such questions would exclude from the public school universe those who think students should also wrestle with forming habits of the heart as well as the mind, should learn to use critical inquiry to amend and expand values and understandings as well as to confirm them, and should go beyond "my country, right or wrong" to embrace the rest of Carl Schurz's famous phrase, "if right, to be kept right; and if wrong, to be set right."

I have spent a fair amount of time in schools of late, witnessing heroic efforts of underfinanced and overregulated teachers to enact both the academic preparation *and* the democracy-building ethos that our schools were meant to embody. If Hess is suggesting that generally left-leaning personal agendas have dominated public school instruction for a generation or more, then we should be able to see around us a widely shared value system that reflects those views. However, when I survey newspapers, polls, elections, and even school reform debates at national and local levels, I see instead an enormous variety of values and priorities. Some may find that diversity of views troubling. What troubles me is not that people disagree but that we seem increasingly incapable of working through our differences to embed public school policies and practices in a conception of the common good that can transcend political perspectives without disrespecting them.

The sort of public conversations about public education that would open minds to a critical look at new ideas would be, as I'm sure Hess would agree, tough to structure and to conduct. Where he and I are likely to disagree is on whether the topic of those conversations will ever be settled and, more important, whether it ever should be. Teaching skills and developing in each generation the social cohesion on which so much else depends will be easier (though never easy) to approach than will matters of values, educational philosophies, social goals, and civic priorities. Moreover, balancing the relative claims of the student, family, community, nation, and the wider world on how and what schools teach is a democratic journey, not a settled destination.

From the start, Hess acknowledges the powerful resonance of the concept of public education. What seems to make him impatient, even exasperated, is that the people who lead what he and some others pejoratively call "government-run schools" aren't listening to him. Not listening can be a stance or a reaction. Seeing it as a *stance*, I join him in his exasperation. The habit of "reflexively shrinking" from a consideration of alternatives hardens the democratic arteries. Seeing it as a *reaction*, I worry that world views (a term I prefer to "ideology") too often appear as righteous opposites, leaving all but the most robust listeners wondering what's the point.

Finding areas of overlap in our views under such conditions isn't easy. Developing the skills of measured and thoughtful dialogue needed to create such overlap is even harder. The challenge of doing so, however, demonstrates why a free nation needs public schools that are set up to make public decision making meaningful at the daily, close-to-home levels, as well as at higher levels. Such deliberative procedures force us to ask not only what we want our own children to learn but also what we want all children to learn. Children are, after all, collectively as well as individually the next generation, and the education we bequeath to them is communal as well as personal.

We need to talk and listen our way into more overlap in our political/philosophical Venn diagrams. Having that running conversation looms large in my definition of what makes the public schools public. Hess seems to argue that, through a few principles and a multitude of entities all claiming the mantle of public education, we can make the need for that conversation go away. I would argue instead that getting better at it should be our number-one priority.

 **NO**

A Response to Frederick Hess: Reimagining Public Education

I heartily agree with Frederick Hess that we need to rethink and reimagine our antiquated American system of public education. But not for the reasons he sets forth.

I also agree with his broad definition of the purposes of public schooling: "that public schools are . . . defined by their commitment to preparing students to be productive members of the social order" (and therefore active citizens of a democratic society) who are able to think and use their minds well and are "aware of their societal responsibilities and respectful of constitutional strictures" (including an understanding of the Constitution and especially the Bill of Rights); "that such schools cannot deny access to students for reasons unrelated to their educational focus" (i.e., no racially, ethnically, or economically segregated schools); "and that the system of public schools available in any community must provide an appropriate placement for each student" (all students and their parents must be offered the kind of schooling they believe is most suitable). But I do not agree that we should seek to create the kind of reimagined system Hess appears to be proposing.

Questions of Definition, Control, and Funding

Throughout most of the history of the U.S., a public school has been defined as a school created, operated, and largely paid for by the citizens of each community through a locally elected board of education. While the Constitution leaves the basic authority for education in the hands of the individual states, and even though such locally controlled schools have, over the past century, received increased funding from both state and federal sources, this tradition of local control has managed to endure more or less intact—at least until the past 25 or so years.

The continued importance of this tradition was underscored in 1973 by the U.S. Supreme Court in its *Rodriguez* decision. The majority opinion put the matter this way:

> In an era that has witnessed a consistent trend toward centralization of the functions of government, local sharing of responsibility for public education has survived. The merit of local control was recognized in both the majority and dissenting opinions in *Wright v. Council of the City of Emporia*. Mr. Justice Stewart stated there that "direct control over decisions vitally affecting the education of one's children is a need that is strongly

felt in our society." The Chief Justice in his dissent agreed that local control is not only vital to continued public support of the schools, but it is of overriding importance from an educational standpoint as well.

The persistence of attachment to government at its lowest level where education is concerned reflects the depth of commitment of its supporters. In part local control means . . . the freedom to devote more money to the education of one's children. Equally important, however, is the opportunity it offers for participation in the decision-making process that determines how those local dollars will be spent. Each locality is free to tailor local programs to local needs. Pluralism also affords some opportunity for experimentation, innovation, and a healthy competition for educational excellence. An analogy to the Nation-State relationship in our federal system seems uniquely appropriate. Mr. Justice Brandeis identified as one of the peculiar strengths of our form of government each state's freedom to "serve as a laboratory; to try novel social and economic experiments." No area of social concern stands to profit more from a multiplicity of viewpoints and from a diversity of approaches than does public education.

Further, Justice William Brennan found in his dissent that "Here, there can be no doubt that education is inextricably linked to the right to participate in the electoral process and to the rights of free speech and association guaranteed by the First Amendment."[1]

During the past quarter century, however, the "consistent trend toward centralization of the functions of government" has run rampant in the field of public schooling. In the name of public school "reform," the states have usurped local control by imposing uniform, authoritarian, "high," "rigorous," one-size-fits-all academic standards and punitive high-stakes standardized testing on all students, all schools, and all school systems.

The federal education establishment, through its No Child Left Behind Act, has carried this intrusive, antidemocratic curricular control and standardized testing program to ludicrous extremes, requiring the testing of all students in grades 3 through 8 and insisting on annual progress in test scores with severe sanctions for schools that fail to show such progress. However, neither the federal government nor the states have provided the financial resources to pay for all this "reform" or to remedy the gross inequities that exist between those school systems that serve the wealthy and those that serve our poor and minority students and parents. I find these events distressing, but none of them appear to worry Hess very much.

If the powerful democratic tradition of local control is to be maintained and if we are to genuinely reimagine our public education system, we will need to do several things. First, we will have to abandon the authoritarian standards and high-stakes testing agenda that currently afflict our public schools and return to the citizens of our local communities the control over what is taught, how it will be taught, and who will teach it. State and federal interference should be limited to ensuring minimum competency in the basic skills of reading, writing, and mathematics.

Second, we will simultaneously need both state and federal governments to guarantee that all of the nation's public schools are fully and equitably funded and that the civil rights of all students and parents—but especially our poor and minority students and parents—are fully protected. Hess does not appear to recommend any of these policies.

The Threat of Vouchers and Privatization

We will also have to erect strong safeguards against the threat of vouchers and any further encroachment of the private corporate sector into the field of public schooling. Now that the Supreme Court has permitted the use of public funds to finance vouchers that can be used to pay tuition at nonpublic, including religious, schools, Hess appears to be saying that we should aim to create a system of public education similar to that of many European countries, where public funding is given directly to all nonpublic schools. Such a proposal would still violate both the First Amendment's separation of church and state and the democratic commitment to local public citizen control.

In addition, Hess proposes that we permit the private, for-profit sector to run both schools and school systems so long as those schools are monitored by some public body—despite the fact that the track record of Edison and other corporate EMOs (education management organizations) is educationally and economically dismal. Hess appears to believe that it is morally legitimate for private corporations to profit from the education of children, rather than being required to plow "profits" back into our chronically underfunded public schools. This thinking parallels the already-established view that it is somehow morally legitimate for corporate HMOs to make a profit out of caring for the sick, rather than being required to plow that money back into the health-care system. Neither of these policies is morally acceptable in any fair, just, and equitable system of democratic government.

A Truly Reimagined, Genuinely Democratic Public System of Diversity and Choice

Hess does raise an issue of fundamental importance when he points out that "there are many ways to provide legitimate public education." I assume that he means that there is no single kind of school—be it rigidly "traditional," wildly "progressive," or something in between—that could possibly serve the diverse educational beliefs of this nation's parents, the equally diverse professional philosophies of our public school educators, and most especially the enormously varied educational needs of our children and young people.

Strangely, however, Hess believes that many "prominent educational thinkers" (among others, he names Frank Smith, Susan Ohanian, Deborah Meier, and Alfie Kohn) have encouraged the public schools to promote "preferred social values" to the American public rather than advocating that all public schools limit themselves to teaching children "the essential skills and knowledge that make for productive citizens." He asserts that the "public schools should teach children . . . to respect our constitutional order and instruct them in the framework of rights and obligations that secure our democracy and protect our liberty." He argues this point as if this educational prescription were not itself an ideology—even if it is one that may be widely shared and one that in its main outlines is most certainly shared by his list of misguided thinkers.

Hess then goes on to advocate not just his own ideological prescription but the basic rule of what I would see as that truly reimagined public system we should be attempting to create. In order to encompass those diverse educational beliefs of parents and professional educators and to meet the varied educational needs of our children and young people, he says that we should "allow families to avail themselves of a range of schools with diverse perspectives, so long as each teaches respect for our democratic and liberal tradition." Thus we need that wide diversity of public schools—ranging from traditional to progressive—from which parents, teachers, administrators, and older students can choose the type of schooling they believe will most benefit each child and young person. As Hess puts it, such strictly public school choice would create "heightened family involvement" and produce "a shared sense of commitment" that would tend to make such "self-selected schools more participatory and democratic."

It is, I believe, the job of our local public school systems, assisted and encouraged by state and federal governments, to provide that diversity of options. But the basic control of what goes on in all of our public schools must always remain solely in the public domain and solidly anchored in the will of the citizens of our local communities.

Note

1. *San Antonio Independent School District* v. *Rodriguez*, U.S. Supreme Court, 411 U.S. 1 (1973).

POSTSCRIPT

Should "Public Schooling" Be Redefined?

In the February 2004 issue of *Phi Delta Kappan*, Frederick M. Hess put forth a rejoinder to his four critics in an article titled "Debating Principles for Public Schooling in a New Century." He lists some significant points of agreement, including that it is necessary and useful to reconsider the essence of "public schooling" in an age marked by radical changes in how education is being provided. However, these critics, Hess contends, attack reforms as "anti-public education" for permitting the same practices that some "public schools" already engage in—for example, schools that are not open to all students when located in an affluent community. He feels that some critics allow the notion of public schooling to become a rhetorical banner for bolstering partisan positions and delegitimatizing opposing ideas. Hess further states that "there is a real danger to the rhetorical strategy of branding objectionable reforms as de facto 'assaults on public schooling.' This device is fruitless and divisive. Perhaps more forebodingly, it excommunicates many who honor public education because they fail to endorse the 'right kind' of public schooling."

John C. Lundt, a professor of educational leadership, says that education is leaving the schoolhouse as technology increasingly makes it an anytime-anywhere activity. In a provocative article in the December 2004 issue of *The Futurist* titled "Learning for Ourselves: A New Paradigm for Education," Lundt concludes that the antiquated structure of today's school was designed to meet the needs of a world that no longer exists, that public schools will not change as long as they monopolize educational funding, and that growing numbers of parents find the activities and values of public schools inappropriate for their children. This basic concern about funding is echoed by reporter Joe Williams in his book *Cheating Our Kids: How Politics and Greed Ruin Education* (2005). Williams examines the impact of special-interest groups on local public school systems (specifically in New York and Milwaukee), finding that most "reform" money only expands already bloated district bureaucracies. He calls for a concerted effort by concerned parents to reclaim power.

Additional challenging ideas may be found in Paul A. Zoch's *Doomed to Fail: The Built-in Defects of American Education* (2004) and Susan Ohanian's "Refrains of the School Critics," *The School Administrator* (August 2005).

On the Internet . . .

School Choice

Pro-voucher site offers reports on a variety of choice plans and provides links to other web sources.

http://www.schoolchoices.org

Home Schooling

Includes feature articles on state laws and regulations governing home schooling, support groups, and successful practices.

http://www.homeschooling.com

Small Schools

Covers nationwide developments in the small school movement with links to articles.

http://smallschools.com

Circle of Inclusion

Offers materials, lessons, and methods for serving learners with disabilities in inclusive school settings.

http://www.circleofinclusion.org

National Association for Bilingual Education

Organization exclusively concerned with the education of language-minority students in American schools.

http://www.nabe.org

Safe Schools

Resource for information on school security, teen violence, bullying, and disruptive behavior.

http://keepschoolssafe.org

From Now On: The Educational Technology Journal

Examines a multiplicity of issues on integrating technology into the content and management of public school programs.

http://www.fno.org

Pay-for-Performance and Merit Pay

National Council on Teacher Quality site explores the issue of improving teacher rewards for excellence.

http://www.nctq.org

PART 3

Current Specific Issues

*T*his section probes specific questions currently being discussed by educators, policymakers, and parents. In most cases, these issues are grounded in the more basic questions explored in Parts 1 and 2. Views are expressed by a wide variety of writers, including Charles L. Glenn, Paul E. Peterson, Michael W. Apple, Brian D. Ray, Rosalie Pedalino Porter, Richard Rothstein, Albert Shanker, and Alfie Kohn.

Issue 11. Has the Supreme Court Reconfigured American Education?

Issue 12. Can Charter Schools Revitalize Public Education?

Issue 13. Is Home Schooling a Danger to American Society?

Issue 14. Is Full Inclusion of Disabled Students Desirable?

Issue 15. Is Size Crucial to School Improvement?

Issue 16. Should Bilingual Education Be Abandoned?

Issue 17. Does School Violence Warrant a Zero-Tolerance Policy?

Issue 18. Should Homework Be Abolished?

Issue 19. Do Computers Negatively Affect Student Growth?

Issue 20. Can Merit Pay Accelerate School Improvement?

Issue 21. Should Alternative Teacher Training Be Encouraged?

ISSUE 11

Has the Supreme Court Reconfigured American Education?

YES: Charles L. Glenn, from "Fanatical Secularism," *Education Next* (Winter 2003)

NO: Paul E. Peterson, from "Victory for Vouchers?" *Commentary* (September 2002)

ISSUE SUMMARY

YES: Professor of education Charles L. Glenn argues that the Supreme Court's decision in *Zelman v. Simmons-Harris* is an immediate antidote to the public school's secularist philosophy.

NO: Professor of government Paul E. Peterson, while welcoming the decision, contends that the barricades against widespread use of vouchers in religious schools will postpone any lasting effects.

In June 2002 the U.S. Supreme Court released its decision of *Zelman v. Simmons-Harris,* which dealt with Ohio's Pilot Project Scholarship Program. This program provides tuition vouchers to certain students in the Cleveland Public School District who wish to transfer from their assigned public school to a participating school of their choosing. The available choices include public schools in adjacent school districts, nonreligious private schools, and religious private schools. Controversy over this program stemmed from the fact that in the 1999–2000 school year, 96 percent of the Cleveland students who were receiving vouchers were enrolled in schools with religious affiliations. Ohio taxpayers (Doris Simmons-Harris et al.) sued state school officials (Superintendent Susan Tave Zelman et al.) to enjoin the program on the grounds that it violated the establishment clause of the U.S. Constitution, which mandates separation of church and state.

The Supreme Court found (by a 5–4 vote) that Ohio's voucher program does not offend the establishment clause, thereby reversing lower courts' judgments that the program is unconstitutional. The majority opinion—delivered by Chief Justice William H. Rehnquist—stated that the program was enacted for the valid secular purpose of providing educational assistance to poor children in a demonstrably failing public school system; that government aid reaches religious institutions only by way of the deliberate choices of individual recipients; and that the only preference in the program is for low-income families, who receive greater assistance and have priority for admission. In dissent, Justice John Paul Stevens queried, "Is a law that authorizes the use of public funds to pay for the indoctrination of thousands of children in particular religious faiths a 'law respecting an establishment of religion' within the meaning of the First Amendment?" He stated, "The voluntary character of the private choice to prefer a parochial education over an education in the public school system seems to me quite irrelevant to the question whether the government's choice to pay for religious indoctrination is Constitutionally permissible. Whenever we remove a brick from the wall that we designed to separate religion and government, we increase the risk of religious strife and weaken the foundation of our democracy."

The history of the Cleveland voucher program and the litigation surrounding it is summarized by Joseph P. Viteritti in "Vouchers on Trial," *Education Next* (Summer 2002). Begun in 1995, the program allows about 4,000 low-income students to attend private schools with up to $2,250 in public support. Since parochial schools were the only nonpublic schools with tuition rates low enough to accommodate voucher students, opponents maintained that the program was indeed an incentive to attend these schools.

Dan D. Goldhaber and Eric R. Eide, in "What Do We Know (and Need to Know) About the Impact of School Choice Reforms on Disadvantaged Students?" *Harvard Educational Review* (Summer 2002), examine empirical evidence and find that school choice programs have little clear-cut impact on either students in the programs or those who remain in their assigned public schools. They do cite evidence that there is greater support for vouchers among African Americans, however. Frederick M. Hess and Patrick J. McGuinn, in "Muffled by the Din: Competitive Noneffects of the Cleveland Voucher Program," *Teachers College Record* (June 2002), contend that the political and legal ambiguity about Cleveland's voucher program dampened the willingness of parochial and independent schools to expand their capacity to receive voucher students. These schools saw voucher programs as a minor threat as far as competitive pressure for reform is concerned. Perhaps the *Zelman* decision will convert this symbolic threat into a true reform movement.

In the following selections, Charles L. Glenn portrays the *Zelman* decision as a harbinger of the emergence of faith-based alternatives to the public school establishment's rampant secularism. Paul E. Peterson admits that *Zelman* is a welcome addition to the pro-voucher arsenal, but he expresses concern about establishment backlash and, even more so, governmental encroachment on religious schools' independence.

Charles L. Glenn  **YES**

Fanatical Secularism

The Supreme Court's majority opinion in the Cleveland voucher case, *Zelman v. Simmons-Harris,* was of course the most newsworthy aspect of the decision, but the dissents were no less revealing. In about 500 words, Justice Stevens managed to use the word "indoctrination" four times and "religious strife" twice. Likewise, Justice Breyer's dissent begins and ends with warnings of "religiously based social conflict" resulting from allowing parents to use public funding to send their children to sectarian schools. Today it is a little startling to encounter these echoes of Justice Black's 1968 dissent in *Board of Education v. Allen,* in which he warned:

> The same powerful sectarian religious propagandists who have succeeded in securing passage of the present law to help religious schools carry on their sectarian religious purposes can and doubtless will continue their propaganda, looking toward complete domination and supremacy of their particular brand of religion. . . . The First Amendment's prohibition against governmental establishment of religion was written on the assumption that state aid to religion and religious schools generates discord, disharmony, hatred, and strife among our people, and that any government that supplies such aids is to that extent a tyranny. . . . The Court's affirmance here bodes nothing but evil to religious peace in this country.

Although the Supreme Court's decision in *Allen* has left no detectable sign of "disharmony, hatred, and strife among our people," the dissenting justices in the Cleveland case seem to believe that the only way to avoid "indoctrination" and religious warfare is to educate children in government-run schools (even though most industrialized countries provide support to religious schools). Concerns over deep entanglements between government and religion have of course haunted the nation from its very beginning. But in the education realm, the sheer hostility toward religious schools is not just a matter of separating church from state. It in part reflects and derives from the self-image of many educators, who like to think of themselves as having been specially anointed to decide what is in the best interest of children. Faith-based schools, they assume, are in the business of "indoctrinating"

From Charles L. Glenn, "Fanatical Secularism," *Education Next* (Winter 2003). Copyright © 2003 by The Board of Trustees of Leland Stanford Junior University. Reprinted by permission of *Education Next.*

their pupils, while public schools are by definition committed to critical thinking and to the emancipation of their pupils' minds from the darkness of received opinions, even those of their own parents.

What I have elsewhere called "the myth of the common school" is a deeply held view with tremendous political resonance, first articulated in the 1830s by Horace Mann and his allies. This myth insists that enlightenment is the exclusive province of public schools, which are thus the crucible of American life and character in a way that schools independent of government could never be.

The actual working out of this powerful idea in the 19th and early 20th centuries was not altogether benign. It included, for example, systematically denying that there were a number of ways to be a good American. Nor was the common school ideal ever fully realized, even in its New England home. Segregation by social class persisted, and black pupils were unofficially segregated in much of the North and West and officially segregated in all of the South. Even the famed "steamer classes" that served immigrant children in the cities of the East and Midwest often did not keep them in school beyond the first year or two.

Nonetheless, the myth of the "common school" deserves credit for many of the accomplishments of public education in this country. It articulated a coherent vision of the American character and of an America-in-process, and it made both convincingly attractive. In recent decades, however, this hopeful myth has been transmuted into an establishment ideology that borrows much of the language and the positive associations of the common school to serve a bureaucratized, monopolistic system that is increasingly unresponsive to what parents want for their children.

The Enlightenment Mission

In *The Myth of the Common School* (1988), a historical account of how the ideology of state schooling emerged, I traced the myth's development in 19th century France, the Netherlands, and the United States. To a great extent the myth was informed by a bias against orthodox religion, often in the name of what was considered a "higher and purer" form of Christianity stripped of "superstitious" elements such as an emphasis on sin and salvation, in favor of a purified morality and faith in progress. State-sponsored schooling was intended to replace religious particularism (whether Catholic or Calvinist) as well as local loyalties and norms with an emerging national identity and culture.

Enlightenment in this form was experienced by many as oppressive rather than liberating. In place of the convictions that had given meaning and direction, and often color and excitement, to their lives, people were offered a diffuse array of platitudes, a bloodless "secular faith" without power to shape moral obligation or to give direction to a life. The effect was to set people free for a new and more oppressive bondage, unrestrained by the custom and ceremony from which, as the Irish poet William Butler Yeats reminded us, innocence and beauty come to enrich our lives.

This political account of the development of public education continues to be helpful in understanding present-day conflicts in Western democracies. If we recognize that the attempt to achieve a government monopoly on schooling was intended to serve political purposes during a period of nation-building, we can see that this monopoly is no longer appropriate—if it ever was.

The case for charter schools, vouchers, and other forms of "marketized" education rests not only on educational performance but also on the claims of freedom of conscience. Parents have a fundamental right—written into the various international covenants protecting human rights—to choose the schooling that will shape their children's understanding of the world. But a right isn't really a right if it can't be exercised. Families who can't afford tuition at a private school or a move to the suburbs should still be able to make choices regarding their children's education.

There is, in other words, a strong argument against attempts by government to use schooling to achieve political or cultural change—or stability, for that matter. John Stuart Mill gave this argument definitive form in 1859, writing:

> All that has been said of the importance of individuality of character, and diversity in opinions and modes of conduct, involves, as of the same unspeakable importance, diversity of education. A general State education is a mere contrivance for moulding people to be exactly like one another; and as the mould in which it casts them is that which pleases the predominant power in the government . . . in proportion as it is efficient and successful, it establishes a despotism over the mind, leading by natural tendency to one over the body.

The same point was made in a lapidary phrase by the U.S. Supreme Court in its 1925 *Pierce v. Society of Sisters* decision: "the child is not the mere creature of the State."

But does this leave nothing to be said for the role of schools in fostering the qualities of civic virtue on which, all moralists agree, the meaningful exercise of freedom depends? Put another way, does a commitment to limiting government's role in the education realm also require that schools refrain from seeking to form the character and worldview of their pupils? This is one of the central dilemmas of a republican form of government, at least in its contemporary form of limited state power. While republics pledge to respect the freedom of their citizens, they also depend on the voluntary adherence of those citizens to often complex norms of civic life. As a result, as Montesquieu pointed out, "It is in republican government that the full power of education is needed." The citizens of a republic must be virtuous since they govern themselves.

Jean-Jacques Rousseau wrote that the teacher must choose whether he will make a man or a citizen. The choice is not so stark, but it is nevertheless real. The state may seek to mold citizens on a particular pattern, but citizens in a free society surely have a right not to be molded, in their opinions and character, by the state. The child is not the mere creature of the state.

Emancipating the Mind

Any account of the tensions between the educational goals of government and of families must consider the third side of the triangle: how teachers and other educators have understood their mission. It is easy to assume that public school teachers line up on the side of the "state project" in education, while teachers in faith-based and other nonstate schools line up on the side of parents. But the reality is much more complex. Indeed, the simple state-versus-parents dichotomy fails to do justice to many educators' perception of themselves as emancipators of the minds of their students.

As noted, education theorists have long contrasted the emancipatory role of the public school with the "indoctrination" they attribute to religious schools. This strikes a note with tremendous cultural resonance. "Emancipation," Jacques Barzun tells us, is "the modern theme par excellence." The most influential of contemporary educators like to think of themselves as liberators of the minds of their pupils rather than as conveyors of "dead" information, such as the traditions of Western culture.

As a result, those who set the pace in the world of American education, and those who follow their lead, look down on the teachers, parents, and policymakers who do not share this understanding of the teacher's mission. Leadership for American education has increasingly been provided by big-city and state superintendents, professors of education, and officials of the education associations and teacher unions who see little need to respond to the uninformed views of the general public and of parents. This was illustrated by a 1997 Public Agenda survey of "teachers of teachers," professors in teacher-training institutions. Of the 900 professors surveyed, 79 percent agreed that "the general public has outmoded and mistaken beliefs about what good teaching means." They considered communication with parents important, but not in order to learn what education parents wanted for their children. Parents were to be "educated or reeducated about how learning ought to happen in today's classroom."

The professors of education surveyed were convinced, for example, that "the intellectual process of searching and struggling to learn is far more important . . . than whether or not students ultimately master a particular set of facts." Sixty percent of them called for less memorization in classrooms, with one professor in Boston insisting that it was "politically dangerous . . . when students have to memorize and spout back." By contrast, according to another Public Agenda study, 86 percent of the public and 73 percent of teachers want students to memorize the multiplication tables and to learn to do math by hand before using calculators.

These are not purely technical questions; they reflect assumptions about the very nature of education. The professors are expressing one form of the "cosmopolitan" values that have been promoted by American schooling over the past century. This perspective has made the exclusion of religion from the public schools seem not a matter of political convenience or respect for societal diversity, but essential to the mission of education. It is also a sign of intellectual laziness. Teaching facts requires knowledge, which is acquired through rigorous study and research. All it takes to teach values is the ability to spout your own beliefs and prejudices.

Platonic Education

The marks of this condescension can be found in the various controversies that swirl around public schooling. State-imposed curriculum frameworks and standardized tests are condemned as distractions from the teaching of "critical thinking." Lecturing is rejected as an unsound practice because it wrongly assumes that the teacher holds some authority. Nor should the teacher stress right and wrong solutions to the problems that she poses; what is important is the pupil's engagement with the search for an answer. This self-censorship on the part of teachers is even more important when it comes to sex education, where talk of "character" and "virtue" is deeply suspect.

So much is this set of attitudes—the priority of "liberation" or "emancipa- tion" as the central metaphor for the teacher's work—taken for granted among American educators that the higher performance of pupils in other countries on international tests in math and science is often dismissed as reflecting other countries' inappropriate stress on drill and memorization. The possibility that a stress on rich curriculum content can result in lively, engaged classrooms is seldom credited. American pupils may not know as much, we are told, but they know how to think and to solve problems creatively.

This complacent assumption rests on a fundamental misunderstanding. Mental "emancipation" can be a very good thing, of course, when it removes the chains of misinformation and when it arouses a thirst for the truth that can be satisfied only by hard, honest mental effort. This is the traditional justification for a "liberal" education.

The classic description of such an emancipation is Plato's parable of prisoners in an underground cavern, convinced that the shadows on the wall are the only reality. One of the prisoners, in a process that Plato explicitly calls an analogy for education, is freed from his chains and brought to a state, literally, of enlightenment.

Plato makes it clear, though, that it is not enough to loose the chains; the prisoner must be forced to turn toward the light and compelled to venture out of the cavern. Only gradually can he bear the light of day, and only after much experience can he look directly at the source of light and truth. Even the gifted youth who are being groomed for leadership, we are told elsewhere in *The Republic*, should not be exposed to the pleasures and rigors of the search for truth through argument until they have mastered the disciplines of music and gymnastics and have matured through responsibility. Otherwise, Plato warns, they will just play with ideas, without any solid foundation or useful result.

While Plato stressed the laborious acquisition of knowledge and under- standing as the means to enlightenment, our impatient age has preferred to think of the emancipation to be achieved through education as simply the removal of the chains of illusion (conventional morality and traditional reli- gious worldviews) without the discipline of seeking truth or the confidence that there is truth to be found.

Critical thinking and creative problem-solving are certainly among the primary goals of a good education, but they are not developed casually in the course of an undirected exploration. Nor should we assume that there is an innate human propensity to rise to that challenge. Most of us are intellectually lazy about large spheres of the world around us. For every person who really wants to know how an automobile engine works, there must be a dozen of us who are content if it starts reliably when we turn the key. This is not necessarily bad. Life would be impossible if we could not take much around us for granted, and even new discoveries rest on the discoveries of others that we do not have to repeat.

Deconstructivism

This is the fundamental wrong-headedness of another classic description of education, Rousseau's Emile. Raised in isolation, denied the use of books and of direct instruction by his tutor, Emile is expected to learn by following his natural inclinations and responding to situations that his tutor secretly creates for him. The boy, Rousseau tells us, "instructs himself so much the better because he sees nowhere the intention to instruct him." His tutor "ought to give no precepts at all; he ought to make them be discovered."

Here is the authentic note of much current pedagogical advice. The article of faith widely held among educators, especially those who have themselves benefited from the most sophisticated education, is that the teacher should never impose anything on his students, nor suggest to them that there are fixed truths that are worth learning or seeking to discover. Instead he should closely observe the interests of his students and create situations in which they are challenged to use those interests as opportunities for learning. In responding to these challenges, the students will "construct" solutions and even meanings that are uniquely their own and will thus be more deeply and validly learned than any that might be suggested by the teacher or by the wider culture and tradition. In the process, students will become autonomous human beings, not the mere creatures of their culture, and will develop capacities of critical judgment that will enable them to participate in creating—"constructing"—a better world.

According to a recent account of "constructivism" in the 2000 yearbook of the National Society for the Study of Education:

> There is to be no notion of correct solution, no external standard of right or wrong. As long as a student's solution to a problem achieves a viable goal, it has to be credited. Nor can relevant educational goals be set externally; they are only to be encountered by the student . . . the constructivistic teacher is to make do without any concept of objective truth or falsehood.

"Even if it were possible to educate children in this way," philosopher Roger Scruton has written, "one thing is certain: that each generation would know less than the one before. . . . And that, of course, is Rousseau's underlying intention—not to liberate the child, but to destroy all intellectual authority, apart from that which resides in the self." As a result, Emile "is the least free of children, hampered at every point in his search for information," and "one can read *Emile* not as a treatise on education, but as a treatise against education." Rousseau's pupil could arrive at a quite incorrect understanding of many natural and social phenomena by relying naively on his experience alone.

Why should we concern ourselves with what Rousseau wrote almost two-and-a-half centuries ago—or indeed with what Plato wrote long before that? Because education is an enterprise, more perhaps than any other save religion, that is shaped by how we choose to think about it.

There is another tradition of thinking about education. It is expressed in the Hebrew scriptures and Jewish practice: "Why do we do these things?" The Passover questions are answered with a story about the experience of a people, a story that has sustained them and given moral direction and meaning to their lives. Does being taught a tradition and taught within a tradition prevent questioning? Of course not; it provides the content that makes questioning fruitful. It can also be found in the classical Greek concept of *paideia* as, in Michael Oakeshott's words, a "serious and orderly initiation into an intellectual, imaginative, moral and emotional inheritance."

"The knowledge-centered teacher," Scruton points out, "is in the business of passing on what he knows—ensuring, in other words, that his knowledge does not die with him." The teacher who loves his subject and cares about his students is concerned that the rising generation not know less than the one that preceded it.

Emancipation is among the elements of a good education; it can help to prepare the way for the exercise of freedom by removing barriers, but it does not of itself make a man or woman free. Education that supports individual freedom and a free society is induction into a culture, not as a straitjacket but as the context of meanings and restraints that make the exercise of real freedom possible. As Philip Rieff has noted, "A culture must communicate ideals . . . those distinctions between right actions and wrong that unite men and permit them the fundamental pleasure of agreement. Culture is another name for a design of motives directing the self outward, toward those communal purposes in which alone the self can be realized and satisfied."

It is for this reason that structural reforms supporting freedom and diversity in education are not enough; they must be paired with a willingness to confront the much more difficult issue of the purposes, the means, and the content of a good education. Diversity and choice must be paired with common standards, and the content of these must be rich and meaningful. This will require an effort for which the schooling we have received in recent decades almost unfits us, to rediscover and give new life and conviction to those elements of history and culture, the virtues, achievements, and consolations, that have at all times shaped and sustained civilization. This is not a plea for a narrowly Western nostalgia trip, but rather an insistence that only a recovery of the permanent things, of humanity's highest accomplishments, can serve as the basis for a worthy education.

Such a happy outcome would be helped along if opponents of school vouchers would refrain from scare tactics based on unfounded stereotypes about faith-based schooling. Schools that teach in ways shown to be harmful to children should be shut down, but the debate over how to organize a pluralistic education system is not helped by worst-case scenarios. Many Western democracies have faced this challenge successfully, finding an appropriate balance between the autonomy of schools and public accountability, and we can do so too, now that the Supreme Court majority has decided in favor of educational freedom.

Paul E. Peterson  **NO**

Victory for Vouchers?

In the most anticipated decision of its recent term, the Supreme Court ruled, in the case of *Zelman v. Simmons-Harris*, that the school-voucher program in Cleveland, Ohio did not violate the Constitution's ban on the "establishment" of religion. Opponents of vouchers—i.e., the use of public funds to help families pay tuition at private schools, including religious schools—were predictably disappointed, but pledged to fight on. As Senator Edward M. Kennedy declared, "Vouchers may be constitutional," but "that doesn't make them good policy."

The policy's sympathizers, needless to say, saw the ruling in a different light. President Bush used the occasion of the Supreme Court's decision to issue a full-throated endorsement of vouchers. *Zelman*, he told a gathering in Cleveland, did more than remove a constitutional cloud; it was a "historic" turning point in how Americans think about education. In 1954, in *Brown v. Board of Education*, the Court had ruled that the country could not have two sets of schools, "one for African-Americans and one for whites." Now, he continued, in ruling as it did in the Cleveland case, the Court was affirming a similar principle, proclaiming that "our nation will not accept one education system for those who can afford to send their children to a school of their choice and one for those who can't." *Zelman*, according to the President, is *Brown* all over again.

But is it?

⁕

Publicly funded school vouchers got their start in Milwaukee, Wisconsin in 1990. Established at the urging of local black leaders and Wisconsin Governor Tommy Thompson (now the Secretary of Health and Human Services), the program was originally restricted to secular private schools and included fewer than a thousand needy students. To accommodate growing demand, religious schools were later allowed to participate, an arrangement declared constitutional in 1998 by the Wisconsin Supreme Court. The Milwaukee program now provides a voucher worth up to $5,785 to over 10,000 students, amounting to more than 15 percent of the school system's eligible population.

In 1999, at the behest of Governor Jeb Bush, Florida also established a publicly funded voucher program, aimed at students attending public schools

From Paul E. Peterson, "Victory for Vouchers?" *Commentary* (September 2002). Copyright © 2002 by The American Jewish Committee. Reprinted by permission of *Commentary* and the author.

that failed to meet state standards. Though just two schools and fewer than a hundred students have participated in the program thus far, ten other schools, with thousands of students, will be eligible to participate this fall. (The Florida program is also noteworthy because it served as amodel for the voucher-like federal scholarship program advocated by George W. Bush during the 2000 presidential campaign—a program subsequently abandoned by the administration in its push for an education bill.)

Though the Milwaukee and Florida programs had until recently received the most public attention, it was the program in Cleveland—the country's only other publicly funded voucher program of any size[1]—That won the opponents of vouchers their day before the Supreme Court. The Cleveland program is relatively small, providing a maximum of $2,250 a year to each of roughly 4,000 students. Parents use the vouchers overwhelmingly for religious schools, which in recent years have enrolled over 90 percent of the program's participants. This, according to lawyers for the teachers' unions, the most powerful foe of vouchers, constituted an obvious violation of the separation between church and state. And they prevailed twice in federal court, winning decisions at the trial and appellate level against Susan Zelman, Ohio's superintendent of public instruction and the official responsible for administering the Cleveland program.

But the five more conservative members of the Supreme Court were not persuaded. In his opinion for the majority in *Zelman*, Chief Justice William Rehnquist pointed to three well-known precedents—*Mueller* (1983), *Witters* (1986), and *Zobrest* (1993)—in which the Court had allowed government funds to flow to religious schools. What these cases had in common, he wrote, and what they shared with the Cleveland voucher program, was that public money reached the schools "only as a result of the genuine and independent choices of private individuals." Under Cleveland's program, families were in no way coerced to send their children to religious schools; they had a range of statefunded options, including secular private schools, charter schools, magnet schools, and traditional public schools. Considered in this wider context, the voucher program was, Rehnquist concluded, "entirely neutral with respect to religion."

The dissenters in *Zelman*, led by Justice David Souter, challenged the majority's reading of the relevant precedents—especially of *Nyquist* (1973), a ruling that struck down a New York State program giving aid to religious schools—and suggested that the choice in Cleveland between religion and non-religion was a mere legal fiction. They saved their most pointed objections, however, for what they saw as the likely social consequences of the ruling. The Court, Souter wrote, was promoting "divisiveness" by asking secular taxpayers to support, for example, the teaching of "Muslim views on the differential treatment of the sexes," or by asking Muslim-Americans to pay "for the endorsement of the religious Zionism taught in many religious Jewish schools." Justice Stephen Breyer suggested that the decision would spark "a struggle of sect against sect," and Justice John Paul Stevens wondered if the majority had considered the lessons of other nations' experience around the world, including "the impact of religious strife . . . on the decisions of neighbors in the Balkans, Northern Ireland, and the Middle East to mistrust one another."

If judicial rhetoric is all that counts, the dissenters in *Zelman* had the better of it. In the majority opinion, by contrast, there is very little that rises to the level of *Brown's* often-cited language about the demands of American equality. Even observers pleased by the ruling were disappointed that the majority's opinion did not go much beyond showing how the facts of the case fit past precedents; no ringing declarations are to be found in Chief Justice Rehnquist's cautious prose.

Only in the concurrences written by two of the Justices does one get a sense of the wider issues at stake. Responding to the worries of the dissenters, Justice Sandra Day O'Connor pointed out that taxpayer dollars have long flowed to various religious institutions—through Pell Grants to denominational colleges and universities; through child-care subsidies that can be used at churches, synagogues, and other religious institutions; through direct aid to parochial schools for transportation, textbooks, and other materials; and, indirectly, through the tax code, which gives special breaks to the faithful. If government aid to religious institutions were such a problem, she suggested, wouldn't American society be torn already by sectarian strife?

What Justice O'Connor failed to answer was the dissenters' obvious disquiet—one shared these days by many Americans—at the prospect of public money going to support the teaching of extremist religious creeds. This is a reasonable concern—though it is hardly clear, as the Justices themselves might have argued, that the best tool for conquering intolerance born of religious zeal is for the government to impose secular enlightenment. The U.S. has achieved religious peace not by depending upon school-based indoctrination of any stripe but by ensuring that the members of all creeds have access to the democratic process and a robust private sphere in which to meet their particular needs.

As an educational matter, several well-designed studies have shown that students who attend private schools in the U.S. are not only just as tolerant of others as their public-school peers but are also *more* engaged in political and community life. Catholic schools have a particularly outstanding record, probably because for more than a century American Catholics have felt compelled to teach democratic values as proof of their patriotism. There are obviously extremist outliers among, for instance, some of the American *madrassas* discovered by journalists since September 11, but there is no reason to doubt that most of the country's religious schools are attempting to prove that they, too, can create good citizens.

As for *Brown* itself, only Justice Clarence Thomas, in his own stirring concurrence, pointed to it as an explicit precedent, quoting Frederick Douglass to argue that today's inner-city public-school systems "deny emancipation to urban minority students." As he observed,

> The failure to provide education to poor urban children perpetuates a
> vicious cycle of poverty, dependence, criminality, and alienation that
> continues for the remainder of their lives. If society cannot end racial dis-
> crimination, at least it can arm minorities with the education to defend
> themselves from some of discrimination's effects.

For Justice Thomas—as for President Bush, whose own remarks were undoubtedly influenced by these passages—vouchers are a civil-rights issue; they promise not to intensify religious strife, as the Court's dissenters would have it, but to help heal the country's most enduring social divide.

.⋅◉⋅.

Whether *Zelman* can in fact meet these high expectations remains very much to be seen. *Brown*, in principle, was self-enacting. Neither state legislatures nor local school boards could defy the ruling without running afoul of the law. George Wallace, Bull Connor, and many other Southern politicians were willing to do just that, but in the end, federal authorities imposed the Supreme Court's decision on the vested interests that opposed it.

Zelman is different. Though it keeps existing voucher programs intact, it does not compel the formation of new ones. Here the barricades to change remain extraordinarily high.

Public opinion does not pose the most serious obstacle; indeed, on this issue it is highly uncertain. Pollsters can get either pro-voucher or anti-voucher majorities simply by tinkering with the wording of their questions and the order in which they are asked. Nor, despite greater exposure for the issue, have the public's views evolved much in recent years; questions asked in 1996 generated basically the same results in 2001.

Vouchers suffer from graver problems among members of the political class. Whether in Congress or at the state level, substantial bipartisan support is usually necessary to get a piece of legislation through the various committees, past a vote in two chambers, and signed into law. For vouchers, such support has never materialized. Whatever the private opinions of Democrats, for most of them, it is political suicide to support vouchers publicly. Teachers' unions have long placed vouchers at the top of their legislative kill list, and they are a key Democratic constituency, providing the party with both substantial financing and election-day shock troops.

Nor can voucher proponents rely on whole-hearted support from the GOP. Most Republicans, especially social conservatives and libertarians who have read their Milton Friedman, support vouchers in principle. Still, an idea whose primary appeal is to black Americans, the most faithful of all Democratic voting blocs, is a hard sell among the Republican rank-and-file. Vouchers simply do not have much resonance with well-heeled suburbanites who already have a range of educational choices. When vouchers came up as state ballot questions in both California and Michigan two years ago, most Republican politicians found a way to dodge the issue—and the proposals lost badly.

Even if this political situation were to change, most states have constitutional restrictions of their own that may be invoked to scuttle attempts to provide vouchers for use at religious schools. Many of these provisions are socalled "Blaine" amendments, dating to the 19th century, when James Blaine, a Senator from Maine and a Republican presidential candidate, sought to win the anti-immigrant vote by campaigning to deny public funds to Catholic schools.

(Blaine is perhaps most famous for describing the Democrats as the party of "Rum, Romanism, and Rebellion.") In its classic version, the Blaine amendment read as follows:

> No money raised by taxation for the support of public schools, or derived from any public fund therefore, nor any public lands devoted thereto, shall ever be under the control of any religious sect; nor shall any money so raised or lands so devoted be divided between religious sects or denominations.

In a number of cases, state courts have interpreted Blaine amendments to mean nothing more than what is required, according to the Supreme Court, by the establishment clause of the First Amendment. On this view, vouchers are safe—but not every state judge necessarily shares this view. Such language-may prove to be a hurdle for the voucher program in Florida, where a trial court has now ruled that the law violates the state constitution. Depending on what finally happens at the state level, the Supreme Court may in time be asked to decide whether, on account of their nativist and anti-Catholic origins, the Blaine amendments themselves are unconstitutional.

<hr>

However much these practical differences may separate *Zelman* from *Brown*, one powerful similarity remains: like the Court's famed ruling against segregation in the schools, the decision to allow vouchers means much more for black students and their families than for other Americans.

For decades, and despite a host of compensatory reforms the sizable gap in educational performance between blacks and whites has remained roughly the same. According to the National Assessment of Educational Progress, black eighth graders continue to score about four grade levels below their white peers on standardized tests. Nor is this gap likely to close as long as we have, in President Bush's words, "one education system for those who can afford to send their children to a school of their choice and one for those who can't."

When parents choose a neighborhood or town in which to live, they also select, often quite self-consciously, a school for their children. That is why various Internet services now provide buyers—and real-estate agents—with detailed test-score data and other information about school districts and even individual schools. But there is a catch: the mobility that makes these choices possible costs money. It is no accident that children lucky enough to be born into privilege also attend the nation's best schools.

African-Americans are often the losers in this arrangement. Holding less financial equity, and still facing discrimination in the housing market, they choose from a limited set of housing options. As a result, their children are more likely to attend the worst public schools. Richer, whiter districts rarely extend anything more than a few token slots to low-income minority students outside their communities.

It is thus unsurprising that blacks have benefited most when school choice has been expanded. In multi-year evaluations of private voucher programs in New York City, Washington, D.C., and Dayton, Ohio, my colleagues and I found that African-American students, when given the chance to attend private schools, scored significantly higher on standardized tests than comparable students who remained in the public schools. In New York, where the estimates are most precise, those who switched from public to private schools scored, after three years, roughly 9 percentage points higher on math and reading tests than their public-school peers, a difference of about two grade levels. If reproduced nationwide, this result would cut almost in half the black-white test-score gap. (Interestingly, there is no evidence that vouchers have improved the academic performance of students from other ethnic groups. In my own research, they had no impact, positive or negative, on the test scores of either whites in Dayton or Hispanics in New York City.)

These findings about the especially positive effects of private schools on African-American students are hardly isolated. One review of the literature, conducted by the Princeton economist Cecilia Rouse, concludes that even though (once again) it is difficult to discern positive benefits for white students, "Catholic schools generate higher test scores for African-Americans." Another, done by Jeffrey Grogger and Derek Neal, economists from the University of Wisconsin and the University of Chicago, finds little in the way of detectable gains for whites but concludes that "urban minorities in Catholic schools fare much better than similar students in public schools."

No less important, in light of concerns about the effect of vouchers on students "left behind," is that school choice also seems to improve the performance of students who remain in the *public* schools. The best data from Milwaukee show strong advances in test scores since the voucher program was put into place there ten years ago, especially at public schools in those low-income neighborhoods where the voucher option was available. As observers in Milwaukee have noted, it was only in the wake of the voucher program's expansion that the public-school system there began to adopt a series of apparently successful reforms.

We do not know precisely what accounts for the gains that black students have made by switching to private schools. The answer is certainly not money, since the private schools they attend are usually low-budget, no-frills operations. The most striking difference, according to my own research, lies in the general educational environment: the parents of these students who reported being much more satisfied with everything from the curriculum, homework, and teacher quality to how the schools communicate with the parents themselves. The classes tend to be smaller, they say, and there is less fighting, cheating, racial conflict, or destruction of property.

⋯

That vouchers can produce such results has been known for some time. The question now is whether the ruling in *Zelman* will have any impact on what the public and politicians think about the issue. If nothing else, the Court's authoritative pronouncement on the constitutionality of vouchers has already conferred new legitimacy on them. Newspaper editors and talk-show hosts have been forced to give the idea more respect, and political opponents cannot dismiss it so easily.

Still, the key to change lies within the black community, and especially with parents, who increasingly know that private schools provide a better education for their children. A 1998 poll by Public Agenda, a nonpartisan research group, found that 72 percent of African-American parents supported vouchers, as opposed to just 59 percent of white parents. A poll conducted two years later by the Joint Center for Political and Economic Studies had similar results, with just under half of the overall adult population supporting vouchers but 57 percent of African-American adults favoring the idea. Perhaps more to the point, blacks constituted nearly half of all the applicants for the 40,000 privately funded vouchers offered nationwide by the Children's Scholarship Fund in 1999, even though they comprised only about a quarter of the eligible population.

Even in the face of such numbers, it is too much to expect that men like Jesse Jackson and Al Sharpton will reconsider their virulent opposition to vouchers; their political tendencies are too well defined. But pressure to support school vouchers is building among black parents, and black leaders will have to act. Howard Fuller, the former superintendent of Milwaukee's public-school system, has formed the Black Alliance for Educational Options, a pro-voucher group that has mounted an effective public-relations campaign and is making waves in civil-rights circles. And young politicians like Cory Booker in Newark have begun to challenge their old-line, machine-style elders, using vouchers as a key dividing point. Responding to these currents—and to the decision in *Zelman*—the city council of Camden, composed entirely of black and Hispanic Democrats, passed a unanimous resolution in July urging the state of New Jersey to establish a voucher program for the city's dysfunctional public schools. Such examples are sure to multiply.

Not even the Supreme Court, it should be recognized, can make educational change come quickly in America. Though *Brown* was handed down in 1954, it took more than a decade before major civil-rights legislation was enacted; Southern schools were not substantially desegregated until the 1970's. Anyone writing about *Brown* ten years after its passage might have concluded that the decision was almost meaningless.

The same may be said about *Zelman* on its tenth anniversary. Perhaps the safest prediction is that, in four or five decades, American education will have been altered dramatically, in ways we cannot anticipate, by the parental demand for greater choice—a demand codified in *Zelman*. Many battles will be fought and lost along the way, to be sure, but the victories will accumulate, because choice, once won, is seldom conceded.

Note

1. New York City, Washington, D.C., and numerous other cities have well-developed *private* voucher programs designed to help low-income families; these currently serve over 50,000 students.

POSTSCRIPT

Has the Supreme Court Reconfigured American Education?

In "Privatizing Education: The Politics of Vouchers," *Phi Delta Kappan* (February 2001), Sheila Suess Kennedy identifies the partisans in the voucher wars. Pro-voucher groups include pro-market libertarians, business organizations, the Christian Right, and the Catholic Church. The anti-voucher side includes the education establishment (teachers' unions, in particular), civil libertarians, church/state separationists, and official African American organizations. Regarding this last group, Michael Leo Owens, in "Why Blacks Support Vouchers," *The School Administrator* (June 2002), states that although urban black America favors school vouchers, its leaders do not. He cites a 1999 survey showing that 68 percent of blacks favor vouchers whereas a similar percentage of black state and local officials do not support voucher plans. Apparently, despite their shortcomings, vouchers offer hope to poor families whose children are trapped in the nation's worst schools. On the contrary, Benjamin O. Canada, in "Black Leadership and Vouchers," *The School Administrator* (June 2002), contends that vouchers cannot systematically expand educational opportunities for blacks—they are a hoax. Interestingly, the first federally funded voucher program has been initiated in the predominantly black District of Columbia schools.

Clearly, the *Zelman* decision has rekindled the debate about breaking up the government monopoly in schooling and giving parents and children new options. So say Lawrence W. Reed and Joseph P. Overton in "The Future of School Choice," *USA Today* (January 2003), who assert, "The empowerment and transformation of parents into active agents is the foundation of educational choice theory." Reed and Overton further contend that the Supreme Court's momentous decision has opened the door to improving schools through the power of choice and competition. In time, they say, it will be seen as a pivotal ruling in the restoration of American education.

In contrast, Peterson's concerns are echoed in Steven Menashi's "The Church-State Tangle: School Choice and Religious Autonomy," *Policy Review* (August & September 2002), in which the author worries that "if voucher laws saddle private schools with the same regulatory regime that now hampers the public education system, school choice will prove an iatrogenic aggravation of the educational crisis."

For further slants on the issue, see the April 2002 issue of *Educational Leadership* and the Winter 2001 issue of *Education Next*.

ISSUE 12

Can Charter Schools Revitalize Public Education?

YES: Chester E. Finn, Jr., Bruno V. Manno, and Gregg Vanourek, from "The Radicalization of School Reform," *Society* (May/June 2001)

NO: Marc F. Bernstein, from "Why I'm Wary of Charter Schools," *The School Administrator* (August 1999)

ISSUE SUMMARY

YES: Former assistant secretaries of education Chester E. Finn, Jr., and Bruno V. Manno, along with Gregg Vanourek, vice president of the Charter School Division of the K12 education program, provide an update on the charter school movement, which, they contend, is reinventing public education.

NO: School superintendent Marc F. Bernstein sees increasing racial and social class segregation, church-state issues, and financial harm as outgrowths of the charter school movement.

"The public education system as currently structured is archaic." So say Diane Ravitch and Joseph Viteritti in "A New Vision for City Schools," *The Public Interest* (Winter 1996). "Instead of a school system that attempts to impose uniform rules and regulations," they contend, "we need a system that is dynamic, diverse, performance-based, and accountable. The school system that we now have may have been right for the age in which it was created; it is not right for the twenty-first century."

Currently, the hottest idea for providing alternatives to the usual public school offering is the charter school movement. Charter schools, which receive funding from the public school system but operate with a good deal of autonomy regarding staffing, curriculum, and spending, began in Minnesota in 1991 through legislative action prompted by grassroots advocates. Charter schools have gained wide support, all the way up to the White House. In the 1998–1999 school year some 1,700 charter schools served about 350,000 students nationwide. The 2000–2001 year saw about 500 additional charters granted.

The movement has certainly brought variety to the school system menu and has expanded parental choice. Community groups, activists, and entrepreneurs seem to be clamoring for available charters for Core Knowledge schools, Paideia schools, fine arts academies, Afrocentric schools, schools for at-risk students and dropouts, technology schools, character education-based schools, job-training academies, and so on.

The National Commission on Governing America's Schools has recommended that every school become a charter school, which would bring an end to the era of centralized bureaucratic control of public school districts. The Sarasota County School District in Florida has already embarked on a decentralized organizationalmodel offering a "100% School Choice Program" through newly conceived "conversion, deregulated, and commissioned schools."

There are obstacles to success, however, and indeed some have already failed. According to Alex Medler in "Charter Schools Are Here to Stay," *Principal* (March 1997), these obstacles include inadequate capital funding and facilities, cash flow and credit problems, regulations and paperwork, disputes with local school boards, and inadequate planning time. A recently released report by the Hudson Institute, *Charter Schools in Action*, indicates wide success in overcoming such obstacles.

Michael Kelly, in "Dangerous Minds," *The New Republic* (December 30, 1996), argues that in a pluralistic society public money is shared money to be used for shared values. He finds that too many of the charter schools are run by extremists who like the idea of using public money to support their ideological objectives. He cites the failed Marcus Garvey School in Washington, D.C., which spent $372,000 in public funds to bring an Afrocentric curriculum to 62 students. However, he notes that this case has not led to a wave of protests against the concept of charter schools.

In fact, *Washington Post* columnist William Raspberry recently declared that he finds himself slowly morphing into a supporter of charter schools and vouchers. "It isn't because I harbor any illusions that there is something magical about those alternatives," he explains. "It is because I am increasingly doubtful that the public schools can do (or at any rate *will* do) what is necessary to educate poor minority children."

An associated topic is privatization. This either involves turning public school management over to private companies, such as Educational Alternatives, Inc., or cooperating with entrepreneurs who want to develop low-cost private alternatives for students currently enrolled in public schools. The most talked-about of the latter is entrepreneur Chris Whittle's Edison Project, an attempt to build a nationwide network of innovative, for-profit schools.

In the following selections, Chester E. Finn, Jr., Bruno V. Manno, and Gregg Vanourek review the charter school movement's progress, seeing it as a potential fulfillment of the basic promise of American education. Contrarily, Marc F. Bernstein sounds a number of warning signals as the public rushes to embrace charter schools as a reform mechanism.

Chester E. Finn, Jr., Bruno V. Manno,
and Gregg Vanourek

 **YES**

The Radicalization of School Reform

Much has changed in the education world since the United States was declared a "nation at risk" in 1983 by the National Commission on Excellence in Education. We've been reforming and reforming and reforming some more. In fact, "education reform" has itself become a growth industry, as we have devised a thousand innovations and spent billions to implement them. We have tinkered with class size, fiddled with graduation requirements, sought to end "social promotion," pushed technology into the schools, crafted new academic standards, revamped teacher training, bought different textbooks, and on and on.

Most of these alterations were launched with good will and the honest expectation that they would turn the situation around. But the problem with much of this reform churning is that the people who courageously addressed this issue in 1983 basically took for granted that the public school system as we knew it was the proper vehicle for making those changes and that its familiar machinery could produce better products if it were tuned up, adequately fueled and properly directed. In short, requisite changes would be made by school boards and superintendents, principals and teachers, federal and state education departments, and would be implemented either in time-honored system-wide fashion or through equally familiar "pilot" and "demonstration" programs.

Yet despite bushels of effort, barrels of decent intentions, and billions of dollars, most reform efforts have yielded meager dividends, with little changing for the better. Test scores are generally flat, and U.S. twelfth graders lag far behind their international counterparts in math and science, although our school expenditures are among the planet's highest. On the reports of the National Education Goals Panel which monitors progress toward the ambitious objectives set by President Bush and the governors in 1989, most years we see the number of arrows that point upward just about equaled by the number pointing down. Combining large budgets and weak performance, American schools can fairly be termed the least productive in the industrial world.

Many in the education establishment excuse the lack of progress by asserting that the reforms we've undertaken still haven't had time to gain traction, haven't been adequately funded, haven't been accompanied by enough "staff development," have been undermined by complacent parents or retrograde political leaders, and so forth. Others explain that families are deteriorating, poverty is spreading, morals are decaying, and it's not realistic to expect schools to do a better job until the whole society is overhauled. A few naysayers still

From *Society*, May/June 2001, pp. 58–63. Copyright © 2001 by Transaction Publishers, Inc. Reprinted by permission.

insist that the "excellence movement" is itself unnecessary, that American schools are doing okay as is, and that the whole flap stems from a right-wing conspiracy to bring down public education by badmouthing it.

Our sense, however, is that the chief explanation for their failure is the essential incrementalism of many of these "reforms"—i.e., the conventional reforms of the past two decades don't fundamentally alter our approach to public education in America. They do not replace the basic institutional arrangements, shift power, or rewrite the ground rules. That is acceptable if one believes the old structures remain sound. But that is not how we read the evidence. We judge that the traditional delivery system of U.S. public education is obsolete.

This view echoes the late 1960s claim of the iconoclastic psychologist Kenneth B. Clark, whose study of the malign effects of school segregation was cited in the Supreme Court's landmark 1954 decision, *Brown v. Board of Education*. Clark called for "realistic, aggressive, and viable competitors" to the public school system that would strengthen "that which deserves to survive," arguing "that public education need not be identified with the present system of organization of public schools." To be sure, there are today some fine schools within the "regular" system and a number of exceptional ones on its periphery. But the system itself is failing because its basic mechanisms and structures *cannot* change in the ways needed to meet today's education needs and societal demands. Its many "stakeholders" and interest groups fight every significant alteration.

Outside the establishment's fortified citadels, however, an important breakthrough can be seen: widening awareness that the American primary and secondary education system as we know it not only needs radical improvement but also that genuine advances will be made only if we rewrite the system's ground rules, replace many of its assumptions, overturn its structures and transform its ancient power relationships. In other words, the present school enterprise is not just doing poorly; it's incapable of doing much better because it is intellectually misguided, ideologically wrong-headed, and organizationally dysfunctional. The spread of this awareness we term the radicalization of school reform.

At day's end, this radicalization defends the principle and function of public education while arguing for a top-to-bottom makeover of its ground rules and institutional practices. It rejects the Hobson's choice that has long paralyzed serious education reform: the choice between a moribund government run system and the chimera of privatization. We are, in fact, seeing signs of a new view of education change, one that welcomes decentralized control, entrepreneurial management, and grassroots initiatives within a framework of publicly defined standards and accountability.

Charter schools are the most prominent manifestation of the radicalization of school reform (though publicly financed vouchers are the most controversial). In fact, charters are the liveliest reform in American education today. Connecticut Democratic Senator Joseph Lieberman writes:

> "School reform is no longer an option—it is a necessity. Competition from charter schools is the best way to motivate the ossified bureaucracies governing too many public schools. This grass-roots revolution seeks

to reconnect public education with our most basic values: ingenuity, responsibility, and accountability."

Before these unconventional independent public schools of choice vaulted into the spotlight in the mid-1990s, education reform in the United States was nearing paralysis—stalemated by politics and interest groups, confused by the cacophony of a thousand fads and pet schemes working at cross purposes, and hobbled by most people's inability to imagine anything very different from the schools they had attended decades earlier. Enter charter schools in 1991, a seedling reform that grew into a robust tree, then a whole grove. The trees are still young, to be sure, and the grove attracts plenty of lightning strikes. But it is steadily expanding and mostly thriving.

Even if the charter forest doesn't come to dominate our education ecosystem, the idea behind it has powerful implications for the entire enterprise of public schooling. In what follows, we explain charter schools, provide an overview of their present status, account for where they came from, and conclude by describing their potential to renew and redefine U.S. public education.

What, Exactly, Is a Charter School?

Few outside the charter movement are clear about the definition of a charter school. A workable starting point is that a charter school is an "independent public school of choice, freed from rules but accountable for results." A charter school is a new species, a hybrid, with important similarities to traditional public schools, some of the prized attributes of private schools—and crucial differences from both familiar forms.

As a public school, a charter school is open to all who wish to attend it (i.e., without regard to race, religion, or academic ability); paid for with tax dollars (no tuition charges); and accountable for its results—indeed, for its very existence—to an authoritative public body (such as a state or local school board) as well as to those who enroll (and teach) in it.

Charter schools are also different from standard-issue public schools. Most can be distinguished by four key features: they can be created by almost anyone; they are exempt from most state and local regulations, essentially autonomous in their operations; they are attended by youngsters whose families choose them and staffed by educators who are also there by choice; and they are liable to be closed for not producing satisfactory results.

Charter schools resemble private schools in two important particulars. First, their independence. Although answerable to outside authorities for their results (far more than most private schools), they are free to produce those results as they think best. They are self-governing institutions. They, like private schools, have wide ranging control over their own curriculum, instruction, staffing, budget, internal organization, calendar, schedule, and much more. The second similarity is that they are schools of choice. Nobody is assigned to attend (or teach in) a charter school. Parents select them for their children, much as they would a private school, albeit with greater risk because the new charter school typically has no track record.

The "charter" itself is a formal, legal document, best viewed as a contract between those who propose to launch and run a school and the public body empowered to authorize and monitor such schools. In charter-speak, the former are "operators" and the latter are "sponsors."

A charter operator may be a group of parents, a team of teachers, an existing community organization such as a hospital, Boys and Girls Club, university or day care center, even (in several states) a private firm. School systems themselves can and occasionally do start charter schools. Sometimes an existing school seeks to secede from its local public system or, in a few jurisdictions, to convert from a tuition-charging non-sectarian private school to a tax-supported charter school. They apply for a charter and, if successful, are responsible for fulfilling its terms. The application spells out why the charter school is needed, how it will function, what results (academic and otherwise) are expected, and how these will be demonstrated. The operator may contract with someone else—including private companies or "education management organizations" (EMOs)—to manage the school, but the operator remains legally responsible to the sponsor.

The sponsor is ordinarily a state or local school board. In some states, public universities also have authority to issue charters, as do county school boards and city councils. If the sponsor deems an application solid, it will negotiate a more detailed charter (or contract) for a specified period of time, typically five years but sometimes as short as one or as long as fifteen.

During that period, the charter school has wide latitude to function as it sees fit. At least it does if its state enacted a strong charter law and did not hobble charter schools with too many of the constraints under which conventional public schools toil. Key features of the charter idea include waivers from most state and local regulations; fiscal and curricular autonomy; the ability to make its own personnel decisions; and responsibility for delivering the results that it pledged.

If a charter school succeeds, it can reasonably expect to get its charter renewed when the time comes. If it fails, it may be forced to shut down. And if it violates any of the unwaived laws, regulations, or community norms during the term of its charter, it may be shut down sooner.

Where Are We Today?

As of early 2001, there are about 2,100 charter schools, located in 34 states and the District of Columbia. Nearly 518,000 youngsters are enrolled in these schools, slightly more than 1 percent of U.S. public school students. Thirty-six states and the District of Columbia have enabling legislation for charter schools and several more are considering it. Fifty-nine charter schools have, for various reasons, ceased operation.

Future growth in the number of charter schools depends in considerable part on state legislation, especially whether limits on the number of charters that can be granted by charter sponsors remain in effect. There is a heated debate now underway in several states (e.g., Kansas, Michigan) over raising these caps, while other states (e.g., Alaska, California, Massachusetts, Texas) have already loosened them due to demand-side pressures. Clearly, the fuel for charter growth will have to come either from amending state laws to lift those caps or from states without real limits (such as Arizona and Texas) or with high limits (like California and New Jersey).

Largely due to these statutory constraints (not lack of interest or demand since 70 percent of all charter schools have waiting lists) charter schools are distributed unevenly. Eleven states account for over 80 percent of them. Arizona alone had 352 in 1999–00; there were 239 in California, 173 in Michigan, 167 in Texas, and 111 in Florida. A large proportion of charters is concentrated in the three states of Arizona, California, and Michigan, but that percentage decreased from 79 percent in 1995–96 to 45 percent in 1999–00.

Charter schools are found in all types of communities: cities, suburbs, and rural areas; industrial towns, deserts, and Indian reservations; ethnic neighborhoods, commuter towns, even in cyberspace. A tour of the charter landscape does not stop at the U.S. border as similar developments can be found around the world, including the United Kingdom, Canada, New Zealand, Australia, Brazil, Chile, and Pakistan.

Numerous cities across the United States have been profoundly affected by charter schools, and in a few we are beginning to glimpse what a system of public education based on the charter principles of autonomy, choice, and accountability might look like. In Washington, D.C. nearly 15 percent of public school students are now enrolled in charter schools; in Kansas City, Missouri, the total is 18 percent; and in Arizona, 4 percent of all youngsters are in charters—which comprise one-fifth of all the state's public schools.

Still, when compared with the vastness of American K–12 education, charters are a flea on the elephant's back, representing 2 percent of all public schools and less than 1 percent of total enrollments. There are about 15 times as many private schools as charter schools. But thus far, the number of charter schools exceeds voucher schools: as of spring 2000, there were only about 150 publicly funded voucher schools compared to nearly 2,000 charter schools.

Charter schools are much studied and intensively scrutinized, so a great deal is known about them. According to the major federal study of these schools, 72 percent of them are new schools, 18 percent are pre-existing district public schools that converted to charter status, and the remaining 10 percent are pre-existing private, non-sectarian schools that have converted. What's more, the percentage of newly created schools is increasing over time: 85 percent of charters opening in 1998–99 were newly created, compared with just over half of the schools that opened in 1994–95 and earlier. Moreover, most charter schools are relatively young—i.e., the average charter school at the end of 1999–2000 was less than three years old.

One can obtain ample information on charter enrollments, demographics, laws, curricula, founders, sponsors, staff, missions, funding, and facilities. According to the Center for Education reform, over half of all charter schools are in urban districts, one-quarter have a back-to-basics curriculum, 40 percent serve dropouts or students at risk of dropping out, and one-quarter are geared to gifted and talented youth. About 10 percent of charter schools are managed by for-profit EMOs, such as Edison Schools, Advantage Schools, and Charter Schools USA.

Most charter schools are small. The federal study estimates their median enrollment at 137 students, compared to the 475-pupil public school average in 27 charter states. Almost two-thirds (65.2 percent) of charters enroll fewer than 200 students. (Just 17 percent of regular public schools are that small.) With small scale comes intimacy and familiarity that are often missing from the larger and more anonymous institutions of public education.

Unfortunately, some schools called "charter schools" are in fact Potemkin charters, displaying the facade but not the reality. So-called "weak" charter laws place constraints on schools' educational, financial, and operational autonomy—e.g., teacher certification requirements, uniform salary schedules, and collective-bargaining agreements. And many charter schools receive less than full per-pupil funding, with no allowance for facilities and other capital expenses. The upshot is that some charter schools are pale shadows of what they are meant to be.

Where Did Charter Schools Come From?

Most charter experts agree that the phrase "charter schools" was first used by the late Albert Shanker, longtime president of the American Federation of Teachers, in a 1988 speech to the National Press Club and a subsequent article. This is ironic, in view of the teacher unions' initial hostility and continuing skepticism to the charter movement. But it was not unusual for the brilliant and venturesome Shanker to suggest education reform concepts well in advance of their time.

Basing his vision on a school he had visited in Cologne, Germany, Shanker urged America to develop "a fundamentally different model of schooling that emerges when we rethink age-old assumptions—the kind of rethinking that is necessary to develop schools to reach the up to 80 percent of our youngsters who are failing in one way or another in the current system."

He contemplated an arrangement that would "enable any school or any group of teachers . . . within a school to develop a proposal for how they could better educate youngsters and then give them a 'charter' to implement that proposal." "All this," Shanker wrote, "would be voluntary."

> No teacher would have to participate and parents would choose whether or not to send their children to a charter school. . . . The school . . . would have to accept students who are representative of other students in the district or building in terms of ability and background. Charter schools also would have to conform to other civil rights guarantees. For its part, the school district would have to agree that so long as teachers continued to want to teach in the charter school and parents continued to send their children there and there was no precipitous decline in student achievement indicators, it would maintain the school for at least 5–10 years. Perhaps at the end of that period, the school could be evaluated to see the extent to which it met its goals, and the charter could be extended or revoked.

Shanker was echoed in a 1989 article by Ray Budde called "Education by Charter." Then a Minnesota legislator named Ember Reichgott Junge resolved to launch this idea in her state, the first to pass charter school legislation in 1991.

Yet that scrap of history doesn't do justice to the many tributaries that fed into the charter idea, both in the education environment and the wider culture. Within the world of education, these ideas include the hunger for higher standards for students and teachers; the realization that education quality would be judged by its results rather than its inputs (e.g., per pupil spending or class size) and its compliance with rules; the impulse to create new and different school designs that meet the needs of today's families; and the movement to give families more choices of schools.

In addition to changes in the education realm, developments in other domains of U.S. society helped clear the path for charter schools. In the corporate sector, traditional bureaucratic arrangements were being restructured, dispensing with middle management and top-down control. In the public sector, the effort to reinvent government was spawned. Both these sectors moved in the direction of a "tight-loose" management strategy: tightly controlled with respect to their goals and standards—the results they must achieve, and the information by which performance is tracked—but loose as to the *means* by which those results get produced.

Besides transformations in education, business, and government, other societal changes helped create a hospitable climate for charter schools. Beginning in the 1960s, there was the broad liberalization of American culture, what political scientist Hugh Heclo grandly terms an "awakening . . . to a plurality of authenticities." Its elements have included, for better or worse, the decline of traditional authority, the exaltation of personal freedom, the rise of tolerance as a supreme value, and the spread of pluralism, multiculturalism, and diversity.

Accompanying these changes has been rekindled interest in the vitality of "civil society," with the civic order recognized as a third path—neither governmental nor strictly private—to meet human needs and solve community problems. Mediating institutions—e.g., churches, Neighborhood Watch groups, and organizations such as the Red Cross and the Girl Scouts—can help solve intractable social problems while strengthening community bonds.

These many tributaries have fed a river of change in public education, which we term "the radicalization of school reform." Charter schools are today's most prominent expression of that process. They change the emphasis from inputs to results by focusing on student achievement. They flip the structure from rule-bound hierarchy to decentralized flexibility by allowing individual schools to shape their own destinies. They constitute education's version of civil society, a hybrid that draws on the best of the public and private sectors. They introduce enterprise, competition, choice, community, and accountability into a weary system.

Reinventing America's Schools

We often think of charters as "reinventing public education." Traditionally, Americans have defined a public school as any school run by the government, managed by a superintendent and school board, staffed by public employees, and operated within a public-sector bureaucracy. "Public school" in this familiar sense is not very different from "public library," "public park," or "public housing" project.

Now consider a different definition: a public school is any school that is open to the public, paid for by the public, and accountable to public authorities for its results. So long as it satisfies those three criteria, it is a public school. Government need not run it. Indeed, it does not matter—for purposes of its "publicness"—who runs it, how it is staffed, or what its students do between 9 a.m. and 10 a.m. on Tuesdays.

Charter schools are the farthest-flung example today of a reinvented—a radicalized—public education. But it is important to bear in mind that they are part of a bigger idea: public education in which elected and appointed officials play a strategic rather than a functional role. Public support of schooling without governmental provision of schools.

What is the nature of the charter approach to radicalizing school reform? Some see the charter idea as a dangerous predator in the education ecosystem, one that will gradually consume and thereby destroy public education. But that isn't the only way to view this dynamic change.

Stephen Jay Gould's discussion of the "cropping principle" in evolution offers a different perspective. The conventional wisdom about the appearance of a new plant- or meat-eating animal—a "cropper"—into a territory is that it shrinks the number of species in the area. But science has found that in nature precisely the opposite occurs. The cropper actually tends to enrich, not decimate, the ecosystem. In Gould's words, "A well-cropped ecosystem is maximally diverse, with many species and few individuals of any single species. Stated another way, the introduction of a new level in the ecological pyramid tends to broaden the level below it." We believe this is the effect that the charter idea will have—indeed is beginning to have—on public education: enriching and broadening the entire ecosystem.

Charter enthusiasts and opponents both tend to depict these schools as a revolutionary change, a policy earthquake, an unprecedented and heretofore unimaginable innovation. The boosters seize on such colorful rhetoric because it dramatizes the historic significance of their crusade. Enemies deploy the same terminology for the opposite purpose: to slow this reform's spread by scaring people into seeing it as radical, risky, and unproven. Both groups tend to stand too close to the objects they are describing.

Viewed from a few inches away, charter schools *do* represent sharp changes in the customary patterns and practices of today's public school systems, especially the large ones. But with more perspective, we readily observe that charter schools embody three familiar and time-tested features of American education.

First, they are rooted in their communities, the true essence of local control of education, not unlike the village schools of the early 19th century and the one-room schoolhouses that could be found across the land through most of the 20th century. They are much like America's original public schools in their local autonomy, their rootedness in communities, their accountability to parents, and their need to generate revenues by attracting and retaining families. Creatures of civil society as much as agencies of government, charter schools would have raised no eyebrows on Alexis de Tocqueville.

Second, charter schools have cousins in the K-12 family. Their DNA looks much the same under the education microscope as that of lab schools, magnet schools, site-managed schools, and special focus schools (e.g., art, drama, science), not to mention private and home schools. Much the same, but not identical. The Bronx High School of Science is selective, while charter schools are not. Hillel Academy and the Sancta Maria Middle School teach religion, while charter schools cannot. The Urban Magnet School of the Arts was probably designed by a downtown bureaucracy and most likely has carefully managed ethnic ratios in its student body, whereas most charter schools do not. Yet the similarities outweigh the differences.

Third, these new schools reveal a classic American response to a problem, challenge, or opportunity: institutional innovation and adaptation. In that respect, they resemble community colleges, which came into being (and spread rapidly and fruitfully) to meet education needs that conventional universities could not accommodate. As an organizational form, then, charter schools are not revolutionary. They are part of what we are and always have been as a nation.

NO

Why I'm Wary of Charter Schools

With its passage of the New York Charter Schools Act of 1998, New York . . . became the 34th state to authorize or implement charter schools.

As a result, roughly two-thirds of the school districts nationwide now are subject to an educational reform that has yet to prove its worth but has raised the most serious practical and philosophical challenges to the viability of public education in our country's history.

In New York, a charter school can be established through an application submitted by teachers, parents, school administrators, community residents or any combination thereof. Though charter schools are subject to the same health and safety, civil rights and student assessment requirements of other public schools, they are exempt from all other state regulations.

The Case for Charters

The case for charter schools is quite simple—the arguments typically revolve around the alleged failure of the public schools. Though many have contested the validity of these charges (educational researchers Gerald Bracey and David Berliner prime among them), the news media, the political establishment and a large segment of the public have become convinced that our schools are failing to serve the children with whom they've been entrusted.

The 15-year diatribe, beginning with the *Nation at Risk* report in 1984, has been translated in recent years into legislative action enabling students to attend alternative charter schools paid for by the school districts that the students would have otherwise attended. Charter schools, by law, are free of most state mandates and are not obligated to conform to teacher union work rules and hours.

Charter school proponents contend the freedom from state regulations and collective bargaining constraints will yield significant advantages:

- Charter schools will permit and encourage a more creative approach to teaching and learning;
- Charter schools will establish models of educational reform for other schools in the same community;

From Marc F. Bernstein, "Why I'm Wary of Charter Schools," *The School Administrator* (August 1999). Copyright © 1999 by The American Association of School Administrators. Reprinted by permission.

- Charter schools will be more reflective of parent and community priorities through the alternative programs that cater to special interests and needs;
- Charter schools will operate in a more cost-effective manner; and
- Charter schools will be governed by boards consisting of parents, teachers and community members, making them more responsive than public schools.

Unrealized Gains

Not only have these benefits not accrued to most of the students attending existing charter schools, but charter school proponents neglect to address three overarching concerns regarding the potential consequences of this movement.

First, the public money used to fund charter schools must come from an existing source and that source is the budget of the public school district.

Second, charter school populations tend to be more homogeneous than most public schools in terms of ethnicity, religion or race. This homogeneity will have a Balkanizing effect when young children are most open to dealing with differences among people.

Third, the constitutional separation between school and religion will be compromised by people of goodwill (and others) who see opportunities to provide alternate education to children in need.

Before elaborating on these concerns, it is instructive to review the formal studies completed to date that have examined the progress of charter schools in fulfilling their stated goals. Charter school advocates, however, seem to show little or no interest in research data about charter schools.

The Case Not Made

In perhaps the most extensive study to date, "Beyond the Rhetoric of Charter School Reform: A Study of Ten California School Districts," researchers at UCLA, led by Professor Amy Stuart Wells, looked at 17 charter schools in 10 school districts. Their selection of districts were chosen for their diversity in order "to capture the range of experiences within this reform movement."

Among its 15 findings, the study concluded that California's charter schools have not lived up to proponents' claims. Four of the findings are most telling:

- California's charter schools, in most instances, are not yet being held accountable for enhanced academic achievement of their students;
- Charter schools exercise considerable control over the type of students they serve;
- The requirement that charter schools reflect the social/ethnic makeup of their districts has not been enforced;
- No mechanisms are in place for charter schools and regular public schools to learn from each other.

Moreover, the researchers found "no evidence that charter schools can do more with less" and that "regular public schools in districts with charter schools felt little to no pressure from the charter schools to change the way they do business." Thus, the UCLA study disputes in the strongest of terms that charter schools raise the academic achievement of their students in a more cost-effective manner and that nearby public schools will do a better job educating their children by adopting the innovations of the charter schools.

In a yearlong study of Michigan's charter school initiative, researchers at Western Michigan University concluded that charter schools may not be living up to their promise of educational innovation and more effective use of public money. The report, which was presented to the pro-charter state board of education . . . , characterized many charters as "cookie-cutter" schools run by for-profit companies and suggested that many administrators and charter school boards were ill-equipped to run a school.

These two studies are clear in their findings, yet the charter movement grows. If the spread of charter schools did not auger the most dangerous consequences, we could ignore it as yet another failed experiment in American education. But the risks here are too great, not only to America's public schools, but to our very society.

The gravest concerns fall into three categories: financial impact, Balkanization and religious intrusion.

Financial Harm

The most direct and immediate impact upon the public schools relates to financing. Money to operate the charter schools comes from the public schools, whether the financing mechanism be that (1) the public school draws a check to the charter; (2) the state forwards a proportion of what the public would have received to the charter; or (3) the state's discretionary resources that could have been used to improve the public schools are budgeted for charter schools.

Regardless of the process, public schools wind up with fewer dollars to improve the education of their students. Such reduced funding likely will lead to poorer academic results, which then will be used to strengthen the case that charter schools (or voucher programs) are the only recourse for failing public schools. Is this Orwellian in intent or merely ignorant in practice?

In New York, where I've worked as a superintendent for 13 years, the public schools are required to pay the charter schools the average operating expenditure per pupil as computed for the most recent school year based on the number of students the charter school claims it will serve in the forthcoming school year. When public school leaders suggested that their schools would be denied a disproportionate amount of money, charter school proponents (and legislators) responded that the money is merely following the student. As such, the public school would have the same percentage of money as students.

This simplistic argument totally ignores the economic concept of marginal cost. It costs less to educate the 24th student in the class than the initial 5, 10, 15 or 20. In my letter to the editor of *The New York Times* on this subject . . . , I wrote: "This means that if 10 students in each grade were to transfer to a charter school from a 1,000-student public elementary school, the public school would lose approximately $500,000. No teacher, custodian or secretary salaries can be eliminated as a result of the reduction in the number of students. However, the public school would have $500,000 less available to educate its remaining students."

Where is the public school to go to recoup this lost $500,000? There are but two choices—raise taxes or reduce programming. Either choice has serious consequences for public education. If we raise taxes, our taxpayers will be paying more to educate fewer students. They won't care to hear about the principle of marginal cost. They will see the public schools as inefficient and will scream for tax relief or increased accountability for the costly public schools. And, if we cut programming or classroom staffing, our parents will demand to know why we are shortchanging their children.

Clearly, the cost of educating some students is greater than it is for others. Few would question that it costs more to meet the needs of a child with disabilities or one who enters public school without speaking English. Research shows it is the knowledgeable parents who do their homework in terms of investigating alternatives to the public school. Therefore, charter schools are more likely to have a sufficient pool of "less costly" applicants leaving the public school with the more costly students to educate.

In addition to penalizing public schools by reducing operating funds, New York state will have fewer total dollars available for educating students.

One provision of the new charter school law requires the state to establish a fund to provide charter schools with loans for furniture, equipment and facilities. The reservoir of available state money is only so large. It can only drain in so many directions. Thus, public schools that are now required to meet higher academic standards will be told that the state lacks the resources to assist.

The only other source of revenue for the public schools is the local taxpayer. Of course, the alternative is to eliminate or cut back nonacademic offerings. Those programs most likely to be dropped or curtailed are those in art or music, the ones for which there is no bottom-line, quantitative assessment.

Either choice results in a no-win situation. We can alienate our taxpayers or we can jeopardize the support of our parents.

Moreover, citizens in this state have the opportunity to register their support or disagreement with a school district's educational program through their vote on the annual school budget. Inasmuch as the charter school's program is solely within the control of its board of directors, is there not a true gap between the public's right of the purse strings and the independence given to charter schools?

A Balkanizing Effect

Can separate be equal?

This question, we thought, had been answered in 1954 by the U.S. Supreme Court in *Brown vs. Board of Education* when racially segregated schools prevailed in parts of our country by the design of governmental entities.

Nearly a half century later, we now have a government-endorsed policy leading us back to that same situation. Surprisingly, charter schools seem to enjoy strong support among minority legislators and advocates, the same groups that rallied behind the Supreme Court's decision that "separate is not equal" in education.

This reversal may reflect the disenchantment of minority parents with America's inner-city schools, which serve the greatest percentage of minority students. For example, a recent poll by the Washington-based Joint Center for Political and Economic Studies reported that blacks are 11 percent less likely than whites to be satisfied with their local public schools.

Though charter school laws in most states attempt to address the matter of potential racial imbalancing, the charter schools nonetheless are becoming increasingly segregated. The Minnesota Charter Schools Evaluation, conducted in 1998 by the University of Minnesota, found that charter schools in that state typically enroll greater numbers of ethnic minorities than the regular schools in their home districts. Half of the charters have student populations that are more than 60 percent children of color.

In Michigan, a statewide study of charters by Western Michigan University identified a segregation pattern in which white children were opting out of local public schools. The percentage of minorities in charters declined by more than 22 percent between 1995 and 1998.

Two other detailed studies—one in North Carolina, the other in Arizona—concluded that their states' charter schools have become increasingly segregated by race. The North Carolina Office of Charter Schools found that 13 of 34 charter schools that opened in 1997 were disproportionately black, compared with their districts. And, the North Carolina Education Reform Foundation, which helps to start charter schools, says at least 9 of the 26 schools that opened last year violate the diversity clause.

Having anticipated the possibility of segregation, North Carolina's charter school law included a diversity clause requiring charter schools to "reasonably reflect" the demographics of their school districts. Even so, the opposite has occurred.

A study titled "Ethnic Segregation in Arizona Charter Schools," issued in January 1999 by Casey Cobb of University of New Hampshire and Gene Glass of Arizona State University, found that nearly half of the state's 215 charter schools (as of 1997) "exhibited evidence of substantial ethnic separation."

These studies describe but one type of segregation—racial—while the term Balkanization connotes the formal division of a geographic area along racial, ethnic and/or religious lines. How unfortunate it would be for our nation's communities to become more fractionalized than they already are.

The limited existing research points to this as a possible outcome as students' attendance is based upon factors other than the schools' academic performance, whether at the parents' choosing or the schools' selection.

America's public schools have as one of their primary goals to acculturate, sensitize and civilize our children to prepare them for their future roles in a democratic society. Will this goal be seriously compromised due to charter schools? I believe it was René Descartes who wrote that the chief cause of human error is to be found in the prejudices picked up in childhood.

Religious Intrusion

Following our state's adoption of a charter school law, New York City religious leaders began enthusiastically preparing themselves to establish charter schools. They already had access to classroom space, an extremely rare commodity, and a significant presence in their communities, which could only help in attracting students. Plus, the religious leaders have been persistent critics of the city's schools.

The most vocal of the clergy, the Rev. Floyd H. Flake of Queens, N.Y., a former U.S. congressman, argued for "skirt(ing) the constitutional barriers between church and state by offering religious instruction outside school hours."

This creative thinking is not limited to New York City. *Education Week* reported . . . that the Rev. Michael Pfleger, a pastor on Chicago's South Side, "has discussed shutting down St. Sabina (its parish school) and, in its place, opening a publicly funded charter school run by a nonprofit board, possibly with links to the parish or the Catholic archdiocese." Both Flake and Pfleger see charter schools as an opportunity to use public money to subsidize their educational and religious efforts.

The U.S. Constitution speaks loudly and clearly against religious intrusion into the public schools. In spite of Supreme Court cases defining the nature of permissible involvements, the issue is never truly resolved. Litigation involving charter schools inevitably will require the court to rule on charter schools' use of church property, the participation of religious leaders on charter school governing boards and the attendance of charter school students at home and afterschool religious education programs when the church's facilities are used to house the charter school.

The court's decisions will significantly affect public school finances and the influence religion will have upon children attending the nation's public schools, whether they are charter or regular public schools.

Constant Monitoring

Though charter schools have yet to prove their academic worth, they are rapidly increasing in number across the country. They provide choices to parents for their children's education and level the playing field between higher and lower socioeconomic classes. Charter schools lend a warm feeling that government is doing something to fix our failing schools by turning the capitalistic engine of competition loose upon the schools.

In reality, charter schools are denying public schools the financial resources they require to address the needs of an increasingly disparate student population. Our communities will be further divided along racial, religious and ethnic lines as children attend their schools of choice, opting to be with children of similar backgrounds. And the never-ending battle to maintain the separation of church and state will suffer another setback as public money moves in the direction of religious (charter) schools, where children receive religious instruction under the guise of attending charter schools.

As educational leaders committed to the values of public education, we must be wary of these unintended consequences. We must continually monitor charter schools' academic performance, use of public money for religious instruction and adherence to diversity provisions.

Undoubtedly, many policymakers have prejudged the success of the charter schools movement. But we must assume the duty to inform the public about this most serious challenge to public education. As part of a professional leadership organization and as career educators, we must monitor the performance of charters in our communities and communicate our concerns to legislators.

POSTSCRIPT

Can Charter Schools Revitalize Public Education?

Charter schools—are they a source of innovation, inspiration, and revitalization in public education or a drain on human and fiscal resources that will leave regular public schools weaker than ever? The debate has just begun, and preliminary results are just beginning to trickle in. But the air is filled with predictions, opinions, and pontifications.

Alex Molnar offers some scathing commentary on the charter school and privatization movements in his article "Charter Schools: The Smiling Face of Disinvestment," *Educational Leadership* (October 1996) and in his book *Giving Kids the Business: The Commercialization of America's Schools* (1996). A more positive assessment is delivered by Joe Nathan in his book *Charter Schools: Creating Hope and Opportunity for American Schools* (1996) and in his article "Heat and Light in the Charter School Movement," *Phi Delta Kappan* (March 1998). Further positive descriptions are provided in James N. Goenner's "Charter Schools: The Revitalization of Public Education," *Phi Delta Kappan* (September 1996) and James K. Glassman's "Class Acts," *Reason* (April 1998).

Additional sources of ideas include *How to Create Alternative, Magnet, and Charter Schools That Work* by Robert D. Barr and William H. Parrett (1997); "Homegrown," by Nathan Glazer, *The New Republic* (May 12, 1997); "Charter Schools: A Viable Public School Choice Option?" by Terry G. Geske et al., *Economics of Education Review* (February 1997); "A Closer Look at Charters," by Judith Brody Saks, *American School Board Journal* (January 1998); "Healthy Competition," by David Osborne, *The New Republic* (October 4, 1999); "Chinks in the Charter School Armor," by Tom Watkins, *American School Board Journal* (December 1999); and Seymour Sarason's *Charter Schools: Another Flawed Educational Reform* (1998).

Some recent provocative publications are Arthur Levine, "The Private Sector's Market Mentality," *The School Administrator* (May 2000); Bruce Fuller, ed., *Inside Charter Schools: The Paradox of Radical Decentralization* (2000); and Bruno V. Manno, "The Case Against Charter Schools," *The School Administrator* (May 2001), in which Manno responds to common complaints.

A few more articles worthy of note are "No Magic Bullet," *The American Teacher* (December 1997); "How to Revive America's Public Schools," *The World & I* (September 1997); "School Reform—Charter Schools," *Harvard Law Review* (May 1997); "The Political Challenge of Charter School Regulation," *Phi Delta Kappan* (March 2004) by Frederick M. Hess; and David Moberg's "How Edison Survived," *The Nation* (March 15, 2004). Multiple articles may be found in *The School Administrator* (August 1999), *Education and Urban Society* (August 1999), and *Phi Delta Kappan* (March 2002).

ISSUE 13

Is Home Schooling a Danger to American Society?

YES: Michael W. Apple, from "The Cultural Politics of Home Schooling," *Peabody Journal of Education* (Vol. 75, Nos. 1 & 2, 2000)

NO: Brian D. Ray, from "Home Schooling for Individuals' Gain and Society's Common Good," *Peabody Journal of Education* (Vol. 75, Nos. 1 & 2, 2000)

ISSUE SUMMARY

YES: Education professor Michael W. Apple examines the larger context of the "conservative restoration" in which much of the home schooling movement is lodged and sounds a number of socio-cultural warnings.

NO: Brian D. Ray, president of the National Home Education Research Institute, feels that in the historical struggle over the control of influences on the younger generation, home schooling has strengthened the side of freedom and democracy.

$\mathbf{T}$he home schooling movement, which has expanded during recent decades to number possibly as high as two million students, is another manifestation of parental concern over the quality and manipulativeness of the governmentally mandated school system. Reasons given for home schooling include concern about the public schools' learning environment, a desire for religion-based moral instruction, and dissatisfaction with academic performance.

Home schooling is legal in every state, but with a wide variety of controls, from states that have no regulations to states that require parents to submit test scores or professional evaluations of their students' progress, to use only state-approved curricula, and to allow home visits by state or local officials. According to Daniel Pink in "School's Out," *Reason* (October 2001), "home schooling has become perhaps the largest and most successful education reform movement of the last two decades." He cites *The Wall Street Journal*'s conclusion that "evidence is mounting that home schooling, once confined to the political and religious fringe, has achieved results not only on a par with public education, but in some ways surpassing it." Pink also contends that one of the great misconceptions about home schooling is that it turns kids into isolated loners. "In fact," he claims, "these children spend more time with adults, more time in the community, and more time with children of varying ages than their traditional-school counterparts."

The National Education Association, on the other hand, believes that home schooling cannot provide students with a comprehensive educational experience. The professional teachers' organization prefers that home instruction be given by persons who are fully licensed, that an approved curriculum be used, and that local public school systems determine credits earned for graduation for students entering from a home school setting.

Home schooling represents a rejection of traditional arguments for public schooling. Originally, according to education historian Joel Spring, the early common-school reformers believed that all children should attend public schools where they would learn to get along with others and learn a common morality and culture. Public schools were to create a community spirit. Home schooling, Spring claims, tosses all of these justifications out the window.

Paul T. Hill, in a balanced appraisal offered in "Home Schooling and the Future of Public Education," *Peabody Journal of Education* (Vol. 75, Nos. 1 & 2, 2000), comes to these conclusions: first, home schooling is part of a broad movement in which private groups and individuals are learning how to provide services that once were left to public bureaucracies; second, as home schooling families learn to rely on one another, many are likely to create new institutions that look something like schools; and third, although many home schooling families are willing to accept help from public school systems, they are far more likely to join the charter and voucher movements than to assimilate back into the conventional public school system.

This leaves a deeper-level question posed by Chris Lubienski in "Whither the Common Good? A Critique of Home Schooling," *Peabody Journal of Education* (Vol. 75, Nos. 1 & 2, 2000): Is home schooling a part of the general trend of elevating private goods over public goods? This is the theme of the two articles presented here, with Michael W. Apple raising warning flags about social and cultural effects of the home education movement and Brian D. Ray offering assurances of positive effects on society as a whole.

YES

Michael W. Apple

The Cultural Politics of Home Schooling

If one of the marks of the growing acceptance of ideological changes is their positive presentation in the popular media, then home schooling clearly has found a place in our consciousness. It has been discussed in the national press, on television and radio, and in widely circulated magazines. Its usual presentation is that of a savior, a truly compelling alternative to a public school system that is presented as a failure. Although the presentation of public schools as simply failures is deeply problematic,[1] it is the largely unqualified support of home schooling that concerns me here. I am considerably less sanguine.

In a relatively short article, I cannot deal at length with all of the many issues that could be raised about the home schooling movement. I want to ask a number of critical questions about the dangers associated with it. Although it is quite probable that some specific children and families will gain from home schooling, my concerns are larger. They are connected to the more extensive restructuring of this society that I believe is quite dangerous and to the manner in which our very sense of public responsibility is withering in ways that will lead to even further social inequalities. To illuminate these dangers, I have to do a number of things: situate home schooling within the larger movement that provides much of its impetus; suggest its connections with other protectionist impulses; connect it to the history of and concerns about the growth of activist government; and, finally, point to how it actually may hurt many other students who are not home schooled.

At the very outset of this article, let me state as clearly as I can that any parents who care so much about the educational experiences of their children that they actively seek to be deeply involved are to be applauded, not chastised or simply dismissed. Let me also say that it is important not to stereotype individuals who reject public schooling as unthinking promoters of ideological forms that are so deeply threatening that they are—automatically—to be seen as beyond the pale of legitimate concerns. Indeed, as I demonstrated in *Cultural Politics and Education* (Apple, 1996), there are complicated reasons behind the growth of antischool sentiments. As I showed there, there are elements of "good" sense as well as bad "sense" in such beliefs. All too many school systems are overly bureaucratic, are apt not to listen carefully to parents'

From *Peabody Journal of Education*, vol. 75, nos. 1 & 2, 2000, pp. 256–271. Copyright © 2000 by Lawrence Erlbaum Associates. Reprinted by permission.

or community concerns, or act in overly defensive ways when questions are asked about what and whose knowledge is considered "official." In some ways, these kinds of criticisms are similar across the political spectrum, with both left and right often making similar claims about the politics of recognition (see Fraser, 1997). Indeed, these very kinds of criticisms have led many progressive and activist educators to build more community-based and responsive models of curriculum and teaching in public schools (Apple & Beane, 1995).

This said, however, it is still important to realize that although the intentions of critics such as home schoolers may be meritorious, the effects of their actions may be less so.

Although there are many home schoolers who have not made their decision based on religious convictions, a large proportion have. In this article, I focus largely on this group, in part because it constitutes some of the most committed parents and in part because ideologically it raises a number of important issues. Many home schoolers are guided by what they believe are biblical understandings of the family, gender relationships, legitimate knowledge, the importance of "tradition," the role of government, and the economy. They constitute part of what I have called the "conservative restoration," in which a tense alliance has been built among various segments of "the public" in favor of particular policies in education and the larger social world. Let me place this in its larger context.

Education and the Conservative Restoration

Long-lasting educational transformations often come not from the work of educators and researchers, but from larger social movements that tend to push our major political, economic, and cultural institutions in specific directions. Thus, it would be impossible to understand fully educational reforms over the past decades without situating them within, say, the long struggles by multiple communities of Color and women for both cultural recognition and economic redistribution (see, e.g., Fraser, 1997). Even such taken-for-granted things as state textbook adoption policies—among the most powerful mechanisms in the processes of defining "official knowledge"—are the results of widespread populist and anti-Northern movements and especially the class and race struggles over culture and power that organized and reorganized the polity in the United States a century ago (Apple, 2000).

It should come as no surprise, then, that education is again witnessing the continued emergence and growing influence of powerful social movements. Some of these may lead to increased democratization and greater equality, whereas others are based on a fundamental shift in the very meanings of democracy and equality and are more than a little retrogressive socially and culturally. Unfortunately, it is the latter that have emerged as the most powerful.

The rightward turn has been the result of years of well-funded and creative ideological efforts by the right to form a broad-based coalition. This new alliance, what is technically called a *new hegemonic bloc,* has been so successful in part because it has been able to make major inroads in the battle over common sense—that is, it has stitched together different social tendencies and commitments creatively and has organized them under its own general leadership in issues dealing with welfare, culture, the economy, and—as many know from personal experience—education. Its aim in educational and social policy might best be described as "conservative modernization" (Dale, 1989). In the process, democracy has been reduced to consumption practices. Citizenship has been reduced to possessive individualism. And a politics based on resentment and a fear of the "Other" has been pressed forward.

There are a number of major elements within this new alliance (for more detailed discussion, see Apple, 1996). The first, *neoliberals,* represent dominant economic and political elites who are intent on "modernizing" the economy and the institutions connected to it. They are certain that markets and consumer choice will solve all of "our" social problems, because private is necessarily good and public is necessarily bad—hence, their strong support of vouchers and privatized choice plans. Although there is clear empirical evidence about the very real inequalities that are created by such educational policies (Lauder & Hughes, 1999; Whitty, Power, & Halpin, 1998), this group is usually in leadership of the alliance. If we think of this new bloc as an ideological umbrella, neoliberals are holding the umbrella's handle.

The second group, *neoconservatives,* are economic and cultural conservatives who want a return to "high standards," discipline, "real" knowledge, and what is in essence a form of Social Darwinist competition. They are fueled by a nostalgic and quite romanticized vision of the past. It is often based on a fundamental misrecognition of the fact that what they might call the classics and "real" knowledge gained that status as the result of intense past conflicts and often were themselves seen as equally dangerous culturally and just as morally destabilizing as any of the new elements of the curriculum and culture they now castigate (Levine, 1996).

The third element is made up of largely White working-class and middle-class groups who mistrust the state and are concerned with security, the family, gender and age relations within the home, sexuality, and traditional and fundamentalist religious values and knowledge. They form an increasingly active segment of *authoritarian populists* who are powerful in education and in other areas of politics and social and cultural policy. They provide much of the support from below for neoliberal and neoconservative positions, because they see themselves as disenfranchised by the "secular humanism" that supposedly now pervades public schooling. They are also often among those larger numbers of people whose very economic livelihoods are most at stake in the economic restructuring and capital flight that we are now experiencing.

Many home schoolers combine beliefs from all three of these tendencies; but it is the last one that seems to drive a large portion of the movement.

Satan's Threat

For many on the right, one of the key enemies is public education. Secular education is turning our children into "aliens" and, by teaching them to question our ideas, turning them against us. What are often accurate concerns about public schooling that I noted earlier—its overly bureaucratic nature; its lack of curriculum coherence; its disconnection from the lives, hopes, and cultures of many of its communities; and more—are here often connected to more deep-seated and intimate worries. These worries echo Pagels's (1995) argument that Christianity historically has defined its most fearful satanic threats not from distant enemies but in relation to very intimate ones. "The most dangerous characteristic of the satanic enemy is that though he will look just like us, he will nevertheless have changed completely" (Pagels, as cited in Kintz, 1997, p. 73).

Some of the roots of this can be found much earlier in the call of conservative activist Beverly LaHaye for the founding of an organization to counter the rising tide of feminism. In support of Concerned Women of America, she spoke of her concern for family, nation, and religion:

> I sincerely believe that God is calling the Christian women of America to draw together in a spirit of unity and purpose to protect the rights of the family. I believe that it is time for us to set aside our doctrinal differences to work for a spiritually renewed America. Who but a woman is as deeply concerned about her children and her home? Who but a woman has the time, the intuition, and the drive to restore our nation? . . . They may call themselves feminists or humanists. The label makes little difference, because many of them are seeking the destruction of morality and human freedom. (as cited in Kintz, 1997, p. 80)

It is clear from this quotation what is seen as the satanic threat and what is at stake here. These fears about the nation, home, family, children's "innocence," religious values, and traditional views of gender relations are sutured together into a more general fear of the destruction of a moral compass and personal freedom. "Our" world is disintegrating around us. Its causes are not the economically destructive policies of the globalizing economy (Greider, 1997), not the decisions of an economic elite, and not the ways in which, say, our kind of economy turns all things—including cherished traditions (and even our children)[2]—into commodities for sale. Rather, the causes are transferred onto those institutions and people that are themselves being constantly buffeted by the same forces—public sector institutions, schooling, poor people of Color, other women who have struggled for centuries to build a society that is more responsive to the hopes and dreams of many people who have been denied participation in the public sphere, and so on.[3]

As I noted at the beginning of this article, however, it is important not to stereotype individuals involved in this movement. For example, a number of men and women who are activists in rightist movements believe that some elements of feminism did improve the conditions of women overall. By focusing on equal pay for equal work and opening up job opportunities that traditionally had been denied to women who had to work for pay, women activists had benefitted many people. However, for authoritarian populists, feminism and secular institutions in general still tend to break with God's law. They are much too individualistic, and they misinterpret the divine relationship between families and God. In so doing, many aspects of civil rights legislation, the public schools' curricula, and so many other parts of secular society are simply wrong. Thus, for example, if one views the Constitution literally as divinely inspired, then it is not public institutions but the traditional family—as God's chosen unit—that is the core social unit that must be protected by the Constitution (Kintz, 1997, p. 97). In a time of seeming cultural disintegration, when traditions are under threat and when the idealized family faces ever more externally produced dangers, protecting our families and our children are key elements in returning to God's grace.[4]

Even without these religious elements, a defensive posture is clear in much of the movement. In many ways, the movement toward home schooling mirrors the growth of privatized consciousness in other areas of society. It is an extension of the "suburbanization" of everyday life that is so evident all around us. In essence, it is the equivalent of gated communities and of the privatization of neighborhoods, recreation, parks, and so many other things. It provides a "security zone" both physically and ideologically. Kintz (1997) described it this way:

> As citizens worried about crime, taxes, poor municipal services, and poor schools abandon cities, the increasing popularity of gated communities, . . . fortress communities, reflects people's desire to retreat. . . . They want to spend more of their tax dollars on themselves instead of others. . . . Further, they take comfort in the social homogeneity of such communities, knowing that their neighbors act and think much as they do. (p. 107)

This "cocooning" is not just about seeking an escape from the problems of the "city" (a metaphor for danger and heterogeneity). It is a rejection of the entire idea of the city. Cultural and intellectual diversity, complexity, ambiguity, uncertainty, and proximity to "the Other"—all these are to be shunned (Kintz, 1997, p. 107). In place of the city is the engineered pastoral, the neat and well-planned universe where things (and people) are in their "rightful place" and reality is safe and predictable.

Yet, in so many ways, such a movement mirrors something else. It is a microcosm of the increasing segmentation of America society in general. As we move to a society segregated by residence, race, economic opportunity, and income, "purity" is increasingly more apt to be found in the fact that upper classes send their children to elite private schools; where neighborliness is determined by property values; where evangelical Christians, ultraorthodox Jews, and others only interact with each other and their children are schooled in private religious schools or schooled at home (Kintz, 1997, p. 108). A world free of conflict, uncertainty, the voice and culture of the Other—in a word I used before, *cocooning*— is the ideal.

Thus, home schooling has many similarities with the Internet. It enables the creation of "virtual communities" that are perfect for those with specialized interests. It gives individuals a new ability to "personalize" information, to choose what they want to know or what they find personally interesting. However, as many commentators are beginning to recognize, unless we are extremely cautious, "customizing our lives" could radically undermine the strength of local communities, many of which are already woefully weak. As Shapiro (1999) put it,

> Shared experience is an indisputably essential ingredient [in the formation of local communities]; without it there can be no chance for mutual understanding, empathy and social cohesion. And this is precisely what personalization threatens to delete. A lack of common information would deprive individuals of a starting point for democratic dialogue. (p. 12)

Even with the evident shortcomings of many public schools, at the very least they provide "a kind of social glue, a common cultural reference point in our polyglot, increasingly multicultural society" (Shapiro, 1999, p. 12). Yet, whether called personalizing or cocooning, it is exactly this common reference point that is rejected by many within the home schooling movement's pursuit of "freedom" and "choice."

This particular construction of the meaning of freedom is of considerable moment, because there is a curious contradiction within such conservatism's obsession with freedom. In many ways this emphasis on freedom, paradoxically, is based on a fear of freedom (Kintz, 1997, p. 168). It is valued but also loathed as a site of danger, of "a world out of control." Many home schoolers reject public schooling out of concern for equal time for their beliefs. They want "equality." Yet it is a specific vision of equality, because coupled with their fear of things out of control is a powerful anxiety that the nation's usual understanding of equality will produce uniformity (Kintz, 1997, p. 186). But this feared uniformity is not seen as the same as the religious and cultural homogeneity sponsored by the conservative project. It is a very different type of uniformity—one in which the fear that "we are all the same" actually speaks to a loss of religious particularity. Thus, again there is another paradox at the heart of this movement: We want everyone to be like "us"—"This is a 'Christian nation'"; "Governments must bow before 'a higher authority'" (Smith, 1998); but we want the right to be different—a difference based on being God's elect group. Uniformity weakens our specialness. This tension between (a) knowing one is a member of God's elect people and thus, by definition, different; and (b) also being so certain that one is correct that the world needs to be changed to fit one's image, is one of the central paradox's behind authoritarian populist impulses. For some home schoolers, the paradox is solved by withdrawal of one's children from the public sphere to maintain their difference. For still others, this allows them to prepare themselves and their children with an armor of Christian beliefs that will enable them to go forth into the world later on to bring God's word to those who are not among the elect. Once again, let us declare our particularity, our difference, to better prepare ourselves to bring the unanointed world to our set of uniform beliefs.

Attacking the State

At the base of this fear both of the loss of specialness and of becoming uniform in the "wrong way" is a sense that the state is intervening in our daily lives in quite powerful ways, ways that are causing even more losses. It is not possible to understand the growth of home schooling unless we connect it to the history of the attack on the public sphere in general and on the government (the state) in particular. To better comprehend the antistatist impulses that lie behind a good deal of the home schooling movement, I need to place these impulses in a longer historical and social context. Some history and theory is necessary here.

One of the keys to this is the development of what Clarke and Newman (1997) have called the "managerial state." This was an active state that combined bureaucratic administration and professionalism. The organization of the state centered around the application of specific rules of coordination. Routinization and predictability are among the hallmarks of such a state. This was to be coupled with a second desirable trait, that of social, political, and personal neutrality rather than nepotism and favoritism. This bureaucratic routinization and predictability would be balanced by an emphasis on professional discretion. Here, bureaucratically regulated professionals such as teachers and administrators still would have an element of irreducible autonomy based on their training and qualifications. Their skills and judgment were to be trusted, if they acted fairly and impartially. Yet fairness and impartiality were not enough; the professional also personalized the managerial state. Professionals such as teachers made the state "approachable" by not only signifying neutrality, but by acting in nonanonymous ways to foster the "public good" and to "help" individuals and families (Clarke & Newman, 1997, pp. 5–7).

Of course, such bureaucratic and professional norms were there not only to benefit "clients." They acted to protect the state by providing it with legitimacy. (The state is impartial, fair, and acts in the interests of everyone.) They also served to insulate professional judgments from critical scrutiny. (As holders of expert knowledge, we—teachers, social workers, state employees—are the ones who are to be trusted because we know best.)

Thus, from the end of World War II until approximately the mid-1970s, there was a "settlement," a compromise, in which an activist welfare state was seen as legitimate. It was sustained by a triple legitimacy. There was (largely) bipartisan support for the state to provide and manage a larger part of social life, a fact that often put it above a good deal of party politics. Bureaucratic administration promised to act impartially for the benefit of everyone. And professionals employed by the state, such as teachers and other educators, were there to apply expert knowledge to serve the public (Clarke & Newman, 1997, p. 8). This compromise was widely accepted and provided public schools and other public institutions with a strong measure of support because, by and large, the vast majority of people continued to believe that schools and other state agencies did in fact act professionally and impartially in the public good.

This compromise came under severe attack as the fiscal crisis deepened and as competition over scarce economic, political, and cultural resources grew more heated in the 1970s and beyond. The political forces of conservative movements used this crisis, often in quite cynical and manipulative—and well-funded—ways. The state was criticized for denying the opportunity for consumers to exercise choice. The welfare state was seen as gouging the citizen (as a taxpayer) to pay for public handouts for those who ignored personal responsibility for their actions. These "scroungers" from the underclass were seen as sexually promiscuous, immoral, and lazy, as opposed to the "rest of us," who were hard-working, industrious, and moral. They supposedly are a drain on all of us economically, and state-sponsored support of them leads to the collapse of the family and traditional morality (Apple, 2000). These arguments may not have been totally accurate, but they were effective.

This suturing together of neoliberal and neoconservative attacks led to a particular set of critiques against the state. For many people, the state was no longer the legitimate and neutral upholder of the public good. Instead, the welfare state was an active agent of national decline, as well as an economic drain on the country's (and the family's) resources. In the words of Clarke and Newman (1997):

> Bureaucrats were identified as actively hostile to the public—hiding behind the impersonality of regulations and "red tape" to deny choice, building bureaucratic empires at the expense of providing service, and insulated from the "real world" pressures of competition by their monopolistic position. Professionals were arraigned as motivated by self-interest, exercising power over would-be costumers, denying choice through the dubious claim that "professionals know best." Worse still, . . . liberalism . . . was viewed as undermining personal responsibility and family authority and as prone to trendy excesses such as egalitarianism, anti-discrimination policies, moral relativism or child-centeredness. (p. 15)

These moral, political, and economic concerns were easily transferred to public schooling, because for many people the school was and is the public institution closest to them in their daily life. Hence, public schooling and the teaching and curricula found within it became central targets of attack. Curricula and teachers were not impartial, but elitist. School systems were imposing the Other's morality on "us." And "real Americans" who were patriotic, religious, and moral—as opposed to everyone else—were suffering and were the new oppressed (Delfattore, 1992). Although this position fits into a long history of the paranoid style of American cultural politics and was often based on quite inaccurate stereotypes, it does point to a profound sense of alienation that many people feel.

As I mentioned previously, there are elements of good sense in the critique of the state made by both right and left. The government has assumed all too often that the only true holders of expertise in education, social welfare, and so forth are those in positions of formal authority. This has led to a situation of overbureaucratization. It also has led to the state being "colonized" by a particular fraction of the new middle class that seeks to ensure its own mobility and its own positions by employing the state for its own purposes. However, there is a world of difference between acknowledging that there are some historical tendencies within the state to become overly bureaucratic and to not listen carefully enough to the expressed needs of the people it is supposed to serve, and a blanket rejection of public control and public institutions such as schools. This not only has led to cocooning, but it also threatens the gains made by large groups of disadvantaged people for whom the possible destruction of public schooling is nothing short of a disaster. The final section of my analysis turns to a discussion of this last point.

Public and Private

We need to think relationally when we ask who will be the major beneficiaries of the attack on the state and the movement toward home schooling. What if gains that are made by one group of people come at the expense of other, even more culturally and economically oppressed groups? As we shall see, this is not an inconsequential worry in this instance.

A distinction that is helpful here is that between a politics of redistribution and a politics of recognition. In the first (redistribution), the concern is for socioeconomic injustice. Here, the political–economic system of a society creates conditions that lead to exploitation (having the fruits of your labor appropriated for the benefit of others), economic marginalization (having one's paid work confined to poorly paid and undesirable jobs or having no real access to the routes to serious and better-paying jobs), and/or deprivation (being constantly denied the material that would lead to an adequate standard of living). All these socioeconomic injustices lead to arguments about whether this is a just or fair society and whether identifiable groups of people actually have equality of resources (Fraser, 1997, p. 13).

The second dynamic (recognition) is often related to redistribution in the real world, but it has its own specific history and differential power relations as well. It is related to the politics of culture and symbols. In this case, injustice is rooted in a society's social patterns of representation and interpretation. Examples of this include cultural domination (being constantly subjected to patterns of interpretation or cultural representation that are alien to one's own or even hostile to it), nonrecognition (basically being rendered invisible in the dominant cultural forms in the society), and disrespect (having oneself routinely stereotyped or maligned in public representations in the media, schools, government policies, or in everyday conduct; Fraser, 1997, p. 14). These kinds of issues surrounding the politics of recognition are central to the identities and sense of injustice of many home schoolers. Indeed, they provide the organizing framework for their critique of public schooling and their demand that they be allowed to teach their children outside such state control.

Although both forms of injustice are important, it is absolutely crucial that we recognize that an adequate response to one must not lead to the exacerbation of the other—that is, responding to the claims of injustice in recognition by one group (say, religious conservatives) must not make the conditions that lead to exploitation, economic marginalization, and deprivation more likely to occur for other groups. Unfortunately, this may be the case for some of the latent effects of home schooling.

Because of this, it is vitally important not to separate out the possible effects of home schooling from what we are beginning to know about the possible consequences of neoliberal policies in general in education. As Whitty et al. (1998) showed in their review of the international research on voucher and choice plans, one of the latent effects of such policies has been the reproduction of traditional hierarchies of class and race—that is, the programs clearly have differential benefits in which those who already possess economic and cultural capital reap significantly more benefits than those who do not. This is patterned in very much the same ways that the stratification of economic, political, and cultural power produces inequalities in nearly every socioeconomic sphere. One of the hidden consequences that is emerging from the expanding conservative critique of public institutions, including schools, is a growing antitax movement, in which those who have chosen to place their children in privatized, marketized, and home schools do not want to pay taxes to support the schooling of "the Other" (Apple, 1996).

The wider results of this are becoming clear—a declining tax base for schooling, social services, health care, housing, and anything "public" for those populations (usually in the most economically depressed urban and rural areas) who suffer the most from the economic dislocations and inequalities that so deeply characterize this nation. Thus, a politics of recognition—"I want to guarantee 'choice' for my children based on my identity and special needs"—has begun to have extremely negative effects on the politics of redistribution. It is absolutely crucial that we recognize this. If it is the case that the emergence of educational markets has consistently benefited the most advantaged parents and students and has consistently disadvantaged both economically poor parents and students and parents and students of Color (Lauder & Hughes, 1999; Whitty et al., 1998), then we need to examine critically the latent effects of the growth of home schooling in the same light. Will it be the case that social justice loses in this equation, just as it did and does in many of the other highly publicized programs of "choice"?

We now have emerging evidence to this effect, evidence that points to the fact that social justice often does lose with the expansion of home schooling in some states. A case in point is the way in which the ongoing debate over the use of public money for religious purposes in education is often subverted through manipulation of loopholes that are only available to particular groups. Religiously motivated home schoolers are currently engaged in exploiting public funding in ways that are not only hidden, but in ways that raise serious questions about the drain on economic resources during a time of severe budget crises in all too many school districts.

Let me say more about this, because it provides an important instance of my argument that gains in recognition for some groups (say, home schools) can have decidedly negative effects in other spheres, such as the politics of redistribution. In California, for example, charter schools have been used as a mechanism to gain public money for home schoolers. Charter school legislation in California has been employed in very "interesting" ways to accomplish this. In one recent study, for example, 50% of charter schools were serving home schoolers. "Independent study" charter schools (a creative pseudonym for computer-linked home schooling) have been used by both school districts and parents to gain money that otherwise might not have been available. Although this does demonstrate the ability of school districts to use charter school legislation strategically to get money that might have been lost when parents withdraw their children to home school them, it also signifies something else. In this and other cases, the money given to parents for enrolling in such independent study charter schools was used by the parents to purchase religious material produced and sold by Bob Jones University, one of the most conservative religious schools in the entire nation (Wells, 1999).

Thus, public money not legally available for overtly sectarian material is used to purchase religious curricula under the auspices of charter school legislation. Yet, unlike all curricula used in public schools that must be publicly accountable in terms of its content and costs, the material purchased for home schooling has no public accountability whatsoever. Although this does give greater choice to home schoolers and does enable them to act on a politics of recognition, it not only takes money away from other students who do not have the economic resources to afford computers in the home, but it also denies them a say in what the community's children will learn about themselves and their cultures, histories, values, and so on. Given the fact that a number of textbooks used in fundamentalist religious schools expressly state such things as Islam is a false religion and embody similar claims that many citizens would find deeply offensive,[5] it does raise serious questions about whether it is appropriate for public money to be used to teach such content without any public accountability.

Thus, two things are going on here. Money is being drained from already hard-pressed school districts to support home schooling. Just as important, curricular materials that support the identities of religiously motivated groups are being paid for by the public without any accountability, even though these materials may act in such a way as to deny the claims for recognition of one of the fastest growing religions in the nation, Islam. This raises more general and quite serious issues about how the claims for recognition by religious conservatives can be financially supported when they may at times actually support discriminatory teaching.

I do not wish to be totally negative here. After all, this is a complicated issue in which there may be justifiable worries among home schoolers that they are not being listened to in terms of their values and culture. But it must be openly discussed, not lost in the simple statement that we should support a politics of recognition of religiously motivated home schoolers because their culture seems to them to be not sufficiently recognized in public institutions. At the very least, the possible dangers to the public good need to be recognized.

Conclusion

I have used this article to raise a number of critical questions about the economic, social, and ideological tendencies that often stand behind significant parts of the home schooling movement. In the process, I have situated it within larger social movements that I and many others believe can have quite negative effects on our sense of community, on the health of the public sphere, and on our commitment to building a society that is less economically and racially stratified. I have suggested that issues need to be raised about the effects of its commitment to cocooning, its attack on the state, and its growing use of public funding with no public accountability. Yet, I also have argued that there are clear elements of good sense in its criticisms of the bureaucratic nature of all too many of our institutions, in its worries about the managerial state, and in its devotion to being active in the education of its children.

In my mind, the task is to disentangle the elements of good sense evident in these concerns from the selfish and antipublic agenda that has been pushing concerned parents and community members into the arms of the conservative restoration. The task of public schools is to listen much more carefully to the complaints of parents such as these and to rebuild our institutions in much more responsive ways. As I have argued in much greater detail elsewhere, all too often, public schools push concerned parents who are not originally part of conservative cultural and political movements into the arms of such alliances by their (a) defensiveness, (b) lack of responsiveness, and (c) silencing of democratic discussion and criticism (Apple, 1996). Of course, sometimes these criticisms are unjustified or are politically motivated by undemocratic agendas (Apple, 1999). However, this must not serve as an excuse for a failure to open the doors of our schools to the intense public debate that makes public education a living and vital part of our democracy.

Luckily, we have models for doing exactly that, as the democratic schools movement demonstrates (Apple & Beane, 1995). There are models of curricula and teaching that are related to community sentiment, that are committed to social justice and fairness, and that are based in schools where both teachers and students want to be. If schools do not do this, there may be all too many parents who are pushed in the direction of antischool sentiment. This would be a tragedy both for the public school system and for our already withered sense of community that is increasingly under threat.

Notes

1. It is important that we remember that public schools were and are a victory. They constituted a gain for the majority of people who were denied access to advancement and to valued cultural capital in a stratified society. This is not to claim that the public school did not and does not have differential effects. Indeed, I have devoted many books to uncovering the connections between formal education and the recreation of inequalities (see, e.g., Apple, 1990, 1995). Rather, it is to say that public schooling is a site of conflict, but one that also has been a site of major victories by popular groups. Indeed, conservatives would not be so angry at schools if public schools had not had a number of progressive tendencies cemented in them.
2. I am thinking here of Channel One, the for-profit commercial television show that is in an increasingly large percentage of our middle and secondary schools. In this "reform," students are sold as a captive audience to corporations intent on marketing their products to our children in schools (see Apple, 2000, and Molnar, 1996).

3. Of course, the very distinction between "public" and "private" spheres has strong connections to the history of patriarchal assumptions (see Fraser, 1989).
4. This is a particular construction of the family. As Coontz (1992) showed in her history of the family in the United States, it has had a varied form, with the nuclear family that is so important to conservative formulations merely being one of many.
5. See Re'em (1998) for an interesting analysis of some of this content.

References

Apple, M. W. (1990). *Ideology and curriculum*. Boston: Routledge & Kegan Paul.
Apple, M. W. (1995). *Education and power* (2nd ed.). New York: Routledge.
Apple, M. W. (1996). *Cultural politics and education*. New York: Teachers College Press.
Apple, M. W. (1999). *Power, meaning, and identity*. New York: Peter Lang.
Apple, M. W. (2000). *Official knowledge* (2nd ed.). New York: Routledge.
Apple, M. W., & Beane, J. A. (Eds.). (1995). *Democratic schools*. Washington, DC: Association for Supervision and Curriculum Development.
Clarke, J., & Newman, J. (1997). *The managerial state*. Thousand Oaks, CA: Sage.
Coontz, S. (1992). *The way we never were: American families and the nostalgia trap*. New York: Basic Books.
Dale, R. (1989). The Thatcherite project in education. *Critical Social Policy, 9*(3), 4–19.
Delfattore, J. (1992). *What Johnny shouldn't read*. New Haven, CT: Yale University Press.
Fraser, N. (1989). *Unruly practices*. Minneapolis: University of Minnesota Press.
Fraser, N. (1997). *Justice interruptus*. New York: Routledge.
Greider, W. (1997). *One world, ready or not*. New York: Simon & Schuster.
Kintz, L. (1997). *Between Jesus and the market*. Durham, NC: Duke University Press.
Lauder, H., & Hughes, D. (1999). *Trading in futures: Why markets in education don't work*. Philadelphia: Open University Press.
Levine, L. (1996). *The opening of the American mind*. Boston: Beacon.
Molnar, A. (1996). *Giving kids the business*. Boulder, CO: Westview.
Pagels, E. (1995). *The origin of Satan*. New York: Random House.
Re'em, M. (1998). *Young minds in motion: Teaching and learning about difference in formal and non-formal settings*. Unpublished doctoral dissertation, University of Wisconsin, Madison.
Shapiro, A. (1999, June 21). The net that binds. *The Nation, 268*, 11–15.
Smith, C. (1998). *American evangelicalism*. Chicago: University of Chicago Press.
Wells, A. S. (1999). *Beyond the rhetoric of charter school reform*. Los Angeles: Graduate School of Education and Information Studies, University of California, Los Angeles.
Whitty, G., Power, S., & Halpin, D. (1998). *Devolution and choice in education*. Philadelphia: Open University Press.

Brian D. Ray

 **NO**

Home Schooling for Individuals' Gain and Society's Common Good

People have been competing to control the education of children since the first *Homo sapiens* was born. Regardless of genteel and resourceful language and rationales promoting consensus building and democratic decision making during the past century and currently, historians of institutional education have revealed that education is typically a realm of contention. Education in the United States is no exception; history supports this claim. In like manner, the discussions about parent-led, home- and family-based education—home schooling—are simply a continuation of the struggle over who will control what goes into the minds and affects the hearts of children—the future full-fledged citizens of any nation.

Whether more persons should choose to home school is, at first glance, an insignificant issue, because currently about 89% of all 52 million U.S. conventional school students in kindergarten through Grade 12 are in state-run institutions, with the other 11% in private schools (U.S. Department of Education, 1998); only another estimated 1.2 million to 1.7 million are home educated (Lines, 1998; Ray, 1999). The issue, however, goes to the core of the centuries-old debate over who should be in the primary position of influence in the educational lives of children and what effect the answer has on society.

Both individual children and society are powerfully affected by today's educational arrangements for the younger generation. In essence, this article is about what is the best educational arrangement that should be promoted in America. An important starting place is to keep in mind that there is nothing that de facto supports the claim that a democratically mandated, tax-funded, and state-run institutional approach to controlling individual children's education is inherently the best approach to education in America. This is the nation made up of a liberty-loving people in a republic that is based on the fundamental premises, among others, that (a) all persons are created equal, (b) all persons are endowed by their Creator with certain unalienable rights (i.e., life, liberty, and the pursuit of happiness), (c) the government shall make law that neither establishes a religion nor prohibits the free exercise of religion, and (d) governments are to be limited in their powers (Declaration of Independence; U.S. Constitution, Article I and X).

From *Peabody Journal of Education*, vol. 75, nos. 1 & 2, 2000, pp. 272–293. Copyright © 2000 by Lawrence Erlbaum Associates. Reprinted by permission.

I am aware that scholars who put their faith in certain theoretical frameworks used for analysis of statements like the preceding (and the ones later in this paragraph) might accuse me of insensitivity and various self-serving, -centric-, myopic-, and power-based interests and paradigms. I am also aware that discussions about education and its reform, both recently and during the 1800s, have been laced with references to the alleged wants and needs of all kinds of particular groups (i.e., arbitrarily and subjectively selected subcategories of the human species). This constant cacophony of discord essentially revolves around what one group wants (or is told by someone else it should have) that another group has. Germane to this article, it should be noted that the preponderance of this debate and jostling for power, position, and entitlement occurs within and around the state-run school system (i.e., financed by individual citizens' tax payments at the county, state, or federal level). Either much less of this kind of debate occurs within the private school community, scholars and the media simply do not report on it, or both. Almost none occurs within the home education community. Considering this background of discord, especially within the state-run school system, the realm of careful thought about education may be helped by putting less emphasis on stereotypical skin color-, ethnic-, class-, gender-, sexuality-, and greed-based language, arguments, and polemics about groups. Rather, individual children and parents might be better served by rationales based on the concepts of the inherent worth of every person's life, altruism motivated by a balance of merit and grace, personal responsibility to help those who are in dire need and have little ability to help themselves, and voluntary giving rather than the government compelling one person to aid another. With these things in mind, I proceed to consider the benefits of home schooling to both individuals and to society.

Contemporary home-based education is not a novel form of education; rather, it is centuries old and both predates and outdates institutional schooling as most American children experience it today (Gordon & Gordon, 1990; Ray, 1999; Shepherd, 1986). Although an age-old practice, home-based education waned to near-extinction by the late 1970s in the United States. Because the institutionalization of education has so completely prescribed and constrained the educational experience and thinking of five generations of Americans, including those scholars, educational practitioners, policymakers, and laypersons today writing about home schooling and reading this article, my task is to make a simple presentation that will stimulate my readers to consider seriously that the schooling and institutions we ourselves have experienced and promoted are likely not the best thing for either individuals or for the ordered society with the least possible intrusion from the state. I think that today, as the millennia change, claims such as "I went to institutional schools and I turned out okay, didn't I . . . ?," "Public schools are what made America great" (Mungeam, 1993; see also Glenn, 1988), "Private education creates more divisiveness," and "We all know that the public common school best serves the common good" are hollow incantations that do little good in addressing the historical and pressing needs of any individual child or nation or humans in general. It is time for education reform-saturated researchers, philosophers, sociologists, teachers, policymakers, and parents to reconsider "the way it is" and consider "the way it might be."

I submit to the reader that five general areas of evidence and reasoning support the claim that home schooling is a good, if not the best, form of education for individuals and for society's common good. These five areas are (a) learned children who become learned adults, (b) children who are psychologically and socially healthy who become adults who are psychologically and socially healthy, (c) hardy and hearty families, (d) liberty in a just society with a nondominant state, and (e) persons with reliable character and value systems.

Learned Children

Discussions about educational reform over the past 20 years frequently have included concepts such as equity, access, race, and gender and ignored or deemphasized academic learning, despite the fact that one of parents' and students' primary interests today—as it has been throughout history—is that children learn how to read, write, compute, and know and understand some basics in the areas of science, history, and geography. It is the ability to read, write, compute, and generally communicate that historically has been one of the primary keys in terms of enabling an individual, in most countries, to do what he or she desires to do and to lead others along a preferred path. In this regard, then, how do the home educated appear to be doing?

The balance of research to date suggests that home-based education has a positive effect on children's academic achievement as compared to the achievement of those in classroom-based institutional schools. A few researchers have found no significant differences between the achievement of the home educated and of those in state-run schools. Most scholars, however, have found the home educated to be outperforming the public schooled whether the study has been local, state-specific, nationwide in the United States (e.g., Ray, 1990, 1997; Rudner, 1999), or in other countries (Priesnitz & Priesnitz, 1990; Ray, 1994; Rothermel, 1999). Typically, the home educated score at the 65th to 80th percentile on standardized achievement tests. More complete reviews of research on academic achievement clearly support the conclusion that the home educated are doing remarkably well (e.g., Ray, 1999; see also Ray, 2000/this issue).

Although these studies have been largely descriptive in nature and not causal comparative, statistical analyses suggest that even when background demographic traits are controlled, students taught mainly by their parents do well (Ray, 1990, 1997; Rudner, 1999; Russell, 1994). Various studies provide evidence that factors such as parent education level, family income, gender of student, degree of regulation of home schooling by the state, and whether the parents ever have been certified teachers show weak relation to these children's achievement. An increase in studies that more carefully control background variables (as did, e.g., Coleman, Hoffer, & Kilgore, 1982) eventually will tell us more about the effect of home schooling on achievement (Cizek, 1993; Ray, 1988; Wright, 1988).

Considering the characteristics that intrinsically may be a part of home schooling (e.g., individualization of curriculum for each student, increased academic engaged time, high levels of social capital, as delineated in Ray, 2000/this issue), it is not surprising that the home schooled do well in terms of the three

Rs, science, history, and geography. As Good and Brophy (1987) noted, private individualized tutoring—which, in many ways, is home-based education—"is the method of choice for most educational purposes, because both curriculum (what is taught) and instruction (how it is taught) can be individualized, and because the teacher can provide the student with sustained personalized attention" (p. 352).

Psychologically and Socially Healthy Persons

Americans, like those in other nations, value psychological and social health for their children in addition to good academic performance. Definitions of psychological and social health are likely to be very dependent on the theoretical orientation of the person doing the defining. Most adults, however, have a general idea of what it means to be healthy in these respects. A general and useful definition is that psychologically and socially healthy persons have (a) an efficient perception of reality, (b) an ability to exercise voluntary control over behavior, (c) positive self-esteem and acceptance by those around them, (d) an ability to form affectionate relationships, and (e) an ability to use their energy productively (Atkinson, Atkinson, Smith, Bem, & Nolen-Hoeksema, 1996, pp. 511–512; see also Meier, Minirth, & Wichern, 1982). Although less research has been performed in the domain of the psychological and social health of the home educated than in the realm of academic achievement, several of the preceding factors have been examined. Four areas of related research on the home educated suggest that they are doing as well or better than their conventionally schooled peers.

First, it should be emphasized that home schooling is actually home- *based* education. The parents are most often the primary decision makers about the daily activities, whether academic or social, of the children, and the majority of younger children's time is spent with their families. These children engage, however, in activities with a wide range of persons and groups and environments outside the confines of the home and family (Medlin, 2000/this issue; Ray, 1990, 1997; Wartes, 1987). In addition, as the children grow older, they spend an ever-increasing amount of time with persons and in places outside the home and family. The research base and my 15 years of close observation of the home schooling community indicate that the vast majority of home-educated children are nowhere near being socially isolated.

Second, research shows that home-educated children are healthy in terms of psychological and emotional health (Carlton, 1999; Medlin, 2000/this issue; Ray, 1999). They apparently have positive self-esteem and self-worth and live in psychologically sound families (Allie-Carson, 1990).

Third, one can infer from the research that those being home educated are doing well socially. Whether their well-being is related to interacting with others (Shyers, 1992), leadership potential (Montgomery, 1989), or being in families that are civically active (Smith & Sikkink, 1999; cf. Traviss, 1998), research indicates the home educated are doing as well or better than those in conventional schools (Medlin, 2000/this issue).

Finally, limited research to date suggests that the home educated are successful as young and older adults (Medlin, 2000/this issue). For example, home-educated girls are becoming young women who develop personal voice and ". . . the strengths and the resistance abilities that give them such an unusually strong sense of self" (Sheffer, 1995, p. 181). More generally, they are doing well in terms of academics just prior to and in college (ACT, 1997; Galloway & Sutton, 1995; Ray, 1997, 1999; Rudner, 1999), and many colleges are recruiting them actively (Ray, 1999). They are doing well in terms of critical thinking (Oliveira, Watson, & Sutton, 1994), leadership in college (Galloway & Sutton, 1995), and general life activities (Knowles & Muchmore, 1994).

In sum, studies indicate that home-schooled children and adults who were home educated are psychologically and socially healthy. As mentioned with regard to research on academic achievement, these studies have been mainly descriptive in nature and not causal comparative.

Hardy and Hearty Families

Humans throughout the centuries have recognized that families (i.e., a father, a mother, and children) are the core functional unit of society (Blankenhorn, 1995; Carlson, 1993; Popenoe, 1996; Wiggin, 1962). Healthy families make for healthy societies. Popenoe (1996) wrote that the empirical evidence "shows that by far the best environment for childrearing is in the home and under the care of the biological parents" (p. 214), and, generally speaking, the main generator of close, warm, and enduring relationships for individuals is marriage and the family. "Numerous studies show now . . . [that] a strong family structure is anti-poverty insurance" (Olasky, 1996, pp. 192–193; see also, e.g., Tucker, Marx, & Long, 1998; White & Kaufman, 1997). Especially pertinent at this time in American history when almost 30% of all children are born out of wedlock, Blankenhorn (1995) emphasized the necessity of parents, fathers in particular, investing energy and resources in their children: "Paternal investment . . . is an essential determinant of child and societal well-being" (p. 251). Furthermore, the research evidence has made clear that parent involvement in a child's life is crucial—perhaps the most significant factor—to a child doing well in the world of schooling and academics (Coleman, 1991; Coleman & Hoffer, 1987; Henderson & Berla, 1994; U.S. Department of Education, 1987, 1994). Of particular interest to those who emphasize the wants and needs of special groups, many researchers have pointed out the special importance of parent involvement in the lives of minority children. For example, Chavkin (1993) reported, "Unfortunately, the educational system has been less successful in educating this growing minority population than it has the majority population" (p. 1); parent involvement clearly improves student academic achievement, and minority students and children from low-income families have the most to gain from such involvement (p. 2).

Not only have members of the modern intellectual class (e.g., researchers) found that strong families are good for children and society, centuries of core belief systems (i.e., religions) have told people that families are important to the well-being of humans. One should note that I am using in this article a functional definition of religion—that is, *religion* generally means a set of beliefs that deal with ultimate concerns. As Baer (1998) explained, "Secular descriptions of reality . . . can function just like supernatural descriptions" (p. 107). With this in mind, one can say that religions have held for millennia that the family is an institution ordained by something or Someone greater than individual humans, and the family—both as an institution and particular groups of persons—is to be promoted and defended against degradation and loss of function.

For example, Christianity and Judaism, two religions significantly related to the history and traditions of the United States, both accord great importance to parents and the family. Meyer (1929/1983) wrote regarding education in ancient Israel:

> All education is at first religious in the sense that religious motives and ideas predominate in the educational efforts of all primitive peoples. . . . Here lies the explanation of the religious-educational character of Hebrew national life, and here, too, the secret of Israel's incomparable influence upon the religious and educational development of the world. The religion of Israel was a vital religion and it was a teaching religion. . . . The home was the only school [including learning to read and write] and the parents the only teachers. (p. 901)

Modern traditional Jewish thinkers concur:

> With respect to education, however, the traditional Jewish sources speak unequivocally, laying down a number of clear principles relevant to the current debate: (1) *Parents must have responsibility and control* . . . (2) *Teachers and schools are agents of parents* . . . control and responsibility remain with the parents. . . . The "education establishment" always remains accountable to parents. (3) *Education should inculcate values as well as knowledge.* Because of this, the Jewish tradition does not see education as purely secular. (Pruzan, 1998, p. 2; see also Lapin, 1993, 1999)

Likewise, traditional Christians today (including both Catholics and evangelicals) concur that parents have the primary and final rights and duties regarding the education of their children (e.g., Adams, Stein, & Wheeler, 1989; Ball, 1994; Clark, 1988; DeJong, 1989; Hardon, 1998; Hocking, 1978; Klicka, 1993; Skillen, 1998).

Based on more limited knowledge, I also understand that traditional Muslims today agree that the primary authority and duty regarding the education of children lies with parents (see, e.g., http://www.ArabesQ.com). Finally, I think it is clear that the large majority of adults in the United States today, regardless of what faith they might espouse (i.e., be it more natural- or supernatural-based), philosophically agree that parents hold the primary right and duty regarding children's education and are, ultimately, the ones best equipped to make educational decisions (cf. Phi Delta Kappa International, 1998).

Research does not yet clearly show whether home schooling creates hardy and healthy families. There is evidence, however, that this may be the case (Allie-Carson, 1990; Carlson, 1993, 1995; Lines, 1994; Romm, 1993; Smith & Sikkink, 1999).

If parent involvement in the lives of children is so critical—based on both research on children's academic success and major religious worldviews—and home-based education is essentially the epitome of parent involvement, then the vast majority of educators, ministers of faith, and parents should be rushing to embrace its practice. During the past 2 decades, in fact, there has been a rush toward home schooling by a relatively significant percentage of parents, but hardly by a majority of educators and ministers of faith. I do not have space in this work to address ministers of faith, but I must take space for the question of why, perhaps, educators are not more ardently advancing the practice of parent-led and home-based education. One might make a good case that the primary reason is the control of a colossal amount of money from taxation (e.g., Brimelow & Spencer, 1993; Lieberman, 1997; Toch, 1991). However, I do not expand on this possibility in this article. Giving educators some benefit of the doubt, I think that at present the answer mainly has to do with their personal conceptions of what is the common good with respect to liberty in a just society with a nondominant state.

Liberty in a Just Society With a Nondominant State

With respect to social and political life, liberty means several things: A person shall not be encumbered with respect to what he believes; the government shall neither try to stop a person from believing something nor try to make a person believe anything (U.S. Constitution). Liberty means that every person is allowed to be as kind and generous as he or she wants to be to any other person or group. A person is not allowed to harm another in any way that clearly violates a clear and unambiguous standard.

Within a freedom-loving nation such as the United States, liberty also entails the idea that a person's rights of life, liberty, and the pursuit of happiness will be guarded in a way that is clear and unambiguous (e.g., all adult persons may vote, any person may sit at the front of a room in a public-access building); it does not mean the government may coerce private persons to give money (e.g., via taxes), jobs, or privileges to other individuals or groups. Liberty means that the government shall not violate the private spaces and relationships of others (e.g., the home, the family, private business) unless there is clear and probable cause that something unlawful is taking place therein. Liberty does not mean, as some believe, license to do whatever one wants to do as long as it does not "clearly harm someone else."

It is clear that society ultimately must make choices of morality on many issues and correspondingly create and uphold law (Bauman, 1999). Each faith tradition, whether more anthropocentric or more theocentric, uses different approaches and standards regarding moral goodness. Judeo-Christian tradition would say that true liberty is attained in thought and action consistent with supernaturally revealed truth that should be the basis of a government's law and is therefore protected by the law. In a freedom-loving nation comprised of individuals with disparate worldviews (e.g., orthodox Jews, Marxists, neoliberals, and New Age adherents), passionate but respectful disagreement about the definition of liberty will continue for a long time. Perhaps more than liberty, justice has been the focus of American thinkers and policymakers during the past 2 decades.

As with the term *liberty,* justice's definition largely depends on one's worldview, one's functional religious presuppositions (see, e.g., Apple, 1993; Skillen, 1998; Welner, 1999). *Justice* has been defined in many ways:

> According to the Romans, justice meant "giving to each its due." Plato and Aristotle conceived of justice as the proper ordering of society, resulting from the rule of reason over passion in public deliberation. The biblical tradition ties justice to righteous conduct—that which is consistent with God's commandments, a proper respect toward the Creator and His creatures. Many today stress the concept of justice as "fairness." (Skillen, 1998, p. 1)

Although I cannot solve the debate here, I suggest that a just society is one in which government officials treat all individuals impartially and in accordance with all law that is constitutional and moral (i.e., good); the government punishes anyone who harms another person (see, e.g., Olasky, 1996, Appendix B; Old Testament, Rom. 13:3–4, New American Standard). A just society is not one in which the government is authorized to force one person or group to give something (e.g., money, a job, more control over capital) to another person or group; that is to say, a just society does not mean one in which those in power—be they political representatives, think-tank sages, university professors, or union leaders—use the force of law and the state to try to create a society that has an absence of differences in things like amount of money earned, kinds of jobs held, or "one's relationship to the control and production of cultural and economic capital" (Apple, 1982, p. 505) when compared by persons' skin color, ethnic background, religion, gender, or sexual practices. For example, a just society is not one that assumes the state has an obligation to meet an indeterminate number of unspecified "needs of all children" (e.g., Clinton, 1996, pp. 128–145; Welner, 1999, p. 2). The nuanced difference between protecting a right and assuring that a person obtains a benefit may be vague, and I again recognize that there may be passionate but respectful disagreement in a constitutional republic about what is a just society.

Fervent wrangling over the definitions of liberty and justice in the context of this nation's and the world's common good will continue. There is often little one can do, in the end, to make another person accept one's own definitions. This is the "nice" thing—the convenient and relaxing thing—about America; everyone may have his or her own opinion. There are many individuals and groups who know, however, that there is a way to ensure that others will accept particular definitions of liberty and justice (or other concepts such as the common good, correct social theory, the best functional religion for a nation). They merely give the state power to create and enforce a system that retains the appearance of noncoercion but effectively guarantees the majority of the population will be under the control of the state and will come to espouse these particular worldviews and notions of liberty and justice. State-controlled schools may be the perfect system to meet these ends.

To the advantage of those who want to use state-run schools to meet their desired ends, I recognize (and I think others hold a similar view; see, e.g., Baer, 1998; Ball, 1994; Everhart, 1982) that the state-run school system has become essentially the "default setting"—the natural, normal, unchallenged choice, so to speak—for most Americans. The implicit assumptions are so pervasive in the thinking and writing of Americans, even among those who are advocates of parental rights, duty, and ultimate authority with respect to children's education, that they often talk about "withdrawing" or "taking children out of" the state school system (e.g., Welner, 1999, p. 2). These terms are even used to describe parents who never sent their children away from themselves and a home-based environment to be taught and directed by the strangers and experts at the state institutions. The practice of sending children to state schools and the language that accompanies it is entrenched in America. It is the "what is," not necessarily the "what ought." Although this language is now ingrained, it is notable that the majority of American parents would choose private or home schooling rather than state-run schools if they thought they genuinely had the choice (Carper & Layman, 1997; Glenn, 1988, p. 284; Havermann, 1998; Phi Delta Kappa, 1998). Of special interest to those who focus on particular groups in the state-run system, Black adults appear to be more interested in authentic choice than do White adults (Glenn, 1988; McDowell, Sanchez, & Jones, 2000/this issue; Phi Delta Kappa, 1998).

Debate about the role of the state in education in America has been strong for well over a century (Arons, 1983; Ball, 1994; Everhart, 1982; Glenn, 1987, 1988; McCarthy, Oppewal, Peterson, & Spykman, 1981; McCarthy, Skillen, & Harper, 1982; Richman, 1994; Spring, 1990; Toch, 1991). I submit that those who promoted voluntary education under the authority of parents and First Amendment free associations and who opposed state-run schooling during the early history of the United States (e.g., the Voluntaryists; Glenn, 1988) were correct; the instruction, education, and indoctrination of children never should have been given over to the state and its agents. The practice of such has caused ceaseless strife among Americans, as Sowell (1993) explained, and it naturally causes the reduction of diverse and free thinking in the people of the United States (Ravitch, 1992). It appears that the desire of many proponents of state-run education over the past 200 years has been to control individuals and "the Other"—individuals or other groups of persons who think differently from oneself—to use the term in a way probably not intended by some (e.g., Apple, 1998).

Historical accounts provide insight regarding the motivations behind advocates of state-run education. For example, McCarthy et al. (1981) explained that Thomas Jefferson had tension in his thought

> between his theoretical commitment to individualism and his pragmatic bent toward collectivism. . . . Jefferson did not take a direct route to the state [guaranteeing societal order]. He turned instead to the school as the primary institution to guarantee the order and freedom he desired in

society. In Jefferson's thought the school gave up its autonomy to the state and became little more than a department of the state. And Jefferson saw nothing wrong with indoctrinating students into a philosophy of government as long as it corresponded to his understanding of orthodoxy.

Benjamin Rush . . . saw that Jefferson's program was but another form of sectarianism. . . . [But] he followed the same route into pragmatic collectivism that Jefferson followed. (p. 85)

Rush unabashedly predicted that "our schools of learning, by producing one general and uniform system of educator, will render the mass of the people more homogeneous and thereby fit them more easily for uniform and peaceable government" (McCarthy et al., 1981, p. 86).

Horace Mann was able to accomplish in the mid-1800s what Jefferson was not able to do in the late-1700s. As McCarthy et al. (1981) wrote, "Mann was successful in that he convinced enough people that a system of public schools which championed a supposedly nonsectarian religion was essential to the well-being of the social, economic, and political order of the state" (p. 86; see also McCarthy et al., 1982). Glenn (1988), likewise, historically and lucidly uncovered much of the thinking that has been behind the advocacy of state-run education in several nations; his findings also corroborate the kinds of thinking exhibited by Jefferson and Rush, as just noted.

It is crucial to recognize that many individuals holding notions that the state should be in control of future adult citizens are from this century, not only from past ones. For example, Wiggin (1962), of the University of Maryland, described herself as liberal in religion and in politics and firmly believes "that the proper place for a child or youth in a republican society is in a public elementary or secondary school" (p. viii) and that state-run schools are "a gigantic moral enterprise" (p. 36) in which society transmits to its citizens the correct answer to questions such as: "Who is an American? . . . What should this American know and what should be his behavior? . . . [and] How may he be a good American citizen?" (p. 36). A professor of education stated in 1981, "Public schools promote civic rather than individual pursuits" and "Each child belongs to the state" (as cited in Richman, 1994, p. 51). Winnie Mandela promised to South Africans in the early 1990s free and compulsory education and stated, "Parents not sending their children to school will be the first prisoners of the ANC [African National Congress] government" (Richman, 1994, p. 51). Apple (1993) explained the struggle that leads up to what becomes the "official knowledge" to be transmitted to future generations of students: "a *selective tradition* operates in which only specific groups' knowledge becomes official knowledge [of texts used in public schools]" (p. 65). A then-advocate of re-Christianizing state-run schools, Simonds (1993) promoted doing "indirect evangelism" in public schools by influencing the selection of curriculum materials that give a biblical view and omitting materials that promote nonbiblical views. He also stated that students "should be taught patriotism and the traditions of Western culture, as well as principles of self-government and democracy," and the "Judeo-Christian philosophy of life . . . should be included in textbooks and the teaching process as a matter of history and the basis for our values, and ethical practices" (p. 109). More recently, an educator and official at the Oregon State Department of Education whose area of authority is home schooling told me that the state, not the parents, should have ultimate authority in making sure that a child receives an education according to the state's demands (D. Perkins, personal communication, May 17, 1999).

Not all persons' desires to use state-run schools for control and social change are as obvious as some of those in the preceding paragraph. For example, a thinker such as Apple (1993, 1996) provides elaborate analyses of the complex issues involved and power being exerted within the realm of America's state-run schools and claims commitment to an ethical and political principle that, among other things, dignifies human life, sees others not as objects to be manipulated, and considers all persons acting as *"co-responsible subjects* involved in the process of democratically deliberating over the ends and means of *all* of their institutions" (Apple, 1993, p. 3). Regarding such seemingly virtuous goals, two very important things must be considered. First, it is common knowledge that a relatively small percentage of citizens—especially parents with school-age children—have ever (especially during the past 50 years) democratically deliberated over the nature and power relationships of state-run schools in any local, meaningful, and effective way. They are not the ones—and never have been, at least in recent history—deciding the nature of state-run schools or the official knowledge being promulgated therein. Second, the same persons who say others should not be manipulated or coerced with power also advocate the state's continuation as the proprietor of indoctrination. As an example, we can read what Apple (1996) had to say about state-controlled schools:

> Many of us have quite ambivalent feelings about the place called school. All of us who care deeply about what is and is not taught, and about who is and is not empowered to deal with these issues, have a contradictory relationship to these institutions. We want to criticize them rigorously and yet in this very criticism lies a commitment, a hope, that they can be made more vital, more personally meaningful and socially critical. If ever there was a love/hate relationship, this is it. . . . I certainly do not want to act as an apologist for poor practices [in schools]. Yet, during an era when—because of rightist attacks—we face the massive dismantling of the gains (limited as they are) that have been made in social welfare, in women's control of their bodies, in relations of race, gender, and sexuality, and in whose knowledge is taught in schools, it is equally important to make certain that these gains are defended. Thus, there is another clear tension in this volume. I want to both defend the idea of a *public* education, and a number of the gains that do exist, and at the same time to criticize many of its attributes. (pp. xv–xvi)

If by those like Apple "public" schools mean tax-funded and state-controlled schools, then there appears to be an inherent self-contradiction in their arguments in favor of peaceful democratic deliberation and against inequalities and dominating powers. On the one hand, they are disturbed that "the Others" (e.g., "rightists") have prevailed at times past in state-run schools and are now prevailing in too many ways (Apple, 1996, 1998, p. xvi), and they argue for nonmanipulative practices in society. On the other hand, they say they are glad they have made gains in certain areas (e.g., women's control over their bodies and whose knowledge is taught in schools) and want to hold on to those gains—gains that often have been attained via powerful political moves and the manipulation of others. My hypothesis (based on what I have read and experiences such as those I have had with educators at professional conferences like the annual meetings of the American Educational Research Association for more than a decade) is that these same persons who advocate state-run schools and the elimination of coercion and manipulation would like to teach children in state-run schools many specific attitudes and beliefs—that these people hold to be true—that are strongly objected to by "the Others" of different worldviews or religious persuasions. In other words, I infer that they are glad when they, or others who believe as they do, prevail in getting their way in the polity, curriculum, and official knowledge of the state-run schools.

Although it is difficult and risky to ascertain the motives of contemporaries, history provides both perspective and motivation to do so. I suggest that many of today's proponents of state-run education are no different from their colleagues of the past. Thankfully, scholars have pointed out that some of the most appalling regimes in memorable history were enamored with using state-run schools to control the thought of children and thus, eventually, the nation (Ravitch, 1992; Richman, 1994). By compelling children to be schooled and then only funding schools that are controlled by the state, a government is inherently acting inequitably toward one group of persons—those who do not want or choose not to put their children under the indoctrinating authority of the government. This coercive use of different scales for different persons is to be detested, and it violates the universally accepted golden rule (Prov. 16:11, 20:23; Matt. 7:12, New American Standard). In addition to other arguments about why state-controlled schools should exist and why children should attend them, some have argued that this is a way to protect children from their parents (e.g., their ineptitude, abuse, narrow-mindedness, crude influence). In response to this line of thought and to the others, it is important to remember certain things, as Skillen (1998) made plain:

> While it is true that public law should not misidentify the family as a totalitarian enclave in which parents may do anything and everything whatever to their children, it is also true that every public-legal attempt to "liberate" minor children from parents makes the minors subject to whatever legal, medical or other authority is then authorized to direct or influence their actions. Thus, not only are the children not liberated from all external authorities, but one of the most important non-governmental institutions of society is thereby weakened by the overwhelming power of the state. The family as an institution suffers injustice, as does the child who was created first for family life and, via the family, for eventual adult maturity and personal independence.
>
> In sum . . . I would argue that the failure to identify human beings correctly as persons-in-community and the family as the foremost community for children, when combined with the failure to discriminate

properly in law between adults and minor children, leads to the publicly unjust treatment of families and children. (pp. 3, 5)

Today's advocates of state-run education view the schools as a way to enact their vision of the good life, the good society, the common good. These schools are a way to keep millions of children (i.e., future adult citizens) under the tutelage of those who can teach them to think and act as they allegedly should.

However, in a nation that claims to be liberty-loving and an advocate of citizens' free thinking, there can be no room for an arrangement in which the state puts its citizens under its own particularistic and value-laden teaching. The functions of instruction, education, and indoctrination should be left in the hands of the private, personal, particular, and peculiar worlds of parents and their families and their volitionally funded and privately managed free associations. Any wrong behaviors that might proceed from teachings of these parents and their free associations would be tempered by clear and consistent law and related punishment for the violation thereof.

But, in the end, perhaps the discussion about who should have the main control over children's instruction and education does not revolve around one's conception of liberty in a just society with a nondominant state and to what extent and how one group should control another. Perhaps the conflict most essentially revolves around which values and beliefs (i.e., faith or religion; McCarthy et al., 1981, p. 111) should prevail in our society.

Persons With Reliable Character and Value Systems

There was a time when I thought—and most people still do think—that all Americans agree on the goodness of some basic traits such as honesty, faithfulness, dependability, kindness, and helpfulness. At this point in American history, and that of Western culture in general, however, it is difficult to say that we can even agree about the absolute goodness of these traits. Intellectual faith systems such as metaphysical naturalism (Johnson, 1995), postmodernism, and sociobiology seem to call into doubt anything of durability and stability in the realm of human ethics and morality. I hope to see an increasing percentage of our society possessing beliefs and expressing behaviors that are good. Among other things, these beliefs include treating all human beings as created equal: "They need no title or qualification beyond their simple humanity in order to command respect for their intrinsic human dignity, their 'unalienable rights'" (Keyes, 1999). But it is now clear that Americans are having great difficulty agreeing on even the character traits that so many once thought were fundamental. Intimately related to this goal, the quintessential issue regarding any child's education actually may be what value system or worldview should be taught to him or her, not what is the socially accepted definition of justice or whether honesty is always the best policy.

Proponents of compulsory schooling law and state-controlled schools, whether "leftists" or "rightists," are working, perhaps unwittingly, to make sure that something called the "common curriculum"—the one approved by those in positions of power—is taught to all (or most) children. Advocates of these government institutions hope they will long be the ones in positions of power. Conversely, most proponents of home schooling and parental choice and authority only want to make sure that their personally chosen curriculum is taught to their children. These folks are not asking the state or anyone else for money or power to teach their curriculum to anyone else. They are asking the state and their neighbors to assume that they, the parents, have the best interests of their children and society's common good in mind. In fact, these parents are only asking the state, and their neighbors and thinkers who empower and influence the agents of the state, to let them go about their lives peaceably and quietly in the privacy of their homes and communities with their children. Advocates of home-based education are familiar with the golden rule and the big issues of liberty and justice for all in society. These parents want the state to allow individual citizens to choose freely when and how they will help other parents.

In Closing

Home schooling allows parents, in a context of nurture and high social capital, to choose freely a unique and effective education for their children. Each year a child grows older gives the parents and the child more opportunity to forge stronger bonds and a richer, relationally developed curriculum. Parents and children in such an arrangement, under no compulsion or coercion from the state, are allowed to escape the hidden curriculum of others and of the state, choose texts for learning, and work together in their communities as they "see work–family–religion–recreation–school as an organically related system of human relationships" (Tyack, 1974, p. 15).

The battles over power and domination that riddle state-run schools cannot sap home schooling parents and their children of their strength, consume their energy, and destroy their zest for learning. Zeal for social justice, liberty, the common good, and being right with one's Creator can be approached from an environment of security, strength, and stability while the ever-maturing child year after year steps out into larger and more expansive spheres of challenge, democratic deliberation, and creative service to others.

The voices of those who are anti-home schooling, anti-parents' rights, and antichoice and of those who assert that home schooling causes "balkanization," "divisiveness," "social anarchy," "narrow-mindedness," "fundamentalism," "segregationism," and "possessive individualism" are increasingly hollow and impotent. Evidence supporting their claims is (and always has been) scarce to nonexistent (e.g., Caldwell, 1999; L. Berg, organizational specialist, National Education Association, personal communication, July 28, 1999). Furthermore—and tragically for this nation's children and to the chagrin of the proponents of state-run schools—the power struggles, illegal drug deals, racism (Greene & Mellow, 1998), violence, philosophical contention, religious censorship, lack of parent involvement, low academic achievement, high dropout rates, premarital sexual activities, teachers' and bureaucratic antiparental power (Baker & Soden, 1998), and greed-based high-stakes labor disputes that are associated with the halls and culture of public schools and so powerfully overshadow the significant incidents of success and joy therein make the common criticisms of parent-led home schooling look very wan and insignificant.

I have explained that the research evidence on home-educated children's learning, psychological and social health, and success in adulthood supports the inference that home schooling has very positive effects. Research and theory also suggest that home schooling is associated with, if not causes, strong and healthy families. I have argued that persons who desire liberty in a just society will embrace and advocate home-based education as the educational option of preference. Also, although several ideas I present and promote in this article may be outside the majority view of contemporary educators, thinkers, and those who publish in the field of education, I have documented that these ideas are certainly neither neoteric nor outside the realm of reasonable and bona fide discourse. Finally, I have posited that although debates over the meanings of and how to advance liberty and justice may continue forever, the issue of how we should make education available to children and youth is essentially a matter of which value system or worldview should be taught to them and who will control the decision; it should be their parents, not the state.

Home schooling is done out of intense care and concern for today's children. Research is clear that home schooling is chosen to (a) assure that children are academically successful, (b) individualize teaching and learning for each child, (c) enhance family relationships, (d) provide children guided and reasoned social interactions with youthful peers and adults, (e) keep children safe in many respects, and (f) transmit particular values and worldviews to the children (Ray, 1999). Parents do not engage in home education, by and large, to aid some group (be it a majority, minority, disadvantaged, or advantaged one). It is done for today's children, knowing that if they benefit, then society as a whole ultimately will benefit and thus the common good will be served.

Home schooling is a potent way of education and a rich social experience that had all but vanished by 1980 from the consciousness of the American people. Family-based and parent-led education is now back in strength and dynamism. Hundreds of thousands of people in America (and other countries) are enthusiastically developing the thesis that it liberates children and families. Home schooling gives parents and children an opportunity to escape the multiple dominating powers and special interest groups who constantly vie for control within the dominion of state-controlled schooling.

Although I have attempted in this article to put relatively little emphasis on subcategories of humans, it is critical to note in this age of such emphasis that both leftists and rightists, light-skinned and dark-skinned, poor and wealthy, those with special needs and those with talented and gifted children, and theists and humanists are joining the ranks of home schooling. Research and anecdotes indicate that involvement of a diversity is presently accelerating.

Home schooling is very open to the public. It frees children and families from the coerced consensus-building processes of the state-run schools. It gives individuals and groups the freedom to help others in direct, personal, immediate, and effective ways. Based on re-search and philosophical reasoning, I believe that in the long run home-based education academically and psychologically benefits children, emancipates persons to choose their social and political lives freely, and advances the common good of any nation.

References

ACT [formerly American College Testing]. (1997). *ACT high school profile; Home schooled composite report; HS graduating class 1997.* Iowa City, IA: Author.

Adams, B., Stein, J., & Wheeler, H. (1989). *Who owns the children? Compulsory education and the dilemma of ultimate authority.* Austin, TX: Truth Forum.

Allie-Carson, J. (1990). Structure and interaction patterns of home school families. *Home School Researcher, 6*(3), 11–18.

Apple, M. W. (1982). Education and cultural reproduction: A critical reassessment of programs for choice. In R. B. Everhart (Ed.), *The public school monopoly: A critical analysis of education and the state in American society* (chap. 14, pp. 503–541). Cambridge, MA: Ballinger.

Apple, M. W. (1993). *Official knowledge: Democratic education in a conservative age.* New York: Routledge.

Apple, M. W. (1996). *Cultural politics and education.* New York: Teachers College Press.

Apple, M. W. (1998). Are markets and standards democratic? *Educational Researcher, 27*(6), 24–28.

Arons, S. (1983). *Compelling belief: The culture of American schooling.* New York: McGraw-Hill.

Atkinson, R. L., Atkinson, R. C., Smith, E. E., Bem, D. J., & Nolen-Hoeksema, S. (1996). *Hilgard's introduction to psychology* (12th ed.). New York: Harcourt Brace.

Baer, R. A. (1998). Why a functional definition of religion is necessary if justice is to be achieved in public education. In J. T. Sears & J. C. Carper (Eds.), *Curriculum, religion, and public education: Conversations for an enlarging public square* (pp. 105–115). New York: Teachers College Press.

Baker, A. J. L., & Soden, L. M. (1998). The challenges of parent involvement research. *ERIC/CUE Digest, 134.* (ERIC Document Reproduction Service No. 419 030 98).

Ball, W. B. (1994). *Mere creatures of the state?: Education, religion, and the courts, a view from the courtroom.* Notre Dame, IN: Crisis.

Bauman, M. (1999). The falsity, futility, and folly of separating morality from law. *Christian Research Journal, 21*(3), 20–23, 36–41.

Blankenhorn, D. (1995). *Fatherless America: Confronting our most urgent social problem.* New York: Basic Books.

Brimelow, P., & Spencer, L. (1993, June 7). The National Extortion Association? *Forbes.*

Caldwell, D. K. (1999, January 30). Death to the schools: Leaders of religious right calling for a Christian exodus out of public education. *Dallas Morning News,* 1G.

Carlson, A. C. (1993). *From cottage to work station: The family's search for social harmony in the industrial age.* San Francisco: Ignatius.

Carlson, A. C. (1995). Preserving the family for the new millennium: A policy agenda. *The Family in America, 9*(3), 1–8.

Carlton, B. (1999). A systemic view of the socialization of home schoolers. *Private School Monitor, 20*(3), 7–9.

Carper, J. C., & Layman, J. (1997, Winter). Black-flight academies: The new Christian day schools. *Educational Forum, 61,* 114–121.

Chavkin, N. F. (Ed.). (1993). *Families and schools in a pluralistic society*. Albany: State University of New York Press.

Cizek, G. J. (1993). The mismeasure of home schooling effectiveness: A commentary. *Home School Researcher, 9*(3), 1–4.

Clark, G. H. (1988). *A Christian philosophy of education* (2nd rev. ed.). Jefferson, MD: Trinity Foundation.

Clinton, H. R. (1996). *It takes a village: And other lessons children teach us*. New York: Simon & Schuster.

Coleman, J. S. (1991). *Policy perspectives: Parental involvement in education*. Washington, DC: U.S. Department of Education, Office of Educational Research and Improvement.

Coleman, J. S., & Hoffer, T. (1987). *Public and private high schools: The impact of communities*. New York: Basic Books.

Coleman, J. S., Hoffer, T., & Kilgore, S. (1982). *High school achievement: Public, Catholic, and private schools compared*. New York: Basic Books.

DeJong, N. (1989). *Education in the truth*. Lansing, IL: Redeemer.

Everhart, R. B. (Ed.). (1982). *The public school monopoly: A critical analysis of education and the state in American society*. Cambridge, MA: Ballinger.

Galloway, R. A., & Sutton, J. P. (1995). Home schooled and conventionally schooled high school graduates: A comparison of aptitude for and achievement in college English. *Home School Researcher, 11*(1), 1–9.

Glenn, C. L. (1987). "Molding" citizens. In R. J. Neuhaus (Ed.), *Democracy and the renewal of public education* (pp. 25–56). Grand Rapids, MI: Eerdmans.

Glenn, C. L. (1988). *The myth of the common school*. Amherst: University of Massachusetts Press.

Good, T. L., & Brophy, J. E. (1987). *Looking in classrooms* (4th ed.). New York: Harper & Row.

Gordon, E. E., & Gordon, E. H. (1990). *Centuries of tutoring: A history of alternative education in America and Western Europe*. Lanham, MD: University Press of America.

Greene, J. P., & Mellow, N. (1998, September). *Integration where it counts: A study of racial integration in public and private school lunchrooms*. Paper presented at the meeting of the American Political Science Association, Boston. (Available at www.schoolchoices.org/roo/jay1.htm)

Hardon, J. (1998). Father Hardon on home schooling. *Seton Home Study School, 15*(11), 4–5.

Havermann, J. (1998, May). A private rescue mission. *Citizen, 12*(5), 16–17.

Henderson, A. T., & Berla, N. (Eds.). (1994). *A new generation of evidence: The family is critical to student achievement*. Washington, DC: National Committee for Citizens in Education.

Hocking, D. L. (1978). The theological basis for the philosophy of Christian school education. In P. A. Kienel (Ed.), *The philosophy of Christian school education* (Rev. ed., pp. 7–28). Whittier, CA: Association of Christian Schools International.

Johnson, P. E. (1995). *Reason in the balance: The case against naturalism in science, law, and education*. Downers Grove, IL: InterVarsity.

Keyes, A. (1999, July 30). The armed defense of liberty. WorldNetDaily.com [Online]. Retrieved July 30, 1999 from the World Wide Web: www.worldnetdaily.com/bluesky_keyes/19990730_xcake_the_armed_.shtml

Klicka, C. J. (1993). *The right choice*. Gresham, OR: Noble.

Knowles, J. G., & Muchmore, J. A. (1994, April). *"Yep? We're grown-up home schooled kids—and we're doing just fine, thank you very much."* Paper presented at the annual meeting of the American Educational Research Association, New Orleans, LA.

Lapin, D. (1993, November). Parents versus the state. *Crisis*.

Lapin, D. (1999). *America's real war*. Sisters, OR: Multnomah.

Lieberman, M. (1997). *The teacher unions*. New York: Free Press.

Lines, P. M. (1994). Homeschooling: Private choices and public obligations. *Home School Researcher, 10*(3), 9–26.

Lines, P. M. (1998). *Homeschoolers: Estimating numbers and growth.* Washington, DC: U.S. Department of Education, Office of Educational Research and Improvement, National Institute on Student Achievement, Curriculum, and Assessment.

McCarthy, R., Oppewal, D., Peterson, W., & Spykman, G. (1981). *Society, state, and schools: A case for structural and confessional pluralism.* Grand Rapids, MI: Eerdmans.

McCarthy, R. M., Skillen, J. W., & Harper, W. A. (1982). *Disestablishment a second time: Genuine pluralism for American schools.* Grand Rapids, MI: Eerdmans.

McDowell, S. A., Sanchez, A. S., & Jones, S. S. (2000/this issue). Participation and perception: Looking at home schooling through a multicultural lens. *Peabody Journal of Education, 75*(1&2), 124–146.

Medlin, R. G. (2000/this issue). Home schooling and the question of socialization. *Peabody Journal of Education, 75*(1&2), 107–123.

Meier, P. D., Minirth, F. B., & Wichern, F. (1982). *Introduction to psychology and counseling.* Grand Rapids, MI: Baker Book House.

Meyer, H. H. (1983). Education. In J. Orr (Ed.), *International standard Bible encyclopedia* (Vol. 2, pp. 900–905). Grand Rapids, MI: Eerdmans. (Original work published 1929).

Montgomery, L. R. (1989). The effect of home schooling on the leadership skills of home schooled students. *Home School Researcher, 5*(1), 1–10.

Mungeam, F. (Executive Producer). (1993, December 5). *Town hall show.* Portland, OR: KATU Television.

Olasky, M. (1996). *Renewing American compassion: How compassion for the needy can turn ordinary citizens into heroes.* New York: Free Press.

de Oliveira, P. C. M., Watson, T. G., & Sutton, J. P. (1994). Differences in critical thinking skills among students educated in public schools, Christian schools, and home schools. *Home School Researcher, 10*(4), 1–8.

Phi Delta Kappa International. (1998). *The 30th annual Phi Delta Kappa/Gallup poll of the public's attitudes toward the public schools* [Online]. Retrieved April 13, 2000 from the World Wide Web: http://www.pdkintl.org/kappan/kp9809-1a.htm

Popenoe, D. (1996). *Life without father: Compelling new evidence that fatherhood and marriage are indispensable for the good of children and society.* New York: Free Press.

Priesnitz, W., & Priesnitz, H. (1990, March). *Home-based education in Canada: An investigation.* Unionville, Ontario: The Alternative Press. (Available from The Alternative Press, 195 Markville Road, Unionville, Ontario L3R 4V8, Canada)

Pruzan, A. (1998). *Toward tradition on educational vouchers/school choice.* Mercer Island, WA: Toward Tradition.

Ravitch, D. (1992). The role of private schools in American education. In P. R. Kane (Ed.), *Independent schools, independent thinkers* (pp. 20–26). San Francisco: Jossey-Bass.

Ray, B. D. (1988). Home schools: A synthesis of research on characteristics and learner outcomes. *Education and Urban Society, 21*(1), 16–31.

Ray, B. D. (1990). *A nationwide study of home education: Family characteristics, legal matters, and student achievement.* Salem, OR: National Home Education Research Institute.

Ray, B. D. (1994). *A nationwide study of home education in Canada: Family characteristics, student achievement, and other topics.* Salem, OR: National Home Education Research Institute.

Ray, B. D. (1997). *Strengths of their own—Home schoolers across America: Academic achievement, family characteristics, and longitudinal traits.* Salem, OR: National Home Education Research Institute.

Ray, B. D. (1999). *Home schooling on the threshold: A survey of research at the dawn of the new millennium.* Salem, OR: National Home Education Research Institute.

Ray, B. D. (2000/this issue). Home schooling: The ameliorator of negative influences on learning? *Peabody Journal of Education, 75*(1 & 2), 71–106.

Richman, S. (1994). *Separating school and state: How to liberate America's families.* Fairfax, VA: Future of Freedom Foundation.

Romm, T. (1993). *Home schooling and the transmission of civic culture.* Unpublished doctoral dissertation, Clark Atlanta University, Atlanta, GA.

Rothermel, P. (1999, Summer). A nationwide study of home education: Early indications and wider implications. *Education Now,* (24), 9.

Rudner, L. M. (1999). The scholastic achievement and demographic characteristics of home school students in 1998. *Education Policy Analysis Archives, 7*(8) [Online]. Retrieved April 13, 2000 from the World Wide Web: http://epaa.asu.edu/epaa/v7n8/

Russell, T. (1994). Cross-validation of a multivariate path analysis of predictors of home school student academic achievement. *Home School Researcher, 10*(1), 1–13.

Sheffer, S. (1995). *A sense of self: Listening to homeschooled adolescent girls.* Portsmouth, NH: Boynton/Cook.

Shepherd, M. S. (1986, September). The home schooling movement: An emerging conflict in American education [Abstract]. *Home School Researcher, 2*(3), 1.

Shyers, L. E. (1992). A comparison of social adjustment between home and traditionally schooled students. *Home School Researcher, 8*(3), 1–8.

Skillen, J. W.(1998). Justice and civil society. *The Civil Society Project, 98*(2), 1–6. (Available from The Civil Society Project, 3544 N. Progress Ave., Suite 101, Harrisburg, PA 17110)

Simonds, R. L. (1993). *A guide to the public schools: For Christian parents and teachers, and especially for pastors.* Costa Mesa, CA: Citizens for Excellence in Education.

Smith, C., & Sikkink, D. (1999, April). Is private schooling privatizing? *First Things, 92,* 16–20.

Sowell, T. (1993). *Inside American education: The decline, the deception, the dogmas.* New York: Free Press.

Spring, J. (1990). *The American school: 1642–1990* (2nd ed.). White Plains, NY: Longman.

Toch, T. (1991). *In the name of excellence: The struggle to reform the nation's schools, why it's failing, and what should be done.* New York: Oxford University Press.

Traviss, M. P. (1998, Fall). Racial integration and private schools: A summary of two of Dr. Jay Greene's articles. *Private School Monitor, 20*(1), 9–10.

Tucker, C. J., Marx, J., & Long, L. (1998, April). "Moving on": Residential mobility and children's school lives. *Sociology of Education, 71,* 111–129.

Tyack, D. B. (1974). *The one best system: A history of American urban education.* Cambridge, MA: Harvard University Press.

U.S. Department of Education. (1987). *What works: Research about teaching and learning* (2nd ed.). Washington, DC: U.S. Government Printing Office.

U.S. Department of Education. (1994). *Strong families, strong schools: Building community partnerships for learning.* Washington, DC: Author.

U.S. Department of Education, National Center for Education Statistics. (1998, February). *Mini-digest of education statistics, 1997.* Washington, DC: Author.

Wartes, J. (1987, March). Report from the 1986 home school testing and other descriptive information about Washington's home schoolers: A summary. *Home School Researcher, 3*(1), 1–4.

Welner, K. M. (1999, April). *Homeschooling and democracy: Exploring the tension between the state and parents.* Paper presented at the annual meeting of the American Educational Research Association, Montreal, Quebec, Canada.

White, M. J., & Kaufman, G. (1997). Language usage, social capital, and school completion among immigrants and native-born ethnic groups. *Social Science Quarterly, 78,* 385–398.

Wiggin, G. A. (1962). *Education and nationalism: An historical interpretation of American education.* New York: McGraw-Hill.

Wright, C. (1988, November). Home school research: Critique and suggestions for the future. *Education and Urban Society, 21*(1), 96–113.

POSTSCRIPT

Is Home Schooling a Danger to American Society?

Michael W. Apple, who is anything but an apologist for government-manipulated schooling, nevertheless sees the expansion of home schooling as a distinct threat to the democratic cultural value of public responsibility. While he lauds most home schooling parents for their good intentions, his main concern is with the effects of the movement as a part of a larger rightward turn in social policy and cultural values. This deeper level of analysis is continued by Brian D. Ray, who finds home educators, seen as liberty-loving people who realize the limitations of governmental power, to be perfectly in tune with America's cultural history. Margaret Talbot, in "The New Counterculture," *The Atlantic Monthly* (November 2001), does not see the movement as a threat to social cohesion. She states, "For ideologically or religiously motivated home schoolers, keeping their kids out of school is not a consumer's whim; it's the exercise of a constitutionally sanctioned right to guide their children's education in accordance with their most deeply held beliefs. And in a democratic society only condsiderations as profound as those are significant enough to outweigh the potential harm of sectarianism."

While this basic argument continues, new developments are diminishing the divide—online high schools, computer curriculum packages, and the allowing of home schooled students to participate in public school activities, services, and special classes. Also more colleges are accepting home schooled candidates for admission.

Additional sources on ideas on the issue include Randall A. Zitterkopf, "Home Schooling: Just Another Silver Bullet," *The School Administrator* (December 2000); Helen Mondloch, "Education Hits Home," *The World & I* (June 2000); George E. Pawlas, "Clearing the Air about Home Schooling," *Kappa Delta Pi Record* (Winter 2001); Sarah Deschenes, Larry Cuban, and David Tyack, "Mismatch: Historical Perspectives on Schools and Students Who Don't Fit Them," *Teachers College Record* (August 2001); Michael H. Romanowski, "Common Arguments about the Strengths and Limitations of Home Schooling," *The Clearing House* (November/December 2001); and Greg Beato, "Homeschooling Alone: Why Corporate Reformers Are Ignoring the Real Revolution in Education," *Reason* (April 2005).

John Taylor Gatto puts the case against government-controlled education this way: "School is like starting life with a twelve-year jail sentence in which bad habits are the only curriculum truly learned."

ISSUE 14

Is Full Inclusion of Disabled Students Desirable?

YES: Richard A. Villa and Jacqueline S. Thousand, from "Making Inclusive Education Work," *Educational Leadership* (October 2003)

NO: Karen Agne, from "The Dismantling of the Great American Public School," *Educational Horizons* (Spring 1998)

ISSUE SUMMARY

YES: Education consultant Richard A. Villa and education professor Jacqueline S. Thousand review the implementation of the Individuals with Disabilities Education Act and suggest strategies for fulfilling its intentions.

NO: Education professor Karen Agne argues that legislation to include students with all sorts of disabilities has had mostly negative effects and contributes to the exodus from public schools.

T he Education for All Handicapped Children Act of 1975 (Public Law 94–142), which mandated that schools provide free public education to all students with disabilities, is an excellent example of how federal influence can translate social policy into practical alterations of public school procedures at the local level. With this act, the general social policy of equalizing educational opportunity and the specific social policy of ensuring that young people with various physical, mental, and emotional disabilities are constructively served by tax dollars were brought together in a law designed to provide persons with disabilities the same services and opportunities as nondisabled individuals. Legislation of such delicate matters does not ensure success, however. Although most people applaud the intentions of the act, some people find the expense ill-proportioned, and others feel that the federal mandate is unnecessary and heavy-handed.

Some of the main elements of the 1975 legislation were that all learners between the ages of 3 and 21 with handicaps—defined as students who are hearing impaired, visually impaired, physically disabled, emotionally disturbed, mentally retarded, or who have special learning disabilities—would be provided a free public education, that each of these students would have an individualized education program jointly developed by the school and the parents, that each student would be placed in the least restrictive learning environment appropriate to him or her, and that parents would have approval rights in placement decisions.

The 1990 version of the original law, the Individuals with Disabilities Education Act (IDEA), has spawned an "inclusive schools" movement, whose supporters recommend that *no* students be assigned to special classrooms or segregated wings of public schools. According to advocates of the act, "The inclusion option signifies the end of labeling and separate classes but not the end of necessary supports and services" for all students needing them.

The primary justification for inclusion, or "mainstreaming," has traditionally resided in the belief that disabled children have a right to and can benefit from inclusion in a regular educational environment whenever possible. French sociologist Emile Durkheim felt that attachment and belonging were essential to human development. If this is the case, then integration of young people with disabilities into regular classrooms and into other areas of social intercourse—as opposed to keeping them isolated in special classrooms—would seem to be highly desirable.

Douglas Fuchs and Lynn S. Fuchs, in "Inclusive Schools Movement and the Radicalization of Special Education Reform," *Exceptional Children* (February 1994), pose this question: How likely is the "inclusive schools" movement to bring special education and general education into synergistic alignment? One viewpoint comes from a five-year government study released in 1994, which found that special-needs students who spend all their time in regular classrooms fail more frequently than those who spend only some. This report, along with the American Federation of Teachers' call for an end to the practice of seeking all-day inclusion for every child, no matter how medically fragile or emotionally disturbed, have helped to keep the issue boiling.

Abigail Thernstrom, in "Courting Disaster in the Schools," *The Public Interest* (Summer 1999), contends that the rights of the disabled stipulated under IDEA have made discipline a "nightmare." The 1997 amendments to IDEA, however, expanded the school's alternatives for dealing with disruptive special needs student. Such students can be suspended for 10 days (or more in some cases); can be placed in an alternative setting for up to 45 days, even over a parent's objection; and can be kept out of the regular classroom for an additional 45 days after a special hearing.

In the selections that follow, Richard A. Villa and Jacqueline S. Thousand contend that with commitment, creative thinking, and effective classroom strategies, inclusion can benefit all students. Karen Agne contends that the inclusion of emotionally disturbed and intellectually unfit students in regular classes robs other students of needed attention, robs teachers of their sanity, and does not serve the special needs students effectively.

Richard A. Villa and
Jacqueline S. Thousand

Making Inclusive Education Work

As an educator, you are philosophically committed to student diversity. You appreciate that learning differences are natural and positive. You focus on identifying and capitalizing on individual students' interests and strengths. But making inclusive education work requires something more: It takes both systems-level support and classroom-level strategies.

Since the 1975 implementation of the Individuals with Disabilities Education Act (IDEA), federal law has stated that children with disabilities have the right to an education in the least restrictive environment (LRE). According to the act, removal from general education environments should occur only when a student has failed to achieve satisfactorily despite documented use of supplemental supports, aids, and services.

During the past 28 years, the interpretation of what constitutes the least restrictive environment has evolved, along with schools' and educators' abilities to provide effective supports. As a result, increased numbers of students with disabilities are now served in both regular schools and general education classes within those schools.

When IDEA was first promulgated in 1975, schools generally interpreted the law to mean that they should mainstream students with mild disabilities—for example, those with learning disabilities and those eligible for speech and language services—into classes where these students could keep up with other learners, supposedly with minimal support and few or no modifications to either curriculum or instruction. In the early 1980s, however, the interpretation of least restrictive environment evolved to include the concept of integrating students with more intensive needs—those with moderate and severe disabilities—into regular classrooms. By the late 1980s and early 1990s, the interpretation evolved into the approach now known as *inclusion*: the principle and practice of considering general education as the placement of first choice for all learners. This approach encourages educators to bring necessary supplemental supports, aids, and services into the classroom instead of removing students from the classroom for those services.

As the interpretation of least restrictive environment has changed, the proportion of students with disabilities included in general education has increased dramatically. By 1999, 47.4 percent of students with disabilities spent 80 percent or more of their day in general education classrooms, compared

From *Educational Leadership*, October 2003, pp. 19–23. Reprinted with permission of the Association for Supervision and Curriculum Development. Copyright © 2001 by ASCD. All rights reserved.

with 25 percent of students with disabilities in 1985 (U.S. Department of Education, 2003).

Although the 1997 reauthorization of IDEA did not actually use the term *inclusion*, it effectively codified the principle and practice of inclusion by requiring that students' Individualized Education Programs (IEPs) ensure access to the general education curriculum. This landmark reauthorization broadened the concept of inclusion to include academic as well as physical and social access to general education instruction and experiences (Kluth, Villa, & Thousand, 2002).

Despite the continued evolution toward inclusive education, however, tremendous disparities exist among schools, districts, and states. For example, the U.S. Department of Education (2003) found that the percentage of students with disabilities ages 6–21 who were taught for 80 percent or more of the school day in general education classrooms ranged from a low of 18 percent in Hawaii to a high of 82 percent in Vermont. Further, the nature of inclusion varies. In some schools, inclusion means the mere physical presence or social inclusion of students with disabilities in regular classrooms; in other schools, it means active modification of content, instruction, and assessment practices so that students can successfully engage in core academic experiences and learning.

Why can some schools and districts implement inclusion smoothly and effectively, whereas others cannot? Three sources give guidance in providing high-quality inclusive practice. First, research findings of the past decade have documented effective inclusive schooling practices (McGregor & Vogelsberg, 1998; National Center on Educational Restructuring and Inclusion, 1995; Villa, Thousand, Meyers, & Nevin, 1996). Second, our own experiences as educators suggest several variables. Third, we interviewed 20 nationally recognized leaders in the field of inclusive education who, like ourselves, provide regular consultation and training throughout the United States regarding inclusive practice.

A Systems Approach

Successful promotion and implementation of inclusive education require the five following systems-level practices: connection with other organizational best practices; visionary leadership and administrative support; redefined roles and relationships among adults and students; collaboration; and additional adult support when needed.

Connection with Best Practices

Inclusive education is most easily introduced in school communities that have already restructured to meet the needs of their increasingly diverse student populations in regular education. Initiatives and organizational best practices to accomplish this aim include trans-disciplinary teaming, block scheduling, multiage student grouping and looping, schoolwide positive behavior support and discipline approaches, detracking, and school-within-a-school family configurations of students and teachers. These initiatives facilitate the inclusion and development of students with disabilities within general education.

School leaders should clearly communicate to educators and families that best practices to facilitate inclusion are identical to best practices for educating all students. This message will help members of the school community understand that inclusion is not an add-on, but a natural extension of promising research-based education practices that positively affect the teaching and learning of all students.

Visionary Leadership

A national study on the implementation of IDEA's least restrictive environment requirement emphasized the importance of leadership—in both vision and practice—to the installation of inclusive education. The researchers concluded,

> How leadership at each school site chose to look at LRE was critical to how, or even whether, much would be accomplished beyond the status quo. (Hasazi, Johnston, Liggett, & Schattman, 1994, p. 506)

In addition, a study of 32 inclusive school sites in five states and one Canadian province found that the degree of administrative support and vision was the most powerful predictor of general educators' attitudes toward inclusion (Villa et al., 1996).

For inclusive education to succeed, administrators must take action to publicly articulate the new vision, build consensus for the vision, and lead all stakeholders to active involvement. Administrators can provide four types of support identified as important by frontline general and special educators: personal and emotional (for example, being willing to listen to concerns); informational (for example, providing training and technical assistance); instrumental (for example, creating time for teachers to meet); and appraisal (for example, giving constructive feedback related to implementation of new practices) (Littrell, Billingsley, & Cross, 1994).

Visionary leaders recognize that changing any organization, including a school, is a complex act. They know that organizational transformation requires ongoing attention to consensus building for the inclusive vision. It also requires skill development on the part of educators and everyone involved in the change; the provision of extra common planning time and fiscal, human, technological, and organizational resources to motivate experimentation with new practices; and the collaborative development and communication of a well-formulated plan of action for transforming the culture and practice of a school (Ambrose, 1987; Villa & Thousand, in press).

Redefined Roles

For school personnel to meet diverse student needs, they must stop thinking and acting in isolated ways: "These are my students, and those are your students." They must relinquish traditional roles, drop distinct professional labels, and redistribute their job functions across the system. To facilitate this role redefinition, some schools have developed a single job description for all professional educators that clearly articulates as expected job functions collaboration and shared responsibility for educating all of a community's children and youth.

To help school personnel make this shift, schools must clarify the new roles—for example, by making general education personnel aware of their legal responsibilities for meeting the needs of learners with disabilities in the least restrictive environment. In addition, schools must provide necessary training through a variety of vehicles, including inservice opportunities, coursework, coteaching, professional support groups, and other coaching and mentoring activities. After clarifying teachers' new responsibilities and providing training, schools should encourage staff members to reflect on how they will differentiate instruction and design accommodations and modifications to meet the needs of all students. School administrators should monitor the degree of collaboration between general and special educators. They should also include implementation of IEP-mandated activities as part of ongoing district evaluation procedures.

Collaboration

Reports from school districts throughout the United States identify collaboration as a key variable in the successful implementation of inclusive education. Creating planning teams, scheduling time for teachers to work and teach together, recognizing teachers as problem solvers, conceptualizing teachers as frontline researchers, and effectively collaborating with parents are all dimensions reported as crucial to successful collaboration (National Center on Educational Restructuring and Inclusion, 1995).

Achievement of inclusive education presumes that no one person could have all the expertise required to meet the needs of all the students in a classroom. For inclusive education to work, educators must become effective and efficient collaborative team members. They must develop skills in creativity, collaborative teaming processes, co-teaching, and interpersonal communication that will enable them to work together to craft diversified learning opportunities for learners who have a wide range of interests, learning styles, and intelligences (Thousand & Villa, 2000; Villa, 2002a; Villa, Thousand, & Nevin, in preparation). In a study of more than 600 educators, collaboration emerged as the only variable that predicted positive attitudes toward inclusion among general and special educators as well as administrators (Villa et al., 1996).

Adult Support

An "only as much as needed" principle dictates best practices in providing adult support to students. This approach avoids inflicting help on those who do not necessarily need or want it. Thus, when paraprofessionals are assigned to classrooms, they should be presented to students as members of a teaching team rather than as people "velcroed" to individual students.

Teaching models in which general and specialized personnel work together as a team are effective and efficient ways of arranging adult support to meet diverse student needs (National Center on Educational Restructuring and Inclusion, 1995; Villa, 2002b). Such models include

- *Consultation.* Support personnel provide assistance to the general educator, enabling him or her to teach all the students in the inclusive class.
- *Parallel teaching.* Support personnel—for example, a special educator, a Title I teacher, a psychologist, or a speech language therapist—and the classroom teacher rotate among heterogeneous groups of students in different sections of the general education classroom.
- *Supportive teaching.* The classroom teacher takes the lead role, and support personnel rotate among the students.
- *Complementary teaching.* The support person does something to complement the instruction provided by the classroom teacher (for example, takes notes on a transparency or paraphrases the teacher's statements).
- *Coteaching.* Support personnel coteach alongside the general education teacher.

Promoting Inclusion in the Classroom

Several curricular, instructional, and assessment practices benefit all the students in the classroom and help ensure successful inclusion. For instance, in a study conducted by the National Center on Educational Restructuring and Inclusion (1995), the majority of the districts implementing inclusive education reported cooperative learning as the most important instructional strategy supporting inclusive education. Some other general education theories and practices that also effectively support inclusion are

- Current theories of learning (such as multiple intelligences and constructivist learning).
- Teaching practices that make subject matter more relevant and meaningful (for example, partner learning, project- and activity-based learning, and service learning).
- Authentic alternatives to paper-and-pencil assessment (such as portfolio artifact collection, role playing, and demonstrations).
- A balanced approach to literacy development that combines whole-language and phonics instruction.
- Thematic/interdisciplinary curriculum approaches.
- Use of technology for communication and access to the general education curriculum.
- Differentiated instruction.

Responding to Diversity

Building on the notion of differentiated instruction (Tomlinson, 1999), universal design provides a contemporary approach to facilitate successful inclusion (Udvari-Solner, Villa, & Thousand, 2002).

In the traditional retrofit model, educators determine both content and instructional and assessment strategies without taking into consideration the special characteristics of the actual learners in the classroom. Then, if a mismatch exists between what students can do and what they are asked to do, educators make adjustments. In contrast, educators using the universal design framework consider the students and their various learning styles first. Then they differentiate curriculum *content*, *processes*, and *products* before delivering instruction.

For example, in a unit on the history of relations between the United States and Cuba, students might access *content* about the Cuban Missile Crisis by listening to a lecture, interviewing people who were alive at that time, conducting Internet research, reading the history text and other books written at a variety of reading levels, or viewing films or videos. The teacher can differentiate the *process* by allowing students to work independently, in pairs, or in cooperative groups. Additional processes that allow learners of differing abilities and learning styles to master standards include a combination of whole-class instruction, learning centers, reflective journal writing, technology, and field trips. Finally, students may demonstrate their learning through various *products*, including written reports, debates, role-plays, PowerPoint presentations, and songs.

Thus, students can use a variety of approaches to gain access to the curriculum, make sense of their learning, and show what they have learned. A universal design approach benefits every student, not just those identified as having disabilities.

Differentiating to enable a student with disabilities to access the general education curriculum requires creative thinking. Four options suggest varying degrees of student participation (Giangreco, Cloninger, & Iverson, 1998).

- First, a student can simply join in with the rest of the class.
- Second, multilevel curriculum and instruction can occur when all students involved in a lesson in the same curriculum area pursue varying levels of complexity.
- Curriculum overlapping is a third option, in which students working on the same lesson pursue objectives from different curricular areas. A student with severe disabilities, for example, could practice using a new communication device during a hands-on science lesson while others focus primarily on science objectives.
- The fourth option, and the last resort, involves arranging alternative activities when a general education activity is inappropriate. For example, a student may need to participate in an activity within his Individualized Education Program, such as employment training in the community, that falls outside the scope of the general education curriculum.

Bridging the Gap

Systems-level and classroom-level variables such as these facilitate the creation and maintenance of inclusive education. Systemic support, collaboration, effective classroom practices, and a universal design approach can make inclusive education work so that students with disabilities have the same access to the general education curriculum and to classmates as any other student and the same opportunity for academic, social, and emotional success.

Inclusive education is a general education initiative, not another add-on school reform unrelated to other general education initiatives. It incorporates demonstrated general education best practices, and it redefines educators' and students' roles and responsibilities as creative and collaborative partners. The strategies described here can bridge the gap between what schools are doing well and what they can do better to make inclusion part and parcel of a general education program.

References

Ambrose, D. (1987). *Managing complex change.* Pittsburgh, PA: The Enterprise Group.

Giangreco, M. F., Cloninger, C. J., & Iverson, V. S. (1998). *Choosing outcomes and accommodations for children (COACH): A guide to educational planning for students with disabilities* (2nd ed.). Baltimore: Paul H. Brookes.

Hasazi, S., Johnston, A. P., Liggett, A. M., & Schattman, R. A. (1994). A qualitative policy study of the least restrictive environment provision of the Individuals with Disabilities Education Act. *Exceptional Children, 60,* 491–507.

Kluth, P., Villa, R. A., & Thousand, J. S. (2002). "Our school doesn't offer inclusion" and other legal blunders. *Educational Leadership, 59*(4), 24–27.

Littrell, P. C., Billingsley, B. S., & Cross, L. H. (1994). The effects of principal support on special and general educators' stress, job satisfaction, school commitment, health, and intent to stay in teaching. *Remedial and Special Education, 15,* 297–310.

McGregor, G., & Vogelsberg, T. (1998). *Inclusive schooling practices: Pedagogical and research foundations.* Baltimore: Paul H. Brookes.

National Center on Educational Restructuring and Inclusion. (1995). *National study on inclusive education.* New York: City University of New York.

Thousand, J. S., & Villa, R. A. (2000). Collaborative teaming: A powerful tool in school restructuring. In R. A. Villa & J. S. Thousand (Eds.), *Restructuring for caring and effective education: Piecing the puzzle together* (2nd ed., pp. 254–291). Baltimore: Paul H. Brookes.

Tomlinson, C. A. (1999). *The differentiated classroom.* Alexandria, VA: ASCD.

Udvari-Solner, A., Villa, R. A., & Thousand, J. S. (2002). Access to the general education curriculum for all: The universal design process. In J. S. Thousand, R. A. Villa, & A. I. Nevin (Eds.), *Creativity and collaborative learning* (2nd ed., pp. 85–103). Baltimore: Paul H. Brookes.

U.S. Department of Education. (2003). *Twenty-third annual report to Congress on the implementation of the Individuals with Disabilities Education Act.* Washington, DC: Author.

Villa, R. A. (2002a). *Collaborative planning: Transforming theory into practice* [Videotape]. Port Chester, NY: National Professional Resources.

Villa, R. A. (2002b). *Collaborative teaching: The coteaching model* [Videotape]. Port Chester, NY: National Professional Resources.

Villa, R. A., & Thousand, J. S. (in press). *Creating an inclusive school* (2nd ed.). Alexandria, VA: ASCD.

Villa, R. A., Thousand, J. S., Meyers, H., & Nevin, A. (1996). Teacher and administrator perceptions of heterogeneous education. *Exceptional Children, 63,* 29–45.

Villa, R. A., Thousand, J. S., & Nevin, A. (in preparation). *The many faces of coteaching.* Thousand Oaks, CA: Corwin Press.

NO

Karen Agne

The Dismantling of the Great American Public School

Everybody's talking about it. Public education, rarely a topic of discussion unless teachers are on strike or tax referendums proposed, is now under review everywhere people gather. The same concerns are being voiced in the checkout line, the dentist's office, the shopping mall. So prevalent is this topic that it's not necessary to take a formal survey to get the data. Just listen and take notes.

> "We took our kids out of public school and put them in Catholic school, and we're not even Catholic. The teacher was taking half the morning to get around to the 'regular' kids."
>
> "I'm staying home now to teach my kids. They weren't learning anything at school. We have a Home-Schooling Mothers group. Do you want to join?"
>
> "We had to move because that school had no program for our child; he's accelerated."
>
> "I'm not a teacher, but I'm home schooling. I got tired of hearing my child cry and complain every day about going to school. She was bored silly."
>
> "I don't want to be teaching. It's hard work and I'm afraid I might not be doing it right, but at least he gets individual attention now."
>
> "Public schools are just for kids with problems."

What happened? How did it all slip away while we weren't looking? "How could this be happening in this country?" parents want to know. In a word, inclusion happened. What does inclusion mean? Take a look:

A kindergarten teacher attempts to explain directions to the tiny charges seated on the rug before her. But a child with Down syndrome, focused on her own agenda, remains the center of attention as she crawls about pinching the bottoms of each child she reaches.

Ear-piercing screams come from a third-grade classroom where a behaviorally disabled child is expressing her displeasure at not being first to observe the science artifact being passed amongst her classmates. Her exhausted teacher says, "Oh, this happens every day. I have to call for help to watch my class while I take her out." The eight-year-old child refuses to walk and continues her high-pitched screams, punching and kicking at her teacher, as she

From Karen Agne, "The Dismantling of the Great American Public School," Educational Horizons (Spring 1998). Copyright © 1998 by Karen Agne. Reprinted by permission.

is carried bodily down the hall. Returning, the teacher offers, "They'll just bring her right back in here and we'll go through this again. This year I just pray to get through each day."

Several children talk or play together in one corner while classmates read or write. "What are they doing?" I ask. "Oh, they don't understand what we're working on," replies the teacher. "I'm told they're supposed to be here. I've tried, but I don't know what to do with them. An aide comes in for half an hour." This scene is repeated throughout the various classrooms of schools in several counties I've observed.

In some elementary schools teachers team up to get through the day. A disruptive, emotionally disturbed child is sent to sit in the other classroom to "calm down," after which time he may return to his assigned classroom. "This helps give the other children a little break from him," the teachers explain.

A special education teacher shares that she is paid to "teach" one student all year. At eleven years of age, this brain-damaged child is confined to a wheelchair. He cannot speak, he must be fed and diapered, and he "has never, in the three years that I've worked with him, ever demonstrated evidence of understanding anything," she explains. But this child is mandated by law to receive regular classroom time. This means that he is wheeled into a classroom each day. Every twenty minutes he begins gasping and must be suctioned to prevent choking. His specially trained teacher says, "I hate having to take him in there. Where's the benefit? He understands nothing. The other kids are frightened by his constant choking, and they can't just ignore the suctioning procedure. I worry about how much of their learning is lost. I worry that he's being used. But if anyone protests, the parents just holler 'Hearing! Hearing!' So there's nothing anyone can do." This single child is granted more than $140,000 per year to meet his special needs.

What I have related here is but a sampling of many such scenarios I have witnessed. How prevalent must this tendency be throughout the country? No one will speak of it, to avoid reproach as cruel, inhuman, or uncaring. The approach described here can hardly be considered advantageous to either the special needs students or their classmates, let alone their teachers. As a result, concerned parents around the country are quietly taking their "unchallenged" children out of our public schools.

While disquieted parents express their disappointment regarding the state of the public school, few ever utter a word suggesting that children with special needs be sent elsewhere, to other rooms or buildings. They lament only that the present approach, with everyone in the same group for academic activities, isn't working for all students; that, indeed, the majority of schoolchildren is falling behind.

Liberty and justice for all, in today's schools, has come to mean that everyone of the same age shall be lumped together in the same classroom, with the same teacher, regardless of a multitude of mental, emotional, and physical needs and requirements.

By analogy, if a horticulturist were to provide the same amount and type of food, water, soil, and light to every one of the hundreds of plants in her care, easily half would not survive. Moreover, it would surely require many years for the same professional to acquire enough varied knowledge and skill to ensure that each plant will survive, much less thrive.

Now, if every ten months each gardener's stock was replaced with a collection of completely new and different plants, only then would his task begin to compare even slightly with that of today's professional teacher. And the hopeful survivor in her care is of significantly deeper complexity; whose survival, yea, whose desired advancement, is of monumental importance in comparison.

Yet regular in-service teachers, already overtaxed and underpaid, are expected to take on even more responsibility and to educate themselves for the expertise necessary to care for these new special needs. Although special education teachers receive years of training and experience designed to prepare them for working with children of diverse learning needs, most regular classroom teachers receive none. Some new in-service recruits may have taken a three-hour course, suggested or required in their preparation. But, as many colleges of education adjust requirements to include a course in special education—a Band-Aid approach to the problem—countless teachers express resentment.

"If I had wanted to teach special education I would have trained for it. I'm not cut out for that. It takes a certain type of person. This isn't fair to me or to the special students assigned to my classroom."

But, wait a minute—if teachers and parents are so opposed to what's happening in public schools, who's responsible for these changes? How did this happen? Who or what, is to blame? And why is nothing being done about it?

How about P.L. 94-142, or IDEA, the well-known mainstreaming law? Heralded by social scientists and inclusion advocates as an educational equalizer, this "one size fits all approach"[1] is anything but equal. It has systematically removed the individual attention required by the most needy few, while simultaneously denying it to the mainstream majority of students. So, why has this faulty approach remained on the education scene? Because it's cheap! Politicians love it. Supporting this movement makes them appear benevolent but allows them to move funding, for which education is in dire need, to more popular, vote-procuring issues. No need to hire the quantity of specialists required to maintain settings in which student-teacher ratios used to be no more than eight to one. No press to provide accelerated programs for gifted students, for we're pretending that all students are gifted these days. No, these requisites no longer mesh with the "one size fits all" plan.

In spite of studies reported by the U.S. Department of Education showing that students with disabilities included in the regular classroom fail more often than do those taught in special settings,[2] proponents continue to press for inclusion. They urge modifying teaching methods and beliefs in ways designed to camouflage the problems and shoehorn all students into one "equal" mold. Some of these changes include the following:

- Knowledge of facts is not important.
- Students needn't know correct grammar, spelling, or punctuation to graduate.

- Memorization, multiple-choice exams, rewards, and competition are all old-fashioned.
- Ability grouping (except for athletics) must be eliminated.
- Honor rolls, advanced or honor classes, valedictorian, and salutatorian recognition must be eliminated.
- Assign group rather than individual grades.
- Use portfolios for "authentic" assessment.
- Raise standards, but don't use tests to detect mastery.
- Cooperative learning should be practiced 80 percent of the time in the classroom.
- Peer tutoring should be encouraged.
- Disruption in classrooms reflects teacher failure.
- Acceleration robs students of "normal" socialization.
- All students are gifted.[3]

A majority of these ideas are being parroted by educationists, 17 percent of whom have never been a classroom teacher and 51 percent of whom have not been a K–12 teacher in more than sixteen years.[4]

A look at our present school system reflects an anti-intellectual society, forged by a misguided, synthetic egalitarianism. The most able students in our society are being taught to devalue their abilities and also themselves. In many cases they are taught little else in today's schools.

Bumper stickers read, "My athlete can beat up your honor student!" Able students purposely underachieve in order to avoid labels like "geek," "nerd," and "dweeb." It's great to be a superior athlete but not even okay to be a superior scholar in an institution established to disseminate learning. Something is wrong with this picture.

A capable student finally drops out of public school, finding no peers, no appropriate programs, and no superintendent who will permit grade acceleration. Cause for great concern? Yes, but when this student can then proceed to pass college entrance exams and be accepted into several college programs without a high school degree, something is definitely amiss in our formula for assessment and decision-making. Clearly, this is not equal educational opportunity, for there is nothing so unequal as equal educational treatment of students with diverse abilities.

When we permit a few educationists to promote the overuse of certain methods as "best for all students"—when in fact these methods (cooperative learning, peer tutoring) obviously exploit the ablest students and systematically prevent their progress—we establish serious consequences in our schools. But when the Office of Gifted and Talented is eliminated; only two cents of every dollar for K–12 education is allotted to serve our most promising students; honors classes are dismantled; and a state rules that only disabled students may receive funding for special education; our public school system, yea, our society is dangerously compromised.[5]

Until we come to realize that education can never be equal unless each student is allowed and enabled to progress at his own highest rate, our efforts to reform our public school system will continue to fail. In our urgency to reform we seem to have fallen into a common trap produced by myopic vision. We can see only one way—either-or. This eliminates the possibility of a flexible middle, a healthy balance that permits commitment to all needs, however diverse.

For instance, regarding the inclusionists' list, much benefit may be afforded memorization capabilities. The fact that all children cannot commit certain information to memory, however, should not dictate eliminating that challenge for others. Many professions depend on rote memorization capability. Indeed, daily life may be enhanced by one's memorized information, selected thoughts, and ideas. There is a special feeling of security that comes with "owning" information. Students love participation in theatrical production, a wonderful way to practice memorization. The activity of brain calisthenics can be fun and rewarding.

Portfolios are not even a good, let alone "best," form of assessment, as Vermont discovered. Several years after the state adopted portfolio assessment, its schools were able to manage only 33 percent reliability.[6] That's because portfolios by nature are purely subjective, making them seriously unreliable for overall assessment purposes. Additionally, they are extremely time-consuming for students and teachers alike, while requiring enormous storage space, a luxury lacking in most schools.

"Authentic assessment," like "inclusion," sounds nice and appears more benevolent, but its purpose is to resolve one of the major problems of inclusion. Many included students cannot pass basic skills tests. But performance-based assessment methods are impractical for large-scale assessment and are not supported by many educational evaluation experts. Major concerns include the neglected issues of reliability and validity, the lack of consensus of how this form of assessment should be used, its ineffectiveness in complex subject areas, and the fear that reliance on such an approach reduces motivation for capable students. A common conclusion of educational psychometricians is that "authentic assessment is a fad that will be of only historical interest" in years to come.[7]

Multiple choice and standardized exams, on the other hand, although highly reliable and useful for determining mastery of basic skills, are certainly inadequate for measuring all human capabilities, especially those deemed most important, such as creativity and high-level problem solving. Shouldn't these factors serve to inform us that both methods are necessary for the most efficient and effective evaluation?

Cooperative learning, which may promote motivation for some students, enhanced socialization, and just plain fun in the classroom, is essential for many learning projects and endeavors. Although currently touted as some great panacea, it's hardly new. Effective teachers have always relied on student grouping, teams, squads, and the like for selected classroom purposes. Too much reliance on group learning, "discovery" methods, and peer teaching, however, can become counterproductive. Misinformation and unnecessary remediation may rob precious learning time. Teachers need to direct as well as facilitate. Students need individual study and on-task time. Each student must also be encouraged to seek her own directions, interests, and challenge levels.

Clearly, none of the various notions, methods, and ideas on the foregoing list of "inclusion-ordered" approaches is, by itself, effective. Each must be varied with the "old-fashioned" methods to ensure "best for all" learning. There must be a balance to serve students of all types and abilities equally.

Students must have some experience with others of like ability. Identical age grouping assumes that all students of the same age can learn together adequately. Yet one common definition of a gifted student is a comprehension level two chronological years beyond his same-age peers. When a child reads at three, circling alphabet letters in kindergarten is clearly not a challenge. When she relishes multiplication computer games at home, we must be prepared to ask more of her than to count to ten. We dare not pretend that there is no such thing as a gifted student or that all children are gifted.

Learners must also have time for individual study. Assigned seats placed in rows may well signal emphasis on control rather than learning, but occasionally this arrangement is perfect for the discerning teacher's purpose. Successful education for all requires appropriate individual challenge and remediation, as well as caring interaction and socialization among students. Most important of all is the teacher/student relationship, which is diminished when teachers must devote excessive time to many children with multiple needs. With distance-learning access on the rise, the opportunity for one-to-one interaction between each learner and her teacher becomes all the more crucial. A healthy mentoring relationship between the teacher and the student has always been and remains a pivotal factor for education excellence.

Successful schools must be prepared to offer all these approaches in order to serve all learners equally. It is not about either-or. People are not designed for either-or treatment. Incredibly, miraculously varied in their needs and capabilities, they also require an education with techniques and methods that can fulfill these unparalleled individual distinctions.

Such an education requires much support, much expertise, varied and multiple personnel needs, and therefore, enormous monetary backing. How much are our children worth? How much is our future worth? How can a nation that currently enjoys such increased prosperity afford not to invest in its children? There can be no either-or. All children must be served.

It is possible to build a great public school system, great because it offers everything needed for all its students; those who learn less easily, those who excel, and all those in between. But we can never achieve this ideal state until fanatical inclusionists and overzealous egalitarians allow a complete portrayal of our students, including encouraging and enabling the very highest capabilities among us.

In a poignant article, the father of a physically handicapped child afflicted with the rare Cornelia de Lange syndrome pleaded,

> The advocates of full inclusion speak glibly of giving teachers training necessary to cope with the immense variety of challenges which handicapped children bring to the classroom. No amount of training could prepare a regular teacher for Mark. The requisite expertise and commitment are found only among teachers who have chosen to specialize in the handicapped. Special education is by no means the unmitigated disaster its critics charge. The drive to ditch this flawed program in favor of a radical alternative will almost certainly result in just such a disaster.

One can only hope that we will not repeat the pattern of sabotaging our genuine achievements in the pursuit of worthy-sounding but deeply wrongheaded ideas.[8]

Notes

1. Albert Shanker, "Full Inclusion Is Neither Free Nor Appropriate," *Educational Leadership* (December/January 1995).

2. Lynn Schnailberg, "E.D. Report Documents 'Full Inclusion' Trend," *Education Week,* 19 October 1994, 17, 19.

3. Robert Slavin, "Cooperative Learning and the Cooperative School," *Educational Leadership* 45, no. 3 (1987): 7–13; Ellen D. Fiedler, Richard E. Lange, and Susan Winebrenner, *Roeper Review* 16 (1993): 4–7; and John Goodlad and Thomas Lovitt, *Integrating General and Special Education* (New York: Merrill, 1993), 171–201.

4. Public Agenda, a nonpartisan, nonprofit organization, *Different Drummers: How Teachers of Teachers View Public Education,* an opinion poll comparing ideas of the general public, in-service teachers, and teacher educators (New York: October 1997).

5. Ellen Winner, *Gifted Children: Myths and Realities* (New York: Basic Books, 1996) and Karen Diegmueller, "Gifted Programs Not a Right, Connecticut Court Rules," *Education Week,* 30 March 1994, 8.

6. Koretz et al., *RAND Corporation* (1992) studied the Vermont statewide assessment program. Average reliability coefficients ranged from .33 to .43. If the reliability of test scores is under .50, there is no differentiation in the performance of an individual student from the overall average performance of students. See also James Popham, *Classroom Assessment: What Teachers Need to Know* (Boston: Allyn and Bacon, 1995), 171–173 and Blaine Worthen, Walter Borg, and Karl White, *Measurement and Evaluation in the Schools* (New York: Longman, 1993), 441–442.

7. Thomas Brooks and Sandra Pakes, "Policy, National Testing, and the Psychological Corporation," *Measurement and Evaluation in Counseling and Development* 26 (1993): 54–58; James S. Terwilliger, "Semantics, Psychometrics, and Assessment Reform: A Close Look at 'Authentic' Tests," ERIC Document Reproduction Service #ED397123, 1996; and Louis Janda, *Psychological Testing: Theory and Applications* (Boston: Allyn and Bacon, 1998), 375.

8. Arch Puddington, "Life with Mark," *American Educator* (1996): 36–41.

POSTSCRIPT

Is Full Inclusion of Disabled Students Desirable?

One wit has stated that P.L. 94–142 was really a "full employment act for lawyers." Indeed, there has been much litigation regarding the identification, classification, placement, and specialized treatment of disabled children since the introduction of the 1975 act.

The 1992 ruling in *Greer v. Rome City School District* permitted the parents to place their child, who has Down's syndrome, in a regular classroom with supplementary services. Also, the decision in *Sacramento City Unified School District v. Holland* (1994) allowed a girl with an IQ of 44 to be placed in a regular classroom full time, in accordance with her parents' wishes (the school system had wanted the student to split her time equally between regular and special education classes). These cases demonstrate that although the aspect of the law stipulating parental involvement in the development of individual education programs can invite cooperation, it can also lead to conflict.

Teacher attitude becomes a crucial component in the success or failure of placements of disabled students in regular classrooms. Some articles addressing this and related matters are "Willingness of Regular and Special Educators to Teach Students With Handicaps," by Karen Derk Gans, *Exceptional Children* (October 1987) and Lynn Miller, "The Regular Education Initiative and School Reform: Lessons From the Mainstream," *Remedial and Special Education* (May–June 1990).

Other noteworthy articles are "Disruptive Disabled Kids: Inclusion Confusion," by Diane Brockett, *School Board News* (October 1994) and multiple articles in *Theory Into Practice* (Winter 1996), *Educational Leadership* (December 1994/January 1995 and February 1996), *Phi Delta Kappan* (December 1995 and October 1996), *Kappa Delta Pi Record* (Winter 1998), and *NASSP Bulletin* (February 2000). Also see Philip Ferguson and Dianne Ferguson, "The Future of Inclusive Educational Practice," *Childhood Education* (Mid-Summer 1998); Susan G. Clark, "The Principal, Discipline, and the IDEA," *NASSP Bulletin* (November 1999); and Jean Mueth Dayton, "Discipline Procedures for Students With Disabilities," *The Clearing House* (January/February 2000).

Of special interest are David Aloyzy Zera and Roy Maynard Seitsinger, "The Oppression of Inclusion," *Educational Horizons* (Fall 2000); Shireen Pavri and Richard Luftig, "The Social Face of Inclusive Education," *Preventing School Failure* (Fall 2000); Nathan L. Essex, "Americans With Disabilities: Are They Losing Ground?" *The Clearing House* (January/February 2002); Lewis M. Andrews, "More Choices for Disabled Kids," *Policy Review* (April & May 2002); Lisa Snell, "Special Education Confidential," *Reason* (December 2002); and Mara Sapon-Shevin, "Inclusion: A Matter of Social Justice," *Educational Leadership* (October 2003).

ISSUE 15

Is Size Crucial to School Improvement?

YES: Patricia A. Wasley, from "Small Classes, Small Schools: The Time Is Now," *Educational Leadership* (February 2002)

NO: Kirk A. Johnson, from "The Downside to Small Class Policies," *Educational Leadership* (February 2002)

ISSUE SUMMARY

YES: Education dean Patricia A. Wasley contends that schools and classrooms must be small if they are to be places where students' personal and learning needs are met.

NO: Policy analyst Kirk A. Johnson, of the Heritage Foundation, argues that while small scale is a popular concept when it comes to class size, the cost is not justified by research findings.

In the early days of American urban public schooling, local authorities, faced with increasing numbers of immigrant children, resorted to "monitorial schools" (based on a British model spawned by the Industrial Revolution) in which one teacher, abetted by monitors, could teach a class of 300 or more students. While this approach may have been expedient at the time, the twentieth century has seen a growing campaign for reduced class sizes at all levels of education.

Another historical trend was the movement toward consolidation of rural and small-town schools. From over 114,000 one-room elementary schools in 1940 to almost none in 1980, and from over 50,000 school districts in the 1950s to about 16,000 in the 1980s, the trend was obviously toward large schools. According to Robert L. Hampel, in "Historical Perspectives on Small Schools," *Phi Delta Kappan* (January 2002), the dominant beliefs were that large schools offer more opportunities for students, attract better teachers and administrators, and counteract provincialism. Since the 1980s, however, there has been a backlash against these beliefs, and advocates of small schools have joined small class proponents in exerting pressure on local, state, and federal authorities to fund size reductions.

While school size reduction has been handled primarily through internal reorganization such as schools-within-schools, the federal government, more than half the states, and countless districts have devised class-size reduction programs. As Jeremy D. Finn points out in "Small Classes in American Schools: Research, Practice, and Politics," *Phi Delta Kappan* (March 2002), the U.S. Department of Education, in an effort to reduce the size of classes in poor urban school districts, has paid the salaries of 29,000 new teachers, and in California alone 28,000 new teachers were hired in the first three years of a statewide class-size reduction initiative. Finn warns, however, that both federal and state efforts have been slowed by the recent economic instability and the shift in priorities brought about by the September 11 attacks.

In "Personalization: Making Every School a Small School," *Principal Leadership* (February 2002), Tom Vander Ark contends that small schools—a benefit enjoyed by affluent private school communities for 200 years—must be brought to inner-city areas to counter the crippling effects of poverty. He cites a Chicago study showing that more personalized small schools can improve attendance, achievement, graduation rates, safety, parent involvement, staff satisfaction, and community engagement. The small learning community strategy includes the forming of houses, academies, school-within-a-school programs, and small autonomous schools.

Positive notes on small classes are sounded by Anke Halbach et al. in "Class Size Reduction: From Promise to Practice," *Educational Leadership* (March 2001), who report on Wisconsin's Student Achievement Guarantee in Education (SAGE) begun in 1996. The program, reducing pupil-teacher ratios to 15 to 1 in disadvantaged K–3 classrooms, was shown to reduce discipline problems, increase instructional time and time for individualization, and support greater flexibility in learning activities. Similarly, Charles M. Achilles, Jeremy D. Finn, and Helen Pate-Bain, in "Measuring Class Size: Let Me Count the Ways," *Educational Leadership* (February 2002), report on positive results in Tennessee's Student Teacher Achievement Ratio (STAR) experiment begun in the 1980s. Contrarily, Eric A. Hanushek, in a recent Fordham Foundation report, "The Evidence on Class Size," maintains that student achievement will be unaffected by class size reductions and that the most noticeable result will be a dramatic increase in the costs of schooling.

In the following selections, Patricia A. Wasley draws on research and personal experience to make the case for small classes and small schools, whereas Kirk A. Johnson cites evidence showing little or no relationship between class size and achievement.

YES

Patricia A. Wasley

Small Classes, Small Schools: The Time Is Now

For many years, educators have debated the effects of class size and school size on student learning. The class size debate centers on the number of students a teacher can work with effectively in any given class period. The school size issue focuses on whether smaller schools encourage optimal student learning and development—and how small a "small school" must be to produce such effects.

. . . To frame the [issue], I want to pose a series of questions:

- Why have issues of class and school size gained prominence?
- What does the research say?
- What does my experience lead me to believe about the impact of class and school size on teaching and learning?

Why Are Class and School Size Important?

Issues of class size and school size have resurfaced as important school improvement ideas for a variety of reasons. First, the standards movement has encouraged the resurgence of the class size and school size debates. All U.S. states but one have academic standards in place. Of those states with standards, 36 use or plan to use test results to make high-stakes decisions about students. Standards enable educators and the public to clarify what they believe students should know and be able to do before the students leave school.

The standards movement has highlighted the fact that schools are largely inequitable places. Students in schools with large populations of disadvantaged students perform least well on standardized assessments. Evidence also suggests that these schools often have the least-experienced teachers (NCTAF, 1996; Roza, 2001). In effect, having standards in place emphasizes that standards are necessary but insufficient in themselves to improve student performance. Unless we change students' learning opportunities, especially for students who are ill-served by their schools, standards alone are unlikely to influence student learning. Educators and policymakers are looking for strategies that will enable students to succeed

From *Educational Leadership*, February 2002, pp. 6–10. Reprinted with permission of the Association for Supervision and Curriculum Development. Copyright © 2001 by ASCD. All rights reserved.

on the new assessments (thereby supporting the standards movement) and, more important, that will enhance students' learning opportunities. Small classes and small schools may be two such strategies.

Second, class size and school size issues have resurfaced because of the increasing consensus among educators and the public that all students can learn. When I began teaching in the early 1970s, teachers generally accepted the notion that some students had an exceptional aptitude for learning and others did not. At that time, my colleagues and I believed that as long as one-fourth of the students in a class performed exceptionally well and another half of the class did reasonably well, we were fulfilling our responsibilities as educators—even if one-fourth of the students in a class failed to learn at an acceptable level. We had been taught that the normal distribution of scores (the "bell curve") was what teachers should aim for and what we should accept as reasonable evidence of accomplishment. In the ensuing years, cognitive scientists, neurological biologists, and educators determined that all students have the capacity to learn. This new, convincing research means that no student should be left behind in the learning process. Educators need to examine all approaches to schooling to determine which strategies are most likely to return gains for students who typically have not done well in schools. Proponents of reduced class size and school size suggest that these factors contribute to the success of a broader swath of learners.

Third, following the events of September 11, educators have a renewed appreciation for the importance of the basic freedoms we enjoy and the advantages that a democracy provides its citizens. We know that a democratic citizenry must value differences among its participants. Schools should strive to develop in students the skills that they need to examine their differences productively and to coexist peacefully while protecting basic freedoms for all (Goodlad, Soder, & Sirotnik, 1990). Schools also have a central responsibility for helping students learn the basic skills of productive citizenry. Both class size and school size influence whether teachers are able to engage students in meaningful discussions of these issues and to help them build these crucial citizenship skills.

Renewed interest in class size and school size is broad-based and nationwide. The Bill & Melinda Gates Foundation has dedicated more than $250 million to reducing the size of U.S. high schools. The U.S. Department of Education has committed $125 million to fund small-school initiatives. In Boston, Chicago, and New York, small-school initiatives are under way. Small-school collaboratives, designed to support the change from comprehensive high schools to smaller learning communities, are springing up everywhere and include New Visions for Learning in New York, the Small Schools Workshop in Chicago (Illinois), the Small Schools Project in Seattle (Washington), and the Bay Area Coalition of Essential Schools in Oakland (California).

Lawmakers in Kentucky, California, Georgia, and Washington have passed legislation to reduce class sizes, believing that teachers will be better able to help all students meet the standards when the teacher-student ratio is substantially reduced.

What Does Research Tell Us?

The United States has had large schools for a relatively short period of time. Until the middle of the 20th century, most U.S. schools were small. In 1930, 262,000 U.S. public schools served 26 million students; by 1999, approximately 90,000 U.S. public schools served about 47 million students (National Center for Education Statistics, 1999). Responding to the recommendations of the Committee of Ten in 1894 and the authors of the Conant Report in 1959, proponents of the school consolidation movement suggested that schools would be more efficient and effective if they were larger. Single plants housing 500–2,000 students presumably could offer greater variety in subject matter, would provide teachers with the opportunity to track their students according to ability, and might put less strain on community resources (Wasley & Fine, 2000).

Research conducted on the validity of the assertions favoring large schools has suggested that less-advantaged students end up in the largest classes, with the least-experienced teachers and the least-engaging curriculum and instructional strategies (Oakes, 1987; Wheelock, 1992). Further research suggests that schools are organized more for purposes of maintaining control than for promoting learning (McNeil, 1988).

Powell (1996) examined independent schools in the United States and learned that private preparatory schools value both small school and small class size as necessary conditions for student success. In 1998, the average private school class size was 16.6 at the elementary level and 11.6 at the high school level. By contrast, the average class size was 18.6 in public elementary schools and 14.2 in public high schools (National Center for Education Statistics, 1999).[1]

Powell also determined that independent elementary schools tend to be small and independent high schools tend to be even smaller—in contrast to public schools, which tend to increase in size as the students they serve get older. In *The Power of Their Ideas,* Meier (1995) suggests that we abandon adolescents just at the time when they most often need to be in the company of trusted adults. . . .

What Has My Experience Taught Me?

Over the years, I have taught students at nearly every level, from 3rd grade through graduate school. As a researcher, I have spent time gathering data on students at every level from preschool through 12th grade. My teaching and research experiences have provided me with data that convince me that both small classes and small schools are crucial to a teacher's ability to succeed with students.

One of my earliest teaching experiences was in a large comprehensive high school in Australia that included grades 7–10. I had more than 40 students in each of seven classes each day. During my second year, I taught Ray Campano. He was a quiet 10th grader who wasn't doing well in English. His parents, aware of his academic weaknesses, came to see me early in the first term. They asked that I keep them informed of the homework required and let them know if Ray was in danger of failing. They wanted to help and were supportive of my efforts on their son's behalf. In the ensuing weeks, I kept track of Ray's progress, but I gradually paid less attention to him. He was pleasant and quiet and well behaved, but there were other students in the class who were not. Other students demanded that I give them individual attention because they wanted to excel. These two groups of students—the rebellious and the demanding—absorbed most of my time, while Ray quietly slipped out of my attention. To be sure, I saw him each day and recorded whether his work was coming in, but I neglected to examine his performance in the midst of competing demands to plan, grade papers, and work with the needier or more demanding students.

When midterm reports came due, I was horrified to realize that I had neglected to keep my eye on Ray's performance, which was less than satisfactory. I met with his parents and explained that I had not kept my end of our bargain. They were angry—and rightly so—but they were fair. Ray's mother asked to come to class for a week to see what was going on. At the end of that week, she said that she thought the work I asked the students to do was appropriate and that I was relatively well organized and focused. Nevertheless, she couldn't imagine how a teacher could manage anything more than a cursory relationship with any given student in so large a classroom. Mrs. Campano confirmed my own experience, which suggested that really knowing all 40 students in each of seven classes was impossible. Despite parental involvement and teachers' good intentions, it is easy for students to get lost in large classes and in large schools.

As Dean of Bank Street College of Education in New York City several years ago, I team-taught 5th and 6th graders in the College's School for Children. We were looking for a course of study that would engage the students in making some contribution to the local community while simultaneously building their reading, computer, writing, and observation skills. After long deliberation and engagement in a number of exploratory activities, our 5th and 6th graders decided that they would tutor younger students in a neighborhood public school. One of the students cried, "How are we supposed to teach reading? We're only kids. We just learned to read ourselves a few years ago!" A heated discussion ensued, during which one of the girls ran up to the chalkboard and said, "I know. Let's map how each of us learned to read."

The students made a chart of how old they were, where they were (home or school), with whom they were engaged in a reading activity, and what activity they were engaged in at the precise moment that they understood that they could read. Seventeen students in the classroom generated 14 different approaches to learning to read. I suggested that the students pick several of the most commonly used approaches and organize a seminar on each approach so that they could learn several methods for working with their reading buddies. They looked at me as if either I had lost my mind or I hadn't been listening. "We can't learn just three approaches, or we'll never learn to help all these kids learn to read! If we needed a bunch of different approaches to learn to read, why wouldn't they?"

This experience reinforced my belief that different students learn differently and that teachers need to build a repertoire of instructional strategies to reach individual students. Small class size is integral to this individualization: Teachers should be responsible for a smaller number of students so that they can get to know each student and his or her learning preferences. It takes time to get to know one's students and to individualize the learning experience, and doing so requires concentration. In a classroom with a large number of students, such attention simply isn't an option.

Colleagues and I recently conducted a study of small schools in Chicago. Part of our time was spent in a small school-within-a-school with eight teachers. Because they were few, they could meet together every day for an hour, work toward common agreements and understandings, and accept shared responsibility for their students. They discussed the curriculum in all subjects, agreed on instructional approaches, and tried to build as much coherence in the curriculum as they could manage. In the larger school, which had some 70 faculty members, a common agenda simply wasn't possible.

The school-within-a-school teachers spent an enormous amount of time talking about their 300 students. They argued about students, challenged one another to see individual students differently, and agreed to work together to communicate to students that math or English or science was important for everyone. By the end of the first year, students in the smaller school-within-a school had outperformed their peers on a number of measures: More of the smaller-school students had stayed in school, completed their courses, and received higher grades than had students in the host school. For example, between September 1998 and September 1999, approximately 11.1 percent of school within-a-school students dropped out of school. By contrast, about 19.8 percent of their host-school peers dropped out during the same period (Wasley et al., 2000).

When we asked the school-within-a-school students why they thought they had achieved such results, they said that their teachers "dog us every day. They're relentless. They call our parents. They really care whether we get our work done. There's no hiding in this school!"

The time is ripe for educators to make the case for what research suggests and what our own experience has been telling us for years: Students do best in places where they can't slip through the cracks, where they are known by their teachers, and where their improved learning becomes the collective mission of a number of trusted adults. We have the resources to ensure that every student gets a good education, and we know what conditions best support their success. It is time to do what is right.

Note

1. The low average class size of public high schools obscures the fact that upper division courses in math and science and Advanced Placement courses are typically smaller, whereas many lower-track courses have more than 30 students.

Kirk A. Johnson  **NO**

The Downside to Small Class Policies

From the attention and financial support given to class size reduction by politicians and the public, one might assume that research has shown small class size to be essential to positive academic outcomes. In fiscal year 2000, the U.S. Congress allocated $1.3 billion for the class size reduction provision of the Elementary and Secondary Education Act (ESEA). During the Clinton administration, class size received a great deal of attention through proposals to pump large sums of money into efforts to increase the number of teachers in public elementary schools, thereby decreasing the ratio of students to teachers (The White House, 2000).

Proponents of class size reduction claim that small classes result in fewer discipline problems and allow teachers more time for instruction and individual attention and more flexibility in instructional strategies (Halbach, Ehrle, Zahorik, & Molnar, 2001).

Do small classes make a different in the academic achievement of elementary school students? Are class size reduction programs uniformly positive, or does a downside exist to hiring and placing more teachers in U.S. public schools?

The California Experience

In 1995, California enacted one of the broadest-reaching laws for ensuring small classes in the early grades. Strong bipartisan approval of the class size reduction measure in the California legislature reflected broad support among constituents for reducing class sizes. The program has been wildly popular over its short lifetime, but it has faced substantial obstacles to success.

California's class size reduction program has suffered from a lack of qualified teachers to fill classrooms. More or less simultaneously, nearly all elementary schools in the state demanded more teachers, and some schools—typically suburban—attracted far more teaching applicants than did those in the inner city.

A consortium of researchers from RAND, the American Institutes for Research (AIR), Policy Analysis for California Education (PACE), EdSource, and WestEd analyzed the effects of California's class size reduction initiative and outlined two basic problems. First, K–3 classes that remained large were

From *Educational Leadership,* February 2002, pp. 27–29. Reprinted with permission of the Association for Supervision and Curriculum Development. Copyright © 2001 by ASCD. All rights reserved.

"concentrated in districts serving high percentages of minority, low-income, or English learner (EL) students" (Stecher & Bohrnstedt, 2000, p. x). Second,

> the average qualifications (that is, education, credentials, and experience) of California teachers declined during the past three years for all grade levels, but the declines were worst in elementary schools. . . . Schools serving low-income, minority, or EL students continued to have fewer well-qualified teachers than did other schools. (p. x)

Do Students Learn More in Small Classes?

Clearly, if billions of dollars are to be spent on reducing class size, tangible evidence should exist that students benefit academically from such initiatives. As yet, evidence of the efficacy of class size reduction is mixed at best.

One of the most frequently cited reports on class size is Mosteller's (1995) analysis of the Project STAR study of elementary school students in Tennessee. Mosteller found a significant difference in achievement between students in classes of 13–17 students per teacher and those in classes of 22–25.

University of Rochester economist Eric Hanushek, however, questioned Mosteller's results, noting that "the bulk of evidence . . . points to no systematic effects of class size reductions within the relevant policy range" (1999, p. 144). In other words, no serious policy change on a large scale could decrease class size enough to make a difference.

The current class size reduction debate often ignores the fact that class sizes have been dropping slowly but steadily in the United States over the course of many years. In 1970, U.S. public schools averaged 22.3 students per teacher; by the late 1990s, however, they averaged about 17 students per teacher—a result of a combination of demographic trends and conscious policy decisions to lower pupil-teacher ratios (U.S. Census Bureau, 1999).

Local and programmatic changes in class size can be illustrative, but does research indicate that, on a national level, students in small classes experience academic achievement gains superior to those of their peers in large classes?

The National Assessment of Educational Progress

The most useful database for analyzing whether small classes lead to better academic achievement is the National Assessment of Educational Progress (NAEP). First administered in 1969, the NAEP measures the academic achievement of 4th, 8th, and 12th graders in a variety of fields, including reading, writing, mathematics, science, geography, civics, and the arts. Students take the math and reading tests alternately every two years. For example, students were assessed in reading in 1998; they were tested in math in 1996 and 2000.

The NAEP is actually two tests: a nationally administered test and a state-administered test. More than 40 states participate in the separate state samples used to gauge achievement within those jurisdictions.

In addition to test scores in the subject area, the NAEP includes an assortment of background information on the students taking the exam, their main subject-area teacher, and their school administrator. Background information includes students' television viewing habits, students' computer usage at home and at school, teacher tenure and certification, family socio-economic status, basic demographics, and school characteristics. By including this information in their assessment of the NAEP data, researchers can gain insight into the factors that might explain differences in NAEP scores found among students.

Results From the Center for Data Analysis

A study from the Center for Data Analysis at the Heritage Foundation examined the 1998 NAEP national reading data to determine whether students in small classes achieve better than students in large classes (Johnson, 2000). Researchers assessed students' academic achievement in reading by analyzing assessment scores as well as six factors from the background information collected by the NAEP: class size, race and ethnicity, parents' education attainment, the availability of reading materials in the home, free or reduced-price lunch participation, and gender.

Class size. The amount of time that a teacher can spend with each student appears to be important in the learning process. To address class size, the Center for Data Analysis study compared students in small classes (those with 20 or fewer students per teacher) with students in large classes (at least 31 students per teacher).

Race and ethnicity. Because significant differences exist in academic achievement among ethnic groups, the variables of race and ethnicity were included in the analysis.

Parents' education. Research indicates that the education attainment of a child's parents is a good predictor of that child's academic achievement. Because the education level of one parent is often highly correlated with that of the other parent, only a single variable was included in the analysis.

The availability of reading materials in the home. The presence of books, magazines, encyclopedias, and newspapers generally indicates a dedication to learning in the household. Researchers have determined that these reading materials are important aspects of the home environment (Coleman, Hoffer, & Kilgore, 1982). Essentially, the presence of such reading materials in the home is correlated with higher student achievement. The analysis thus included a variable controlling for the number of these four types of reading materials found at home.

Free and reduced-price lunch participation. Income is often a key predictor of academic achievement because low-income families seldom have the resources to purchase extra study materials or tutorial classes that may help their children perform better in school. Although the NAEP does not collect data on household income, it does collect data on participation in the free and reduced-price school lunch program.

Gender.   Although data on male-female achievement gaps are inconsistent, empirical research suggests that girls tend to perform better in reading and writing subjects, whereas boys perform better in more analytical subjects such as math and science.

After controlling for all these factors, researchers found that the difference in reading achievement on the 1998 NAEP reading assessment between students in small classes and students in large classes were statistically insignificant. That is, across the United Sates, students in small classes did no better on average than those in large classes, assuming otherwise identical circumstances.

Such results should give policymakers pause and provoke them to consider whether the rush to hire more teachers is worth the cost and is in the best interest of students. In terms of raising achievement, reducing class size does not guarantee success.

When Irwin Kurz became the principal of Public School 161 in Brooklyn, New York, well over a decade ago, the schools' test scores ranked in the bottom 25th percentile of schools in Brooklyn's 17th District. Today, P.S. 161 ranks as the best school in the district and 40th of 674 elementary schools in New York City, even though a majority of its students are poor. The pupil-teacher ratio at P.S. 161 is 35 to 1, but the teachers make neither class size, nor poverty, nor anything else an excuse for poor performance. As Kurz likes to say, "better to have one good teacher than two crummy teachers any day."

References

Coleman, J., Hoffer, T., & Kilgore, S. (1982). *High school achievement.* New York: BasicBooks.

Halbach, A., Ehrle, K., Zahorik, J., & Molnar, A. (2001, March). Class size reduction: From promise to practice. *Educational Leadership, 58*(6), 32–35.

Hanushek, E. (1999). Some findings from an independent investigation of the Tennessee STAR experiment and from other investigations of class size effects. *Educational Evaluation & Policy Analysis, 21*(2), 143–164.

Johnson, K. (2000, June 9). *Do small classes influence academic achievement? What the National Assessment of Educational Progress shows* (CDA Report No. 00–07). Washington, DC: Heritage Foundation.

Mosteller, F. (1995). The Tennessee study of class size in the early school grades. *The Future of Children, 5*(2), 113–127.

Stecher, B., & Bohrnstedt, G. (Eds.). (2000). *Class size reduction in California: The 1998–99 evaluation findings.* Sacramento: California Department of Education.

U.S. Census Bureau. (1999). *Statistical abstract of the United States.* Washington, DC: Government Printing Office.

The White House (2000, May 4). President Clinton highlights education reform agenda with roundtable on what works [Press release].

POSTSCRIPT

Is Size Crucial to School Improvement?

$\mathbf{E}$ric Hanushek, a professor of economics and public policy and Hoover Institution fellow, has asserted in various publications that extensive statistical investigations show no relationship between class size and student performance, that the modest gains shown during Tennessee's STAR experiment were only in kindergartens, and that there is no firm foundation for pouring huge amounts of money into class size reduction on a nationwide basis. Others have raised questions about the validity of some of the statistics cited by researchers on both sides of the issue, arguing that pupil-teacher ratio is an administrative figure not reflective of actual class size figures. According to some analysts, the approximate difference between the two figures on a nationwide basis is 10 (if a school's pupil-teacher ratio is 17 to 1, then its teachers will average about 27 students per class).

The benefits of small schools have been more clearly demonstrated by researchers in major urban areas. Most of these schools develop a unique culture that nourishes interpersonal relationships and constructively interacts with the surrounding community. But there are many barriers to be overcome. Wasley and Richard J. Lear, in "Small Schools, Real Gains," *Educational Leadership* (March 2001), for example, cite these barriers: the tightly woven structure of high schools makes real change difficult, some small schools try too hard to act like large schools, the focus is too often on short-term goals, and many educators lack a clear image of what a small school can be.

When such barriers are successfully overcome, the resulting connectedness that the small school fosters can have a positive effect on student behavior. A recent federally funded survey, the National Study of Adolescent Health, showed that students who attend small junior and senior high schools are less likely to engage in violence, drug use, and early sexual activities, with the primary causative factor being a sense of connectedness to their teachers and to their fellow students.

Other slants on these combined issues can be found in Anne Reynolds, "Less Is More: What Teachers Say About Decreasing Class Size and Increasing Learning," *American School Board Journal* (September 2001); Craig Howley and Robert Bickel, "The Influence of Scale: Small Schools Make a Big Difference for Children of Poor Families," *American School Board Journal* (March 2002); Mary Anne Raywid, "The Policy Environments of Small Schools and Schools-Within-Schools," *Educational Leadership* (February 2002); and 10 articles on "Small Learning Communities" in *Principal Leadership* (February 2002).

ISSUE 16

Should Bilingual Education Programs Be Abandoned?

YES: Rosalie Pedalino Porter, from "The Politics of Bilingual Education," *Society* (September/October 1997)

NO: Richard Rothstein, from "Bilingual Education: The Controversy," *Phi Delta Kappan* (May 1998)

ISSUE SUMMARY

YES: Rosalie Pedalino Porter, director of the Research in English Acquisition and Development Institute, offers a close examination of the major research studies and concludes that there is no consistent support for transitional bilingual education programs.

NO: Richard Rothstein, a research associate of the Economic Policy Institute, reviews the history of bilingual education and argues that, although many problems currently exist, there is no compelling reason to abandon these programs.

T he issue of accommodating non-English-speaking immigrants by means of a bilingual education program has been controversial since the late 1960s. Events of the past decades have brought about one of the largest influxes of immigrants to the United States in the nation's history. And the disadvantages that non-English-speaking children and their parents experience during the childrens' years of formal schooling has received considerable attention from educators, policymakers, and the popular press.

Efforts to modify this type of social and developmental disadvantage have appeared in the form of bilingual education programs initiated at the local level and supported by federal funding. Approaches implemented include direct academic instruction in the primary language and the provision of language tutors under the English for Speakers of Other Languages (ESOL) program. Research evaluation of these efforts has produced varied results and has given rise to controversy over the efficacy of the programs themselves and the social and political intentions served by them.

A political movement at the national and state levels to establish English as the official language of the United States has gained support in recent years.

Supporters of this movement feel that the bilingual approach will lead to the kind of linguistic division that has torn Canada apart.

Perhaps sharing some of the concerns of the "official English" advocates, increasing numbers of educators seem to be tilting in the direction of the immersion approach. In *Forked Tongue: The Politics of Bilingual Education* (1990), Rosalie Pedalino Porter, a teacher and researcher in the field of bilingual education for over 15 years, issues an indictment of the policies and programs that have been prevalent. One of her central recommendations is that "limited-English children must be placed with specially trained teachers in a program in which these students will be immersed in the English language, in which they have as much contact as possible with English speakers, and in which school subjects, not just social conversations, are the focus of the English-language lessons from kindergarten through twelfth grade."

Amado M. Padilla of Stanford University has examined the rationale behind "official English" and has also reviewed the effectiveness of bilingual education programs (see "English Only vs. Bilingual Education: Ensuring a Language-Competent Society," *Journal of Education*, Spring 1991). Padilla concludes that "the debate about how to assist linguistic minority children should focus on new educational technologies and not just on the effectiveness of bilingual education or whether bilingualism detracts from loyalty to this country."

Recent treatments of the problem, prompted by state initiatives and congressional bills, include "English Über Alles," *The Nation* (September 29, 1997); "Ingles, Si," by Jorge Amselle, *National Review* (September 30, 1996); and "Should English Be the Law?" by Robert D. King, *The Atlantic Monthly* (April 1997), in which the author contends that proponents of "official English" are tearing the nation apart. Another provocative portrayal of the dilemma is presented in Laurie Olsen's "Learning English and Learning America: Immigrants in the Center of a Storm," *Theory Into Practice* (Autumn 2000).

Linguistics professor Donaldo Macedo, in "English Only: The Tongue-Tying of America," *Journal of Education* (Spring 1991), maintains that the conservative ideology that propels the movement against bilingual education fails to recognize the need to prepare students for the multicultural world of the twenty-first century and relegates the immigrant population to the margins of society.

In the first of the selections that follow, Rosalie Pedalino Porter exposes the political assumptions behind governmental efforts to help non-English-speaking school children gain language competency. She finds the "politically correct" native-language instruction approach to be mired in a record of poor results. In the second selection, Richard Rothstein looks at the complexities of the problem, cites historal precedents and modern research findings, and makes a plea for removing the debate from the political realm.

YES

Rosalie Pedalino Porter

The Politics of Bilingual Education

In the United States, the efforts being made and the money being invested in the special programs to help immigrant, migrant, and refugee school children who do not speak English when they enter U.S. schools is still largely misguided. The current population of limited-English students is being treated in ways that earlier immigrant groups were not. The politically righteous assumption is that these students cannot learn English quickly and must be taught all their school subjects in their native language for three to seven years while having the English language introduced gradually. Twenty-seven years of classroom experience with this education policy and a growing body of research show no benefits for native-language teaching either in better learning of English or better learning of school subjects. These facts have hardly dented the armor of the true believers in the bilingual education bureaucracy.

Yet some changes and improvements have occurred in this most contentious area of public education. Research reports contribute additional evidence on the poor results of native-language instruction as the superior road to English-language competency for classroom work. But the successful results from programs emphasizing intensive English are beginning to appear, now that some small measure of funding is being allocated to these so-called alternative model programs.

All too often, it remains almost impossible to voice criticism of bilingual education programs without being pilloried as a hater of foreigners and foreign languages and of contributing to the anti-immigrant climate. Another area in which little positive change has occurred in the past few years is in reducing the established power of state education departments to impose education mandates on local school districts. The power of the bilingual education bureaucracy has hardly diminished, even in states like California where the state bilingual education law expired in 1987. However, there are counterforces opposing the seemingly settled idea that native-language programs are the single best solution for limited-English students, and these challenges are growing at the local school level.

Updating the Research

The basic questions posed in the early years of bilingual education still have not found clear-cut answers. Are there measurable benefits for limited-English students when they are taught in their native language for a period of time,

From Rosalie Pedalino Porter, "The Politics of Bilingual Education," *Society* (September/October 1997). Copyright © 1997 by Transaction Publishers. Reprinted by permission.

both in their learning of the English language for academic achievement and in their mastery of school subjects? Has a clear advantage emerged for a particular pedagogy among the best-known models—transitional bilingual education, English as a Second Language [ESL], structured immersion, two-way, dual immersion, or developmental bilingual programs? There is no more consensus on the answers to these questions than there was five years ago. However, there is growing evidence of an almost total lack of account-ability in states that have invested most heavily in bilingual education for the past fifteen or twenty years and have not collected data or evaluated pro-grams to produce answers to the questions raised above. The research that has been published in recent years includes a study by the General Account-ing Office, the ALEC [American Legislative Council] Study, a review of the El Paso Bilingual Immersion Project, a longitudinal study of bilingual students in New York, a report of a two-year study of California's bilingual education programs, and a report of a state commission on Massachusetts's bilingual education.

The GAO Study

Every year since the late 1970s, the school enrollment of limited-English stu-dents has increased at a faster rate than the rest of the school population, and the costs of special programs nationwide are beginning to be tallied. The U.S. General Accounting Office (GAO) published a study in January 1994 titled *Limited-English Proficiency: A Growing and Costly Educational Challenge Facing Many School Districts* at the request of the Senate Committee on Labor and Human Resources. The GAO study provides an overview of the serious prob-lems confronting U.S. public schools in meeting the needs of limited-English students, new demographics on where these students are concentrated, and a detailed description of five representative school districts with rapidly growing limited-English proficient (LEP) populations.

Briefly, the GAO report highlights these problems in the five districts that are common to all public schools with LEP students:

- Immigrant students are almost 100 percent non-English speaking on arrival in the U.S.
- LEP students arrive at different times during the school year, which causes upheavals in classrooms and educational programs.
- Some high school students have not been schooled in their native lands and lack literacy skills in any language.
- There is a high level of family poverty and transiency and a low level of parental involvement in students' education.
- There is an acute shortage of bilingual teachers and of textbooks and assessment instruments in the native languages.

The information gathered by the GAO study is valuable to educators, researchers, and policy makers. An alarming fact reported in this study is men-tioned only in passing and never explained: *Immigrant children account for only 43 percent of the limited-English students in our schools.* Who, then, make up the other 57 percent and why are such large numbers of native-born children classified as limited- or non-English proficient and placed in native-language instruction programs? In a private conversation with one of the GAO regional managers, I was unable to get an explanation for the high percentage of native-born students classified as limited-English. I was told that the GAO had not found an agreed upon definition of what a "limited-English person" is and that they have included in this category children who speak English but who may not read and write it well enough for schoolwork. In that case, there surely are a large number of students who are wrongly enrolled in programs where they are being taught in another language when what they urgently need is remedial help in reading and writing in English. . . .

The ALEC Study

The ALEC Study makes a bold attempt to unravel the mysteries of exactly how many students are served by special programs that aim to remove the language barrier to an equal education, what kinds of programs they are enrolled in, where these students are concentrated—by state—and how much is actually being spent in this special effort. As a former school administrator, I know firsthand that it is quite possible to account for special costs. In the Newton, Massachusetts, public schools annual budget there is an account for bilingual/ESL programs that covers all the costs incurred for the LEP students: teachers, teacher aides, books, materials, transportation, and administration. One knew what was spent each year, over and above the school costs for general education, and in Newton this averaged about $1,000 per student per year for LEP students. Not all school districts keep such information, and it is not collected consistently by all state education departments because this is not required by the federal government.

Analyzing data from the National Center for Education Statistics, the Office of Bilingual Education and Minority Languages Affairs (OBEMLA), and various other federal and state sources, the ALEC study synthesizes the data to arrive at these conclusions for the 1991–1992 school year:

- On average, all federal funding for education amounts to 6 percent; state and local sources provide roughly 47 percent each.
- Federal funding for bilingual education, $101 million in 1991 and $116 million in 1992, was mostly allocated to native-language instruction programs, giving only 20–30 percent to ESL programs.
- There were 2.3 million limited-English students enrolled in U.S. public schools while only 1.9 million were enrolled in any special language program, leaving 450,000 LEP students without any special language help.
- Of the 1.9 million students in special programs, 60 percent were enrolled in bilingual programs, 22 percent in ESL, and 18 percent in a category labeled "unknown" because states could not describe their special language programs.
- Candidly explaining the difficulties of collecting strictly accurate data, the costs of programs for LEP students are estimated to be $5.5 billion

(56 percent) for bilingual programs, $1.9 billion (20 percent) for ESL, and $2.4 billion (24 percent) for unknown programs, totaling $9.9 billion for 1991–1992.

- Projecting that increases in enrollments in 1993 would be the same as recent increases, spending on special language programs would amount to $12 billion in 1993.

The ALEC study draws some tenable conclusions from the data summarized above while it admits that the approximate cost figures may be overand underestimations of what is actually spent. Both federal and state agencies do give preference to native-language instruction programs over ESL in funding decisions by a wide margin, even though "there is no conclusive research that demonstrates the educational superiority of bilingual education over ESL." Even if the ALEC cost estimates were overestimated, this is only one of several recent reports that point out the widespread lack of accountability in bilingual education. Twenty-seven years of heavy investment in mainly bilingual programs has not produced exact data on how much these programs cost or how successful they are in realizing their goals in student achievement. . . .

The El Paso Bilingual Immersion Project

In 1992, the Institute for Research in English Acquisition and Development (READ) published a monograph by Russell Gersten, John Woodward, and Susan Schneider on the final results of the seven-year longitudinal study of the Bilingual Immersion Project; the results were summarized by Gersten and Woodward in *The Elementary School Journal* in 1995. This evaluation clearly demonstrates advantages for the immersion approach over the transitional bilingual education (TBE) model.

- The Iowa Test of Basic Skills (in English) results for grades 4 and 5 do show superior performance in all academic areas for students in the immersion program over students in the transitional bilingual program.
- By grade 6, 99 percent of immersion students were mainstreamed; at end of 7th grade, 35 percent of TBE students are still in the bilingual program.
- Well-designed bilingual immersion leads to more rapid, more successful, and increased integration of Latino students into the mainstream, with no detrimental effects in any area of achievement for students who took part in this program. The increased integration may lead to a decrease in high school dropout rates among Hispanic students. Subsequent research is needed to explore the possibility of this effect of immersion programs.
- The major strengths of the bilingual immersion program are its use of contemporary thinking on language acquisition and literacy development and its relatively stress-free approach to the rapid learning of English in the primary grades.
- Teacher questionnaires revealed much greater satisfaction with the early, systematic teaching of English in the immersion program than with the slow introduction of English in the bilingual program.

- Student interviews indicated no significant differences in reactions to the two programs. No evidence emerged, from students, parents, or teachers, that native-language teaching produces a higher level of selfesteem or that early immersion in a second language is more stressful, two of the common beliefs promoted by bilingual education advocates.

Research such as that conducted in El Paso is invaluable in the ongoing debate on program effectiveness. Because the comparison was made between two radically different teaching methods in the same school district with the same population of limited-English students, this study provides incontrovertible proof of the benefits to students of early second-language learning. More recently, the New York City public schools published a report that threw a metaphorical bombshell into the bilingual education camp.

The New York Study

Educational Progress of Students in Bilingual and ESL Programs: A Longitudinal Study, 1990–1994, was published in October 1994 by the Board of Education of the City of New York. New York City invested $300 million in 1993 in bilingual programs where the instruction was given in Spanish, Chinese, Haitian Creole, Russian, Korean, Vietnamese, French, Greek, Arabic, and Bengali—an investment that was not only misguided but harmful to the student beneficiaries, as the results of the longitudinal study show.

The New York City study is important because, like the El Paso study, it examines student achievement in basically different programs in large, urban school districts and because it charts student progress over a period of years. The criteria of student success measured included number of years served in a special language program before exiting to a mainstream classroom, reading level in English, and performance in math. The two groups of limited-English students whose achievement was monitored were (1) Spanish speakers and speakers of Haitian Creole who were enrolled in bilingual classrooms where they received mostly native-language instruction in reading, writing, and school subjects, with brief English-language lessons, (2) students from Russian, Korean, and Chinese language backgrounds who were placed in ESL classes where all instruction is provided through a special English-language curriculum. The study included children who entered school in fall 1990: 11,320 entering kindergarten, 2,053 entering 1st grade, 841 entering 2nd grade, 797 entering 3rd grade, 754 entering 6th grade, and 1,366 entering 9th grade.

As any disinterested observer might have anticipated, there is strong evidence showing that the earlier a second language is introduced, the more rapidly it is learned for academic purposes. Surprising? Not at all, but it flies in the face of the received wisdom of Jim Cummins's theories that were developed, after the fact, to justify bilingual education: the facilitation theory and the threshold hypothesis. With appropriate teaching, children can learn a new language quickly and can learn subject matter taught *in* that language. Reading and writing skills can be mastered, and math can be learned successfully in a second language; here are the proofs from thousands of New York City schoolchildren.

The most riveting outcome of this research reported in the New York study is the fact that "at all grade levels, students served in ESL-only programs exited their programs faster than those served in bilingual programs." The three-year exit rates were as follows: For ESL-only programs, the exit rates were 79.3 percent, 67.5 percent, and 32.7 percent for students who entered school in grades kindergarten, 2, and 6, respectively; for bilingual programs, the exit rates were 51.5 percent, 22.1 percent, and 6.9 percent, respectively.

The three-year exit rates for LEP students who entered kindergarten from different language groups, whether they were in ESL or bilingual programs, [were] reported as follows: 91.8 percent for Korean, 87.4 percent for Russian, 82.6 percent for Chinese, 58.7 percent for Haitian Creole, and 50.6 percent for Spanish.

Differences among language groups remained steady even for students entering the New York schools in the higher grades. Critics of the study, including Luis O. Reyes of the New York City School Board, allege that Korean, Russian, and Chinese background students are from middle-class families and that the social class difference invalidates the study. Socioeconomic data is not reported in the study. We do not know how many of the children in any of the language groups are from poor, working-class, or middle-class families, and we should not make unwarranted assumptions. One could hazard a guess that most immigrant, migrant, and refugee children attending the New York City public schools do not come from affluent families. The undeniable facts are that children from Spanish and Haitian Creole speaking families are mostly funneled into bilingual classrooms, and children from other language groups are mostly assigned to ESL classrooms. I firmly believe that the type of schooling these children receive makes a large difference in their ability to achieve at their own personal best. I believe, even more firmly, that Haitian and Latino children would succeed in mastering English-language skills better and faster and, therefore, join their English-speaking peers in mainstream classes much sooner than is now the case *if they were given the same opportunity given to Russian, Korean, and Chinese students.*

Exiting the special program classrooms more expeditiously is not only a cost consideration but a matter of integration and opportunity. Remaining in substantially segregated bilingual classrooms for several years does not equip students to compete in the broader life of the school and community—in fact it has the opposite effect. . . .

The California Study and Others

. . . New York City's willingness actually to monitor the progress of LEP students and report the results to the public is much to be praised when we survey the lack of accountability in other parts of the country. The State of California, with 1.2 million limited-English students (43 percent of all LEP students in the United States) and a twenty-year history of involvement with bilingual education, commissioned an evaluation of educational programs for these students. *Meeting the Challenge of Language Diversity: An Evaluation of Programs for Pupils with Limited Proficiency in English,* the published report of a two-year study, 1990–1992, shows generally poor results for bilingual education programs in California and essentially evades the legislature's requirement that it provide "information to determine which model for educating LEP pupils is most effective and cost effective."

Major findings of this study are the following:

1. California public schools do not have valid assessments of the performance for students with limited proficiency in English. Therefore, *the state and the public cannot hold schools accountable for LEP students achieving high levels of performance* (emphasis added).
2. Many schools do not reclassify students (that is, move them from the bilingual programs with appropriate skills to work in mainstream classrooms), keeping them in native-language classrooms well beyond the time when they are fluent in English. "It is not surprising that many students may wait years to be formally retested for program exit and that many others may never be reclassified, going on to the middle school still bearing the LEP label."
3. Junior and senior high school LEP students do not have access to core academic subjects through Sheltered English or ESL. Long stays in bilingual programs in elementary schools delay the effective learning of the English-language literacy skills that are so important for secondary school work.

Meeting the Challenge presents a bleak picture of the disappointing results of twenty years of bilingual education in California. When the Chacon-Moscone Bilingual Bicultural Act of 1976 expired in 1987, the California State Department of Education sent notification to each school district that the intent of the act would still be promoted by state regulations, principally, "that the primary goal of all [bilingual] programs is, as effectively and efficiently as possible, to develop in each child fluency in English." *Meeting the Challenge* fails to tell us how or if this goal is being properly met but offers a variety of excuses for not fulfilling its mission. The weaknesses in this giant instructional system for limited-English students—one out of every five students in California—are of huge proportions. The fact that the State Department of Education has allowed school districts to evade their responsibility to assess and report on student progress shows an unconscionable lack of accountability by this powerful bureaucracy. If we cannot hold the schools responsible for program outcomes after twenty years, then perhaps the responsibility for this failure rests squarely on the state agency that has forcefully promoted the bilingual education policy.

California's high school dropout rates reported in June 1995 amounted to a statewide average of 5 percent per year, or a four-year average of 20 percent of students leaving school before graduation. Discouraging as that seems, the dropout rate for Latino students statewide is even higher—28 percent, compared to 10 percent for Asian students and 12 percent for white students. The four-year dropout rate for the Los Angeles Unified School District, the district enrolling the highest percentage of LEP students in the state, is a shocking 43.6 percent.

In 1993 the Los Angeles Unified School District embarked on a plan to improve its bilingual education programs, partly through expanded teacher training in the native languages of the students (actually, in Spanish only). Clearly, the increased emphasis on native-language instruction has not had any positive effect on the dropout rates for LEP students in the Los Angeles schools. The latest Los Angeles figures on dropout rates by ethnic breakdown, as reported by the State Department of Education in October 1994 for the 1993–1994 school year, are 44.4 percent for Hispanic students, *three-fourths of whom are enrolled in bilingual classes in the district.* . . .

Massachusetts Revisited

Ironically, the Commonwealth of Massachusetts, which passed the first state law mandating native-language teaching in 1971, Chapter 71–A, has an even more dismal record than California in the area of public accountability. Efforts to reform the Transitional Bilingual Education law have been successfully resisted, even though there can hardly be one legislator who has any documented proof for the effectiveness of bilingual education in Massachusetts. A state commission was appointed by Governor Weld to survey the status of bilingual education in the state, and in December 1994 it reported this conclusion:

> We do not know, on the basis of measured outcomes, whether TBE programs in Massachusetts produce good results or poor results. There are no comprehensive data that evaluate the performance of TBE pupils compared with pupils from other groups. This specialized program which accounts for 5% of all pupils in Massachusetts public schools and 17% of all pupils in Boston public schools is not held separately accountable for its performance.

Apparently, the commission has recommended that the state department of education develop new guidelines on accountability as soon as suitable tests are developed. As a veteran Massachusetts educator who has seen many a set of "guidelines" arrive with a flourish and disappear without a trace, I reserve judgment on the latest pronouncements.

Massachusetts probably leads the country in zany educational experiments. I reported earlier on the Cape Verdean project to try to encourage the use of a nonstandard dialect as the classroom language of instruction. The Boston public school system, in its infinite wisdom, now maintains a K–12 bilingual program in Kriolu, a dialect of Portuguese spoken in the Cape Verde Islands that has no alphabet, no written language, and no books. Massachusetts is thought to be the only place in the world to have schoolrooms in which Kriolu is the language of instruction, with Kriolu programs in Boston, Brockton, and New Bedford schools. Portuguese is the official language of education in Cape Verde.

Aside from the minor matters of alphabets, a written language, or books, there are these exquisite complications. Cape Verdean students may speak one of many dialects and not understand Kriolu, as explained by a science teacher in the Dearborn School, Boston, who says: "Sometimes a student gets upset because he's not understanding the Fogo dialect so you have to go back and help him in Kriolu or Portuguese." Communication between the schools and Cape Verdean parents is not improved either. Massachusetts law requires that all paperwork be sent to parents in the student's native language. A teacher at the Condon School, Eileen Fonseca, says it frustrates parents to receive a notice written in Kriolu: "When we send home report cards and matriculation papers in Kriolu, parents complain. This is new to them. They have to have it read three times, or they just ask for Portuguese or English, often so it can be read to them by family or friends." One parent made this comment: "They sent me a letter apparently to tell me something. I never understood what it was trying to say. I called to say that if the intent of the letter is to communicate, it would be better in Portuguese."

The Kriolu Caper makes an amusing, now-I've-heard-everything anecdote, but the enormity of such folly in education policy is no laughing matter. This program neither helps students learn the language or acquire the literacy skills necessary for school achievement, nor does it facilitate communication between school and family. What it does do is foster resentment in the Cape Verdean community, which does not feel respected or understood, a situation similar to the misguided attempt to make black English the language of instruction for African-American schoolchildren two decades ago. The Peoples Republic of Massachusetts is in serious need of a reality check.

Let me conclude with the review of a chapter in *The Emperor Has No Clothes: Bilingual Education in Massachusetts* by Christine Rossell and Keith Baker that summarizes the major studies on the effectiveness of bilingual education and analyzes those studies that are methodologically acceptable.

Social science research in education is, at best, an approximation of true scientific research. Schoolchildren cannot be isolated in laboratory test tubes and studied under pristine conditions, controlling for minute variables. In the area of bilingual education research, the quality of the product is generally acknowledged to be especially low. The elements of a scientifically valid evaluation of a special effort must include, at the minimum:

- random assignment of subjects to avoid self-selection bias
- a control group to compare with the group receiving the special program (treatment)
- pretesting to establish that students in different groups are starting with the same traits—i.e., that all are limited or non-English speakers—or statistical adjustments to account for pre-treatment differences
- posttesting to determine the effect of different treatments
- assurance that one group does not receive extra benefits, aside from the difference in treatments, such as after-school programs or a longer school day.

In the area of bilingual education research, there is the added problem that the label is applied to a range of educational varieties, from the classic model, in which native language instruction is given 80–90 percent of the school day, to the other extreme, in which the teacher may use a word or two of another language on occasion. This complicates the work of analyzing the effects of bilingual programs.

Rossell and Baker read over five hundred studies, three hundred of which were program evaluations. The authors found seventy-two methodologically acceptable studies, that is, studies that show the effect of transitional bilingual education on English-language learning, reading, and mathematics, compared to (1) "submersion" or doing nothing, (2) English as a Second Language, (3) structured immersion in English, and (4) maintenance bilingual education. The authors' overall finding, which is of crucial importance as this is the most current, comprehensive analysis of the research, is that *"there is still . . . no consistent research support for transitional bilingual education as a superior instructional practice for improving the English language achievement of limited-English-proficient children"* (emphasis added).

NO

Richard Rothstein

Bilingual Education: The Controversy

Bilingual education, a preferred strategy for the last 20 years, aims to teach academic subjects to immigrant children in their native languages (most often Spanish), while slowly and simultaneously adding English instruction.[1] In theory, the children don't fall behind in other subjects while they are learning English. When they are fluent in English, they can then "transition" to English instruction in academic subjects at the grade level of their peers. Further, the theory goes, teaching immigrants in their native language values their family and community culture and reinforces their sense of self-worth, thus making their academic success more likely.

In contrast, bilingual education's critics tell the following, quite different, story. In the early 20th century, public schools assimilated immigrants to American culture and imparted workplace skills essential for upward mobility. Children were immersed in English instruction and, when forced to "sink or swim," they swam. Today, however, separatist (usually Hispanic) community leaders and their liberal supporters, opposed to assimilation, want Spanish instruction to preserve native culture and traditions. This is especially dangerous because the proximity of Mexico and the possibility of returning home give today's immigrants the option of "keeping a foot in both camps"—an option not available to previous immigrants who were forced to assimilate. Today's attempts to preserve immigrants' native languages and cultures will not only balkanize the American melting pot but hurt the children upon whom bilingual education is imposed because their failure to learn English well will leave them unprepared for the workplace. Bilingual education supporters may claim that it aims to teach English, but high dropout rates for immigrant children and low rates of transition to full English instruction prove that, even if educators' intentions are genuine, the program is a failure.

The English First Foundation, a lobbying group bent on abolishing bilingual education, states that most Americans "have ancestors who learned English the same way: in classrooms where English was the only language used for all learning activities."[2] According to 1996 Republican Presidential nominee Bob Dole, the teaching of English to immigrants is what "we have done . . . since our founding to speed the melting of our melting pot. . . . We must stop the practice of multilingual education as a means of instilling ethnic

From Richard Rothstein, "Bilingual Education: The Controversy," *Phi Delta Kappan* (May 1998). Adapted from *The Way We Were?* (Century Foundation Press, 1998). Copyright © 1998 by The Century Foundation, Inc. Reprinted by permission.

pride, or as a therapy for low self-esteem, or out of elitist guilt over a culture built on the traditions of the West."[3]

Speaker of the House Newt Gingrich chimed in as well:

> If people had wanted to remain immersed in their old culture, they could have done so without coming to America. . . . Bilingualism keeps people actively tied to their old language and habits and maximizes the cost of the transition to becoming American. . . . The only viable alternative for the American underclass is American civilization. Without English as a common language, there is no such civilization.[4]

This viewpoint has commonsense appeal, but it has little foundation in reality.

Bilingual Education: The History

Despite proximity to their homeland, Mexican Americans are no more likely to reverse migrate than were Europeans in the early 20th century. One-third of the immigrants who came here between 1908 and 1924 eventually abandoned America and returned home.[5]

What's more, the immigrants who remained did not succeed in school by learning English. During the last great wave of immigration, from 1880 to 1915, very few Americans succeeded in school, immigrants least of all. By 1930, it was still the case that half of all American 14- to 17-year-olds either didn't make it to high school or dropped out before graduating. The median number of school years completed was 10.

Far from succeeding by immersing themselves in English, immigrant groups did much worse than the native-born, and some immigrant groups did much worse than others. The poorest performers were Italians. According to a 1911 federal immigration commission report, in Boston, Chicago, and New York 80% of native white children in the seventh grade stayed in school another year, but only 58% of Southern Italian children, 62% of Polish children, and 74% of Russian Jewish children did so. Of those who made it to eighth grade, 58% of the native whites went on to high school, but only 23% of the Southern Italians did so. In New York, 54% of native-born eighth-graders made it to ninth grade, but only 34% of foreign-born eighth-graders did so.[6]

A later study showed that the lack of success of immigrants relative to the native-born continued into high school. In 1931, only 11% of the Italian students who entered high school graduated (compared to an estimated graduation rate of over 40% for all students). This was a much bigger native/immigrant gap than we have today.

While we have no achievement tests from that earlier period by which to evaluate relative student performance, I.Q. tests were administered frequently. Test after test in the 1920s found that Italian immigrant students had an average I.Q. of about 85, compared to an average for native-born students of about 102. The poor academic achievement of these Italian Americans led to high rates of "retardation"—that is, being held back and not promoted (this was the origin of the pejorative use of the term "retarded").

A survey of New York City's retarded students (liberally defined so that a child had to be 9 years old to be considered retarded in the first grade, 10 years old in the second grade, and so on), found that 19% of native-born students were retarded in 1908, compared to 36% of Italian students. The federal immigration commission found that the retardation rate of children of non-English-speaking immigrants was about 60% higher than that of children of immigrants from English-speaking countries.[7] The challenge of educating Italian immigrant children was so severe that New York established its first special education classes to confront it. A 1921 survey disclosed that half of all (what we now call) "learning disabled" special education children in New York schools had Italian-born fathers.[8]

As these data show—and as is the case today—some groups did better than others, both for cultural reasons and because of the influence of other socioeconomic factors on student achievement. If Italian children did worse, Eastern European Jewish children did better. This is not surprising in light of what we now know about the powerful influence of background characteristics on academic success. In 1910, 32% of Southern Italian adult males in American cities were unskilledmanual laborers, but only one-half of 1% of Russian Jewish males were unskilled. Thirty-four percent of the Jews were merchants, while only 13% of the Italians were. In New York City, the average annual income of a Russian Jewish head-of-household in 1910 was $813; a Southern Italian head-of-household averaged $688.[9]

But even with these relative economic advantages, the notion that Jewish immigrant children assimilated through sink-or-swim English-only education is a nostalgic and dangerous myth. In 1910, there were 191,000 Jewish children in the New York City schools; only 6,000 were in high school, and the overwhelming majority of these students dropped out before graduating. As the Jewish writer Irving Howe put it, after reviewing New York school documents describing the difficulties of "Americanizing" immigrant children from 1910 to 1914, "To read the reports of the school superintendents is to grow impatient with later sentimentalists who would have us suppose that all or most Jewish children burned with zeal for the life of the mind."[10] There may have been relatively more such students among the Jewish immigrants than in other immigrant communities, Howe noted, but they were still a minority.

Immersing immigrants in an English-language school program has been effective—usually by the third generation. On the whole, immigrant children spoke their native language; members of the second generation (immigrants' native-born children) were bilingual, but not sufficiently fluent in English to excel in school; members of the third generation were fluent in English and began to acquire college educations. For some groups (e.g., Greek Americans), the pattern more often took four generations; for others (e.g., Eastern European Jews), many in the second generation may have entered college.

This history is not a mere curiosity, because those who advocate against bilingual education today often claim that we know how to educate immigrant children because we've done it before. However, if we've never successfully educated the first or even second generation of children from peasant or unskilled immigrant families, we are dealing with an unprecedented task, and history can't guide us.

To understand the uniqueness of our current challenge, compare the enormous—by contemporary standards—dropout rate of New York City Jewish students in 1910 with that of Mexican students in the Los Angeles school district today. Like New York in 1910, Los Angeles now is burdened with a rising tide of immigrants. In 1996, there were 103,000 Hispanic students in grades 9–12 in Los Angeles (out of the city's total K–12 Hispanic population of 390,000). Hispanic high school students were about 26% of the total Hispanic student population in Los Angeles in 1996,[11] compared to 3% for Jews in New York in 1910 (only 6,000 high school students out of 191,000 total Jewish enrollment). In Los Angeles today, 74% of Mexican-born youths between the ages of 15 and 17 are still in high school; 88% of Hispanic youths from other countries are still in attendance.[12] More than 70% of Hispanic immigrants who came to the United States prior to their sophomore year actually complete high school (compared to a 94% high school completion rate for whites and a 92% rate for blacks).[13] English immersion programs for Jews early in this century (and certainly similar programs for Italians) cannot teach us anything that would help improve on today's immigrant achievement or school completion, much of which may be attributable to bilingual education programs, even if imperfectly administered.

If the notion is misleading that English immersion led previous generations of immigrants to academic success, so too is the claim that bilingual education repudiates the assimilationist approach of previous immigrants. In reality, today's Hispanics are not the first to seek bicultural assimilation. Some 19th- and early 20th-century European immigrants also fought for and won the right to bilingual education in the public schools.[14] Native-language instruction was absent from 1920 until the mid-1960s only because a fierce anti-German (and then anti-immigrant) reaction after World War I succeeded in banishing it from American classrooms. Even foreign-language instruction for native-born students was banned in most places. If Chicago's Bismarck Hotel found it necessary to rename itself the "Mark Twain," it should not be surprising that bilingual education programs were also abolished.

Before World War I, immigrant groups often pressed public schools to teach children in their native language. The success of these groups depended more on whether adult immigrant activists had political power than on a pedagogical consensus. The immigrants' objective, as it is today, was to preserve a fragment of ethnic identity in children for whom the pull of American culture seemed dangerously irresistible. In this, they were supported by many influential educators. William Harris, the school superintendent in St. Louis and later U.S. commissioner of education, argued for bilingual education in the 1870s, stating that "national memories and aspirations, family traditions, customs and habits, moral and religious observances cannot be suddenly removed or changed without disastrously weakening the personality." Harris established the first "kindergarten" in America, taught solely in German, to give immigrant students a head start in the St. Louis schools.[15]

Nineteenth-century immigrant parents were often split over the desirability of bilingual education, as immigrant parents are split today. Many recognized that children were more likely to succeed if schools' use of the native language validated the culture of the home. But others felt that their children's education would be furthered if they learned in English only.

The first bilingual public school in New York City was established in 1837 to prepare German-speaking children for eventual participation in regular English schools. The initial rule was that children could remain in German-language instruction only for 12 months, after which they would transfer to a regular school. But the German teacher resisted this rule, believing that, before transferring, the children needed more than the limited English fluency they had acquired after a year of German instruction. The record is unclear about how often the rule was stretched.

Many immigrant children, not just Germans, did not attend school at all if they could not have classes in their native language. In his 1840 address to the New York legislature, Gov. William Seward (later Lincoln's secretary of state) explained that the importance of attracting immigrants to school—and of keeping them there—motivated his advocacy of expanded native-language instruction: "I do not hesitate to recommend the establishment of schools in which [immigrant children] may be instructed by teachers speaking the same language with themselves." Only by so doing, Gov. Seward insisted, could we "qualify . . . [them] for the high responsibilities of citizenship."

Buoyed by Seward's endorsement, Italian parents in New York City demanded a native-language school as well, and in 1843 the Public School Society established a committee to determine whether one should be established. The committee recommended against an Italian-language school, claiming the Italian community was itself divided. "Information has been obtained," the committee stated, "that the more intelligent class of Italians do not desire such a school, and that, like most [but not, apparently, all] of the better class of Germans, they would prefer that those of their countrymen who come here with good intentions should be Americanized as speedily as possible."[16]

Bilingual education, though sometimes controversial, was found nationwide. In Pennsylvania, German Lutheran churches established parochial schools when public schools would not teach in German; in 1838, Pennsylvania law converted these German schools to public schools. Then, in 1852, a state public school regulation specified that "if any considerable number of Germans desire to have their children instructed in their own language, their wishes should be gratified."[17]

In 1866, succumbing to pressure from politically powerful German immigrants, the Chicago Board of Education decided to establish a German-language school in each area of the city where 150 parents asked for it. By 1892 the board had hired 242 German-language teachers to teach 35,000 German-speaking children, one-fourth of Chicago's total public school enrollment. In 1870, a public school established in Denver, Colorado, was taught entirely in German. An 1872 Oregon law permitted German-language public schools to be established in Portland whenever 100 voters petitioned for such a school. Maryland, Iowa, Indiana, Kentucky, Ohio, and Minnesota also had bilingual education laws, either statewide or applying only to cities with large immigrant populations. In Nebraska, enabling legislation for bilingual education was enacted for the benefit of German immigrant children as late as 1913.[18]

There was considerable variation in how these programs arranged what we now call the "transition" to English. In St. Louis, Harris' system introduced English gradually, beginning in the first grade. The 1888 report of the Missouri supervisor of public instruction stated that "in some districts the schools are taught in German for a certain number of months and then in English, while in others German is used part of the day and English the rest. Some of the teachers are barely able to speak the English language." Ohio's 1870 rules provided that the lower grades in German-language public schools should be bilingual (half the instructional time in grades 1 through 4 could be in German), but in grades 5 through 8 native-language instruction had to be reduced to one hour a day. Baltimore permitted public schools in the upper grades to teach art and music in German only, but geography, history, and science had to be taught in both English and German. In some midwestern communities, there was resistance to any English instruction: an 1846 Wisconsin law insisted that public schools in Milwaukee must at least teach English (as a foreign language) as one academic subject.[19]

While Germans were most effective in demanding public support for native-language instruction, others were also successful. In Texas in the late 19th century, there were seven Czech-language schools supported by the state school fund. In California, a desire by the majority to segregate Chinese children seemed to play more of a role than demands by the Chinese community for separate education. San Francisco established a Chinese-language school in 1885; the city later established segregated Indian, Mongolian, and Japanese schools.[20]

San Francisco's German, Italian, and French immigrants, on the other hand, were taught in their native languages in regular public schools. Here, bilingual education was a strategy designed to lure immigrant children into public schools from parochial schools where they learned no English at all. According to San Francisco's school superintendent in 1871, only if offered native-language instruction could immigrant children be brought into public schools, where, "under the care of American teachers," they could be "molded in the true form of American citizenship."[21]

Support for bilingual education was rarely unanimous or consistent. In San Francisco, the election of an "anti-immigrant" Republican school board majority in 1873 led to the abolition of schools in which French and German- had been the primary languages of instruction and to the firing of all French and German-speaking teachers. After protests by the immigrant community, bilingual schools were reestablished in 1874. In 1877, the California legislature enacted a prohibition of bilingual education, but the governor declined to sign it. William Harris' bilingual system in St. Louis was dismantled in 1888, after redistricting split the German vote and the Irish won a school board majority.[22]

In 1889, Republican Gov. William Hoard of Wisconsin sponsored legislation to ban primary-language instruction in public and private schools, claiming the support of German immigrant parents. The *Milwaukee Sentinel* published a front-page story about "a German in Sheboygan County . . . who sent his children away to school in order that they might learn English." The father, reported the *Sentinel*, complained that "in the public schools of the town,

German teachers, who . . . did not know English . . . had been employed . . . , [and] he felt it essential to the welfare of his children, who expected to remain citizens of this country, to know English."[23]

But both the newspaper and Wisconsin's Republican politicians had misjudged the immigrants' sentiments. In response to the anti-bilingual law, enraged German Americans (who had previously supported Republican candidates) mobilized to turn the statehouse over to Democrats and to convert the state's 7-to-2 Republican majority in Congress to a Democratic majority of 8-to-1. The Democrats promptly repealed the anti-bilingual education law.

An almost identical series of events took place in Illinois, where formerly Republican German American voters mobilized in both East St. Louis and Chicago to elect a liberal Democrat, Peter Altgeld, governor in 1890, largely because of his bilingual school language policy. These upheavals in two previously safe Republican states played an important role in the election of Democrat Grover Cleveland as President in 1892. Nonetheless, the controversy continued, and in 1893 the *Chicago Tribune* began a new campaign against German-language instruction. In a compromise later that year, German instruction was abolished in the primary grades but retained in the upper grades, while Chicago's mayor promised German Americans a veto over future school board appointments to ensure that erosion of primary-language instruction would not continue.[24]

But these controversies ended with World War I. Six months after the armistice, the Ohio legislature, spurred by Gov. James Cox, who was to be the Democratic Presidential candidate in 1920, banned all German from the state's elementary schools. The language posed "a distinct menace to Americanism," Cox insisted. The *New York Times* editorialized in 1919 that, although some parents "want German to be taught [because it] pleases their pride . . . , it does not do their children any good." Within the following year, 15 states in which native-language instruction had flourished adopted laws requiring that all teaching be in English. By 1923, 35 states had done so.[25] Only when Nebraska went so far as to ban native-language instruction in parochial as well as public schools did the Supreme Court, in 1923, strike down an English-only law.[26]

During the next 30 years, bilingual instruction had its ups and downs, even where English was not the native language. In 1950, Louisiana first required English, not French, to be the language of public school instruction. In the Southwest, where teaching in Spanish had long been common, the practice continued in some places and was abolished in others. Tucson established a bilingual teaching program in 1923, and Burbank established one in 1931. New Mexico operated bilingual schools throughout most of the 20th century, up until the 1950s. The state even required the teaching of Spanish to English-speaking children in elementary school. But in 1918, Texas made teaching in Spanish a crime, and, while the law was not consistently enforced (especially along the Mexican border), as recently as 1973 a Texas teacher was indicted for not teaching history in English.[27] In the same year, Texas reversed itself andadopted bilingual education as its strategy.

When bilingual education began to reemerge in the 1970s—spurred by a Supreme Court finding that schools without special provisions for educating language-minority children were not providing equal education—the nation's memory of these precedents had been erased. Today many Americans blithely repeat the myth that, until the recent emergence of separatist minority activists and their liberal supporters, the nation had always immersed its immigrant children in nothing but English and this method had proved its effectiveness.

Bilingual Education: Mixed Evidence

This mixed history, however, does not prove that bilingual education is effective, any more so than English immersion or intense English-language instruction. To an unbiased layperson, the arguments of both advocates and opponents of bilingual education seem to make sense. On the one hand, it's reasonable to insist that children who don't speak English continue their education in a language they understand in history, literature, math, and science, while they learn English. It's also reasonable to expect, however, that this might make it too tempting to defer English-language instruction. Moreover, the best way to do something difficult—e.g., making the transition to English—is simply to do it without delay. It makes sense to acknowledge that children may adapt better to school if the school's culture is not in conflict with that of the home. But some immigrant parents may be more intent on preserving native culture for their children than are the children themselves.

Modern research findings on bilingual education are mixed. As with all educational research, it is so difficult to control for complex background factors that affect academic outcomes that no single study is ultimately satisfying. Bilingual education advocates point to case studies of primary-language programs in Calexico, California; Rock Point, Arizona; Santa Fe, New Mexico; New Haven, Connecticut; and elsewhere that show that children advance further in both English and other academic subjects when native-language instruction is used and the transition to English is very gradual. Opponents point to case studies in Redwood City and Berkeley, California; in Fairfax, Virginia; and elsewhere that prove that immersion in English or rapid and intensive English instruction is most effective.[28] Overall, the conflicting evidence from these case studies does not suggest that abolition of bilingual education or even the substitution of parental choice for pedagogical expertise in determining whether bilingual approaches should be used would improve things much.

The problem is especially complex because not only economic factors but also generational variation apparently affects the achievement of immigrant youths. In 1936, the principal of a high school in New York City that enrolled large numbers of Italian immigrants wrote:

> The problem of juvenile delinquency . . . baffles all the forces of organized society. . . . The highest rate of delinquency is characteristic of immigrant communities. . . . The delinquent is usually the American-born child of foreign-born parents, not the immigrant himself. Delinquency, then, is fundamentally a second-generation problem. This intensifies the responsibility of the school.[29]

The same is true today. The challenge now facing immigrant educators is that academic achievement for second-generation Hispanic and Asian children is often below that of children who arrive in the U.S. as immigrants themselves.[30] Many of these children of the second generation seem to speak English, but they are fully fluent in neither English nor their home language. Many of their parents, frustrated that their own ambition has not been transmitted to their children, may become convinced that only English immersion will set their children straight, while others seek bilingual solutions to prevent the corruption of American culture from dampening their children's ambition.

In the absence of persuasive evidence, the issue has become politicized. In a country as large as ours, with as varied experience, there is virtually no limit to the anecdotes and symbols that can be invoked as substitutes for evidence.

Opponents of bilingual education promote Hispanic parents to the media when they claim they want their children to learn English without bilingual support; the clear implication is that only liberal ideologues and separatists support native-language instruction. These claims, like those circulated by the *Milwaukee Sentinel* a century ago, may not reflect the feelings of most parents. And the technology of teaching a new language to immigrant children is complex; both bilingual education advocates and opponents claim their goal is full English literacy as rapidly as possible. But there's no reason to expect that politicized parent groups are the best judges of language acquisition research.

There are also successful adult immigrants who brag of their English fluency, acquired either with or without bilingual education. As always, such anecdotal evidence should be treated with caution. Richard Rodriguez' autobiography, *Hunger of Memory*, describes his successful education in an English-only environment. But Rodriguez, unlike most immigrants, was raised in a predominantly English-speaking neighborhood and was the only Spanish speaker in his class.[31] His experience may be relevant for some immigrants, but not relevant for many others.

Whichever method is, in fact, more effective for most immigrant children, there will be many for whom the other method worked well. It may be the case that immigrant children's social and economic background characteristics should affect the pedagogy chosen. Even if some Russian Jewish immigrants did not require bilingual education to graduate from high school, perhaps Italians would have progressed more rapidly if they'd had access to bilingual instruction. Today, the fact that some (though not all) Asian immigrants seem to progress rapidly in school without native-language support provides no relevant evidence about whether this model can work well for Mexican or Caribbean children, especially those low on the ladder of socioeconomic status and those whose parents have little education. Nor does it tell us much about what the best pedagogy would be for Asians who generally do less well in school, such as Hmong, Laotian, and Cambodian children.[32]

It is certain, however, that the American "melting pot" has never been endangered by pluralist efforts to preserve native languages and cultures. Bilingual instruction has never interfered with the powerful assimilationist influences that overwhelm all children whose parents migrate here. And this is equally true of Spanish-speaking children today.

After the last 20 years of bilingual education throughout America, Spanish-speaking children continue to assimilate. From 1972 to 1995, despite rapidly accelerating immigration (more Hispanic youths are first-generation immigrants today than 20 years ago), the Hispanic high school completion rate has crept upward (from 66% to 70%). Hispanic high school graduates who enroll in college jumped from 45% to 54% (for non-Hispanic whites, it's now 64%). And the number of Hispanic high school graduates who subsequently complete four years of college jumped from 11% to 16% (for non-Hispanic whites, it's now 34%).[33] A study of the five-county area surrounding Los Angeles, the most immigrant-affected community in the nation, found that from 1980 to 1990, the share of U.S.-born Hispanics in professional occupations grew from 7% to 9%, the share in executive positions grew from 7% to 10%, and the share in other administrative and technical jobs grew from 24% to 26%.[34] Overall, 55% of U.S.-born Hispanics are in occupations for which a good education is a necessity, in an area where bilingual education has been practiced for the last generation.

Perhaps we can do better. Perhaps we would do better with less bilingual education. But perhaps not. All we can say for sure is that the data reveal no apparent crisis, and the system for immigrant education with which we've been muddling through, with all its problems, does not seem to be in a state of collapse.

The best thing that could happen to the bilingual education debate would be to remove it from the political realm. Sound-bite pedagogy is no cure for the complex interaction of social, economic, and instructional factors that determine the outcomes of contemporary American schools.

Notes

1. Technically, "bilingual education" refers to all programs designed to give any support to non-English-speaking children, including programs whose main focus is immersion in English-speaking classrooms. In public debate, however, the term generally refers to only one such program, "transitional bilingual education (TBE)," in which native-language instruction in academic subjects is given to non-English speakers. In this article, I use the term in its nontechnical sense to refer only to "TBE" programs.

2. Web site, English First Foundation: http://englishfirst.org.

3. Mark Pitsch, "Dole Takes Aim at 'Elitist' History Standards," *Education Week*, 13 September 1995, p. 18.

4. Newt Gingrich, *To Renew America* (New York: HarperCollins, 1995), pp. 161–62.

5. Irving Howe, *World of Our Fathers* (New York: Simon and Schuster, 1983), p. 58.

6. Michael R. Olneck and Marvin Lazerson, "The School Achievement of Immigrant Children: 1900–1930," *History of Education Quarterly*, Winter 1974, pp. 453–82, Tables 3, 5, 6.

7. David K. Cohen, "Immigrants and the Schools," *Review of Educational Research*, vol. 40, 1970, pp. 13–27.

8. Seymour B. Sarason and John Doris, *Educational Handicap, Public Policy, and Social History* (New York: Free Press, 1979), pp. 155–56, 340–51.

9. Olneck and Lazerson, Tables 11 and 12.

10. Howe, pp. 277–78.

11. *Fall 1995 Preliminary Ethnic Survey* (Los Angeles: Information Technology Division, Los Angeles Unified School District, Publication No. 124, 1996).

12. Georges Vernez and Allan Abrahamse, *How Immigrants Fare in U.S. Education* (Santa Monica, Calif.: RAND Corporation, 1996), Table 3.2.

13. These figures are not strictly comparable; estimates are based on data in Vernez and Abrahamse, Table 4.2, and in National Center for Education Statistics, *Dropout Rates in the United States: 1995* (Washington, D.C.: Office of Educational Research and Improvement, U.S. Department of Education, NCES 97–473, 1997), Table 9.

14. Native-language instruction in public schools was also common in the Southwest, particularly in Texas, New Mexico, and Arizona, which were formerly part of Mexico and whose native populations, not their immigrants, were originally Spanish-speaking Mexicans. It was also common in Louisiana, where French-language public schools were established well after the Louisiana Purchase to preserve native French culture.

15. Diego Castellanos, *The Best of Two Worlds: Bilingual-Bicultural Education in the United States* (Trenton: New Jersey State Department of Education, CN 500, 1983), pp. 23–25.

16. Sarason and Doris, pp. 180–81, 194.

17. Heinz Kloss, *The American Bilingual Tradition* (Rowley, Mass.: Newbury House, 1977), pp. 149–50.

18. Ibid., pp. 61, 86, 180; Castellanos, p. 19; and Mary J. Herrick, *The Chicago Schools: A Social and Political History* (Beverly Hills, Calif.: Sage, 1971), p. 61.

19. Kloss, pp. 69, 86, 158–59, 190; and Castellanos, pp. 24–25.

20. Kloss, pp. 177–78, 184.

21. Castellanos, p. 23; and Paul E. Peterson, *The Politics of School Reform, 1870–1940* (Chicago: University of Chicago Press, 1985), p. 55.

22. Peterson, pp. 55–56; Castellanos, p. 25; and James Crawford, Bilingual Education: History, Politics, Theory, and Practice (Trenton, N.J.: Crane Publishing Company, 1989), p. 22.

23. "The School Question," *Milwaukee Sentinel*, 27 November 1889.

24. Herrick, p. 61; Kloss, p. 89; Peterson, pp. 10, 58; William F. Whyte, "The Bennett Law Campaign in Wisconsin," *Wisconsin Magazine of History,* vol. 10, 1927, pp. 363–90; and Bernard Mehl, "Educational Criticism: Past and Present," *Progressive Education,* March 1953, p. 154.

25. Crawford, pp. 23–24; and David Tyack, "Constructing Difference: Historical Reflections on Schooling and Social Diversity," *Teachers College Record,* Fall 1993, p. 15.

26. *Meyer v. Nebraska*, 262 US 390 (1923).

27. Castellanos, pp. 43, 49; Crawford, p. 26; and idem, *Hold Your Tongue* (Reading, Mass.: Addison-Wesley, 1992), p. 72.

28. See, for example, Rudolph Troike, "Research Evidence for the Effectiveness of Bilingual Education," *NABE Journal,* vol. 3, 1978, pp. 13–24; *The Bilingual Education Handbook: Designing Instruction for LEP Students* (Sacramento: California Department of Education, 1990), p. 13; Iris Rotberg, "Some Legal and Research Considerations in Establishing Federal Bilingual Policy in Bilingual Education," *Harvard Educational Review,* May 1982, pp. 158–59; and Rosalie Pedalino Porter, *Forked Tongue: The Politics of Bilingual Education* (New York: Basic Books, 1990) p. 141.

29. Leonard Covello, "A High School and Its Immigrant Community—A Challenge and an Opportunity," *Journal of Educational Sociology,* February 1936, p. 334.

30. Ruben G. Rumbaut, "The New Californians: Research Findings on the Educational Progress of Immigrant Children," in idem and Wayne Cornelius, eds., *California's Immigrant Children: Theory, Research, and Implications for Educational Policy* (San Diego: Center for U.S.-Mexican Studies, University of California, 1995).

31. For a discussion of Rodriguez as prototype, see Stephen D. Krashen, *Under Attack: The Case Against Bilingual Education* (Culver City, Calif.: Language Education Associates, 1996), p. 19.

32. Rumbaut, Table 2.6.

33. *Dropout Rates in the United States: 1995,* Table A–37; and National Center for Education Statistics, *The Condition of Education 1997* (Washington, D.C.: U.S. Department of Education, NCES 97–388, 1997), Indicators 8, 22.

34. Gregory Rodriguez, *The Emerging Latino Middle Class* (Malibu, Calif.: Pepperdine University Institute for Public Policy, 1996), Figure 22.

POSTSCRIPT

Should Bilingual Education Programs Be Abandoned?

Research comparing the effectiveness of the several approaches to help-ing linguistically disadvantaged students remains inconclusive. At the same time, the effort is clouded by the political agendas of those who champion first-language instruction and those who insist on some version of the immersion strategy. Politics and emotional commitments aside, what must be placed first on the agenda are the needs of the students and the value of native language in a child's progress through school.

Some books to note are Jane Miller's *Many Voices: Bilingualism, Culture and Education* (1983), which includes a research review; Kenji Hakuta's *Mirror of Language: The Debate on Bilingualism* (1986); *Bilingual Education: A Source-book* by Alba N. Ambert and Sarah E. Melendez (1985); *Sink or Swim: The Politics of Bilingual Education* by Colman B. Stein, Jr. (1986); and *Teaching Other People's Children: Literacy and Learning in a Bilingual Classroom* by Cynthia Ballenger (1999). Thomas Weyr's book *Hispanic U.S.A.: Breaking the Melting Pot* (1988) presents a detailed plan of action in light of the prediction that "by the year 2000 as many people in the U.S. will be speaking Spanish as they will English."

A number of pertinent articles may be found in the March 1989 issue of *The American School Board Journal,* the March 1988 issue of *The English Journal,* the Summer 1988 issue of *Equity and Excellence,* and the Autumn 2000 issue of *Theory Into Practice.* Some especially provocative articles are "Bilingual Education: A Barrier to Achievement," by Nicholas Sanchez, *Bilingual Education* (December 1987); "'Official English': Fear or Foresight?" by Nancy Bane, *America* (December 17, 1988); and "The Language of Power," by Yolanda T. DeMola, *America* (April 22, 1989).

More recent articles include David Hill's "English Spoken Here," *Teacher Magazine* (January 1998); Jerry Cammarata's "Tongue-Tied," *American School Board Journal* (June 1997); and Glenn Garvin's "Loco, Completamente Loco," *Reason* (January 1998). Donaldo Macedo offers a wide-ranging critique of current educational practices in "Literacy for Stupidification: The Pedagogy of Big Lies," *Harvard Educational Review* (Summer 1993). Also see his book *Literacies of Power: What Americans Are Not Allowed to Know* (1994).

Of especial note are "Americanization and the Schools," by E. D. Hirsch, Jr., *The Clearing House* (January/February 1999); Lynn W. Zimmerman's "Bilin-gual Education as a Manifestation of an Ethic of Caring"; Gail L. Thompson's "The Real Deal on Bilingual Education," *Educational Horizons* (Winter 2000); and Christine H. Rossell's "The Near End of Bilingual Education," *Education Next* (Fall 2003).

ISSUE 17

Does School Violence Warrant a Zero-Tolerance Policy?

YES: Albert Shanker, from "Restoring the Connection Between Behavior and Consequences," *Vital Speeches of the Day* (May 15, 1995)

NO: Alfie Kohn, from "Safety from the Inside Out: Rethinking Traditional Approaches," *Educational Horizons* (Fall 2004)

ISSUE SUMMARY

YES: Albert Shanker, president of the American Federation of Teachers (AFT), advocates a "get tough" policy for dealing with violent and disruptive students in order to send a clear message that all students are responsible for their own behavior.

NO: Alfie Kohn, author of numerous books on education, contends that heavy-handed disciplinary procedures fail to get at the causes of aggression and are detrimental to the building of a school culture of safety and caring.

$\mathbf{B}$eyond basic classroom discipline and general civility lies the more serious realm of violence in schools: unpredictable acts of violence against students and teachers and what Jackson Toby refers to as everyday school violence fueled by a disorderly educational and social atmosphere. Toby, in "Everyday School Violence: How Disorder Fuels It," *American Educator* (Winter 1993/1994), states, "The concept of 'school disorder' suggests that schools, like families, also vary in their cohesiveness and effectiveness. What school disorder means in concrete terms is that one or both of two departures from normality exists: A significant proportion of students do not seem to recognize the legitimacy of the rules governing the school's operation and therefore violate them frequently; and/or a significant proportion of students defy the authority of teachers and other staff members charged with enforcing the rules." Toby and other experts feel that teachers lost much of their authority, especially in inner-city high schools, during the 1960s and 1970s when school systems stopped standing behind teachers' disciplinary actions and many teachers became afraid of confronting aggressive student behavior.

A 1978 report to Congress by the National Institute of Education, *Violent Schools—Safe Schools,* documented widespread incidents of theft, assaults, weapon possession, vandalism, rape, and drug use in America's schools. These findings helped lead to the current period of security guards metal detectors, book bag searches, locker raids, and pursuit of armed teenagers in school halls. "Zero tolerance" emerged as a rallying cry of the 1990s—zero tolerance for any weapons in school (handguns, semiautomatics, knives, and, in a few cases, fingernail files) and zero tolerance for any drugs in school (crack cocaine, pot, alcohol, and, in some cases, Midol or Tylenol).

These measures have sparked a heated debate over the conflict between students' rights and the need to protect students and professionals from violence. We pride ourselves on being a tolerant society, but it has become obvious that new lines must be drawn. Daniel Patrick Moynihan, senior senator from New York, in "Defining Deviancy Down," *The American Scholar* (Winter 1993), contends that we have become accustomed to alarming levels of criminal and destructive behavior and that the absence of meaningful punishment for those who commit violent acts reinforces the belief that violence is an appropriate way to settle disputes among members of society.

Congressional passage of the Gun-Free Schools Act in 1994 placed an automatic one-year expulsion on weapon-carrying students and demanded referral of offenders to the criminal justice or juvenile delinquency system after due process procedures are carried out. According to Kathleen Vail, in "Ground Zero," *American School Board Journal* (June 1995), some child advocates, educators, and parents feel that such zero-tolerance policies do not allow enough room for exceptions, especially when young children are involved. There is also a concern that get-tough measures weaken the implementation of conflict-resolution strategies aimed at uncovering deeper explanations of aggressive behavior.

A flurry of articles on school violence has appeared in recent years. Among the best are Jackson Toby's "Getting Serious About School Discipline," *The Public Interest* (Fall 1998); "The Dark Side of Zero Tolerance," by Russ Skiba and Reece Peterson, *Phi Delta Kappan* (January 1999); Abigail Thernstrom's "Courting Disorder in the Schools," *The Public Interest* (Summer 1999); Michael Easterbrook's "Taking Aim at Violence," *Psychology Today* (July/August 1999); "Zero Tolerance for Zero Tolerance," by Richard L. Curwin and Allen N. Mendler, *Phi Delta Kappan* (October 1999); W. Michael Martin's "Does Zero Mean Zero?" *American School Board Journal* (March 2000); and two articles on the controversial practice of profiling potentially violent students in *The School Administrator* (February 2000).

The American Federation of Teachers (AFT) has strongly supported zero-tolerance policies. In the first of the following selections, the late Albert Shanker, former AFT president, makes the case for tough measures to restore safety and confidence in the public schools and thereby stem the exodus of concerned parents. In the second selection, Alfie Kohn calls for a refocus on the human element of violence that goes beyond punishment and technical fixes.

 **YES**

Restoring the Connection Between Behavior and Consequences

I can't think of a more important topic. . . . [T]here have been and will be a number of conferences on this issue. I can assure you, all of the other conferences resemble each other, and this one will be very different. It will have a very different point of view.

We have had, over the last decade or more, a national debate on the issue of school quality. And there is a national consensus that we need to do a lot better. We are probably doing better than we used to, but we're not doing as well as other industrial countries. And in order to do well, we are going to have to do some of the things that those other countries are doing, such as develop high standards, assessments related to those standards, and a system of consequences so that teachers and youngsters and parents know that school counts. School makes a difference, whether it's getting a job or getting into a college or getting into a training program.

We're well on the way. It's going to take time, but we're on the way to bringing about the improvement that we need. But you can have a wonderful curriculum and terrific assessments and you can state that there are consequences out there but none of this is going to do much good in terms of providing youngsters with an education if we don't meet certain basic obvious conditions. And those conditions are simply that you have to have schools that are safe and classrooms where there is sufficient order so that the curriculum means something. Without that, all of this stuff is nonsense. You can deliver a terrific curriculum, but if youngsters are throwing things, cursing and yelling and punching each other, then the curriculum doesn't mean anything in that classroom. The agenda is quite different.

And so we have a very interesting phenomenon. We have members of Congress and governors and state legislators talking about choice and vouchers and charter schools, and you know what the big incentive is for those issues. Parents are not really pushing for these things, except in conditions where their children seem to be unsafe or in conditions where they can't learn. And then they say, well, look, if you can't straighten things out here, then give me a chance to take my youngster somewhere else. And so we're about to put in place a ridiculous situation. We're going to create a system of

From Albert Shanker, "Restoring the Connection Between Behavior and Consequences," *Vital Speeches of the Day* (May 15, 1995). Copyright © 1995 by Albert Shanker. Reprinted by permission of The American Federation of Teachers.

choice and vouchers, so that 98 percent of the kids who behave can go someplace and be safe. And we're going to leave the two percent who are violent and disruptive to take over the schools. Now, isn't it ridiculous to move 98 percent of the kids, when all you have to do is move two or three percent of them and the other 98 percent would be absolutely fine?

Now this is a problem which has a number of aspects and I want to talk about them. First, there is, of course, the problem of extreme danger, where we are dealing with violence or guns or drugs within the school. And, as we look to the schools, what we find is that the schools seem to be unable to handle this. We had headlines here in DC . . . saying that the mayor and school officials say they don't know what else to do. In other words, they've done everything that they can, and the guns, and the knives, and the drugs are still there. So, it just happens that they have actually said it, but that is, in fact, how many school administrators and school boards across the country behave. They treat violence as a fact of life, that's what society is like, and they just go through a couple of ritual efforts to try to show that they're doing something. But, basically they give up.

What we have is what amounts to a very high level of tolerance of this type of activity. Now, of course, the violence and the guns and the drugs have to be distinguished from another type of activity. This other type isn't deadly in the sense that you are going to read tomorrow morning that some youngster was stabbed or shot. And that's the whole question of just plain out-and-out disruption: the youngster who is constantly yelling, cursing, jumping, fighting, doing all sorts of things, so that most of the time the other students in the class and the teacher is devoted, not to the academic mission of the schools, but to figuring out how to contain this individual. And in this area, we have an even higher tolerance than we do in the area of violence, where occasionally youngsters are suspended or removed for periods of time. . . .

Last year when Congress was debating the Goals 2000 education program, there were an awful lot of people who said, you know, in addition to having different kinds of content standards—what you should learn—and performance standards—how good is good enough—you ought to have opportunity-to-learn standards. It's not fair to hold kids to these standards unless they've had certain advantages. It's not fair, if one kid has had early childhood education and one hasn't, to hold them to the same standard. It's not fair, if at this school they don't have any textbooks or the textbooks are 15 years old, and in that school they have the most modern books. It's not fair, if in this school they've got computers, and in that school kids have never seen a computer.

Well, I submit to you that if you want to talk about opportunity-to-learn standards, there are a lot of kids who've made it without the most up-to-date textbooks. It's better if you have them. There are a lot of kids who've made it without early childhood education. It's a lot better if you've got it, and we're for that. Throughout history, people have learned without computers, but it's better if you've got them. But nobody has ever learned if they were in a classroom with one or two kids who took up 90 percent of the time through disruption, violence, or threats of violence. You deprive children of an opportunity to learn if you do not first provide an orderly situation within the classroom and within the school. That comes ahead of all of these other things.

Now, I said that this conference was going to be different from every conference that I've been to and every conference that I've read about. I have a report here that was sent to me by John Cole [President of the Texas Federation of Teachers], who went to The Scholastic Annual Summit on Youth Violence on October 17 [1994]. I'm not going to read the whole thing, but I'll just read enough that you get the flavor of what these other conferences are like:

> "So start with the concept that the real victims of violence are those unfortunate individuals who have been led into lives of crime by the failure of society to provide them with hope for a meaningful life. Following that logic, one must conclude that society has not done enough for these children and that we must find ways to salvage their lives. Schools must work patiently with these individuals offering them different avenues out of this situation. As an institution charged with responsibility for education, schools must have programs to identify those who are embarking on a life of crime and violence and lift them out of the snares into which they have fallen. Society, meanwhile, should be more forgiving of the sins of these poor creatures, who through no real fault of their own are the victims of racism and economic injustice.
>
> "Again and again and again, panelists pointed out that the young people we are talking about, to paraphrase Rodney Dangerfield, 'don't get no respect.' The experts assured us that young people take up weapons, commit acts of violence, and abuse drugs because this enables them to obtain respect from their peers. I found myself thinking that we aid and abet this behavior when we bend over backwards to accommodate those young people who have bought into this philosophy. By lavishing attention on them, we may even encourage a spread of that behavior. Many of these programs are well meaning but counterproductive.
>
> "I don't want to condemn this conference as a waste of time. Obviously, we do need programs to work with these young people, and we should try to salvage as many as we can. However, we must somehow come to grips with the idea that individuals have responsibility for their own actions. If we assume that society is to blame for all of the problems these young people have, may we then assume that society must develop solutions that take care of these young people's problems? We take away from each individual the responsibility for his or her own life. Once the individual assumes that he or she has lost control of his own destiny, that individual has no difficulty in justifying any act because he or she feels no responsibility for the consequences."

Now with that philosophy, the idea is not that we want to be punitive or nasty, but essentially schools must teach not only English and mathematics and reading and writing and history, but also teach that there are ways of behaving in society that are unacceptable. And when we sit back and tolerate certain types of behavior, we are teaching youngsters that certain types of behavior are acceptable, which eventually will end up with their being in jail or in poverty for the rest of their lives. We are not doing our jobs as teachers.

And the system is not doing its job, if we send youngsters the message that this is tolerable behavior within society. . . .

All we ask of our schools is that they behave in the same way that a caring and intelligent parent would behave with respect to their own children. I doubt very much, if you had a youngster who was a fire bug or a youngster who used weapons, whether you would say, well, I owe it to this youngster to trust him with my other children to show him that I'm not separating him out or treating him differently. Or I'm going to raise his self-esteem by allowing him to do these things. All of these nutty things that we talk about in school, we would not do. So the starting point of this conference, which is different from all of the others, is that I hope that you people join withme in a sense of outrage that we have a system that is willing to sacrifice the overwhelming majority of children for a handful. And not do any good for that handful either. And we need to start with that outrage, because without that we're not going to change this system.

That outrage is there among parents. That outrage was partly expressed in the recent election as people's anger at the way government was working. Why can't government do things in some sort of common sense way? And this is one of the issues that's out there. Now, what are some of the things that enter into this? Well, part of it is that some people think of schools as sort of custodial institutions. Where are we going to put the kids? Put them here. Or they think the school's job is mostly socialization. Eventually troubled kids will grow up or grow out of this, and they're better off with other youngsters than they are separated. Of course, people who take that point of view are totally ignoring the fact that the central role of schools, the one that we will be held accountable for, is student academic achievement. We know the test scores are bad. And we know that our students are not learning as much as youngsters in other countries. So we can't just say we know we are way behind, but, boy, are we good custodians. Look at how socialized these youngsters are.

People are paying for education and they want youngsters who are going to be able to be employed and get decent jobs. We want youngsters who are going to be as well off or in better shape than we are, just as most of us are with respect to our parents and grandparents. And the academic function is the one that's neglected. The academic function is the one that's destroyed in this notion that our job is mainly custodial.

So our central position is that we have to be tough on these issues, and we have to be tough because basically we are defending the right of children to an education. And those who insist on allowing violence and disruptive behavior in the school are destroying the right to an education for the overwhelming majority of youngsters within our schools.

Two years ago or three years ago, I was in Texas at a convention of the Texas Federation of Teachers. I didn't know this was going to happen, but either just before I got there or while I was there, there was a press conference on a position the convention adopted, and they used the phrase "zero tolerance." They said that with respect to certain types of dangerous activities in schools, there would be zero tolerance. These things are not acceptable and there are going to be consequences. There might be suspension, there might be expulsion, or there might be something else, but nevertheless, consequences will be clear. Well, that got picked up by radio, television, legislators. I was listening to a governor the other night at the National Governors Association, who stood up and came out for zero tolerance. It is a phrase which has caught on and is sweeping the country.

I hope it is one that all of you will bring back to your communities and your states, that there are certain types of activities that we will not tolerate. We will not teach youngsters bad lessons, and we're going to start very early. When a youngster does something that is terribly wrong, and all of the other youngsters are sure that something is going to happen to him because he did something wrong, we had better make sure that we fulfill the expectations of all those other youngsters that something's going to happen. And they're all going to say, "Thank God, I didn't do a terrible thing like that or I would be out there, and something would be happening to me." That is the beginning of a sense of doing something right, as against doing wrong.

And we have to deal with this notion that society is responsible, social conditions are responsible. The AFT does not take second place to anybody in fighting for decent conditions for adults and for youngsters and for minorities and for groups that have been oppressed. We're not in a state of denial; we're not saying that things have been wonderful. But when your kids come home and say "I'm doing these terrible things because of these conditions," if you're a good parent, you'll say, "That's no excuse." You are going to do things right, because you don't want your youngster to end up as a criminal or in some sort of horrible position. . . .

Now what should schools do? Schools should have codes of conduct. These codes can be developed through collective bargaining or they can be mandated in legislation. I don't think it would be a bad idea to have state legislation that every school system needs to have a code of discipline that is very clear, not a fuzzy sort of thing, something that says these things are not to be done and if this happens, these are the consequences. A very clear connection between behavior and consequences. And it might even say that, if there is a legitimate complaint from a group of parents or a group of teachers or a group of students that clearly shows the school district doesn't have such a code or isn't enforcing it, there would be some sort of financial penalty against the district for failing to provide a decent education by allowing this type of violence and disruption to continue.

Taxpayers are sending money into the district so that the kids can have an education, and if that district then destroys the education by allowing one or two youngsters to wipe out all of the effects that money is supposed to produce, what the hell is the point of sending the money? If you allow these youngsters to so disrupt that education, you might as well save the money. So there's a reason for states to do this. And, by the way, I think that you'll find a receptive audience, because the notion of individuals taking responsibility for their actions is one of the things fueling the political anger in this country—that we have a lot of laws which help people to become irresponsible or encourage them not to take responsibility for their own actions.

Now, enforcement is very important. For every crime, so to speak, there ought to be a punishment. I don't like very much judgment to be used, because once you allow judgment to be used, punishments will be more severe for some kids than for others and you will get unfairness. You will get prejudice. The way to make sure that this is done fairly and is not done in a prejudiced way is to say, look, we don't care if you're white or Hispanic or African-American or whether you're a recent immigrant or this or that, for this infraction, this is what happens. We don't have a different sanction depending upon whether we like you a little more or a little less. That's how fairness would be ensured, and I think it's very important that we insist on that. . . .

One of the big problems is school administrators. School administrators are concerned that, if there are a large number of reports of disruptions and violence in their schools, their reputations will suffer. They like to say they have none of those problems in their schools. Now, how do you prove that you have none of these problems in your school? Very simple. Just tell the teachers that if they report it, it's because they are ineffective teachers. If you tell that to one or two teachers, you will certainly have a school that has very little disruption or violence reported. You may have plenty of disruption and violence. So, in many places we have this gag rule. It's not written, but it's very well understood.

As a teacher, I myself faced this. Each time I reported something like this, I was told that if I knew how to motivate the students properly, this wouldn't happen. It's pretty universal. It wasn't just one district or just my principal. It's almost all of them. Therefore, I think that we ought to seek laws that require a full and honest reporting of incidents of violence and extreme disruption. And that would mean that, if an administrator goes around telling you to shut up or threatening you so that you're not free to report, I think that there ought to be penalties. Unless we know the extent of this problem, we're never going to deal with it adequately.

Of course, parents know what the extent of it is. What is the number one problem? It's the problem of violence and order in the schools. They know it. The second big problem and obstacle we face is, what's going to happen if you put the kid out on the streets? It reminds me of a big campaign in New York City to get crime off the streets, and pretty soon they were very successful. They had lots of policemen on the streets, and they drove the criminals away. The criminals went into the subways. Then they had a campaign about crime in the subways, and they drove them back up into the streets. So the business community, parents, and others will say, you can't just throw a kid out and put them on the streets. That's no good. But you could place some conditions on it. To return to school, students would have to bring with them a parent or some other grown-up or relative responsible for them. There is a list of ways in which we might handle it. But we can't say that we're going to wait until we build new schools, or build new classrooms, or have new facilities. The first thing you do is separate out the youngster who is a danger to the other youngsters.

Now, let me give an example. And I think it's one that's pretty close. We know that, when we arrest adults who have committed crimes and we jail them, jail will most likely not help those who are jailed. I don't think it does, and I don't think most people do. However, most of us are pretty glad when someone who has ommitted a pretty bad crime is jailed. Not because it's going to do that person any good, but because that person won't be around to do the same thing for the next ten or fifteen years. And for the separation of youngsters who are destroying the education of others, the justification is the same. I'm not sure that we can devise programs that will reach those youngsters that will help them. We should try. But our first obligation is to never destroy the education of the twenty or twenty-five or thirty because you have an obligation to one. Especially when there's no evidence that you're doing anything for that one by keeping him there.

Now, another big obstacle is legal problems. These are expensive and time consuming. If a youngster gets a lawyer and goes to court, the principal or some other figure of authority from the school, usually has to go to court. They might sit a whole day and by the end of the first day, they decide not to hear it. And they come a second day, and maybe it's held over again. It might take three or four days for each youngster. So if you've got a decent-sized school, even if you're dealing with only two or three percent of the youngsters, you could spend your full time in court, instead of being in school. Well, I wouldn't want to do that if I were the principal of the school. And then what does the court do when you're all finished? The court says, well, we don't have any better place to put him, so send him right back. So, that's why a lot of teachers wouldn't report it, because nothing happens anyway. You go through all of this, you spend all of that time and money, and when you're all finished, you're right back where you started. So we need to change what happens with respect to the court, and we have two ideas that we're going to explore that have not been done before.

One of the things we need to do is see whether we can get parents, teachers, and even perhaps high school students to intervene in these cases and say, we want to come before the judge to present evidence about what the consequences are for the other children. When you go to court now, you have the lawyer for the board of education, the lawyer for the youngster, and the youngster. And the youngster, well, he's just a kid and his lawyer says, "This poor child has all of these problems," and the judge is looking down at this poor youngster. You know who is not there? The other 25 youngsters to say, this guy beats me up every day. If I do my homework, I get beat up on the way to school because he doesn't want me to do my homework. So instead of first having this one child standing there saying, "Poor me, let me back in school, they have kicked me out, they have done terrible things to me," you also have some of the victims there saying, "Hey, what about us?" You'll get a much fairer consideration if the judge is able to look at both sides, instead of just hearing the bureaucrat from the board of education. None of these board of education lawyers that I've met talk about the other students. They talk about the right of the board of education under the law to do thus, and so what you have is a humane judge who's thinking of the bureaucrat talking about the rights of the board of education as against the child. I think we need to balance that.

Now, there's a second thing we are going to explore. We are all familiar with the fact that most of our labor contracts have a provision for grievance procedures. And part of that grievance procedure is arbitration. Now, you can take an arbitration award to court and try to appeal it, but it's very, very difficult to get a court to overthrow an arbitrator's award. Why? Because the court says, look, you had your day, you went to the arbitrator and you presented all your arguments, the other side presented all their arguments. In order for me to look into that arbitration and turn it over, you're going to have to prove to me that something in this arbitration was so terrible that we have to prove that the arbitrator was absolutely partial or that he broke the law. You've got to prove something outrageous. Otherwise, the judge is going to say, "You've had your day in court."

Now, why can't school districts establish a fair, inexpensive, due-process arbitration procedure for youngsters who are violent or disruptive? So that when the youngster goes to court, they can say, "Hey, we've had this procedure. We've had witnesses on both sides, and here was the determination. And, really, you shouldn't get into this stuff unless you can show that these people are terribly prejudiced or totally incompetent or something else." In other words, we don't have to use the court. We could create a separate school judicial system that had expertise and knowledge about what the impact is on students and teachers and the whole system of these kinds of decisions. Arbitration is a much cheaper, much faster system, especially if you have an expedited arbitration system. There is a system in the American Arbitration Association of expedited arbitration that says how many briefs you're allowed to write and how much time each side can take, and all of that. So we have a legal team and we're going to explore the notion of getting this stuff out of the courts and creating a system that is inexpensive and fair to the youngster and fair to the other youngsters in the school.

Now, let me point out that a lot of the tolerance for bad behavior is about to change, because we are about to have stakes attached to student academic outcomes. In other words, in the near future, we are going to have a situation where, if you don't make it up to this point, then you can't be admitted into college. Or if you don't make it here, then you will not get certified for a certain type of employment. But in Chapter I schools, this is going to start very soon. There is a provision in the new Chapter One, now called Title I, and very soon, if Title I schools do not show a substantial progress for students, the school's going to be punished. And one of the punishments is reconstitution of the school. The school will be closed down, teachers will go elsewhere, students will go elsewhere, and the school will open up with a new student body, slowly rebuild. That's one of the punishments. There are other punishments as well. So if you've got a bunch of these disruptive youngsters that prevent you from teaching and the other students from learning, it won't be like yesterday, where nobody seems to care, the kids are all going to get promoted anyway and they can all go to college, because there are no standards. There are no stakes.

Now, for the first time, there will be stakes. The teachers will know. The parents will know, hey, this school's going to close. I'm going to have to find a way of getting my kid to some other school because of the lack of learning that comes from this disruption. Teachers are going to say, hey, I'm not going to have my job in this school a couple of years from now because they're going to shut it down. I don't know what the rules are, what happens to these teachers, whether other schools have to take them or not. But we are entering a period where there will be consequences and parents and teachers are going to be a lot more concerned about achievement.

Now, one of the other issues that has stood in the way of doing something here is a very difficult one to talk about in our society, and that's the issue of race. And whenever the topic of suspension or expulsion comes up, there's always the question of race. Cincinnati is a good example. The union there negotiated a good discipline code as part of a desegregation suit. And the question was raised, "Well, is there a disparate impact, with more minority kids being suspended than others?" And who are the teachers who are suspending them? Do you have more white teachers suspending African-American kids?

Our position on that is very clear. In any given school, you may have more white kids with infractions or you may have more African-American kids, or you may have more Hispanic kids. We don't know. I don't think anybody knows. But we handle that by saying, "Whatever your crime is and whoever you are, you're going to get exactly the same punishment." If we do that, I'm sure that the number who will be punished will end up being very, very small. Because, as a young kid, if you see that there is a consequence, you will change your behavior. . . .

Now we have another very big problem, and we're going to try to deal with this in legislation. Under legislation that deals with disabled youngsters, we have two different standards. Namely, if a youngster in this class is not disabled and commits an infraction, you can do whatever is in that discipline code for that youngster. But if the youngster is disabled and is in that same class (for instance, the youngster might have a speech defect), you can't suspend that youngster while all of the proceedings are going on because that's a change in placement. It might take you a year-and-a-half in court, and meanwhile that youngster who is engaged in some threatening or dangerous behavior has to stay there. This makes no sense. We have a lot of support in the Congress on this, and we think we have a good chance of changing this. . . .

Well, that's the whole picture. And to return to the theme at the beginning, we have a cry for choice, a cry for vouchers, a cry for charters. It's not really a cry for these things. People really want their own schools, and they want their kids to go to those schools, and they want those schools to be safe and orderly for their youngsters.

It is insane to set up a system where we move 98 percent of our kids away from the two percent who are dangerous, instead of moving the two percent away from the 98 percent who are OK. We need to have discipline codes, we need to have a new legal system, we need to have one standard for all students. We need to have a system where we don't have to wait for a year or a year-and-a-half after a student has perpetrated some terrible and atrocious crime before that student is removed for the safety of the other students. How are we going to do this? We are going to do this, first of all, by talking to our colleagues within the schools. Our polls show that the overwhelming majority accepts these views.

The support of African-American parents for the removal of violent youngsters and disruptive students is higher than any other group within our society. Now very often when youngsters are removed, it's because some parents group or some committee starts shouting and making noise, and the school system can't resist that. Now I think that it's time for us to turn to business groups, it's time for us to turn to parents' groups. When youngsters commit such acts, and when they've had a fair due-process within the system, we need to have a system of public support, just as we have in the community when someone commits a terrible crime. People say, send that person to jail, don't send him back to us. We need to have a lot of decent people within our communities, when you have youngsters who are destroying the education of all the others, who will stand up and say, "Look, we don't want to punish this kid, but for the sake of our children, you're going to have to keep that one away, until that one is ready to come back and live in a decent way in society with all of the other youngsters."

I'm sure that if we take this back to our communities, and if we work on it, the appeal will be obvious. It's common sense. And we will save our schools and we will do something which will give us the basis for providing a decent education for all of our children.

Safety from the Inside Out: Rethinking Traditional Approaches

For many people, the idea of safety in an educational context brings to mind the problem of school violence, and specifically the string of shootings at schools across the country in recent years. Let's begin, then, by noting that the coverage of those events has obscured several important facts:

- The real horror is that young people die, not where they die. To be sure, there's something deeply unsettling about the juxtaposition of the words "violence" and "schools." But keep in mind that the vast majority of young homicide victims are killed at home, on the streets, or somewhere else other than school. During one three-year period in the 1990s, for example, about eighty homicides took place on school grounds—while more than 8,000 children were killed elsewhere. This is important to keep in mind, both so that we recognize the full extent of the problem and so we don't exaggerate how dangerous schools really are.
- There is a tendency, upon hearing about stunning cases of school violence, to infer that adolescents are Public Enemy No. 1. But Mike Males, a sociologist, urges us to focus our attention on the "far more common phenomenon of adults killing kids." He points out that Americans blame teenagers too easily, and usually inaccurately, for what's wrong with our society.[1]
- When school violence does occur, low-income students of color are disproportionately likely to be the victims, Columbine and other notorious school-shooting incidents notwithstanding. If that fact is surprising, it may be because of the media's tacit assumption that any problem—crime, drugs, violence—is more newsworthy when white people in the suburbs are affected.

Yet another series of mistaken assumptions comes into play when educators and policymakers try to respond to violence—or to their fear of it. Questionable beliefs often lead to wrongheaded policies.

First, we Americans love to imagine that *technical fixes* will take care of complicated problems. (Remember the V-chip, which was supposed to be the

Copyright 2004 by Alfie Kohn. Reprinted from *Educational Horizons*, Fall 2004, pp. 33–41, with the author's permission. For more information, please see www.alfiekohn.org.

solution to children's exposure to violent television programming?) Some people still cling to the hope that schools can be made safer if we just install enough surveillance cameras and metal detectors. In reality, though, it's simply not feasible to guard every doorway or monitor every screen. The number of cameras at one Washington, D.C., high school was recently doubled, from thirty-two to sixty-four, but the principal admitted that it's hard to keep guns "on the outside of the school unless we become armed camps, and I don't think anyone wants to send their child to an armed camp." His comments were reported in a newspaper article that was aptly headlined "Trust, Not Cameras, Called Best Prevention."[2]

Pedro Noguera, who teaches at New York University, put it this way: "Design and staffing of schools are driven by security concerns, but no thought is given to how these designs and atmospheres make students and [teachers] feel. If we use prisons as our models for safe schools—well, prisons are not safe places, right? Safety comes from human relations. I'd say we'd do much better to invest in counselors than armed guards."[3]

Second, when we do focus on the human element of violence prevention, we often assume that students just need to be taught the appropriate *skills*.[4] This model is so simple and familiar to us that we don't even think of it as a model at all. It seems a matter of common sense that if children don't pay attention to what someone else is saying, they would benefit from some remedial listening skills. If they fail to lend a hand to someone in distress, they need to hone their helping skills. If they're reluctant to stand up for themselves, they're candidates for assertiveness training. Thus, by analogy, if violence keeps breaking out, all we need to do is teach students the skills of conflict resolution.

Unfortunately, skills are not enough. Most kids already know how to listen, how to help, and how to assert themselves. The question is why they sometimes lack the *disposition* to act in these ways. It's much the same with efforts to raise academic achievement: a skills-based approach has its limits if we ignore the question of how interested students are in what they're being taught. Such efforts may even do more harm than good if an emphasis on teaching basic skills makes school downright unappealing. The same goes for literacy in particular: consider how many children know how to read, but don't. In short, what matters is not only whether people can learn, or act, in a particular way, but whether they have the inclination to do so.

Why, then, do we spend so much time teaching skills? For one thing, this implies that it's the students who need fixing. If something more complicated than a lack of know-how is involved, we might have to question our own practices and premises, which can be uncomfortable. Moreover, a focus on skills allows us to ignore the structural elements of a classroom (or school or family). If students hurt one another, it's easier for us to try to deal with each individual's actions than it is to ask which elements of the system might have contributed to the problem.

A skills-based approach is also compatible with behaviorism, whose influence over our schools—and, indeed, over all of American society—is difficult to overstate. Behaviorism dismisses anything that can't be reduced to a discrete set of observable and measurable behaviors. This dogma lies behind segmented instructional techniques, as well as many of the most popular approaches to character education, classroom management, and our practices with students who have special needs.

When we're preoccupied with behaviors, we're less likely to dig deep in order to understand the reasons, values, and motives that give rise to those behaviors. We end up embracing superficial responses, such as trying to improve the climate of a school by forcing students to dress alike. (Among other limitations of such a policy, our assumption seems to be that we can reduce aggression by borrowing an idea from the military.) But any time we talk about changing students' "behaviors," we run the risk of ignoring the students-who are doing the behaving. We lose the human beings behind the actions. Thus, we may come to see students as computers that can be reprogrammed, or pets that can be retrained, or empty receptacles that can be refilled—all dangerously misleading metaphors. We offer behavioral instruction in more appropriate ways to express anger, but the violence continues because we haven't gotten anywhere near where the problem is.

❧

It often doesn't work, then, to employ technical fixes or to teach skills. But there's a third response that isn't merely ineffective—it's actively counterproductive. I have in mind the policies that follow from assuming we can stamp out violence—or create safety—by *coercive means*. In her book *A Peaceable School*, Vicky Dill remarked that while it can be bad to have no plan for dealing with school violence, "it can be much worse to have a simplistic, authoritarian policy."[5]

A reliance on old-fashioned discipline, with threats of punishments for offenders, not only distracts us from dealing with the real causes of aggression, but in effect *models* bullying and power for students. Many school officials fail to understand that fact and end up throwing fuel on the fire by responding to signs of student distress with ever-harsher measures. Consistent with the tendency to ignore the structural causes of problems, they seem to think sheer force will make the bad stuff go away; if students are made to suffer for doing something wrong, they will see the error of their ways. When that proves ineffective, it's assumed that *more* punishment—along with tighter regulations and less trust—will do the trick.[6]

The shootings at Columbine provoked a general panic in which hundreds of students across the country were arrested, while "countless others were suspended or expelled for words or deeds perceived as menacing."[7] The fear here is understandable: administrators wondered whether their districts, too, might be incubating killers. But we need to understand the difference between *overreaction*, such as closing down a school to search for bombs after a student makes an offhand joke, and *destructive reactions*, such as coercive policies.

A particularly egregious example of the latter is the so-called "zero tolerance" approach, which is based on the premise that harsh punishment works better if it's meted out indiscriminately—indeed, in robotic fashion. It took a few years before this strategy began to attract critical attention in the media[8] Research, meanwhile, has been accumulating to confirm that it makes no sense at all. One study discovered that students in schools with such a policy "actually report feeling less safe . . . than do students in schools with more moderate policies."[9] That subjective impression is supported by objective evidence: another analysis showed that "even after schools with zero tolerance policies had implemented them for more than four years, those schools were still less safe than schools without such policies."[10] Moreover, zero tolerance doesn't affect everyone equally: African-American and Latino students are more likely than their white counterparts to be targeted by this sort of punitive discipline[11] As a society, we seem to have a lot more tolerance for the misbehavior of white children.

The finding that schools become less safe as a result of adopting zero-tolerance policies will sound paradoxical only to those readers who believe that threats and punishment can create safety. In reality, safety is put at risk by such an approach. A safe school environment is one where students are able to really know and trust—and be known and trusted by—adults.[12] Those bonds, however, are ruptured by a system that's about doing things *to* students who act inappropriately rather than working *with* them to solve problems. "The first casualty" of zero-tolerance policies "is the central, critical relationship between teacher and student, a relationship that is now being damaged or broken in favor of tough-sounding, impersonal, uniform procedures."[13]

Zero tolerance is bad enough, but the situation becomes even worse when the punishments in question are so harsh that students are turned into criminals. Across the country, the *New York Times* reported in early 2004, schools "are increasingly sending students into the juvenile justice systems for the sort of adolescent misbehavior that used to be handled by school administrators."[14] Apart from the devastating effects that turning children over to the police can have on their lives, the school's climate is curdled because administrators send the message that a student who does something wrong may be taken away in handcuffs and, in effect, exiled from the community. Here we see the *reduction ad absurdum* of trying to improve schools by relying on threats and fear.

There are many explanations for this deeply disturbing trend, including the loss of school-based mental health services due to budget cuts. But Mark Soler of the Youth Law Center, a public interest group that protects at-risk children, observes that these days "zero tolerance is fed less by fear of crime and more by high-stakes testing. Principals want to get rid of kids they perceive as trouble" because doing so may improve their school's overall test results.[15] School safety is at risk, that is, not merely because some educators wrongly believe that stricter or more consistent application of punitive discipline will help, but because of the pressure to raise test scores.

What's more, that same pressure, which leads some people to regard students in trouble as disposable commodities, also has the effect of squeezing out efforts to help them avoid getting into trouble in the first place. Programs to promote conflict resolution and to address bullying and other sorts of violence are being eliminated because educators are themselves being bullied into focusing on standardized test results to the exclusion of everything else. Scott Poland, a school psychologist and expert in crisis intervention, writes: "School principals have told me that they would like to devote curriculum time to topics such as managing anger, violence prevention and learning to get along with others regardless of race and ethnicity, but . . . [they are] under tremendous pressure to raise academic scores on the state accountability test."[16]

Thus, argues Margaret McKenna, the president of Lesley University, "Some of the most important lessons of Columbine have been all but forgotten—left behind, so to speak, in no small measure because of . . . the No Child Left Behind Act. The law's narrow focus on yearly improvement in test scores has [made schools] . . . even less conducive to teachers' knowing their students well." To drive home the point that our priorities have become skewed, she observes that "the test scores at Columbine High were among the highest in Colorado."[17]

∙◄❀►∙

Even in cases where a student's actions pose a significant risk to the safety of others, an educator's first response should not be "Have we used sufficient force to stamp out this threat?" but "What have we done to address the underlying issues here? How can we transform our schools into places that meet students' needs so there is less chance that someone will be moved to lash out in fury?"

Here's another way to look at it: we need to stop talking primarily about creating peaceful schools, which is not a particularly ambitious or meaningful goal. Schools, after all, are completely peaceful at 3 a.m. Similarly, a classroom full of docile, unquestioning students may be peaceful, even if they aren't learning much of value, don't care much about one another, and would rather be someplace else. What we need to work for is the creation of schools that are *peaceable*—that is, committed to the value of peace and to helping students feel safe, in all senses of that word.[18]

Physical safety, the most obvious kind, has understandably been the priority, particularly where it seems to be in short supply. But intellectual and emotional safety matter, too—in their own right and also because they're related to physical safety. Bullying and other violent acts are less likely to happen in a school that feels like a caring community, a place where children experience a sense of connection to one another and to adults, a place where they come to think in the plural and feel a sense of belonging. That's the polar opposite of a school where kids are picked on for being different or uncool, to the point that they fear entering certain hallways or sections of the cafeteria. Caring school communities don't let that happen: they regard any evidence of nasty cliques or hurtful exclusion as serious problems to be addressed. They do everything possible so that no one fears being laughed at, picked on, or humiliated.

These efforts take place in individual classrooms and also as a matter of school policy. Proactive efforts to build community and resolve conflicts are important, but so too must educators focus on what gets in the way of safety and community. Thus, teachers not only hold class meetings on a regular basis so that students can participate in making decisions; they also use these meetings to address troubling things that may be going on. One teacher spoke up after a math lesson, for example, to talk with her students about

> something I *don't* like and I *don't* want to hear because it makes me feel bad, and if it makes me feel bad it probably makes someone else in here feel bad. It's these two words. (She writes "That's easy" on the chalkboard and draws a circle around the phrase.) . . . When I am struggling and trying so hard, [hearing that phrase] makes me feel kind of dumb or stupid. Because I am thinking, gosh, if it's so easy why am I having so much trouble with it? . . . And what's one of our rules in here? It's to be considerate of others and their feelings.[19]

Such an intervention may be motivated not only by a general commitment to ensuring that students don't feel bad, but also by a desire to promote high-quality learning. There are intellectual costs when students don't feel safe to take risks. A classroom where kids worry that their questions will be thought silly is a classroom where unself-conscious engagement with ideas is less likely to take place. (Of course, students often are unwilling to ask questions or acknowledge that they're struggling for fear of the reaction from the teacher, not just from their classmates.)

On a schoolwide level, intellectual and emotional safety require that students are freed from being rated and ranked, freed from public pressure to show how smart they are—or even worse, how much smarter they are than everyone else. Awards assemblies and honor rolls are very effective ways to destroy the sense of safety that supports a willingness to learn. Some schools that pride themselves on their commitment to high standards and achievement have created a climate that really isn't about learning at all—let alone about caring. Such places are more about results than about kids. Their students often feel as though they're in a pressure cooker, where some must fail in order that others can succeed. The message students get is that other people are potential obstacles to their own success.[20]

There is much more to be said, of course, about how and why to build community, to meet kids' needs, to create a culture of safety and caring.[21] The benefits of doing so are most pronounced in schools that have more low-income students,[22] yet such schools are often distinguished instead by punitive discipline and a climate of control. However, schools in affluent areas may also feel unsafe in various ways. Columbine High School was reportedly a place where bullying was common and a sharply stratified social structure was allowed to flourish, one in which athletes were deified. (Some of these sports stars taunted other students mercilessly "while school authorities looked the other way."[23]) In some suburban schools, the curriculum is chock full of rigorous advanced placement courses and the parking lot glitters with pricey SUVs, but one doesn't have to look hard to find students who are starving themselves, cutting themselves, or medicating themselves, as well as students who are taking out their frustrations on those who sit lower on the social food chain.

Even in a, school free of weapons, children may feel unsafe and unhappy. And that's reason enough to rethink our assumptions, redesign our policies, and redouble our commitment to creating a different kind of educational culture.

Notes

1. Mike Males, "Who's Really Killing Our Schoolkids?" *Los Angeles Times,* May 31, 1999. Also see other writings by Males, including his book *The Scapegoat Generation: America's War on Adolescents* (Monroe, Maine: Common Courage Press, 1996).

2. The article, by Debbi Wilgoren, appeared in the *Washington Post* on February 3, 2004: A-7.

3. Pedro A. Noguera, "School Safety Lessons Learned: Urban Districts Report Progress," *Education Week,* May 30, 2001: 15.

4. This section is adapted from my article "The Limits of Teaching Skills," *Reaching Today's Youth,* Summer 1997, which is available at <www.alfiekohn.org/teaching/lts.htm>.

5. Vicky Schreiber Dill, *A Peaceable School. Creating a Culture of Non-Violence* (Bloomington, Ind.: Phi Delta Kappa, 1997), 24. Also see Irwin A. Hyman and Pamela A. Snook, *Dangerous Schools* (San Francisco: Jossey-Bass, 1999), an excerpt from which appeared in the March 2000 issue of *Phi Delta Kappan.*

6. This section is adapted from my article "Constant Frustration and Occasional Violence: The Legacy of American High Schools," *American School Board Journal,* September 1999, which is available at <www.alfiekohn.org/teaching/cfaov.htm>. For more on the counterproductive effects of—and some alternatives to—punitive "consequences" and rewards, see my book *Beyond Discipline: From Compliance to Community* (Alexandria, Va.: Association for Supervision and Curriculum Development, 1996).

7. Caroline Hendrie, "Schools, A Sigh of Relief as Tense Spring Draws to a Close," *Education Week,* June 23, 1999.

8. For example, see Dirk Johnson, "Schools' New Watchword: Zero Tolerance," *New York Times,* December 1, 1999; and Jesse Katz, "Taking Zero Tolerance to the Limit," *Los Angeles Times,* March 1, 1998.

9. This quotation is from Robert Blum of the University of Minnesota. The study, to which he contributed, was published in the *Journal of School Health* and summarized in Darcia Harris Bowman, "School 'Connectedness' Makes for Healthier Students, Study Suggests," *Education Week,* April 24, 2002: 16.

10. John H. Holloway, "The Dilemma of Zero Tolerance," *Educational Leadership,* December 2001/January 2002:84. The analysis summarized here was published by the National Center for Education Statistics in 1998. Also see an excellent review of the effects of such policies in Russ Skiba and Reece Peterson, "The Dark Side of Zero Tolerance: Can Punishment Lead to Safe Schools?" *Phi Delta Kappan,* January 1999: 372–76, 381–82.

11. A report by a civil rights group called The Advancement Project, based on an analysis of federal statistics, was described in Kenneth J. Cooper, "Group Finds Racial Disparity in Schools 'Zero Tolerance'," *Washington Post,* June 15, 2000.

12. For example, see Deborah Meier, *In Schools We Trust* (Boston: Beacon Press, 2002).

13. William Ayers and Bernadine Dohrn, "Have We Gone Overboard with Zero Tolerance?" *Chicago Tribune,* November 21, 1999.

14. Sara Rimer, "Unruly Students Facing Arrest, Not Detention," *New York Times,* January 4, 2004: A-1.

15. That explanation also makes sense to Augustina Reyes of the University of Houston: "If teachers are told, 'Your [test] scores go down, you lose your job: all of a sudden your values shift very quickly. Teachers think, 'With bad kids in my class, I'll have lower achievement on my tests, so I'll use discretion and remove that kid.'" Both Reyes and Soler are quoted in Annette Fuentes, "Discipline and Punish," *The Nation,* December 15, 2003: 17–20.

16. "The Non-Hardware Side of School Safety," *NASP* [National Association of School Psychologists] *Communique* 28:6 (March 2000). Poland made the same point while testifying at a congressional hearing on school violence in March 1999—a month before the shootings at Columbine.

17. Margaret A. McKenna, "Lessons Left Behind," *Washington Post,* April 20, 2004:A-19.

18. The distinction between peaceful and peaceable was popularized by Bill Kreidler, who worked with Educators for Social Responsibility and wrote several books about conflict resolution. He died in 2000 at the unripe age of forty-eight.

19. Paul Cobb, Erna Yackel, and Terry Wood, "Young Children's Emotional Acts While Engaged in Mathematical Problem Solving." In *Affect and Mathematical Problem Solving: A New Perspective,* ed. D. B. McLeod and V. M. Adams (New York: Springer-Verlag, 1989), 130–31.

20. Our culture's uncritical acceptance of the ideology of competition is such that even people who acknowledge the damaging effects of an "excessive" emphasis on winning may continue to assert that competition *per se* is inevitable or productive. If this assertion is typically unaccompanied by evidence, that's probably because the available data support exactly the opposite position—namely, that a win/lose arrangement tends to hold us back from doing our best work and from optimal learning. I've reviewed some of that evidence in *No Contest: The Case Against Competition* (Boston: Houghton Mifflin, 1986).

21. See my article "Caring Kids: The Role of the Schools," *Phi Delta Kappan,* March 1991: 496–506 (available at <www.alfiekohn.org/teaching/cktrots.htm>); and chapter 7 ("The Classroom as Community") of *Beyond Discipline,* op. cit. Many other writers, of course, have also addressed this question.

22. Victor Battistich, Daniel Solomon, Dong-il Kim, Marilyn Watson, and Eric Schaps, "Schools as Communities, Poverty Levels of Student Populations, and Students' Attitudes, Motives, and Performance: A Multilevel Analysis," *American Education Research Journal* 32 (1995): 627–58.

23. Lorraine Adams and Dale Russakoff, "Dissecting Columbine's Cult of the Athlete," *Washington Post,* June12, 1999:A-1.

POSTSCRIPT

Does School Violence Warrant a Zero-Tolerance Policy?

How can the aggressive drive be harnessed so that it provides young people with the energy to live productively in American society rather than being unleashed in the form of violence? This question is posed by Lorraine B. Wallach in "Violence and Aggression in Today's Schools" in the Spring 1996 issue of *Educational Horizons*. Wallach contends that "children who accumulate an overload of anger, hate, or jealousy or feel worthless are more likely to be violent, particularly when these feelings are combined with poor inner controls." The building of internal controls and the channeling of normal aggressiveness must begin, of course, in the home and at the presecondary levels of schooling.

Related articles of interest include "What to Do About the Children," by William J. Bennett, *Commentary* (March 1995), in which the author discusses the governmental role in dealing with crime, immorality, and uncivilized behavior; "Waging Peace in Our Schools: Beginning With the Children," by Linda Lanteiri, *Phi Delta Kappan* (January 1995); and "Ganging Up on Gangs," by Reginald Leon Green and Roger L. Miller, *American School Board Journal* (September 1996). An excellent array of articles may be found in *The School Administrator* (February 1996); the *NASSP Bulletin* (April 1996); and the *Harvard Educational Review* (Summer 1995), which features Janie V. Ward on cultivating a morality of care, Pedro A. Noguera on violence prevention, and interviews with Noam Chomsky and Peggy Charren. Students who will soon enter the teaching profession may also profit from reading *Safe Schools: A Handbook for Practitioners*, which was released in 1994 by the National Association of Secondary School Principals.

Other articles of interest are Roger W. Ashford, "Can Zero Tolerance Keep Our Schools Safe?" *Principal* (November 2000); Charlene M. Alexander, "Helping School Counselors Cope With Violence," *USA Today Magazine* (January 2002); Reece L. Peterson and Russell Skiba, "Creating School Climates That Prevent School Violence," *The Clearing House* (January/February 2001); Cherry Henault, "Zero Tolerance in Schools," *Journal of Law and Education* (July 2001); Catherine Seipp, "Asthma Attack: When 'Zero Tolerance' Collides With Children's Health," *Reason* (April 2002); Jean Hannon, "No Time for Time Out," *Kappa Delta Pi Record* (Spring 2002); Annette Fuentes, "Discipline and Punish," *The Nation* (December 15, 2003); and Pedro A. Noguera, "Rethinking Disciplinary Practices," *Theory into Practice* (Autumn 2003).

ISSUE 18

Should Homework Be Abolished?

YES: Etta Kralovec and John Buell, from "End Homework Now,"
Educational Leadership (April 2001)

NO: David Skinner, from "The Homework Wars," *The Public Interest*
(Winter 2004)

ISSUE SUMMARY

YES: Learning specialist Etta Kralovec and journalist John Buell
attack the assignment of homework as a pedagogical practice,
claiming that it disrupts family life and punishes the poor.

NO: Editor David Skinner negatively reacts to Kralovec and Buell's
book, *The End of Homework*, citing research to undermine their
position.

One of the more controversial books on the subject of education to appear in
recent years was *The End of Homework: How Homework Disrupts Families, Overburdens Children, and Limits Learning* by Etta Kralovec and John Buell. The book rekindled arguments concerning the use and misuse of homework that have flared
periodically in America during the twentieth century. In a well-documented
review of the controversy, Brian P. Gill and Steven L. Schlossman, in "Parents
and the Politics of Homework: Some Historical Perspectives," *Teachers College
Record* (June 2003), claim that in the first half of the century, "the vast majority
of educational commentary on homework attacked its central place in
schooling." Many school districts limited how much homework could be
assigned at various levels of schooling and some cities even abolished
homework altogether.

In the second half of the century, however, international technological
and economic competition and the perceived weaknesses in American academic
performance (as documented in *A Nation at Risk*) shifted the national consensus
on homework to "the more, the better." The George W. Bush administration's
emphasis on standards and testing has strengthened the role of homework
in promoting student achievement. But the issue is not settled. As Gill and
Schlossman concede, "Over the course of the twentieth century we have
found little agreement about homework among experts, teachers, and parents."
Perhaps only the students hold a near-unanimous opinion on the matter.

Education officialdom has periodically expressed concern about the value and effects of homework requirements. For example, the American Educational Research Association has stated that "whenever homework crowds out social experience, outdoor recreation, and creative activities, and whenever it usurps time that should be devoted to sleep, it is not meeting the basic needs of children and adolescents." The National Education Association has recommended that children in the early elementary school period have no homework specifically assigned, that an hour or less per day be introduced in the middle school years, that in secondary school no more than one-and-a-half hours a night be expected, and that homework be limited to four nights a week. Kralovec and Buell contend that these recommendations have been ignored by school administrators and policy makers. On the other side of the ledger, the U.S. Department of Education cites research that shows that, among high school students, there is a correlation between length of time spent on homework and proficiency scores in reading, mathematics, literature, history, and geography.

A somewhat middle-ground position was struck by Harris Cooper, a leading researcher on the issue. In "Homework for All—in Moderation," *Educational Leadership* (April 2001), Cooper, after reviewing recent studies on the effects of homework, concludes that "flexible homework policies should let individual schools and teachers take into account the unique needs and circumstances" of students. Given this, another aspect that must be addressed is the quality of the assignments. They can be "busywork." They can be meted out as "punishment." Or they can be creative, constructive, and even fascinating. Homework can be a "Grind" done (or not done) in isolation, or it can be an opportunity for collaboration among students or members of the family.

In weighing the value of homework, an important question arises: Is the assignment a reasonable extension of the work done in class? An embellishment and encouragement of further inquiry or creative expression? Does the assignment of homework construct a bridge between school and home, an opportunity for parents to make a connection with their children's academic development?

In the following articles, Etta Kralovec and John Buell summarize the position developed in *The End of Homework*, emphasizing the growing burden of homework on the lives of children and youths, while David Skinner finds that most students are not overburdened by excessive homework, that the overworked American student is not at all typical.

YES

Etta Kralovec and
John Buell

End Homework Now

Parents say that teachers require it. Teachers say that parents demand more of it. Politicians call for grading parents on their ability to help with it. Citizens run for school board seats on no-homework platforms. The National Parent Teacher Association and the National Education Association set guidelines. Some dismiss the current anti-homework outcry as just the latest swing of the opinion pendulum. School boards and politicians dictate homework policies for political rather than pedagogical reasons. Teachers say that they are increasingly uncomfortable about handing over to parents the learning for which teachers are accountable. Welcome to the homework wars.

When the school board in Piscataway, New Jersey, voted earlier this fall to limit homework in the elementary grades to half an hour each night and high school homework to two hours a night, the *New York Times* ran a front-page article on the school (Zernike, 2000) and national television networks followed suit. Homework is controversial, not only because of legitimate questions about its efficacy. Concern about homework is also part of a growing apprehension in the United States about the time pressures that both adults and children now face. Unstructured family time is shrinking in the face of longer workweeks and more hours of homework than ever before (Hofferth & Sandberg, in press).

In the early 1990s, we discovered the impact of homework on students' lives when we helped conduct a study of alternative schools for Maine's Department of Education, aiming to find out why these schools had been so successful in helping former high school dropouts graduate from high school (Antonnuci & Mooser, 1993). We spoke with parents, school personnel, and school board members and conducted in-depth interviews with more than 45 at-risk students enrolled in these schools, asking them to identify when they had known they were going to drop out of school. Students told us about chaotic family lives, cramped living quarters, and parents who worked at night. They also kept mentioning their inability to complete homework as a factor in the decision to leave school.

Surprised that homework contributed so dramatically to students' dropping out of school, we analyzed research reports and talked with hundreds of teachers, parents, high school dropouts, and high school students. Instead of focusing narrowly on homework's impact on academic achievement or its presumed role in developing self-discipline and good work habits, we examined homework in the context of the lives of students, families, and communities.

From *Educational Leadership*, April 2001, pp. 39–42. Reprinted with permission of the Association for Supervision and Curriculum Development. Copyright © 2001 by ASCD. All rights reserved.

From this perspective, we found that homework often disrupts family life, interferes with what parents want to teach their children, and punishes students in poverty for being poor. Perhaps more significantly for educators are the serious limitations of homework's pedagogical prowess (Kralovec & Buell, 2000).

In the past 20 years, family life in the United States has undergone dramatic demographic and economic changes. More mothers work, more single parents run households, and more parents work longer—all contributing to a decrease in unstructured family time (Hofferth & Sandberg, in press). White middle-class parents in the past decade have increased their time at work by nearly six full-time weeks a year. African American middle-income families log an average of 4,278 hours per year, almost 500 hours per year more than white families (Mishel, Bernstein, & Schmitt, 2001).

Homework squeezes family life. All parents have educational agendas for their children. They want to pass on their cultural heritage, religious beliefs, and important life skills. They want to teach their children how to be good citizens and how to share in the responsibilities of running a home. More homework makes parents put their own agendas on hold even as they often struggle to help their children cope with homework assignments. Additionally, families need time to constitute themselves as families. According to a 1998 survey by Public Agenda, nearly 50 percent of parents reported having a serious argument with their children over homework, and 34 percent reported homework as a source of stress and struggle. Parents often have conflicting feelings about homework, viewing it as a way for their children to succeed but also as imposing serious limits on family time.

Homework reinforces the social inequities inherent in the unequal distribution of educational resources in the United States. Some students go home to well-educated parents and have easy access to computers with vast databases. Other students have family responsibilities, parents who work at night, and no educational resources in their homes. A principal once told us that he had solved the homework problem for students in poverty simply by not assigning them homework. This curious solution raises troubling questions: Either homework is of no educational value—in which case why is anyone doing it—or we are committing the worst form of educational discrimination by differentiating academic programs on the basis of economic class.

The poor person's version of the emblematic soccer mom is the burger mom—the mother who works nights in a fast food restaurant while her children sit in a booth waiting for her to help them with homework. Close to 20 percent of children in the United States live in poverty, and homework further exacerbates their academic problems. Well-meaning parents cannot overcome their lack of resources, including the time needed to make sure that their children complete school assignments.

Homework: The Black Hole

The call for greater accountability in education, with its increased focus on test scores and outcomes, puts homework on the line. When we leave a sizable portion of learning to parents, how can we hold schools and teachers responsible for meeting higher standards? To teach to standards means to teach in a more tightly controlled system, leaving no room for an unknown variable—the black hole of homework—in the education process. Moreover, how can teachers know the level of their students' learning if they don't know how students are getting their assignments done at home?

Cognitive scientists have contributed to a revolution in learning theory, building on the foundation laid by Jean Piaget and Lev Vygotsky. Educators accept that students have unique cognitive structures that determine their abilities to solve problems at different points in their development. We know that we must scaffold new learning onto existing mental frameworks to build new knowledge. Understanding students' mistakes is a crucial part of the teaching process. When work goes home, teachers have little understanding of the mistakes that students have made on the material and little control over who does the work. Teachers wonder, Did the students do their own work? Did they exchange answers with friends over the phone or before school? Did they send homework by e-mail to their grandparents, who did the work and returned it early the next morning? Did they download the paper they are handing in? Homework is a black hole in the learning process, leaving teachers unaware of each student's true educational level or progress and unable to scaffold new knowledge for the students.

Homework Myths

Three homework myths have persisted during the past century, making us unwilling to ask for solid evidence on the benefits of homework and acquiescent in accepting claims about its efficacy.

Myth: Homework increases academic achievement. Even supporters of homework acknowledge the problems of research on homework. Homework supporter Harris Cooper acknowledges that "the conclusions of past reviewers of homework research show extraordinary variability. . . . the reviews often directly contradict one another" (1989, p. 28). Most researchers now concede that homework does not improve academic achievement for elementary students (Cooper, 1994). Recently, homework advocates have shifted their focus from homework's questionable impact on student achievement to homework's alleged importance in developing traits like self-discipline and time management. According to these views, developing homework habits early means that a student will be more disciplined about completing homework in high school and beyond.

According to Piaget, however, asking children to perform tasks before they are developmentally ready proves counterproductive to development. We need to ask ourselves whether homework falls into this category. Lacking solid evidence, homework supporters ask us to take on faith the notion that homework can instill desirable character traits.

Myth: If our students don't do lots of homework, their test scores will never be competitive internationally. Comparisons of student test scores often pit U.S. students against students from other countries. Ironically, the 1995 Third International Math and Science Study (TIMSS) found that 8th graders in

Japan and Germany are assigned less homework but still outperform U.S. students on tests (National Center for Educational Statistics, 2001). Japanese schools spend a greater portion of their budgets on professional development and organize their school days so that teachers can work collaboratively. Teachers in Japan are at school eight to nine hours a day, but they teach only four hours a day. In addition, the Japanese school calendar has longer school days, longer school years, longer lunches, and longer recess periods. The Japanese classroom is a sacred space that does not allow interruptions. We can learn many lessons from the Japanese system (Rohlen & LeTendre, 1995).

Myth: Those who call homework into question want to dilute the curriculum and kowtow to the inherent laziness of students. By calling homework into question, we are not questioning the work of homework, but rather the value of students completing that work at home. Students need to complete long-term, independent projects as part of a rigorous academic program. They need to learn many skills through drill and practice. They need time to make new learning their own. Professional educators need to design rigorous academic work, scaffold new knowledge, and coach new study habits. The place for such work is in the school.

Focus on Genuine Reforms

Educators are under the gun as never before to improve student achievement. With national attention now focused on school reform, education leaders have a valuable opening for educating the public about how to improve schools in the United States. Rather than defending the practice of homework, educators should direct national discussion to more important issues.

- After close to 20 years of school reform measures, we now have some proven practices for increasing academic success. A recent RAND study of academic achievement compared 1993–1996 state test results and found that the states with higher test results shared three important characteristics: smaller class size, more pre-K education, and more resources for teachers (Grissmer, Flanagan, Kawata, & Williamson, 2000). A call for more school funding should be the mantra of our profession.
- The rush to fund and build after-school programs is now a major policy initiative with the potential to solve some of the homework problems we face (Miller, 2000). Education leaders should seek to ensure that after-school learning programs are academically rigorous and work closely with the community organizations that provide after-school services.
- Research on learning suggests the importance of physical movement in the learning process (Jensen, 2000). Beyond the back problems associated with heavy backpacks, students who sit all day in a classroom and then for hours to complete homework at night face a potential health threat. Turning up the pressure to achieve, instituting high-stakes testing programs, cutting physical activities, and piling on the homework are recipes for disaster. Educators should help parents and politicians understand how an overemphasis on testing will result in one-dimensional learning.

Piling on homework and arguing for its value are cheaper and less politically risky strategies, but educators need to inform the public about the real levers of school improvement. Do we have the courage to call for adequate school funding? Are we willing to declare an eight-hour workday for both students and teachers? Are we willing to commit ourselves to the professional development that teachers need to teach effectively in their classrooms? Are we willing to staff our after-school programs with professionals who can support student learning? Educators need to consider these questions before answering calls about homework from parents and the local news media.

References

Antonnuci, F., & Mooser, E. (1993). *Research report: Assessment of alternative programs.* Augusta: Maine State Department of Education.

Cooper, H. (1989). *Homework.* New York: Longman.

Cooper, H. (1994). *The battle over homework: An administrator's guide to setting sound and effective policies.* Thousand Oaks, CA: Corwin Press.

Grissmer, D., Flanagan, A., Kawata, J., & Williamson, S. (2000). *Improving student achievement: What the NAEP test scores tell us.* Santa Monica: RAND Corporation.

Hofferth, S., & Sandberg, J. (in press). Changes in American children's time, 1981–1997. In T. Owens & S. Hofferth (Eds.), *Children at the millennium: Where have we come from, Where are we going?* New York: Elsevier Science.

Jensen, E. (2000). Moving with the brain in mind. *Educational Leadership, 58*(3), 34–37.

Kralovec, E., & Buell, J. (2000). *The end of homework: How homework disrupts families, overburdens children, and limits learning.* Boston: Beacon Press.

Miller, B. (2000). The power of the hours: The changing context of after school. *School-Age Review, 2*(1), 18–23.

Mishel, L., Bernstein, J., & Schmitt, J. (2001). *The state of working America, 2000–2001.* New York: Cornell University Press.

National Center for Educational Statistics. (2001). *Pursuing excellence: Comparison of international 8th grade mathematics and science achievement from a U.S. perspective, 1995 and 1999* [Online]. Available: nces.ed.gov/pubs2001/2001028.pdf

Public Agenda. (1998). *Playing their parts: What parents and teachers really mean by parental involvement* [Online]. Available: www.publicagenda.org/specials/parent/parent.htm

Rohlen, T., & LeTendre, G. (1995). *Teaching and learning in Japan.* Boston: Cambridge University Press.

Zernike, K. (2000, October 10). Homework: What's enough? *New York Times,* pp. A1, A29.

David Skinner  **NO**

The Homework Wars

The American child, a gloomy chorus of newspapers, magazines and books tells us, is overworked. All spontaneity is being squeezed out of him by the vice-like pressures of homework, extracurricular activities, and family. "Jumping from Spanish to karate, tap dancing to tennis—with hours of homework waiting at home—the overscheduled child is as busy as a new law firm associate," reports the *New York Times*. The article goes on to describe a small counter-trend in which some parents are putting a stop to the frenzy and letting their children, for once in their little harried lives, simply hang out or, as one of the insurgent parents explains, enjoy an informal game of pickup.

What's this? A game of catch is news? And this is said to be sociologically significant? Something must be amiss in the state of childhood today. The common diagnosis is that too much work, too much ambition, and an absence of self-directedness are harming American children. In an influential 2001 article in the *Atlantic Monthly*, David Brooks, author of *Bobos in Paradise*, christened the overachieving American child the "Organization Kid." Reporting on the character of the generation born in the early 1980s, in which he focused on those attending some of America's most prestigious colleges, Brooks found a youth demographic of career-oriented yes-men, with nary a rebel in the bunch. Called team players and rule-followers, they are best captured by a 1997 Gallup survey Brooks cites in which 96 percent of teenagers said they got along with their parents.

In this hyper-productive, overachieving setting, a curious educational debate has broken out. The parents of the younger K-12 worker-bees are revolting against the reportedly increasing amounts of homework assigned their children. A major lightning rod for this debate has been *The End of Homework*, a book by Etta Kralovec and John Buell, whose argument found an appreciative audience in *Time, Newsweek*, the *New York Times, People* magazine, and elsewhere. For a novel polemic against a long-established educational practice, such a widespread hearing suggests that the issue has struck a chord with many American families. Understanding the book's argument—its strengths and weaknesses—is not necessary to understanding the debate over homework, but it is helpful to understanding the overall tenor of this controversy.

Reprinted with permission of the author from: THE PUBLIC INTEREST, No. 154 (Winter 2004), pp. 49–60. Copyright © 2004 by National Affairs, Inc.

The End of Homework

What makes *The End of Homework* stand out is that it was written by academics. Etta Kralovec holds a doctorate in education from the Teachers College at Columbia University and, for over 12 years, she directed teacher education at the College of the Atlantic. John Buell, too, has spent time on the faculty at the College of the Atlantic. Now a newspaper columnist, the onetime associate editor of *The Progressive* has authored two books on political economy. In an afterword, the authors say *The End of Homework* grew out of a series of interviews with high school dropouts, many of whom cited homework as a reason they discontinued their education. This snapshot of homework's dire effect, unfortunately, requires much qualification.

Kralovec and Buell show little restraint when describing the problems brought on by the reported increase in home-work. Attacking the proposition that homework inculcates good adult habits, the authors cite the historical trend in psychology away from viewing children as miniature adults, but then quickly lose perspective. "In suggesting that children need to learn to deal with adult levels of pressure, we risk doing them untold damage. By this logic, the schoolyard shootings of recent years may be likened to 'disgruntled employee' rampages." Nor do Kralovec and Buell inspire confidence by quoting a report attributing a spate of suicides in Hong Kong to "distress over homework." The report they cite is from the *Harare Herald* in Zimbabwe, not exactly a widely recognized authority on life in Hong Kong.

The End of Homework's alarmist tone is best captured, however, in its uncritical acceptance of a 1999 report from the American Association of Orthopedic Surgeons (AAOS) "that thousands of kids have back, neck, and shoulder pain caused by their heavy backpacks." The book's cover photo even shows two little kids straining like packmules under the weight of their bookbags. It so happens that orthopedic professionals themselves, at the AAOS no less, dispute the report. To pick a recent example, a study presented at the 2003 meeting of the AAOS, based on interviews with 346 school-age orthopedic patients, found only one patient who attributed his back pain to carrying a bookbag.

Kralovec and Buell's case against homework is further diminished by the book's clear political agenda. Indeed, the telltale signs of an overriding left-wing social critique are sadly abundant. Twice inside of 100 pages, the same unilluminating quotation is trotted out from "the great radical sociologist C. Wright Mills," whose influence on this book, however, pales next to that of Harvard economist Juliet B. Schor. Schor is most famous for her controversial 1992 bestseller *The Overworked American: The Unexpected Decline of Leisure*, which argued that American adults were losing their disposable time to the steady encroachments of longer work schedules. But the book's primary findings were contradicted by existing research and just about every mainstream expert asked to offer an opinion on the subject.

Nevertheless, Schor's laborite call for a new consensus on the proper number of hours and days that should be devoted to employment (approximately half of current levels) finds an echo in *The End of Homework*'s call to

American families to throw off their homework shackles and reclaim the evenings for family time. Indeed, one notices in this book more than a little overwrought socialist rhetoric. For example, after bemoaning the failure of standards-based reforms to improve achievement scores, the authors comment that the continued emphasis on homework "fits the ideological requirement of those who maintain the status quo in our economy and politics" and that homework "serves the needs of powerful groups within our society."

The book's other patron saint is Jonathan Kozol, the influential left-wing author of *Savage Inequalities* who has done more than anyone to swamp mainstream education debate with radical social criticism. In the style of Kozol, whom they cite a dozen or so times, Kralovec and Buell binge on the theme of equality when they should be carefully picking over social science data, insisting that homework "pits students who can against students who can't." And when they're not raising the specter of class warfare, Kralovec and Buell are lecturing readers on their unwillingness to recognize its insidious influence: "We suspect that many Americans may be unwilling to acknowledge the existence of an entrenched class system in the United States that serves to constrain or enhance our children's life chances." Economic inequalities, the authors inveigh, fly in the face of "our most cherished values, such as democracy and freedom." Typical of their tempestuous approach to this discrete pedagogical question, Kralovec and Buell devote their final chapter to "Homework in the Global Economy."

Hidden amid the authors' polemic, however, is a persuasive and warranted case against an educational practice of limited value. Homework, in some cases, deserves to be attacked, which makes it all the more a pity that Kralovec and Buell couldn't confine themselves to their primary subject. Their opinion that "homework is almost always counterproductive for elementary schoolchildren" is not the product of some left-wing fever swamp and deserves further consideration.

How Much

. . . University of Missouri professor of psychological sciences Harris Cooper, whose research on homework is widely cited by critics on both sides of the debate, including Kralovec and Buell, offers conditional support for the practice. "Is homework better than no homework at all?" he asks in a 1980s literature review. On the basis of 17 research reports examining over 3,300 students, Cooper found that 70 percent of comparisons yielded a positive answer. In terms of class grades and standardized test scores, he found that "the average student doing homework in these studies had a higher achievement score than 55 percent of students not doing homework." Break down such average findings, however, and this modest advantage gained through homework is lost through other variables.

Perhaps the most commanding factor in deciding the homework question is age or grade level. "Older students benefited the most from doing homework," writes Cooper. "The average effect of homework was twice as large for high school as for junior high school students and twice as large again for junior high school students as for elementary school students." This raises interesting questions about homework's distribution among age groups.

Much of the homework controversy is fueled by stories of very young children burdened with lengthy assignments and complicated projects that require extensive parental involvement. Searching for evidence that such work is important to their child's education and development, the parent of a fifth grader will find only cold comfort in the research examined by Cooper. "Teachers of Grades 4, 5, and 6 might expect the average student doing homework to outscore about 52 percent of equivalent no-homework students." A 2 percentile-point advantage gained by a practice that could be interrupting dinner, stealing family time, and pitting child against parent hardly seems enough to justify the intrusion.

For high school students, however, homework can do a lot of good. "If grade level is taken into account," Cooper finds, "homework's effect on the achievement of elementary school students could be described as 'very small,' but on high school students its effect would be 'large.'" If the average fourth- through sixth-grade student who does homework can expect only a 2 percentile-point advantage over one who does none, junior high school students doing homework can expect a 10 percentile-point advantage and high school students a 19 percentile-point advantage. What's more, this effect translates into high achievement not only in class grades—which more readily reflect a positive homework effect—but also on standardized tests, which are quite significant to a student's educational future.

What Kind

There are other wrinkles worth attending to. For one, Cooper himself still favors homework, but possibly not the kind that is causing the most heartache and the most headaches. "Not surprisingly, homework produced larger effects if students did more assignments per week. Surprisingly, the effect of homework was negatively related to the duration of the homework treatment—treatments spanning longer periods produced less of a homework effect." Which is to say, homework comprised of short regular assignments is probably the most effective.

One underlying lesson here should cause many enemies of homework to groan. Kralovec and Buell, for example, marshall the classic complaint, usually made by children, that homework is boring, repetitive, and basically has nothing to do with the developing child's true self. Interesting homework—the fun stuff that allows a child to express himself, that supposedly promotes "creativity" and "critical thinking" and "planning skills"—does not come off well in Cooper's study. Examining broad national and statewide studies of the relationship between time spent on homework and its effects, Cooper found that the correlations between time spent and positive effects increased "for subjects for which homework assignments are more likely to involve rote learning, practice, or rehearsal. Alternately, subjects such as science and social studies, which often involve longer-term projects, integration of multiple skills, and creative use of non-school resources show the smallest average correlations." Note the collision of opposing pedagogical trends: improving standards by increasing homework and the movement away from rote learning. Indeed, there may be nothing more unhelpful to a student than a teacher of high standards who doesn't want to bore his students.

Interestingly, no one involved in the fight over homework has argued that parents might consider encouraging their children to put in less effort on homework that is overly time-consuming and pedagogically unproductive. Which seems a pity. Why shouldn't a parent tell his overworked fifth-grader to spend less time on that big assignment on American subcultural narratives? Or occasionally have him not do his homework at all? A little civil disobedience might be a useful way of sending a message to a teacher whose assignments are overly ambitious. And if the child gets a lower grade as a result, then it's a small price to pay. It's not as if his entire educational future is on the line.

The homework critics never suggest such a course of action, needless to say, but not because it might undermine teachers' authority, a result they otherwise happily pursue. Odd as it sounds, the fight against homework is largely about achievement, specifically about setting the price of officially recognized excellence at an acceptable rate. Reading Kralovec and Buell and the many newspaper and magazine articles depicting the rebellion against homework, one comes away with an impression in keeping with David Brooks's "Organization Kid," but with an egalitarian twist. The whole movement reflects an organization culture that wants high grades to be possible for all kids, regardless of their varying levels of ability or willingness to work, regardless of what other commitments these children have made, regardless of the importance of family.

Time and Homework

A significant underlying question remains to be addressed. The evidence that there is a widespread homework problem—that too many students are carrying too heavy a homework load—is largely anecdotal. There are some empirical indications of a modest increase in homework over the last 20 years or so, but other indications suggest the problem is being overstated. While some parents and families may have rather serious homework problems, these would generally appear to be private problems, hardly in need of national or even local solutions.

At least there is a consensus on standard reference points. One constant in this debate are the data gathered from the University of Michigan's 1997 Child Development supplement to the Panel Study of Income Dynamics and 1981 Study of Time Use in Social and Economic Accounts, a collection of time-use studies of children. Often appearing in the press cheek-by-jowl with quotes from overstretched parents, most reporting on the study suggests its findings support the conclusion that American children lack for leisure time amid demands imposed on them by parents and school. But the study's authors, who arguably know more than anyone about how American children are actually spending their time day-in and day-out, do not see the story this way. In fact, in a *New York Times* article, the study's primary researcher, Sandra L. Hofferth, dismissed the whole notion that the American child is over-worked and overoccupied. "I don't believe in the 'hurried child' for a minute. . . . There is a lot of time that can be used for other things."

On the question of homework, Hofferth and co-author John F. Sandberg reject the claim that homework has seen a significant general increase. The average amount of time spent studying for 3- to 12-year-olds has increased from 1981 to 1997, but the vast majority of those increases (studying and reading are measured separately) are concentrated among 3- to 5-year-olds (reading) and 6- to 8-year-olds (studying). "The main reason for the increase in studying among 6- to 8-year-olds was an increase in the proportion who did some studying at all, from one-third to more than one-half. The fact that significant increases in reading occurred among 3- to 5-year-olds probably reflects parents' increasing concern with preparing children for school."

Which is to say, homework appears to be increasing most where there was no homework before, and among age groups for whom it will do the least good. Far from a situation of the straw breaking the camel's back, we see many unburdened camels taking on their first tiny handfuls of straw, and a number of others carrying little if any more than they did in the past. This is where the story of the debate over homework takes a major turn. While arguably some American children have been turned into walking delivery systems for wicked educators bent on upsetting the home life of innocent American families, this is clearly not true across the board. In fact, one might say that a good number of American children and teenagers are already deciding how much time they want to spend on homework, and the amount of work they've opted for is not exactly back-breaking.

The Brookings Institution recently weighed in on the homework debate on this very point, arguing that "almost everything in this story [of over-worked students] is wrong." Like Hofferth and Sandburg, Tom Loveless, the Brookings author, points out that most of the increase noted in the University of Michigan study is concentrated among the youngest subjects who are reading earlier and being introduced to homework at a younger age. The most telling finding in the Brookings report, however, is that "the typical student, even in high school, does not spend more than an hour per day on homework." Needless to say, this picture is quite different from the homework situation described by Kralovec and Buell, to say nothing of the dire drama described over and over in newspaper and magazine stories.

The 1997 University of Michigan time-use studies do report average increases for time spent on homework against a 1981 benchmark, but analysis by the Brookings Institution shows these increases are nearly negligible. The amount of time 3- to 5-year-olds spent studying increased from 25 minutes per week in 1981 to 36 minutes per week in 1997. This translates to an increase of two minutes a night if studying takes place five nights a week. The next group, 6- to 8-year-olds, as mentioned, saw the biggest increase, from 52 minutes a week to 2 hours and 8 minutes a week, which translates to an average increase of 15 minutes a night, bringing average homework time to a grand total of 25 minutes or so a night. The oldest group, 9- to 12-year-olds, saw only an increase of 19 minutes on average per week, an increase of less than four minutes a night. Other data culled by Brookings from the University of Michigan study show that over one-third of 9- to 12-year-olds reported doing no homework. Indeed, half of all 3- to 12-year-olds said that they were doing no homework whatsoever, despite data showing a small average increase in homework for this group.

Other research supports these findings. The National Assessment of Education Progress (NAEP) reports that a significant number of 9- and 13-year-olds are assigned no homework at all. Between 1984 and 1999, at least 26 percent and as much as 36 percent of 9-year-olds reported receiving no homework assignments the day before filling out the questionnaire. Among 13-year-olds, the numbers show a relatively large and increasing number of students assigned no homework: 17 percent in 1988, increasing to 24 percent in 1999. As for older students, the 1999 National Center for Education Statistics (NCES) reports that 12 percent of high school seniors said they were doing no homework during a typical week. Of the remaining 88 percent, most said they spent less than 5 hours a week doing homework. This, remember, is in high school, where teachers assign more work, students are expected to do more work, and homework is agreed to have the most benefits. And yet, the above NCES number tells us that most high school students who do homework spend less than an hour a day, five days a week, doing it. According to the NAEP, only about a third of 17-year-olds have more than one hour of homework a night.

What about examining the homework habits of students who go on to college, thus controlling for the downward pull of low performers in high school? In the national survey of college freshmen performed by the University of California at Los Angeles, a surprising number report having worked no more than one hour a night as high school seniors. In 1987, only 47 percent of college freshmen surveyed said they had done more than five hours of homework a week. By 2002, that number had fallen to 34 percent—meaning only about one-third of American college freshman said they'd spent more than one hour a night on homework as high school seniors. As the Brookings report comments, such a homework load makes American high schoolers look underworked compared with their peers in other developed nations.

Pleased with Ourselves

The evidence suggests that while a significant portion of students are not carrying an insupportable burden of homework, a small percentage of students work long hours indeed—and some of them not for any good reason. We are giving the wrong kind of homework and in increasing quantities to the wrong age groups. As the Brookings report notes, 5 percent of fourth graders have more than 2 hours of homework nightly. Whether such a figure is surprising or not may merely be a question of expectations, but it hardly seems reasonable to expect 9-year-olds to be capable of finishing such quantities of after-school work. Still, that a small percentage of students are unnecessarily overworked does not justify the national press coverage and research interest this story has generated.

Why the homework controversy has received the attention it has may result from our national preference for stories that make our children seem one and all to be high achievers. Also, it's no secret that many professional and upper-class parents will undertake extraordinary measures to help their children get ahead in school in order to get ahead in the real world: These children are sent to elite schools that liberally assign homework, even as they are signed up for any number of organized activities in the name of self-improvement. And, of course, this segment of the population does more than its share to direct and set the tone for press coverage of news issues of interest to families. That surely helps explain spectacular headlines like "The Homework Ate My Family" (*Time*), "Homework Doesn't Help" (*Newsweek*), and "Overbooked: Four Hours of Homework for a Third Grader" (*People*).

So, while the overworked American child exits, he is not typical. Strangely enough, he seems to be more of an American ideal—drawn from our Lake Woebegone tendency of imagining that we're so good and hard-working, we might be too good and too hard-working. Thus do we ask ourselves why Johnny is doing so much homework, when in fact he is not.

POSTSCRIPT

Should Homework Be Abolished?

In Etta Kralovec's 2003 book, *Schools That Do Too Much: Wasting Time and Money in Schools and What We Can All Do About It*, she offers ideas for restructuring schools, with particular emphasis on time use. Re-emphasizing her end-homework-now theme, she states that "the all-important principle that should guide a redesigned schedule is that all assigned schoolwork should be completed at school, where all students have equal access to educational resources." Besides phasing out homework, Kralovec suggests moving athletics and drama programs into the community, ripping out all loud speakers in school, throwing out student fund-raising, making schools "no-construction zones" during instructional hours, and keeping the local community informed of school activities and intentions. By following these suggestions (each of which can be discussed as an issue in itself), schools will move toward Kralovec's goal of becoming "sacred places dedicated to learning."

Kralovec's position on homework and time utilization echoes the thoughts of Ted and Nancy Sizer in their 1999 book *The Students Are Watching*. They contend that "in a rushed school, already carrying the burden of too many functions, homework is often used as a way to extend the demands of the school without extending school hours. The increasing amount of homework may not be helping students to learn more; indeed, it often undermines the student's health, the development of personal interests, and the quality of family life." These comments raise questions about the extensiveness of the curriculum and the structure of the school day. In times past, the curriculum was narrower and, at least at the secondary level, students were provided more time, through study halls and homeroom periods, to work on class assignments.

Additional books for exploration of this and allied issues are Susan Ohanian's *What Happened to Recess and Why Are Our Children Struggling in Kindergarten?* (2002), Janine Bempechat's *Getting Our Kids Back on Track: Educating Children for the Future* (2000) (particularly chapter four), and John Merrow's *Choosing Excellence* (2001) (particularly the chapter on homework and home learning).

It is obviously time to weigh the positive and negative effects of homework. Among positive aspects pointed out by researcher Harris Cooper are better retention of factual knowledge, increased understanding, better critical thinking, and greater self-discipline and self-direction. The negatives he cites are loss of interest in academic material, physical and emotional fatigue, cheating, and the increase in differences between students from affluent and low-income families.

ISSUE 19

Do Computers Negatively Affect Student Growth?

YES: Lowell Monke, from "The Human Touch," *Education Next* (Fall 2004)

NO: Frederick M. Hess, from "Technical Difficulties," *Education Next* (Fall 2004)

ISSUE SUMMARY

YES: Lowell Monke, an assistant professor of education, expresses deep concerns that the uncritical faith in computer technology in schools has led to sacrifices in intellectual growth and creativity.

NO: Frederick M. Hess, while sharing some of Monke's observations, believes that the tools of technology, used appropriately, can support innovation and reinvention in education.

The schools have not always used or responded to new media constructively, so it is crucial that media experts help teachers, administrators, and curriculum designers carve out appropriate strategies for dealing with new technologies. Some experts—while seeing many exciting possibilities in computer-based instruction, particularly in the realm of individualization and self-pacing—caution that we need far more sophisticated understanding of the processes of learning, human motivation, and factors involved in concentration. Others fear the controlling force of computer programs because it could lead to the diminution of the spontaneity and instinctive responses of the learner. The ultimate effect of the new technology could be a complete transformation of learning and the conception of organized education—but similar predictions were made with the advent of television and even radio.

In 1984 MIT professor Seymour Papert predicted, "There won't be schools in the future; I think that the computer will blow up the school." But Larry Cuban, in "Revolutions That Fizzled," *The Washington Post* (October 27, 1996), warns that the persistent urge to reengineer the schools has continually failed to transform teaching practices. Papert, writing in the same issue, counters that the computer makes possible John Dewey's depiction of learning through experimentation and exposure to the real world of social experience. Computer enthusiasts Jim Cummins of New York University and Dennis Sayers of the Ontario Institute for Studies in Education, in their 1996 book *Brave New Schools*, urge heavy investment in an Internet-wired nationwide school system.

On the negative side, Richard P. Lookatch, in "The Ill-Considered Dash to Technology," *The School Administrator* (April 1996), warns that "hardware hucksters have found K–12 schools to be open landfills for outdated central processing units, while software pushers find technology-zealous media specialists ideal targets for software, much of which ultimately ends up in a storage cabinet because it is either too frustrating, too complicated, or too poorly correlated to the curriculum." His position is that educational media offer no unique benefits and may well lead to inequity, lower standards, and wasted financial resources.

In "The Emperor's New Computer: A Critical Look at Our Appetite for Computer Technology," *Journal of Teacher Education* (May–June 1996), David Pepi and Geoffrey Schuerman pose several crucial questions, including the following:

- Is technology an effective catalyst for educational reform?
- Are past, current, and anticipated uses of technology consistent with contemporary theories of learning?
- Is using computers synonymous with good teaching?
- Does technology promote critical thinking?
- Does technology build cooperation?
- How much information can we tolerate?

In considering responses to such questions, the authors draw on Neil Postman's 1993 book *Technopoly*, in which "technopoly" is defined as a culture in which all aspects of human life must find meaning in terms of the current technology and in which there is no tolerance of alternative worldviews. It is Postman's opinion that we are moving toward that culture.

Books addressing the issue include Jane M. Healy's *Failure to Connect* (1998); Frederick Bennett's *Computers as Tutors: Solving the Crisis in Education* (1999); Clifford Stoll's *High Tech Heretic* (1999); Andrea A. DiSessa's *Changing Minds: Computers, Learning, and Literacy* (2000); Larry Cuban's *Oversold and Underused* (2001); and Seymour Papert's *The Connected Family* (1996). In his book, Papert states, "Despite frequent predictions that a technological revolution in education is imminent, school remains in essential respects very much what it has always been, and what changes have occurred (for better or for worse) cannot be attributed to technology."

The opinions that follow pit Lowell Monke, who feels that the computer's emphasis on information acquisition reconstitutes learning and shifts our values, against Frederick Hess, who holds out hope that the efficiencies of computer technology can free students and teachers for more creative exploration.

YES

Lowell Monke

The Human Touch

In 1922 Thomas Edison proclaimed, "I believe the motion picture is destined to revolutionize our educational system and that in a few years it will supplant largely, if not entirely, the use of textbooks." Thus began a long string of spectacularly wrong predictions regarding the capacity of various technologies to revolutionize education.

What betrayed Edison and his successors was an uncritical faith in technology itself. This faith has become a sort of ideology increasingly dominating K–12 education. In the past two decades, school systems, with generous financial and moral support from foundations and all levels of government, have made massive investments in computer technology and in creating "wired" schools. The goal is twofold: to provide children with the computer skills necessary to flourish in a high-tech world and to give them access to tools and information that will enhance their learning in subjects like mathematics and history.

However, in recent years a number of scholars have questioned the vast sums being devoted to educational technology. They rarely quibble with the need for children to learn how to use computers, but find little evidence that making technology more available leads to higher student achievement in core subjects. As Stanford University professor Larry Cuban writes in *Oversold and Underused*, "There have been no advances (measured by higher academic achievement of urban, suburban, or rural students) over the past decade that can be confidently attributed to broader access to computers. . . . The link between test-score improvements and computer availability and use is even more contested."

While it is important to examine the relationship between technology and learning, that debate often devolves into a tit-for-tat of dueling studies and anecdotes. The problem with framing the issue merely as a question of whether technology boosts test scores is that it fails to address the interaction between technology and the values learned in school. In short, we need to ask what kind of learning tends to take place with the computer and what kind gets left out.

The Need for Firsthand Experience

A computer can inundate a child with mountains of information. However, all of this learning takes place the same way: through abstract symbols, decontextualized and cast on a two-dimensional screen. Contrast that with the way

From *Education Next,* Fall 2004, pp. 10–14. Copyright © 2004 by Education Next. Reprinted by permission.

children come to know a tree—by peeling its bark, climbing its branches, sitting under its shade, jumping into its piled-up leaves. Just as important, these firsthand experiences are enveloped by feelings and associations—muscles being used, sun warming the skin, blossoms scenting the air. The computer cannot even approximate any of this.

There is a huge qualitative difference between learning about something, which requires only information, and learning from something, which requires that the learner enter into a rich and complex relationship with the subject at hand. For smaller children especially, that relationship is as physical as it is mental. Rousseau pointed out long ago that the child's first and most important teacher is his hands. Every time I walk through a store with my sons and grow tired of saying, "Don't touch that!" I am reminded of Rousseau's wisdom.

What "Information Age" values tempt us to forget is that all of the information gushing through our electronic networks is abstract; that is, it is all representations, one or more symbolic steps removed from any concrete object or personal experience. Abstract information must somehow connect to a child's concrete experiences if it is to be meaningful. If there is little personal, concrete experience with which to connect, those abstractions become inert bits of data, unlikely to mobilize genuine interest or to generate comprehension of the objects and ideas they represent. Furthermore, making meaning of new experiences—and the ideas that grow out of them—requires quiet contemplation. By pumping information at children at phenomenal speed, the computer short-circuits that process. As social critic Theodore Roszak states in *The Cult of Information,* "An excess of information may actually crowd out ideas, leaving the mind (young minds especially) distracted by sterile, disconnected facts, lost among the shapeless heaps of data."

This deluge of shapeless heaps of data caused the late social critic Marshall McLuhan to conclude that schools would have to become "recognized as civil defense against media fallout." McLuhan understood that the consumption and manipulation of symbolic, abstract information is not an adequate substitute for concrete, firsthand involvement with objects, people, nature, and community, for it ignores the child's primary educational need—to make meaning out of experience.

Simulation's Limits

Of course, computers can simulate experience. However, one of the byproducts of these simulations is the replacement of values inherent in real experience with a different set of abstract values that are compatible with the technological ideology. For example, "Oregon Trail," a computer game that helps children simulate the exploration of the American frontier, teaches students that the pioneers' success in crossing the Great Plains depended most decisively on managing their resources. This is the message implicit in the game's structure, which asks students, in order to survive, to make a series of rational, calculated decisions based on precise measurements of their resources. In other words, good pioneers were good accountants.

But this completely misses the deeper significance of this great American migration, which lies not in the computational capabilities of the pioneers but in their determination, courage, ingenuity, and faith as they overcame extreme conditions and their almost constant miscalculations. Because the computer cannot traffic in these deeply human qualities, the resilient souls of the pioneers are absent from the simulation.

Here we encounter the ambiguity of technology: its propensity to promote certain qualities while sidelining others. McLuhan called this process amplification and amputation. He used the microphone as an example. The microphone can literally amplify one's voice, but in doing so it reduces the speaker's need to exercise his own lung power. Thus one's inner capacities may atrophy.

This phenomenon is of particular concern with children, who are in the process of developing all kinds of inner capacities. Examples abound of technology's circumventing the developmental process: the student who uses a spell checker instead of learning to spell, the student who uses a calculator instead of learning to add—young people sacrificing internal growth for external power.

Often, however, this process is not so easily identified. An example is the widespread use of computers in preschools and elementary schools to improve sagging literacy skills. What could be wrong with that? Quite a bit, if we consider the prerequisites to reading and writing. We know that face-to-face conversation is a crucial element in the development of both oral and written communication skills. On the one hand, conversation forces children to generate their own images, which provide connections to the language they hear and eventually will read. This is one reason why reading to children and telling them stories is so important. Television and computers, on the other hand, generally require nothing more than the passive acceptance of prefabricated images.

Now consider that a study reported in *U.S. News & World Report* estimated that the current generation of children, with its legions of struggling readers, would experience one-third fewer face-to-face conversations during their school years than the generation of 30 years ago. It may well be that educators are trying to solve the problem of illiteracy by turning to the very technology that has diminished the experiences children need to become literate.

Obsolete Lessons

But students need to start using computers early in order to prepare for the high-tech future, don't they? Consider that the vast majority of students graduating from college this past spring started kindergarten in 1986, two years after the Macintosh was invented. If they used computers at all in elementary school, they were probably command-line machines with no mouse, no hard drive, and only rudimentary graphics. By the time these students graduated from college, whatever computer skills they picked up in primary school had long been rendered obsolete by the frenetic pace of technological innovation.

The general computer skills a youth needs to enter the workplace or college can easily be learned in one year of instruction during high school. During the nine years that I taught Advanced Computer Technology for the Des Moines public schools, I discovered that the level of computer skills students brought to the class had little bearing on their success. Teaching them the computer skills was the easy part. What I was not able to provide were the rich and varied firsthand experiences students needed in order to connect the abstract symbols they had to manipulate on the screen to the world around them. Students with scant computer experience but rich ideas and life experiences were, by the end of the year, generating sophisticated relational databases, designing marketable websites, and creating music videos. Ironically, it was the students who had curtailed their time climbing the trees, rolling the dough, and conversing with friends and adults in order to become computer "wizards" who typically had the most trouble finding creative things to do with the computer.

Certainly, many of these highly skilled young people (almost exclusively young men) find opportunities to work on computer and software design at prestigious universities and corporations. But such jobs represent a minuscule percentage of the occupations in this nation. And in any case, the task of early education is not merely to prepare students for making a living; it is to help them learn how to make a life. For that purpose, the computer wizards in my class seemed particularly ill prepared.

So why is it that schools persist in believing they must expose children to computers early? I think it is for the same reason that we take our children to church, to Fourth of July parades, and indeed to rituals of all types: to initiate them into a culture—in this case, the culture of high technology. The purpose is to infuse them with a set of values that supports the high-tech culture that has spread so rapidly across our society. And this, as we shall see, is perhaps the most disturbing trend of all.

The Ecological Impact of Technology

As the promise of a computer revolution in education fades, I often hear promoters fall back on what I'll term the neutrality argument: "Computers are just tools; it's what you do with them that matters." In some sense this is no more than a tautology: Of course it matters *how* we use computers in schools. What matters more, however, is that we use them *at all*. Every tool demands that we somehow change our environment or values in order to accommodate its use. For instance, the building of highways to accommodate the automobile hastened the flight to the suburbs and the decline of inner cities. And over the past 50 years we have radically altered our social landscape to accommodate the television set. In his seminal book *Autonomous Technology*, Langdon Winner dubbed this characteristic "reverse adaptation."

Consider the school personnel who already understand, intuitively, how this principle works: the music teacher whose program has been cut in order to fund computer labs; the principal who has had to beef up security in order to protect high-priced technology; the superintendent who has had to craft an "acceptable use" agreement that governs children's use of the Internet (and for the first time in our history renounces the school's responsibility for the material children are exposed to while in school). What the computers-are-just-tools argument ignores is the ecological nature of powerful technologies—that is, their introduction into an environment reconstitutes all of the relationships in that environment, some for better and some for worse. Clinging to the belief that computers have no effect on us allows us to turn a blind eye to the sacrifices that schools have made to accommodate them.

Not only do computers send structural ripples throughout a school system, but they also subtly alter the way we think about education. The old saw, "To a man with a hammer everything looks like a nail," has many corollaries (the walls of my home once testified to one of my favorites: to a four-year-old with a crayon, everything looks like drawing paper). One that fits here is, "To an educator with a computer, everything looks like information." And the more prominent we make computers in schools (and in our own lives), the more we see the rapid accumulation, manipulation, and sharing of information as central to the learning process—edging out the contemplation and expression of ideas and the gradual development of meaningful connections to the world.

In reconstituting learning as the acquisition of information, the computer also shifts our values. The computer embodies a particular value system, a technological thought world first articulated by Francis Bacon and Rene Descartes four hundred years ago, that turns our attention outward toward asserting control over our environment (that is essentially what technologies do—extend our power to control from a distance). As it has gradually come to dominate Western thinking, this ideology has entered our educational institutions. Its growing dominance is witnessed in the language that abounds in education: talk of empowerment, student control of learning, standards, assessment tools, and productivity. Almost gone from the conversation are those inner concerns—wisdom, truth, character, imagination, creativity, and meaning—that once formed the core values of education. Outcomes have replaced insights as the yardstick of learning, while standardized tests are replacing human judgment as the means of assessment. No tool supports this technological shift more than computers.

In the Wrong Hands

There are some grave consequences in pushing technological values too far and too soon. Soon after my high-school computer lab was hooked up to the Internet, I realized that my students suddenly had more power to do more damage to more people than any teenagers in history. Had they been carefully prepared to assume responsibility for that power through the arduous process of developing self-discipline, ethical and moral strength, compassion, and connection with the community around them? Hardly. They and their teachers had been too busy putting that power to use.

We must help our young people develop the considerable moral and ethical strength needed to resist abusing the enormous power these machines give them. Those qualities take a great deal of time and effort to develop in a child, but they ought to be as much a prerequisite to using powerful computer tools as is learning how to type. Trying to teach a student to use the power of computer technology appropriately without those moral and ethical traits is like trying to grow a tree without roots.

Rather than nurture those roots, we hand our smallest children machines and then gush about the power and control they display over that rarefied environment. From the earliest years we teach our children that if they have a problem, we have an external tool that will fix it (computers are not the only tools; Ritalin, for example, is a powerful technology that has been scandalously over-prescribed to "fix" behavior problems). After years of this training, when our teenagers find themselves confused, angry, depressed, or overwhelmed, we wonder why so many of them don't reach out to the community for help or dig deep within themselves to find the internal strength to persevere, but rather reach for the most powerful (and often deadly) tool they can find to "fix" their problems. Our attempts to use powerful machines to accelerate or remediate learning are part of a pattern that sacrifices the growth of our children's inner resources and deep connectedness to community for the ability to extend their power outward into the world. The world pays a high price for the trade-off.

The response that I often hear to this criticism—that we just need to balance computer use in school with more "hands-on" activities (and maybe a little character education)—sounds reasonable. Certainly schools should help young people develop balanced lives. But the call for balance within schools ignores the massive commitment of resources required to make computers work at all and the resultant need to keep them constantly in use to justify that expense. Furthermore, that view of balance completely discounts the enormous imbalance of children's lives outside of school. Children typically spend nearly half their waking life outside of school sitting in front of screens. Their world is saturated with the artificial, the abstract, the mechanical. Whereas the intellectual focus of schools in the rural society of the 19th century compensated for a childhood steeped in nature and concrete activity, balance today requires a reversal of roles, with schools compensating for the overly abstract, symbolic, and artificial environment that children experience outside of school.

Technology with a Human Purpose

None of this is to say that we should banish computers from all levels of K–12 education. As young people move into subject areas like advanced mathematics and chemistry that rely on highly abstract concepts, computers have much to offer. Young people will also need computer skills when they graduate. But computer-based learning needs to grow out of years of concrete experience and a fundamental appreciation for the world apart from the machine, a world in which nature and human beings are able to speak for and through themselves to the child. Experiences with the computer need to grow out of early reliance on simple tools that depend on and develop the skills of the child rather than complex tools, which have so many skills already built in. By concentrating high technology in the upper grades, we honor the natural developmental stages of childhood. And there is a bonus: the release of massive amounts of resources currently tied up in expensive machinery that can be redirected toward helping young children develop the inner resources needed to put that machinery to good use when they become adults.

There remains a problem, however. When Bacon began pushing the technological ideology, Western civilization was full of meaning and wretchedly short on the material means of survival. Today we face the reverse situation: a society saturated in material comforts but almost devoid of meaning. Schools that see their job as preparing young people to meet the demands of a technology-driven world merely embrace and advance the idea that human needs are no longer our highest priority, that we must adapt to meet the demands of our machines. We may deliver our children into the world with tremendous technical power, but it is rarely with a well-developed sense of human purpose to guide its use.

If we are to alter that relationship, we will have to think of technological literacy in a new way. Perhaps we could call it technology awareness. Whatever its name, that kind of study, rather than technology training, is what needs to be integrated into the school curriculum. I am currently working with the Alliance for Childhood on a set of developmental guidelines to help educators create technology-awareness programs that help young people think about, not just with, technology. This is not the place to go into the details of those guidelines. What I want to emphasize here is that they share one fundamental feature: They situate technology within a set of human values rather than out in front of those values. They do not start by asking what children need to do to adapt to a machine world, but rather, which technologies can best serve human purposes at every educational level and how we can prepare children to make wise decisions about their use in the future.

The most daunting problems facing our society—drugs, violence, racism, poverty, the dissolution of family and community, and certainly war—are all matters of human purpose and meaning. Filling schools with computers will not help find the answers to why the freest nation in the world has the highest percentage of citizens behind bars or why the wealthiest nation in history condemns a sixth of its children to poverty.

So it seems that we are faced with a remarkable irony: that in an age of increasing artificiality, children first need to sink their hands deeply into what is real; that in an age of light-speed communication, it is crucial that children take the time to develop their own inner voice; that in an age of incredibly powerful machines we must first teach our children how to use the incredible powers that lie deep within themselves.

Frederick M. Hess  **NO**

Technical Difficulties

In 2000, at the height of the technology boom, Maine governor Angus King made a splash by proposing to give laptops to all of the state's 7th graders. His stated purpose was to "do something different from what everybody else is doing." Missing from the $50 million proposal, however, was any rationale related to school performance. No evident thought had been put into how this major investment in new technology would make schools more efficient, produce future savings, or enhance the learning process.

King's proposal was typical of the way in which technologies like the personal computer and the Internet have been used in public education. The tendency has been to sprinkle computers and Internet connections across classrooms in the pleasant hope that teachers will integrate them into their lessons. The purpose is seldom to make teachers more productive or to rethink the way in which lessons are delivered. Indeed, PCs often serve as little more than high-priced typewriters, sitting in the back of classrooms unused for most of the school day.

This state of affairs stands in sharp contrast to how technology is used by business and government enterprises that engage in competition with other manufacturers and service providers. To them, technology is not an end in itself, something to be adopted merely because it exists, but a tool for self-improvement. A competitive enterprise adopts new technologies when these enable workers to tackle new problems or to do the *same thing* as before, but in a *cheaper and more efficient* fashion. For example, technology investments enabled the U.S. Postal Service, under heavy competitive pressure from United Parcel Service and Federal Express, to trim its workforce by 16,000 in 2003. These cuts followed layoffs of 23,000 employees over the preceding two years. The cuts were made possible not by reducing service, but by substituting technology in areas where people were performing either routine tasks or roles that automated machines could handle more efficiently.

At a broader level, in recent years the nation's 100 largest companies improved productivity so rapidly that in 2003 it took only nine workers to do what ten workers had done in 2001. Economists have long recognized that the potential for growth in productivity is more limited in service sectors like education than in manufacturing or retail. Nonetheless, even the service

From *Education Next*, Fall 2004, pp. 15–19. Copyright © 2004 by Education Next. Reprinted by permission.

sector has witnessed productivity gains of about 1 percent a year during the past three decades.

Public schools, by contrast, have steadily *added* to the ranks of teachers and reduced class sizes even as they make ever-larger investments in new technologies. Spending on technology in public schools increased from essentially zero in 1970 to $118 per student in 2002 and $89 per student in 2003, according to *Education Week*. In 1998 there were 12.1 students for every computer connected to the Internet; by 2002, the ratio had dropped to 4.8 students per computer, according to the Department of Education. In the past five years alone, the nation has spent more than $20 billion linking schools and classrooms to the Internet through the federal E-rate program with little to show for it in the way of instructional changes or improved outcomes. Meanwhile, despite these huge new investments in technology, massive increases in the workforce of teachers drove the student-teacher ratio from 22 students per teacher to 16 students per teacher between 1970 and 2001.

Cultural Bias

Why have public schools failed so far to put all this fancy new technology to good use? One clear reason is that they face no pressure to do so. Organizations like the Postal Service make effective use of technology because they must keep up with FedEx, UPS, and other delivery services. Competitive enterprises are on a constant search for ways of boosting their productivity, holding down their costs, and developing innovative products—because they know that their competitors are always on the lookout for similar advantages. No executive wants to adopt a painful course like downsizing the workforce or imposing wrenching change. They take these steps only when compelled.

Public schools, however, are insulated from the pressures of competition. They thus have no reason to regard technology as a tool to trim their workforce or to rethink the ways in which they deliver education. This problem is compounded by the fact that collective-bargaining agreements between school districts and employee unions have made using technology to displace workers or reinvent processes extraordinarily difficult.

There is also a bias within the culture of education against ideas that seem too "businesslike." Indeed, the very words "efficiency" and "cost-effectiveness" can set the teeth of parents and educators on edge. Proposals to use technology to downsize the workforce, alter instructional delivery, or improve managerial efficiency are inevitably attacked by education authorities as part of an effort to, in the words of Henry Giroux, "Transform public education . . . [in order] to expand the profits of investors, educate students as consumers, and train young people for the low-paying jobs of the new global marketplace." The notion that the responsible use of public money is the work of some shadowy global conspiracy evinces a fundamental lack of seriousness about educating children.

Traditionalists insist that it is impossible to educate children more efficiently, that there is no way technology can be substituted for anything that educators do. They frequently compare the act of teaching to the arts: where the act of creation itself is the end product, it can be difficult or impossible to use technology to improve performance. As the late Daniel Patrick Moynihan, the legendary U.S. senator, was fond of saying, producing a Mozart quartet two centuries ago required four musicians, four stringed instruments, and, say, 35 minutes. Producing the same Mozart quartet today requires the same resources. Despite breathtaking technological advances, productivity has not changed.

In the case of schooling, however, this analogy is incomplete and ultimately misleading. In the arts, what has changed over two centuries is that, through radio, CDs, television, and digital media, the number of people able to *hear and appreciate* a given performance has increased dramatically, at an ever-decreasing cost. Improved technology has now made available to the general public what was once the preserve of the elite.

The spread of the Internet and other technological advances has created similar opportunities in education. For instance, during the 2002–03 school year, the Florida Virtual School enrolled more than 6,800 students in its 75 course offerings. Florida Virtual is a public entity that provides instruction to students in schools and districts throughout the state. The school provides web-based classes, instruction, and assessments to students in a variety of academic subjects and electives. Like virtual schools operating in 15 other states, Florida Virtual allows faculty to provide courses to a scattered student population. Programs like Florida Virtual may make it possible to provide some academic instruction more cheaply and more effectively, freeing up resources for other needs.

At the university level, nearly 2 million students took at least one course online in the fall of 2003. In a national survey of nearly 1,000 college administrators conducted by the Sloan Consortium, 57 percent of the administrators reported that Internet-based courses were already at least equivalent to traditional courses in quality. And a third of the administrators thought that the web-based courses would be superior to in-class instruction within three years. Such improvements are to be expected among the many colleges and universities now competing for students' distance-learning dollars. However, efforts to use the Internet in an effective manner are few and far between among K-12 public schools.

Technology and Data Management

Used wisely, information technology does have the capacity to help schools become dramatically more effective. Data systems that track information on individual students permit teachers to quickly check the performance of individual students on specific tasks. Information technology can also give school-site personnel unprecedented control over budgets and hiring and can increase their flexibility regarding resource allocation. The Learning First Alliance, a consortium that includes the National Education Association and the American Federation of Teachers, has highlighted how this has worked in districts like Long Beach and Chula Vista, California, and Aldine, Texas.

Outside of schooling, a compelling illustration of how accountability and technology can together improve public services comes from the remarkable success that New York City and other cities enjoyed using new tools to combat crime in the 1990s. The New York City Police Department introduced a system called CompStat, short for "comparative statistics." CompStat compiled data from police reports, crime complaints, arrests, and crime patterns. Over time, the system was broadened to include 734 categories of concern, measuring even the incidence of loud parties and of police overtime.

In the first five years after the 1993 introduction of CompStat, the number of homicides in New York City fell from 1,946 to 629—a rate of decrease three times that of the nation as a whole. Similar results were experienced in other cities that implemented the system, from Philadelphia to Los Angeles. Why did the system work? It helped to hold officers accountable, to pinpoint areas of concern, and to provide the information that can help all police focus on using their skills. In New York City, precincts were required to update their crime statistics on a weekly or daily basis, rather than on the monthly or quarterly basis that had traditionally been the norm. New software allowed department officials to precisely map clusters of crimes, correlating them with drug sale sites, areas of gang activity, schools, public housing, and other relevant locations, and to share the information department-wide within seconds.

In K–12 education, by contrast, we generally manage most information the same way stores managed inventory in the 1960s. Almost unbelievably in this day and age, the typical district spends 40 or more minutes a year per student collecting, processing, and reporting the data required by the U.S. Department of Education under the No Child Left Behind Act. That equates to more than 6,000 hours of employee time in a district with 10,000 students. The tremendous delays in processing data and the staff time consumed are the consequence of districts' having personnel fill out written forms and retyping data from one software package to another. Simply equipping districts to report data electronically and acquire data from existing databases is a daunting challenge.

When principals or teachers are asked for this information, those that have it available almost inevitably turn to large binders rather than more nimble electronic interfaces. When asked if he could pull some data on teacher absenteeism or staff training costs, one veteran principal in a well-regarded district spluttered, "Do you know what I do if I want substitute teacher data? I have [my secretary] go through the files and tally it up. She keeps a running total on a piece of graph paper for me. . . . If I want to check on a supply order, I call the deputy [superintendent] for services because we're old friends, and I know he'll actually have someone pull it for me."

Modern information technology offers a wealth of straight-forward, time-tested ways to make the necessary data widely and instantly available. There is an array of systems, produced by firms like Scantron and IntelliTools, that allow teachers to call up simple graphs detailing the performance of individual students at the push of a button. However, using these systems requires the consistent collection of information on student learning. Assigning paper-based quizzes ensures that almost all of the information on student mastery will be lost, while the software produced by a dozen or more firms is able to quickly read the results from electronically administered tests into an evolving protfolio of data that tracks student learning.

Ultimately, to be useful, this information has to be at people's fingertips. This is an eminently solvable technical challenge. Huge, complicated organizations, from Wal-Mart to the Internal Revenue Service, routinely track productivity figures, costs, and evaluative measures.

A New Role for Teachers

How else can technology support innovation and reinvention in education? Consider that, historically, teachers have been expected to perform a wide range of responsibilities. Each teacher is expected to design lesson plans, lecture, run class discussions, grade essays and exams, mentor colleagues, supervise homeroom, and patrol the cafeteria. Every year our high schools have tens of thousands of teachers giving variations of the same lectures on the Civil War, the digestive system, and the properties of quadratic equations. In fact, the job description of a teacher today is pretty similar to that of a teacher in 1950.

In medicine, by contrast, progress has been marked by specialization. Doctors with different types of training have taken on more precisely defined roles while less expensive professionals like registered nurses and physical therapists are now performing tasks that don't require a doctor's training. Similarly, 16-year-old volunteers using handheld scanners are able to track medical supplies and hospital inventory with a precision that would have been unimaginable even in the best-managed enterprise just two decades ago.

Imagine a hospital with no nurses or physicians' assistants or physical therapists, where doctors performed every task. We would need a slew of additional doctors, each would have less time to devote to any particular specialty, and costs would skyrocket.

How can technology enable teachers to specialize in the same manner as, say, doctors? Let's consider one classroom example in order to understand how technology can help teachers use their time more productively. Teachers know it is useful to have students write on a regular basis. When I taught high-school social studies, like so many of my colleagues, I required students to write at least three pages a week commenting on what we had read and discussed in class.

The problem is that, at a minimum, this meant my 150 students would turn in 450 pages a week of writing. A teacher who reads, marks, and comments on each student's weekly work in just five minutes will spend more than 12 hours a week simply providing feedback on such writing assignments. Most of this time isn't spent providing particularly cerebral feedback, but instead flagging obvious grammatical and structural problems and reminding students to write in complete sentences. Meanwhile, teachers also need to prepare for teaching, assess other assignments, assist and advise students, and lead a personal life. The result is often that teachers provide limited feedback, read student work sporadically, or (most commonly) assign less writing than might be ideal.

Once, such compromises were unavoidable. That is no longer the case. Today, for instance, there is essay-grading software, commercially available from companies like Vantage Learning or the Educational Testing Service, that can quickly and efficiently analyze pieces of writing on dimensions such as sentence construction, language, and mechanics. Several of these programs match the scores given by expert human raters more than 90 percent of the time, which is actually *higher* in some cases than the rate of agreement among multiple human readers. How can this be? In most cases, we're not talking about evaluating Proustian prose; we're talking about helping the typical 4th grader learn to write clearly and effectively. Most of the mistakes that students make and most of the feedback they need are pretty predictable.

Clearly technological tools cannot imitate the full range of skills that a teacher brings when reading a student's essay. Technology cannot gauge a student's growth, analytic prowess, possible interests, or unexpected developments. However, assessment software can replicate the routine elements of evaluation, providing more complete feedback on the essentials while freeing up teachers to make fuller use of their expertise. The result is that teachers spend less time on trivia while adding more value. Rather than requiring hundreds of thousands of teachers to spend hundreds of hours a year circling dangling participles or errant commas, the sensible substitution of technology can help ensure quality feedback while allowing teachers more time for preparation, instruction, and tutoring.

Human ingenuity is the most expensive commodity in the developed world. People are costly to employ; no well-run organization hires reams of bodies when it is possible to hire more selectively and use employees more thoughtfully. This is why efforts to reduce class size are a static, unimaginative, and inefficient way to improve schooling. These efforts presume that teachers need to perform all the duties and tasks now in place; helping them accomplish these tasks more effectively thus requires shrinking the number of students they must teach. However, if we were to retool the teacher's role in a way that used scarce resources like teachers' time and expertise more carefully, teachers could spend more time on the areas where they add value even while working with larger classes of students. If grading essays or examining student performance on weekly quizzes took only half as much time as it currently does, a teacher could work with more students and still have *more* instructional time for each student in that class.

A Tool, Not a Miracle Cure

The nation continues to blithely operate schools in a fashion that was dated in the 1970s and that today would be deemed irresponsible in a toothpaste factory. Rather than demand that education dollars be invested with particular care, we pour money into technology with little thought to how these tools might be used most sensibly.

The ability to instantly share full information on student performance, school performance, and costs across vast distances permits a focus on results that was simply not feasible until the most recent decade. The information technology that makes the easy sharing of information possible is the engine that makes tough-minded accountability, school choice, and visionary leadership a possibility.

Using new technological tools to relieve educators of routine functions will help them focus on those roles that add substantial value—enhancing their contribution, making the organization more productive, and thereby increasing both the benefit to the customer and the resources available to reward employees. Reducing rote demands allows people to focus on what they do best and reduces the number of talented workers who need to be hired—which, in turn, allows us to pay employees more.

Ultimately, if leaders lack the tools to increase efficiency, streamline their workforce, or sensibly reallocate resources, they won't. Technology is not a miracle cure. It is a tool. Used wisely, it can help professionals to take full advantage of their skills, slash the time spent on rote tasks, and concentrate resources and effort where they are needed most.

POSTSCRIPT

Do Computers Negatively Affect Student Growth?

A few years ago educational reformer John I. Goodlad declared that "school" should be considered a concept rather than a place and that this formulation would seem to be an appropriate keynote for education in the twenty-first century. Certainly, advocates of computerization and global networking would be comfortable with the idea. But today, as more school systems are being "wired," questions of initial cost, hardware obsolescence, variable availability, software quality and appropriateness, teacher reluctance, and productive utilization remain to be discussed and resolved.

Help in exploring these and related questions may be found in Gary Kidd's "Using the Internet as a School," *The Educational Forum* (Spring 1996); "Unfilled Promises," by Jane McDonald, William Lynch, and Greg Kearsley, *The American School Board Journal* (July 1996); Frederick Bennett's *Computers as Tutors* (1999); Leon Botstein's "A Brave New World?" *The School Administrator* (March 2001); Craig A. Cunningham's "Improving Our Nation's Schools Through Computers and Connectivity," *Brookings Review* (Winter 2001); R. W. Burniske's "When Computer Literacy Goes Too Far," *Phi Delta Kappan* (March 2001); and Frederick Bennett's "The Future of Computer Technology in K-12 Education," *Phi Delta Kappan* (April 2002). The April 1996 issue of *The School Administrator* contains a number of articles on such topics as Internet access and technology's usefulness in the inclusion of disabled students. Other journal issues devoted to the controversy include *Educational Leadership* (November 1997), *Contemporary Education* (Winter 1997), *NASSP Bulletin* (November 1997), *Theory Into Practice* (Winter 1998), *The School Administrator* (April 1999), *NASSP Bulletin* (May 1999 and September 1999), *Principal* (January 2000), *The Futurist* (March–April 2000), *Educational Leadership* (October 2000), *Kappa Delta Pi Record* (Fall 2000), *American Educator* (Fall 2001), *The School Administrator* (October 2001), *NASSP Bulletin* (November 2001) and *The School Administrator* (August 2005). Recent sources of special interest include Todd Oppenheimer's *The Flickering Mind: The False Promise of Technology in the Classroom and How Learning Can Be Saved* (2003), Gene I. Maeroff's *A Classroom of One: How Online Learning Is Changing Our Schools and Colleges* (2002), and Jane M. Healy's "Young Children Don't Need Computers," *Principal* (May–June 2003).

Finally, educational psychologist Richard P. Lookatch has argued that multimedia use in school offers students the opportunity to interact with the images behind a glass screen, but the looming danger is that it replaces students' interaction with each other and their environment.

ISSUE 20

Can Merit Pay Accelerate School Improvement?

YES: Steven Malanga, from "Why Merit Pay Will Improve Teaching," *City Journal* (Summer 2001)

NO: Al Ramirez, from "How Merit Pay Undermines Education," *Educational Leadership* (February 2001)

ISSUE SUMMARY

YES: Steven Malanga, a senior fellow of the Manhattan Institute, draws on examples from the corporate world and from public school systems in Cincinnati, Iowa, and Denver to make his case for performance-based merit pay for teachers.

NO: Associate professor of education Al Ramirez contends that merit pay programs misconstrue human motivation and devalue the work of teachers.

The issue of merit pay, or pay-for-performance, for teachers is certainly not new, but as Steven Malanga, one of the combatants presented in the pairing offered here, says, it is "one of the bitterest controversies in today's school reform debate." The current push to improve public education, particularly in impoverished areas, and to hold individual schools more accountable for achieving desired results has rekindled the argument over merit pay as a replacement for a reward system based primarily on seniority and earned course credits.

Although some forms of merit plans were widely used in the early part of the twentieth century, the economic depression of the 1930s prompted conversions to uniform pay scales. Teachers' unions, which gained strength throughout the remainder of the century, were not supportive of incentive pay schemes. They expressed doubts about the fairness of various evaluation methods and concerns about possible threats to collegiality and the standardization of teaching practices. Since the 1980s, and particularly since the passage of the "No Child Left Behind" legislation, pressure for an accountability system containing specific rewards for teachers and schools that meet desired outcomes has vastly increased.

The matter of how to appropriately and fairly evaluate teacher performance remains a major stumbling block in the adoption of merit pay plans. Local socioeconomic factors and the unevenness of support structures among school systems and states add complexity to the process. According to Sandra McCollum, in "How Merit Pay Improves Education," *Educational Leadership* (February 2001), merit pay programs are often discontinued because of one or more of the following reasons: they are unfairly implemented, teachers' unions refuse to endorse them, they create poor teacher morale, legislators who support them leave office, and they are simply too costly and difficult to administer.

An economist's view is offered by Darius Lakdawalla in "Quantity Over Quality," *Education Next* (Fall 2002). He contends that schools have been hiring more teachers in an effort to reduce class sizes but have not been rewarding them for quality performance. In the past few decades, serious opportunities outside teaching have opened up, and school systems have not risen to challenge the competition. The problem of retaining and attracting top-quality teachers is addressed in Marge Scherer, "Improving the Quality of the Teaching Force: A Conversation With David C. Berliner," *Educational Leadership* (May 2001). Berliner states that 7 of 23 nations surveyed exceed the United States in starting salaries for teachers and that 9 of 21 nations exceed the United States in top teacher salaries. In the realm of pay, status, and working conditions, says Berliner, "The U.S. is saying to its educators that they are not really important; if we thought they were important, we'd pay them a larger share of our gross domestic product, as other nations do." Yet Berliner is also worried that a merit pay plan based primarily on student achievement could lead to teachers' doing the wrong thing in their classrooms—cheating and narrowing the curriculum.

Some guidelines for the fair evaluation of teacher performance are put forth by Thomas R. Hoerr in "A Case for Merit Pay," *Phi Delta Kappan* (December 1998). In Hoerr's view, there must be trust between the administration and the faculty, judgments must be treated with confidentiality, there must be recognition that both what is valued and how it is measured will vary by context, and teachers who do not perform satisfactorily and do not respond to supportive intervention should not be rehired. Getting rid of ineffective teachers, however, is so arduous and expensive that many school systems do not attempt it. So says Peter Schweizer in "Firing Offenses," *National Review* (August 17, 1998). He analyzes the companion issue of teacher tenure, a system that was originally designed to protect the best teachers from wrongful termination but that Schweizer says now protects the worst teachers from rightful termination.

In the following selections, Steven Malanga argues that merit pay is essential to meaningful teacher evaluation and school improvement, while Al Ramirez contends that merit pay is a misguided policy with numerous unintended consequences.

Steven Malanga

 **YES**

Why Merit Pay Will Improve Teaching

One of the bitterest controversies in today's school-reform debate is merit pay—rewarding teachers not for seniority and the number of ed-school credits they've piled up, as public schools have done since the early 1920s, but for what they actually achieve in the classroom. Education reformers argue that merit pay will give encouragement to good teachers and drive away bad ones, and thus improve under-performing public schools. But most teachers' unions adamantly oppose the idea. We don't have reliable means to measure a teacher's classroom performance, the unions charge, so merit plans will inevitably result in supervisor bias and favoritism: "Just too many cliques in the system," one teacher typically complains in a recent survey.

Nowhere is the incentives debate raging more fiercely than in New York City, where teachers' contract negotiations have been at an impasse for months. Mayor Rudolph Giuliani has demanded that merit pay for individual teachers be part of any deal; the teachers' union response (at least so far): fuh-geddaboudit.

Missing from the argument, though, are lessons from the private sector, where sophisticated, effective performance-based compensation has been *de rigueur* since the 1980s—part and parcel, experts believe, of corporate America's hugely successful restructuring. Also ignored are experiments with comprehensive merit-pay plans that are under way in a few innovative school districts across the country—districts burdened with much less political resistance than Gotham.

To get a sense of what merit pay could do for the public schools, consider the benefits it has showered on American industry over the last two decades. Before the eighties, merit pay in U.S. firms—if it existed at all—was pretty simple: the boss gave you a fat bonus if you (or your unit) met sales or production goals. But as international economic competition pummeled them in the early 1980s, U.S. corporations, desperate to regain their competitiveness, began to experiment with measuring individual worker performance. They established pay incentives to improve it in formerly hard-to-measure categories of output and in previously intangible areas like customer service

From Steven Malanga, "Why Merit Pay Will Improve Teaching," *City Journal*, vol. 11, no. 3 (Summer 2001). Copyright © 2001 by *City Journal*. Reprinted by permission.

or product quality. Of course, the bottom line was still the bottom line, but these intangibles, companies now reasoned, mattered to the long-term economic health of the firm, even if they didn't show up right away in the quarter-by-quarter numbers.

Familiar today, the new performance criteria—and the multi-faceted compensation plans built on their foundation—were strikingly original at the time. Retailers hired "mystery" shoppers to check out how employees treated customers, and based salaries, in part, on what they found. Businesses built into sales contracts "integrity" clauses that gauged not just how many widgets an employee sold but how long clients stuck with him. Banks remunerated loan officers not just for the lending they brought in but for the long-term quality of their loan portfolios. Some auto dealers tied part of salesmen's pay to how customers rated them in follow-up surveys. Companies combined these kinds of individualized incentives with rewards for everybody if the whole firm did well. Airlines, for example, gave the entire crew bonuses if the fleet's on-time performance improved.

Predictably, when U.S. businesses first introduced these innovations, workers grumbled, especially in heavily unionized industries like auto manufacturing, where any change threatened cushy labor arrangements. "They said that you couldn't measure some things, that the pay systems were too subjective, that supervisors were too subjective—in short, everything that teachers today are saying," observes Alan Johnson, a New York-based compensation consultant. Many efforts stumbled at first, too, and companies had to discard or overhaul them. Creating effective programs, it became clear, would not be an overnight fix. "Even today, with all we know, it takes three years to start up an effective incentive-pay program," cautions Martha Glantz, a compensation expert with Buck Consultants in Manhattan. "You can spend the first year just deciding what the company's goals and missions are, and collecting the data."

But American firms, needing to change or perish, forged ahead, winning over employees who liked the challenge of incentive pay and, through trial and error, developing pay plans that worked. By the mid-1990s, half of all major American corporations used such incentives. "It's no longer credible to say you can't measure something or that the only thing you can measure is a simple output," says Johnson. Merit pay played a crucial role, most observers believe, in generating the zooming productivity gains and superior product quality that American firms began recording in the late 1980s and that have been central to the nation's economic prosperity ever since.

⊷⊙⊶

The public education monopoly has long resisted merit pay with the same ferocity with which private-sector workers at first greeted it. Opponents have constantly invoked previous attempts that failed—though their only examples have been two experiments that are over 100 years old, and another from the 1960s, before modern notions of performance pay emerged. The conventional wisdom among educators had long been that any attempt to pin down exactly what makes for good teaching, let alone measure and reward it fairly, was doomed to fail. "There was a general feeling that you were either gifted as a teacher or you weren't, and that good teaching wasn't something you could define," says Charlotte Danielson, an expert on teaching at the Educational Testing Service in New Jersey. As a last-ditch defense, some educators even argued that factors outside school, especially a student's socioeconomic and family situation, had a much greater impact on student performance than teachers did, so that using merit pay based on student performance to promote good teaching, even if it could be defined, wasn't fair. The unasked question was why teachers should ever receive salary hikes if what they do doesn't matter.

Over the last decade, these views have utterly collapsed, undermining the intellectual case—weak as it was—against merit pay. A key figure has been University of Tennessee statistician William Sanders, who discovered how to measure a teacher's effect on student performance. Rather than try to filter out the myriad sociological influences on pupils, a nearly impossible task, Sanders used complex statistical methods to chart the progress of students against themselves over the course of a school year and measure how much "value" different teachers added. Now called the Tennessee Value-Added Assessment System, Sanders's approach proved what every parent already knew: not only did teachers matter, but some were lots better than others. Other education experts, including Danielson, author of several popular books on pedagogy, developed widely accepted criteria to judge good teaching, which put paid to the absurd notion that it was too elusive to define.

⋅◆⋅

If the 1990s helped re-establish the centrality of teaching in the education debate, however, that victory hasn't melted away the teachers' unions' political opposition to merit pay. Even so, a small number of school systems across the country, under intense pressure from parents, politicians, and administrators to improve student performance, have turned to merit pay to promote better teaching. And, after some give-and-take, they've managed to get the teachers' unions on board.

Cincinnati's public school system, the first to experiment with performance incentives, persuaded its teachers' union in 1997 to do a test run of merit pay. Two years later, a ten-school pilot program, designed by administrators and teachers, got under way. Essential to union support was the pilot's proposed use of peers to evaluate teachers. "The peer evaluators, who have no stake in how teachers are judged, are important to the perception of the fairness of the system," observes Kathleen Ware, associate superintendent of Cincinnati schools. Using Danielson's criteria of good teaching—they include class preparation and clarity of presentation—the principals and peer evaluators devoted 20 to 30 hours to assessing every teacher in the ten chosen schools. Based on how they scored, teachers then wound up in one of five salary categories, with "novices" making the least money and "accomplished" teachers the most.

The pilot proved successful. A majority of teachers involved found it fair and judged the standards used as appropriate for the whole school district. The city's board of education adopted it in the spring of 2000, and, in a subsequent election, union members signed on. Teachers will go through evaluations every five years, though those looking to move up quickly can request an appraisal after just two years. New teachers and one-fifth of all experienced teachers [had] evaluations done [in 2001], but no one [started] getting paid under the new system until 2002.

Unfortunately, Cincinnati's new program doesn't directly use student test scores in its evaluations. Bringing in scores would have generated too much union hostility for the plan to gain acceptance, reports school superintendent Steven Adamowski. And in all likelihood, tying pay solely to test scores is a bad idea; nobody would call meritorious a teacher who boosted scores but left his students psychological wrecks because of his bullying. Yet leaving tests out altogether also makes no sense. After all, what better way to determine how well students are doing—the only reason for the concern over teaching quality in the first place—than test scores? Cincinnati's program recognizes this implicitly. The district will monitor test results of students whose teachers score the highest ratings. If those students don't show substantial improvement, school officials will toughen the program's standards. In addition, the district will rely on student tests to award bonuses to all teachers in a school whose kids take big strides.

✎◎✐

One major benefit of merit systems is that they enable schools to pay teachers—especially young and ambitious teachers—fatter salaries. That's the overriding rationale behind Iowa's new incentives program, enacted by the state legislature to keep better-paying nearby states from spiriting away top teachers. The state has anted up $40 million for salary increases, but, in a program similar to Cincinnati's, Iowa will now evaluate teachers thoroughly to make sure the extra dough goes only to the good classroom performers, not the duds. "We believe this system will help us retain the best people by re-professionalizing teaching," enthuses John Forsyth, chief executive of the Des Moines-based Wellmark Blue Cross and Blue Shield. Forsyth helped the state dream up the new system, looking to the market for inspiration. "We know good teachers make a difference," he continues, "and we're going to pay those who do make a difference." How much more reasonable this is than the New York union's claim that, because a few city teachers jump to higher-paying suburban schools each year, all teachers—the good and the bad alike—need equal raises to make them stay.

In Iowa's new system, good teachers will now be able to reach higher salary levels much earlier in their careers than before. "The private pay consultants who looked at our old seniority system thought it must have been designed specifically to keep teacher pay low and save school districts money," says Ted Stilwill, director of Iowa's Department of Education. "The only way for teachers to get paid more under that system was for them to stick it out for years." As in Cincinnati, union opposition means that Iowa won't rely on test scores to evaluate teachers—at least not directly. But in addition to paying teachers based on their performance evaluations, the state will also offer modest yearly bonuses to all teachers in a school whose students do well on standardized tests, with the biggest bonuses going to the school's best instructors, rather than all teachers getting equal rewards.

Helping to develop Iowa's plan has been an eye-opener for the state's education chief. "Private-sector compensation experts taught me that businesses use pay as a way of getting everyone to follow common goals," Stilwill says. "Being in the public sector most of my life, I never understood that."

⋯⊙⋯

Though Cincinnati and Iowa have skirted the controversy of using student test scores, Denver is confronting it head-on. The city has launched two pilot plans that link pay directly to scores. One pilot program uses student scores in standardized tests of basic skills; another relies on scores in specific subjects. Principals and teachers agree at the beginning of the school year on what kinds of improvements in test scores they'll shoot for and then face evaluation at the end of the year to see if they've met their goals. Denver is also instituting a third merit-pay pilot program that instructs teachers in the principles of good teaching and then evaluates their teaching skills and rewards them accordingly. Denver will later measure how their students perform on tests to see if its criteria for good teaching really produce results. Through these experiments, Denver hopes to figure out what motivates teachers best and what works best for students.

Denver's teachers' union, surprisingly, has contributed mightily to developing the pilots; the head of the project's design team, Brad Jupp, is a union negotiator. He says the union is participating because the demand to make schools more accountable is so intense that teachers would rather help create performance systems than have them imposed from above. "If you believe that your union members are doing a good job—and we do—then you want a system that accurately measures that," says Jupp.

Experiences from the private sector suggest that it will take several years before these imaginative programs work out all their kinks. In the meantime, controversy will dog the new programs. Critics will pounce on their every mistake as evidence that paying teachers for performance is a bad idea. And unions are likely to push for watered-down plans in order to deflect criticism without giving up too much.

This last is exactly what's happening in New York. The teachers' union has offered the mayor a compromise: pay every teacher in a school or district a bonus if the school's or district's test scores rise. A trial run of such a system, supported by Gotham's business community, is under way in two urban districts; other states, including California and Georgia, already have school-based bonuses.

But group bonuses will never substitute adequately for true performance pay, compensation experts believe, since they don't single out good and bad teachers. All they're likely to do is to frustrate first-rate teachers working in schools with mediocre staffs. "If you have four workers doing well in a unit that is not otherwise performing, over time those four will leave the company and go somewhere that they can be rewarded for their superior work," says consultant Glantz. And since schoolwide bonuses don't put any pay at risk—poor performance doesn't mean less money—they won't help rid schools of lousy teachers either. By contrast, teachers who score poorly in, say, Cincinnati, now find themselves shunted into the lowest salary level, discouraging them from sticking around. Mayor Giuliani, rightly, has rejected the union's offer.

Of course, smaller cities like Cincinnati are far removed from the we don't-do-windows union obstructionism of a New York or a Los Angeles. For 15 years, Cincinnati's teachers' union has accepted some kind of peer evaluation of teachers; it's easily one of the nation's most flexible teachers' unions. Unions in New York and Los Angeles, conversely, have fought almost every education reform tooth and nail. Last year in Los Angeles, thousands of teachers ferociously protested against a proposed merit-pay plan, eventually killing it. Moreover, in the current public school monopoly, there's nothing really comparable to the outside economic pressure that forced American industry to develop its merit programs—one more argument for school choice.

Without individualized merit pay, teacher evaluations will remain perfunctory at best. Today, New York principals fail less than 1 percent of all teachers in annual evaluations. New York hopes to get principals to crack down on bad teaching by rewarding them financially when their schools do well. That will eliminate one of the main objections to teacher merit pay—that it leads to supervisor favoritism: even if a principal hates an effective teacher's guts, he's not going to want to lose someone who's helping him sweeten his own salary. But until teachers are part of any performance-pay system, the impact of such innovations will be severely limited—and students will continue to get shortchanged, regardless of how much their teachers take to the bank.

Al Ramirez

How Merit Pay Undermines Education

Proposals for merit pay, including pay-for-performance, continue to surface as policymakers search for ways to motivate administrators and teachers to be more effective—and to make educators do what policymakers want them to do. These types of remuneration plans are different from paying a teacher extra for taking on additional duties, such as running an after-school computer laboratory or serving as a mentor or master teacher. Instead, these merit pay policies give individual employees extra compensation, above and beyond the base salary, for work and contributions that exceed some pre-established criteria. These criteria often include achieving higher student test scores on standardized tests.

Carrots and Sticks

Why can't teachers and administrators be "incentivized" like aluminum-siding salespeople? Not all lawyers in a legal firm take home the same annual salary and bonuses, so why can't policymakers for public education find a way to pay similar classifications of employees different rates of pay on the basis of their job performance? Professional sports teams pay their players on the basis of their performance and perceived potential value to the team, so why can't school districts do the same?

But do compensation decisions really reflect employees' contributions? As Rosabeth Moss Kanter (1987) points out, "Status, not contribution, has traditionally been the basis for the numbers on employees' paychecks. Pay has reflected where jobs rank in the corporation hierarchy—not what comes out of them" (p. 60). Despite centuries of experience with employee compensation plans, status still wins out over contribution. Contrast the pay of corporate CEOs in the United States, some of whom earn more than 600 times as much as their typical non-management employees, to the much smaller differential between the pay of employees and CEOs in Europe and Japan. Do American corporate boards know something about compensation plans that their foreign competitors don't?

From *Educational Leadership*, February 2001. Reprinted with permission of the Association for Supervision and Curriculum Development. Copyright © 2001 by ASCD. All rights reserved.

In fact, the seemingly logical link between employee production and compensation is often debatable and highly subjective. We can understand why new approaches to determining pay are so difficult to establish in public school districts today if we look at the historical development of educators' most common compensation approach—uniform salary schedules with steps and lanes. This compensation system rewards professionals for their years of experience on the job and level of educational attainment. Incentives are structured to encourage teachers and some administrators to remain loyal to the school district and to improve their skills and knowledge by pursuing additional training, usually by attending approved workshops and courses or earning graduate degrees.

In the ideal situation, this system rewards a teacher or principal who, for example, participates in a workshop, typically on his or her own time, about the educational uses of computers. This employee is building on a knowledge base and thus is able to make a greater contribution to the school district's mission to prepare students for success in our democratic society. In theory, this compensation system motivates employees to get better at their jobs. Critics argue that the theory behind this system doesn't hold up. They point to the lack of linkage between the incentive system and outcomes in schools and classrooms. They also challenge the abuses in such systems, where employees are rewarded for taking courses in wok cooking or given graduate credit by diploma mills for signing up for the walking tour of downtown Los Angeles.

But the tenacious attachment to this system has deep roots. In the past, policy leaders set up teacher compensation systems according to criteria that they felt were justified and appropriate, and boards of education, city councils, and other similar deliberative bodies used democratic means to arrive at pay policies. Nonetheless, some of these decisions look strange to us today. Consider the Chicago school system in the early 1900s. As the school system matured, policymakers moved to standardize the employee compensation system. One of the components of their system was a substantial pay differential between male and female employees (Peterson, 1985), and the gender pay differential continued even when women started to assume administrative roles. At the beginning of the 20th century, pay differentials in Atlanta, Georgia, were based on race. Although the African American community had managed to secure minimal services from the Atlanta school board, the dual system of education determined that African American and white teachers would not have the same rate of pay (Peterson, 1985). History has demonstrated that governing bodies are capable of establishing unfair practices. The legacy of such compensation systems in public education has been to elevate one criterion—fairness—as the paramount consideration in all pay decisions.

Logic would dictate that a teacher's years of experience in the classroom and level of educational attainment are somewhat related to the academic performance of students. In theory, a first-year chemistry teacher fresh out of college is not as effective with high school students as is a 10-year veteran with a master's degree in science teaching or organic chemistry. But critics counter that empirical evidence doesn't support such logic. They assert that a teacher's training is irrelevant and that experience counts for nothing. What matters, they say, are the results a teacher gets with students; outcomes, not inputs, should determine rewards. Using an outcome-based criterion, they claim, is the only fair approach to rewarding teachers.

Educators point out that such proposals for output-based compensation are not fair, reverting once again to the fairness issue. How can teachers be held accountable for school conditions that they cannot control? Unless all inputs are equalized for all teachers and administrators, how can policymakers judge the value of the outcome? Educators further argue that their jobs involve more than teaching academic subjects and often extend beyond the measurable—for example, consoling a child whose parents are going through a divorce or advising a student about options for college.

Understanding Human Motivation

The problem with both the input-reward system and the outcome-reward system is that they ignore the basic dynamics of what motivates human beings. The approach of focusing on fairness above all else has inhibited the contribution of some members of the group—for example, those with exceptional abilities who may not fit the mold. In contrast, the outcome-centered motivation system devalues the significance of an individual's contribution and oversimplifies the role of the educator. Neither system considers the body of research related to the psychology of human motivation.

Consider the work of Frederick Herzberg (1987) and his studies of employee motivation. He and his colleagues identified a series of more than 3,000 items that either motivated workers or diminished employees' enthusiasm for their jobs. The "satisfiers" and "dissatisfiers" will surprise policymakers who view money as the sole motivator on the job. Organizational policy and administrative procedures, supervisory practices, employee-employer relations, working conditions, and salary proved to have greater potential to be dissatisfiers than satisfiers. These dissatisfiers are important and need the attention of employers. But the satisfiers—the motivators that are essential to spurring performance to higher levels—included achievement on the job, recognition for one's contribution or for a job well done, the work itself, job responsibility, opportunities for career advancement, and professional growth.

Abraham Maslow's (1970) study of human motivation should also inform policymakers who are intent on lighting a fire under professional educators. Maslow bases his theory on a hierarchy of needs to which all humans respond. This hierarchy ascends from basic needs (water, shelter, and food) to complex needs (advancement, growth, and achievement). Money, benefits, and job security appear at the lower end of the hierarchy. Merit pay systems that attempt to use money alone as a lever for improvement are more likely to cause educators who have other employment options to leave the school district than to strive for the desired results of their supervisors.

William Glasser (1997) presents an articulate explanation of human motivation through his Choice Theory. Glasser points out that all people are motivated to meet their needs for belonging to groups, maintaining a sense of self-efficacy or power, and having fun. These are natural and intrinsic needs that humans are driven to meet. When institutions use extrinsic motivation devices to manipulate their members, they often divert their members from meeting these intrinsic human needs. The frustration and anger that often result are destructive to the organization. Ill-conceived reward systems that diminish employee loyalty and increase resentment toward management can cause incalculable productivity losses in organizations. Here again, money alone does not work as a motivator.

Perhaps no one has been more eloquent than the late W. Edwards Deming (1993) in addressing the destructive nature of extrinsic reward systems

> that squeeze out from an individual, over his lifetime, his innate intrinsic motivation, self-esteem, dignity. They build into him fear, self-defense, extrinsic motivation. We have been destroying our people, from toddlers on through the university, and on the job. (p. 124)

According to Deming, the forces of destruction include grade rankings; merit systems, particularly ones that categorize people; contrived competition among people within organizations; schemes for incentive pay and pay-for-performance; and numerical goals, targets, and quotas—without any guidelines on how to achieve them. These forces suboptimize the system and cause humiliation, resentment, and fear. Using such approaches also shifts the burden to produce results from management to the employees. Deming asserts that such practices belie the fact that more than 90 percent of the organization's outcomes are the result of the leadership and governance structure of the organization and not the effort of individual workers who work in the system.

Extrinsic reward systems create the illusion of employer control but at the expense of the full involvement and commitment of dedicated, enthusiastic employees. Extrinsic reward systems divert resources and energy from what is much more likely to move the organization to higher levels of performance. They discard the most valuable resources in the organization: the brainpower, problem-solving ability, and innovative thinking that every employee brings to the job.

Dud Silver Bullets

A growing number of legislators, governors, mayors, superintendents, school board members, and business people advocate programs for merit pay or pay-for-performance. Their good intentions to make schools better often lead them to quick-fix solutions and seemingly obvious, but wrong, answers. Perhaps one of the biggest ironies encountered by school leaders is the ill-informed advice they receive, often unsolicited, from business leaders who proffer "real-world" solutions—like merit pay—to fix school problems. These business leaders are ignorant of the research literature that does not support such practices; ironically, these findings often come out of business leaders' own university-based business colleges. In some cases, unfortunately, the political leaders know better but cannot resist the temptation to scapegoat the less powerful members of the organization—teachers—and pander to an ignorant public and news media. And in the worst cases, leaders are so cynical about the public education system that they blame and punish employees as a way of diverting attention from the real, and typically more costly, issues confronting the schools.

Donald Campbell, Kathleen Campbell, and Ho-Beng Chia (1998) conducted a thorough investigation of merit pay systems. They concluded that pay-for-performance programs raise problematic issues related to measurement, performance appraisal and feedback, and the desirability of the rewards. For example, questions arise about the validity either of the instrument used to measure performance or the nature of the work. Attempts to address these issues through training or better measures fall short. Additionally, the researchers found that employees tend to reject most or all of the evaluation systems, regardless of what adjustments are made. Money, the key factor in such systems, is usually in short supply, so the potential impact of rewards is minimal and does not outweigh the negative effects of the merit pay system. Finally, the authors conclude that the implementation of merit pay systems becomes unwieldy, contributes to mission drift, and often leads to unintended consequences, such as enormous pay differentials between subordinates and supervisors, or the ignoring of work assignments that do not earn consideration for merit.

Questions to Ask

Policymakers and school leaders are supposed to make changes that improve the education systems for which they are responsible. The penchant to move to action and make sweeping changes without proper policy analysis and policy development techniques contributes to the dysfunction of many school systems. The one-step-forward-two-steps-back method of creating education policy, so common today, is certainly irresponsible, if not unethical. Flashy or feel-good policies make the system worse. Policymakers, leaders, and deliberative bodies that are interested in investigating the value of merit pay systems should ask themselves these questions:

- Do I understand the nature of human motivation? Why have our teachers and administrators chosen to work in our school district? It is often difficult to tap into the employee's motivation for employment, and some appraisal and reward systems may even reduce enthusiasm for the job and productivity.
- Can a school district be run like a business? Do business practices readily transfer to a publicly held organization run by highly trained professionals with an educational mission? Do the culture and structure of a school district support or deter the use of business-like evaluation and merit systems?
- Is this evaluation and reward system fair? How would I feel if my employer instituted such a program at my job? Fairness in the design and implementation of appraisal and reward systems is both crucial and complex. The fairness issue will permeate any proposed

system and must apply to the employee, the appraiser, the organization, and the organizational stakeholders, including students, parents, and taxpayers.

- Can my organization find an evaluation and compensation system that is not excessively burdensome and that operates effectively? Do I understand that some important job functions may not be measurable? Do I understand that some elaborate evaluation systems may distract staff from their duties?
- Have I explored the unintended consequences of a new system? Organization leaders must be careful about what is rewarded in a merit pay system—because they will get it! Have I considered what won't get done because it doesn't count for merit pay? The goal is to move forward, not to suboptimize the organization.
- Am I clear about whom to reward? This central question must be part of policymakers' considerations. Will the system reward individuals or teams? Enterprises that are highly collaborative should be cautious about setting compensation systems in motion that promote destructive competition.

A candid discussion of these questions among policymakers, school leaders, and stakeholders will go a long way toward forming sound education policy. Employee evaluation and reward systems are complicated matters that require thoughtful deliberation. They have the potential to be as destructive as they are constructive. Our schools are too important to operate with misguided policies.

References

Campbell, D. J., Campbell, K. M., & Chia, H. B. (1998). Merit pay, performance appraisal, and individual motivation: An analysis and alternative. *Human Resources Management, 37*(2), 131–146.

Deming, W. E. (1993). *The new economics for industry, government, education.* Cambridge, MA: Massachusetts Institute of Technology Center for Advanced Engineering Study.

Glasser, W. (1997). A new look at school failure and school success. *Phi Delta Kappan, 78*(8), 596–602.

Herzberg, F. (1987). One more time: How do you motivate employees? *Harvard Business Review, 65,* 109–120.

Kanter, R. M. (1987, March/April). Attack on pay. *Harvard Business Review, 65,* 60–67.

Maslow, A. H. (1970). *Motivation and personality.* New York: Harper & Row.

Peterson, P. E. (1985). *The politics of school reform, 1870–1940.* Chicago: University of Chicago Press.

POSTSCRIPT

Can Merit Pay Accelerate School Improvement?

After the Soviet Union's challenge to America's technological superiority manifested itself in the late 1950s, financial incentives were given to present and recruited teachers of math and science under a federal initiative. Currently, the "crisis" focus is on underperforming public schools located primarily in districts with high percentages of minority students. Some critics have made the argument that a maximum federal effort should be directed at schools with the greatest need in order to close the existing achievement gaps. This idea is elaborated upon by Cynthia D. Prince in "Attracting Well-Qualified Teachers to Struggling Schools," *American Educator* (Winter 2002). "Today," she explains, "both the ATF [American Federation of Teachers] and the NEA [National Education Association] favor offering locally-developed financial incentives to qualified teachers who choose to work in hard-to-staff schools."

In "The Teacher Shortage: A Case of Wrong Diagnosis and Wrong Prescription," *NASSP Bulletin* (June 2002), Richard M. Ingersoll offers an analysis of reasons why large numbers of qualified teachers are departing their jobs for reasons other than retirement. In "Why Are Experienced Teachers Leaving the Profession?" *Phi Delta Kappan* (September 2002), Barbara Benham Tye and Lisa O'Brien report on their survey of teachers who have already left the profession and those who are considering leaving. They found that those who had left ranked the pressure of increased accountability (high-stakes testing and standards) as the number one reason. Salary considerations ranked seventh. Of those who were considering leaving, however, salary considerations ranked first.

A stinging indictment of merit pay can be found in Maurice Holt's "Performance Pay for Teachers: The Standards Movement's Last Stand?" *Phi Delta Kappan* (December 2001). In it, Holt states, "Having done their best to demoralize schools and give the phrase 'testing to destruction' a new meaning, there's one last aspect of civilized education that the Standardistos have in their sights: the sense of trust and cooperation among teachers." Their ammunition: "competitive salary structures."

Further resources on the topic of merit pay for teachers include Lawrence Hardy, "What's a Teacher Worth?" *American School Board Journal* (August 2002); Allan Odden, "New and Better Forms of Teacher Compensation Are Possible," *Phi Delta Kappan* (January 2000); Cynthia D. Prince, "Higher Pay in Hard-to-Staff Schools: The Case for Financial Incentives," *The School Administrator* (June 2002); and Allan Odden, Dale Ballou, and Michael Podgursky, "Defining Merit," *Education Matters* (Spring 2001).

ISSUE 21

Should Alternative Teacher Training Be Encouraged?

YES: Robert Holland, from "How to Build a Better Teacher," *Policy Review* (April & May 2001)

NO: Linda Darling-Hammond, from "How Teacher Education Matters," *Journal of Teacher Education* (May/June 2000)

ISSUE SUMMARY

YES: Public policy researcher Robert Holland argues that current certification programs are inadequate, especially given the growing shortage of teachers.

NO: Educational professor Linda Darling-Hammond offers evidence of failure among alternative programs and responds to criticism of standard professional preparation.

The quality and appropriateness of teacher preparation programs have long been topics of discussion in academic and professional circles, as well as in the media. From the appraisals by educators James Bryant Conant, Sterling McMurrin, and James Koerner in the 1960s to recent critiques by James Coleman, Ernest Boyer, John I. Goodlad, and William J. Bennett, the education of future teachers has consistently been under careful scrutiny. Rita Kramer called for the closing of all schools of education in her 1991 book *Ed School Follies: The Miseducation of America's Teachers*. Education dean Donald J. Stedman, in "Re-inventing the Schools of Education," *Vital Speeches of the Day* (April 15, 1991), recommended a serious restructuring of teacher preparation to replace the current bureaucratic rigidity with a flexible interdisciplinary approach.

In 1985 the Carnegie Forum released its agenda for wide-ranging improvements, and the American Association of Colleges of Teacher Education published *A Call for Change in Teacher Education*. Of greater impact was the formation of the Holmes Group by deans of education schools at almost all of the leading universities in the country. In 1986 a report released by this organization entitled *Tomorrow's Teachers* called for a stronger preparation in the liberal arts and academic majors and for moving teacher certification courses to the master's degree level. A National Board of Professional Standards was established in 1987, offering the prospect of a higher level of certification and status enhancement for teachers. In 1995 the Holmes Group, in *Tomorrow's Schools of Education*, supported the concept of professional development schools run jointly by universities and public school systems and fueled by applied research. A firm message was sent: "Reform—or get out of business!"

While many internal reforms have been carried out in the past two decades, pressures from the outside for alternatives to the usual paths of entry into the profession have been steadily building. Frederick M. Hess, in "Break the Link," *Education Next* (Spring 2002), contends that anyone who has not completed the specified training is unsuited to enter a classroom and must be prohibited from applying for a job, regardless of any other qualifications. About 10 years ago, Wendy Kopp launched Teach for America in an attempt to bring bright and dedicated teacher candidates into disadvantaged schools by providing an abbreviated training program. In her 2001 book *One Day All Children . . . The Unlikely Triumph of Teach for America and What I Learned Along the Way*, she explains the program and offers a self-appraisal.

The growing undersupply of teachers has created more urgent calls for change. The 1998 report of the National Center for Education Information, *Alternative Teacher Certification—An Overview*, documents the evolution of alternative routes and the rapid growth in the number of individuals pursuing them. Articles that examine this issue include Linda Darling-Hammond, "The Challenge of Staffing Our Schools," *Educational Leadership* (May 2001); Mary E. Diez, "The Certification Connection," *Education Next* (Spring 2002); Arthur E. Wise, "Creating a High-Quality Teaching Force," *Educational Leadership* (December 2000–January 2001); and Richard M. Ingersoll, "Holes in the Teacher Supply Bucket," *The School Administrator* (March 2002).

In the following selection, Robert Holland reviews the criticism of traditional teacher certification programs, critiques the profession's attempts at internal reform, and suggests a "value-added" approach. In the second selection, Darling-Hammond presents evidence that internal reforms have strengthened the programs and that alternatives such as Teach for America are woefully inadequate.

YES

Robert Holland

How to Build a Better Teacher

Americans schools need more teachers. American schools need better teachers. Practically everyone with a stake in the education debate agrees with those two premises. However, there is sharp disagreement as to whether more regulation or less is the way to go.

The differences of perspective begin over just how vital to transmitting knowledge a teacher is. No one is more certain about the overriding importance of a teacher in a child's academic progress than Tennessee statistician William Sanders, who has developed a value-added instrument that might revolutionize how good teachers are found and rewarded for productive careers. Speaking before the metropolitan school board in Nashville in January [2001], Sanders risked friendly fire when he disputed the connection much of the education world makes between poverty and low student performance: "Of all the factors we study—class size, ethnicity, location, poverty—they all pale to triviality in the face of teacher effectiveness."

That flies in the face of a widespread conviction in the education world that poverty is such a powerful depressant on learning that even the greatest teachers may only partially overcome its effects. As Diane Ravitch documents in her recent book *Left Back* (Simon & Schuster), education "progressives" long have believed that many children shouldn't be pushed to absorb knowledge beyond their limited innate capacities; that they are better off with teachers who help them get in touch with their feelings and find a socially useful niche.

But Sanders has volumes of data to back up his contention. While at the University of Tennessee, he developed a sophisticated longitudinal measurement called "value-added assessment" that pinpoints how effective each district, school, and teacher has been in raising individual students' achievement over time. His complex formula factors out demographic variables that often make comparisons problematic. Among other things, he found that students unlucky enough to have a succession of poor teachers are virtually doomed to the education cellar. Three consecutive years of first quintile (least effective) teachers in Grades 3 to 5 yield math scores from the thirty-fifth to forty-fifth percentile. Conversely, three straight years of fifth quintile teachers result in scores at the eighty-fifth to ninety-fifth percentile.

From Robert Holland, "How to Build a Better Teacher," *Policy Review* (April & May 2001). Copyright © 2001 by The Board of Trustees of the Leland Stanford Junior University. Reprinted by permission of *Policy Review*.

The state of Tennessee began using value-added assessment in its public schools in 1992, and Sanders is in demand in many other states where legislators are considering importing the system. The "No Excuses" schools identified by an ongoing Heritage Foundation project—high-poverty schools where outstanding pupil achievement defies stereotypes about race and poverty–buttress Sanders' contention that the quality of teaching is what matters most. Consider, for instance, Frederick Douglass Academy, a public school in central Harlem that has a student population 80 percent black and 19 percent Hispanic. The *New York Times* recently reported that all of Frederick Douglass's students passed a new, rigorous English Regents exam last year, and 96 percent passed the math Regents. The Grades 6-12 school ranks among the top 10 schools in New York City in reading and math, despite having class sizes of 30 to 34.

And what makes the difference? "Committed teachers," said principal Gregory M. Hodge—teachers, he said, who come to work early, stay late, and call parents if children don't show up for extra tutoring. The disciplined yet caring climate for learning set by Hodge and principals of other No Excuses schools also is due much credit.

Those who believe in deregulation of teacher licensing see in value-added assessment a potential breakthrough. Principals (like Hodge) could hire and evaluate their teachers not necessarily on the basis of credit-hours amassed in professional schools of education but in terms of objective differences instructors make when actually placed before classrooms of children. The Thomas B. Fordham Foundation published in April 1999 a manifesto on teacher quality that argues strongly for a "results-based accountability system," disaggregated by teacher, along the lines of what Sanders has devised.

However, much of the education establishment—those in and around education school faculties nationwide, the professional development specialists at teacher unions and associations, state and local boards of education, and education specialists in much of the foundation world—takes a very different view. They argue that what is needed is much more centralized control of teacher preparation and licensing to ensure that teachers are better and more uniformly qualified when they enter the classroom. They propose to ensure this by placing professional licensing under the aegis of a single accreditation body, one that would be controlled to a great extent by the teachers themselves—or, more precisely, their national unions.

Which side prevails in this dispute over how to get the best teachers into schools—the Sanders model of ongoing evaluation of effectiveness or the establishment preference for centralized credentialing—may tell us more than anything else about the quality of instruction American pupils and their parents can expect from their schools for a generation. This is the key battleground in public education today.

Teacher Certification: A Primer

The one point on which both camps agree is that the existing system of teacher certification badly needs reform. Hence, a brief survey of that system may be helpful. Currently, state departments of education and collegiate schools of education are the gatekeepers to teaching careers in America's public schools. This is a collaboration dedicated to the use of government power to standardize and centralize education, or, in the economists' term, "regulatory capture." Government licensing agencies that are charged with protecting the public interest are effectively controlled by the interests—in this case, the teacher-trainers—they are supposed to be regulating.

As a result, an aspiring teacher typically must complete a state-approved program of teacher education that is heavy on how-to-teach or pedagogical courses. All 50 states require new teachers to obtain a bachelor's degree, and all 50 require course work in pedagogy. In some states, the teacher's degree must be in education, while other states require an academic major but specify that within that degree there must be a considerable number of education courses (about a semester's worth) and also a period of student teaching (another semester). In addition, many teacher colleges tack on additional training requirements, so that fulfilling requirements for the study of pedagogy can consume well over a year of college. Most states require prospective teachers to pass one or more subject-area tests, but these often ask for regurgitation of nostrums taught by education professors.

Critics of the schools of pedagogy are legion. Seventy years ago, H.L. Mencken (never one to mince words) asserted that most pedagogues "have trained themselves to swallow any imaginable fad or folly, and always with enthusiasm. The schools reek with this puerile nonsense."

In the early 1990s, Rita Kramer took a nationwide tour of leading schools of education, from Teachers College at Columbia to the University of Washington, and reported in *Ed School Follies* on the intellectual emptiness of teacher preparation—hours spent on how to teach Tootles the Locomotive with the proper attitude, but precious little depth in history, mathematics, science, or literature. Recently Heather Mac Donald took a close look at ed schools for *City Journal* and summed up teacher educators' dogma in the phrase "Anything But Knowledge." She found teachers of teachers still holding fast to the doctrine laid out in 1925 by Teachers College icon William Heard Kilpatrick: Schools should instill "critical thinking" in children instead of teaching them facts and figures, which (he surmised) they could always look up for themselves as they became "lifelong learners." Today, Teachers College mandates courses in multicultural diversity and has students act out ways to "usurp the existing power structure."

Jerry Jesness, a special education teacher in a south Texas elementary school, observes that "every profession has its gatekeepers, the college professors who not only teach, but also sift out the slow, the lazy, and the mediocre, those unfit to practice the profession for which they are preparing. One must have intelligence, drive, and stamina, especially to get through schools of engineering, law, or medicine.

"In colleges of education, the reverse seems to be the case. After a few weeks of Ed 101, the students most possessed of those qualities begin to slip away. By the time education students begin their semester of student teaching, the best and brightest have already defected to other disciplines. Colleges and departments of education separate the wheat from the chaff, but unlike those of the other disciplines, they then throw away the wheat."

The current system does allow for a semblance of public accountability. At least in theory, citizens—by their votes for governors and state legislators, and in some states, the state education boards and superintendents of public instruction—can pressure education bureaucrats to adopt more sensible rules for preparing and employing teachers. One state in which the political process has recently yielded reform is Georgia, where Democratic Gov. Roy Barnes last year won legislative approval for eliminating seniority-based teacher tenure.

At the center of the school of thought that believes tighter national regulation is key to reformis a foundation-funded entity called the National Commission on Teaching and America's Future (NCTAF). NCTAF is the latest incarnation of a Carnegie Corporation commission—the first was the 1986 Carnegie Task Force on Teaching as a Profession—advocating a centralized, national system of teacher licensing controlled by private organizations with stakes in the process. With North Carolina Gov. James Hunt as its chairman and Stanford education professor Linda Darling-Hammond as its director, NCTAF issued its report, "What Matters Most: Teaching for America's Future," in 1996. (The Rockefeller Foundation joined Carnegie in bankrolling the commission.) NCTAF, which stayed active to lobby for its proposals, drew raves in the press for its "action agenda" to reform the training and certifying of teachers. Little ink went toward exploring the deeper implications of nationalizing control of teaching.

NCTAF called for, among other things:

- Mandatory accreditation by an organization called the National Council for Accreditation of Teacher Education (NCATE) of all teacher training programs in the country.
- National Board for Professional Teaching Standards (NBPTS) certification of more than 100,000 "master" teachers.
- Formation of "independent" professional boards in each state to set policies on teacher preparation, testing, and licensing, in tune with the nationalized policy.

In December 1999, Linda Darling-Hammond forcefully stated the case for the pro-regulatory proposition that education credentials do make a difference. "It stands to reason," she wrote, "that student learning should be enhanced by the efforts of teachers who are more knowledgeable in their field and are skillful at teaching it to others. Substantial evidence from prior reform efforts indicates that changes in course taking, curriculum content, testing, or textbooks make little difference if teachers do not know how to use these tools well and how to diagnose their students' learning needs."

The Union Interest

The National Education Association [NEA], the nation's largest teacher union, has emerged as a leading advocate of the NCTAF model of "reforming" the system by stripping control of teacher certification from the state departments of education. The NEA touts this as "professionalization," meaning self-regulation by teachers or benign-sounding "peer review." But critics dispute how much rank-and-file teachers would be empowered. Education Consumers Clearinghouse founder John Stone, a professor of education at East Tennessee State University, believes "the parties serving up these bold proposals represent the interests that have governed teacher training and licensure all along. Since publication of *A Nation at Risk* in 1983, teacher training and licensure have undergone repeated rewrites, none of which has produced any noticeable improvements in schooling."

The NEA likes the idea of all teachers having to graduate from a teacher training program certified by NCATE. This is perhaps unsurprising, given that NCATE has been tightly linked to the NEA since the former's founding in 1954. NCATE's director, Arthur E. Wise, also heads the NEA's 31-year-old nonprofit subsidiary, the National Foundation for the Improvement of Education. Meanwhile, NEA president Robert F. Chase chairs the Executive Committee of NCATE. Furthermore, Wise sat on the national commission, NCTAF, that would grant NCATE control of all teacher accreditation that it has not been able to gain on a voluntary basis over the past 40 years.

An important link in the pro-regulatory reformers' plan is the National Board for Professional Teaching Standards (NBPTS), an outgrowth of the 1986 Carnegie report. NBPTS subsequently received Carnegie Corporation outlays of several million dollars. In the 1990s, the federal government also began subsidizing the NBPTS heavily, at the urging of President Clinton. The board is a key element in today's strategy to centralize control of the gates to teaching. The privately operated NBPTS confers national certification on teachers who submit portfolios (videotapes of the teaching, lesson plans, samples of student work) for evaluation. The teachers also must pay a $2,300 application fee, but sometimes their school boards pay it for them.

The NBPTS purports to identify excellence through this process, but economists Dale Ballou of the University of Massachusetts and Michael Podgursky of the University of Missouri—who called "professionalization" into question after careful analysis—point out that there has been no evidence to show that students of NBPTS-certified teachers learn any more than students of other teachers. Researchers at the Consortium for Policy Studies at the University of Wisconsin at Madison recently found that NBPTS-certified teachers tend to become more reflective about their teaching, but their principals found it difficult to link any improvements in student achievement to the teachers' national certification.

From the perspective of economists Ballou and Podgursky, "The activities over which the profession seeks control—accreditation of teacher education programs and teacher licensing—are well-recognized means of restricting supply," which puts upward pressure on salaries. They add there can be no doubt that teacher unions see the professionalization movement "as a means to increase salaries." For further evidence of how tightly linked some of the regulatory reform is, consider that NEA president Chase serves as a member of NCTAF, which seeks to greatly augment the powers of NCATE, on which Chase is a major power—and all this would confer more economic muscle on the NEA.

NCTAF was remarkably successful using the rhetoric of reform to persuade business leaders and the media that its program actually was a "scathing indictment" of the system for training and certifying teachers. The *New Republic* begged to differ: "Forcing teachers," the journal's editors commented, "to attend NCATE certification programs that douse them with pedagogical blather (NCATE's 'vision of quality' seeks to promote 'equity' and 'diversity' but says nothing about academic achievement) will likely scare off math and science specialists in droves."

The NEA stepped up its campaign in spring 2000. Chase and his associates unveiled revised NCATE standards for accreditation at a Washington news conference. NCATE stated that schools of education it accredits will have to meet "rigorous new performance-based standards" in order to win NCATE accreditation.

By focusing on "candidate performance," said NCATE president Wise, the "standards represent a revolution in teacher preparation." But skeptics wonder how "revolutionary" it is to assess candidates largely according to videotaped activities, portfolios of projects, personal journals, or their compatibility with a team. That's the emphasis of the NBPTS, but portfolio assessment relies heavily on subjective judgment, as opposed to testing a teacher's knowledge of the subject being taught.

"In spite of claims to the contrary," notes Podgursky, "at present there exists no reliable evidence indicating whether or not graduates of NCATE accredited teacher training programs are better teachers." Although several states have responded by mandating NCATE accreditation, Podgursky added, "mandatory accreditation would almost certainly restrict the supply of teachers and exacerbate teacher shortages, yet its effect on the teacher quality pool is uncertain. It may also stifle promising state-level experiments with alternative teacher certification and the entry of new teacher-training institutions into the market."

For his part, Wise claims: "As more institutions meet NCATE's national professional standards, more qualified teacher candidates will be available, since candidates from accredited institutions pass licensing examinations at a higher rate than do those from unaccredited institutions or those with no teacher preparation." Wise based that assertion on a recent Educational Testing Service (ETS) study of the rates at which teacher candidates pass the Praxis II licensing exams. However, the same study shows that the SAT and ACT scores of NCATE graduates who passed licensing exams are lower than those of non-NCATE peers. In addition, Podgursky observed that the released ETS data are so flawed as to make any comparisons problematic. For instance, 14 percent of the sample of Praxis II test-takers never enrolled in a teacher-training program—yet the researchers sorted them into NCATE categories based on the colleges they attended. The study also failed to take into account wide variations in how states test prospective teachers.

The new standards condense NCATE's 1995 version of standards from 20 categories into six. Examiners will look at teacher-candidates' knowledge, skills, and "dispositions"; the school's assessment system; the inclusion of field experience and clinical practice; the institution's devotion to "diversity"; how faculty model "best practices"; and unit governance, including the wise use of information technology.

Actually, notes Professor Stone, the "new" standards implement mostly old ideas about teaching from existing standards. As for the portfolios, classroom observations, and emphasis on Praxis II, "performance on these various assessments reflects nothing more than a grasp of the same old faulty teaching practices that education professors have been espousing right along."

Most parents—the primary consumers of education—want schools to stress academic achievement, as studies by the nonpartisan Public Agenda have shown. However, as Public Agenda's surveys also reveal, many education professors believe "best practice" is a teacher not teaching, but facilitating in the progressive tradition, while children construct their own meaning, an approach called constructivism. "Social justice" is valued more highly than achievement. Arguably, that's the approach NCATE accreditation would enshrine.

As Podgursky and Ballou note in a recent Brookings Institution paper, public education already is a regulated monopoly. In most school districts, parents have little or no choice of their children's schools or teachers. In addition, unlike in medicine or other service markets, education consumers lack the protection of antitrust or malpractice lawsuits. Within this structure, the teacher unions already exercise enormous economic power as their well-organized affiliates bargain with fragmented local school boards.

If, next, teacher unions win control of the gates to teaching through their domination of such organizations as NCATE, they arguably would possess "market power not enjoyed by producers or unions in any major industry in our economy." That would not bode well for efforts to expand consumer choice and to get fresh blood into the teaching profession. Moreover, when a monopoly can restrict supply, prices will rise—in this case, teacher salaries. That would fulfill a primary objective of the teacher unions, but without any guarantee of increased quality.

Another Approach

What kind of persons might be attracted to teaching were the doors to teaching careers open to people with a wide variety of backgrounds that didn't necessarily include sitting through hundreds of hours of education courses, whether NCATE-accredited or not? Suppose principals could hire their own teaching staffs without having to follow the credits-hours prescribed by education bureacracies?

Well, there would be more teachers like Scott (Taki) Sidley, who taught English at T.C. Williams High School in Alexandria, Va., the past three years, but ran athwart the state bureaucracy's insistence that he take additional prescribed courses in order to be "certified." In a piece of Sunday commentary in the *Washington Post* (June 25, 2000), long-time teacher Patrick Welsh lamented the "bureaucratic narrow-mindedness" that pushes people like Sidley out of teaching.

Welsh noted that Sidley, a University of Virginia graduate who has served in the Peace Corps, won acclaim from students and parents and was considered "one of our [T.C. Williams'] finest teachers." But he must leave the young people he was teaching so well because he lacks on his resume 30 credit-hours that regulators insist he must have—one being a low-level composition course, even though he took 48 graduate hours in creative writing at U.Va. and the university exempted him from introductory composition because of his Advanced Placement English score in high school.

Many young teachers like Sidley, Welsh notes, "see the petty adherence to the certification rules as symptomatic of a pervasive problem." For an alternative vision, he quoted Dave Keener, head of the school's science department and the 1998 Virginia winner of the Presidential Award for Excellence in Science and Mathematics Teaching: "The process of getting the best has to be streamlined. Individual high schools should be given the power to advertise positions and do their own recruiting. . . . Principals, with advice of teachers, should be able to do all the hiring on the spot without having to get approval from the central office, which often takes weeks. De-emphasize the education courses. Once we get the kind of people we want, we could train them in the schools."

That's the sensible approach that one kind of education reform, the charter school, facilitates. Organizers of charter schools—often teachers with a common vision— receive waivers from certification and other bureaucratic rules. In exchange for independence, they agree to be accountable for academic results. Many charter schools freely hire teachers who know their subjects but haven't been through the education-school mill. Only a small fraction of charter school teachers choose to belong to the national teacher unions.

In its 1996 report, NCTAF gave the impression with its sharp attack on the current state-controlled certification system that it wanted a thoroughgoing reform that would bring bright young teachers into the classroom. But as Professors Ballou and Podgursky observe, NCTAF focuses not on recruiting more talented individuals but on beefing up the system of teacher training— and shifting its control from political bodies to organizations, like NCATE, that may also reflect private agendas, such as the NEA'S.

There are a few small-scale programs designed to deepen the pool of teaching talent by going outside the certification routine. One is Teach for America, which places liberal arts graduates in high-need urban and rural districts. Another is Troops to Teachers, which assists retiring military personnel in becoming teachers. In both instances, the newly minted teachers obtain provisional certification and then work toward obtaining enough professional education credits to gain full certification.

New Jersey is one state that has taken seriously the desirability of offering alternative routes to teaching. In 1984, the state reduced the number of education courses required for traditional certification, while putting new teachers under the tutelage of a mentor teacher. At the same time, it allowed teachers to recruit liberal arts graduates who hadn't been through education schools at all. These teachers were also put under the supervision of a mentor. They would get on-the-job training in applied teaching. The new approach has resulted in higher scores on licensing tests, a lower attrition rate, and a more diverse teaching force, notes former New Jersey Education Commissioner Leo Klagholz in a Fordham Foundation paper.

Such programs are fine as far as they go—but they don't go nearly far enough nationwide. Strict regulation of K-12 teaching has yielded pervasive mediocrity. It is time to deregulate and to emphasize results. Instead of screening teachers according to courses taken and degrees earned, school administrations should free principals to hire the most intellectually promising material— English majors to teach English, history majors to teach history—and then let the schools assimilate them in the nitty-gritty of preparing lesson plans and monitoring lunchrooms.

Value-Added Assessment

The quest for reform based on proof of good teaching brings us back to William Sanders and the Tennessee Value-Added Assessment System (TVAAS), which generates annual reports of gains in student achievement produced by each teacher, school, and school district. Progress is broken down by core subject, and gains are compared to national, state, and local benchmarks.

Professor John Stone explains the significance of using such a system:

> By comparing each student's current achievement to his or her past performance and aggregating the results, value-added assessment statistically isolates the impact of individual teachers, schools, and school systems on the average progress of the students for which they are responsible. Not incidentally, value-added assessment can also be used by education's decisionmakers to isolate and assess the effectiveness of everything from the latest curricular innovations, to the preparedness of novice teachers, to the quality of the programs in which teachers were trained.

Here, in short, is a real-world way to assess the performance of teachers—as opposed to the paperwork realm of NCATE, which deems credentials and licensure hoops to be the equivalent of quality assurance.

The most thoroughgoing reform of teacher licensing and hiring could come through a combination of the New Jersey and Tennessee approaches. Schools could hire teachers with liberal-arts educations and/or valuable working-world experiences, then give them on-the-job mentoring, and finally evaluate their teaching prowess according to a value-added assessment.

It's known from Sanders's research, the No Excuses schools, and plain common sense that teachers make a profound difference in students' lives. Deregulated teacher hiring combined with value-added assessment could bring an infusion of fresh talent into teaching and provide a basis for rewarding those teachers who do the most to help children learn. Such a system also could quickly identify teachers who needed extra training, or those who ought to be pursuing a different line of work. Such a change would deserve to be called reform; mandatory accreditation locking in the status quo in teaching preparation does not.

Three days into his administration, President George W. Bush unveiled an accountability plan for federal education spending that sparked hope for a fresh approach to bringing good teachers to K–12 schools. He proposed that Congress revise Title II of the Elementary and Secondary Education Act so that school districts can come up with alternative ways to certify teachers. And he would reserve a chunk of funding for grants to states that develop systems to measure teacher effectiveness according to student academic achievement.

That's value-added, and it may turn out to be the most significant education tool since chalk.

How Teacher Education Matters

Over the past decade, public dissatisfaction with schools has included dissatisfaction with teacher education. Education schools have been variously criticized as ineffective in preparing teachers for their work, unresponsive to new demands, remote from practice, and barriers to the recruitment of bright college students into teaching. In more than 40 states, policy makers have enacted alternative routes to teacher certification to create pathways into teaching other than those provided by traditional 4-year undergraduate teacher education programs. Whereas some of these are carefully structured postbaccalaureate programs, others are little more than emergency hiring options. Upon his election in 1988, President Bush's only education proposal was the encouragement of alternative teacher certification. In 1995, Newt Gingrich proposed the elimination of teacher certification rules as his major education initiative. In 1999, Chester Finn and the Thomas B. Fordham Foundation issued a manifesto arguing against teacher education requirements as a "barrier" to entering teaching.

Voices of dissatisfaction have been raised from within the profession as well (Goodlad, 1990; Holmes Group, 1986). These voices, however, have urged the redesign of teacher education to strengthen its knowledge base, its connections to both practice and theory, and its capacity to support the development of powerful teaching. Proposals at the far ends of this continuum stand in stark contrast to one another. One approach would replace university-based preparation with on-the-job training that focuses on the pragmatics of teaching, whereas the other would expand professional training to prepare teachers for more adaptive, knowledge-based practice, while simultaneously tackling the redesign of schools and teaching. Which of these routes holds the most promise? What are the implications for teachers' capacities, and, most important, for the education of children?

Although the debates on these questions have been largely ideological, there is a growing body of empirical evidence about the outcomes of different approaches to teacher education and recruitment. This research suggests that the extent and quality of teacher education matter for teachers' effectiveness, perhaps now even more than before. The expectations that schools teach a much more diverse group of students to much higher standards

From Linda Darling-Hammond, "How Teacher Education Matters," *Journal of Teacher Education,* vol. 51, no. 3 (May/June 2000). Copyright © 2000 by The American Association of Colleges for Teacher Education. Reprinted by permission of Corwin Press, Inc., a Sage Publications Company.

create much greater demands on teachers. Teaching for problem solving, invention, and application of knowledge requires teachers with deep and flexible knowledge of subject matter who understand how to represent ideas in powerful ways [and] can organize a productive learning process for students who start with different levels and kinds of prior knowledge, assess how and what students are learning, and adapt instruction to different learning approaches.

Do Education Schools Help Teachers Learn?

Even if one agrees that there are desirable knowledge and skills for teaching, many people believe that anyone can teach, or, at least, that knowing a subject is enough to allow one to teach it well. Others believe that teaching is best learned, to the extent that it can be learned at all, by trial and error on the job. The evidence strongly suggests otherwise. Reviews of research over the past 30 years have concluded that even with the shortcomings of current teacher education and licensing, fully prepared and certified teachers are generally better rated and more successful with students than teachers without this preparation (Ashton & Crocker, 1986; Evertson, Hawley, & Zlotnik, 1985; Greenberg, 1983; Haberman, 1984; Olsen, 1985).

In fields ranging from mathematics and science to vocational education, reading, elementary education, and early childhood education, researchers have found that teachers who have greater knowledge of teaching and learning are more highly rated and are more effective with students, especially at tasks requiring higher order thinking and problem solving. (For a review of this literature, see Darling-Hammond, 1996b.) Interestingly, whereas subject-matter knowledge is often found to be an important factor in teaching effectiveness, it appears that its relationship to teaching performance is curvilinear; that is, it exerts a positive effect up to a threshold level and then tapers off in influence. Furthermore, measures of pedagogical knowledge, including knowledge of learning, teaching methods, and curriculum, are more frequently found to influence teaching performance and often exert even stronger effects than subject-matter knowledge (Ashton & Crocker, 1986; Begle & Geeslin, 1972; Byrne, 1983; Evertson et al., 1985; Ferguson & Womack, 1993; Guyton & Farokhi, 1987; Monk, 1994; Perkes, 1967–1968). It seems logical that pedagogical skill would interact with subject matter knowledge to bolster or undermine teacher performance. As Byrne (1983) suggests,

> insofar as a teacher's knowledge provides the basis for his or her effectiveness, the most relevant knowledge will be that which concerns the particular topic being taught and the relevant pedagogical strategies for teaching it to the particular types of pupils to whom it will be taught. (p. 14)

Meanwhile, studies of teachers admitted with less than full preparation find that recruits tend to be less satisfied with their training and have greater difficulties planning curriculum, teaching, managing the classroom, and diagnosing students' learning needs. They are less able to adapt their instruction to promote student learning and less likely to see it as their job to do so, blaming students if their teaching is not effective. Principals and colleagues rate these teachers less highly on their instructional skills, and they leave teaching at higher-than-average rates. Most important is that their students learn less, especially in areas such as reading, writing, and mathematics, which are critical to later school success (Darling-Hammond, 1999b).

Illustrating these findings, Gomez and Grobe's (1990) study of the performance of alternate certification (AC) candidates in Dallas, who receive a few weeks of summer training before they assume full teaching responsibilities, found that their performance was much more uneven than that of traditionally trained entrants who had equivalent scores on the state's subject matter exams. From 2 to 16 times as many AC recruits were rated "poor" on each teaching factor evaluated, and their students showed significantly lower achievement gains in language arts and writing.

Perhaps it is not surprising that alternate route teachers from short-term programs report less satisfaction with their preparation and less commitment to remaining in teaching than other recruits (Darling-Hammond, Hudson, & Kirby, 1989; Lutz & Hutton, 1989). Problems resulting from inadequate preparation headed the list of complaints of the 20% of Los Angeles AC candidates who quit before they completed their summer training programs in 1984 and 1985, as well as many of those who remained but voiced dissatisfaction (Wright, McKibbon, & Walton, 1987). Stoddart's (1992) analysis reveals that 53% of these recruits had left teaching within the first 6 years of program operation. Among AC candidates in Dallas, only half successfully "graduated" to become full-fledged teachers after their first year as interns. Only 40% said that they planned to stay in teaching, as compared to 72% of traditionally trained recruits (Lutz & Hutton, 1989).

Even very intelligent people who are enthusiastic about teaching find that they cannot easily succeed without preparation, especially if they are assigned to work with children who most need skillful teaching. The best-publicized program founded on this idea is Teach for America (TFA), created to recruit bright college graduates to disadvantaged schools en route to careers in other professions. If anyone could prove the claim that teachers are born and not made, these bright eager students might have been the ones to do it. Yet, four separate evaluations found that TFA's 3-to-8-week summer training program did not prepare candidates adequately (Grady, Collins, & Grady, 1991; Popkewitz, 1995; Roth, 1993; Texas Education Agency, 1993), despite the intelligence and enthusiasm of many of the recruits. Many recruits knew that their success—and that of their students—had been compromised by their lack of access to the knowledge needed to teach. Yale University graduate Schorr (1993) was one of many to raise this concern:

> I—perhaps like most TFAers—harbored dreams of liberating my students from public school mediocrity and offering them as good an education as I had received. But I was not ready. . . . As bad as it was for me, it was worse for the students. Many of mine . . . took long steps on the path toward dropping out.... I was not a successful teacher and the loss to the students was real and large. (pp. 317–318)

These feelings contribute to the program's high attrition rate. Even though many recruits report that they initially entered the program with the intention of exploring teaching as a career, many also indicate that they left in discouragement because they felt unsuccessful. TFA statistics show that of those who started in 1990, 58% had left before the third year, a 2-year attrition rate nearly three times the national average for new teachers. The Maryland State Department of Education found that 62% of corps members who started in Baltimore in 1992 left within 2 years.

Aside from high attrition, studies of short-term alternative programs have also noted that what little pedagogical training they provide tends to focus on generic teaching skills rather than subject-specific pedagogy, on singular techniques rather than a range of methods, and on specific, immediate advice rather than research or theory (Bliss, 1992; Stoddart, 1992; Zumwalt, 1990).

The lack of traditional coursework and student teaching in these programs are generally supposed to be compensated for by intensive mentoring and supervision in the initial months of full-time teaching. Ironically, however, most studies have found that promised mentors did not often materialize (Darling-Hammond, 1992).

Unfortunately, the least well-prepared recruits are disproportionately assigned to teach the least advantaged students in high-minority and low-income schools (National Commission on Teaching and America's Future [NCTAF], 1996). In the aggregate, this can make a substantial difference in what children learn. Recent multivariate studies of student achievement at the school and district level have found a substantial influence of teachers' qualifications on what students learn. Ferguson's (1991) analysis of Texas school districts found that teachers' expertise, including their scores on a licensing examination measuring basic skills and teaching knowledge; master's degrees' and experience accounted for more of the interdistrict variation in students' reading and mathematics achievement in grades 1 through 11 than student socioeconomic status. The effects were so strong, and the variations in teacher expertise so great, that after controlling for socioeconomic status, the large disparities in achievement between Black and White students were almost entirely accounted for by differences in the qualifications of their teachers. This finding contravenes the common presumption that students' school achievement is largely a function of their socioeconomic status and that school variables make little difference in educational outcomes.

A more recent Texas study (Fuller, 1999) found that students in districts with greater proportions of fully licensed teachers were significantly more likely to pass the Texas state achievement tests after controlling for student socioeconomic status, school wealth, and teacher experience. Similar to this, a North Carolina study (Strauss & Sawyer, 1986) found that teachers' average scores on the National Teacher Examinations measuring subject matter and teaching knowledge had a large effect on students' pass rates on the state competency examinations. A 1% increase in teacher quality (as measured by NTE scores) was associated with a 3% to 5% decline in the percentage of students failing the exam.

A recent school-level analysis of mathematics test performance in California high schools (Fetler, 1999) found a strong negative relationship between average student scores and the percentage of teachers on emergency certificates, after controlling for student poverty rates. Another California study found that across all income levels, elementary students' reading achievement is strongly related to the proportions of fully trained and certified teachers (Los Angeles County Office of Education, 1999), much more so than to the proportion of beginners in the school. The study concluded that "this supports the finding that differing test scores are a teacher training issue and not merely due to new teachers' lack of classroom experience."

Responses to Critiques of Traditional Teacher Education

Lest schools of education become sanguine, however, there are grounds for concern about traditional preparation programs as well. The often-repeated critiques of traditional teacher education programs include the pressure of inadequate time within a 4-year undergraduate degree, which makes it hard to learn enough about both subject matter and pedagogy; the fragmentation of content and pedagogical coursework and the divide between university- and school-based training; the weak content of many courses that pass on folklore instead of systematically developed knowledge; the lack of adequate clinical training; and the lack of resources in many education programs that serve as "cash cows" for their universities, which perpetuates much of the above.

Over the past decade, many schools of education and school districts have begun to change these conditions. Stimulated by the efforts of the Holmes Group and the National Network for Educational Renewal, more than 300 schools of education have created programs that extend beyond the confines of the traditional 4-year bachelor's degree program, thus allowing more extensive study of the disciplines to be taught along with education coursework that is integrated with more extensive clinical training in schools. Some are 1- or 2-year graduate programs that serve recent graduates or midcareer recruits. Others are 5-year models that allow an extended program of preparation for prospective teachers who enter teacher education during their undergraduate years. In either case, because the 5th year allows students to devote their energies exclusively to the task of preparing to teach, such programs allow for year-long school-based clinical experiences that are woven together with coursework on learning and teaching.

Many of these programs have joined with local school districts to create professional development schools where novices' clinical preparation can be more purposefully structured. Like teaching hospitals in medicine, these schools aim to provide sites for state-of-the-art practice that are also organized to support the training of new professionals, extend the professional development of veteran teachers, and sponsor collaborative research and inquiry. These approaches resemble reforms in teacher education abroad. Countries such as Germany, Belgium, France, and Luxembourg have long required from 2 to 3 years of graduate-level study in addition to an undergraduate degree for prospective teachers, including an intensively supervised internship in a school affiliated with the university.

A number of recent studies have found that graduates of extended programs (typically 5-year programs) are not only more satisfied with their preparation, they are viewed by their colleagues, principals, and cooperating teachers as better prepared, are as effective with students as much more experienced teachers, and are much more likely to enter and stay in teaching than their peers prepared in traditional 4-year programs (Andrew, 1990; Andrew & Schwab, 1995; Arch, 1989; Denton & Peters, 1988; Dyal, 1993; Shin, 1994). In fact, the entry and retention rates of these programs are so much higher than those of 4-year programs—which are, in turn, much higher than short-term alternative programs—that it is actually less expensive to prepare career teachers in this way once the costs of preparation, recruitment, induction, and replacement due to attrition are taken into account (Darling-Hammond, 1999a).

These new programs typically engage prospective teachers in studying research and conducting their own inquiries through cases, action research, and the development of structured portfolios about practice. They envision the professional teacher as one who learns from teaching rather than one who has finished learning how to teach, and the job of teacher education as developing the capacity to inquire sensitively and systematically into the nature of learning and the effects of teaching. This is an approach to knowledge production like the one that Dewey (1929) sought, one that aims to empower teachers with greater understanding of complex situations rather than to control them with simplistic formulas or cookie-cutter routines for teaching:

> Command of scientific methods and systematized subject matter liberates individuals; it enables them to see new problems, devise new procedures, and in general, makes for diversification rather than for set uniformity. (p. 12)

> This knowledge and understanding render (the teacher's) practice more intelligent, more flexible, and better adapted to deal effectively with concrete phenomena or practice. . . . Seeing more relations he sees more possibilities, more opportunities. His ability to judge being enriched, he has a wider range of alternatives to select from in dealing with individual situations. (pp. 20–21)

Dewey's notion of knowledge for teaching is one that features inquiry into problems of practice as the basis for professional judgment grounded in both theoretical and practical knowledge. If teachers investigate the effects of their teaching on students' learning, and if they study what others have learned, they come to understand teaching to be an inherently nonroutine endeavor. They become sensitive to variation and more aware of what works for what purposes in what situations. Access to contingent knowledge allows them to become more thoughtful decision makers.

Training in inquiry also helps teachers learn how to look at the world from multiple perspectives, including those of students whose experiences are quite different from their own, and to use this knowledge in developing pedagogies that can reach diverse learners. Learning to reach out to students, those who are difficult to know as well as those who are easy to know, requires boundary crossing, the ability to elicit knowledge of others, and to understand it when it is offered. As Delpit (1995) notes, "We all interpret behaviors, information, and situations through our own cultural lenses; these lenses operate involuntarily, below the level of conscious awareness, making it seem that our own view is simply 'the way it is'" (p. 1512). Good teachers must develop an awareness of their perspectives and how these can be enlarged to avoid a "communicentric bias" (Gordon, 1990), which limits their understanding of those whom they teach.

Developing the ability to see beyond one's own perspective, to put oneself in the shoes of the learner and to understand the meaning of that experience in terms of learning, is perhaps the most important role of universities in the preparation of teachers. One of the great flaws of the "bright person myth" of teaching is that it presumes that anyone can teach what he or she knows to anyone else. However, people who have never studied teaching or learning often have a very difficult time understanding how to convey material that they themselves learned effortlessly and almost subconsciously. When others do not learn merely by being told, the intuitive teacher often becomes frustrated and powerless to proceed. This frequently leads to resentment of students for not validating the untrained teacher's efforts. Furthermore, individuals who have had no powerful teacher education intervention often maintain a single cognitive and cultural perspective that makes it difficult for them to understand the experiences, perceptions, and knowledge bases that deeply influence the approaches to learning of students who are different from themselves. The capacity to understand another is not innate; it is developed through study, reflection, guided experience, and inquiry.

Among the tools teacher educators increasingly use for this purpose are inquiries that engage prospective teachers in investigating learning and the lives of learners and evaluating the many different outcomes of teaching. These include prospective teachers conducting case studies of children while studying development and learning, thus coming to better understand the children's thinking and experiences; conducting community studies that investigate local neighborhoods in ways that illuminate culture, customs, and life experiences of different groups of people; conducting investigations of student learning, like the National Board for Professional Teaching Standards' student learning commentaries that evaluate artifacts of the learning of 3 diverse students over time; assembling portfolios that use artifacts of teaching and learning to analyze the effects of practice; and pursuing problem-based inquiries that seek to identify problems of practice and understand them through action research coupled with reviews of others' research. These tools allow the application of theoretical principles to problems in specific contexts while appropriately complicating efforts to draw generalizations about practice. A small but growing body of research suggests that such strategies can help teachers understand more deeply the many variables that influence their work. For example, in the case of cases and portfolios that require teachers to examine student learning in relation to their teaching, teachers claim that the process of engaging in such analysis ultimately enriches their ability to understand the effects of their actions and helps them better meet the needs of diverse students. (For a review of this literature, see Darling-Hammond and Snyder, in press.) One of the ways in which this occurs is through the process of trying to view teaching and classroom events from the perspectives of the students who experience them. As teachers look beyond their own actions to appreciate the understandings and experiences of their students, and evaluate these in light of their self-developed knowledge of individual learners and their professional knowledge of factors influencing development and learning, they grow wiser about the many ways in which learning and teaching interact.

A commitment to open inquiry, the enlargement of perspectives, and the crossing of boundaries are critical features of the ideal of university education. In fact, the basis of the very earliest universities was that they tried to bring together scholars from all over the known world. They sought to create ways to share diverse perspectives from various geographic areas, cultures, and disciplines as the basis for developing knowledge and finding truth. If universities are to continue to make the important contribution to the education of teachers that they can make, they need to pursue these ideals of knowledge building and truth finding by creating a genuine praxis between ideas and experiences, by honoring practice in conjunction with reflection and research, and by helping teachers reach beyond their personal boundaries to appreciate the perspectives of those whom they would teach.

References

Andrew, M. (1990). The differences between graduates of four-year and five-year teacher preparation programs. *Journal of Teacher Education, 41,* 45–51.

Andrew, M., & Schwab, R. L. (1995). Has reform in teacher education influenced teacher performance? An outcome assessment of graduates of eleven teacher education programs. *Action in Teacher Education, 17,* 43–53.

Arch, E. C. (1989, April). *Comparison of student attainment of teaching competence in traditional preservice and fifth-year master of arts in teaching programs.* Paper presented at the annual meeting of the American Educational Research Association, San Francisco.

Ashton, P., & Crocker, L. (1986). Does teacher certification make a difference? *Florida Journal of Teacher Education, 3,* 73–83.

Begle, E. G., & Geeslin, W. (1972). *Teacher effectiveness in mathematics instruction.* (National Longitudinal Study of Mathematical Abilities Reports No. 28). Washington, DC: Mathematical Association of America and National Council of Teachers of Mathematics.

Bliss, T. (1992). Alternate certification in Connecticut: Reshaping the profession. *Peabody Journal of Education, 67*(3), 35–54.

Byrne. (1983). *Teacher knowledge and teacher effectiveness: A literature review, theoretical analysis, and discussion of research strategy.* Paper presented at the meeting of the Northeastern Educational Research Association, Ellenville, NY.

Darling-Hammond, L. (1992). Teaching and knowledge: Policy issues posed by alternative certification for teachers. *Peabody Journal of Education, 67*(3), 123–154.

Darling-Hammond, L. (1999a). *Solving the dilemmas of teacher supply, demand, and standards: How we can ensure a competent, caring, and qualified teacher for every child.* New York: National Commission on Teaching and America's Future.

Darling-Hammond, L. (1999b). *Teaching quality and student achievement: A review of state policy evidence.* Seattle, WA: Center for the Study of Teaching and Policy, University of Washington.

Darling-Hammond, L., Hudson, L., & Kirby, S. (1989). *Redesigning teacher education: Opening the door for new recruits to science and mathematics teaching.* Santa Monica, CA: RAND.

Darling-Hammond, L., & Snyder, J. (in press). Authentic assessment of teaching in context. *Journal of Teaching and Teacher Education.*

Denton, J. J., & Peters, W. H. (1988). *Program assessment report: Curriculum evaluation of a non-traditional program for certifying teachers.* College Station, TX: Texas A & M University.

Dewey, J. (1929). *The sources of a science of education.* New York: Horace Liveright.

Dyal, A. B. (1993). *An exploratory study to determine principals' perceptions concerning the effectiveness of a fifth-year preparation program.* Paper presented at the annual meeting of the Mid-South Educational Research Association, New Orleans, LA.

Evertson, C., Hawley, W., & Zlotnick, M. (1985). Making a difference in educational quality through teacher education. *Journal of Teacher Education, 36*(3), 2–12.

Ferguson, R. F. (1991). Paying for public education: New evidence on how and why money matters. *Harvard Journal on Legislation, 28*(2), 465–498.

Ferguson, P., & Womack, S. T. (1993). The impact of subject matter and education coursework on teaching performance. *Journal of Teacher Education, 44*(1), 55–63.

Fetler, M. (1999, March 24). High school staff characteristics and mathematics test results. *Education Policy Analysis Archives, 7* [Online]. Available: http://epaa.asu.edu.

Fuller, E. J. (1999). *Does teacher certification matter? A comparison of TAAS performance in 1997 between schools with low and high percentages of certified teachers.* Austin: Charles A. Dana Center, University of Texas at Austin.

Gomez, D. L., & Grobe, R. P. (1990, April). *Three years of alternative certification in Dallas: Where are we?* Paper presented at the Annual Meeting of the American Educational Research Association, Boston.

Goodlad, J. (1990). *Teachers for our nation's schools.* San Francisco: Jossey-Bass.

Gordon, E. W. (1990). Coping with communicentric bias in knowledge production in the social sciences. *Educational Researcher, 19.*

Grady, M. P., Collins, P., & Grady, E. L. (1991). *Teach for America 1991 Summer Institute evaluation report.* Unpublished manuscript.

Greenberg, J. D. (1983). The case for teacher education: Open and shut. *Journal of Teacher Education, 34*(4), 2–5.

Guyton, E., & Farokhi, E. (1987, September–October). Relationships among academic performance, basic skills, subject matter knowledge and teaching skills of teacher education graduates. *Journal of Teacher Education,* 37–42.

Haberman, M. (1984, September). *An Evaluation of the rationale for required teacher education: Beginning teachers with or without teacher preparation.* Paper prepared for the National Commission on Excellence in Teacher Education, University of Wisconsin-Milwaukee.

Holmes Group. (1996). *Tomorrow's teachers: A report of the Holmes Group.* East Lansing, MI: Author.

Los Angeles County Office Of Education. (1999).

Lutz, F. W., & Hutton, J. B. (1989). Alternative teacher certification: Its policy implications for classroom and personnel practice. *Educational Evaluation and Policy Analysis, 11*(3), 237–254.

Monk, D. H. (1994). Subject matter preparation of secondary mathematics and science teachers and student achievement. *Economics of Education Review, 13*(2), 125–145.

National Commission on Teaching and America's Future. (1996). *What matters most: Teaching for America's future.* NY: Author.

Olsen, D. G. (1985). The quality of prospective teachers: Education vs. noneducation graduates. *Journal of Teacher Education, 36*(5), 56–59.

Perkes, V. A. (1967–1968). Junior high school science teacher preparation, teaching behavior, and student achievement. *Journal of Research in Science Teaching, 6*(4), 121–126.

Popkewitz, T. S. (1995). Policy, knowledge, and power: Some issues for the study of educational reform. In P. Cookson & B. Schneider (Eds.), *Transforming schools: Trends, dilemmas and prospects.* Garland Press.

Roth, R. A. (1993). *Teach for America 1993 summer institute: Program review.* Unpublished report.

Schorr, J. (1993, December). Class action: What Clinton's National Service Program could learn from "Teach for America." *Phi Delta Kappan,* 315–318.

Shin, H.-S. (1994). *Estimating future teacher supply: An application of survival analysis.* Paper presented at the annual meeting of the American Educational Research Association, New Orleans, LA.

Strauss, R. P., & Sawyer, E. A. (1986). Some new evidence on teacher and student competencies. *Economics of Education Review, 5*(1), 41–48.

Stoddart, T. (1992). An alternative route to teacher certification: Preliminary findings from the Los Angeles Unified School District Intern Program. *Peabody Journal of Education, 67*(3).

Texas Education Agency. (1993). Teach for American visiting team report. Meeting minutes of Texas State Board of Education Meeting (Appendix B), Austin.

Wright, D. P., McKibbon, M., & Walton, P. (1987). *The effectiveness of the teacher trainee program: An alternate route into teaching in California.* Sacramento: California Commission on Teacher Credentialing.

Zumwalt, K. (1990). Alternate routes to teaching: Three alternative approaches. New York: Teachers College, Columbia University.

POSTSCRIPT

Should Alternative Teacher Training Be Encouraged?

The present shortage of teachers, which has brought about the admission of college graduates without indoctrination in "methods," is an opportunity not to be missed. Liberal arts majors, if their courses were truly liberal, will be free of crippling ideas about how to teach.

—Jacques Barzun

This sentiment, of course, is in direct contrast to Darling-Hammond's position expressed in *The Right to Learn* (1997): "Many people sincerely believe that anyone can teach, or, at least, that knowing a subject is enough to allow one to teach it well. Others believe that teaching is best learned, to the extent that it can be learned at all, by trial and error on the job. The evidence, however, strongly suggests otherwise."

Further argumentation on this basic issue can be found in the following sources: Chester E. Finn, Jr., and Kathleen Madigan, "Removing Barriers for Teacher Candidates," *Educational Leadership* (May 2001); Carol Tell, "Making Room for Alternative Routes," *Educational Leadership* (May 2001); David C. Berliner, "A Personal Response to Those Who Bash Teacher Education," *Journal of Teacher Education* (November/December 2000); and Susan Moore Johnson, "Can Professional Certification for Teachers Reshape Teaching as a Career?" *Phi Delta Kappan* (January 2001).

Articles related to the Wendy Kopp alternative include Molly Ness, "Lessons of a First-Year Teacher," *Phi Delta Kappan* (May 2001); Sara Mosle, "Mrs. Ed: Teach for America's Misguided Critics," *The New Republic* (January 23, 1995); and Margaret Raymond and Stephen Fletcher, "The Teach for America Evolution," *Education Next* (Spring 2002). Molly Ness has recently expanded her ideas into book form with *Lesson To Learn: Voices from the Front Lines of Teach for America* (2004).

Special theme issues may be found in *Educational Horizons* (Fall 1999 and Spring 2000), *Kappa Delta Pi Record* (Spring 2000), *The School Administrator* (January 2001), *Educational Leadership* (March 2002), and *Education Next* (Spring 2002).

In the midst of all of this wrangling about the components and length of teacher preparation, perhaps what is needed is a reconceptualization of teaching as a career. We need to address what is needed before entry into the profession, what is needed in the formative stages of the developing professional, and, most important, what is needed in the various fulfillment stages along the path to retirement and beyond.

On the Internet . . .

Discovery Institute

Site offering a wide range of material justifying the "intelligent design" viewpoint as well as previews of upcoming conferences on the topic.

http://www.discovery.org

Understanding Evolution

A one-stop source for information on evolution featuring articles aimed at teachers and the general public, sponsored by the University of California and its Museum of Paleontology.

http://evolution.berkeley.edu

Gurian Institute

Site providing training materials for teachers and parents concerned about gender factors in learning and behavior.

http://www.gurianinstitute.com

Education Sector

Site of an independent education policy think tank devoted to developing-solutions to pressing problems in education, founded in 2005.

http://www.educationsector.org

PART 4

Bonus Issues

*T*he *two debates presented in this part represent issues that have become particularly contentious since the fourteenth edition of this book went to press, although both have been discussed in one form or another by educators and policymakers for a number of years. The first issue, brought into the news in December 2005 with a Pennsylvania court decision in* Kitzmiller v. Dover Area School District, *deals with attempts there and elsewhere to insert alternative explanations into the teaching of evolution in the science curriculum of public schools. The second issue, brought to public attention by a January 30, 2006,* Newsweek *cover story, "The Boy Crisis," and a declaration of special interest in the education of boys by Laura Bush, examines the evidence on the achievement patterns of boys on a nationwide basis.*

- Is "Intelligent Design" a Threat to the Curriculum?

- Is There a Crisis in the Education of Boys?

ISSUE 22

Is "Intelligent Design" a Threat to the Curriculum?

YES: Mark Terry, from "One Nation, Under the Designer," *Phi Delta Kappan* (December 2004)

NO: Dan Peterson, from "The Little Engine That Could . . . Undo Darwinism," *The American Spectator* (June 2005)

ISSUE SUMMARY

YES: Biology teacher and science department administrator Mark Terry warns of the so-called Wedge Strategy being employed by the Discovery Institute to incorporate the "intelligent design" approach into the public school science curriculum.

NO: Attorney Dan Peterson presents fact-based arguments that separate "intelligent design" from previous campaigns for inclusion of "creation science" in the biology curriculum and cause evolution theorists to possibly adjust their standard positions.

For the past few years, fresh challenges in the old debate over the teaching of evolution in America's schools have emerged. Most of these challenges have been orchestrated by proponents of "intelligent design" who desire, at a minimum, the inclusion of supernatural explanations of biological origins to be added to the science curriculum as a companion to instruction about the theory of evolution.

Much of the impetus for this renewed campaign comes from early 1980s' concerns by religious fundamentalists about the domination of secular humanism in the public school curriculum. Members of organizations such as Rev. Jerry Falwell's Moral Majority expressed the view that humanism and naturalism indoctrinate the young with ideas and attitudes that are contrary to traditional religious teachings. A focal point of the campaign against secular humanist influences was an effort to include "creation science" in the curriculum and its textbooks. George E. Hahn, in "Creation-Science and Education," *Phi Delta Kappan* (April 1982), claimed that nearly 1,500 scientists felt that creationism was not only scientifically legitimate but actually superior to the evolution-science perspective. Legislative efforts were initiated at the state and local levels to bring science instruction into a more balanced format by injecting religious interpretations of data examined. Such efforts in California, Arkansas, Louisiana, and other locales, however, were curtailed by adverse judicial rulings.

In the 1990s, religious leaders such as Ralph E. Reed, Jr. of the Christian Coalition and Robert L. Simonds of Citizens for Excellence in Education rekindled public concern about the unquestioned acceptance of the theory of evolution and the exclusion of religion in public schools. In the political arena, support for the ideas of these and like groups came from the Heritage Foundation and luminaries such as Newt Gingrich, William J. Bennett, and Rush Limbaugh. On the other side, in this phase of the so-called culture wars, stood the National Education Association, People for the American Way, and various organizations championing the separation of church and state. By the early 2000s, the strategy of the Christian right had switched from creation science, which had been consistently prohibited by the courts, to arguments grounded in the concept of "intelligent design," which suggests that some organisms in the natural world are far too complex to have developed by evolutionary processes alone. Charles Haynes of the Freedom Forum believes that intelligent design has the best chance of making inroads into the curriculum and that the majority of Americans want to see a reasonable alternative to evolution in science courses.

Spearheading recent attempts to get public schools to move away from teaching evolution as an incontrovertible "truth" are scientists affiliated with the Seattle-based Discovery Institute. It is their contention that teachers should learn the scientific arguments for, and against, modern evolutionary theory. These scientific arguments against Darwinism are presented without specific religious underpinnings, but in December 2005 the federal judge presiding in *Kitzmiller v. Dover Area School District* in Pennsylvania disallowed the intelligent design alternative, stating that it is a religious rather than scientific view, "an extension of the Fundamentalists' view that one must either accept the literal interpretation of Genesis or else believe in the godless system of evolution." This judicial setback, however, will not diminish the contentious disputes likely to persist at state and local levels of policymaking.

In the following selections, Mark Terry warns of religious incursions into the science curriculum, while Dan Peterson pleads for a widening of the science curriculum to include "design" theories and evidence.

YES

Mark Terry

One Nation, Under the Designer

If you're not a high school biology teacher, you may be missing some of the current excitement in American education. There has been a sea change in the tactics of the anti-evolution forces, whose efforts have waxed and waned ever since the Scopes Trial. Before you dismiss this topic as of no interest to you as a history, English, or social studies teacher or as an administrator, watch out for the Wedge. For the Wedge is looking for you, too. Evolution is simply the initial target of opportunity, and there is a special emotional attachment to rooting it out. But make no mistake: if the first dangerous weed, modern science, can be removed from the garden, your area will be ripe for replanting as well.

Back to the Future

The sea change is taking us back to mid-19th-century Europe, a period whose intellectual history I love but never expected to relive. Pre-Darwin, or one might better say pre-Huxley, English secondary and university education, with all of its advancements, was still in the hands of clerics. The Church of England provided the lion's share of instructors and professors, and the colleges were built physically and philosophically around religious centers, a logical extension of the origin of the universities in the Middle Ages.

But a rigid scholasticism had also been retained, and this became particularly obvious in the sciences. Geology and, in its very infancy, biology were busy discovering phenomena and hazarding theories that seemed to have no relationship to scripture. Yet most of the early researchers and thinkers were religious and would often base part of their teaching on religious texts. Tensions grew. And it began to appear that, for science and other educational enterprises to progress, to admit to unknowns and to explore those unknowns, references to Christian scriptures would have to take a back seat. It was not a question of abandoning Christianity itself, but rather any limiting hold it had over the study of the natural world.[1]

Enter T. H. Huxley. A commoner, Huxley was practical and down-to-earth, but he nonetheless remained somewhat idealistic and saw one arena in which change was essential: science teaching. A wonderfully complex fellow, he saw that the teaching of science was lagging far behind developments in science itself and even farther behind the promise and potential of science. Science had to be done. This meant schools had to have labs where students

---

From *Phi Delta Kappan*, December 2004, pp. 265–270. Copyright © 2004 by Phi Delta Kappan. Reprinted by permission of the publisher and Mark Terry.

could gain direct experience. From direct experience, real learning would come; from real learning would spring new questions and, ultimately, greater progress. Scriptural limitations on the understanding of the natural world must be left behind. And for all of this to happen, new instructors, themselves practically trained scientists, not clerics, needed to be placed in charge of those new science classrooms.

Huxley is known as Darwin's bulldog because he was such a great popularizer of the idea of evolution. But perhaps his most important and lasting legacy was a revolution in science education. After publication of *On the Origin of Species*, while Darwin was at Down House quietly pursuing further evolutionary questions, Huxley was politicking on the London School Board. Great institutions, and great expectations, were initiated throughout British education in the pursuit of free and open inquiry into the processes of science and the study of history. The hold of the Church of England was loosened. Science was to be pursued for science's sake and for the sake of improving the lot of humankind, without constant reference to a deity or to scripture. And the same was to hold true for education in general.[2]

In the century and a half since Huxley, we have assumed that both science and education should be pursued in this way. Of course, it's fine if members of a religiously committed group wish to pursue science and education within the confines of their beliefs, doctrines, or scriptures in their own institutions. That's what religious schools are for. But, given the separation of church and state that Huxley promoted and that the U.S. is founded upon, public education and public science must be free of religious orientation.

Back to the Present

I've been teaching biology for over 30 years, and I always used to enjoy the creationist/evolutionist tension. Each decade's version of the controversy allowed me to say to my biology students, "See, this topic is not buried on some 19th-century shelf. It's here, and it's vital to those folks in Arkansas or Louisiana." And each time, as the courts ruled against creationism—then against creation science—it all seemed instructive and worth discussing in the classroom. It was not in the least threatening.[3] I used to think my colleagues who taught physics or chemistry must be jealous. What wouldn't they give for a headline-generating controversy to put an edge on, say, the periodic table or the wave-particle nature of light? But there are no religio-political factions—at least none that I'm aware of—willing to lobby state legislatures or to stack school boards with arguments either for or against the role of electrons or photons. Only in biology and earth science can we count on one of our core concepts being labeled controversial, even dangerous.

For most of my career I've been teaching about evolution in an integrated curriculum that joins biology and the humanities. It has been a delight to be able to place evolution in a historical and cultural context, while at the same time studying its scientific content and its current application. My colleagues and I have made sure that students see their humanities teachers grappling with the science and their biology teachers working to interpret the cultural scene.

The history of the public's perception of evolution and the controversies that continue to swirl around it have themselves arrested our attention. Students and teachers of all sorts of religious or nonreligious persuasions have enjoyed and benefited from this study, which has never been aimed at challenging anyone's religious beliefs, though we have examined the fact that some people feel that their beliefs are challenged by the very idea of evolution itself.

These days, I teach in an independent school, where the freedom to develop and carry out such a curriculum is a tremendous asset. But I know of plenty of public school biology teachers who have also done excellent work over the years. Evolution became a strong component of a terrific group of high school textbooks in the 1960s, and there have been many fine additions to that list in the decades since.[4]

But a couple of years ago I began to sense something new in the air. The school where I work is just a couple of blocks up the hill from downtown Seattle, and, in one of the nearby high-rises, a great searchlight seemed to be scanning the country. If only it had been a light designed to illumine and promote great science teaching! But no. I began to see that the search was for efforts to revise statewide science standards, so that the forces of the Discovery Institute might weigh in on the side of weakening or eliminating evolution and substituting something called "Intelligent Design." This was not restricted to Arkansas or Louisiana; this was a national campaign, directed from the home of Starbucks, Microsoft, and a highly sophisticated biomedical research complex.

Creation science always sounded a little foolish, trying to establish the scientific basis for religious writings that are thousands of years old. Intelligent Design (ID), however, is not about Biblical literalism. In fact, in their public battles ID proponents try to shift the entire discussion away from religion. Their claim is that science has discovered evidence of the work of a "designer" and that they have mathematical formulae and scientific-sounding "concepts" to back this up.[5]

Not only is ID not about Biblical literalism, but almost all talk of God has been carefully removed from the discussion. In an apparent nod to the failure of "scientific creationism," ID makes no reference to scripture and proudly proclaims that some of its advocates are nonbelievers. No proof of God's existence is offered—just that of an "Intelligent Designer." Students are not to be taught who this Designer is, just that the evidence shows that the Designer exists. Presumably, they can take it from there.

This gives the newspaper op-ed pieces and public forums a new twist. All the would-be reformers can now claim to be calling for nothing more than "better science teaching." Biology and earth science teachers are portrayed as just not knowing enough about what's going on in their own fields. If this is true, of course, then state standards must be redrafted to bring everybody up to speed with the latest "science," which is Intelligent Design.[6]

Of course, it's not true. There is no such scientific revolution under way.[7] But if the public can be convinced that such a revolution exists, science teachers who object can be portrayed as the reactionary, closed-minded ones. It's as though they must answer the question, "Have you stopped teaching stale, incorrect science?" The ID proponents challenge with, "We only want you to teach more about evolution, including this ultra-modern idea that is sweeping biology." The public is left to wonder what all the fuss is about. Why shouldn't our science teachers get on with teaching all this cutting-edge stuff?

The fuss, of course, is that it isn't science. The supposed "scientific revolution" is a creation of public relations. A science teacher cannot go to any major science journal or scientific organization and find out about all this new research—because there is none. In the fall of 2004 an ID article by a Discovery Institute Fellow appeared in the *Proceedings of the Biological Association of Washington*, a venerable but formerly obscure journal dealing with subtle taxonomic issues. The flurry of responses to the article gives a good picture of the current state of ID as science: the governing council of the journal almost immediately disavowed the article's publication. The National Center for Science Education (NCSE) and the Discovery Institute websites provide contrasting views of the publication and its retraction.[8] Of course, there are several religious journals, such as the *Journal of Interdisciplinary Studies*, and journals created specifically to carry the work of the Intelligent Design movement's own authors. There is also a spate of books and articles outlining the philosophical positions that underlie Intelligent Design, and there are some buzz phrases that are meant to sound quantifiable and solidly scientific, such as "irreducible complexity."[9] Finally, and undeniably, there is the Wedge Strategy.

Watch Out for the Wedge

The Wedge Strategy, which derives from the writings of Berkeley law professor Phillip Johnson, proposes nothing less than "the salvation of Western Civilization" by, among other things, the removal of evolution from science education and the institution of a Christian belief system throughout American society.[10]

In their more aggressive postures, the advocates of Intelligent Design have proposed a reestablishment of "proper science," science that will always take into account the work of a Supreme Being, an Intelligent Designer, or even, if you catch them in an unguarded moment, God.[11] The restoration of the science that was being pursued in England prior to the Darwin/Huxley revolution—all to the greater glory of God and mindful of His great works—is central to the Wedge Strategy. And, of course, this very aim gives the lie to proclamations of a purely scientific revolution. Proponents need to have science itself redefined to include the supernatural if they are to conduct their revolution.

It's a strange scientific revolution that seeks to establish its position in secondary school curricula before the research itself has been accomplished. But this obvious impediment is removed if the revolution is based on a *redefinition* of science rather than on new research.

Additional evidence of the true purpose of this so-called scientific revolution may be found in the history of Seattle's Discovery Institute and the backgrounds of its major figures. The Discovery Institute used to feature the Wedge Strategy on its website, and Phillip Johnson was a founding advisor of its Center for the Renewal of Science and Culture. This center, the anti-evolution arm of the Discovery Institute, originally had a very apt logo: Michelangelo's magnificent representation of God passing the spark of life to Adam. When the Wedge Strategy document was removed from the website, so too were the logo and name of the center. Now, it is simply the Center for Science and Culture, and the logo is a beautiful Hubble image that is also somewhat suggestive of an eye.[12]

The Fellows of the Center for Science and Culture have an impressive array of degrees, but you won't find a leading biologist among them. Many have degrees in philosophy, divinity, mathematics, or the law. Most have some active connection to evangelical Christian institutions. One who does have a Ph.D. in biological sciences from the University of California, Berkeley, has proclaimed his intention to follow the commission he received from the Rev. Sun Myung Moon to root out the evil of evolution. In fact, that's why he worked to earn a Ph.D. in biology.[13] But the publications and press releases of the Center for Science and Culture are "designed" to look as if they are reporting on nothing but a dispute among scientists that any up-to-date science teacher had better include in his or her teaching—or a great scientific revolution will leave the poor students behind.

Hammering the Wedge

Though the Wedge Strategy is no longer posted on the website of the Discovery Institute, its recommendations are clearly being followed. For example, the strategy details a simultaneous assault on state boards of education and on the print and broadcast media, which the Discovery Institute is carrying out. In some state battles, these Intelligent Design folks have been found out, and their efforts have been temporarily thwarted. But their tactics are sophisticated, and they understand that all publicity is good and that no defeat is real. They are more than willing to back off—even to cease advocating for the inclusion of ID— and just make sure that all science teachers are required to portray evolution as a "theory in crisis." The strategy is to move, relentlessly, from standards battles, to curriculum writing, to textbook adoption, and back again—doing whatever it takes to undermine the central position of evolution in biology.[14]

These people have money, political sophistication, experience, patience, and a wonderful user-friendly website.[15] Their carefully orchestrated campaign is designed to leave the science establishment looking close-minded, as if it is attempting to hide some dirty linen. How likely is it, after all, that the public will consult the current scientific literature or contact major scientific organizations, which would inform them that evolution is alive and well— indeed, central to virtually all biology and medicine—and not in any crisis?

In 2002, during the flap that ID advocates created surrounding the revision of the Ohio state science standards, redefining science to include God was proposed to the Ohio legislature, so that the legislature would then be able to get behind a new set of standards that would, naturally, include Intelligent Design. Imagine a state legislature defining science! Imagine a state legislature mandating the inclusion of religious content in science classes![16] Behind the elaborate ID façade, this effort was simply an attempt to bring a religious orientation into the public schools via, of all places, the science classroom. And that was just a step in the overall plan to put the U.S. on a course toward the theocracy envisioned in the Wedge Strategy.

Back to the Classroom

Intelligent Design was very much alive and well in Darwin's day, though it was then known as "natural theology." But science—through Darwin, Alfred Russel Wallace, and others—discovered a naturalistic theory by which to work, evolution by natural selection (and other mechanisms discovered over time), and, ever since the Enlightenment, has pursued scientific research without reference to religion. Scientists, of course, may be religious people, but science itself is not a religious endeavor. Science says nothing against adopting the ID outlook as a personal philosophy, but that doesn't make ID science.[17]

Meanwhile, good science is hard to teach. A teacher needs a solid background in science, sufficient time, a measure of creativity, a supportive administration, decent equipment, and sound texts. Those were the very things that T. H. Huxley was arguing for in the late 19th century, as he tried to free British science education from control by the Church of England. And those are *still* the things that science teachers need to succeed in their work, not a stealth religious agenda resurrected from Huxley's time.

But the ID folks—especially those from the Discovery Institute—make headway almost everywhere they go, because not only students and parents but teachers themselves are so poorly educated about science in general and about religion, philosophy, the history of ideas, and evolution that they have no ready defenses against the attack. It sounds so good. The major proponents of ID have doctorates, possess great media savvy, and exhibit supreme confidence. What's an educator or concerned citizen to do? Here are a few possibilities.

1. *As usual, there's no substitute for being informed.* Regularly visit the Discovery Institute's website and follow the news updates posted on the website of the NCSE, an organization that has been dedicated for over 20 years to helping teachers, administrators, school districts, and communities deal intelligently, humanely, and effectively with assaults on the teaching of evolution.[18] View the videos supported and inspired by the Discovery Institute, Icons of Evolution and Unlocking the Mystery of Life, preferably before they are shown in your area. Chances are that they are already in heavy demand at your local library, and several public broadcast stations have shown them around the country. They are excellent propaganda pieces, made up to look like NOVA-style science videos. Read the detailed critiques of these videos available through the NCSE journal and website.[19] Read an account of the history of Intelligent Design and of the Discovery Institute. Barbara Forrest's summary article is the quickest way to learn important details, and if you want more background, you can find a gold mine in *Creationism's Trojan Horse*, which she co-authored with Paul Gross.[20]

2. *Consider some ideas to improve the teaching of evolution in your school(s).* Make no mistake about it, the ID movement and the Discovery Institute, in particular, will seize the initiative wherever possible. To prevent being always in a posture of reaction and defense, you'll need to do the best job possible of teaching real evolutionary science.[21]

3. *Learn more about religions, history, and the humanities in general, and make use of that knowledge.* One of the most significant

opportunities to increase understanding of this issue is to be found in the humanities. Most students are woefully ignorant of the histories of the world's great religions, let alone the smaller ones. This makes meaningful discussions of the differences between scientific and religious thought next to impossible. Consider the example of the Scopes Trial. The fundamentalist movement is highly significant in American history and politics, and understanding its historical context helps to show how evolutionary biology, an activity of science, came to be such a target of fundamentalist ire. The "Trial of the Century" in little Dayton, Tennessee, makes all kinds of sense when the economics, politics, and Chamber of Commerce mentality of rural Tennessee are known. And William Jennings Bryan's role also makes sense in light of the struggles of the fundamentalist movement to gain the initiative in the pulpits of America. Public school science classrooms and evolution were seized upon as an attention-getting target for this denominational skirmish.[22] The proper separation of church and state makes sense only if one is aware of the great variety of religions that exist today in our communities and have existed throughout the history of this country.

Oddly, if religion could be accorded a position of greater respect and importance in our humanities curricula, it could well be less threatening—even to fundamentalists—for students to learn in their science courses what scientists are up to. While scientists are undertaking all this evolution-based research, fundamentalists are clearly entitled to believe in a literal Biblical account. People should be strong in their faith. Meanwhile, they ought to learn what those modern biologists are doing, because it's exciting in its own right.

4. *Examine the teaching of evolution at the introductory level in colleges, especially as manifested in teacher preparation programs.* There needs to be better preparation at this level for all teachers, since this is likely to be the only background in the subject that they'll ever get. The genuine revolution in molecular biology that has taken place over the last four decades has squeezed aside such "whole organism" topics as evolution in many introductory college programs—to the delight of the anti-evolutionists.

5. *Check out the so-called Santorum Amendment.* This is believed to be a very big gun in the ID movement's arsenal, and it is easily portrayed as a federal mandate to "teach the controversy" and include Intelligent Design as a legitimate scientific theory. In reality, the "Santorum Amendment" is only some language tucked away in an obscure text that was part of the discussions during debate on the No Child Left Behind Act. Besides being emphatically ambiguous, it never became law.[23]

6. *Prepare to be challenged if any standards writing or statewide curriculum development is about to go on.* The Discovery Institute is on the lookout for all such activity, and some of their "Fellows" are likely to show up. Consult the NCSE for local resources to help in the battle as soon as you know that any aspect of science teaching will be on the table.

An American Education

In the end, shouldn't it to be possible for fundamentalists, mainstream believers, agnostics, and atheists to have a rich understanding of, let us say, Islam, Buddhism, or any religion? It is possible to understand a great deal about these religions without adopting their belief systems. Likewise, both believers and nonbelievers could have a rich understanding of what evolutionary researchers are up to. They can understand the processes and findings of the sciences, and they need not abandon their religious or philosophical positions. They could learn that many religions promote the notion that God is an active Designer, but that many others don't. They could learn that science is silent on the subject of God.

Where I teach, the Intelligent Design movement, as a 21st-century echo of the natural theology of the mid-19th century, adds one more interesting facet to our discussions of the cultural context in which the science of evolution continues to develop.[24] But across the country, in the battles on the revision of state standards, in curriculum writing, and in textbook adoptions, Intelligent Design, especially as promoted by the Discovery Institute of Seattle, is causing great confusion. Those who care must not stand idly by. It is time for science educators and their colleagues in the humanities and in religious education to join with administrators and get into the discussions and on the appropriate committees.

And if readers who do not teach biology have gotten this far, sit back and think about the implications if the Wedge Strategy should succeed. What if science is redefined to make consistent reference to the supernatural? What if the "Intelligent Designer" becomes central to the biology curriculum in the lab down the hall? If this Designer could fabricate the basal complex of a bacterial flagellum, one of the ID supporters' favorite images, it would seem a trivial exercise for the Designer to influence the outcome of a war or a political campaign. If we apply ID to human history, will we not find that some societies are obviously chosen by the Designer over others because of their "correct" beliefs? And to ensure continuing favor with the Designer, will we not have to institute public displays of understanding so that the Designer will know that we're ready to work with Him? Her? It? A morning rendition of the Pledge of Allegiance will seem quaint and trivial compared to the dedication of public schools to the work of following the Designer's design.

References

1. John Hedley Brooke, *Science and Religion: Some Historical Perspectives* (Cambridge: Cambridge University Press, 1991).

2. Adrian Desmond, *Huxley: From Devil's Disciple to Evolution's High Priest* (Reading, Mass.: Perseus Books, 1997); Adrian Desmond and James Moore, *Darwin* (New York: Norton, 1991); and William Irvine, *Apes, Angels, and Victorians* (New York: Time, Inc., 1963).

3. Edward J. Larson, *Trial and Error: The American Controversy over Creation and Evolution* (Oxford: Oxford University Press, 2003); and Dorothy Nelkin,

The Creation Controversy: Science or Scripture in the Schools (Boston: Beacon Press, 1982).

4. *BSCS Biology: A Molecular Approach*, 8th ed. (Columbus, Ohio: Glencoe/McGrawHill, 2001); *BSCS Biology: An Ecological Approach*, 9th ed. (Dubuque, Ia.: Biological Sciences Curriculum Study, Kendall/Hunt, 2002); Ken Miller and Joe Levine, *Biology* (Old Tappan, N.J.: Prentice-Hall, 2004); and George B. Johnson, *The Living World* (New York: McGraw-Hill, 2003).

5. Robert T. Pennock, ed., *Intelligent Design: Creationism and Its Critics* (Cambridge, Mass.: MIT Press, 2001).

6. *Icons of Evolution: Dismantling the Myths* (Colorado Springs, Colo.: Focus on the Family Films, 2002).

7. Barbara Forrest and Paul R. Gross, *Creationism's Trojan Horse: The Wedge of Intelligent Design* (London: Oxford University Press, 2003).

8. Stephen C. Meyer, "The Origin of Biological Information and the Higher Taxonomic Categories," *Proceedings of the Biological Society of Washington*, vol. 117, 2004, pp. 213–39. . . .

9. Michael J. Behe, *Darwin's Black Box: The Biochemical Challenge to Evolution* (New York: Free Press, 1996); William A. Dembski, *No Free Lunch: Why Specified Complexity Cannot Be Purchased Without Intelligence* (Lanham, Md.: Rowman & Littlefield, 2002); and John Angus Campbell and Stephen C. Meyer, eds., *Darwinism, Design, and Public Education* (East Lansing: Michigan State University Press, 2003).

10. Barbara Forrest, "The Wedge at Work: How Intelligent Design Creationism Is Wedging Its Way into the Cultural and Academic Mainstream," in Pennock, pp. 5–53.

11. Phillip E. Johnson, *The Wedge of Truth: Splitting the Foundations of Naturalism* (Downers Grove, Ill.: InterVarsity Press, 2000).

12. Glenn Branch, "Evolving Banners at the Discovery Institute," *Reports of the National Center for Science Education*, 12 September 2002. . . . Since this article was written, the layout and logo of the institute have changed again, and the Wedge Strategy is once more available on the website. The introductory article "The Wedge Document: So What?" asserts that the Wedge Strategy does not represent some behind-the-scenes conspiracy. But whether or not the effort is conspiratorial has little to do with whether Intelligent Design qualifies as science.

13. Jonathan Wells, "Darwinism: Why I Went for a Second Ph.D.,". . . .

14. Mark Terry and Scott Linneman, "Watching the Wedge: How the Discovery Institute Seeks to Change the Teaching of Science," *Washington State Science Teachers' Journal*, March 2003, pp. 12–15.

15. . . . .

16. Forrest and Gross, pp. 231–39.

17. Kenneth R. Miller, *Finding Darwin's God: A Scientist's Search for Common Ground Between God and Evolution* (New York: HarperCollins, 1999); and Michael Ruse, *Darwin and Design: Does Evolution Have a Purpose?* (Cambridge, Mass.: Harvard University Press, 2003).

18. . . . .

19. Illustra Media, *Unlocking the Mystery of Life: The Case for Intelligent Design* (Colorado Springs: Focus on the Family Films, 2002); . . . See also *Icons of Evolution*; and Mark Terry, "Icons of Deception," *Reports of the National Center for Science Education* (in press, 2004).

20. Forrest, op. cit.; and Forrest and Gross, op. cit.

21. See, for example, Paul Farber, "Teaching Evolution and the Nature of Science," *American Biology Teacher*, May 2003, pp. 347–54; Brian J. Alters and Sandra M. Alters, *Defending Evolution in the Classroom* (Sudbury, Mass.: Jones and Bartlett, 2001); Mark Terry, "Art and Evolution," *Science Teacher*, 2005, in press. . . .

22. Edward Larson, *Summer for the Gods: The Scopes Trial and America's Continuing Debate over Science and Religion* (New York: Basic Books, 1997).

23. Glenn Branch, "Farewell to the Santorum Amendment," *Reports of the National Center for Science Education*, vol. 22, nos. 1–2, 2002, pp. 12–14. . . .

24. Robert T. Pennock, *Tower of Babel: The Evidence Against the New Creationism* (Cambridge, Mass.: MIT Press, 1999); and Ruse, op. cit.

Dan Peterson

 **NO**

The Little Engine That Could . . . Undo Darwinism

Imagine a nanotechnology machine far beyond the state of the art: a micro-miniaturized rotary motor and propeller system that drives a tiny vessel through liquid. The engine and drive mechanism are composed of 40 parts, including a rotor, stator, driveshaft, bushings, universal joint, and flexible propeller. The engine is powered by a flow of ions, can rotate at up to 100,000 rpm (ten times faster than a NASCAR racing engine), and can reverse direction in a quarter of a rotation. The system comes with an automatic feedback control mechanism. The engine itself is about 1/100,000th of an inch wide—far smaller than can be seen by the human eye.

Most of us would be pleasantly surprised to learn that some genius had designed such an engineering triumph. What might come as a greater surprise is that there is a dominant faction in the scientific community that is prepared to defend, at all costs, the assertion that this marvelous device could not possibly have been designed, must have been produced blindly by unintelligent material forces, and only gives the appearance—we said *appearance!*—of being designed.

As you may have guessed, these astonishingly complex, tiny, and efficient engines exist. Millions of them exist inside you, in fact. They are true rotary motors that drive the "bacterial flagellum," a whip-like propulsion device for certain bacteria, including the famous *E. coli* that lives in your digestive system.

Oddly enough, this intricate high-speed motor is at the center of a controversy that has been kindling in scientific circles for a decade, and is now igniting hot debate outside those circles. That's because, even more oddly, the implications of whether this little engine was designed are incalculably profound. They involve questions such as: What constitutes science? Did living things "just happen" by natural causes or were they designed by an intelligence? And what follows from those two competing alternatives—in morality, education, culture, and science itself?

The controversy stems from the work of a growing cadre of scientists, mathematicians, and scholars in the field of "intelligent design," or ID for short. In the life sciences, the proponents of intelligent design are challenging the reigning orthodoxy that life developed entirely by the blind operation of natural forces. Their arguments are essentially of two kinds.

From *The American Spectator,* vol. 38, no. 5, June 2005, pp. 34–38, 42–43. Copyright © 2005 by American Spectator, LLC. Reprinted by permission.

First, building on recent discoveries in cell biology, molecular genetics, and other disciplines, they contend that life, and the complex processes by which cells do their work, cannot have been produced by that combination of chance and necessity known as Darwinian evolution. Second, using the analytical techniques of information theory, they contend that the kind of information embodied in things that are designed can only be produced by an intelligent agent, not by undirected material causes. Design, they say, is empirically detectable—and it is detectable, in fact, in living things. (Some of the ID proponents have demonstrated that the physical laws of the universe also show overwhelming evidence of being designed. For reasons of space rather than interest, I can only discuss here the work that ID is doing in the biological sciences.)

Of course, if the hypothesis that the universe and life are designed is true, the ready inference is that this designer has to be an incomprehensibly potent and awesome Intelligent Agent. A lot of influential people in science, the media, the schools, and other institutions don't much like the notion of the Big Intelligent Agent. Hence the controversy over ID, and the slanted treatment of it that is often seen.

Among certain sectors of the media, for example, it's an article of faith that those who believe in God, or advocate principles supporting that belief, are just a mob of Bible-thumping, knuckle-dragging, Scripture-spouting, hellfire and brimstone-preaching, rightwing, gun-toting, bigoted, homophobic, moralistic, paternalistic, polyester-wearing, mascara-smeared, false-eyelashed, SUV-driving, Wal-Mart shopping, big hair, big gut, fat butt, holy-rolling, snake-handling, Limbaugh-listening, Bambi-shooting, trailer-park-dwelling, uneducated, ignorant, backwater, hayseed, hick, inbred, pinhead rubes—mostly from the South, or places no better than the South—who voted for Bush.

So, many of the news stories refer to intelligent design theory as "creationism" and ignore the science behind it. They imply that ID is just religion in disguise: "Creationism in a cheap tuxedo," as one headline put it. Let's look at the science, then, because the truth about the intelligent design school could not be more different from those stereotypes. The proponents of ID base their arguments on biological and physical data generally accepted in science. They use the same kinds of analytical methods and mathematical tools as other scientists. The ID theorists do not reason from religious premises. Neither do they attempt to prove the truth of Scripture, or of any particular religious views. As a rule, they do not contest that life on Earth is billions of years old, or that evolution has occurred in the sense of "change over time" in biological forms.

What they do contest is that undirected material causes alone can explain life's origin and development. Instead, they argue that design is the best *scientific* explanation for the stunning complexity of the cellular processes that underlie life, and for the evidence of how life actually developed. That conclusion, if true, certainly has religious implications. But, as will become evident, the reasoning and methods used by the ID proponents are fact-based and scientific.

Before getting to the science, though, let's take a moment to see who the ID proponents are. Many of the prominent ID theorists are affiliated with the Center for Science and Culture (CSC) at the Seattle-based Discovery Institute (most of them hold day jobs, too). Some background on the individuals whose work is mentioned in this article may be helpful in deciding if the ID movement is really just a confederacy of dunces allied against the enlightened.

The most prolific of the ID proponents is William Dembski. A bespectacled, youthful-looking man, Dembski has a Ph.D. in mathematics from the University of Chicago, a Ph.D. in philosophy from the University of Illinois, and a Master of Divinity from Princeton Theological Seminary. He has done postdoctoral work in mathematics at MIT, in physics at the University of Chicago, and in computer science at Princeton, as well as being a National Science Foundation doctoral and postdoctoral fellow. He is the leading thinker in applying information theory in the field of intelligent design, and has written or edited ten books.

Michael Behe, who popularized the flagellar motor as an example of intelligent design, is a professor of biochemistry at Lehigh University in Pennsylvania, with more than 35 articles in refereed scientific journals (and many popular works) to his credit. Stephen Meyer, director of the Discovery Institute's CSC, has undergraduate degrees in physics and geology, and a Ph.D. in the history and philosophy of science from Cambridge University in England for his dissertation on the history of origin of life biology.

Jonathan Wells holds a Ph.D. in molecular and cell biology from the University of California at Berkeley, and another Ph.D. in religious studies from Yale University. He got double 800s on his SATs. Phillip Johnson, whose advocacy will be mentioned in a moment, is professor of law at the University of California-Berkeley. He graduated first in his law school class at the University of Chicago Law School, clerked for Chief Justice Earl Warren on the United States Supreme Court, and published scores of articles and several books during his career.

Highly educated journalists may be forgiven for looking down their noses at hopeless dummies like these. To the rest of us, their credentials may suggest that they could be fairly intelligent men, whose arguments may be worth considering. In fact, they and others like them have put the Darwinist establishment on the defensive in the battle of ideas.

There is good reason for that, when you think about it. Throughout most of the history of Western civilization, the fact that life was designed by God was beyond any serious dispute. Genesis told the story of how God created the heavens, earth, and life. The complexity, beauty, and order we see in life and the cosmos was confirming evidence of his hand at work, and a reflection of his glory. There was no other plausible, competing explanation of how life could be so perfectly designed to fit the environment, and how the environment could be so perfect for life. But in the mid-19th century, Darwin changed all that.

Darwin posited that a purely materialist account, dispensing with God, could explain the origin of species. His central mechanism was natural selection acting on random variation. When variations in living things naturally occurred by chance, those variations that were harmful to the organism's survival would be ruthlessly weeded out. Variations that were conducive to survival or reproduction, however, would gradually come to prevail. The organisms that possessed them would, over time, outcompete those with less adaptive characteristics. This purely naturalistic mechanism—wholly devoid of any foresight, design, or purpose—could, in Darwin's view, explain the development of life and why different species were apparently so well designed for their environment.

Darwin thus provided a "creation story" for a naturalistic or materialistic view of the world. Richard Dawkins—Oxford zoologist, militant atheist, and leading exponent of materialistic Darwinism—has declared that "although atheism might have been *logically* tenable before Darwin, Darwin made it possible to be an intellectually fulfilled atheist." But if atheistic materialism is true, life on Earth by definition cannot have been designed by an intelligence (except perhaps by space aliens, whose own design would remain unexplained). Dawkins therefore asserts that "biology is the study of complicated things that give the *appearance* of having been designed for a purpose." He refers to living beings as "designoid" objects. "Designoid objects look designed," Dawkins contends, "so much so that some people—probably, alas, most people—think they are designed. These people are wrong."

Dawkins' view that we, and all life forms, are only apparently designed has been the emphatically enforced orthodoxy among biologists since not long after Darwin. But, as it turns out, increasing knowledge over the past few decades about the immensely complicated processes and structures within the cell, the operation of DNA, the fossil record of the development of species, and other pertinent evidence has not confirmed Darwinism, but radically undermined it.

Enter the intelligent design theorists. Severe difficulties with the Darwinian theory were becoming increasingly obvious by the 1980s, and some scientists began to state openly that design should be considered as an alternative theory. Then in 1991 Phillip Johnson (the Berkeley law professor mentioned above) published a powerful critique of Darwinism entitled *Darwin on Trial*. In that volume Johnson marshaled the extensive scientific evidence against Darwinism. More importantly, he showed that Darwinism has essentially become a faith in naturalism that is immune to refutation by any set of facts. Arguments or conclusions that are not Darwinian are automatically ruled out of bounds by the scientific establishment. Within the Darwinian fold, wild conjectures, surmises unsupported by facts, and arguments lacking in explanatory power are accepted as legitimate, so long as they permit a "naturalistic" explanation.

Johnson also had the temerity to point out that many of the "classic" examples of Darwinian evolution, including those often presented in textbooks, were either distorted or outright fakes. ID proponent Jonathan Wells later took up this theme in his book *Icons of Evolution*. (See also the article by Wells, "Survival of the Fakest," *TAS*, December 2000/January 2001.) Often the Darwinists knew of these falsifications, but managed to forgive themselves for the good of their mutual cause. Johnson and Wells didn't cut them any slack.

The Darwinists were outraged by Johnson, but there was worse to come. In 1996, Michael Behe (the Lehigh biochemistry professor) published a blockbuster called *Darwin's Black Box*. In that book, he explored the mind-boggling complexity of biochemical activities within the body and the cell. Some complex structures or processes, known as *cumulatively complex*, may continue to function if some part is taken away. An army, for example, is highly complex, but it can lose soldiers, vehicles, or even whole units, and still be able to perform its function of fighting, although progressively less well. But Behe demonstrated that the molecular machines existing inside cells, and other biological processes, are sometimes *irreducibly complex*. An irreducibly complex machine or process is one that has multiple parts, and will not function if any one of the fundamental parts is taken way. All of the parts must be there, all at once, for any function to occur.

Behe's most famous example is the bacterial flagellum described above. If you take away the driveshaft from the flagellar motor, you do not end up with a motor that functions less well. You have a motor that does not function at all. All of the essential parts must be there, all at once, for the motor to perform its function of propelling the bacterium through liquid.

Why is that important? Because that is precisely what Darwinian evolution cannot accomplish. Darwinian evolution is by definition "blind." It cannot plan ahead and create parts that might be useful to assemble a biological machine in the future. For the machine to be assembled, all or nearly all the parts must already be there and be performing a function. Why must they already be performing a function? Because if a part does not confer a real, present advantage for the organism's survival or reproduction, Darwinian natural selection will not preserve the gene responsible for that part. In fact, according to Darwinian theory, that gene will actually be selected *against*. An organism that expends resources on building a part that is useless handicaps itself compared to other organisms that are not wasting resources, and will tend to get outcompeted.

Darwin himself said that "if it could be demonstrated that any complex organ existed which could not possibly have been formed by numerous, successive, slight modifications, my theory would absolutely break down." But an irreducibly complex system cannot evolve in that way, according to Behe. By definition, if an irreducibly complex system were missing just one of its essential parts, it would not function. How or why, then, would blind, purposeless evolution have created the other parts that had no prior function, just waiting for the final part to fall into place? Answer: it wouldn't. Irreducibly complex systems, which do not function if any core part is missing, can only be created by an intelligent designer who plans ahead. . . .

But why should scientists reject design as a matter of principle? And why should they do so when naturalistic explanations are lacking or deeply flawed, and the evidence of design is becoming more and more compelling?

That's the question being asked by the intelligent design theorists. William Dembski, whom we met above (the bespectacled guy with the bookcase full of advanced diplomas), has developed powerful arguments based on mathematics and information theory to show that design can be detected scientifically. He also demonstrates that as a matter of principle blind necessity—that is, the laws of nature—cannot produce design of the kind life exhibits. Neither can that kind of design be produced by the interaction of chance and necessity—that is, by the Darwinian principle of random variation filtered through the laws of nature. Only intelligence can produce what Dembski refers to as "complex specified information," and life exhibits complex specified information (or "specified complexity") to an extraordinary degree. . . .

How could this vast amount of complex specified information come about without intelligence? The problem for Darwinian theory is particularly acute with respect to the origins of life. But even after life gets underway, random variation and natural selection can't conceivably generate the magnitude of information necessary, the ID theorists argue.

To take just one example, a well-known (and unsolved) problem for Darwinism is the Cambrian Explosion. As noted by Stephen Meyer in the book *Debating Design*, this event might be better called the Cambrian Information Explosion. For the first three billion years of life on Earth, only single-celled organisms such as bacteria and bluegreen algae existed. Then, approximately 570 million years ago, the first multi-cellular organisms, such as sponges, began to appear in the fossil record. About 40 million years later, an astonishing explosion of life took place. Within a narrow window of about 5 million years, "at least nineteen and perhaps as many as 35 phyla (of 40 total phyla) made their first appearance on Earth. . . ." Meyer reminds us that "phyla constitute the highest categories in the animal kingdom, with each phylum exhibiting unique architecture, blueprint, or structural body plan." These high order, basic body plans include "mollusks (squids and shellfish), arthropods (crustaceans, insects, and trilobites), and chordates, the phylum to which all vertebrates belong."

These new, fundamental body plans appeared all at once, and without the expected Darwinian intermediate forms. The amount of new biological information necessary to create these abruptly emerging body plans is staggering. Meyer states that sponges such as those that existed right before the Cambrian explosion probably required about five basic cell types. More complex animals like the arthropods would have required 50 basic cell types. These in turn are dependent on new and different proteins. Citing recent research, he notes that the more complex kinds of single cell organisms might require about a million DNA base pairs to manufacture the necessary proteins. But a complex, multicellular organism such as an arthropod would require "orders of magnitude" more coding instructions. The modern fruit fly is an arthropod, and it has about 120 million base pairs. The odds that this quantity of information could be generated by random variation filtered through natural selection quickly surpass the "universal probability bound." It's not going to happen. Not even once, in the entire universe, in its whole history.

But it did happen. The preceding paragraph of this article also happened, even though the odds of it being produced by chance also far exceed the universal probability bound. That's because it's not difficult for an intelligence to produce complex specified information that would otherwise be vanishingly improbable. That's also why the ID theorists contend that only an intelligence could possibly produce the vast and detailed information base that is required for life in all its amazing complexity and variety.

This is not an "argument from ignorance" or for a "God of the gaps." The ID theorists are not saying "We don't know how something occurred, therefore God must have done it." Rather, it is an "inference to the best explanation." Naturalistic explanations have turned out to be wholly insufficient, in principle and in practice, to explain the specified complexity that characterizes life at the cellular and molecular level. We know that intelligent agents can generate complex specified information. As a matter of both experience and theory, it appears that complex specified information can *only* be generated by intelligence. So when we find living organisms that exhibit specified complexity, the best explanation is that the information was produced by an intelligent agent, and that the organism was, in fact, designed.

How has the scientific establishment reacted to the ID challenge? Variously. Some scientists have reconsidered their views, and become sympathetic to intelligent design. Others have engaged the ID theorists in debate, ranging in character from cordial to caustic.

Richard Dawkins refuses to debate Dembski, and a couple of years ago published an unfinished letter to the late Stephen Jay Gould, the renowned evolutionist from Harvard. In that letter, Dawkins proposed that they not debate "latter day creationists" who only want to share a platform with a "real scientist" (such as, presumably, himself). Dawkins is a true believer in the Darwinian faith, who characterizes his role as "Advocate for Disinterested Truth." He refers to religion as a "virus of the mind," and explicitly affirms that he is both "contemptuous" and "hostile" towards it. According to Dawkins, "It is absolutely safe to say that, if you meet somebody who claims not to believe in evolution, that person is ignorant, stupid or insane (or wicked, but I'd rather not consider that)."

It is plain to see that there is more than a disagreement over scientific techniques or reasoning here. Dawkins' commitment to materialism and atheism is a philosophical position, not a scientific one. Those who challenge materialism's creation story must be anathematized. Unfortunately, the American Association for the Advancement of Science has taken a similar position. In a board resolution adopted in 2002, that organization charges the "so-called" ID movement with, among other things, claiming "that contemporary evolutionary theory is incapable of explaining the origin of the diversity of living organisms." In other words, ID proponents are charged not merely with being wrong, but with committing heresy against contemporary evolutionary theory."

Richard M. von Sternberg holds two Ph.D.s in the area of evolutionary biology, and is not himself an advocate of intelligent design. When serving as the managing editor of the *Proceedings of the Biological Society of Washington*, he allowed a scholarly paper by the Discovery Institute's Stephen Meyer to be published in that journal. Although he had followed standard peer review procedures, the full brunt of the Darwinian establishment's wrath was brought down on him. . . . Dembski summarizes the strident reaction to ID by parts of the scientific community (and presents strategies for handling it) in "Dealing with the Backlash against Intelligent Design,". . .

The controversy has for several years been spilling into the public schools. The ID proponents do not contend that their theory ought to be taught in the public schools. All they claim is that students should be made aware that there is a controversy here. But the supporters of Darwinism are adamant. Only the Darwinian orthodoxy can be taught, and no theory critical of it can even be mentioned.

All of this suggests that what is at stake here are two competing philosophical visions: one that automatically rules out the possibility of God (and therefore a designer) as a matter of principle, and one that affirms God, or is at least willing to entertain the possibility of a designer. That division, to a great extent, underlies the "culture wars" and much else in our public life.

It is precisely because intelligent design relies upon scientific methods and evidence that it is regarded by the materialists as so extraordinarily dangerous. It threatens to allow religion to escape from the ghetto assigned to it by the dominant 19th- and 20th-century materialism. It actually claims to be true, on the same level that all science claims to be true.

If intelligent design makes good its claims, it might change the definition of science. It might change the assumptions on which we conduct our public discourse and education. It might change conceptions about whether there is an objective moral order. It might help open minds that would otherwise be closed.

It might *be* true, and be able to prove it.

POSTSCRIPT

Is "Intelligent Design" a Threat to the Curriculum?

According to Sam Harris in *The End of Faith: Religion, Terror, and the Future of Reason* (2004), "Our world is fast succumbing to the activities of men and women who would stake the future of our species on beliefs that should not survive an elementary school education. That so many of us are still dying on account of ancient myths is as bewildering as it is horrible and our own attachment to these myths, whether moderate or extreme, has kept us silent in the face of developments that could ultimately destroy us." These strong words are aimed at religious extremism as a threat to reason and could, by some, be applied to some aspects of the issue discussed here. For a more conciliatory position on the educational implications of this broader concern, see Columbia University professor Kent Greenawalt's 2005 book *Does God Belong in Public Schools?*, and for litigation background, see Martha M. McCarthy's "The Legal Evolution of Intelligent Design," *Educational Horizons* (Spring 2006). Another good review of the problem can be found in Vicki D. Johnson's "A Contemporary Controversy in American Education: Including Intelligent Design in the Science Curriculum," *Kappa Delta Pi Record* (Spring 2006).

A wealth of books has appeared in recent years that exemplify the depth of the controversy. Among the best are *Darwinism, Design, and Public Education* (2003), edited by John Angus Campbell and Stephen C. Meyer; Phillip E. Johnson's *The Wedge of Truth: Splitting the Foundations of Naturalism* (2000); *Darwin and Design: Does Evolution Have a Purpose?* (2003) by Michael Ruse; *Intelligent Design: Creationism and Its Critics* (2001), edited by Robert T. Pennock; *Creationism's Trojan Horse: The Wedge of Intelligent Design* (2003) by Barbara Forrest and Paul R. Gross; and *The Ancestor's Tale: A Pilgrimage to the Dawn of Evolution* (2004) by Richard Dawkins.

Some journal articles to add fuel to the fire are Donald K. Sharpes and Mary M. Peramas, "Accepting Evolution or Discarding Science," *Kappa Delta Pi Record* (Summer 2006); Gary K. Clabaugh, "Teaching Intelligent Design and the 'Bush Doctrine'," *Educational Horizons* (Spring 2006); Robert George Sprackland, "Teaching About Origins: A Scientist Explains Why 'Intelligent Design' Isn't Science," *American School Board Journal* (November 2005); and Chris Mooney, "Inferior Design," *The American Prospect* (September 2005).

ISSUE 23

Is There a Crisis in the Education of Boys?

YES: Michael Gurian and Kathy Stevens, from "With Boys and Girls in Mind," *Educational Leadership* (November 2004)

NO: Sara Mead, from "The Truth About Boys and Girls," An Education Sector Report (June 2006)

ISSUE SUMMARY

YES: Michael Gurian and Kathy Stevens, researchers in gender differences and brain-based learning at the Gurian Institute, contend that our schools, structurally and functionally, do not fulfill gender-specific needs and that this is particularly harmful to boys.

NO: Sara Mead, a senior policy analyst at Education Sector in Washington, D.C., assembles long-term data from the federally sponsored National Assessment of Educational Progress to show that the "crisis" emphasis is unwarranted and detracts from broader social justice issues.

The importance of gender in the process of education has permeated professional discourse for quite a few years. Stereotyping, which often begins in the home and is heavily reinforced in the commercial realm (pink for girls, blue for boys; dolls for girls, guns for boys), typically continues during the years of schooling. Boys and girls have been steeredtoward certain areas of the curriculum and have been prompted to follow certain career paths. Individual teachers are often guilty of gender bias and often fail to see beyond the stereotypes and biases to recognize their effects on the aspirations and achievements of the learner.

In the early 1990s, the spotlight was clearly on the female gender. The 1992 report issued by the American Association of University Women (AAUW), *How Schools Shortchange Girls,* called for reforms and legislative action to reverse prevailing patterns of discrimination and to bolster the self-esteem of girls and increase the breadth and depth of their vocational and professional aspirations. Many of the findings of the AAUW report were given support in research-based books such as Myra and David Sadkers' *Failing at*

Fairness: How America's Schools Cheat Girls and Judy Mann's *The Difference: Growing up Female in America*. The Sadkers' research revealed vastly different gender expectations on the part of teachers, leading to great differences in the way they interact with male and female students, with most of the negative effects being felt by girls.

There was a backlash against this campaign by those who saw it as part of the wider feminist movement and who questioned the need for more gender equity legislation. Diane Ravitch, then U.S. assistant secretary of education, contended that great strides had already been made in the previous quarter-century to redress historical patterns of discrimination that squelched female opportunity. A further turn was taken in 2000 by Christina Hoff Sommers in her book *The War against Boys: How Misguided Feminism Is Harming Our Young Men*. In that work, she declared that the research supporting claims of male privilege is riddled with errors, that in actuality boys are on the weak side of the education gender gap. The typical boy, Sommers claimed, is behind the typical girl in reading and writing, is less committed to school, and is less likely to go to college.

Greater specificity in the concern about boys was brought to public and professional attention by Michael Gurian and fellow brain researchers at the Gurian Institute who published their findings in *The Wonder of Boys, Boys and Girls Learn Differently,* and *The Minds of Boys*. In his article "Learning and Gender," *American School Board Journal* (October 2006), Gurian claims that boys make up about 90 percent of discipline referrals, 70 percent of learning disabled children, and at least 66 percent of children on behavioral medication. They receive two-thirds of the Ds and Fs, and on average are a year-and-a-half behind girls in literacy skills. Earlier in 2006, *Newsweek* featured a cover story on "The Boy Crisis," claiming that at every level of schooling, they are falling behind. The Gurian Institute has enrolled some 15,000 educators in its seminars on brain-based strategies, and a representative of the Gates Foundation has declared that "helping underperforming boys has become part of our core mission." Not everyone has jumped on the bandwagon, however. In "The Myth of 'The Boy Crisis'" in *The Washington Post* (April 9, 2006), Caryl Rivers and Rosalind Chait Barnett take the position that "obsessing about a boy crisis or thinking that American teachers are waging a war on boys" is not helpful.

In the following articles, Michael Gurian and Kathy Stevens present their case for "boy-friendly" classrooms, while Sara Mead counters with evidence that gender is not the crucial factor.

YES

**Michael Gurian and
Kathy Stevens**

With Boys and Girls in Mind

Something is awry in the way our culture handles the education needs of boys and girls. A smart 11-year-old boy gets low grades in school, fidgets and drifts off in class, and doesn't do his homework. A girl in middle school only uses the computer to instant-message her friends; when it comes to mastering more essential computer skills, she defers to the boys in the class.

Is contemporary education maliciously set against either males or females? We don't think so. But structurally and functionally, our schools fail to recognize and fulfill gender-specific needs. As one teacher wrote,

> For years I sensed that the girls and boys in my classrooms learn in gender-specific ways, but I didn't know enough to help each student reach full potential. I was trained in the idea that each student is an individual. But when I saw the PET scans of boys' and girls' brains, I saw how differently those brains are set up to learn. This gave me the missing component. I trained in male/female brain differences and was able to teach each individual child. Now, looking back, I'm amazed that teachers were never taught the differences between how girls and boys learn.

New positron emission tomography (PET) and MRI technologies enable us to look inside the brains of boys and girls, where we find structural and functional differences that profoundly affect human learning. These gender differences in the brain are corroborated in males and females throughout the world and do not differ significantly across cultures.

It's true that culture affects gender role, gender costume, and gender nuances—in Italy, for example, men cry more than they do in England—but role, costume, and nuance only affect some aspects of the learning brain of a child. New brain imaging technologies confirm that genetically templated brain patterning by gender plays a far larger role than we realized. Research into gender and education reveals a mismatch between many of our boys' and girls' learning brains and the institutions empowered to teach our children.

We will briefly explore some of the differences, because recognizing these differences can help us find solutions to many of the challenges that we experience in the classroom. Of course, generalized gender differences may not apply in every case.

From *Educational Leadership* by Michael Gurian and Kathy Stevens, pp. 21–26. Copyright © 2004 by Association for Supervision & Curriculum Development. Reprinted by permission. The Association for Supervision and Curriculum Development is a worldwide community of educators advocating sound policies and sharing best practices to achieve the success of each learner. To learn more, visit ASCD at www.ascd.org

The Minds of Girls

The following are some of the characteristics of girls' brains:

- A girl's corpus callosum (the connecting bundle of tissues between hemispheres) is, on average, larger than a boy's—up to 25 percent larger by adolescence. This enables more "cross talk" between hemispheres in the female brain.
- Girls have, in general, stronger neural connectors in their temporal lobes than boys have. These connectors lead to more sensually detailed memory storage, better listening skills, and better discrimination among the various tones of voice. This leads, among other things, to greater use of detail in writing assignments.
- The hippocampus (another memory storage area in the brain) is larger in girls than in boys, increasing girls' learning advantage, especially in the language arts.
- Girls' prefrontal cortex is generally more active than boys' and develops at earlier ages. For this reason, girls tend to make fewer impulsive decisions than boys do. Further, girls have more serotonin in the bloodstream and the brain, which makes them biochemically less impulsive.
- Girls generally use more cortical areas of their brains for verbal and emotive functioning. Boys tend to use more cortical areas of the brain for spatial and mechanical functionisng (Moir & Jessel, 1989; Rich, 2000).

These "girl" brain qualities are the tip of the iceberg, yet they can immediately help teachers and parents understand why girls generally outperform boys in reading and writing from early childhood throughout life (Conlin, 2003). With more cortical areas devoted to verbal functioning, sensual memory, sitting still, listening, tonality, and mental cross talk, the complexities of reading and writing come easier, on the whole, to the female brain. In addition, the female brain experiences approximately 15 percent more blood flow, with this flow located in more centers of the brain at any given time (Marano, 2003). The female brain tends to drive itself toward stimulants—like reading and writing—that involve complex texture, tonality, and mental activity.

On the other hand, because so many cortical areas are used for verbal-emotive functioning, the female brain does not activate as many cortical areas as the male's does for abstract and physical-spatial functions, such as watching and manipulating objects that move through physical space and understanding abstract mechanical concepts (Moir & Jessel, 1989; Rich, 2000). This is one reason for many girls' discomfort with deep computer design language. Although some girls excel in these areas, more males than females gravitate toward physics, industrial engineering, and architecture. Children naturally gravitate toward activities that their brains experience as pleasurable—"pleasure" meaning in neural terms the richest personal stimulation. Girls and boys, within each neural web, tend to experience the richest personal stimulation somewhat differently.

The biological tendency toward female verbal-emotive functioning does not mean that girls or women should be left out of classes or careers that use spatial-mechanical skills. On the contrary: We raise these issues to call on our civilization to realize the differing natures of girls and boys and to teach each subject according to how the child's brain needs to learn it. On average, educators will need to provide girls with extra encouragement and gender-specific strategies to successfully engage them in spatial abstracts, including computer design.

The Minds of Boys

What, then, are some of the qualities that are generally more characteristic of boys' brains?

- Because boys' brains have more cortical areas dedicated to spatial-mechanical functioning, males use, on average, half the brain space that females use for verbal-emotive functioning. The cortical trend toward spatial-mechanical functioning makes many boys want to move objects through space, like balls, model airplanes, or just their arms and legs. Most boys, although not all of them, will experience words and feelings differently than girls do (Blum, 1997; Moir & Jessel, 1989).
- Boys not only have less serotonin than girls have, but they also have less oxytocin, the primary human bonding chemical. This makes it more likely that they will be physically impulsive and less likely that they will neurally combat their natural impulsiveness to sit still and empathically chat with a friend (Moir & Jessel, 1989; Taylor, 2002).
- Boys lateralize brain activity. Their brains not only operate with less blood flow than girls' brains, but they are also structured to compartmentalize learning. Thus, girls tend to multitask better than boys do, with fewer attention span problems and greater ability to make quick transitions between lessons (Havers, 1995).
- The male brain is set to renew, recharge, and reorient itself by entering what neurologists call a *rest state*. The boy in the back of the classroom whose eyes are drifting toward sleep has entered a neural rest state. It is predominantly boys who drift off without completing assignments, who stop taking notes and fall asleep during a lecture, or who tap pencils or otherwise fidget in hopes of keeping themselves awake and learning. Females tend to recharge and reorient neural focus without rest states. Thus, a girl can be bored with a lesson, but she will nonetheless keep her eyes open, take notes, and perform relatively well. This is especially true when the teacher uses more words to teach a lesson instead of being spatial and diagrammatic. The more words a teacher uses, the more likely boys are to "zone out," or go into rest state. The male brain is better suited for symbols, abstractions, diagrams, pictures, and objects moving through space than for the monotony of words (Gurian, 2001).

These typical "boy" qualities in the brain help illustrate why boys generally learn higher math and physics more easily than most girls do when those subjects are taught abstractly on the chalkboard; why more boys than girls play video games that involve physical movement and even physical destruction; and why more boys than girls tend to get in trouble for impulsiveness, shows of boredom, and fidgeting as well as for their more generalized inability to listen, fulfill assignments, and learn in the verbal-emotive world of the contemporary classroom.

Who's Failing?

For a number of decades, most of our cultural sensitivity to issues of gender and learning came from advocacy groups that pointed out ways in which girls struggled in school. When David and Myra Sadker teamed with the American Association of University Women in the early 1990s, they found that girls were not called on as much as boys were, especially in middle school; that girls generally lagged in math/science testing; that boys dominated athletics; and that girls suffered drops in self-esteem as they entered middle and high school (AAUW, 1992). In large part because of this advocacy, our culture is attending to the issues that girls face in education.

At the same time, most teachers, parents, and other professionals involved in education know that it is mainly our boys who underperform in school. Since 1981, when the U.S. Department of Education began keeping complete statistics, we have seen that boys lag behind girls in most categories. The 2000 National Assessment of Educational Progress finds boys one and one-half years behind girls in reading/writing (National Center for Education Statistics, 2000). Girls are now only negligibly behind boys in math and science, areas in which boys have historically outperformed girls (Conlin, 2003).

Our boys are now losing frightening ground in school, and we must come to terms with it—not in a way that robs girls, but in a way that sustains our civilization and is as powerful as the lobby we have created to help girls. The following statistics for the United States illustrate these concerns:

- Boys earn 70 percent of *D*s and *F*s and fewer than half of the *A*s.
- Boys account for two-thirds of learning disability diagnoses.
- Boys represent 90 percent of discipline referrals.
- Boys dominate such brain-related learning disorders as ADD/ADHD, with millions now medicated in schools.
- 80 percent of high school dropouts are male.
- Males make up fewer than 40 percent of college students (Gurian, 2001).

These statistics hold true around the world. The Organisation for Economic Co-operation and Development (OECD) recently released its three-year study of knowledge and skills of males and females in 35 industrialized countries (including the United States, Canada, the European countries, Australia, and Japan). Girls outperformed boys in every country. The statistics that brought the male scores down most significantly were their reading/writing scores.

We have nearly closed the math/ science gender gap in education for girls by using more verbal functioning—reading and written analysis—to teach such spatial-mechanical subjects as math, science, and computer science (Rubin, 2004; Sommers, 2000). We now need a new movement to alter classrooms to better suit boys' learning patterns if we are to deal with the gaps in grades, discipline, and reading/writing that threaten to close many boys out of college and out of success in life.

The Nature-Based Approach

In 1996, the Gurian Institute, an organization that administers training in child development, education, and male/female brain differences, coined the phrase *nature-based approach* to call attention to the importance of basing human attachment and education strategies on research-driven biological understanding of human learning. We argued that to broadly base education and other social processes on anything other than human nature was to set up both girls and boys for unnecessary failure. The institute became especially interested in nature-based approaches to education when PET scans and MRIs of boys and girls revealed brains that were trying to learn similar lessons but in widely different ways and with varying success depending on the teaching method used. It became apparent that if teachers were trained in the differences in learning styles between boys and girls, they could profoundly improve education for all students.

Between 1998 and 2000, a pilot program at the University of Missouri–Kansas City involving gender training in six school districts elicited significant results. One school involved in the training, Edison Elementary, had previously tested at the bottom of 18 district elementary schools. Following gender training, it tested in the top five slots, sometimes coming in first or second. Statewide, Edison outscored schools in every subject area, sometimes doubling and tripling the number of students in top achievement levels. Instead of the usual large number of students at the bottom end of achievement testing, Edison now had only two students requiring state-mandated retesting. The school also experienced a drastic reduction in discipline problems.

Statewide training in Alabama has resulted in improved performance for boys in both academic and behavioral areas. Beaumont Middle School in Lexington, Kentucky, trains its teachers in male/female brain differences and teaches reading/writing, math, and science in separate-sex classrooms. After one year of this gender-specific experiment, girls' math and science scores and boys' Scholastic Reading Inventory (SRI) scores rose significantly.

The Nature-Based Classroom

Ultimately, teacher training in how the brain learns and how boys and girls tend to learn differently creates the will and intuition in teachers and schools to create nature-based classrooms (see "Teaching Boys, Teaching Girls" for specific strategies). In an elementary classroom designed to help boys learn, tables and chairs are arranged to provide ample space for each child to spread out and claim learning space. Boys tend to need more physical learning space than girls do. At a table, a boy's materials will be less organized and more widely dispersed. Best practice would suggest having a variety of seating options—some desks, some tables, an easy chair, and a rug area for sitting or lying on the floor. Such a classroom would allow for more movement and noise than a traditional classroom would. Even small amounts of movement can help some boys stay focused.

The teacher can use the blocks area to help boys expand their verbal skills. As the boys are building, a teacher might ask them to describe their buildings. Because of greater blood flow in the cerebellum—the "doing" center of the human brain—boys more easily verbalize what they are doing than what they are feeling. Their language will be richer in vocabulary and more expansive when they are engaged in a task.

An elementary classroom designed to help girls learn will provide lots of opportunities for girls to manipulate objects, build, design, and calculate, thus preparing them for the more rigorous spatial challenges that they will face in higher-level math and science courses. These classrooms will set up spatial lessons in groups that encourage discussion among learners.

Boys and Feelings

An assistant principal at a Tampa, Florida, elementary school shared a story of a boy she called "the bolter." The little boy would regularly blow up in class, then bolt out of the room and out of the school. The assistant principal would chase him and get him back into the building. The boy lacked the verbal-emotive abilities to help him cope with his feelings.

After attending male/female brain difference training, the assistant principal decided to try a new tactic. The next time the boy bolted, she took a ball with her when she went after him. When she found the boy outside, she asked him to bounce the ball back and forth with her. Reluctant at first, the boy started bouncing the ball. Before long, he was talking, then sharing the anger and frustration that he was experiencing at school and at home. He calmed down and went back to class. Within a week, the boy was able to self-regulate his behavior enough to tell his teacher that he needed to go to the office, where he and the assistant principal would do their "ball routine" and talk. Because he was doing something spatial-mechanical, the boy was more able to access hidden feelings.

Girls and Computers

The InterCept program in Colorado Springs, Colorado, is a female-specific teen mentor-training program that works with girls in grades 8–12 who have been identified as at risk for school failure, juvenile delinquency, and teen pregnancy. InterCept staff members use their knowledge of female brain functioning to implement program curriculum. Brittany, 17, came to the InterCept program with a multitude of issues, many of them involving at-risk behavior and school failure.

One of the key components of InterCept is showing teenage girls the importance of becoming "tech-savvy." Girls use a computer-based program to consider future occupations: They can choose a career, determine a salary, decide how much education or training their chosen career will require, and even use income projections to design their future lifestyles. Brittany quite literally found a future: She is entering a career in computer technology.

TEACHING BOYS, TEACHING GIRLS

For Elementary Boys

- Use beadwork and other manipulatives to promote fine motor development. Boys are behind girls in this area when they start school.
- Place books on shelves all around the room so boys get used to their omnipresence.
- Make lessons experiential and kinesthetic.
- Keep verbal instructions to no more than one minute.
- Personalize the student's desk, coat rack, and cubby to increase his sense of attachment.
- Use male mentors and role models, such as fathers, grandfathers, or other male volunteers.
- Let boys nurture one another through healthy aggression and direct empathy.

For Elementary Girls

- Play physical games to promote gross motor skills. Girls are behind boys in this area when they start school.
- Have portable/digital cameras around and take pictures of girls being successful at tasks.
- Use water and sand tables to promote science in a spatial venue.
- Use lots of puzzles to foster perceptual learning.
- Form working groups and teams to promote leadership roles and negotiation skills.
- Use manipulatives to teach math.
- Verbally encourage the hidden high energy of the quieter girls.

The Task Ahead

As educators, we've been somewhat intimidated in recent years by the complex nature of gender. Fortunately, we now have the PET and MRI technologies to view the brains of boys and girls. We now have the science to prove our intuition that tells us that boys and girls do indeed learn differently. And, even more powerful, we have a number of years of successful data that can help us effectively teach both boys and girls.

The task before us is to more deeply understand the gendered brains of our children. Then comes the practical application, with its sense of purpose and productivity, as we help each child learn from within his or her own mind.

References

American Association of University Women. (1992). *AAUW Report: How schools shortchange girls.* American Association of University Women Foundation.

Baron-Cohen, S. (2003). *The essential difference: The truth about the male and female brain.* New York: BasicBooks.

Blum, D. (1997). *Sex on the brain: The biological differences between men and women*. New York: Viking.

Conlin, M. (2003, May 26). The new gender gap. *Business Week Online*. Available: www.businessweek.com/magazine/content/03_5f21/b3834001_4fm2001.htm.

Gurian, M., Henley, P., & Trueman, T. (2001). *Boys and girls learn differently! A guide for teachers and parents*. San Francisco: Jossey-Bass/John Wiley.

Havers, F. (1995). Rhyming tasks male and female brains differently. *The Yale Herald, Inc.* New Haven, CT: Yale University.

Marano, H. E. (2003, July/August). The new sex scorecard. *Psychology Today*, 38–50.

Moir, A., & Jessel, D. (1989). *Brain sex: The real difference between men and women*. New York: Dell Publishing.

National Center for Education Statistics. (2000). *National Assessment of Educational Progress: The nation's report card*. Washington, DC: U.S. Department of Education.

Organisation for Economic Co-operation and Development. (2003). *The PISA 2003 assessment framework*. Author.

Rich, B. (Ed.). (2000). *The Dana brain daybook*. New York: The Charles A. Dana Foundation.

Rubin, R. (2004, Aug. 23). How to survive the new SAT. *Newsweek*, p. 52.

Sommers, C. (2000). *The war against boys*. Simon and Schuster.

Taylor, S. (2002). *The tending instinct*. Times Books.

Sara Mead  **NO**

The Truth about Boys and Girls

If you've been paying attention to the education news lately, you know that American boys are in crisis. After decades spent worrying about how schools "shortchange girls," the eyes of the nation's education commentariat are now fixed on how they shortchange boys. In 2006 alone, a *Newsweek* cover story, a major *New Republic* article, a long article in *Esquire*, a "Today" show segment, and numerous op-eds have informed the public that boys are falling behind girls in elementary and secondary school and are increasingly outnumbered on college campuses. A young man in Massachusetts filed a civil rights complaint with the U.S. Department of Education, arguing that his high school's homework and community service requirements discriminate against boys. A growth industry of experts is advising educators and policymakers how to make schools more "boy friendly" in an effort to reverse this slide.

It's a compelling story that seizes public attention with its "man bites dog" characteristics. It touches on Americans' deepest insecurities, ambivalences, and fears about changing gender roles and the "battle of the sexes." It troubles not only parents of boys, who fear their sons are falling behind, but also parents of girls, who fear boys' academic deficits will undermine their daughters' chances of finding suitable mates.

But the truth is far different from what these accounts suggest. The real story is not bad news about boys doing worse; it's good news about girls doing better.

In fact, with a few exceptions, American boys are scoring higher and achieving more than they ever have before. But girls have just improved their performance on some measures even faster. As a result, girls have narrowed or even closed some academic gaps that previously favored boys, while other long-standing gaps that favored girls have widened, leading to the belief that boys are falling behind.

There's no doubt that some groups of boys—particularly Hispanic and black boys and boys from low-income homes—are in real trouble. But the predominant issues for them are race and class, not gender. Closing racial and economic gaps would help poor and minority boys more than closing gender gaps, and focusing on gender gaps may distract attention from the bigger problems facing these youngsters.

The hysteria about boys is partly a matter of perspective. While most of society has finally embraced the idea of equality for women, the idea that

From *Education sector,* June 2005. Copyright © 2006 by Sara Mead. Reprinted by permission.

women might actually surpass men in some areas (even as they remain behind in others) seems hard for many people to swallow. Thus, boys are routinely characterized as "falling behind" even as they improve in absolute terms.

In addition, a dizzying array of so-called experts have seized on the boy crisis as a way to draw attention to their pet educational, cultural, or ideological issues. Some say that contemporary classrooms are too structured, suppressing boys' energetic natures and tendency to physical expression; others contend that boys need more structure and discipline in school. Some blame "misguided feminism" for boys' difficulties, while others argue that "myths" of masculinity have a crippling impact on boys. Many of these theories have superficially plausible rationales that make them appealing to some parents, educators, and policymakers. But the evidence suggests that many of these ideas come up short.

Unfortunately, the current boy crisis hype and the debate around it are based more on hopes and fears than on evidence. This debate benefits neither boys nor girls, while distracting attention from more serious educational problems—such as large racial and economic achievement gaps—and practical ways to help both boys and girls succeed in school.

A New Crisis?

"The Boy Crisis. At every level of education, they're falling behind. What to do?"

—*Newsweek* cover headline, Jan. 30, 2006

Newsweek is not the only media outlet publishing stories that suggest boys' academic accomplishments and life opportunities are declining. But it's not true. Neither the facts reported in these articles nor data from other sources support the notion that boys' academic performance is falling. In fact, overall academic achievement and attainment for boys is higher than it has ever been.

Long-Term Trends

Looking at student achievement and how it has changed over time can be complicated. Most test scores have little meaning themselves; what matters is what scores tell us about how a group of students is doing relative to something else: an established definition of what students need to know, how this group of students performed in the past, or how other groups of students are performing. Further, most of the tests used to assess student achievement are relatively new, and others have changed over time, leaving relatively few constant measures.

The National Assessment of Educational Progress (NAEP), commonly known as "The Nation's Report Card," is a widely respected test conducted by the U.S. Department of Education using a large, representative national sample of American students. NAEP is the only way to measure national trends in boys' and girls' academic achievements over long periods of time. There are two NAEP tests. The "main NAEP" has tracked U.S. students' performance in reading, math, and other academic subjects since the early 1990s. It tests students in grades four, eight, and 12. The "long-term trend NAEP" has tracked student performance since the early 1970s. It tests students at ages 9, 13, and 17.

Reading

The most recent main NAEP assessment in reading, administered in 2005, does not support the notion that boys' academic achievement is falling. In fact, fourth-grade boys did better than they had done in both the previous NAEP reading assessment, administered in 2003, and the earliest comparable assessment, administered in 1992. Scores for both fourth- and eighth-grade boys have gone up and down over the past decade, but results suggest that the reading skills of fourth- and eighth-grade boys have improved since 1992.

The picture is less clear for older boys. The 2003 and 2005 NAEP assessments included only fourthand eighth-graders, so the most recent main NAEP data for 12th-graders dates back to 2002. On that assessment, 12th-grade boys did worse than they had in both the previous assessment, administered in 1998, and the first comparable assessment, administered in 1992. At the 12th-grade level, boys' achievement in reading does appear to have fallen during the 1990s and early 2000s.

Even if younger boys have improved their achievement over the past decade, however, this could represent a decline if boys' achievement had risen rapidly in previous decades. Some commentators have asserted that the boy crisis has its roots in the mid- or early-1980s. But long-term NAEP data simply does not support these claims. In fact, 9-year-old boys did better on the most recent long-term reading NAEP, in 2004, than they have at any time since the test was first administered in 1971. Nine-year-old boys' performance rose in the 1970s, declined in the 1980s, and has been rising since the early 1990s.

Like the main NAEP, the results for older boys on the long-term NAEP are more mixed. Thirteenyear-old boys have improved their performance slightly compared with 1971, but for the most part their performance over the past 30 years has been flat. Seventeen-year-old boys are doing about the same as they did in the early 1970s, but their performance has been declining since the late 1980s.

The main NAEP also shows that white boys score significantly better than black and Hispanic boys in reading at all grade levels. These differences far outweigh all changes in the overall performance of boys over time. For example, the difference between white and black boys on the fourth-grade NAEP in reading in 2005 was 10 times as great as the improvement for all boys on the same test since 1992.

And while academic performance for minority boys is often shockingly low, it's not getting worse. The average fourth-grade NAEP reading scores of black boys improved more from 1995 to 2005 than those of white and Hispanic boys or girls of any race.

Math

The picture for boys in math is less complicated. Boys of all ages and races are scoring as high—or higher—in math than ever before. From 1990 through 2005, boys in grades four and eight improved their performance steadily on the main NAEP, and they scored significantly better on the 2005 NAEP than in any previous year. Twelfthgraders have not taken the main NAEP in math since 2000. That year, 12th-grade boys did better than they had in 1990 and 1992, but worse than they had in 1996.

Both 9- and 13-year-old boys improved gradually on the long-term NAEP since the 1980s (9-yearold boys' math performance did not improve in the 1970s). Seventeen-year-old boys' performance declined through the 1970s, rose in the 1980s, and remained relatively steady during the late 1990s and early 2000s. As in reading, white boys score much better on the main NAEP in math than do black and Hispanic boys, but all three groups of boys are improving their math performance in the elementary and middle school grades.

Other Subjects

In addition to the main and long-term NAEP assessments in reading and math, the NAEP also administers assessments in civics, geography, science, U.S. history, and writing. The civics assessment has not been administered since 1998, but the geography and U.S. history assessments were both administered in 1994 and 2001; the writing assessment in 1998 and 2002; and the science assessment in 1996, 2000, and 2005.

In geography, there was no significant change in boys' achievement at any grade level from 1994 to 2001. In U.S. history, fourth- and eighth-grade boys improved their achievement, but there was no significant change for 12th-grade boys. In writing, both fourth- and eighth-grade boys improved their achievement from 1998 to 2002, but 12th-grade boys' achievement declined. In science, fourth-grade boys' achievement in 2005 improved over their performance in both 1996 and 2000, eighth-grade boys showed no significant change in achievement, and 12th-grade boys' achievement declined since 1996.

Overall Long-Term Trends

A consistent trend emerges across these subjects: There have been no dramatic changes in the performance of boys in recent years, no evidence to indicate a boy crisis. Elementary-school-age boys are improving their performance; middle school boys are either improving their performance or showing little change, depending on the subject; and high school boys' achievement is declining in most subjects (although it may be improving in math). These trends seem to be consistent across all racial subgroups of boys, despite the fact that white boys perform much better on these tests than do black and Hispanic boys. Evidence of a decline in the performance of older boys is undoubtedly troubling. But the question to address is whether this is a problem for older boys or for older students generally. That can be best answered by looking at the flip side of the gender equation: achievement for girls.

The Difference Between Boys and Girls

To the extent that tales of declining boy performance are grounded in real data, they're usually framed as a decline relative to girls. That's because, as described above, boy performance is generally staying the same or increasing in absolute terms.

But even relative to girls, the NAEP data for boys paints a complex picture. On the one hand, girls outperform boys in reading at all three grade levels assessed on the main NAEP. Gaps between girls and boys are smaller in fourth grade and get larger in eighth and 12th grades. Girls also outperform boys in writing at all grade levels.

In math, boys outperform girls at all grade levels, but only by a very small amount. Boys also outperform girls—again, very slightly—in science and by a slightly larger margin in geography. There are no significant gaps between male and female achievement on the NAEP in U.S. history. In general, girls outperform boys in reading and writing by greater margins than boys outperform girls in math, science, and geography.

But this is nothing new. Girls have scored better than boys in reading for as long as the long-term NAEP has been administered. And younger boys are actually catching up: The gap between boys and girls at age 9 has narrowed significantly since 1971—from 13 points to five points—even as both genders have significantly improved. Boy-girl gaps at age 13 haven't changed much since 1971—and neither has boys' or girls' achievement.

At age 17, gaps between boys and girls in reading are also not that much different from what they were in 1971, but they are significantly bigger than they were in the late 1980s, before achievement for both genders—and particularly boys—began to decline.

The picture in math is even murkier. On the first long-term NAEP assessment in 1973, 9- and 13-year-old girls actually scored better than boys in math, and they continued to do so throughout the 1970s. But as 9- and 13-year-olds of both genders improved their achievement in math during the 1980s and 1990s, boys *pulled ahead* of girls, opening up a small gender gap in math achievement that now favors boys. It's telling that even though younger boys are now doing better than girls on the long-term NAEP in math, when they once lagged behind, no one is talking about the emergence of a new "girl crisis" in elementary- and middle-school math.

Seventeen-year-old boys have always scored better than girls on the long-term NAEP in math, but boys' scores declined slightly more than girls' scores in the 1970s, and girls' scores have risen slightly more than those of boys since. As a result, older boys' advantage over girls in math has narrowed.

Overall, there has been no radical or recent decline in boys' performance relative to girls. Nor is there a clear overall trend—boys score higher in some areas, girls in others.

The fact that achievement for older students is stagnant or declining for both boys and girls, to about the same degree, points to another important element of the boy crisis. The problem is most likely not that high schools need to be fixed to meet the needs of boys, but rather that they need to be fixed to meet the needs of *all* students, male and female. The need to accurately parse the influence of gender and other student categories is also acutely apparent when we examine the issues of race and income.

We Should Be Worried About Some Subgroups of Boys

There are groups of boys for whom "crisis" is not too strong a term. When racial and economic gaps combine with gender achievement gaps in reading, the result is disturbingly low achievement for poor, black, and Hispanic boys.

But the gaps between students of different races and classes are much larger than those for students of different genders—anywhere from two to five times as big, depending on the grade. The only exception is among 12th-grade boys, where the achievement gap between white girls and white boys in reading is the same size as the gap between white and black boys in reading and is larger than the gap between white and Hispanic boys. Overall, though, poor, black, and Hispanic boys would benefit far more from closing racial and economic achievement gaps than they would from closing gender gaps. While the gender gap picture is mixed, the racial gap picture is, unfortunately, clear across a wide range of academic subjects.

In addition to disadvantaged and minority boys, there are also reasons to be concerned about the substantial percentage of boys who have been diagnosed with disabilities. Boys make up twothirds of students in special education—including 80 percent of those diagnosed with emotional disturbances or autism—and boys are two and a half times as likely as girls to be diagnosed with attention deficit hyperactivity disorder (ADHD). The number of boys diagnosed with disabilities or ADHD has exploded in the past 30 years, presenting a challenge for schools and causing concern for parents. But the reasons for this growth are complicated, a mix of educational, social, and biological factors. Evidence suggests that school and family factors—such as poor reading instruction, increased awareness of and testing for disabilities, or over-diagnosis—may play a role in the increased rates of boys diagnosed with learning disabilities or emotional disturbance. But boys also have a higher incidence of organic disabilities, such as autism and orthopedic impairments, for which scientists don't currently have a completely satisfactory explanation. Further, while girls are less likely than boys to be diagnosed with most disabilities, the number of girls with disabilities has also grown rapidly in recent decades, meaning that this is not just a boy issue. . . .

The Source of the Boy Crisis: A Knowledge Deficit and a Surplus of Opportunism

It's clear that some gender differences in education are real, and there are some groups of disadvantaged boys in desperate need of help. But it's also clear that boys' overall educational achievement and attainment are not in decline—in fact, they have never been better. What accounts for the recent hysteria?

It's partly an issue of simple novelty. The contours of disadvantage in education and society at large have been clear for a long time—low-income, minority, and female people consistently fall short of their affluent, white, and male peers. The idea that historically privileged boys could be at risk, that boys could be shortchanged, has simply proved too deliciously counterintuitive and "newsworthy" for newspaper and magazine editors to resist.

The so-called boy crisis also feeds on a lack of solid information. Although there are a host of statistics about how boys and girls perform in school, we actually know very little about why these differences exist or how important they are. There are many things—including biological, developmental, cultural, and educational factors—that affect how boys and girls do in school. But untangling these different influences is incredibly difficult. Research on the causes of gender differences is hobbled by the twin demons of educational research: lack of data and the difficulty of drawing causal connections among multiple, complex influences. Nor do we know what these differences mean for boys' and girls' future economic and other opportunities.

Yet this hasn't stopped a plethora of so-called experts—from pediatricians and philosophers to researchers and op-ed columnists—from weighing in with their views on the causes and likely effects of educational gender gaps. In fact, the lack of solid research evidence confirming or debunking any particular hypothesis has created fertile ground for all sorts of people to seize on the boy crisis to draw attention to their pet educational, cultural or ideological issues.

The problem, we are told, is that the structured traditional classroom doesn't accommodate boys' energetic nature and need for free motion—or it's that today's schools don't provide enough structure or discipline. It's that feminists have demonized typical boy behavior and focused educational resources on girls—or it's the "box" boys are placed in by our patriarchal society. It's that our schools' focus on collaborative learning fails to stimulate boys' natural competitiveness—or it's that the competitive pressures of standardized testing are pushing out the kind of relevant, hands-on work on which boys thrive.

The boy crisis offers a perfect opportunity for those seeking an excuse to advance ideological and educational agendas. Americans' continued ambivalence about evolving gender roles guarantees that stories of "boys in crisis" will capture public attention. The research base is internally contradictory, making it easy to find superficial support for a wide variety of explanations but difficult for the media and the public to evaluate the quality of evidence cited. Yet there is not sufficient evidence—or the right kind of evidence—available to draw firm conclusions. As a result, there is a sort of free market for theories about why boys are underperforming girls in school, with parents, educators, media, and the public choosing to give credence to the explanations that are the best marketed and that most appeal to their pre-existing preferences.

Unfortunately, this dynamic is not conducive to a thoughtful public debate about how boys and girls are doing in school or how to improve their performance.

Hard-Wired Inequality?

One branch of the debate over gender and education has focused on various theories of divergence between male and female brains. Men and women are "wired differently," people say, leading to all kinds of alleged problems and disparities that must be addressed. There's undoubtedly some truth here. The difficulty is separating fact from supposition.

The quest to identify and explain differences between men's and women's mental abilities is as old as psychology itself. Although the earliest work in this genre began with the assumption that women were intellectually inferior to men, and sought both to prove and explain why this was the case, more recent and scientifically valid research also finds differences in men's and women's cognitive abilities, as well as in the physiology of their brains.

It's important to note that research does not find that one gender is smarter than the other—on average, men and women score the same on tests of general intelligence. But there are differences between men's and women's performance in different types of abilities measured by intelligence tests. In general, women have higher scores than men on most tests of verbal abilities (verbal analogies being an exception), while men have higher scores on tests of what psychologists call "visual-spatial" abilities—the ability to think in terms of nonverbal, symbolic information, measured through such tasks as the ability to place a horizontal line in a tilted frame or to identify what the image of an irregular object would look like if the object were rotated. Quantitative or mathematical abilities are more even, with men performing better on some types of problems—including probability, statistics, measurement and geometry—while women perform better on others, such as computation, and both genders perform equally well on still others.

Much of this research is based on studies with adults—particularly college students—but we know that gender differences in cognitive abilities vary with development. Differences in verbal abilities are among the first to appear; vocabulary differences, for example, are seen before children are even 2 years old, and by the time they enter kindergarten, girls are more likely than boys to know their letters and be able to associate letters with sounds. Male advantages in visual-spatial abilities emerge later in childhood and adolescence.

The research identifying these differences in male and female cognitive abilities does not explain their cause, however. There may be innate, biologically based differences in men and women. But gender differences may also be the result of culture and socialization that emphasize different skills for men and women and provide both genders different opportunities to develop their abilities.

Researchers have investigated a variety of potential biological causes for these differences. There is evidence that sex hormones in the womb, which drive the development of the fetus's sex organs, also have an impact on the brain. Children who were exposed to abnormal levels of these hormones, for example, may develop cognitive abilities more like those of the opposite sex. Increased hormone levels at puberty may again affect cognitive development.

And performance on some types of cognitive tests tends to vary with male and female hormonal cycles.

In addition, new technologies that allow researchers to look more closely into the brain and observe its activities have shown that there are differences between the sexes in the size of various brain structures and in the parts of the brain men and women use when performing different tasks.

But while this information is intriguing, it must be interpreted with a great deal of caution. Although our knowledge of the brain and its development has expanded dramatically in recent years, it remains rudimentary. In the future, much of our current thinking about the brain will most likely seem as unsophisticated as the work of the late 19th and early 20th century researchers who sought to prove female intellectual inferiority by comparing the size of men's and women's skulls.

In particular, it is notoriously difficult to draw causal links between observations about brain structure or activity and human behavior, a point that scientists reporting the findings of brain research often take great pains to emphasize. Just as correlation does not always signify causation in social science research, correlations between differences in brain structure and observed differences in male and female behavior do not necessarily mean that the former leads to the latter.

But these caveats have not prevented many individuals from confidently citing brain research to advance their preferred explanation of gender gaps in academic achievement.

Proponents of different educational philosophies and approaches cherrypick findings that seem to support their visions of public education. And a growing boys industry purports to help teachers use brain research on gender differences to improve boys' academic achievement. But many of these individuals and organizations are just seizing on the newest crisis—boys' achievement—to make money and promote old agendas. Scientific-sounding brain research has lent an aura of authority to people who see anxiety about boys as an opportunity for personal gain. Many have also added refashioned elements of sociology to their boys-in-crisis rhetoric.

Dubious Theories and Old Agendas

"Girl behavior becomes the gold standard. Boys are treated like defective girls."

—Psychologist Michael Thompson, as quoted in *Newsweek*

Thompson is just one of many commentators who argue that today's schools disadvantage boys by expecting behavior—doing homework, sitting still, working collaboratively, expressing thoughts and feelings verbally and in writing—that comes more naturally to girls. These commentators argue that schools are designed around instructional models that work well with girls' innate abilities and learning styles but do not provide enough support to boys or engage their interests and strengths. While female skills like organization, empathy, cooperativeness, and verbal agility are highly valued in schools, male strengths like physical vigor and competitiveness are overlooked and may even be treated as problems rather than assets, the argument goes.

Building from this analysis, a wealth of books, articles, and training programs endeavor to teach educators how to make schools more "boy friendly." Many of these suggestions—such as allowing boys to choose reading selections that appeal to their interests—are reasonable enough.

But many other recommendations are based on an inappropriate application of brain research on sex differences. Many of these authors draw causal connections between brain research findings and stereotypical male or female personality traits without any evidence that such causality exists, as the sidebar demonstrates. These analyses also tend to ignore the wide variation among individuals of the same sex. Many girls have trouble completing their homework and sitting still, too, and some boys do not.

Members of the growing "boys industry" of researchers, advocates, and pop psychologists include family therapist Michael Gurian, author of *The Minds of Boys, Boys and Girls Learn Differently!*, and numerous other books about education and gender; Harvard psychologist William Pollack, director of the Center for Research on Boys at McLean Hospital and author of *Real Boys*; and Michael Thompson, clinical psychologist and the author of *Raising Cain*. All of these authors are frequently cited in media coverage of the boy crisis. A quick search on Amazon.com also turns up Jeffrey Wilhelm's *Reading Don't Fix No Chevys*, Thomas Newkirk's *Misreading Masculinity: Boys, Literacy and Popular Culture*, Christina Hoff Sommers' *The War On Boys*, Leonard Sax's *Why Gender Matters*, and *Hear Our Cry: Boys in Crisis*, by Paul D. Slocumb. A review of these books shows that the boys industry is hardly monolithic. Its practitioners seem to hold a plethora of perspectives and philosophies about both gender and education, and their recommendations often contradict one another.

Some focus on boys' emotions and sense of self-worth, while others are more concerned with implementing pedagogical practices—ranging from direct instruction to project-based learning—that they believe will better suit boys' learning style. Still others focus on structural solutions, such as smaller class sizes or single-sex learning environments. But all are finding an audience among parents, educators, and policymakers concerned about boys.

It would be unfair to imply that these authors write about boys for purely self-serving motives—most of these men and women seem to be sincerely concerned about the welfare of our nation's boys. But the work in this field leaves one skeptical of the quality of research, information, and analysis that are shaping educators' and parents' beliefs and practices as they educate boys and girls. Perhaps most tellingly, ideas about how to make schools more "boy friendly" align suspiciously well with educational and ideological beliefs the individuals promoting them had long before boys were making national headlines. And some of these prescriptions are diametrically opposed to one another.

A number of conservative authors, think tanks, and journals have published articles arguing that progressive educational pedagogy and misguided feminism are hurting boys. According to these critics, misguided feminists have lavished resources on female students at the expense of males and demonized typical boy behaviors such as rowdy play. At the same time, progressive educational pedagogy is harming boys by replacing strict discipline with permissiveness, teacher-led direct instruction with student-led collaborative learning, and academic content with a focus on developing students' self-esteem. The boy crisis offers an attractive way for conservative pundits to get in some knocks against feminism and progressive education and also provides another argument for educational policies—such as stricter discipline, more traditional curriculum, increased testing and competition, and single-sex schooling—that conservatives have long supported.

Progressive education thinkers, on the other hand, tend to see boys' achievement problems as evidence that schools have not gone far *enough* in adopting progressive tenets and are still forcing all children into a teacher-led pedagogical box that is particularly ill-suited to boys' interests and learning styles. Similarly, the responses progressive education writers recommend—more project-based and hands-on learning, incorporating kinetic and other learning styles into lessons, making learning "relevant," and allowing children more self-direction and free movement—simply sound like traditional progressive pedagogy.

More recently, critics of the standards movement and its flagship federal legislation, the No Child Left Behind Act (NCLB), have argued that the movement and NCLB are to blame for boys' problems. According to *Newsweek*, "In the last two decades, the education system has become obsessed with a quantifiable and narrowly defined kind of academic success, and that myopic view, these experts say, is harming boys." This is unlikely, because high-school-age boys, who seem to be having the most problems, are affected far less by NCLB than elementary-school-age boys, who seem to be improving the most.

Further, many of the arguments NCLB critics make about how it hurts boys—by causing schools to narrow their curriculum or eliminate recess—are not borne out by the evidence. A recent report from the Washington, D.C.-based Center for Educational Policy showed that most schools are not eliminating social studies, science, and arts in response to NCLB. And, a report from the U.S. Department of Education found that over 87 percent of elementary schools offer recess and most do so daily. More important, such critics offer no compelling case for why standards and testing, if harmful, would have more of a negative impact on boys than on girls.

In other words, few of these commentators have anything new to say— the boy crisis has just given them a new opportunity to promote their old messages. . . .

POSTSCRIPT

Is There a Crisis in the Education of Boys?

In an article in *Principal* (March/April 2005), David Sadker and Karen Zittleman address the issue at hand in "Closing the Gender Gap—Again!". The authors observe that gender bias, once considered to affect only girls, continues to impact both girls and boys in ways often difficult to detect. They conclude that "the gender gap is the one demographic that challenges [all] schools, urban and rural, wealthy and poor."

This brings up some companion issues. First, the education of black boys. A provocative book by Jawanza Kunjufu, *Countering the Conspiracy to Destroy Black Boys*, written in 1982, perhaps was a springboard to the serious treatment of this problem. Jonathan Kozol and others have clearly and forcefully documented the sad state of many urban schools. Rosa A. Smith, in "Saving Black Boys," *The School Administrator* (January 2005), addresses the situation specific to black boys—expulsions, dropouts, low graduation rates, juvenile incarceration, and unemployment. Smith says "school success for black male students . . . depends on leaders willing to distance themselves from business as usual. . . . For these students, it is a matter of life and death."

Two other good sources on this subissue are Carla R. Monroe's "African American Boys and the Discipline Gap: Balancing Educators' Uneven Hand," *Educational Horizons* (Winter 2006) and Rosa A. Smith's "Building a Positive Future for Black Boys," *American School Board Journal* (September 2005).

Another subissue is single-sex education. Dr. Leonard Sax, founder of the National Association for the Advancement of Single-Sex Public Education, contends that the learning styles of boys and girls differ in ways that are now fairly well understood. Because of this, he states in "Single-Sex Education: Ready for Prime Time?" in *The World & I* (August 2002), that "for the first time in thirty years teachers and administrators are at liberty to offer single-sex education to students in public schools." Other perspectives on this subissue include Karen Stabiner's book *All Girls: Single-Sex Education and Why It Matters* (2002) and Michael Ruhlman's *Boys Themselves: A Return to Single-Sex Education* (1996). Also see Kathleen Vail's "Same-Sex Schools," *American School Board Journal* (November 2002) and Mary Ellen Flannery's "No Girls Allowed," *NEA Today* (April 2006).

Finally, another interesting subissue is the effect of teacher gender on on interactions with students. For this, see "The Why Chromosome: How a Teacher's Gender Affects Boys and Girls" by Thomas S. Dees in *Education Next* (Fall 2006).

Contributors to This Volume

EDITOR

JAMES WM. NOLL has retired from his professorial position in the College of Education at the University of Maryland in College Park, Maryland, where he taught philosophy of education and chaired the Social Foundations of Education unit. He has been affiliated with the American Educational Studies Association, the National Society for the Study of Education, the Association for Supervision and Curriculum Development, and the World Future Society. He received a B.A. in English and history from the University of Wisconsin-Milwaukee, an M.S. in educational administration from the University of Wisconsin, and a Ph.D. in philosophy of education from the University of Chicago. His articles have appeared in several education journals, and he is coauthor, with Sam P. Kelly, of *Foundations of Education in America: An Anthology of Major Thought and Significant Actions* (Harper & Row, 1970). He also has served as editor and editorial board member for McGraw-Hill/Dushkin's *Annual Editions: Education series.*

STAFF

Larry Loeppke	Managing Editor
Jill Peter	Senior Developmental Editor
Susan Brusch	Senior Developmental Editor
Beth Kundert	Production Manager
Jane Mohr	Project Manager
Tara McDermott	Design Coordinator
Nancy Meissner	Editorial Assistant
Lori Church	Pemissions Coordinator
Julie J. Keck	Senior Marketing Manager
Mary S. Klein	Marketing Communications Specialist
Alice M. Link	Marketing Coordinator
Tracie A. Kammerude	Senior Marketing Assistant

AUTHORS

MORTIMER J. ADLER (1902–2001), during a long and distinguished career, taught philosophy at the University of Chicago, served on the board of the *Encyclopedia Britannica*, founded the Institute for Philosophical Research and the Aspen Institute, and co-edited *The Great Books of the Western World*. His books include *Six Great Ideas* (1981), *Mind Over Matter* (1990), and an autobiography, *Philosopher at Large* (1977).

KAREN AGNE is an assistant professor of education in the Center for Educational Studies and Services at the State University of New York at Plattsburgh and is director of the Adirondack Advocacy for Gifted Education.

MICHAEL W. APPLE is the John Bascom Professor of Curriculum and Instruction and Educational Policy Studies at the University of Wisconsin-Madison. He is author of *Cultural Politics and Education* and *Official Knowledge*.

RAY BACCHETTI is a scholar in residence at the Carnegie Foundation for the Advancement of Teaching at Stanford, California. He is a former vice-president for planning and management at Stanford University.

MARC F. BERNSTEIN is superintendent of the Bellmore-Merrick Central High School District in North Merrick, New York.

JOHN BUELL is a freelance journalist and author of *Closing the Book on Homework: Enhancing Public Education and Freeing Family Time* (2004).

JAMIN CARSON is an assistant professor at East Carolina University after completing his doctorate in curriculum studies at the University of Texas at Austin. His research interest is in the philosophical foundations of education.

EVANS CLINCHY is a senior consultant at the Institute for Responsive Education at Northeastern University in Boston. He is editor of *Transforming Public Education* and *Reforming American Education*.

LINDA DARLING-HAMMOND is the Charles E. Ducommun Professor of Education at Stanford University and executive director of the National Commission on Teaching and America's Future. She has also been co-director of the National Center for Restructuring Education, Schools, and Teaching. Among her publications is *The Right to Learn: A Blueprint for Schools That Work* (1997).

JOHN DEWEY (1859–1952) was a philosopher and leader in the field of education. He taught at the University of Michigan, the University of Chicago (where he founded a laboratory school to test his ideas), and Columbia University (where he spawned the progressive education movement). Among his many books are *The School and Society* (1899) and *Democracy and Education* (1916).

EDD DOERR is executive director of Americans for Religious Liberty in Silver Spring, Maryland. He is also a columnist for *The Humanist* and is the author of *The Case Against School Vouchers* (1996).

DAVID ELKIND is a professor of child development at Tufts University where he conducts research in cognitive, perceptual, and social growth of children based on the theories of Jean Piaget. Among his books are *The Hurried Child* and *Miseducation.*

CHESTER E. FINN, JR. is president of the Thomas B. Fordham Foundation and a senior fellow at the Manhattan Institute. He served as assistant U. S. secretary of education from 1985 to 1988, and he was a member of the National Assessment Governing Board from 1988 to 1996.

ERICA D. FRANKENBERG is a doctoral student at Teachers College, Columbia University.

CHARLES L. GLENN is professor of administration, training, and policy studies and fellow of the University Professors Program at Boston University. He formerly was director of urban education and equity efforts for the Massachusetts Department of Education.

MICHAEL GURIAN is a co-founder of the Gurian Institute in Colorado Springs, Colorado, which carries on research and develops training programs on gender differences and brain-based learning. His most recent book is *The Minds of Boys,* co-authored with Kathy Stevens.

FREDERICK M. HESS is a resident scholar at the American Enterprise Institute in Washington, D. C. His most recent book is *Common Sense School Reform.*

ROBERT HOLLAND is a senior fellow of the Lexington Institute in Arlington, Virginia. A journalist, he served as op-ed page editor for the Richmond *Times-Dispatch.*

JOHN HOLT (1923–1985) was an educator and a critic of public schooling. He authored several influential books on education, including *How Children Fail* (1964) and *Instead of Education: Ways to Help People Do Things Better* (1976).

NINA HURWITZ was a high school teacher in Westchester County, New York for 23 years. She and her husband, Sol, have written many articles on education and student health care.

SOL HURWITZ is an education consultant and a freelance writer. He has also served as a board member of the Albert Shanker Institute.

ROBERT M. HUTCHINS (1879–1977) was chancellor of the University of Chicago, co-compiler of *The Great Books of the Western World* and director of the Center for the Study of Democratic Institutions. Among his books are *The Higher Learning in America* (1936) and *University of Utopia* (1964).

KIRK A. JOHNSON is a senior policy analyst at the Center for Data Analysis at the Heritage Foundation in Washington, D.C. He was previously affiliated with the Center for Economic Studies at the U.S. Census Bureau.

KEN JONES is the director of teacher education at the University of Southern Maine, Gorham.

ALFIE KOHN writes and lectures widely on education and human behavior. His books include *Punished by Rewards* (1993), *Beyond Discipline: From*

Compliance to Community (1996), *The Schools Our Children Deserve* (1999), and *The Case Against Standardized Testing* (2000).

ETTA KRALOVEC is vice president for learning with Training and Development Corporation in Maine. She is a former classroom teacher and was director of teacher education at the College of the Atlantic.

CHUNGMEI LEE is a research associate with the Civil Rights Project at Harvard University.

STEPHEN MACEDO is professor of politics and director of the University Center for Human Values at Princeton University. He is the author of *Diversity and Distrust: Civic Education in a Multicultural Democracy.*

STEVEN MALANGA is a contributing editor at *City Journal* and a senior fellow at the Manhattan Institute for Policy Research.

BRUNO V. MANNO is a senior program associate with the Annie E. Casey Foundation and a former U. S. assistant secretary of education.

SARA MEAD is a senior policy analyst at Education Sector, a Washington, D.C. think tank founded in 2005 by Andrew Rotherham and Thomas Toch. Prior to joining Education Sector, she was an education policy analyst with the Progressive Policy Institute.

LOWELL MONKE is an assistant professor of education at Wittenberg University in Springfield, Ohio, where he teaches courses on philosophical and social perspectives in education.

JOE NATHAN is director of the Center for School Change in the Hubert H. Humphrey Institute of Public Affairs at the University of Minnesota, Minneapolis.

LINDA NATHAN is headmaster of the Boston Arts Academy, a public high school for the visual and performing arts.

WARREN A. NORD is director of the Program in the Humanities and Human Values and teaches philosophy of religion at the University of North Carolina, Chapel Hill. He is the author of *Religion and American Education* (1995) and co-author, with Charles Haynes, of *Taking Religion Seriously Across the Curriculum* (1998).

GARY ORFIELD is a professor of education and social policy in the Harvard Graduate School of Education and the Kennedy School of Government. He is co-director of the Civil Rights Project and is co-author, with Susan E. Eaton, of *Dismantling Desegregation.*

PAUL E. PETERSON is the Henry Lee Shattuck professor of government and director of the Program on Education, Policy, and Governance at Harvard University. He is a senior fellow at the Hoover Institution and editor-in-chief of *Education Next: A Journal of Opinion and Research.* He is co-author of *The Education Gap: Vouchers and Urban Schools.*

DAN PETERSON is an attorney and writer who claims to have been designed to live in Northern Virginia.

ROSALIE PEDALINO PORTER is chairman of the board of the Research in English Acquisition and Development (READ) Institute in Amherst, Massachusetts. She served in bilingual and ESL programs in the Newton public schools for ten years and has lectured widely on the subject of bilingualism. She is the author of *Forked Tongue: The Politics of Bilingual Education* (1996).

AL RAMIREZ is an education professor at the University of Colorado at Colorado Springs, specializing in the leadership program. He formerly was the chief state school officer in Iowa.

BRIAN D. RAY is the founder and president of the National Home Education Research Institute in Salem, Oregon and long-time editor of the *Home School Researcher*, an academic journal.

CARL R. ROGERS (1902–1987), a noted psychologist and educator, taught at the University of Chicago and the University of Wisconsin-Madison. He introduced the client-centered approach to psychotherapy in 1942, and he was the first psychologist to record and transcribe therapy session verbatim. He authored *On Becoming a Person* (1972), among many other influential works.

ANDREW ROTHERHAM is director of educational policy at the Progressive Policy Institute in Washington, D. C. He also served as director of the institute's 21st Century Schools Project and has been a White House adviser.

RICHARD ROTHSTEIN is a research associate at the Economic Policy Institute in Washington, D. C., a senior correspondent for *The American Prospect,* a national education columnist for *The New York Times,* and an adjunct professor of public policy at Occidental College. He is author of *The Way We Were? Debunking the Myth of America's Declining Schools* (1998).

PETER SCHRAG is a journalist with a long time affiliation with the Sacramento Bee. Among his books are *Final Test: The Battle for Adequacy in America's Schools and Practice Lost: California's Experience; America's Future.*

ALBERT SHANKER (1928–1997) was president of the American Federation of Teachers in Washington, D. C., which gave teachers a union alternative to National Education Association membership. A leader in the educational reform movement, he was the first labor leader elected to the National Academy of Education. His Sunday *New York Times* column "Where We Stand" brought educational issues to a wide audience.

B. F. SKINNER (1904–1990), a noted psychologist and exponent of behaviorism, held the William James Chair in the Department of Psychology at Harvard University. His major works include *About Behaviorism* (1976) and *Reflections on Behaviorism and Society* (1978). His most widely read book is *Walden Two* (1948).

DAVID SKINNER is the assistant managing editor at *The Weekly Standard* and former managing editor at *The Public Interest.* He also edits the journal *Doublethink.*

KATHY STEVENS is director of the Gurian Institute Training Division and the Women's Resource Agency, both located in Colorado Springs, Colorado.

MARK TERRY is chair of the science department at the Northwest School in Seattle, Washington. He has been a teacher in public and independent schools for over three decades.

JACQUELINE S. THOUSAND is a professor in the College of Education at California State University at San Marcos. She has been a coordinator of special education programs and is co-author of *A Guide to Co-Teaching*.

GREGG VANOUREK is vice president of the Charter School Division at K12 in McLean, Virginia.

RICHARD A. VILLA is president of Bayridge Consortium, Inc. in San Marcos, California. He has been a classroom teacher, special education administrator, and director of instructional services. He is co-author of *A Guide to Co-Teaching*.

PATRICIA A. WASLEY is dean of the College of Education at the University of Washington in Seattle and former dean of the Graduate School of Education at the Bank Street College of Education.

JUAN WILLIAMS is a journalist and political commentator who worked for 23 years at *The Washington Post* and who expresses his ideas on National Public Radio and FOX News. He is author of *Eyes on the Prize: America's Civil Rights Years, 1954–1965* and, most recently, *I'll Find a Way or Make One: A Tribute to Historically Black Colleges and Universities.*

Index